Reduced

CROMARTIE:
HIGHLAND LIFE 1650–1914

Planting potatoes, crofters in Wester Ross, mid-nineteenth century.

CROMARTIE:
HIGHLAND LIFE 1650-1914

Eric Richards and Monica Clough

ABERDEEN UNIVERSITY PRESS

First published 1989
Aberdeen University Press
A member of the Pergamon Group

© Eric Richards and Monica Clough 1989

All Rights Reserved. No part of this publication may be reproduced, stored in a retrieval system or transmitted in any form or by any means: electronic, electrostatic, magnetic tape, mechanical, photocopying, recording or otherwise, without permission in writing from the copyright holders.

British Library Cataloguing in Publication Data
Richards, Eric
   Cromartie: Highland life 1650–1914.
   1. Scotland. Highland region. Cromarty. Country estates.
Cromartie Estate, history
   I. Title   II. Clough, Monica
941.1′72

ISBN 0-08-037732-7

PRINTED IN GREAT BRITAIN
THE UNIVERSITY PRESS
ABERDEEN

Contents

List of Illustrations and Maps	vii
The Mackenzies of Tarbat and Cromartie	xi
Glossary	xii
Abbreviations	xiii
Preface	xv

Part One   The Making of Cromartie and the Road to Disaster 1650-1745

1	The Triumphing Sword of the Mackenzies and the Origins of the Cromartie Estate	3
2	Winning an Earldom	12
3	The Workings of a Highland Estate: the Managers	26
4	Estate Life and its Productions	38
5	Prelude to Disaster	51
6	Losing Everything: Cromartie and the 'Forty-Five	57

Part Two   Dispossession and Restoration 1746-1784

7	Annexation 1746-1786	71
8	State Enterprise and Infant Industries	85
9	Count MacLeod and the Recovery of the Cromartie Estate	96

Part Three   A Highland Estate in the Age of the Clearances

10	Cromartie Restored and the Context of Change	111
11	The Broken Succession 1789-1801	129
12	The Vicissitudes of a Highland Laird, 1801-1825	143
13	Economic Malaise, Above and Below	165
14	Measures of Highland Change: the 1830s	182
15	Emigration, Famine and the Impecunious Landlord	200

Part Four Cromartie and the Aristocratic Merger, 1849-1880

16	A Vital Marriage and the Seeds of Touble 1849-1854	219
17	Rebellion at Coigach	236
18	Paradoxical Aristocratic Finances	246
19	Rich and Poor on a Highland Estate: the 1860s	252
20	Strathpeffer Spa 1850-80	269
21	The Social Volcano	284
22	The Shock of the Crofters' Revolt	297
23	The Voice of the Crofter	312
24	Managerial Atitudes	324
	Appendix: a month in the life of a Factor: August 1882	342
25	The Tenantry 1830-1914	344

Part Five Adjustments of a New Era, 1880-1914

26	Cromartie Finances in Travail: the 1880s	363
27	The Hazards of Inheritance 1888-1896	378
28	Cromartie Alone 1896-1914	394

Epilogue 415

Appendices

A. Rents on Cromartie Estate	431
B. The Population of the Cromartie Estate	439
C. The Oral Testimony of Morag Shaw Mackenzie, 1982	442
D. Maps	445
Note on the Pedigree and Titles of the Earls of Cromartie	452
Bibliography	454
Notes	461
Index	506

List of Illustrations and Maps

	Frontispiece. Planting potatoes, Wester Ross, mid-nineteenth century. Courtesy of Ethnological Archive, National Museums of Scotland	ii
1	The Triumphing Sword.	5
2	Sir Rorie Mackenzie of Tarbat. *The Earls of Cromartie*, by William Fraser, Edinburgh, 1876.	9
3	George Mackenzie of Tarbat, First Earl of Cromartie. *The Earls of Cromartie*.	13
4	Castle Leod. *The Earls of Cromartie*.	17
5	Royston House. *The Earls of Cromartie*.	19
6	Tarbat House c. 1700. *The Earls of Cromartie*.	30
7	John, Second Earl of Cromartie. *The Earls of Cromartie*.	33
8	Portmahomock. Courtesy of Historic Buildings and Monuments, Scottish Development Department.	35
9	Prince Charles' letter to Cromartie. *The Earls of Cromartie*.	58
10	George, Third Earl of Cromartie and Isabella Gordon, Countess of Cromartie. *The Earls of Cromartie*.	63
11	Fishing boats off Ross. Courtesy of National Museums of Scotland.	89
12	Count MacLeod. *The Earls of Cromartie*.	97
13	*Pier at Tanera, Loch Broom. A Voyage round Great Britain . . . with a series of views . . . drawn and engraved by William Daniell*, Vol 1, Richard Ayton, London, 1814. Courtesy of the Trustees of The National Library of Scotland.	106
14	*Dingwall in 1824*. Courtesy of Dingwall Museum. Photograph by Ian Rhind.	117
15	Highland Mowing. *Wild Sports and Natural History of the Highlands*, Charles St John, London, 1893.	126

16	(a) and (b) Roads were late in reaching Wester Ross: contemporary writers warned sportsmen about difficult conditions. (a) *Field Sports*, by William Henry Scott, London, 1818. (b) *Wild Sports and Natural History of the Highlands*.	134, 5
17	Maria Mackenzie, wife of Edward Hay-Mackenzie. *The Earls of Cromartie*.	145
18	Edward Hay-Mackenzie. *The Earls of Cromartie*.	148
19	John Hay-Mackenzie.	152
20	Ballone, one of 'two ruined castles' which George Taylor saw 'commanding a view of the Sutherland coast'. *The Earls of Cromartie*.	172
21	Tarbat, Nigg, from a chart of the Firth of Cromartie from 'A survey by George Buchanan, civil engineer, Edinburgh, 1836'. Courtesy of Mr Donald Matheson, Cromarty.	214
22	Anne Hay-Mackenzie.	220
23	Sketch of Knockfarrel allotments.	223
24	Detail from sketch of Knockfarrel allotments.	224
25	Agricultural landscape, Strathpeffer. Courtesy of Scottish Field Studies Association (Annual Report 1963) and of *Scottish Studies* (Vol 9 Pt 1, 1965) 'Easter Ross: A Residual Crofting Area', Joy Tivy.	230
26	An illustration entitled, 'An Interloper', from *Shooting*, by Lord Walsingham and Sir Ralph Payne-Gallway, London, 1893.	242
27	Castle Leod, mid-nineteenth century. *Strathpeffer Spa Medical Guide*, by W Bruce, Dingwall, 1910. Courtesy of the Trustees of The National Library of Scotland.	249
28	Countess of Cromartie, Duchess of Sutherland. *The Earls of Cromartie*.	253
29	Raven cottage in 1900, the last of the estate houses still to be thatched, engulfed by smart villas.	266
30	Lithograph of the projected Spa, and plans for the Spa feus, 1868, by William Devey.	270
31	The Pavilion. *Strathpeffer Spa Medical Guide*.	277
32	The wells and baths, at noon. *Strathpeffer Spa Medical Guide*.	277
33	Strathpeffer Spa. Aperient Salts label.	279
34	Strathpeffer in summer and winter, c. 1907. Courtesy of Mrs Spark, The Pharmacy, Strathpeffer.	282
35	Pony cart, used to steady the open sack being filled with the wool-clip. Courtesy of the Scottish Ethnological Archive, National Museums of Scotland.	303
36	John Rose of Inchvannie and his wife, c. 1870.	317

List of Illustrations and Maps

37	John Mackenzie, pony-man and Inchvannie crofter, 1912.	318
38	Tarbat House, built 1796.	321
39	MacLean, the deaf and dumb tailor and his wife, c. 1870.	329
40	Francis, Earl of Cromartie.	366
41	The *Lady Sibell* in which the family cruised to the Mediterranean.	384
42	(a) and (b) Captain Walter Blunt and Countess Sibell in the year of their marriage, 1890.	386
43	**Strathpeffer Spa.** Treatment by electricity. Courtesy of Mrs Spark, the Pharmacy, Strathpeffer.	388
44	Treatment by water. Courtesy of Mrs Spark, the Pharmacy, Strathpeffer.	388
45	The Peat Bath. *Strathpeffer Spa Medical Guide.*	389
46	The Douche. *Strathpeffer Spa Medical Guide.*	389
47	The Nicholson Memorial Mineral Hospital. *Strathpeffer Spa Medical Guide.*	390
48	The Pavilion, Strathpeffer, as an American convalescent hospital in 1917. Courtesy of Ian Grant, Blairninich.	390
49	Ben Wyvis Hotel, exterior. Courtesy of Mrs Spark, the Pharmacy, Strathpeffer.	391
50	Ben Wyvis Hotel, interior. Courtesy of Mrs Spark, the Pharmacy, Strathpeffer.	391
51	The orchestra in the Square, Strathpeffer. *Strathpeffer Spa Medical Guide.*	392
52	Queen Victoria's Diamond Jubilee celebrated in Strathpeffer by the local inhabitants. Courtesy of Ian Grant, Blairninich.	393
53	Grain stacks and the teams of horses required, on the farm of Rhinie, parish of Fearn about 1900. Courtesy of the Scottish Ethnological Archive, National Museums of Scotland.	400
54	Scything storm-flattened oats, about 1905, on a farm near Culbokie, Easter Ross. Courtesy of the Scottish Ethnological Archive.	400
55	Threshing mills did the rounds in winter in Easter Ross: a steam mill with straw-elevator at work near Conon Bridge, 1905. Courtesy of the Scottish Ethnological Archive.	401
56	Herring-gutters at work in Ullapool, early 1900s. Courtey of the Scottish Ethnological Archive.	401
57	Patriotism was strong: the victorious tug o' war team from the Heights in 1905 and 1906. Courtesy of Dr Newton, Heights of Inchrannie.	409

58	The Countess and her sons Roderick (Rorie) and Walter at the door of Castle Leod, 1916.	410

Three Families: 1.
    The Cromarties.

59	Lord Tarbat's welcome home party in 1928. Courtesy of Alex G Matheson, Delny.	421
60	Family at the celebrations for Lord Tarbat's return from India. Courtesy of Alex G Matheson, Delny.	421

Three Families: 2.
    The Grants, Gamekeepers of Tarbat, Strathpeffer.

61	John Grant, born in 1800, photographed about 1870. Courtesy of I Grant, Blairninich.	422
62	Colin Grant organizing a big shoot on the low ground at Castle Leod. Courtesy of I Grant, Blairninich.	422
63	Ian Grant and the stalkers celebrating bringing in a Royal. Courtesy of I Grant, Blairninich.	423
64	Lord Cromartie presenting long service medals to Estate staff in 1964. Courtesy of I Grant, Blairninich.	423

Three families: 3.
    The MacDonalds, crofters on the Heights of Inchvannie, Strathpeffer.

65	The MacDonald family at the gate of their house on the Heights of Inchvannie. Courtesy of Dr Newton, Heights of Inchvannie.	424
66	The MacDonald family outside their croft house, about 1911. Courtesy of Dr Newton.	425
67	A MacDonald family occasion on the Heights, July 1906. Courtesy of Dr Newton, Heights of Inchvannie.	425
68	Cromartie Estates forestry staff, Castle Leod, 1912.	426

Appendix D: Maps

Cromartyshire	446
Scotland, showing mainland Ross and Cromarty	447
Barony of Tarbat, from Avery's 1727 map. Courtesy of Inverness Museum and Art Gallery	448
Barony of Strathpeffer from Avery's map	449
Coigach, from May's 1755 map	450
Coigach, from May's map	451

THE MACKENZIES OF TARBAT AND CROMARTIE

See Note on the pedigree and titles of the Earls of Cromartie p. 452.

SEAFORTH LINE

John, of Killin, Tenth Chief of Mackenzie b(c) 1482 d1561. Obtained Crown charters for lands of Kintail, Eilean Donan, Castle Leod and Kinnellan, Strathpeffer

Kenneth, Eleventh Chief d1568

Colin 'Cam' 12th Chief d1568

Kenneth, 13th Chief d1611 cr 1st Lord of Kintail

TARBAT LINE

I Sir Rory (Roderick) of Castle Leod, Tarbat and Coigach, 14th Chief d1628 m Margaret MacLeod, Heiress of Lewes

II Sir John d1654 m Margaret Erskine of Innerteil

III Sir George b1632 d1714 Sheriffdom and regality of Cromarty 1684. cr Viscount Tarbat, Lord MacLeod and Castlehaven 1684, cr Earl of Cromartie 1703 m (1) Anne Sinclair d1699 (2) Margaret, Countess of Wemyss d1704

IV John, 2nd Earl b(c) 1660 d1731 m (1) Lady Eliza Gordon (2) Hon Mary Murray (3) Hon Anne Fraser by (2)

V George, 3rd Earl b(c) 1704 d1761 m Isabella Gordon. Attained and estates forfeited 1745

Roderick b(c) 1706

Capt Kenneth (VII)

VI John, Lord MacLeod/MP Major-Gen'l and Count of Sweden. Recovered estates but not title 1784 d1789sp

Isabella (VIII)

VII Capt Kenneth Mackenzie, grandson of 2nd Earl succeeded to estates 1789 d1796sp

VIII Lady Isabella Mackenzie b(c) 1728 d1801 eldest d of 3rd Earl m George, 6th Lord Elibank, succeeded to estates 1796

IX Hon Maria Murray Mackenzie b1763 d1858 m Lord Edward Hay of Newhall, who became Mr Edward Hay-Mackenzie

X John Hay-Mackenzie 'Cromartie' d1849 m Ann Gibson-Craig

XI Anne Hay-Mackenzie d1888 m George Granville William 3rd Duke and 21st Earl of Sutherland. cr Countess of Cromartie, Viscountess of Tarbat, Baroness Castlehaven and Baroness MacLeod of MacLeod all in her own right with reversion to her second surviving son

XII Francis, Earl of Cromartie etc d1893 m Lilian Macdonald

XIII Sibell Lilian Mackenzie, Countess of Cromartie etc b1878 d1962 m 1899 Lt Col Edward Walter Blunt-Mackenzie b1860 d1949

XIV Roderick Grant Francis Mackenzie, Earl of Cromartie etc b1904 m (1) Dorothy Downing Porter (2) Olga Mendoza Stuart Laurance (3) Lilias Janet Garvie MacLeod

John Ruaridh Mackenzie, Viscount Tarbat b1948 m (1) Helen Murray (2) Janet Harley by (2)

Colin Ruaridh b1987

Glossary

Abulziements, garments, attire.
Bere, bear, beer-barley, an earlier variety of barley, with four or six rows of ears. Modern barley has two rows of ears.
Black mail, A payment in return for protection from injury or plunder such as the stealing of cattle.
Boll, a dry measure, amounting for grain to about 6 bushels. The 'Great Boll of Tarbat' was bigger, though its size is not known exactly.
Bowman, a man or tenant in charge of a 'bow' or herd of cattle.
Brog-maker, a maker of brogues or shoes of untanned hide and thongs.
Cart tramms, the shafts of a cart.
Cateran, a Highland marauder, or a gang of them.
Cess, the land or king's tax.
Chalder, a measure of capacity, amounting for grain to 16 *bolls*.
Customs, customary rents and services forming part of the payment for a lease.
Feu, originally feudal tenure of land where the vassal or *feu(a)r* made a return in grain and money in lieu of performing military service; later a heritable holding for which feu duty was paid to a superior.
Firlot, the fourth part of a *Boll*.
Girnel(l), a chest or barrel for storing grain; (2) a specially built warehouse or granary.
Grassum, a sum paid by a tenant or *feu(a)r* on renewal of rent, or, according to a written obligation, at fixed intervals of a number of years.
Kiln, a chamber heated by a fire for drying grain prior to sale or grinding.
Lippie, a quarter of a *Peck*.
Mailer, mealer, a small tenant, paying rent or 'mail'.
Money rent, the proportion of a rent, or the rent, paid in money.
Multure, a proportion of grain or meal paid to the tenant or proprietor of a mill for corn ground in it.
Peck, a quarter of a *Firlot*.
Policy, the park or enclosed grounds of a large house (usually plural).
Port, bearing, deportment.
Rantle, a wooden bar, also in the form *rant*, which seems to be a back-formation.
Rappee, coarse snuff.
Scallag, a farm-labourer, later a 'boy'.
Services, tenant's obligations as part of his lease, e.g. a stated number of days' labour, carriages, etc.
Silver mail, -meal, portion of rent paid in money.

Soum, souming, unit of pasturage that will support a fixed number of beasts; the number of animals that can be supported by a *soum(ing)*.
Tack, lease, tenancy agreement.
Tacksman, a major lease-holder, often with sub-tenants, responsible to the proprietor.
Tenement, land held in tenure and built on; a holding.
Victual rents, parts of rents paid in kind, in grain, milk products, poultry, eggs, etc.
Wadset, a mortgage of property, with a conditional right of redemption by the *wadsetter,* or holder of the mortgage.
Wayne rants, wooden spars forming part of a wain or wheeled vehicle.
Yeald, of an animal, barren or dry.

Abbreviations

C.P.	Cromartie Papers.
D.N.B.	Dictionary of National Biography.
Fraser	Sir William Fraser, *The Earls of Cromartie, Their Kindred, Country and Correspondence* (2 vols, Edinburgh, 1876).
N.L.S.	National Library of Scotland.
N.S.A.	*New Statistical Account of Scotland.*
O.S.A.	*Old Statistical Account of Scotland.*
S.C.	Sutherland Collection D593, Stafford County Record Office.
S.R.O.	Scottish Record Office.
T.G.S.I.	*Transactions of the Gaelic Society of Inverness.*

'I hope the Reader will not take it ill, that for their Diversion I have planted that Void with some Hints and Fragments of history.'
George, first Earl of Cromartie, *c.*1704

Preface

In the history of the Scottish Highlands there are few studies of particular districts or estates to set beside the well-known general outline of that story. There are, it is true, studies of families and clans, of certain economic and military themes, of emigration and famine, and other specific topics. But the main organising unit of social, economic and political life, that is the great estate, has been somewhat neglected. English and Irish estates are better known.

Cromartie is a longtitudinal study of such an estate and of its land, people and owners. The story is about the amassing of territory and political control in the hands of a major branch of the Mackenzie family and is a relatively unusual attempt to find lines of continuity and change over three centuries of estate life. It is about the great continuities in the struggle not only for the control of the land but also in the winning of subsistence and wealth from that land which comprises a well-defined but broken band of country stretching east to west across the northern Highlands. It is about the rise and fall of industries and of populations, and about the varying fortunes of the component strata of estate society. It is about social and political leadership, state and private enterprise, and about economic change which, at different times, provided excellent opportunities for advancement and also withdrew them with little warning. It is a study which is also about the personalities and propensities of the people who governed and managed more than a dozen generations of Highland life. It treats the estate both as a business operation and as a social system, being concerned with the fissures and connections within the estate fabric and the capacity of the estate to respond to severe economic and political change.

In reality many of these questions are, for long stretches of historical time, simply unanswerable. The documentary record is at times utterly silent for decade upon decade. The people of the Cromartie estate often simply do not speak for posterity, some of them remaining unheard even into the present century. Sometimes even the owners of the Cromartie estate are barely visible or audible—for instance there is little surviving personal correspondence for much of the nineteenth century. Sometimes the entire record is very poor, for example, in the decades immediately before the '45 and in the 1820-50 period. The primary documentation for this study is derived essentially from the detritus of the Cromartie estate office over three centuries, supplemented wherever possible by other sources. This, of course, creates its own serious biasses and we have tried to avoid the dangers of writing history simply from the viewpoint of the factor's office window.

The survival of documentation over such a long period is often either random, or eccentric, or skewed in favour of certain sections of society. To present the Cromartie story as 'the Highland experience' is, therefore, both inaccurate and immodest. Nevertheless it is a proper ambition and the sorts of evidence we use take us further in this direction than is possible in broader-gauge studies. Here, at least, it is possible to trace the emergence of what one nineteenth century laird described as 'the small people' into the surviving historical record. The common Highlander was invisible in 1600, a blurred image in 1700, a clearer silhouette in 1800, and a fully three-dimensional actor in the process of social revolution by 1900.

Consequently the story as presented here seeks out the material foundations of life, the organising principles of social, economic and political existence, and the manner in which the Cromartie estate supported its landlord and its people. In following these questions we have encountered, inevitably, the great historical passages of Highland life: the long evolution of landownership, the slow ending of 'feudalism', the relations between Highlands and Lowlands, the Jacobite uprisings, the intervention of the Hanoverian government and the intrusion of classical political economy, the invasion of southern and colonial capital, the impact of agrarian transformation and the clearances, and finally the emergence and politicisation of the crofting community in the 1880s. All this runs parallel with the story of aristocratic finances and, more exotically, the development of a medico-tourist resort at Strathpeffer in the midst of a resolutely Highland environment.

Nomenclature poses some problems in this study. In a formal sense the Cromartie estate did not exist as a single unit until the creation of the Sheriffdom in 1686. For purposes of simplicity and clarity we refer to the three constituent baronies—Coigach, Tarbat and Strathpeffer—as 'Cromartie' throughout even though, until 1686, they were owned by the first Earl of Cromartie's predecessors, the Mackenzie Lairds of Tarbat. Similarly there is confusion in the spelling of Cromartie, in previous centuries often spelled Cromertie or Cromarty. We have adopted the modern spelling almost everywhere.

When this study began the main corpus of documents, the Cromartie Papers, was located at Castle Leod near Strathpeffer, and in the loft of the old stables at the former factor's residence at Nutwood, nearby. The present Earl of Cromartie, himself a productive and critical historian, has since deposited this material in the Scottish Record Office.[1] In the meantime one of the authors has also migrated, like some of the people of the study itself, to Australia. We are extremely grateful to the Earl and his family not only for access to his large and rich collection of papers, but also for their patience, encouragement and lively conversation at Strathpeffer.

We are keenly conscious of another historian who also worked in the muniments at Castle Leod. A hundred years and more ago Sir William Fraser edited two large and sumptuous volumes called *The Earls of Cromartie*. They provide a valuable and meticulous anthology of documents from the collection and they have undoubtedly eased our own passage into the story. Fraser was the doyen of Victorian family historians serving the aristocracy, and his work is well acknowledged. But his purposes were primarily genealogical and antiquarian. Fraser's splendid volumes contain scarcely a breath of reference to the people of the Cromartie estate. Even where he discusses economic matters Fraser confines himself exclusively to the financial problems of the family to which his researches were devoted. Our new book, while benefitting from his, is entirely different in scope and intent.

We have received help not only in Strathpeffer but also from the staff of the National Library of Scotland, the Scottish Record Office, the County Record Office in Stafford, the County Library of Ross and Cromarty and the Museums in Inverness and Dingwall; from Mr G.D. Finlayson of the North of Scotland Hydro-Electric Board, and from Mr Roderick Richard who now lives in Nairn. The Flinders University of South Australia has supported a period of study leave in Strathpeffer in the sharp winter months of 1975, and the Australian Research Grants Committee has also promoted this research. We also wish to thank Mr Hugh Campbell in Tasmania, Mrs Jane Durham in Easter Ross, Miss Anne Riches, Principal Inspector, Historic Buildings, Scotland and Mr James Miller, Inverness for information and Mrs Joan Hancock and Ms Robin Haines for expert research assistance. Mrs Joan Stephenson processed every word in this book and, not unreasonably, looked for revelations in the Epilogue; and Mrs Isobel Miller typed all Monica Clough's work. For photographs and much useful information we have to thank Dr Paddy Newton, daughter of Colin Macdonald, Heights of Inchvannie; Mr Ian Grant, Blairninich; Mr Alex G. Matheson, Delny, and Mrs Sparks, Strathpeffer. Other illustrations are the property of the Cromartie Estates and we reiterate our sense of gratitude. We also thank our families for their patience and encouragement over a long period.

In terms of responsibility for this volume, we started out with formal plans: the earliest period covered, from about 1650 to about the return of the estates from the long Annexation to the Crown in 1784, was to be Monica Clough's section. From the late eighteenth century to the outbreak of the Great War was to be Eric Richards' field. In fact we found that the overlapping and interweaving of the estates' histories was a good deal more complex. We have both researched, criticised one another and colluded over the whole period covered. The final draft, in the interests of unity of style and a certain antipodean distancing, has been the work of Eric Richards.

If it were possible this book should give off the confusing aromas of peat smoke, salt fish, the gun-room, human sweat, smallpox, sheep grease, sulphuretted hydrogen, whisky, mountain air, and cattle dung. Sadly such evocative fragrances must be filtered through words, some of which have been dried out in pigeon lofts and archives for too many decades. The odours of history are easily lost. This book derives from a world which must have reeked of such smells. If *Cromartie* conjures up some of those realities of the Highland past one of its main purposes will have been fulfilled.

Eric Richards,
Brighton,
South Australia.

Monica Clough,
Drumnadrochit,
Inverness.

PART ONE

The Making of Cromartie and the Road to Disaster 1650–1745

CHAPTER 1

The Triumphing Sword of the Mackenzies and the Origins of the Cromartie Estate

I

Before industrialisation most people in the British Isles lived in the shadow, even under the protection, of large landowners. The ownership and control of the land was a central influence upon the social and political structure, the source of political cohesion and, equally, of antagonism and rivalry. Social relations and economic security were shaped, to a large degree, by the traditions of landownership, the values embodied in the dominance of hereditary proprietorship over the densely-layered rurality beneath. Great estates evolved in all parts of the British archipelago. In the Scottish Highlands the forging of stable landownership was part and parcel of the imposition of primitive order upon a notably anarchic territory. By 1600 the kaleidoscope of Highland landownership seems to have settled, at least temporarily, into some identifiable patterns of firm control. One of the emergent estates with claims to territorial dominance was that of Cromartie, held by a particularly vigorous branch of the Mackenzies.

There can be no question that the accumulation and survival of great landed estates is one of the critical themes of British history in the last thousand years. In the Scottish Highlands the dominance of proprietorship—of chieftainship itself—has been legendary. Most of Highland history is written in terms of the greatness of its landowners and the solidarity of its clans. So powerful has been this tradition that many of the people of the estates, the clansmen and others, have only recently struggled from beneath the historiographical burden to emerge in their own right. Nor do we fully understand the extent to which the Highlands differed from the rest of the British Isles. We tend to believe that there was a different civilisation in the north, based upon the clan and its masters. We tend to think also that only in the late eighteenth century, after Culloden, did the Highlands merge fully into the wider and overwhelming homogeneity of the British system of landownership and economic society. On all these issues there is scope for debate, and Cromartie is a test of such propositions. Here indeed was one of the more remote zones of estate control, geographically far from the main currents of national life.

In the Scottish Highlands, as far as is known, the control of the land and its wealth has practically always rested in the hands of great landed magnates, aristocratic or otherwise. Primitive communalism has occupied little role in this society. No doubt there has been a changing hierarchy of owners—a minority of vast territorial empires, more medium and smaller accumulations, and some tiny independences. By force, by diplomacy, by marriage, by luck, certain families came to control, own and govern large agglomerations of land. Often the fortunes of these families described an arc, rising to power and distinction and then collapsing or subsiding when, perhaps, they lost favour, or produced too many dependents, or else ran out of luck. The Mackenzies of the Cromartie Estate conformed to this rough recurrent pattern over the centuries 1550 to 1850.

II

The Mackenzies of Tarbat and Cromartie were part of the greater family of kinship dominated by Mackenzie of Kintail, the Seaforth connection, itself one of the greatest landowners in the Highlands.[1] The cadet branch developed a strength of its own, and achieved its greatest prominence in Scottish affairs, culminating in the Cromartie Earldom, in the years 1650-1714. In the subsequent decades, soon after the death of the first Earl in 1714, the family was wracked by financial and political problems. These culminated in ruin and humiliation. The family was virtually destroyed by the Jacobite debacle after Culloden in 1746. Stripped of its estates and title, the family languished almost to extinction in the mid-eighteenth century.

The road to recovery was tortuous and painful; its ultimate achievement was close to heroic. First the reputation of the family was rescued by extraordinary public service to the Hanoverian monarchy, through the raising of a regiment of Foot, and then the estates were recovered and with them some of the family pride. By the end of the eighteenth century the Cromartie line was back in power as a substantial estate owner in Ross and Cromarty—as a landowner with political influence once more, building a fine new residence and possessing again the moral and economic authority to raise a regiment. Once again a senior branch of the Mackenzies was in a position to maintain a decent enough port and to exert a substantial influence in the district. Their financial underpinnings remained precarious as their living standards rose, but this was not unusual among their caste.

More glamour, and a life-saving injection of capital, was achieved when, out of the blue in 1849, the daughter and only child of the family contracted to marry the heir to perhaps the greatest aristocratic fortune in Britain. This timely alliance with the House of Sutherland brought a glittering future to the Cromartie estates, and the aspect of life changed radically in half a generation. For three decades the Cromartie estates became a satellite of the vast Sutherland empire and in many ways benefitted from its capital investment and modern management.

The impact of the Sutherland alliance, nevertheless, was relatively brief. By the end of the nineteenth century the Cromartie estate resumed a more modest aspect, and essentially withdrew into more constrained circumstances. By the early twentieth century Cromartie, in company with most other purely agricultural estates, was unable to counter the impact of redistributive legislation. There followed, in each generation, the almost inevitable erosion of the territorial base of the Earldom. Its influence was

1   The Triumphing Sword: carried by the Third Earl for Prince Charles Edward in 1745.

diminished in every respect. Where once it possessed land and power without a title, in the twentieth century it found itself with a title and not much else to sustain its older role and position.

III

The arc of the Cromarties' fortunes extended over the everyday life of Highland communities which were subject to longer and deeper influences than the familial vicissitudes of their successive landlords. The sound, the smell, the feel of life were realities of a different level, barely observed in the documents of the day. Nevertheless the longitudinal line of ownership helped to give continuity to social and economic relations for, possibly, twenty-five generations of landlords and their people.

At no time was the Cromartie estate in the top rank of Highland or Scottish estates, but it was well beyond the average in both extent and income. In reality the estate was a decidedly odd aggregation of property, a curious scattering of fragments of land of highly variable value and quality, east to west across the land mass of the northern Highlands. In the nineteenth century the Cromartie estate amounted to about 200,000 acres. The diversity of its location and condition made it a useful cross section of a region itself as remarkable for its geographical variety as for its unity.

The estate of Cromartie was for a century and a half, effectively coterminous with the county of Cromartyshire, a legislative construct well known as an anomalous and inefficient arrangement. It was highly unusual for an estate to be fashioned into a county to suit the ambitions of a proprietor. It was essentially a measure of the political ascendancy of the family in Scottish affairs between 1685 and 1703 when the first Earl obtained by Act of Parliament 'the privilege of having his various estates, large and small, throughout Ross, erected into a new county of Cromarty, consisting of fourteen detached pieces.' This peculiar fantasy was maintained until demolished by the Building Commissioners in 1891.[2] The county and estate of Cromarty was essentially a set of fragments in the fabric of the parent county of Ross.

Altogether an odd geography, the fourteen bits of Cromartie appear to have begun with an original ownership of Mackenzie lands in Strathpeffer and in the Easter Ross parish of Tarbat. In the seventeenth century, during the rise of the Mackenzies of Tarbat and Cromarty, the estate grew rapidly, that is, augmented by the addition of diverse parcels of land stretching from the Summer Isles in the west to the untamed fastnesses of Fannich and Ben Wyvis in the centre of the northern Highlands, across to Tarbat in the east.

The accumulation of lands reached nearly its maximum point in about 1626: this territory, despite its untidy geography, then remained the core of the Cromartie estate for the next four centuries, with the addition of Cromarty itself in 1684. By 1626 the basic form of the estate had been established. It was, in essence, three considerable Baronies: Strathpeffer, Easter Aird (later New Tarbat) and Coigach. The forging of the estate had been a tortuous process, itself a good reflection of Highland history. The estate evolved out of a wider Mackenzie empire of the fourteenth and fifteenth centuries. One of the starting points appears to have been the granting of a charter, in 1463, for some of the lands of Castle Leod. Rebuilt in 1606-16, Castle Leod was the main residence and administrative centre of the tripartite estates for much of the succeeding centuries.

Of the baronies the most easterly was Easter Aird, dominated in the early seventeenth century by the castle of Ballone and extending to the fertile though rocky peninsula of Tarbat. Here were the small harbours of Castlehaven and Portmahomack and some good fertile farms (Wilkhaven, Tarrell and Arball). More land was acquired (from Sir Robert Dunbar) and a new residence built—facing the sands of Nigg to the port of Cromarty and with good access to the sheltered waters of the Cromarty Firth. Then were good farms—Blackhall, Priesthill, Meddatt and more—added, together with the planted village of Milton. A marriage in 1654 produced as a dowry the adjacent Abbey lands of Fearn. These properties, together, became the most prosperous and lucrative part of the estate, fine grain-growing lands typical of the favoured portions of Easter Ross. They were amalgamated into one Barony: New Tarbat. It supported a large residence in the late seventeenth century, and a new but less ambitious edifice, Tarbat House, in 1785.

The second Barony of the Cromartie Estate was Strathpeffer, a marvellous and beautiful alliance of severe Highland terrain and lush lowland pastures. Here were excellent corn lands full of potential for improvement which rapidly merged into highland grazing and wild country. Strathpeffer itself was a low lying, poorly drained valley which led towards the inconsiderable town of Dingwall. The valley possessed broad arable acres and supported a relatively numerous tenantry administered from Castle Leod, a well-fortified landmark in the region. It was surrounded by other castles and landed houses and set in what was frequently regarded as 'the fairest district of the Highlands'.[3] The Peffer burn ran sluggishly through the Town Moss of Dingwall before joining the sea. Behind the strath was Ben Wyvis which dominates the northern skies and provided important grazing to the communities of the valleys. There were a number of remote and difficult routes to the west through the passes about Wyvis. The main route ran through Garve: but east-west traffic was always difficult and the tripartite division of the Cromartie estate was reinforced by the mountain terrain that separated the parts. There was no wheeled transport to the west until 1790.

The third barony was Coigach in Wester Ross, divided by mountains from Strathpeffer, and itself characteristically West Highland: remote, rocky and mainly inaccessible. Coigach had changed hands with the changing fortunes of Highland nobility through the Middle Ages, belonging in turn to Macleod, Mackay of Strathnaver, the Earl of Ross and again to Macleod of Lewes. It was disputed territory until the early seventeenth century; the claims of the Macleods and the Mackenzies for both Coigach and Lewis remained unsettled until a key marriage resolved the issue (and, indeed, the armed conflict) and Coigach became the westernmost extremity of the Mackenzie estates. The formal contract for the wedding of Sir Rorie Mackenzie with Margaret Macleod was made in Dingwall in May 1605, and the Coigach Charter was confirmed by the Crown in 1609 and was then held in the family for the next four centuries. Coigach was totally different in character from the fat corn lands of Tarbat or from the moderate prosperity of Strathpeffer. It was mainly grazing country and the people of Coigach ran stock—cattle, sheep and goats; they bred horses, and wove and fished. The district never grew enough grain for its own requirements, and until the middle of the eighteenth century there was no corn mill anywhere in Coigach. The landlord never maintained a family mansion house in Coigach: on rare visits he would be accommodated by the local manager, the main tacksman. Coigach was an entirely Gaelic-speaking area, and its customs and way of life were little touched by events in the rest of Scotland. Its natural focus was westwards and its connections were maritime. Stornoway was the nearest centre of administration, and Lochbroom provided a remarkable harbour for future development. Ben Mhor Coigach rose directly from the shores of Loch Broom, a bare rocky peak with pockets of good grazing on its shoulders. In the seventeenth century the whole interior was covered by a thick forest of oak and native Scots pine.

The Tarbat estate—the three baronies of New Tarbat, Strathpeffer and Coigach—was welded into a stable unit by 1626 but did not become 'Cromartie' until 1684. Its boundaries thereafter changed relatively little,[4] though the acquisition of the head port and sheriffdom of Cromarty and later earldom much enhanced its status. An administrative unity had been established, forming a settled framework for generations of tenants, and also the basis for the upward status and political mobility of its owners, the Mackenzies. The estate had achieved this stability by service to the Crown, by astute and timely marriages, and by sheer tenacity in a region repeatedly unsettled by internecine conflict.

IV

Credit for the accumulation and stabilisation of the Cromartie estate is usually attributed to Sir Rorie Mackenzie who was born about 1579: a vigorous, influential and strong-armed character who established the foundations of a new dynasty partly by subduing rivals of the Crown in the western Highlands and Islands. It was, in Scotland, an age still 'bedevilled by long and recurrent royal minorities', plagued, especially in the Highlands, 'by a baronage of unexcelled rapacity and unreliability'.[5] Little is known of Sir Rorie. When the Victorian antiquarian, Sir William Fraser, searched the Cromartie Charter Chest he had to report:

> there is not a single scrap of writing of the famous Sir Rorie Mackenzie who was the founder of the Cromartie Family. He has the reputation of having been a great warrior, and I have thought that he was probably so much occupied with subduing the wild men of Lewes that he had little time for writing.[6]

It was a reputation confirmed in 1739 when Lord Lovat visited the Earl of Cromartie, bringing with him what he described as 'the triumphing sword of your great and worthy ancestor, and, my great grand uncle, Sir Rory, tutor of Kintail'.[7]

Rorie Mackenzie was the second son of the Chief of the Kintail Mackenzies, who later became the Earls of Seaforth. He inherited in his own right the lands of Castle Leod in Fodderty parish which gave him a base in the eastern Highlands. Then, in 1605, he married Margaret Macleod, heiress of Torquil Macleod of the Lewis. She was a woman of considerable fortune and brought to the marriage the lands of Coigach. The alliance was equally significant in another respect because it brought to an end the armed

2 Sir Rorie Mackenzie of Tarbat.

conflict in the west between branches of the Mackenzies and the Macleods. Mackenzie and his brother were now considerable magnates in the west: on the death of his elder brother Mackenzie became Tutor of Kintail during the minority of his brother's heir, Colin, the clan chief. It was a position of immense authority and responsibility in Lewis and elsewhere on the west coast. Mackenzie was engaged in the brutal pacification of Lewis and adjacent areas on behalf of his nephew. He also worked for the Crown: by sword and fire he subdued Mull, Morvern and Tiree. These were notable services: they suppressed much of the dynastic rivalry of the warring factions in the west and allowed the Stuarts to extend their effective suzeraignty in the region. In effect Mackenzie was an instrument in the Royal campaign to bring the Highlands into the polity of Scotland. It gave Mackenzie further ambitions to claim leadership of the Macleods of Lewis and even the Lordship of the Isles.

These events, which saw the transfer of lands from the Macleods of Lewis to the Mackenzies, have been described as

> one of the most pitiful [stories] in Highland history. As soon as the Mackenzies obtained the island [of Lewis], they promptly restored order; the remaining members of the Macleod family were murdered or driven out under the commission of fire and sword.

Mackenzie was 'terrible and ruthless', and a Gaelic proverb says that 'there are two things worse than the Tutor of Kintail, frost in spring and mist in the dog-days'.[8]

Rorie Mackenzie was rewarded with title and lands by James VI. In 1619 he was given a knighthood. In addition he acquired lands in many places—in Inverness-shire, at Torresay, the island of Barra, East Aird, Easter Tarbat, Downilarne and Meikle Tarbat. Some of these were connected into the Barony of New Tarbat in 1623. Within a generation Sir Rorie Mackenzie had created a substantial estate and a position of political prominence. In 1606 he rebuilt Castle Leod to match his status: nearly four hundred years later this building was described as 'the best-preserved specimen of the dwellings of our Highland territorial families'.[9] Mackenzie's career also cemented the allegiance of his family to the Stuart monarchy, a relationship recognised in many ways: most important, Mackenzie had achieved official and legal recognition in Edinburgh for his control of the remote west coast. In every generation from the time of the Tutor leading members of the Mackenzies were to be found holding high office under the crown in the judiciary of Scotland. Their rights to land were fixed in charters and the Mackenzie hegemony was fully established by the beginning of the seventeenth century—in lands and castles describing a wide sweep from Tarbatness to the Black Isle and back through Ross to Kintail, Gairloch, Applecross and Lochbroom. The greatest holding of the fourteen great Mackenzie castellans was that of the Earl of Seaforth, but Sir Rorie Mackenzie had carved a fine territorial base in his own right and was second in rank to Seaforth himself. Thus emerged, by sword and marriage, one of the key apparatchiks of Stuart control in the Highlands.

V

On his death in 1626 Sir Rorie was succeeded by his under-age son, Sir John Mackenzie of Tarbat. Sir John sat in Parliament for Inverness-shire from 1628 to 1633 and in 1639-40. He was made a Knight Baronet of Nova Scotia in 1628 and received a grant of 16,000 acres in the colony. His many children ultimately created a network of marital connections with influential Scottish families, and links into both Court and Parliament during the subsequent half century. His daughters, for instance, married respectively the Earl of Seaforth, Alexander Mackenzie of Gareloch, Lord Lovat and Sir Colin

Campbell of Aberuchil. It was said that Sir John Mackenzie 'excelled in the polite Arts, and was accounted one of the most accomplished Gentlemen of his Age'. But he held a 'mistaken loyalty' to Charles I. He became heavily involved in the Civil War: first as a Covenanter and a ruling Elder in the Presbytery of Tain, and as a vigorous debater and—in the Glasgow Assembly of 1648—critic of the 'Divine Rights' of kings. Like many of his class he experienced difficulty in maintaining a straightforward allegiance, particularly when the Kirk party appeared to threaten the very principle of monarchy. In 1648 Mackenzie made a break from the Estates; he ceased to be M.P. for Inverness-shire and became unambiguously allied to the Royal cause. By the end of 1650 Mackenzie and his eighteen year old son George both held commissions from Charles II as colonels of foot.[10] By then, of course, Mackenzie had completed a total reversal of his original position *vis à vis* the monarchy. There were local factors which reinforced the decision but Mackenzie had moved in sympathy with many of the northern nobility who had turned against the grim Covenanting ministers by 1650. By aligning themselves with the Stuarts, Mackenzie and son followed a course exactly replicated 95 years later by his Jacobite descendant and his equally young son.

Mackenzie paid heavily for his allegiance to the Crown. The new Parliament of 1649 passed an Act which imposed a series of fines and other onerous financial obligations on several families: among them were those placed on the estates of Sir John Mackenzie. The amounts extracted by the government rose sharply, especially after Glencairn's Rising, and much of the cost was shouldered by the various Mackenzie estates. These were substantial (but unquantified) burdens which created problems of liquidity and capital preservation for Sir John Mackenzie's estates. For a generation there were severe difficulties, and the ensuing accumulations of debt almost caused the extinction of the estate. This was not all. In pursuit of such debts, it seems, Cromwell caused Mackenzie (and others) to be incarcerated in prison in his new citadel of Inverness in 1654. The imprisonment was brief: in September of 1655 Sir John Mackenzie was dead, after a short illness, in his castle at Ballone in the East Aird of Tarbat.

The position of the Cromartie estate in 1655 therefore was not favourable. Debt hung about its neck; the family's allegiance to the Stuarts, once the source of its rapid ascendancy in the Highlands, now disqualified it from the centres of power; the son and heir was still a youth of 25, and now undeniably glued to the apparently lost cause of the Stuarts. It seemed to indicate the rise and fall of a Highland family in two generations. It also seemed to demonstrate the primacy of politics in the fate of the Mackenzies. Meanwhile, however, the life of the people and society of the landed estates remained, in essence, unrecorded. For them the great volumes of Cromartie documents compiled by Sir William Fraser in 1876 are totally mute.

CHAPTER 2

Winning an Earldom

I

In the mid 1650s, the heir to the Tarbat estates was gripped firmly in the jaws of financial ruin and political humiliation. Sir George Mackenzie of Tarbat, the new laird, was totally embroiled in the Civil Wars. He, like his father, had tied his colours to the Royalist mast. In 1654 he found himself totally identified with the wrong side at the wrong time. He was forced to flee the country.

Within relatively few years, Mackenzie was able to resurrect the fortunes of his family. He eventually acquired a bagful of titles (including a viscountcy in 1685, an earldom in 1703, and a sherriffdom also) and ultimately occupied a place in Scottish affairs which enabled him to influence the future of the nation. It was a great exercise in political survival and ascendancy; it was, of course, a story which ran parallel with the fate of the Stuarts. Indeed, in the first instance, Mackenzie's recovery depended entirely upon the restoration of the Royal House. The Earldom would be the eventual reward for loyalty. Subsequently, after the second fall of the Stuarts, Mackenzie shifted towards a more pragmatic and flexible perception of political realities. His descendants in the eighteenth century however returned to the most catastrophic variety of Jacobitism. Consequently a full revolution in the family affairs was turned within one hundred years.

II

The fugitive heir in 1655 was Sir George Mackenzie of Tarbat. Born in 1630[1] he was educated at St. Andrews and King's College, Aberdeen from whence he graduated in 1646. In 1655 on the death of his father he inherited lands in Inverness, Ross, Elgin and Fife, and in 1662 he inherited further land from his grandmother in the barony of Duart in Argyllshire.[2] The core of his wealth, however, was the three baronies of his father in Ross-shire.

Mackenzie was described as 'an excellent scholar, and cultivated both literature and science' and, as his later career demonstrated, he was easily the most urbane and gifted of all the Cromarties. However, it is also clear that 'politics absorbed his chief interests'.

3 George Mackenzie of Tarbat, First Earl of Cromartie.

While little more than a youth he became 'a passionate courtier' and committed himself to the cause of Charles II. His political life, for the next half century, was a set of complex variations on the theme of loyalty to the Stuarts. Mackenzie and his cousin were at one stage described as 'furious Cavaliers' and Mackenzie was praised for his 'unfaltering loyalty to the king'. His faith was perhaps more malleable; he opposed the extreme Presbyterian forms of church government but remained a staunch episcopalian. Like many of his caste his monarchist principles were at ease in a regime of bishops and the *Book of Common Prayer* but was severely embarrassed by the fear of Catholicism and by the excesses of the Presbyterian zealots.

The year 1653 was fateful for Mackenzie. Clan chiefs in the north of Scotland were in touch with Charles II in Europe. They promised to rise in his support on the assumption that they could gain foreign supplies of arms and money. This was the making of the Glencairn Rising—itself the prototype of all subsequent Jacobite risings during the next ninety years. The same clans were involved, the same internal feuds subverted the campaign, and the same lack of support from the Stuart contingent abroad was central in the ultimate defeat of the clans. Even more critical, however, was the fact that, for the first time in Scottish history, the central Commonwealth government possessed a large army in the form of the efficient New Model.[3] This was the indispensable requirement for the imposition of law and order in the Highlands. Consequently the Glencairn Rising was a watershed in the history of the north, a decisive moment in the spread of central authority. Mackenzie, whose grandfather had been instrumental in assisting the process in the western isles, now played a central part in the Stuart resistance.

Glencairn's Rising, in the event, assumed some of the forms of a guerrilla war in which small bodies of armed men were supported tacitly by a large proportion of the population of central and lowland Scotland. It had begun in 1652 when Charles II sent a secret agent to instigate active support. Seaforth held a meeting at Glenelg to muster forces: the Stuarts were hoping to take advantage of the outbreak of Anglo-Dutch hostilities and to create danger in the north. Charles appointed General Middleton, a landed aristocrat and soldier who had also changed sides in the conflict, to command the Highland host. But first Middleton was ordered to raise supplies in Europe, and his appearance in the Highlands was much delayed.

Meanwhile William Cunningham, ninth Earl of Glencairn initiated a series of guerrilla strikes, some with marked success. Lightning raids were carried as far south as Galloway and Carlisle. They even defied the Commonwealth and raised cess or tax from most of the north. Middleton eventually arrived in Scotland at the end of February 1653. He landed at Tarbatness in the barony of New Tarbat which indeed belonged to the northern estate of Sir George Mackenzie. His intention was to march westwards, towards Assynt in north.west Sutherland, following friendly Mackenzie territory throughout. Glencairn was constrained to place his own successful troops under Middleton's command at Dornoch. Immediately there were further rifts in the leadership and they were insufficiently prepared to meet the might of Cromwell's northern forces.

They met their defeat, at the hands of Monck in the pass of Dalnaspidal in 1654 and the cause of Charles II in the Highlands was rapidly neutralised. Seaforth treated, in effect, for a surrender at Inverness to Colonel Monck. Nevertheless the Rising had demonstrated the potential for Highland resistance, and Cromwell met the challenge with a combination of force and diplomacy. Conciliation of the nobles and gentry came in the form of the Act of Pardon and Grace of 1654. Suppression was achieved by a series of forts built at key locations in the Highlands. Moreover Cromwell made the chiefs 'stand surety for their clans and their neighbours'.[4] Seaforth and his followers had to find £6000 sterling to guarantee his clan's peaceable behaviour; the castle of Eilan Donan was surrendered, and the arms were given up at Inverness within 20 days of the treaty.

Defeat was attended by some concessions to local realities. Although the private armies were required to disband, the chiefs were nevertheless allowed to carry arms 'for their own defence against broken men and thieves within their own bounds'. Favourable arrangements were made for certain estates which had suffered devastation, 'which are all burnt or destroyed', in the Rising. This included Lochbroom and suggests that the local consequences in Coigach were probably severe.[5] Though the financial impositions on the rebellious Highland estates were onerous, they fell short of full retribution. Monck's policy suggests an ambivalence—between subjugation and conciliation—which may have encouraged the recurrent lapses into rebellion which dislocated Highland life until their final suppression in 1746.

The role of Sir George Mackenzie in the Glencairn Rising and its aftermath is not entirely clear. He was described as 'the chief confidant and tool' of Middleton—as though he were in some sense manipulated into rebellion. He apparently raised a contributory force to the Rising and 'was forced into an honourable capitulation' at Lochgaw. He escaped in a party that included Lord Balcarres and Sir Robert Moray. First they went to Eilan Donan, and then all three began a long journey round the western isles during which Mackenzie developed his observations in Natural Philosophy (to become the basis of his later contributions to the Royal Society). Mackenzie's movements between the end of 1655 and the Restoration of 1660 are obscure. He was on the continent for some of the time, met Charles II, and it is possible that he studied at one of the protestant universities; he also practised law in Edinburgh. More particularly he cultivated good relations with Protectorate officials in the north and his liaisons with the clans were soon valued: his connections between the country and the capital, and with the Royal court itself, would be important in his future political ascent.

III

Mackenzie was a man well known for his charm and address; he obviously possessed a considerable measure of personal charisma. He had been extravagantly loyal to the Stuarts and knew Charles II personally. These advantages were rewarded in the Restoration in 1660: Mackenzie's star rose with the Stuarts. For the following fifty years his political loyalties shifted from decade to difficult decade. He kept his footing and became one of the most influential men in Scotland: he also developed a reputation for opportunism and changeability which spoke either of deviousness or sophisticated political judgement, or both.

On the return of Charles II in 1660 the affairs of Scotland remained unclarified for some time. The Restoration was generally welcomed by Scotland and when the arrangement of the country was settled the royalists did well. Mackenzie was among them. Lord Lauderdale, a presbyterian and an 'engager' (one who had agreed to support the crown on condition that Presbyterian Church government was imposed), became Secretary of State for Scotland. Middleton was given an Earldom and made King's commissioner for Parliament. Glencairn himself became Lord Chancellor. The Scottish Kirk was given an episcopalian form, with bishops chosen by the king. George Mackenzie attached himself to Middleton and in 1661 was made Lord of Session with the courtesy title Lord Tarbat. He was also elected member of the Estates of Ross-shire. Already his talents at the political centre were noted: he was regarded as 'one of the most extraordinary men that Scotland had produced'.[6] Tarbat was well placed to scale the heights of Scottish political life.

The trouble was that he had connected himself with Middleton who was clearly bent on ousting Lauderdale who was unpopular with the most zealous Cavaliers. Some said that Tarbat was merely Middleton's cat's-paw, and Tarbat claimed subsequently that he simply carried out his instructions. Tarbat was involved in complex negotiations between Holyrood and London in 1661 and again in 1664, concerning office-holding in Scotland and the authority of both Crown and Parliament. There was no doubt that Middleton (through Tarbat's instrumentality) was conspiring to eliminate Lauderdale from the Government—most notably and transparently with the so-called Billeting Act in 1662, a convoluted attempt to disqualify Lauderdale from office. The entire exercise backfired: the King was furious and Lauderdale was reinforced in his authority. Middleton was effectively banished to Tangier. Tarbat was also humiliated and in 1664, after his defence was heard, he was stripped of the 'public trusts he did enjoy in that our kingdom'. He lost his place in the College of Justice.[7]

Tarbat, therefore, began his public career in disaster. He held no public offices for the next ten years; nevertheless he continued to sit in the Scottish Parliament as member for Ross. It may have been a time too for the repair of his finances which were certainly stretched by the costs of his political careerism in Holyrood. He remained active in committees and began to develop a reputation for a specialist political knowledge of Highland affairs. His correspondence of 1665, for example, shows him offering intelligence on the suppression of robbery and lawlessness in the Highlands. He advocated that the Earls of Moray and of Seaforth—two great men of the north—should be made lieutenants of the 'broken Highlands', that is the anarchic area. The chiefs and landlords would then be directly responsible to the lieutenants—thereby creating a practical line of command and a communication with Edinburgh and London. It was good advice but less effective because he was still a man in political disgrace.

The history of the people of the Cromartie estates hardly begins even to emerge until after the period of the Restoration. Whether these generations of dependents were protected, subdued, fathered, terrorised, or neglected, by the Mackenzie family, is practically unknown. Mostly the record is silent. The people of the Highlands until about 1650 are no better documented than, say, African peoples of the same period: their history depends mainly on genealogical recollection handed down through each generation.

4 Castle Leod.

IV

During the eight years of his political eclipse, from 1664 to the end of 1672, there is meagre direct information about Mackenzie of Tarbat or his estates. In those years he concentrated on his estate affairs and lived mainly in the north: consequently there was little correspondence with his chamberlain (this being a disadvantage of resident landowners, for historians). But he still practised some law in Edinburgh and continued to sit in parliament as member for Ross: his legal work may have aided the finances of the northern estates but was never enough to make any large impact on the problems created by his political and economic ventures. In 1672 Tarbat was still only 40 years of age, a veteran of the Civil Wars, a beneficiary of the Stuart Restoration, but his career had been tarnished and almost broken by his association with the defeated and vanquished Middleton. For all his charm and connections, and luminous intelligence[8], he had so far made little enough impact on national affairs.

In that year, 1672, Tarbat seems to have decided to live in Edinburgh[9] and to return to the politics of the nation's capital. His rehabilitation was smoothed by James Sharp, Archbishop of St. Andrews who had repeatedly spoken on his behalf to the Duke and Duchess of Lauderdale at Ham House. Sharp recognised in Tarbat a sincere and able ally on the side of episcopacy: the bishops certainly needed allies in Scotland. But in parliament Tarbat continued to identify with the complicated opposition to Lauderdale's hegemony in Scottish affairs. He needed to bide his time for any larger preferment.

Full restitution was achieved at the end of 1678. Tarbat was restored to Royal favour. The King wrote a long letter of pardon. It began by recapitulating Tarbat's original error and the reasons for his dismissal from office. The King then delivered his resolution:

> But now, considering how before that, and even in the worst of times he had on all occasions evidenced an entire loyalty and fidelity to us, and that since he hath not only showed a dutiful acquiescence to our will and his grief for the wrong he had committed in that affair [i.e. the Billeting Act with Middleton] but also that he hath laid hold on all fit opportunities to demonstrate his contact duty and loyalty to us and affection to our Minister [Lauderdale] whom he hath injured.[10]

How exactly Tarbat had demonstrated his reformed character and proper loyalty is not known. A good word from the bishop probably helped, and also the influence of his cousin, Mackenzie of Rosehaugh, who had been made Advocate General a year earlier.

The royal pardon, handsomely expressed, was the signal for the rapid blossoming of Tarbat's career. Within a month he was appointed Lord Justice General of Scotland (in October 1678) to which was attached a pension of £200: it made him second in the ranks of the Scottish law lords. After another month Tarbat was admitted and sworn in to the Privy Court. He was now remarkably well placed in the affairs of Scotland: set for a continuous career in politics in both Edinburgh and Whitehall. Indeed he would be in public office for most of the remainder of his long life. It was a commitment which took him away not only from his Ross-shire estates, but also from local politics which were repeatedly dislocated by religious conflict.

At the time of the King's pardon, Tarbat received a letter from his young nephew,

Seaforth, from the Mackenzie stronghold, Brahan Castle. It predicted a rapid advance for Tarbat and also contained a suggestion of envy about his elevation. He wrote 'I have not much to say but to congratulate the kindness you have from the Duke of Lauderdale. I know your merit will bring you to preferment and if you get any title of honour, I hope will not interfere with me.'

Tarbat's ascent accelerated with the demise of Lauderdale who, old and ill in 1680, was urged out of office. The administration of the King's business in Scotland passed to James, Duke of York, to the Earl of Moray and eventually to Tarbat himself. James, of whom most people suspected the worst, was banished to Edinburgh. It was an exile from London where his overt Catholicism had created a storm. In Edinburgh James set about the revival of the court of Holyrood which had stood empty and neglected since the start of the century. He revived the nobility of Scotland and attempted to rejuvenate both Cavalier and episcopalian fortunes. He even thought he could revitalise the Catholic Church in Scotland. He generated great antagonism and unpopularity yet, for the while, survived various efforts to exclude him from the succession. Tarbat found himself closely connected with these complex events; in 1681 he became Lord Clerk Register and Lord of Session, part of his increasing accumulation of offices. In effect Tarbat came

5   Royston House (now Caroline Park), Edinburgh.

to be, until 1688, the chief manager of Scots affairs. His office practically required him to live in Holyrood Palace, in very considerable style, virtually in the royal party itself. There were substantial additional benefits. In 1683 Tarbat's ownership of the Cromartie estates was definitively confirmed, and his lands were erected into a separate Sheriffdom of Cromartie under the Great Seal.[11] It was said that he was inundated with honours, and that his close personal rapport with the monarch counted for as much as the services he performed. While Tarbat revelled in his rapid political ascent his career was paralleled by that of his older cousin, George Mackenzie of Rosehaugh who was responsible for the military suppression of the Bothwell Brig rising in 1672. Rosehaugh founded the Advocates' Library in Edinburgh, his cousin founded the Register of Sasins. At much the same time Tarbat bought the Barony of Royston, at the edge of Edinburgh—a further clear indication of rising fortunes. But it all depended on the security of James and his succession, an improbable foundation for political conservation.

The accession of James VII and II was achieved in 1685 and Tarbat was better placed than ever to reap political returns. He was granted a further pension—this time £400 a year—by the new King, and then, in April 1685, as was widely predicted, he was raised to the Peerage: he became Viscount Tarbat, Lord Macleod and Castlehaven. It suggested a political assiduity well recompensed. Soon after, Tarbat began the reconstruction of Royston House, after the manner of Ham House, Lauderdale's residence outside London. It was an enterprise of great pretension and elegance, perhaps the most ambitious town-house of its day in Edinburgh. It was also a financial quagmire which would cost Tarbat more than £6000 sterling, and eventually was to jeopardise the solvency of his estates.

V

Through nearly all the reign of James VII and II Tarbat was held in high esteem, and was in office as a Privy Councillor, Lord Clerk Register, and an ordinary Lord of Session. As unofficial manager for Scotland a great deal of business passed through his hands—this included about 250 known registered grants by the Crown which no doubt brought with them 'considerations' or commissions.

Tarbat did well under James' kingship. He even considered conversion to the Catholic faith. He decided against this cause, but his son joined the Catholic church. Tarbat tried to dissuade his heir from deserting the protestant and episcopalian beliefs in which he had been raised—he couched his advice in a manner which demonstrated his own essential credo—that is, that political pliancy does not necessarily require an inconstancy of faith.

Yet Tarbat emerged in this period, and the more so later, as a man with very loose and changeable principles, a man whose career was 'more variable and inconsistent than that of any other Scottish statesman of his time.'[12] Certainly he was prepared to act as the instrument of James's dangerous popish policies. For instance, among Tarbat's papers is a draft of James's proposals for the refounding of the Order of the Thistle, 'in the name of Our Blissed Lady and the Holy Apostles', a blatantly anti-protestant exercise.

Such pro-Catholic policies were regarded as especially provocative and dangerous in Scotland and Tarbat seems to have made himself active in the support of these policies, for example, the first Test Act. When James made stronger moves to encourage Catholicism, in the sweeping second Test Act, Tarbat is known to have demurred and advised against further incitement of religious violence. Nevertheless he did his ultimate reputation no good at all: an historian, writing in 1834, described him unsympathetically as 'the most submissive servant of every government.'[13]

The so-called 'Glorious Revolution of 1688', the triumph of Protestantism under William and Mary was considered far from glorious in Scotland. It should have terminated the career of Tarbat, that 'obsequious flatterer of King James.'[14] He was fifty-eight and utterly identified with the Stuart dynasty which now represented a continuing threat to the State. It seems likely also that, just prior to the Orange invasion, Tarbat wavered and was undecided as to which way to jump. Some evidence suggests he was about to raise troops for James only three weeks before William's landing.[15]

Yet Tarbat effectively salvaged a remarkable proportion of his public reputation. Disregarding his association with the Jacobite regime, Tarbat acted adroitly, and did all he could to smooth the transfer of power to the Revolution government of the House of Orange. In this he took important practical steps which eased the establishment of King William's government and, of course, helped to secure his own position with the new rulers. Tarbat was in some personal danger during the transition and he made public noises, to recommend the disbanding of the military, which were clearly designed to assist the new rulers in Scotland. Nevertheless he was tainted by his association with the previous regime (and by his son's open support of James and Catholicism) and was not fully exonerated until January 1690.

Meanwhile Tarbat made every effort to prove his allegiance to the Revolution. A later comment was that he 'wisely changed with the times, and was as zealous a Defender of the Revolution as any man. He made himself necessary to the Revolution Ministry.'[16] His greatest asset in this his second political rehabilitation was his experience and skill in Scottish affairs and particularly his expertise in Highland matters. The insecurity of the new regime in the north, and in Ireland, provided Tarbat with ample opportunity to demonstrate his utility to William. As evidence of his loyalty he sent a shipload of bere-barley to help provision the king's army in Ireland in 1690.

The stability of the Highlands was indispensable to the King. On April 25, 1689 he wrote to Melville the new Secretary of State for Scotland, that Tarbat could be used to good purpose:

> Since you think my Lord Tarbat can be serviceable in quieting the North, I hope you will encourage his going thither, and to that end I have sent you his discharge in the form it is desired, which you make use of or not, as you see opportunity. A distribution of money among the Highlanders being thought the likeliest way to satisfy them, I have given orders for 5 or 6 thousand pounds to be sent to Major General Mackay for those purpose, and also for 2 frigates to cruize on the north-east coast as you desire, and hope in some time our affairs will be in so good a posture that we shall not apprehend an invasion from Ireland but rather be in a condition to send over some sufficient force to support the British interest there.

Despite the King's confidence Tarbat was still under suspicion; one of the first acts of General Mackay on taking up his northern command was to arrest Tarbat's son, as well as Lord Lovat. They were placed under the surveillance of the Lord of Balnagowan. Tarbat's son was imprisoned in Inverness for several weeks despite his protestation that his only wish was to 'live peaceably and with all submission to the present government under King William and Queen Mary.' Tarbat's son was a well known Catholic in Easter Ross and the target of some local prejudice from rival presbyterian landowners in the district. Old scores were being settled. The Highlands were effectively under military rule and a great deal of acrimony was generated by questions such as the cost of billeting the occupying troops. There was endless fear of a Highland uprising.

Residual suspicions notwithstanding, Tarbat's abilities were fully engaged in 1690 in the effort to bring order to the persistently turbulent Highlands. Indeed the allegiance of the entire north was in grave doubt throughout these years, and the perambulating tours of Mackay's troops were not enough to generate general unity and loyalty. Tarbat was engaged to negotiate with the Highland chiefs in the period 1690-2 in an effort to pacify the region. William recognised in Tarbat a 'secular authority', a professional politician and manager who was of greater value than the extreme Presbyterians. As Rosalind Mitchison says, 'He was reported to be corrupt, almost certainly with good reason. He was valuable because he understood the chiefs' and was able to devise practical plans to bring peace to the Highlands. Tarbat's plan required some selective buying out of interests in dispute between opposing factions of whom the Campbells were the most aggressive. In 1691 Tarbat was authorised to 'treat with the highlanders in rebellion' and empowered to offer up to £2000 to 'any chieff and tribe' to submit to the Crown.[17] Unfortunately the execution of his ideas was mismanaged. The peace formula broke down badly and the eventual consequence was the catastrophe at Glencoe. The modern historian P.W.J.Riley judges that Tarbat's efforts to bring order to the Highlands were a total failure. Tarbat's efforts 'were inconspicuously though effectively sabotaged. Too many people wanted to see him fail, particularly those with a vested interest in the existing Highland situation, however disturbed.' Tarbat's erratic health did not help, and he was clearly unable to counter the anarchic forces in the north.[18]

Tarbat was nevertheless fully assimilated into the Williamite government of Scotland. In 1692 he recovered his position as Lord Clerk Register and was again accumulating the pensions and perks of office. In 1695, however, he was discovered 'grossly mal-verising' in both public and private business, that is engaging in the corrupt misuse of office. He was required to resign his registership. At another time he was alleged to have falsified the record of Parliament, and was compared in his opinions to 'an eel'. Yet he was awarded another large pension, of £400, in 1696 and was doing well enough to continue the reconstruction of Royston House and to incur large new expenses at Tarbat House during this decade. It was said that he was personally very popular, and gifted with the most diverting conversation.

Tarbat bounced back, as always, and emerged at the turn of the century, as the elder statesman of Scotland. His capacity for survival in decades of political turbulence, worthy of Talleyrand himself, was the basis of his profitable career of state service. At the accession of Queen Anne he became Secretary of State for Scotland and in 1703 was created Earl of Cromartie. Once more he was branded as a trimmer—'he turned as great a Whig as the best of them' said Lockhart, and was eventually 'so magotty and unsettled he was not to be much relyed upon'. Another hostile commentator called him 'A veteran instrument of arbitrary authority'. Bishop Burnet observed too that the Earl had 'great notions of virtue and religion, but they were only notions.' But the evidence of his role in the making of the Union of 1707 suggests a man of great energy and conviction. He was indeed an able and strenuous supporter of the Union of the Crowns, and praised for his cogent and judicious advocacy, in his votes, speeches and numerous writings. He was one of the first of that 'influential nucleus of opinion' to advocate Union (as early as 1698) as 'the only way to Tame the factions which made Scotland ungovernable'. He was a prime advocate of the vital economic advantages which would accrue from an incorporating union. He saw no future for Scotland in anything less than a full-blooded arrangement with England and he remained constant in his powerful advocacy throughout the difficult negotiations that followed. As Secretary of State for Scotland Cromartie was a key analyst of the political situation in the north and an eloquent spokesman for a vision of a United Kingdom. In 1705, for instance, he wrote to Mar, 'God send a Solid Union in, and of, Brittaine!—for I am sorly afraid, and firmly perswaded, that such will, only will, secure Brittaine, and deliver old Scotland from its many complaints'.[19] Though he was roundly abused by his anti-unionist opponents, and though he made insistent demands for a lucrative reward for his services, his advocacy was persuasive and influential to the success of the negotiations. His pleasure and pride in the outcome was unqualified and genuine. It was Cromartie's role in the making of the Union that gave him his reputation as a statesman, and one commentator said that it atoned 'for much that was foolish and inconsistent in his career.' In one of his pamphlets he explained his enthusiasm for the Union:

> 'I am old, and in long experience of slavery and now of poverty, and I wish to leave the nation free of the first, and at least on the road to leave the other.'[20]

Despite his advanced age he was made Lord Justice Clerk again in 1705. But he was not elected as one of the sixteen representative peers of Scotland and he soon passed into relative political obscurity. The Union delivered, and age creeping on, he eventually decided to retire from the scene in 1712.

Cromartie's was a cultivated and philosophical mind[21] and he accumulated a considerable reputation not only in politics, but in science and philosophy also. As one of the original Fellows of the Royal Society, in 1660, he was the author of several contributions to its august proceedings. Mackay described him as 'A gentleman of very polite learning and good parts; hath a great deal of wit, and is the pleasantest character in the world; a great master in philosophy, and much esteemed by the Royal Society of London. He hath been very handsome in person, is tall, fair complexioned, and now past 70 years old.' His writing on natural history included climatological observations, descriptions of the Hebrides, and a disquisition on Scottish mosses. His political writing charted his own career—pamphlets in praise of the Protestant settlement 1689, in favour of Union in 1702, and pro-Episcopalian in 1703. He also cultivated some historical investigations including a history of the Mackenzies.

According to Dean Swift, Cromartie retired to New Tarbat in 1712:

> 'after four score years he went to his country house in Scotland with a resolution to stay six years and live thriftly in order to save up money that he might spend it on London.'[22]

Here was good evidence of Cromartie's financial difficulties which were to cast a gloom over the lives of his successors. It also suggests a much developed taste for the consuming attractions of London, as well as a somewhat cavalier attitude to the uses of estate income. It may suggest that Cromartie believed that the surplus of estate income was designed for landlordly consumption rather than the development of the sources of his wealth. For most of the previous three decades Cromartie's estates had been left in the hands of his chamberlains. His first wife, who bore eight children, had also been involved, and had helped managerial affairs with a degree of practical competence while her husband had been tied up in statesmanship in London and Edinburgh. Six months after her death, in 1700, Cromartie had married the dowager Countess of Wemyss which was the prelude to much increased expenditure. Royston House was refurbished for her, and she accompanied him to London to the Court of Queen Anne in the best style. He lavished upon her expensive clothes and jewellery and on her death in 1704 commissioned a lavish memorial. She had been wealthy in her own right but her estates then passed to her son David.

Towards the end of his life Cromartie became increasingly strident and bitter in his attempts to recoup what he claimed were arrears of salary from his service to the Crown. He endlessly chivvied the Earl of Mar, his successor as Secretary of State, to recover £1100 sterling which he claimed was owed to him. In the process he emphasised his role in the creation of the Union and in the restoration of the monarchical principle to the country. In 1705 he outlined his financial plight to Mar and said that he was being forced into more debt because of the non-payment of salary due: 'I beg you lay these before the Queen, and I hope shee will doe whats just and favourable for ane old calm Torie.' One year later the refrain was repeated, equally plaintively:

> the Queen may be pleased to know that I with humility think I am barbarously used, and, I deserved no riches, yet I must say I never deserved such unusual hardship from the Crown nor royale family. For I frankly owne to your Lordship that, if the £1100 due to me at Mertinmas last be not soone payed, and very soone, I must runn for shelter ... Necessity presses me to press thus.

As his frustration rose so also did the extent of his demands—his creditors in London were chasing him while his salary was still unpaid. He drew attention to the fact that he had served nearly sixty years and benefited very little in comparison with his contemporaries. During that time his expenses of living in London had been enormous and unavoidable. He even offered to make over his Royston property to the government as part of the settlement of his claims, but to no avail. In 1707 he became shriller: 'I may, and cannot but say that I have been used like a cast dogg.'

Cromartie obtained no satisfaction of his claims against the government. By 1713 his demands had grown to a figure of £4214 for the loss of salary and allowances. He was by now desperate enough to address the Queen directly in a series of passionate pleas for financial relief. In so doing he claimed recognition for services a half a century before and for a sum of £1000 he had advanced to General Monck at the time of the Revolution. In one letter to the Queen he remarked:

> I have now served the Crown above 54 years, and in that tyme I never plunged into any faction, nor ever changed my principles, which keept me poor, when others, by other methods, have doubled their estates; but I envy not those.

It was a remarkable, even incredible, claim made by a man who had performed a succession of political somersaults in his life in politics. He also pointed out that he had been 'instrumental with all my possible (and not yet very ineffectual) zeal, in carrying on the Union of Britain.' More specifically, in another petition, he asserted

> that now, after sixty years publick service, he hath not added sixty crowns to his private fortune, albeit he never did live at a lower rate as when he was in publick service. He did enjoy for some while the Register's office, which was lucrative, but five other cowes did devour and eat up that fat one—nor did that cure the leanness.

But for all his splendid turn of phrase Cromartie received no compensation and his estate plunged further towards financial crisis.

In fact Cromartie lived neither to recover his fortune nor to see London again. He died in the north in 1714 at the age of 84.[23] He had served six monarchs and had survived no less than five political traumas; his estates had been consolidated into a county; he was regarded as the elder statesman of his country and one of the architects of the Union. He had achieved the remarkable transition from the traditional role of a minor highland chieftain to that of a cultivated statesman and courtier, in Whitehall. He had won an Earldom for his family. But the economic foundations of the Cromartie ascendancy, the subject of the next two chapters, were insecure.

CHAPTER 3

The Workings of a Highland Estate: the Managers

I

In the hundreds of surviving fragments of evidence about the Cromartie estates before the Jacobite Rebellion of 1745 there are enough clues to reconstruct the basic apparatus of land management. It is possible to see its estate administration system, at least in outline; similarly the financial vicissitudes of the Mackenzie family become apparent, especially in the legal papers and financial documents which chart their relations with generations of debtors and creditors. Equally exposed is the machinery of local government and the lines of administration from Edinburgh to the local community. Even some of the economic foundations—the systems of production upon which the entire edifice of the landed society ultimately depended—much of this, too, is visible in the mundane detail of estate administration. Thus the economic relations between the social strata of the Highlands may be revealed, even if somewhat blurred and static in form. Some of the external economic connections may be defined: the directions of inter-estate and inter-regional trade and settlement are to be perceived in the residues of seventeenth century estate management records. All of this is important in any reconstruction of local and national history.

Yet it remains a restricted and selective story which is mainly innocent of genuine connection with the overwhelming majority of the actual population of this, or indeed any other, estate. The documentation of the Cromartie estate is generous on the machinery of government and the apparatus of family finances; it is, in the same degree, weak in its penetration of the foundations of society. The record is populated by members of the Cromartie family, its relations and its hierarchy of managers; but the people below, the producers and the peasantry, are almost entirely invisible, anonymous or, at best, abstractions in the process of producing rents, surpluses, armed forces or consumers. Until the 1750s we do not even know their numbers,[1] we hardly know their fate in war and famine, and virtually nothing of their welfare, religion, politics and culture. Such people emerge into this historical account very slowly, as though shy of attention. Only in the late nineteenth century do they emerge with any full degree of individuality. It is a common enough problem in all pre-modern, pre-literate history. As Ian Whyte has said, only recently,

> The material [of private estate papers] relates almost entirely to the preoccupations of the landowners and their officers who were concerned with estate management, such preoccupations need not have been, and in most cases probably were not, shared by the bulk of the population ... the conditions, aspirations and fears of people below the tenant class are hardly recorded at all.[2]

This archival dilemma reflects accurately enough the realities of the times. Society was clearly pyramidal in structure, and dominated utterly by landowners. It was to a considerable degree (though not entirely) a peasant society in which most production did not enter a recognisable market. Land itself was the basis of political power and economic strength; it also conferred prestige and honour. Its precise military significance, in a transitional age, is less easily determined. Land certainly signified political authority through parliamentary representation and the prosecution of the law. Land was both a measure, and a source of political power. The relationship ran in both directions as the careers of the Cromartie Mackenzies demonstrate with great clarity: land provided the basis for political careers in Edinburgh and London, and it was the sine qua non of involvement in government. A political life was expensive (especially in Holyrood House as Tarbat discovered) and political status required the maintenance of a style and generosity of life (and especially housing) which could only grow out of an independent income. But a political career itself might prove lucrative and eventually subsidise an estate and the further aggrandisement of its owner in both territorial and honorific terms. Political advancement was often well rewarded.

Indeed one of the more salient questions on Scottish historiography in this period is the extent to which financial status affected political allegiance. Specifically it is frequently suggested that Jacobite support was fuelled by the opportunism of landowners in various degrees of economic desperation, if not actual bankruptcy.

Another political implication of a dearth of archival matter about the lower echelons of society is the notion that the people in general lived under the sway, and moral dominance, of the landowner. The very silence of the people tends towards the nineteenth century assumption that such local societies were entirely stable and that the relationship between the chief and his people was one of unquestioning even childlike, loyalty and allegiance. Similarly it is easy to believe such relations were uncommercialised, dependent upon 'traditional' obligations and measured by considerations unaffected by the market. Lack of evidence tends to encourage notions of a primitive simplicity unsullied by capitalist modes of economic relationship, a society in which chieftainly leadership was broadly accepted by the mass of the people. On most of the questions there is remarkably little direct evidence and it may distort the picture to assume that each sign of, for instance, the money economy or popular independence, was the beginning of a new age. More useful may be a picture of certain demonstrable realities of estate life in the late seventeenth century.

II

The Cromartie estate had, by 1660, become large and diverse enough to require an elaborate system of management. This body of managers was indispensable, but particularly so in the absence of the owner on political and social duties in Edinburgh. Other members of the family sometimes participated directly in estate management, but generally they were not relied upon. A hierarchy of managers, a small bureaucracy in its own right, presided over the rise of the Cromartie fortunes, and then (after 1707) wrestled with the problems of financial decline. A high proportion of their business was of a legal nature, but they were also close to the productive process—the yield mainly of food from the land.

The apparatus of estate management, in 1660, was headed by a lawyer in Elgin in the county of Moray, followed by the chamberlains (one for each section of the estate, and also known as factors or doers), local officers and the Baron Baillie Deputes. The estate probably employed other personnel about the residences, and certainly paid the salaries of church ministers, a few schoolmasters, foresters and others. The management system was not new and indeed there seems to have been an hereditary succession of some of the officers. Relatives of the Mackenzie family were somewhat favoured in the system. The lawyers and the chamberlains generated most of the documentation that survives; it was richer during the absence of Tarbat when accountability depended primarily on correspondence.

The Dallas family, a legal partnership in Elgin, had served the Tarbats for at least three generations. They had themselves married into the Lowther family which had acted for the Mackenzie family (as Writers and agents) since at least the early seventeenth century. Hugh Dallas was the head of the firm and his brother also managed business for the Cromartie estates. They provided similar services to other landowners in Moray and Easter Ross. The Dallases piloted substantial acquisitions of land for the family, and held legal documents—writs and charters. A great deal of their work concerned the settling of debts with the many partners with whom the family engaged—in trade, in rents, in land settlements, in family arrangements. In addition were the more strictly legal entanglements which, on occasion, seem to throttle all enterprise on Highland estates. During Tarbat's long absences in Edinburgh Hugh Dallas was described as the chief 'Manager of his affairs'. It is clear that he took primary responsibility for the business activities of the estate, and communicated directly with the chamberlains on the one hand, and the landlord on the other. In professional terms, however, the Dallases were, foremost, legal advisors; they were not estate improvers or agricultural men; they were not resident technical innovators or agronomists. In that sense they clearly differed from some of their nineteenth century successors.

Nevertheless the lawyers were involved closely in the daily matters of the estate: in 1692, for instance, Dallas had to seek crown rents from tenants on the estates; he pursued matters in detail, and he negotiated all debts sustained by his master, for example with a London bookseller. He also appraised the prospects of income from the fishing on the River Conan which was the largest single tack on the estate at that time. Most of all he watched over the general finances of the estate, the sources of its income and the scale and direction of its expenditures. It was here that a close and candid relationship with the proprietor was indispensable. Dallas cultivated a personal informality which was expressed in some of his letters—for instance, in March 1694, he commiserated with the Tarbats over their difficulties (moral and financial) with their sons. Dallas agreed that the sons were lazy, expensive and troublesome but advised patience and good humour in their parental dealings. Most of his work as 'your good old servant' and 'factor to Lord Tarbat' was mundane and repetitive: accounting payments of Bishop's rents, stipends for ministers in parishes under Tarbat's patronage, the levying of taxes (or cess), crown dues, as well as small-time legal exercises such as precepts of poinding and other legal bread-and-butter business. When Dallas was appointed Commissary Clerk to the counties of Ross and Cromarty much of that type of business was streamlined and simplified. More complex and commercially testing would be Dallas's responsibilities in the development of trade, especially in grain, following the personal directions of Lord Tarbat from Edinburgh.

Though the functions of the late seventeenth century factor were not fundamentally different from those of his successors two centuries later, there were two important aspects worth comment. In the absence of the proprietor he probably exerted rather more discretionary authority—over tenants, debtors and in negotiations with contiguous landowners. A seventeenth century Highland estate, in any case, possessed greater local autonomy than its descendant, and its managers were, consequently, more powerful. Second, the personal business of the lawyer-factor seems to have overlapped or mingled with that of his master in a more informal and confusing manner than his more systematic equivalent in Victorian times. Partly it was a function of distance and accounting procedures—monies were not settled and balanced so quickly, much business was not concluded for several years (notably the rentals). More particularly, and more dangerously, the factor-lawyer engaged in loans for, or on behalf of, his principal. This appears to have been common practice. Certainly Tarbat borrowed money, in fairly modest amounts, from Dallas; there was, for instance, a Bond for £556 Scots to George Dallas in 1687. Dallas also arranged wadsets (a certain form of reverse mortgage from tenant to landlord common in Scots land law). Inevitably such arrangements led to an intimacy, and even an interdependence, between servant and master. Complicated debt arrangements and multi-lateral legal business all created a web of connections and trust which was tenuous yet central to efficient estate administration.

When Hugh Dallas died, about 1710, the Cromartie estate business passed once more to the family, to his sons, John, William and Robert Dallas. But in 1712 the longstanding arrangement with the Dallases came to an abrupt termination—in effect Tarbat, now Earl of Cromartie, sacked them in circumstances which suggest financial confusion. William Dallas, apparently, was caught in some measure of peculation. In an account of the case the tried and trusted character of the old relationship was stressed: for more than a century the Dallases and the Lowthers had served the Mackenzies of Tarbat: 'they acting with kindness and honesty to him as their predecessors had done to his'. Hundreds of papers and accounts it was argued, demonstrated that Hugh Dallas was always 'faithful and diligent'; when he died Tarbat had felt complete confidence in passing the commission on to his sons, 'they being in a manner his hereditary trustees'. Thus was his sense of outrage the greater when, in 1712, the Earl found that in his absence in Edinburgh, William Dallas had commenced an action against him on an old Bond granted in 1673 to the Bishop of Ross. The allegation was that Dallas was taking undue advantage of his client's age and rising financial difficulties for his own personal financial gain. Given the great quantity of papers held in the firm's hands the opportunities of malfeasance were always considerable.

Dallas's response to these allegations is not known. But the outcome was clear. The firm did no further business for the Earl of Cromartie. A century-old connection was instantly severed. Their place, at a time of worsening financial problems for the estate, was taken by a succession of lawyers, also from Elgin or Edinburgh. They were beset by many difficulties, not least of which were the contradictory instructions emanating from the second and third Earls. Moreover they remained somewhat divorced from the detailed business of the estate, and indeed rarely crossed the Firth to visit. The actual management of the estate devolved directly on the chamberlains, sometimes also known as factors.

III

Chamberlains were appointed for each Barony of the Cromartie estate (i.e. New Tarbat, Strathpeffer and Coigach). They were usually selected from the leading tacksmen (i.e. leaseholders) and were often kinsmen of the landlord. Their salaries came out of rents and this was central to the conventional method of estate management: they were entitled to a percentage from the rents collected which, naturally, was an incentive for diligent collection.

Their work was heavy and wide ranging. They acted for the Lord, advised on the allocation of tacks and tenancies, and executed evictions when required. Many of the functions of informal local government fell on their shoulders. Their burdens were greater than their nineteenth century counterparts in one particular aspect: much of the rental income was derived in the form of victuals (and some services). This greatly compounded the business not only of collection but also of processing and disposal. It created much added work, and it also placed an entrepreneurial responsibility on the landlord by way of his chamberlain. On the Cromartie estate the taking of victual rents caused the landlord to involve himself thoroughly in the grain trade of north east Scotland.

Victual rents were taken twice a year, corn at Candlemas and beasts at Martinmas: on the eastern estate grain was collected as well as small amounts of money-rent ('silver mail') and 'customs'. The chamberlain then was responsible for the good condition of the grain and arrangements for its storage, processing and sale to purchasers locally or to a distant market (see below). The tenantry was certainly sensitive to market forces as, for instance, in 1690 when excellent grazing conditions caused a sharp fall in cheese prices at Dingwall. In bad years, when prices were high, the tenants were prodded by the chamberlains to produce to their limits. The quasi-barter economy was in no sense insulated from such pressures. In the summer months the chamberlains were required to supervise a number of service rents (or customs): tenants were required to cut and carry peats, to make hay and later to harvest the barley-bere. There were complicated labour requirements connected with the delivery of grain, and road-work was likely too. In the western barony, Coigach, there were further responsibilities because rent was taken mainly in the form of silver (i.e. cash), wedders, butter and woven plaids. In Coigach this entailed a long ride across hill passes and, often, an energetic round-up of the recalcitrant tenants along the rocky shores. Sometimes the collection of a rent took

The Workings of a Highland Estate: the Managers

6 Tarbat House c.1700.

a fortnight—the chamberlain was accompanied by an officer or two, and a piper was always present at a collection. In 1704, for example, it was recorded that 'the officer and the piper' were paid 40 merks, and two years' rent was collected.[3]

Little is known about the subordinate officers in the estate management. They were, in effect, the 'non-commissioned' overseers of the routine stages in estate affairs. They were illiterate—in the Judicial Rental of 1755 none of them could sign their names, though they could probably keep a tally and worked hard. Specialist functions were required in the Forest of Fannich—a big uninhabited area of central Ross, lightly forested and covered with good grazing between the deep bogs, lochans and crags. Here a forester was engaged, mainly to police the woods against illicit fuel gathering. There was also a 'Yeald Bowman' who was responsible for cattle, particularly the barren cows and heifers before their first calving, sent to Fannich from Coigach for the summer grazing. Fannich was ancilliary to the normal sheiling arrangements at Coigach; the Bowman's pay was meagre, a mere three bolls of bere per annum. But by 1783 two bowmen were being employed and this reflected the increased value of good grazing in the West Highlands already evident in its rental value.

Finally, in the structure of estate management, was the central role of the Depute Baron Baillie, usually undertaken by one of the chamberlains. He acted in the name of the Baron, in fact the landlord, Tarbat, as magistrate of the Barony courts in each barony and as Sheriff of Cromartyshire. He tried local disputes and minor matters of law. The jurisdiction extended only to the tenantry of the estate, and estate disputes constituted a high proportion of the cases before the court. It was an arrangement heavily weighted in the landlord's favour.

IV

The recruitment and careers of the early chamberlains are not well documented. Alexander Merchant of Wilkhaven served for the barony of Easter Aird for several decades. He was described as tacksman of the mills and kiln of Ballone. He appeared in estate business in the 1670s, and was responsible for construction work at Portmahomack in 1698, and for grain movements. In 1707 he complained about inadequate instructions from Cromartie to deal with victual rents. Soon thereafter he was replaced and there were allegations that Merchant had not finalised payments to Cromartie of dues and victuals.

After 1707, during years of great financial stringency and confusion, an important Cromartie chamberlain was McLeod of Cadboll, the son of an Edinburgh lawyer. He was a distant blood relative of the Cromartie family and was probably favoured for this reason. He himself delegated the actual chores of grain collection, for example, to humbler members of his immediate family. Cadboll strove hard to keep the second Earl's head above the sea of debts which threatened to overwhelm him. Unlike his principal, Cadboll's family went on to become prosperous and influential in Easter Ross. In particular Cadboll acquired the lands of Easter Aird by means of a wadset; he made loans to his landlord and in 1707 took over the tack of Castle Leod and the Barony of

Strathpeffer for seven years as the means of retrieving his money. It was a further sign of financial embarrassment on the estate.

Similar types of arrangements governed the chamberlaincy of the Mackenzies of Meddat who served their landlord for three generations. They too were probably kin of the landlord, and also tacksmen or tenants of a large and prosperous farm in New Tarbat. There survives an inventory of buildings of Meddat for 1666 and this indicates some of the capital equipment of the seventeenth century chamberlain: it included millbarns, byres, a girnell (granary), a boll (a measure for grain) and various locks—all clearly designed for the reception and storage of victual rents. His house was equipped with glass windows, a sure sign of prosperity in Ross-shire in the 1660s. Meddat was described as a Notary Public and he and his son both performed the office of Baron Baillie Depute for many years in the Tarbat court. They were also required to collect rents and held Baron courts in distant Coigach, itself a major expedition across the

7 John Second Earl of Cromartie.

mountains. Meddat lent money to Tarbat as early as 1667 and such loans probably reinforced the interdependence of chamberlain and master. Total loyalty was expected in the relationship: thus John Mackenzie of Meddat was left in charge of the estates when the third Earl joined Charles Edward Stuart in 1745. He remained in charge through the Uprising and then, remarkably, became trusted aide of the Factor of the Annexed Estate until his death in 1783. Through these difficult years Meddat not only continued to send money and food parcels to the Earl in the Tower of London, and in his later banishment, but also to retain the trust of the occupying Factor, Forbes of New. He provided the evidence necessary in the confirmation of the depositions of all the tenants of Coigach, Strathpeffer, and New Tarbat at the Judicial Rental of 1755.[4] More significantly the Mackenzies of Meddat provided a line of continuity from the time of the Revolution of 1688, through the financial rise and fall of the Cromarties, through the Uprising of 1745, the Annexed estates, through to the eve of the return of the estates to the third Earl's son in 1785.

V

Missing from surviving accounts of Cromartie in these years is much evidence of the texture of life, of the priorities and social needs of the community. In this only clues remain, hints merely of a lost world. The centrality of religion is clear enough, and so is the sustained 'democratic' element in church matters. Each parish sought to install a minister of the persuasion of its chief landowners (the Heritors), and the parishioners seldom disagreed, acquiescing in the Jacobite-episcopalian slant of the MacKenzies or the Whig and presbyterian preferences of the lairds of Foulis and Balnagowan. They did however riot often and hard at any threat to 'intrude' ministers of the opposite political and religious complexion. It was perhaps the liveliest popular debate of the eighteenth century in Ross. Nevertheless, despite such a clear commitment by landlord and community to the needs of the church, educational and religious standards—in Rosskeen, Logie Easter and Kilmuir—were abysmal. Complaints in 1718 blamed the low stipends of ministers and teachers as the root cause of the problem.[5]

The benefits of Cromartie's fame and fortune were not prominent on the social welfare of the northern estates. But some charitable payments were recorded. For instance by 1686 the Earl was responsible for several mortifications for distribution annually in various parishes, including one in Fife in memory of his second wife, 'for the behoof of poor colliers'. The recipients were required to adopt certain forms of behaviour—to attend regularly Divine service, and to remain innocent of blasphemy, lying, drunkenness, fornication, and disrespect to the Crown and the Church. The first and second offence were punished by an admonishment by the minister, the third time the offender was reported to the Trustees, and disqualified from further benefit.[6]

Local rivalries seem to have been overlaid with religious elements which often operated together in civil disorder. Thus in 1704 a great riot took place at Dingwall which echoed the accumulated bad feeling between Balnagowan and local Whigs on the one hand, and the Mackenzie Tories on the other. But the occasion of the riot was the death (after 50 years service) of the Episcopalian minister of Dingwall parish church,

8   Portmahomack: the construction of the harbour and girnel-house (centre) was the work of the mason Stronach, for the first earl in 1699.

John McCrae. Within 24 hours Balnagowan and a party of armed men attempted to force their way into the church to install a Presbyterian minister of their choice—in total defiance of the authority of the Sheriff. The interference of Balnagowan provoked a violent response from the local people, especially the womenfolk, and Balnagowan and his 60 armed men were forced to retreat. Injuries were incurred, some by the women, and Balnagowan was subsequently fined for a breach of the peace. Balnagowan was involved in several such episodes in the district and complained that the local J.P.s were making no effort to thwart the 'barbarian Jacobite mobs, the Papist rabbles'. In 1710 again the people of the parish of Rosemarkie successfully resisted the induction of a new minister under the patronage of the Earl of Cromartie. As much as anything these episodes are eloquent testimony of the powerful and divisive force of religion, and the tradition of popular resistance to unwanted inductions. On one occasion there was a threat made to Balnagowan that '200 men in women's cloathes' would tear his own forces to pieces—an early example of transvestitism in the record of popular resistance in the Scottish Highlands.[7]

Another part of the subterranean life of this society emerged, briefly only, in further reports about problems of law and order. In 1682 for instance, strong measures were instituted in Ross-shire against beggars and thieves. It is clear also that the blight of cattle thieving, on a large scale, was undiminished in the 1690s and remained serious as late as 1723. In 1697 Tarbat was himself complaining that although he had spent £600 Scots in 'watch-money' a cattle raid had taken place within three miles of his own house 'having guarded the more distant places with greater care. It may be easily concluded that the vulgar will blame the government.'[8] Alcohol was regarded as undermining public order too—there were 44 brewers reported in the Black Isle in 1711, and an evident rash of illicit distilling as well. The threatened severity of the law (and society) in cases of immorality and petty crime was no less in Ross than elsewhere; an adultress, by law, might be strangled to death for her sin, almost Moslem fashion, and a thief was, in theory, hangable for his offence.[9] Such ferocious deterrents did not prevent crime and even innocent travellers were at risk as, for instance, the hapless McIntaggart who, in 1720, was stripped of his clothes and letters while delivering a message to the Earl of Cromartie.[10] In the same year there was a reported precognition taken against witches in Tarbat Parish and it is thought that this district was indeed one of the last in the British Isles to witness witch burning.[11]

Presbyterian historians of religion in the late nineteenth century tended to interpret the record of religious conflict in the Highlands as the desperate struggle of the people against the theological oppression of their landlords. Certainly the episodes of resistance and ejection are consistent with a recurrent cleavage between the landlords' will and the collective notions of the community. The Reverend John Kennedy in 1861 was able to cite a stream of cases in Easter Ross[12]—from the conflict of Rev'd John McKilligan in Fodderty in 1655-63 to the remarkable contest which pitted the 'factious opposition' of the lairds against 'the free choice of the people' in 1725. Such contests clearly galvanised the local community and defined the limits both of domination and dependence.

In reality these parochial conflicts exposed several other layers of social division. They were, for instance, part of a long standing struggle between local magnates attached respectively to Episcopalianism and to Presbyterian forms of worship. Inevitably these struggles took on a political colouring especially when the government imposed new regulations governing lay patronage. The assertion of patronage was, therefore, an expression of local political power as well as a measure of social and religious control. Many of the induction riots at the beginning of the eighteenth century were commentaries on the seething conflict between Presbyterian and Episcopalian ambitions in which popular feeling and landlord pressure were deeply confused. The spread of Presbyterian forms became virtually inescapable by the 1720s and, for the Cromarties, the decline of Episcopalianism paralleled their own loss of control over their estate finances. The second Earl of Cromartie was himself a Catholic, which made his position still more complex. The total identification of the Episcopal wing with the Jacobite cause sent open Episcopalianism under ground and eventually into almost total eclipse. There were therefore varied antagonisms at work in these rural communities and the subsequent oppresive rule of the Presbyterians probably encouraged an undergrowth of resistance and reaction which fed the erratic career of Jacobitism. In the course of these social transitions the Earls of Cromartie had lost much of their social control and it was not entirely surprising that Tarbat became a safe house for clandestine priests.[13]

Legal proceedings in 1722 revealed some of the tensions and armed thuggery that continued to dislocate local society even into the eighteenth century. There were allegations that elections were rendered farcical by the intervention, at Dingwall, of unlawful convocations of 'some hundreds of Men at Arms' under the instruction of various local magnates. They were alleged to have carried off, bodily, three councillors on the annual election day 'with the intent to overcome and influence the Election of the Burgh'. The accused denied this allegation and said that they had been framed. In a series of counter-allegations further revelations about armed bands marauding the citizenry were made, including the assembly of 300 to 400 Highlanders, armed and threatening. In one incident, actually on the Cromartie estate near Milton of New Tarbat, 'a mob speedily gathered of Men in Women's Cloathing, and other disorderly persons', attacked officials from Dingwall. From these reports the only clear point was the existence of a persistent level of near-anarchy that could burst forth from moment to moment. Much of the problem derived from 'notions of power lodged in the Hands of those who call themselves Heads of Clans and Families, superior to and dispensing with the Laws', and indeed remained a threat to government. From this fragmentary evidence comes a picture of social turbulence, of banditti, and rebellious Highlanders causing 'heats of divisions', erratically incited to kidnapping and 'meddling with Elections'. The thinness of central authority was clearly a fact of life.[14]

CHAPTER 4

Estate Life and its Productions

I

In the management of the Cromartie properties the early chamberlains always made the basic distinction between 'my lord's lowland estates and my lord's highland estates'. The Highland component was Coigach in the far west of the county, the long fiord-like Lochbroom, the Atlantic-facing sands of Achnahaird, and the mountainous grazing lands of the interior. Coigach was Highland in more than the geographic sense: all the inhabitants in the late seventeenth century were primarily Gaelic speakers, whereas their lowland counterparts in the east were already becoming anglicised. In Coigach the people were not so much settled farmers as pastoral people with only a few patches of cultivation and a greater reliance on fishing and cattle rearing. The old warlike traditions seemed to have persisted longer in the west too: during the rising of the '45 Coigach was the best source of recruits for Cromartie's regiment, and it had the same reputation in 1777 when Lord Macleod raised the 73rd Foot. There were far more recruits from Coigach than the two lowland baronies. The way of life and the methods of agriculture remained distinctive throughout the eighteenth century. It was most obvious, almost symbolic, in ploughing: Coigach men used the cas-chrom, the ancient breast-plough, for tillage, late into the nineteenth century—yet, even in 1757, it was virtually unknown in the eastern baronies.[1] Coigach was a different world.

Evidence about the social structure, even the population, of Coigach is extremely sparse before the eighteenth century. There survives a 'List of the Pollable of Coaygach' for 1695 with 208 names, almost all Gaelic, attached. Unfortunately this provides little guide to the demography of the area since it offers no clue as to family size or number of servants per family. It does however indicate a social hierarchy headed by the tacksmen and descending through various categories, especially 'mailers', and includes a series of occupational groups including 'Murd. pyper' and 'Rory the Wright'. Prominent in the highest echelon was the 'minister' whose social role was probably at a premium since there was no landlord's residence in the vast district of Coigach.

In the east were the lowlands of the Cromartie estate, a semi-circle of arable farms along the Moray Firth, facing east and south and in close communication with the rest of Scotland, including the capital. The New Tarbat estate was accumulated from old holdings and new acquisitions in the late seventeenth century, and stretched over several parishes about the Cromarty Firth. Here was built New Tarbat House, the main residence of the family in the north. A great deal was spent on its building and furnishings.

The Hearth Tax returns of 1690-91 provide a primitive guide to the composition of the Tarbat estate. Tarbat House itself returned 15 hearths, plus an oven in the brew house. There were thirty-two other named householding tenants nearly all with single hearths, and then further anonymous mailers, servants, cottars and fishers who, in aggregate, made a total of 203 hearths for the Tarbat lands. The chamberlain (Meddat) accounted for seven hearths; mailers were also prominent in the lists, paying tax on kilns (for grain-drying) which demonstrates the importance of arable farming on the estate. Alex Mackenzie, a blacksmith, paid for 'house, smiddie, kiln and mailers, six hearths'. A big farm at Priesthill accounted for ten hearths. Six of the main householders were Mackenzies. Few of the remainder had any Gaelic connotations. Around the great house at New Tarbat the hearth tax returns suggest a predominantly agricultural community with some service occupations (e.g. gardeners) together with numerous millers, fishers and a smith. New Tarbat was the source of much of the grain export from the estates. Further to the east landownership was more variegated in a densely populated zone, and in East Tarbat there was an ancilliary list of 'the poor who are unable to pay tax', nine men and forty-five women. It was a society with a pyramidal structure, already dominated by consolidated landownership and large tenant farmers. The third estate, Strathpeffer, was located in mid Ross, on the margin between lowlands and highlands. It was more mixed both in its production and in its accompanying social structure.

At the base in each parish was a large class of poor whose existence hardly surfaces in the remainder of the estate documentation.[2] For instance in Fearn lived Christian McCounchie, 'a poor woman in a poor way', and at Little Tarrell 'there also is three poor pensioners that lives on the Charity of the Church'. At Ballamuckie 'there is also four poor widows and three poormen not worth fourteen shillings Scots'. Little can be deduced from most of the lists of names in the Hearth Tax Returns, but there is a striking disproportion of the sexes in the lists of the poor—61 per cent were women in Fearn, and 85 per cent in Tarbat. The sex bias may reflect the distribution of wealth in this society; it may also reflect the greater longevity of women and the conventional association of age with poverty.

II

Social leadership in the north of Scotland in the seventeenth century, however elaborate the structure of management, could not be entirely delegated to the factors and chamberlains. Local circumstances and the turbulence of Highland politics and defence were too complicated for the secondhand authority of underlings. In this matter the Cromartie family may have incurred social costs on their own estates to set beside their considerable gains in metropolitan life in Edinburgh and London. Communications from north to south were poor. In the early eighteenth century the overland journey from Edinburgh to Ross-shire, a mere 170 miles, still required eight days travelling time. Only the first eleven miles could be reached by coach. For much of the journey there were no wheeled vehicles and even horsemen were liable to be stranded by mud. Mail was carried by messengers on foot.[3] The sea passage from Leith was preferred in summer.

In the 1690s there were many complaints about Lord Tarbat's absence both by tenants on his estate and by local landowners. He had little time for local administrative tasks even though the Highlands were in a state of turmoil. Local authority had passed to Ross of Balnagowan as Sheriff who was accused of strong-arm tactics and of favouritism. The politically disturbed conditions gave rival landowners the opportunity to make local gains and to settle old scores. Balnagowan used all his authority for assisting arrests, searching houses and, particularly, the requisition of property during recurrent crises. Often this involved extracting stocks of meal, numbers of horses and labour services. Most contentious of all was the quartering of troops on the local population, a grave strain on resources especially during the poor harvest years and political unrest of the early 1690s. At one time 100 men were garrisoned at Castle Leod and required 40 bolls of oats, 16 bolls of bere; horses were taken over and cows killed for food as well as supplies of candles, crockery and cutlery, and 700 loads of peat.[4] The quartering of troops was no new event in the north: whenever times were unsettled the populace had to support such army units as the government chose to send. This method continued into the eighteenth century until the government adopted Cromwell's old tactic of building military citadels (at Fort William, Fort George and Fort Augustus) for the accommodation of their forces.

One of Tarbat's neighbours told him in 1690 that 'I have often regretted your absence from this country but more especially have I cause to do now when we are ruled by the Lord of Balnagowan as Sheriff.'[5] Balnagowan seems to have revelled in his power to demand service from local people; moreover any objection could easily be branded as disloyalty to the Crown. Quartered troops could eat their way through local resources, consuming meal, cattle, chickens, butter, eggs and anything else on which they could lay their hands. The burden included taxes on the heritors and the provision of troops and horses, and straw for the animals. One tenant had his entire stock of meal requisitioned by troops at this time. Bitterness arose not only because the demands jeopardised the subsistence of the community but also because the burden was not spread evenly and equitably. Moreover the 'depredations' of the Sheriff's men were compounded by the increase of cattle thefts during the northern turmoil. Tarbat was warned in 1693 'that Balnagowan's men will beggar the tenants of Coigach unless your Lordship prevent it'. It was one of many embittered comments at this time. Examples of oppression were cited, notably the case of a widow of Achshachall who had lost ten cows to the troops. The entire period was disrupted by the political climate which no doubt also impeded the development of the estate economy.

Ultimately such local dislocations were reflected in the estate finances. In 1691 Robert Dunbar, factor to Tarbat in Cromarty town, wrote to his master reporting the poor income of the property and saying that it was not his fault that the rent was not paid. The harvest of 1689 had been poor, various tenants had failed to pay their rents, ministers were arguing about their stipends, and the demands of quartering had been particularly onerous: there had been no repayment to the people for goods commandeered. The troops had taken horses, and had forced labourers to go to Inverness, Badenoch and Cromdale. Tenants had also been required to take weekly consignments of corn and straw to Inverness, incurring as well the cost of the ferry. 'The people are poor', said Dunbar, 'the poor people never stood in more need, considering the badness of the crop'. If they were not recompensed they would 'be broken'. Similarly a tenant told Tarbat that the country was in a most unsettled state. Writing in September 1691 he complained 'I am not tranquil', and that 'conditions here do not allow me to go away from home', and told Tarbat candidly that his services were required in the north and that it was time for him to 'show his love for his country'. Tarbat was tied up in Edinburgh and his efforts to moderate Balnagowan's demands were not particularly successful.

III

The output of the Cromartie estate was clearly reflected in the rentals.[6] In the west, at Coigach, the tenantry was required to pay rent in cash together with lesser demands in the form of sheep, butter, cheese and plaids. A 1679 rental suggests that the rent of Coigach was then about 2120 merks, (£59 sterling), but the evidence is fragmentary and may be misleading. At Coigach (and in the eastern parts of the estate) the land seems to have been let out on five year leases (tacks), often in large tracts, presumably for subdivision to the lesser tenantry. The form of rental payment clearly indicates a grazing economy which depended on cattle sales which yielded money income—a paradox in that the west coast was, in most other aspects, well insulated from the rest of the world. Surprisingly all the rents from the west coast were received in silver coin, certainly from 1660 onwards, and this was derived from the sale of cattle at the great cattle fair of Beauly, and from the sale of salt herring through dealers in Stornoway. In the late seventeenth century there is evidence of a direct exchange of products between Coigach and the eastern estate. Meal was despatched from Strathpeffer and New Tarbat by ship to Coigach while bullocks and wedders were driven eastwards over the mountains by labour services, namely 'vassalage carriage'. Cattle were highly negotiable commodities and were used for the discharge of Bonds and other debts. Their portability was an advantage, particularly during the great shortage of coin in the decades about the Act of Union. Coigach seems to have benefitted from the expansion of the cattle trade in the late seventeenth century (and more after 1707), and this was the period when much of the covering of oak and Scots pine was removed for timber and fuel. It was also a time when the western tenantry complained loudly about the fluctuations in the availability and value of the currency.

In the east, at New Tarbat and Strathpeffer, the rents were paid almost exclusively in kind—primarily in bere-barley, the very basis for the expanding grain trade in which the landlord played a large commercial role. Victual rents remained in force throughout the eighteenth century (despite doctrinaire opposition from improvement thinkers), and efforts towards commutation were resisted on the landlord side. The new managers at the time of Annexation (in 1754) regarded the victual rents as unambiguously advantageous to the landlord.[7]

To a substantial degree the landlord acted as an entrepreneur for the agricultural output of his eastern estates: necessarily this involved his managers in great commercial responsibilities and expertise. Estate management employed a pre-modern system of rent-obligation for clearly capitalistic purposes.

Easter Ross had developed as a grain export region, particularly in the early seventeenth century. It had been sending grain to Aberdeen and to Norway from at least the beginning of the century as evidenced by shipments of bere-barley to Bergen in 1621.[8] Easter Ross, a favoured agricultural area, had some of the best yields of bere-barley in the whole of Scotland, and produced large surpluses beyond local requirements. Though he was energetic and innovating in the trade, Tarbat did not invent the trade,[9] nor was he the only landowner to see rich opportunities for grain exports to the developing urban markets in Edinburgh and the Forth basin. The 'Merchant Lairds of Orkney' were renowned for their enterprise, and other Easter Ross landowners (even quite small owners) were involved in the trade (often through intermediary agents). The grain trade was part of a remarkably extensive trading pattern established in and beyond the Highlands by 1700. The Earls of Cromartie, in company with other Highland lairds, demonstrated considerable business acumen since many of them were directly involved in the daily detail of the commerce. As William Mackay long ago remarked, 'The old Highland chiefs and lairds have been painted as far above traffic of this kind, but the truth is that they had a keen eye for business, and were experts at a bargain.'[10]

Tarbat's efforts were notably systematic and thoroughly organised. Between 1662 and 1672 Tarbat and his chamberlains set about the creation of a mechanism of export to the southern lowlands; by the time he went to live in Edinburgh in 1672 Tarbat's scheme was already working smoothly. The estate victual rents, in the form of bere-barley, came in at Candlemas (February 2nd), usually about 600 bolls of the Tarbat measure.[11] Then an agent in Edinburgh was told of the available surplus in order to arrange a contract of sale with a master brewer-burgess of Edinburgh. Another contract was signed with a charter skipper of Leith or one of the Fife ports for the conveyance of the grain. The chamberlain may also have been instructed to buy up any balance on the open market. Then the estate officials set about the drying, bagging and shipping under the supervision of a chamberlain at the little ports of Easter Ross.[12] Contemporaries claimed that the grain of Easter Ross was as good as the best produced in the Lothians. Certainly the grain trade was the principal source of income from the estates and produced an average of £1200 Scots per annum in the late seventeenth or early eighteenth century. Methods of settlement between the several parties involved in the trade were slow, and much legal business and correspondence was generated in the process.

Having established the commercial connections for this grain trade, Tarbat then extended the infrastructure and the scale of his operations. Shipments were made through the Royal Burghs of Dingwall, Cromarty or Tain, at which ports shipping dues were levied by law. After much lobbying Tarbat managed to convert his own ports viz. New Milton and Portmahomack, into burghs and ports of barony. He also invested in capital equipment for the trade: at Portmahomack he began the construction of a harbour wall and a secure, substantial grain store, which were completed in 1689 (and still stand three centuries later).[13] To crown his expansion into the grain trade, he also bought his way into the royal burgh of Cromarty, and adjoining cornlands, and on completion immediately built a new girnel to service his head port. His ships were then able to take grain from both the Black Isle and from Strathpeffer, and moved across to the Sands of Nigg to lie offshore and take on board the crop of New Tarbat, and as owner of the former Royal burgh he paid no customs dues. Gaining possession of Cromarty was the apex of his career as a landowner, politician in Ross, and merchant. When Queen Anne honoured Tarbat after her accession in 1703 he became Earl of Cromartie.

Thus, so far as his capital would allow him, Tarbat was a precocious improving landlord. While his boats sailed to Edinburgh with bere-barley for malting and grain for northern European ports, he was also introducing new techniques to Easter Ross. He imported Dutch experts to reclaim the low lying lands below Meddat.[14] In April 1691 Andrew Fletcher of Saltoun asked him for advice on 'all the new improvements in husbandry' and suggested that he 'buy the books of that kynd for your shelf and for me'. He asked for specific detailed advice on converting from arable to pasture, and also about suitable rotations.[15] Tarbat corresponded with Sir William Binning on turnip cultivation. The eastern Cromartie estates were, therefore, at the forefront of agricultural improvement, but progress was slow. Easter Ross had become a grain export district but, for another century and a half, it remained vulnerable to sudden seasonal shortfalls. Famine remained a recurrent threat to the community. The year 1741, for instance, saw a severe scarcity here as elsewhere. In Tarbat 1741 was remembered because 'Many were then found dead on the highways and in the fields, and others, through long-fasting, expired as soon as they tasted food.' Corn rents were then being exported but only 'till the mob put a stop to this by breaking up a sloop laden with oat meal for Greenock'.[16] There was no government intervention at that time.

Half a century earlier the construction of new port facilities at Portmahomack had been paralleled by other major work in the building of New Tarbat House, a very substantial mansion close to the port and built on a scale to match Tarbat's rising status. The building continued over several decades and the accounts of its construction have survived in some detail. One technological detail in methods employed stood out, perhaps as a mark of the relatively advanced character of economic operations in late seventeenth century Easter Ross. In 1686 the accounts mention the purchase of twelve pairs of birch rails from Inverness for the use of 'cart trams and wayne rants', as well as 18 pairs of 'cart trams' and payment of 'carters for the stone-waggons'.[17] This was almost certainly evidence of a wagonway to transport stone from the quarries to the site of the new house: the contracted mason was required to win the stone, but Tarbat was obliged to load the stone to the construction site. Wagonways had been developed in parts of England as early as 1603-4 but were extremely rare in Scotland and Tarbat's facility is surprising in a relatively remote area. It may have reflected Tarbat's own progressive and enquiring attitude to technology and new industry.[18]

There were other sources of income on the estate though they were generally somewhat unreliable in character. In the seventeenth century there were substantial sales of timber, notably from the distant area of Inverchassely which provided oak timber for shipbuilding and for house construction, together with birch and fir for deals. In 1707 Cadboll reported that the 'woods of Strathcarron is altogether destroyed by storm', but timber sales, especially from Coigach, continued through the eighteenth century.

More elaborate was the extremely lucrative income from fishing on the River Conan, purchased from the Urquhart Estate—this involved complicated systems of weirs and nets into which swam the spawning salmon. The catches were either smoked in a croft or, more generally, cleaned and packed into barrels with salt, for export. The owner of the fishing always leased it out to an agent and took a percentage of sales. The Conan fishing was, apparently, big business, but for more than a century there were tedious legal controversies about its ownership. In 1688 the sales of salmon were depressed by the curtailment of trade with France, clearly an important market for the fish. Consignments were also sent to Aberdeen. Tarbat appears to have paid the fishermen in kind—in bolls of barley-bere, and was also responsible for stores of salt and barrels. Salt was a special problem and sometimes the catch was lost for want of it: salt came from France, Inverness or Leith, depending on the quality required.

Fishing in the Conan dropped out of the estate correspondence in 1714 and appears to have been on wadset to a merchant of Inverness, Provost Duff. When Peter May surveyed the Conan Fishing in 1754 he found the weirs in a broken down state, and eventually recommended that they be rebuilt on the old scheme.[19] On the west coast, fishing at Lochbroom was also leased on an annual rent; in the early eighteenth century the enterprise appears to have been confined to salmon netting. Success eluded various leaseholders; one Aberdeen merchant fell into debt through his attempts to export the fish. Further efforts to develop the herring fishery at Ullapool by Tarbat were also modest and only small progress was made for half a century.

Though his own enterprise was not notably successful Tarbat was an eloquent advocate for the national development of fisheries in Scotland and pressed the question in the Scottish Parliament before the Union. He, like many of his countrymen, believed that fishing (currently mainly in Dutch hands) was a vital matter for Scottish development, for wealth and employment. A true mercantilist, Tarbat believed that fishing could accumulate capital in Scotland as the basis for 'planting and sustaining a colony on probable and solid grounds'. In his *Short Proposal for African Company and Fishing* (c.1698) he argued that the profits generated by a Scottish colonial venture should first be employed to finance busses to operate off the Scottish coasts. He made the point that 'mines of gold and silver in the earth do not renew their treasure ... whereas the mines of the fish in the sea are yearly renewed'. In his *Overtures for the Advantages of Fishing* he advocated bounties on the herring fishery, and went into more substantial detail in 1712 with his *Proposals made by the Earl of Cromartie on the Fishing*.

Tarbat, unable to activate government assistance, made several attempts to generate his own fishing enterprise at Lochbroom (many decades before the entry of the British Fishery Society into the field). As early as 1698, in association with Sir William Binning, he set in motion a prototype fishing station at Ullapool with the intention of developing the export of salt herrings from Wester Ross to Stockholm, London and France. The effort was renewed a dozen years later. In 1712 he expressed his frustrations—pointing out that herrings were so abundant in Lochbroom that the people were using them for manure, yet hardly a Scottish boat was to be seen. Capital, transport and the salt tax were the great impediments to development. In fact it was not until the growth of Glasgow as a port, and as an exporter of salt and dried fish across the Atlantic for the slave trade, that the commercial fishing of the remote north-west became feasible. But this is not to say that there was no commercial fishing in Coigach before 1790. The correspondence between Baillie John Steuart of Inverness and Lord Cromartie in the 1720s and 1730s indicates a continuing trade in cured cod and herrings. The reality, however, was that the scale was small and that the potential for development had not been tapped.[20]

All the primary production of the Cromartie estate was subject to two hazards: the long range and intermittent management of the owner and his chamberlains, and the problems of weather and crop failure. It was also subject to the effects of prices, and sudden gluts in the various markets. Though little evidence survives of the economic viability of the trades, it is nevertheless clear that the estate did not lack incentive or enterprise in developing saleable output from the north. The crisis in estate finances, after 1720, was not the result of inertia or indolence so much as excessive expenditure and incompetence in other directions.

There were other signs of an enterprising spirit activating estate affairs, certainly in the 1690s, possibly linked to the buoyant income of Tarbat during his political ascendancy in Edinburgh. He entertained many ideas for both Highland and national development including a Proposal for an University in Inverness.[21] In 1694 he bought twelve shares in the new Paper Manufactory of Scotland in Edinburgh, promoted by Nicholas Deray, whose linen manufacturing he also supported. Tarbat was clearly prominent in the new enterprise and his shares were worth £3 sterling each. He was also one of the promoters of the Leith Glass Works which began operation in 1689: the glass works, initially, prospered with a monopoly of manufacture in Scotland (and was also protected by a prohibition of glass imports). Tarbat had energetically promoted the enterprise as an infant industry both by the enabling legislation and by private investment. It built up a custom in green glass bottles from Kirkwall to Aberdeen, and among many medical practitioners. But it began to fail sometime before the final collapse in 1708—partly a consequence of taxes and the billetting of troops on the works. More particularly, however, it seems likely that the Leith company was undercut by English manufacturers (possibly with the connivance of a crooked customs official at Arbroath), and the Leith Glass Works were not revived till the last quarter of the eighteenth century. The proprietors of the Leith Glass Works, in a petition of 1701, complained bitterly that 'The Master of the Glass Manufactures of England on purpose to break our trade send in great quantities of the said glass bottles to undersell and ruin our manufacture'. They warned that the ultimate object of the English competition was the eradication of Scots production and the imposition of a new monopoly price for glass set in England. The eventual failure of the Leith Works in the face of English mercantilist practice may have further persuaded Tarbat of the wisdom of union.[22]

Tarbat was also connected with the promotion and ultimately the spectacular failure of the much more ambitious enterprise known as the Darien Scheme. In 1693 he was active in the pressure groups seeking opportunity to develop Scottish trade with Africa and India and later America. Tarbat believed passionately that the Scots were severely disadvantaged by their effective exclusion from American colonisation and from the great English markets.[23] At one point he remonstrated with the king that Scots merchants were being driven by their poverty into scandalous acts of piracy.[24] It was not surprising therefore that he should follow his own logic and advocacy and involve himself directly in the Darien scheme to promote Scotland's own colonisation. His brother Roderick Lord Prestonhall became secretary of the Company, and Tarbat and his sons invested £2500 Scots. The outcome was an unmitigated disaster. Tarbat's own finances were already in disrepair, and the collapse of the Darien scheme was a blow not only to his pride but also to his pocket. His mercantilist convictions remained—the policy of government should be 'to enrich Scotland so as it may thrive in trade without being beholden to other nations for loans.' Soon, of course, the solution of Scotland's economic problems took the shape of union with England, into which course Cromartie threw most of his remaining political energies.

IV

Tarbat's successful ventures in the grain trade between Easter Ross and Edinburgh depended to some degree on his acquisition of property in the region. Contained in the legal documents of the period 1660-1700 is the intricate, indeed byzantine, story of the means taken to dismember and swallow up the smaller but important estate of Urquhart. It was a case-study in the internecine life of Scottish estates. The family of Urquhart had owned land on the eastern tip of the Black Isle, including the west Sutor, the cliff guarding the narrow entrance to the sheltered waters of the Cromarty Firth, since the fourteenth century. The small township and port of Cromarty was a Royal burghal place and existed as an enclave within the Urquhart territory. Urquhart was an old-established family, part of the network of Moray and Ross magnates, many of whom were connected by kinship.

The Urquharts fell on very hard times by the mid seventeenth century. When Sir Thomas Urquhart (1611-1660) inherited in 1647, it was already described as 'a craizied estate', that is a much weakened property, creaking and groaning and ready to fall to pieces. The family finances were weakened by accumulating debts and Sir Thomas was not the man to rescue the inheritance: his main fame was as a prolific and idiosyncratic author whose translation of Rabelais was reckoned more bawdy than the original. He is said to have died in Paris of a seizure of joy and mirth on hearing the news of the Restoration in 1660. The estates passed in three rapid successions to his descendants and by 1680 they were exceedingly run down and the castle vandalised.

The passage of the Urquhart estates to Tarbat was by way of a carefully articulated series of loans and legal arrangements[25] which eventually throttled the original owners. It was a process which extended over a quarter of a century and involved a consortium of creditors who re-scheduled their loans until complete control was achieved. It was a common enough process between landowners and one which eventually (in the eighteenth century) confronted the Cromartie estate itself. Much of the exercise was arbitrated by the Dallases who did legal business for various parties involved, including the Urquharts. The informal consortium of creditors comprised three landowners—Tarbat, his cousin Mackenzie of Rosehaugh,[26] and an introverted old Presbyterian called Alexander Brodie.

The Urquhart estate, already heavily encumbered with other debts, engaged in further loans from this partnership—even by 1660 it was said that Urquhart had borrowed from every friendly laird, and from nobles in Inverness and Edinburgh. There was endless dispute and confusion over the status of debts and claims, and they thickened significantly in the early 1670s. At that time Tarbat, in political eclipse, was in the north and able to concentrate his strategy. Moreover the estates' potential was enhanced by the expansion of his grain trade, and this clearly motivated his acquisitive attitude in the district. It was a ripe plum ready for the picking. Tarbat was best placed to make a catch. Partly it was a consequence of the ineptitude and extravagance of the heirs; in 1677 the incumbent was said to possess 'much of vanity and affectation', and the heir committed suicide the following year. Another member of the family thanked Tarbat in 1687, saying he was 'Only left with the matter of seven pounds' and hoped 'God Almighty will repay you for being kind to me as you has been'. By then the estates, through the mechanism of long running debt and mortgage, had passed into Tarbat's hands. In 1683 Tarbat was secure in the ownership of the Urquhart estate; he had made himself responsible to the creditors attached to the estate revenues, in particular to the other people in the partnership.[27] In the course of the next dozen years Tarbat also gained rights over the burgh of Cromarty. While thus enhancing his capacity in the grain trade Tarbat appears also to have been motivated in his acquisition of Cromarty by the idea eventually of providing for his second son: when, in 1704, Kenneth became a baronet he also came into the possession of the burgh estate of Cromarty.[28]

Tarbat by this predatory strategy had complemented his political success in Edinburgh with appropriate territorial aggrandisement in his ancestral homelands. But he had not achieved this without financial strain and eventually his ambitions were counterpoised with growing financial problems both in the capital and the north.

V

There is never a moment in Tarbat's career when the surviving papers make it possible to draw up a straightforward profit and loss account, nor is it clear the degree to which his income from his political offices was channelled into the finances of the northern estates. In fact the health and future of the estate finances was concealed in the relationship between its creditors and debtors. These were contained in complex webs of 'bonds' which measured a huge range of money transactions, loans and obligations. Nearly two thousand such documents survive, as relating to the period 1640 to 1745. Such documents were encrusted with legal problems—the wadset arrangement was probably the most vexatious. It was small wonder that the law provided so lucrative a living for the Scottish middle classes, nor that many lairds sent their sons to study law before they took up their inheritance.

Before the time of formal banking, the Bond was an extraordinarily versatile financial mechanism. For borrowing or lending, the transfer of capital, raising mortgages, paying annuities, salaries, school bills or the tailor, the Bond was the means of payment. There was no alternative system but bonds for banking or transfer of cash or of liability. (It also applied to bonds of good behaviour or political compliance.) They were the universal means of financial transaction[29] and through them is written the history of early modern estates. The central problem, however, is that most were cancelled and destroyed. The surviving evidence tends to reflect transactions which were not settled in the conventional fashion.[30] Some claims via Bonds were sustained over generations—for instance John Macleod of Talisker advanced a claim against the Cromartie estate in 1753, offering as documentation a bond dated 1661.[31]

Tarbat eventually took control of the Urquhart estate by amassing Bonds against its hereditary owners until they were finally bankrupt. His own estate came under similar assault, mainly after his own death in 1714. But the mechanism was much the same, and a single example illustrates the insidious process, essentially by Bond of Wadset. A wadset consisted of an initial loan of money from a tacksman or tenant to his landlord, the loan being secured by lowered rents. However, if the principal was not paid off as agreed, the whole transaction graduated into a transfer of the land—in effect a forced sale to the tacksman. The role of wadsetter also conferred status, sometimes in the form of voting rights. Aeneas Macleod of Cadboll performed precisely these moves as the result of a wadset for bonds entered into with the first and second Earls of Cromartie 'when they were distressed by their creditors'. Macleod thus became owner of parts of the Easter Aird of the Tarbat Estates. Wadsets and other bonds created a tangle of obligations which, unless perfectly managed, could easily overwhelm an estate. The embarrassment of the Cromartie estate after 1714 provides a perfect example.

The Cromartie estate was a fine property by the standards of northern Scotland; in the 1680s and 90s its victual rents were worth £1300 Scots per annum, on average, and there were other cash crops. As an estate it often yielded very good surpluses which found excellent vent in the cattle trade of the west, and the grain trade of the east. The proprietor's flourishing practice at the Scottish Bar brought in large but unspecified sums; his service for the State was, on the face of it, well rewarded with pensions and salary. Yet the family was too often 'distressed by their creditors'. The particular reasons cannot be quantified, but they boil down to an old story: the Earls of Cromartie and their dependents had expensive tastes (and obligations) which outran their handsome income. The symptoms were not difficult to identify.

Tarbat spent an imprudent amount of money to gain possession of the Urquhart property in Cromarty, and he was a master of conspicuous expenditure. He inherited two substantial though antiquated houses. Castle Leod, rebuilt by his grandfather, needed little attention. The castle at New Tarbat, however, was in the medieval and run-down state left by the previous owner, Dunbar. The Earl rebuilt Tarbat House, with the probable aid of his friend Sir William Bruce and local labour, laying out gardens and orchards, and furnishing the interior with marble and fine furniture.

> Here he introduced the sash-window into the Scottish Highlands within about a decade of its very first appearance in Britain, and here he commissioned work by the exceptionally renowned plasterer George Dunsterfield, fresh from his superb achievements at Holyroodhouse. The gardens were equally outstanding, but unfortunately none of this now stands.[32]

He also acquired the rights to the small barony of Royston on the outskirts of Edinburgh where he built between 1683 and 1690 a most elegant town villa on the remains of an earlier courtyard-house. Royston had money lavished on its building and furnishing.

In addition Tarbat's appearances at Whitehall entailed the elaborate wardrobe and wigs of late Stuart times, a coach and four, although the Scottish roads scarcely could carry them; portraits painted by Lely, silver plate, including 'twa tay pots' which were amongst the earliest in Scotland; and a library of fine books for which he sent to the Royal Printers of the Louvre as well as to London. The first Earl had very fine taste, judging from the surviving pieces of furniture and from the detailed inventories of his clothes, books and possessions. Unfortunately his style of living outstripped his resources, and the estate was in severe difficulties when he died in 1714. Two clear symptoms showed the extent of the problem: the extension of wadsets over several parts of the estate, and the rapid consumption of the forested reserves of the land, especially in Coigach. Both undermined the future income of the estate.

It is evident also that the first Earl's ambitious plans for new enterprise in the Cromarty Firth (beyond the elaborate reconstruction of New Tarbat) over-extended his finances. There was a plaintive note in the exchanges between Cromartie and his creditors—for instance with Alexander Stronach the building mason who contracted to erect the great new pier at Portmahomack. In July 1701 Stronach presented Tarbat (presumably after many earlier attempts) with his final account for his work. He complained that the money and meal owed to him had not been paid, emphasising the fact that, should he not receive his payments soon, he would be 'necessitated to forsake my family and country through the urgent importunity of other workmen who finished the work with me'. The web of indebtedness was wide: in this case Stronach was compelled to accept settlement in kind in the form of the inferior local barley-bere grain instead of the much more expensive oatmeal as originally specified. Another clear indication of the parlous state of the family fortunes was a contract signed in 1707 between the Earl and his son, Lord Macleod, in which it stated that Macleod had outspent his allowance, and that the Earl agreed to pay his debts off 'in order to save the Estate'.[33]

Much of the financial damage to the estate was a consequence of the waywardness of the heir: his attempts to influence the management of the estates had caused offence among the chamberlains; when he was sent to the Low Countries in 1694 (to recover his health and his reputation) he ran up alarming expenses, and contracted impossible transactions in grain to the further embarrassment of the estate agents. He incurred expenses with a stylish insouciance which eventually persuaded his father to entail the estate to prevent its future wastage. In 1695 another son showed a similar nonchalance— he arrived in London, reporting that 'I found that before I touched land I had spent five guineas ... I am afraid I cannot live so cheap here as at Oxford.' The heir's first wife spent her way through a good fortune and was divorced mainly on those grounds. In 1707 the heir was in total financial confusion. His own father remarked that only a fool would lend him money,[34] but the Earl himself had established substantial annuities and obligation on the estate for the support of his large family, all of which further mortgaged future income.

The old Earl, to meet this, the most severe financial crisis of his career, mustered his relatives and senior tacksmen, who deliberated at Castle Leod, and wrote a number of papers on the subject. Eventually the Earl persuaded his kinsman MacLeod of Cadboll to take a seven year tack of Strathpeffer Barony and his other kinsman, Mackenzie of Inchculter, to oversee Coigach, the cattle trade, and to act as political manager. Both showed reluctance, but worked well once confirmed by documents. Cadboll's price for this and for lending a large sum of money was the wadset of the best cornlands of the easter Aird properties; Tarrel, Arboll and Wilkhaven among them. This transaction started Cadboll on the upward path, while beginning the slow decline of the Cromartie estates. The reason assigned by the Earl for the crisis was the extravagance of his son John, but it seems obvious that his own expenditure had been far too heavy as well. A number of debtors in Edinburgh headed by Blackwood, a banker/tailor, had bonded together to raise a joint action against the earl and his heir. However the Earl blamed John entirely. In a complex and savage legal document he disinherited his eldest son from the Estate, which he entailed onto his eldest grandson, then a few years old. John was to have a life-rent of Tarbat House and to live on the jointure for his wife, 40 chalder of bere barley of the growth of Tarbat Barony. He was expressly barred from the sale of any property or land. His son, the Heir En Tailzie, was to inherit the three Baronies intact, and three Tutors were appointed: his father, his mother's brother, Lord Elibank, and his uncle, Lord Royston. There seems no doubt that if this drastic measure had not been taken, and confirmed in the Will of the first earl, the second would have sold much of the estates before his death in 1731.

But it would be a mistake to charge the Earl's heir and his siblings with all the dilapidation of the estate's finances. The first Earl himself had been an extravagant spender—in buildings, in investments, in land, in the very style of life which his political prominence entailed. Most particularly his expenditures at Royston were glaringly ill-considered, particularly if he assumed that his successor would aspire to a comparable standard of ostentation. Tarbat had bought Royston in 1683 and it was developed in the most expensive and ornate style over the following ten years.[35] It was, according to modern commentators, 'a villa of the grandest sort, designed to display the owner's importance to those in business in Edinburgh ... whilst affording the necessary privacy for political intrigue'. In 1705, when his debts were mounting and the house had become a liability he tried in vain to sell Royston to the government as a residence for the Secretary of State. He asked £4000 sterling for a house which had cost £6000 sterling. It was a measure of his growing financial embarrassment.[36]

There is still, over a door at Royston House, a wise inscription which reads 'riches unemployed are of no use, but made to circulate are productive of much good.'[37] Yet Royston itself was a neutralisation of the family's capital, and the first Earl's attempts to employ creatively his capital in investments were almost all unsuccessful. For this was a classic case of a northern laird adopting, even leading, new cosmopolitan standards of life in the capital: in the long run such landlord behaviour could be sustained only by draining the cash income of the estate sources—the production of the Highland people themselves. For the most part there continued to be, in the surviving records of the Cromartie estate, virtually no direct reference to the existence of these people.

CHAPTER 5

Prelude to Disaster

I

The second Earl of Cromartie, John Mackenzie (c.1656-1731) was almost sixty years of age when he succeeded to the earldom in 1714. The new Earl had neither the resources nor the personality to sustain the prominence his illustrious father had given the family in national politics. When his father was raised to the earldom in 1703 his heir took the title Lord McLeod and Master of Tarbat. He had been M.P. for the County of Ross in 1685 but his political career was permanently blighted by his involvement in the attempted Rising for King James. Nor did his reputation benefit when, in August 1691, he was tried with two others before the Court of Justiciary for murder. Apparently he had been involved in a scuffle or skirmish in the Kirkgate of Leith: in the brawling confusion in a tavern Elias Poiret, a French Protestant refugee, and a Gentleman of the King's Guard, had been killed in a darkened bedchamber. All the protagonists had been drunk and the Master of Tarbat was naked. In his defence Tarbat said that the Frenchman had been killed by mistake in the dark by his own friends. He seems to have been believed because the Court acquitted him, the charge was not proven and he went free. The episode had been profoundly embarrassing to the family and a good deal more dangerous than its outcome seemed. The Master of Tarbat's behaviour could easily have been construed as treasonable: that of a young Jacobite sprig in mortal combat with a French Protestant in the service of the King. He was lucky not to have been pursued much further. It was a narrow shave, and young Tarbat was pushed off on a prolonged tour of the Low Countries in 1693, after a period of rustication at Tarbat House. He seems never to have visited Edinburgh again during his father's lifetime.

When John Mackenzie became second Earl of Cromartie in 1714 he inherited a mountain of financial problems. The position was probably already irretrievable and as soon as he took control of the estates the creditors flocked about him in increasingly predatory formation. The financial crisis was the product of excessive expenditure by his father, and by the weight of relatives living off the estate revenues. This was, indeed, a recurrent dilemma for landed estates north and south of the border. On the elevation of the first Earl in 1704 his two other sons were made Baronets. Long before, arrangements had been made that the estates would eventually be divided to provide both with wealth appropriate to their status, and this undoubtedly weakened the central finances of the Cromartie estate.

The financial history of the first Earl was a sorry story and had reached its nadir in the pathetic efforts he made before his death to extract 'debts' directly from the Crown (see above, Chapter Three). Almost all the responsibility for the problem derived from the unrestrained consumption behaviour led by the Earl himself but taken to an extreme in the careers of his sons. Each of them, but especially the heir, consumed their way into great debt and caused grave embarrassment to the family. The first Earl had been unable to control their extravagance and even his wills are full of despair for their future. One of them, in 1707, referred to the 'overplus of debt' which now deterred all prospective creditors to him or his heir. He concluded miserably that

> during the Earl of Cromartie's lifetime the Lord McLeod, his lady and family, have not one groat to live upon. And no wise man can lend him any, who doth not resolve to gift him the money ... This is the best view that Lord McLeod's estate can be considered in. During his life the heir and the rest of the children will not have a groat.

He predicted that after MacLeod's own death the creditors would pursue his widow and children 'and the rest must begg'.[1] It was in that year, 1707, that Cromartie made a contract with his son in which it was stated that MacLeod had spent more than his allowance and thus the Earl had been required to intervene and pay off his debts, the terms of which were agreed by Lady MacLeod.[2] His wife indeed was central to the problem.

The second Earl, inheriting in 1714, had married first Lady Elizabeth Gordon, daughter of the Earl of Aboyne. The marriage was a disaster. His wife, according to him, was remarkably extravagant and contracted large debts for 'meat, drink, cloaths, abulziments, rings, bracelets, and jewels of great value'. She was curbed by 'letters of inhibition' in 1696, to protect the estate and was soon after divorced; her own defence was that her husband had left her as surety—in pawn—in Holland while he tried to raise funds in Scotland. During these years the heir appears to have raised loans on his expectation of succeeding and on the family home. These accumulating debts caused major family crises of indebtedness in 1685, 1690, and again in 1707-12. Lands in Coigach and Strathpeffer were set in tack to Cadboll for seven years to pay off the 1707 debts, an arrangement repeated in 1714 for the same reason. Cromartie's second wife was the Hon. Mary Murray, third daughter of Lord Elibank, with whom he had six children; a third wife, Anna, third daughter of Lord Lovat, also bore six children. It was a large family which extended by marriage the network of contacts into the landed classes of Scotland, but it also accumulated further financial obligations which ultimately depended on the net revenues of the Cromartie estate.

The Cromartie estate was therefore overloaded with debts and obligations to family members. Its future earnings had long been mortgaged away. The symptoms of decline could be seen even in the Earl's own household. In 1716, for instance, an order was sent to an apothecary in Inverness for arsenic to kill off the rats which were devouring the Earl of Cromartie's books. In the following year there were reports that Castle Leod was in a ruinous state and the policies surrounding it 'in bad condition'.[3] A crisis was gathering and there appeared little solution available.

In September 1717 Cromartie's estate chamberlain pleaded with the Earl to winter at the house at New Tarbat 'where I am sure your Lordship will be much easier than in the hurry of the city'.[4] In fact the financial benefits of residence on the estate were vital but, presumably, not enough. In 1717 creditors of the Cromartie estates banded together to apply concerted pressure to the second Earl. The crisis dragged on without resolution for several years. Various schemes were concocted to retrieve the family's fortunes. In 1722 Lord Elibank, tutor to the under-age owner, George, Lord Tarbat, was involved as adviser to the family and warned him that it was a 'very critical time for the preservation of your family and your own welfare and settlement'. He implored Tarbat to take seriously his predicament. One solution required the sale of assets and the departure of the heir abroad. Another was that the estates be put out to a farmer at £5 per boll 'to extinguish those debts that your grandfather left the estate burdened with'. Tarbat was summonsed for consultations with Elibank in Edinburgh and warned directly

> your own interest and the preservation of your family intirely depend on it. Be sure to bring with you a full and compleat rentall of all your estate, both victual and money rent, with rents, salmon fishing and kens and everything else.[5]

In the outcome the solution to the financial morass of the Cromartie family came in two stages. The first was the actual sequestration of the estate in 1723. That is, control was forfeited and the appropriate income diverted to the prior satisfaction of the claims of the creditors of the estate. John MacBean, writer in Inverness, was appointed to collect the rents for this purpose. The Earl was required to live in Tarbat House and on '40 chalder of victual secured as his wife's portion'. But he continued to build at New Tarbat and to sell off moveable property, especially the timber of Coigach despite ambiguity about his legal title.[6] It was during the period of sequestration that complaints were made against Macbean's administration. In 1730 it was alleged that he employed too many agents to collect the rent. The agents were reported as 'pretending to be in danger of their lives', but, it was pointed out, Easter Ross was as peaceful and accessible as Midlothian.[7]

The sequestration had been prompted in 1723 by the actions of Cromartie's creditors. MacBean was empowered to 'uplift' the Cromartie rents until the debts were paid off. MacBean's position was undoubtedly made difficult by a certain degree of mutiny on the part of some of the tenantry who resisted his authority. They refused to meet his messengers and refused to pay rents, and they repossessed their cattle after they had been poinded. The resistance of the tenantry to the demands of Cromartie's creditors may suggest a degree of solidarity between the tenantry and either the dispossessed laird or with his son, but it may simply reflect a degree of opportunism among the people.[8] Either way it did Cromartie little good in terms of his debts.

The second stage of the financial re-stabilisation of the Cromartie estate came in the form of an extraordinarily favourable marriage contracted between the heir to the estate and 'Bonnie Bell Gordon' in 1724. Isabel Gordon was the daughter of Sir William Gordon, a wealthy London banker and also Private Secretary to Frederick, Prince of Wales. Gordon was delighted by the match and showed extraordinary generosity to his new in-laws by way of financial assistance. He began paying off some of the debts and, eventually, rescheduling others until he was a great creditor of the Cromartie estates.

In 1724, at the time of the marriage, he expressed his good feeling thus: 'No arguments were necessary to induce me to go as far in money as my circumstances could at present allow me in favour of the young lord, of whom I have very great expectation'. He realised the importance of his intervention for the family, in 'retrieving the present weights and intricacies under which it labours'.[9]

This, however, was only the beginning of a rescue operation. In October 1725 the Earl of Cromartie, his estates sequestrated still, was continuing to evade his creditors. Indeed his ability to avoid legal action was a measure of the continuing autonomy of Highland jurisdiction. Cromartie was hereditary sheriff and able to protect himself and no effective action could be taken against him. Lord Islay, effectively the government's manager for Scotland, regarded this as further proof of the persistent ungovernability of the north under the prevailing legal system:

> The Highlands can never be civilised, so long as any person is tolerated in the giving publick defiance to the courts of the Law, and the difficultys that attends the execution of the Law in the Highlands seems to be the very essence of their barbarity.

Islay suggested that General Wade take action in the case but the latter had no appetite to take on the functions of a bailiff.[10] Cromartie however was able to gain further relief from Sir William Gordon who, in 1726, entered a heritable bond to lend the Earl £42,083 Scots. It was a transaction rendered complex by existing wadset over parts of Coigach[11] but was clearly another mark of Gordon's wealth and generosity to the family into which his attractive daughter had married.

II

The second Earl died in 1731 and was succeeded by George Mackenzie whose fortunate marriage and relatively prudent conduct had saved the estate from complete extinction. The third Earl was born about 1703 and is said to have been educated solely in the Protestant church and that, until the actual rising in 1745, had shown no suspicion of unorthodox or Jacobite views. In a retrospective evaluation of his personality it was said: 'The Earl of Cromartie's private character is very amiable; he is esteemed a polite nobleman, and affable in his temper and behaviour, and has little or nothing of that austere pride and haughtiness so peculiar to most highland chiefs.'[12] Mackenzie had acted as Grand Master of the Freemasons in 1737-8 and, perhaps more significantly, was an intimate friend of Simon Fraser, Lord Lovat, his cousin and prominent agent in the conspiracies which preceded the Rising. Cromartie's policy towards estate administration is barely documented but he was adventurous enough to introduce southern colliers to investigate the possibilities of an outcrop of coal near Castle Leod. The vein of coal was only twelve inches thick and proved a disappointment. He made efforts also to develop fishing and agriculture and may have shored up the finances of the estate on a temporary basis, but the general result was frustrating. As a sign of his seriousness in agricultural matters he was a member of the important Society of Improvers.[13]

In broad terms, therefore, the third Earl ended the years of poor management on the Cromartie estates and introduced several new improvements and renovated the decaying mansion houses of New Tarbat and Castle Leod. He brought new crop rotations of barley, wheat, peas and beans to Strathpeffer. His grandfather had introduced turnips, as a garden crop, as early as 1690. Much hedging and ditching was undertaken and the third Earl planted 100 acres of timber at Strathpeffer. He also embarked on schemes of consolidation, including enclosures at the Castle Leod mains. The Earl collected higher rents, set tacks of 15-year periods, and wadsetted major parts of the property as a means of recovering other debts. There is also fragmentary evidence to suggest that Cromartie, in company with other Highland proprietors, was already attempting to circumvent and therefore undermine the tacksmen. This is indicated by the increasing use of direct tenancies. In 1730 only 24 small tenants held leases directly from the Earl. By the late 1740s the number had tripled,[14] which must have diminished the status and control of the tacksmen. The available evidence suggests that the old subtenancy system, the most important single element in 'Highland feudalism', was under assault in the early eighteenth century. Nevertheless much of the system managed to cling on for a further one hundred years.

Despite such evident dedication to agricultural development and the revival of the estate economy, the Earl's efforts were only partially successful. The lapse of the estate into famine in 1741 was one vivid demonstration of its fundamental backwardness.[15] Another sign was the continuing debt problem of the Earl. The evidence of bills outstanding at the death of his father indicated the scale of the problem. Thirteen years later the problem remained: Cromartie's financial state was exposed in his letters to Lord Tweeddale in 1743 and 1744. They echoed the desperate pleas of his grandfather four decades before. He pleaded that 'without vanity I can say I have done as good services as many that have greater marks of favour'. He asked for his case to be placed before the Chancellor of the Exchequer.[16]

Cromartie's desperate pleas for the remission of Crown Rents obscured a much more serious deficiency in his financial relationship with the Crown. By the fateful year 1745 the Earl of Cromartie was almost swamped in debt. He and his managers, with some difficulty, had managed to stave off the demands of the Crown since he inherited his lands in 1731. Indeed Cromartie had paid off many other debts handed down to him from his grandfather's and father's times. But, by 1745, the Crown Debt had accumulated to the huge sum of £5498.9.3 sterling. This was five times the gross rental income of the estate: rents were about £1103 sterling per annum; Cromartie's personal estate was worth about £3770 sterling (mostly in the form of houses on the estate). He was clearly very close to bankruptcy, not in itself a new thing for the family but, in 1745, connected with more threatening circumstances. In fact, in June 1745, Cromartie's 'Petition for a stay of Execution on the Crown Rents' was rejected by the Lords of the Treasury. Indeed the response of the Lords was unambiguous—Cromartie had rendered no account for any year since 1733, and he automatically forfeited a bond of £1000. Thus, it must be said, the Earl of Cromartie was profoundly and, perhaps, irretrievably in debt to the Crown at the very moment when Jacobitism emerged in such spectacular confrontation with the Hanoverian crown in the west Highlands.

III

Many of the Scots leaders involved in the Jacobite Risings of the eighteenth century were practically insolvent. Two questions arise. One concerns the degree of financial desperation and opportunism which activated a large implication in the Rebellions. The other is about the typicality of the Jacobites: were they more or less prone to financial instability than their non-Jacobite peers? Both questions remain largely unanswered though most historians now resist the notion that there was a simple correlation between economic failure and disaffection. Nevertheless it is clear that the clans which joined the Hanoverian side were predominantly the more prosperous of their class. Bruce Lenman has remarked that 'it is certainly the case that a surprisingly high proportion of those chiefs who committed themselves unequivocally to Prince Charles in 1745 can be shown to have been in a parlous state financially'—it was, he claims, 'essentially a conservative backlash led by disgruntled lairds and nobles'. Rosalind Mitchison, reflecting directly on the case of Cromartie, writes, 'the belated Jacobitism of the bankrupt Earl of Cromarty [sic] reminds us that bringing the chiefs into the orbit of other landed society was apt to increase their expenses and that there was a marked correlation between bankruptcy and rebellion'.[17] While neither perfect nor conclusive[18] the correlation is difficult to avoid.

There is no doubt that Cromartie was in dire financial circumstances at the moment he and his son chose to join the Jacobite movement in 1745. Their kinsmen were similarly stricken by financial ineptitude. Cromartie's cousin, Sir George Mackenzie, who had inherited the extensive estate of Cromarty, fell bankrupt in 1741 and was forced to sell his estate to William Urquhart of Meldrum. Another cousin had inherited Royston but, lacking capital resources, was forced to sell it to the Duke of Argyll in 1739 for about £7,000. There was no financial assistance to be had from any of the Mackenzie side of the family.

The fact that the Earl of Cromartie was terminally insolvent at the time of his defection to the Jacobite Prince may, of course, have no connection with his decision to follow such a course. There is not a single iota of direct evidence of such a line of motivation. Yet the probabilities must be considered. It is not unlikely that a large, legal and unpayable, demand, at such a critical juncture, would have tipped the scales away from loyalty to George II and towards a sporting gamble with the heir of the house of Stuart. After all it was evident that the English peers who made the last rebellion against the Crown, in 1688, had been well rewarded. The Cromarties themselves had prospered from ancient benefits derived ultimately from the Stuart monarchs. The arrival of a final debt demand from the Hanoverian and Whig Lords of the Treasury, at the precise moment of rebellion in 1745, could not have been far from Cromartie's mind when he decided to throw in his lot with the Prince. But no such mundane or mercenary thought was ever allowed to cast a shadow over his subsequent defence in the months after the disaster of Culloden.

CHAPTER 6

Losing Everything: Cromartie and the 'Forty-Five

I

It would be difficult to exaggerate the consequences of Lord Cromartie's decision to join the Jacobite uprising in late 1745. It led to almost perfect disaster. He achieved relatively little glory in his military capacity and entirely missed the awful climax of Culloden. In his trial Cromartie was reduced to particular humiliation and was sentenced to death. He came within an inch or so of losing his life. He was banished from Scotland to live in abject poverty and total obscurity for the rest of his life. His family too were reduced to conditions of near-beggary and his son, who served with his father in the Uprising, chose to hide his shame by taking employment abroad. The Cromartie estates were confiscated by the Crown. The degradation was complete.

The manner in which the third Earl of Cromartie was drawn into the events of 1745 was a matter of critical importance in the subsequent interpretation of his role, and judgement on his guilt. In his defence at his trial in 1747 it was said that, disappointed by his failure to receive a commission in the government forces,[1] Cromartie had fallen into a sloth of despair. Worse still he got totally drunk, lost control of his reason, and committed himself to the Pretender under the influence of pressing (and presumably more sober) friends. He had been tricked into complicity, and had been excessively influenced by his friend Simon Lovat. In his own words, 'I was unhappily seduced from that loyalty in an unguarded moment by the arts of desperate and designing men.'[2] It was not a particularly likely story.[3]

For many years there had been rumours that the house of Stuart was about to venture a last throw for the throne of Britain. Such rumours were made more plausible and more threatening in 1743 when England and France came into armed conflict in the Low Countries. The possibility of French support for a Stuart invasion of Scotland, thought to be indispensable, now became a living issue. Highland landowners were alive to the possibility of invasion. It was a critical juncture, wrote the Earl of Sutherland in 1744: 'all that can be dear to any Briton has been threatened with an invasion'. Sutherland told the commander-in-chief for Scotland, Sir John Cope, that he would undertake to raise 500 men to keep the public peace. He warned that though the Highlands officially had been disarmed, those elements 'disaffected in the Highlands' were actually 'in general very well armed'.

Borrodel, Aug. y.e 8th 1745

Having been well inform'd of y.r Principles and Loyalty, I cannot but expect y.e Assistance at this juncture, that I am come with a firm resolution to retrieve the King my Father or perish in y.e attempt. I know the interest you have among those of y.r Name, and I depend upon you to exert it to y.e utmost of y.r Power. I have some reasons not to risk any application to y.e Earl of Seaforth without y.r advice, wch I shou'd Desire you to give me sincerely. I intend to set up y.e Royal Standard at Glenfinnen on monday y.e 19.th instant, and then I be very glad to see you on that occasion. If time does not allow it, I still depend upon your joyning me with all convenient speed. In y.e mean time you may be assured of the particular esteem and friendship I have for you.

Charles P.R.

9 Prince Charles' letter to Cromartie.

Prince Charles Edward Stuart landed at Moidart in August 1745, lacking the anticipated French backing. He lost no time in writing to possible adherents to his standard, notably Lord Lovat and the Earl of Cromartie. He reminded himself of their tradition of allegiance to the Stuarts. From Borradaile in Moidart on August 8 the Prince addressed Cromartie: 'I cannot but expect your assistance at this juncture'. No immediate reply has been traced. Cromartie managed to delay his response for many weeks, and indeed consulted several parties on the government side including Duncan Forbes of Culloden, the Lord President. Forbes was engaged in the effort to hold the Highlands to the government, and offered various incentives for their loyalty. For instance, in Cromartie's case, Forbes offered his son Lord MacLeod a captain's commission.[4] This was on the 23rd of September (more than a month after the Prince's overture): Cromartie's delay to Forbes' offer caused Forbes 'great unease'. Indeed three days later Cromartie seemed to show his hand by refusing Forbes' offer on the ground that the terms of the commission were unsatisfactory. Cromartie told Forbes:

> I cannot desire him, nor is it his own inclination, to accept of it on these terms, as it disables him from doing the service as he would wish; and if he is thought less capable than others, who are offered greater priviledges, it is no less to lay him aside.[5]

This response may simply have been a smokescreen behind which Cromartie was able to extricate his son from an earlier commitment to the government. The day-to-day circumstances remain obscure but Cromartie was already in the process of enrolling men for service with the Prince.

During these critical days Cromartie continued to prevaricate in his correspondence with Forbes and other loyalists. On 13th October Lord Macleod's refusal to accept a company was being interpreted as disaffection[6] but six days later Cromartie was still protesting his loyalty to the Hanoverian cause and his readiness to serve their cause. He claimed that he had been much misrepresented. Two days later Forbes wrote to Cromartie asking for a clear declaration of his loyalty and a denial of his rumoured defection to the Prince. Forbes said that he was disturbed by 'the Makers and Retailers of News in thy Country' and the rumours were damaging Cromartie's reputation. He could not believe such reports which were 'flatly contradictory to the hourly declarations of your Zeal for his Majestie's Service which your Ldp made to me when I last had the honour to see you at this place.'[7] By 24th October Forbes thought he had received such an assurance in which Cromartie had contradicted 'the many lies made of him, and assuring me that all the steps taken by him were only to provide men for the service of the government'.[8]

In truth Cromartie had been raising troops for the opposite purpose. The role of Lord Lovat, whom Cromartie had described as 'my best friend',[9] was critical. On 6th November 1745 Cromartie and his son visited Lovat at Beaufort and three days later they proceeded openly to join the Prince. In the process they had recruited about 150 Mackenzies, allegedly 'debauched' from their chief, Lord Fortrose, himself now a well known Hanoverian and the man who had accepted Forbes' commission ahead of Cromartie's son. Lovat told Forbes that he and Cromartie were on their way to join the Prince:

> So you see that the wise and worldly people of the Mackenzies are infected, so that it is no wonder that the Frasers, that were never thought worldly or wise should be infected with a contagion, tho' never so foolish and dangerous.

It is clear at least that Cromartie had been in two minds: the prolonged discussion with Forbes of Culloden indicated a great deal of vacillation. His allegiances were torn two ways—other Mackenzies had opted for the Government (against past precedent), and his wife's family had clear Hanoverian connections. He was thought still to be supporting the government in mid-October 1745. Only after this delay did Cromartie—and his son Lord Macleod, aged only 18—enter the Stuart forces, and join the second army, then gathering at Perth. Thereafter there can be no doubt about his total commitment to the war.[10]

Cromartie raised his own contingent to the Jacobite Army which was eventually assembled at both Perth and Alloa in the lowlands. At some considerable time before the end of October he had let it be known that he was raising a regiment but did not make it clear in whose interest he was acting. Cromartie and Lovat made a joint recruiting foray in Glen Urquhart and beyond and then openly declared for the Prince. Lord Macleod was also active in recruitment and on the 8th November he was reported to be rendezvous-ing with his father who had already raised 100 men. Macleod was expecting to raise the Mackenzies and Macleods in the west, in Lochbroom and Assynt.[11]

Cromartie had recruited more than 80 men from his own eastern estates and these were augmented by others (including many Mackenzies) from the Redcastle estate and further north. His success in raising local troops in this region was significant because most of the county of Ross was generally lukewarm towards the Stuarts if not actually in support of the government. Nevertheless Cromartie was not able to recruit all the Mackenzies and was clearly unable to command total loyalty in his own region.[12] Cromartie and his son were more obviously successful in the west at Coigach and the surrounding district where they raised more than 200 men, which must have been a high proportion of the total able-bodied male population.

There were contradictory accounts and much subsequent controversy surrounding the scale and force of Cromartie's regimental recruitment. The numbers involved are unclear and so is the degree of inducement exerted. It is known that Cromartie toured his districts in the company of a piper and fiddler from Strathpeffer and it is not unlikely that great moral pressure was applied to the tenantry. An unsympathetic contemporary account, by Daniel Munro, minister of Tain (later described as 'an uncouth man, a monster of unpiety, wickedness, and ill nature') described the forces created by Cromartie. They included a force of 400 Mackenzies, a substantial body of 'Banditti Highlanders'. Munro alleged that Cromartie 'affected to be chief of the Mackenzies' and 'threatened Military Execution against Mackenzie of Scatwell ... if he did not give his men also'. He also levied money from the estates in Ross for the support of the troops. Another post-rebellion commentary said that Cromartie raised about 200 men on the West Coast, 'and of his Tenants in East Ross he raised about 100 who were dragged much against their own inclination to the Rebellion.'[13] In the west, at Assynt, it was claimed that the few Mackenzies there recruited 'were obliged to go with him to the Rebellion'. In Coigach itself the local minister James Robertson used his pulpit to oppose

Cromartie's recruitment. He was initially successful but the arrival of Lord Macleod caused the people to change their minds. A second recruitment was made by Macleod in mid-March 1746. Robertson, who remained faithful to the government and later defended the people, said of Macleod:

> He unexpectedly surprised the poor people snatching some out of their beds. Others who thought their old age would excuse them, were dragged from their ploughs, while some were taken off the highways. One I did myself see overtaken by speed of foot, and when he declared he would rather die than be carried to the rebellion, was knocked to the ground by the butt of a musket and carried away all bleed [sic].[14]

Robertson's testimony was part of his post-Culloden effort to exculpate his parishioners and he may have been tempted to bend the truth of the matter.

Cromartie's Regiment was almost entirely officered by Mackenzies of minor or cadet families, or by younger sons; the great houses of Gairloch, Scatwell and Coull kept aloof, following the lead of Fortrose (Seaforth) who accepted command of a government regiment of Fencibles. All had suffered heavily from involvement in previous Jacobite risings, and the clan Mackenzie was in consequence deeply divided internally. The best of the existing records[15] gives the names of 46 officers and 238 men, though the total size of the regiment fluctuated and records are sketchy. Of those we can identify, more than half the total came from Lochbroom, and over a third were of the name of Mackenzie.

II

Cromartie and his regiment were billeted through the winter in Dunblane in Perthshire to guard the crossing of the Forth. They were also required to reinforce the cateran forces of clan Macgregor who had entered the neighbourhood. Cromartie, second in command to the aged Locheil, commanded several inconclusive forays into Fife in attempts to collect the cess and horses. His enemies later accused him of a lack of zeal in prosecuting the Fife lairds to pay up.

After taking part in the victory of Falkirk and the ineffective siege of Stirling Castle, Cromartie's Regiment marched north again, detached now from the two main groups of the Highland army. Late in January 1746 Cromartie was sent to Ross and the Earl was designated as Commander-in-Chief with 1500 men north of the Beauly River. He was charged with three tasks—to hold down Loudon's Regiment which was policing the north on behalf of the government; second, to rendezvous with one of the oft-promised consignments of French gold and arms understood to be aboard the Hazard; third, to collect cess and corn across the northern territories.[16]

Cromartie, during this time, billeted himself in his own mansion at New Tarbat and his appearance at Dingwall with a party of troops caused consternation to Loudon and Forbes of Culloden who quickly dispersed their troops and went into hiding themselves.[17] Since these were the last bastions of King George's government based in Inverness, Cromartie's apparent success gave heart to the Prince's army. The success however was strictly temporary. Cromartie's effort to secure the Hazard was beaten by

Lord Reay's troops in the north who got to it first when the ship was driven ashore. Cromartie claimed that his command in the north was hampered by a mass of contradictory orders from the Prince's headquarters, a claim supported by the many surviving orders, sometimes three in a day.[18] Contemporaries blamed him for being a poor soldier and for lacking sufficient determination in the collection of funds for the Prince's cause. Whatever the reason, the loss of the Hazard was followed by an even more humiliating disaster in Sutherland. On April 15th, the day before the battle of Culloden, Cromartie and his troops were surprised and taken prisoner at Dunrobin Castle in east Sutherland. Cromartie's forces were routed, 50 of them killed, and 165 taken prisoner, and only 30 managed to escape. It was later claimed that Cromartie and his son, Macleod, were tricked into surrender at Dunrobin Castle. In a letter written in 1754[19] the Earl blamed his capture on his brother Roderick Mackenzie for basely betraying him, and giving him and his other friends up for one thousand pounds. For this claim there is no existing corroboration. However, regardless of the particular causes, the Cromarties' fate was sealed by the collapse of the Rising at Culloden: thereafter their only realistic alternatives were capture or exile. Cromartie and son were taken into custody at Dunrobin the day before Culloden and then sent from Inverness in H.M.S. Hound for trial in London.[20]

From the moment he joined the Rising, Cromartie's estates were automatically forfeit and passed into the hands of the Commissioners for Forfeited Estates, and were subsequently annexed by the Act of 1752. From the time of his arrest Cromartie was known as the Late Earl, and a little later on as The Attaindered Person. In formal terms he had no further part in the conduct of his estates.

III

Cromartie and other Jacobite rebels were committed to the Tower (Lady Cromartie was allowed to share her husband's prison) and on 23 July 1746 were tried before a Grand Jury for High Treason. Also on trial, 'a most solemn and fine' occasion in the Rufus Hall of Westminster, were the Earl of Kilmarnock, Lord Lovat, and Lord Balmerino. Cromartie's defence advocate was Adam Gordon, a member of his wife's family who stood staunchly by the Cromartie connection at this time. Cromartie pleaded 'guilty and pray'd for Mercy'. According to one gloss, 'Cromartie, without dignity or self-possession, disappointed half the audience by pleading guilty'. They were at once removed, Cromartie almost swooning.'[21] In reality there was singularly little that Cromartie could do for his defence: he was obviously guilty and there were no mitigating circumstances apart from a palpably thin story of his drunkenness at the time of his induction into the Stuart cause.

The sentence was not surprising. All four prisoners were convicted. On 1st August 1746 they were each sentenced to death for high treason, their estates and peerages to be forfeited, and their titles attainted. They were to be taken to a place of execution:

> when you come there, you must be hanged by the Neck, but not till you are Dead; for you must be cut down alive; then your Bowels must be taken out, and burnt before your

Faces; then your Heads must be severed from your Bodies; and your Bodies must be divided each into four quarters; and these must be at the King's disposal. And God Almighty be merciful to your Souls.[22]

Cromartie's response to the Judgement of Death was that his 'unhappy case' be brought before the King 'in consideration of his numerous Family'. Apparently he had a substantial prepared speech 'in very many words' but was not able to deliver it though it was later printed.[23] It was reported that: 'He really appeared at the Bar under so deep a grief, that he could scarcely utter the few words he did.' According to Hugh Walpole, Cromartie was 'an indifferent figure, much dejected, and rather sullen.'[24] Meanwhile Lady Cromartie, who had joined him in the Tower, had sent north to Tarbat House for various items including '12 window curtains damask, cushion and stool covers, the hammer-cloth and mournings of a Hearse in three pieces'—to be prepared to give the Earl's execution some semblance of dignity.

Kilmarnock and Balmerino met their fate as did Lovat, later—in the manner of the time and amid much melodrama, gore and public excitement, they were ceremoniously beheaded at Tyburn. For Cromartie a Dutch woodcut of his beheading was prepared, and his 'last words' were being sold on the streets on the eve of his execution. Cromartie, however, avoided this termination. The story is that his neck was saved by the extraordinary behaviour of his extraordinary wife. Of this there were several accounts. She

10   George Third Earl of Cromartie and Isabella Gordon Countess of Cromartie.

was a strikingly handsome woman already far into yet another pregnancy. She waited personally on members of the Cabinet:

> On the Sunday after sentence was passed upon him, she went to Kensington Palace, dressed in deep mourning, accompanied by Lady Stair, to make a personal appeal to His Majesty for Royal Clemency.

Despite her great fortitude she eventually broke down in front of the King:

> Taking her stand, surrounded by her ten [sic] young children, in the entrance of the Chapel through which the King had to pass, she awaited his arrival, and as he approached she fell on her knees, seized him by the coat-tails, presented her petition, and fainted at his feet.

The King raised her up, and with further persuasion from the Princess of Wales and friends, eventually provided her husband with a royal reprieve. The eldest son, John, captured along with his father, had also pleaded guilty.[25] He too received a conditional pardon (in 1748) and went abroad, entering the service of the Swedish crown, eventually becoming colonel and *aide-de-camp* to the King of Sweden. Father and son had been extraordinarily lucky, they had escaped not only the executioner's axe but also transportation to America. Many of their kinsmen were far less fortunate.

IV

The fate of many of Cromartie's followers is less easy to determine. The statistical registers are unreliable and much of the post-Culloden evidence was clearly designed to demonstrate that the prisoners had been forced to take any part in the Uprising. This was undoubtedly their best defence and endlessly invoked. It is also known that soon after Culloden a naval party descended on Loch Broom to weed out any remaining supporters of the Prince.

Of the survivors of the debacle at Dunrobin most were taken south to London with their leaders. It has been suggested, though not demonstrated, that a fifth of them died en route in conditions of ship-board squalor and neglect.[26] Roderick McCulloch, laird of Glastullich in Coigach and a captain in Cromartie's Regiment, was tried in London on 15th November 1746 and sentenced to death but not executed.[27] In all the surviving letters of the Earl of Cromartie (during and after his own imprisonment) and in the memoirs of his son, there was no mention of fellow-prisoners. Nor was their any reference to the subsequent fate of other officers or their men. In January 1747 his own kinsman, Meddat, tried to persuade Cromartie to take more interest in the fate of his men, without apparent success.[28] This suggests little of the fabled loyalty and democratic spirit that was said to have moved the Highlanders in the Uprising. Much more communal solidarity (and Christian forgiveness) was exhibited in the heroic efforts of the Rev. James Robertson who had tried to dissuade the original enlistment of the Coigach recruits back in 1746. Robertson, the Hanoverian loyalist throughout, followed the captured men of Coigach first to Carlisle where they faced the English authorities. At great personal sacrifice and with much eloquence he pleaded for their lives. At Carlisle Gaol he gave the Coigach prisoners moral support and interpreted from the Gaelic at their ensuing trial. Robertson also followed the prisoners to London and made further intercessions on their behalf. Robertson's influence was probably enhanced by the fact that he had served Loudon during the Uprising and had been in direct communication with Cumberland after Culloden. He saved at least one life by sheer persistence.[29] In the outcome most of the prisoners were transported to America.

Some of the Cromartie prisoners, not surprisingly, claimed that they had acted under pressure. One of them, for example, said he had been under Cromartie's orders but had nevertheless done 'all in his power to restrain the barbaritys and abuses ... by the Highlanders'. At Falkirk he had saved the lives of 'severall of the King's troops and was to challenge the Highlanders for their barbarity'. He claimed that he had persuaded Lady Cromartie to influence her husband against acts of plundering against his uncooperative tenantry.[30]

The 'Lists of Persons concerned in the Rebellion' compiled by Commissioners of Excise after the event, included none of the Coigach men.

Nevertheless, among the 2500 names some 48 may be attributed to the Cromartie districts of Easter Ross. In the aftermath of the rebellion it was common for soldiers to claim that they had been forced into treason. It was said, for instance, that John Erskine, 'Officer of excise in Dingwall, who was at Falkirk and Sutherland with the rebels [had] threatened to burn houses in Dingwall to force the possessors into rebel service'. Alexander Mackenzie, 'late grieve' was 'employed in forcing out men into the Rebellion ... by his late master's orders'. Several Cromartie tenants were identified, some 'with the Rebels in Sutherland, now lurking in the country.'

The subsequent statistical record of 'The Prisoners of the '45'[31] brings us much closer to the background and ultimate fate of the men in Cromartie's Regiment, and even some of the faces emerge in the sea of imprisoned men. Of something like 3400 Jacobite prisoners 218 appear to have come from the Cromartie Regiment. Many of them came directly from the Cromartie Estate and a disproportionate number from the Lochbroom district. One source suggests that about 200 men had been recruited on the Coigach estate itself which, if correct, must have constituted a very high proportion of the able-bodied manhood of the district (in 1756 there was a total of 238 men over the age of 17 in Coigach).[32] The suggestion (probably attributable to Forbes of Culloden) that the Cromartie Mackenzies were no longer 'much inclined to follow their Chief, Neither are they in Use, or Very Apt to Armaments in that Country of Ross, of late they are much come to Independency' is not well borne out by the events of 1745.[33]

There was a surprisingly wide geographical recruitment—from as far distant as Caithness, Elgin, Sutherland and Skye, so that the regiment was considerably less homogeneous than might be expected. Among the Cromartie prisoners the ages ranged from 10 to 65, but the large number who reported ages of 20, 30, 40, etc., suggests that these people were generally careless or ignorant of their precise ages. Among the occupations specified for these men it is hardly surprising that most were rural folk—farmers, husbandmen, labourers, servants, ploughmen. A few were more exotic—a brogmaker (shoemaker), a weaver, several blacksmiths, some drovers, a forester, a dairyman, tailors, a snuff seller and a fiddler. But the range clearly reflects an overwhelmingly rural society.

The treatment of these men was rigorous both before and after the trials. In the aftermath of Culloden there was 'a calculated reign of terror in the Highlands' and the fleeing rebels were pursued ruthlessly through the northern districts and the marines scoured and devastated various west coast settlements, including Lochbroom. W.A. Speck says that 'the rebels were widely regarded as subhuman, as animals or vermin, fit only to be hunted down and destroyed.' A contemporary described the Highlanders as 'a ragged, hungry rabble of Yahoos', and another said they were 'a hungry, rapacious and uncivilised crew of ungrateful villains, savages and traitors'.[34] Rosalind Mitchison has suggested that the prisoners were treated with great severity and inhumanity which reflected the profound rift between the two cultures. Certainly the conditions in which the prisoners were kept in Carlisle were atrocious, in appalling squalor.[35] It is also true that Lord President Forbes had recommended the wholesale transportation of clans to America—a policy in which Cumberland himself agreed—'that while they remain in this island their rebellious and thievish nature is not to be kept under without an army within reach of them.' The initial reaction had been even stronger—in the form of demands for blood and vengeance. But, as Speck points out, 'once the victorious forces had expiated their vengeance on the battlefield and in the glens, the actual treatment of the rebels by the government was mild in contrast with the earlier threats of severity.' Indeed of 3400 Jacobite rebels, only 120 were put to death and of those, 40 were deserters from the Hanoverian army itself.[36]

Many of these points are reflected in the experience of the Cromartie prisoners. Most of them seem to have ended up in London, at Tilbury in the hulks moored off-shore, perhaps after trial in London or Inverness; relatively few seemed to have been dealt with in Carlisle. Practically all those who survived to the point of trial were transported to America. But many are unaccounted for and probably died in captivity, presumably from the awful conditions under which they were held. A subsequent report (in 1754) stated that 'the tenants of Coigach were generally all in the Rebellion, and many of them were taken prisoners during that time, and were transported to America, by which means a great part of that barony was wasted for several years.'[37] A substantial number turned King's Evidence and were acquitted though where they went thereafter is not known. Some avoided transportation (or possibly execution) by accepting enlistment in British regiments. More than a few claimed that they had been forced into the Rebellion—but this plea seems to have been generally discounted since such prisoners were transported regardless.

The evidence of the prisoners also reveals the social distinctions in the regiment and the society from which they had been recruited. Alexander McKenzie was described as 'a gentleman', a Lieutenant in Cromartie's force. He had been a steward or factor to Lord Cromartie, holding the tack of Corry in Coigach at £25 a year 'and reported to be a man of considerable credit and substance'. He was 40 years of age, originally from Thurso in Caithness and had been captured in the engagement at Dunrobin Castle. He was tried in January 1747 and sentenced to death—from which he was reprieved and, instead, two months later transported. In contrast Hector McKenzie, an Ensign in Cromartie's Regiment, was a farmer and undertenant 'a low Man, and has no Estate'—

in fact a forester in Lochbroom, aged 45. He claimed he had been recruited under duress and had made frequent attempts to escape. This man was pardoned on condition that he left the country permanently and transported himself to America.

John Gray was a 57 year old drover, imprisoned in Carlisle and London, who gave evidence against leaders in the Jacobite army and was pardoned and discharged. Donald Fraser was 19, from Logie Easter, a tailor by trade—and though he gave evidence against Lord Macleod was nevertheless transported. Among the prisoners there were 90 Mackenzies and no less than a dozen with the Christian name Alexander. One of the latter, a grieve of Coul was alleged to have been 'employed in forcing out men into the Rebellion ... by his late master's [Mackenzie of Coull] order'. He claimed to have had nothing to do with the Rebellion and that he was the victim of the ill will of a neighbour—an appeal which was rejected and he too was transported. William Maclean of Lochbroom had the support of his minister who said he had been forced to join, and had surrendered—but this too cut no ice and Maclean was also transported. The later suggestion that none of the New Tarbat people had been involved in the Rebellion is not borne out by the evidence—for instance Donald McIntyre of Milton, Kilmuir, was a servant to Cromartie in the Rebellion, and three other tenants from Milton also 'carried arms in Cromarty's Rebel Regiment'.[38]

Random denouncing in Ross was less than that recorded in the Jacobite regions to the south. It is clear that many of those who wished to plead mitigating circumstances for their involvement naturally claimed that they had been forced out. There was probably some public satisfaction in pinpointing those who were alleged to have forced out tenants—it is noticeable, for example, that those so denounced were standard unpopular characters: the exciseman of Dingwall, and the figure of the ground officer and grieve. The defence that many men were forced into service as rebel soldiery may also have reflected the genuine insecurity of Highland tenancy and the status of dependency with which it went. It is indeed impossible to disentangle those who were Jacobite by conviction, or by religious inspiration, from those who followed unthinkingly the military call of their landlords and clan superiors, and those who were reluctant or even 'forced'. In the excitement and fear of the Rising all motives were likely to be mixed and even contradictory.

V

Undoubtedly, the '45 and its aftermath were together an unmitigated catastrophe for the Cromartie Mackenzies. The life of the Earl had been saved: but lost was the dignity of the family, its lands, its income,[39] its title and many of its people. In the desperation of August 1746 the Countess had abased herself in the most pathetic fashion. Thereafter the family lived in a degradation of totally Hogarthian proportions.

The former Earl, now George Mackenzie and his son John Macleod, remained in the Tower for another eighteen months. He was then, in February 1748, permitted to leave on condition that he lodged at the house of a messenger.[40] In August of the same year he received permission to live at Layhill in Devonshire.[41] In September Cromartie wrote from Layhill to seek permission to seek better housing on the grounds that his 'house is in a manner ruinous, not even necessary furniture in it, hardly a chair to sit on'.[42] In

October 1749 he was pardoned[43] under the Privy Seal, but ordered to remain wherever the King determined. He now resided at Northcote near Honiton, Devon. Mackenzie and his large family had virtually no visible means of support and probably depended upon relatives for most of the time. His wife, apparently, was in 1749 voted a pension of £200 out of the rents of the Forfeited Estates, but this was paid irregularly. Moreover she was denied her jointure until the death of her husband.

The exiled Earl was not happy in Devon, and he pined for his native land. In November 1748 he wrote 'this place ... is in the heart of a very fine county ... but for all that I would much rather live at the foot of Peenonish and be better pleased with an oaten cake, and the Strathpeffer or Milntoun bere than with the finest bread, the finest cyder, and all the other necessarys of life which this country is remarkable for beyond any other in England.'[44] He received little sympathy from kinsmen in the north of Scotland. When in May 1749 Meddat sought financial aid for Cromartie from Sir Alexander Mackenzie of Gairloch the response was negative. He said he was sorry that Cromartie was obliged to solicit the aid of 'small gentlemen' such as himself: 'I much rather he had dyed sword in hand even where he was ingaged then be necessitate to act such a pairt.'[45] Cromartie was thus reduced to beggary, and it was reported of his eldest daughter that she was 'not too proud to perform the most menial tasks for the comfort of her parents and their younger children'.[46]

Mackenzie was reduced to very poor conditions in his last years. In 1751 he complained to Meddat 'we are most excessively pinched for want of money'. In July 1758 Cromartie was in desperate straits, pleading for help from Lord Hardwicke through to the Duke of Newcastle. His debts were so pressing that he was in danger of eviction from his house and the expropriation of his goods—and his creditors were about to descend upon him. It was caused by the withholding of the £200 annuity during the previous five years 'which his Majesty was most graciously pleased to order for me'. Without it there was no hope of paying off the creditors 'who are every day more and more impatient'.[47] In 1759 he again wrote of his 'miserable situation' and the burden of his 'load of debts'. He said that 'We were never more put to it than at present. Every year grows worse and worse for us, as every year increases the load of our debts.' He complained bitterly: 'We feel daily the miserable situation we are in. I am afraid we shall be put to the utmost extremity soon, perhaps not to have a house to go into or a bed to lie on, and no hopes of any amendment in this our distressed situation for some time.'[48] According to the Victorian historian, Alexander Mackenzie, 'His Lordship lived for several years in seclusion and poverty, supported mainly by the contributions of his old tenants and retainers on the forfeited estates.'[49]

The Jacobite Earl died at Poland Street in London in September 1766.[50] His wife's pension was increased to £400. But the position of the family remained doleful. They lived in the hope of legislation to restore their estates and titles. Meanwhile the children had, mostly, married, moving into army or mercantile connections. It was however in the life and work of the disinherited heir, the former Jacobite John, Lord Macleod, that the family would eventually achieve a phoenix-like return to the class of lairds in Highland Scotland. Before that, though, the Cromartie estates, the foundation of all the family's pretensions, political and aristocratic, had themselves passed through various transformations.

PART TWO

Dispossession and Restoration 1746-1784

CHAPTER 7

Annexation 1746-1784

'... the ruins of New Tarbat, once the magnificent seat of an unhappy nobleman, who plunged into a most ungrateful rebellion, destructive to himself and family. The tenants, who seem to inhabit it gratis, are forced to shelter themselves from the weather in the very lowest apartments, while swallows make their nests in the bold stucco of some of the upper.' (Thomas Pennant, 1769)

I

In the twentieth century radical opinion in the Highlands has commonly advocated that the land should be nationalised or, better still, returned to 'the people'. In recent decades state enterprise has taken the lead in the provision of capital and direction in the development of the Highland economy. Two centuries before, in the aftermath of Culloden, the Highlands experienced a thoroughly co-ordinated experiment in state enterprise—under the authority of the Commissioners of the Forfeited and the Annexed Estates. Cromartie was one of the annexed estates. For 38 years it was administered by the state on behalf of the nation, itself a circumstance extremely unusual in the history of the land in Britain. The benefits and the costs of this interlude are uncertain but one clear advantage emerged—the estates were never before so well documented.

As soon as Cromartie joined the Rising in 1745 his estates were automatically forfeited to the Crown. The processes of dispossession and rearrangement, however, worked slowly. It was not until 1754 that the administration of the estates was regularised under government control. Thereafter Cromartie, in common with the estates of other Jacobite rebels, was firmly in the hands of officials charged with precise instructions to maximise social and economic change in the formerly mutinous parts of the Highlands. The estates became thus part of a substantial experiment in economic and social engineering.

During the years of annexation the dispossessed laird languished in southern England, reduced to a condition close to penury. The former Earl had no viable future. His son Macleod, however, was made of stern material: he was a man of action who carved for himself a remarkable career in foreign and colonial service. His efforts were sufficiently illustrious that the idea of re-instatement in the ancestral lands of Cromartie became a feasible climax to his career. It was an astonishing recovery of esteem made possible by Macleod's own energy and connections and also by the opportunities which lay open to men of initiative in the world of European expansion in the third quarter of the eighteenth century. In the meantime, of course, the Scottish Highlands were thoroughly tamed, at least to the tastes of the Hanoverian government.

II

In the ugly and bloody days after Culloden, parts of the Highlands were laid waste by Cumberland's troops. Cattle were driven away and woods fired. In Skye, for instance, Lord Loudon was told 'to drive the cattle, burn the ploughs and destroy what you can belonging to all such as are and have been in the rebellion, and burning the houses of the chiefs.'[1] Coigach was the obviously Jacobite quarter of the Cromartie estate and the Hanoverian troops took their revenge there—in a district already robbed of the flower of its male youth by the transportation to America of a large proportion of the prisoners of the Forty Five.

The punishment of Coigach after Culloden is poorly documented and the only available description dates from an entry in the *New Statistical Account* a century after the event, probably reliant upon oral testimony. It was said that, soon after the defeat, a squadron of the King's vessels, under the command of Ferguson, appeared off the Lochbroom coast and dropped anchor

> A strong party landed there and proceeded up the Strath as far as the residence of Mr Mackenzie of Langwell, who was married to a near relative of Earl George of Cromartie. Mr Mackenzie got out of the way; but the lady was obliged to attend some of her children, who were confined by smallpox. The house was ransacked, a trunk containing valuable papers, and among them a wadset of Langwell and Inchvannie, from the Earl of Cromartie, was burned before her eyes; and about fifty head of black cattle were mangled by their swords, and driven away to the ships. Similar depredations were committed in the neighbourhood without discrimination of friends or enemies, during eight days that they remained upon the coast.[2]

Contemporary references to the 'wasting' of Coigach go far to sustain the report. The revenge taken in 1746 soured the defeated districts and made them less easy to regulate in the coming decades of forfeiture. It contrasted too with the subsequent post-rebellion policy of the government which was devoted to the business of 'civilisation'.

The Cromartie estates came under the authority of the Scottish Court of Exchequer. Forfeiture covered 'all and every Land, Heritages, Debts or Sums of Money, Goods or Chattels whatsoever'.[3] Most of the other forfeited estates were sold off by public auction but thirteen—the most obviously Jacobitical and therefore including Cromartie—were permanently annexed to the Crown by the Act of 1752. The object was unambiguous—the Act was 'for Purposes of Civilising the Inhabitants of the Said Estates and other parts of the Highlands and Islands of Scotland'. In 1754 the estates passed from the Barons of Exchequer to the Commissioners of the Annexed Estates—who were not appointed until March 1755. They retained control for the following three decades.

In the period of nine years before Annexation the Cromartie estates remained in a somewhat suspended condition. The legal and financial status of the property in this interim period was ambiguous particularly because there appear to have been few clear directives from Edinburgh or London. The consequence was that legal tangles between the estate and its creditors and tenants simply worsened. Immediately after the Rising factors on the Jacobite estates were faced with the problem of collecting rents from tenants who were without the means of payment. Others could not easily stomach the idea of paying rent to anyone other than their traditional landlord or indeed to him. According to Meddat, the resident factor, 'ingrate tenants' at Strathpeffer had sold their barley-bere before he could attend to collect his due. Not unexpectedly there was passive opposition to factors' efforts to control the property—in its more active form it occasioned the death of the factor in the infamous Appin murder. On the Cromartie estates even the allocation of rental income was unclear: presumably income was siphoned off to the Crown, but Lady Cromartie was due a pension of £200 per annum, and some of the loyal tenants seem to have made informal payments to their vanquished patron now in the south of England. The tenantry, especially in Coigach, was in a poor condition from difficult economic conditions and the loss of the youth and muscle of the community in the rebellion and its aftermath.

During these interim years the Cromartie estates were administered piecemeal by local factors appointed or confirmed by the Lords of the Treasury. One of the common managerial mistakes of these years was the use of non-resident factors, 'a state of affairs which resulted in reliance on sub-factors, who were more often than not the friends, kinsmen or even former factors of the forfeiting persons'.[4] For Cromartie the central authorities appear to have placed considerable trust in Mackenzie of Meddat, the factor and tacksman of the Cromartie family, a man acknowledged by all parties to be both honest and dispassionate. He appears to have acted as the bridge between the old family administration and the slowly coordinating new management of the state. It was not until May 1748 that the first major intrusion of the Commissioners was seen—Hugh Munro of Teanninich, a staunch Hanoverian, was directed to survey the eastern portions of the estate and to draw up a Judicial Rental. This was evidently a systematic preparation for a more thorough-going takeover of estate administration. Teanninich, during his survey, reported favourably about the cooperation of Meddat who had been 'very obliging upon me in the course of my office, and gave all the necessary assistance that I could ask or expect.'[5] The tenantry however was not always so pliant.

The Gordons of Invergordon—related by marriage—had acted as caretakers for the Cromartie family during these years. For instance they had taken into safekeeping the documents and valuables of the family. When Munro of Teanninich came to examine the old Cromartie mansion houses (at Castle Leod and New Tarbat) he reported: 'I searched both but found nothing of value in either of them'. The Gordons appear also to have employed solicitors to serve the residual legal rights of their defeated kinsmen. Mackenzie of Meddat continued to collect rents and provide factorial services even when new factors were appointed. It seems that Cromartie continued to receive some estate income as late as 1752, but official payments from the Forfeited Estate Commissioners were far from regular.[6] Lady Cromartie was entitled to a pension of £200 from the rents but neither was this nor her other financial dues to be relied upon. The manner in which her husband's life had been spared by the intervention of Frederick, Prince of Wales, was said to have caused a grudge which the administration held against

Lady Cromartie. Indeed she had to wait until the death of her husband, in 1766, before any of her jointure was paid, even though her husband had totally ceased to support her or her family. Other Jacobite ladies all received their marriage portions but, despite many petitions, the King refused to grant Lady Cromartie her legal rights. Consequently the family lived off £200 a year and anything that Meddat and other friends could scrape together. Yet though they may have been objects of pity in these years they nevertheless received an income vastly in excess of the common people of their former estates.

The Cromarties were lucky to get anything at all from their estates in these years. The tenantry, certainly in the west, were disaffected and dismally poor. At moments there appeared almost to be a rent strike in operation. In January 1747 when the Earl was still in the Tower of London, Meddat transmitted local news. He congratulated the Earl on the Royal Pardon that had saved his life. But in Coigach, he had to report 'Most of the people of this place are quite unquiet and unmanageable, and think they should pay nothing; any little I can scrape together shall be sent by the next post'—by which he probably referred to informal payments to the Earl (as opposed to the official rents). The local minister was also experiencing difficulties, probably over the payment of teinds. Even in the east, at Strathpeffer, some of the tenants were also 'ingrate'. Nevertheless some individual tenants still believed that they should make payments to the Cromarties, a sign that the bonds of tradition exceeded the legal requirement of the moment.[7] But poverty was the inescapable condition of society—Meddat described the condition of Coigach as unstable, and the Crown Rents were forty five years in arrears. Some stability was achieved however by the registration of a tack for the district under Mackenzie of Achilty.[8]

From his first arrest until he died Cromartie continued to send Meddat instructions about estate matters though Meddat did not always take notice. A full correspondence continued—for instance elaborate details on the policies and gardens at Tarbat and Castle Leod were transmitted from the west of England—at a time when Cromartie complained of living in great poverty. Throughout this time, even into the late 1750s, the Cromarties continued to expect gifts and money from old tenants and friends. As one of their begging letters put it, it was 'a hard struggle to keep our heads above water, we have met with credit and forebearance ... but their patience is near wore out'. The former Earl said in March 1759, reproachfully, financial assistance from 'some friends in the north' was quite necessary and that 'a little from several individuals would not hurt them'. The trickles of aid continued into the 1760s—in 1761 Mackenzie of Meddat acknowledged the payment of £44-6-0 sterling to Lord Cromartie from Coigach at a time when the assessed rental of the entire district was only £151.9.1d sterling.[9] It was a substantial sum raised among an appallingly poor tenantry and, perhaps, a significant measure of the old patriarchal ties.

III

The Act of Annexation was a process of formal expropriation by the state. The government's resolution since 1746 had not wavered: there would be no repetition of the experience after the Rebellion of 1715 when many estates found their way back into rebel hands. Annexation put paid to the idea that the Cromarties might return home. It was the abrupt and ostensibly final termination of all hope for the retrieval of the estates; similarly the title was equally lost 'forever'. Annexation was much more drastic than mere Forfeiture.

'Though not in any way vindictive', says T.C. Smout of the Commissioners, a committee of mainly Edinburgh lawyers, 'they worked on the assumption that Highland peasants were ignorant, idle and culturally savage, and they therefore strove to do all they could to eliminate the mores of the clan'.[10] The whole process was activated by an ungovernable contempt for and fear of the essence of Highland life. In practice Annexation was more a matter of social and political engineering than financial development, foreshadowing later Indian and colonial development policies. In the history of the Cromartie estate over these three decades, the ultimate authority, the Treasury, seemed to have taken only small interest in the financial needs of the property. The Act itself was long delayed in its execution and there was no full meeting of the Commissioners until 1755. The administration was invested with little sense of urgency or direction: the new masters had difficulty even raising quorums for their meetings in Edinburgh. Their local factors were required to report to the capital and the Commissioners showed great reluctance in visiting their far-flung territories—of which Cromartie was indeed the furthest from the centre.

A central assumption seemed to inform the basic administration of the Annexed Estates: that without the burden of landlords and their great houses and retinues to support, the estate revenues would be able to finance their own capital development. Instead of their capital surpluses filling the pockets of the landlords, the revenues would fructify the estate economy to the benefit and modernisation of the entire region. Moreover the Highlanders, under such generous circumstances, would be won over by the valuable improvements initiated from the benevolent agencies in London and Edinburgh. Sadly the basic thinking was flawed: in reality estate income was soaked up by the high expenses of management, by the costs of administration and premises in Edinburgh, and by the continuing requirement to pay off the accumulated debts which hung upon the forfeited estates.[11] Moreover family obligations and widow's portions continued to make effective claims against estate rentals. Consequently there was remarkably little surplus of capital for capital investment in the estates, and little injection of new capital from London either.

The estates appear therefore to have been starved of capital. Moreover the Commissioners gained the reputation as lenient landlords, kinder than the average run of Highland proprietors, partly to win loyalty for the Crown, partly from a lack of resolve. The government wanted to win loyalty by way of a lenient administration but this approach itself created problems of estate discipline. Factors faced endless trouble from litigious tenants egged on by energetic lawyers. Such attitudes also undermined ideas of rational development since they failed to maximise income or to set a high premium on the growth of income. Certainly there was no wish to see the former owners regain possession, and there was an unambiguous resolve to eradicate the distinctive and deplorable features of old Highland society. As Rosalind Mitchison says, the estates 'were put in the hands of a commission of London gentry which attempted to turn them from debt-ridden little despotisms to modern and industrious units.'[12] It was a process already under way before 1745 but the Commissioners attempted to accelerate the process, hamstrung in part by objective circumstances, in part by the fallibility of their own planning.

One of the most recent historians of the Annexed Estates, Dr Annette Smith, has demonstrated effectively the distance between the developmental/philanthropic purposes of government policy and the actual execution of that policy. As the case of Cromartie reveals, many of the schemes for development ran out of luck and capital; the administrative system was cumbersome; economic conditions were often adverse, and the geography of the estates was a great disadvantage. While the destruction of the worst features of the old feudalism of the chiefs was a high priority, the positive aspects of the new era were not to be doubted. Annexation entailed 'the attempted alleviation of social and economic ills and modernisation with the help of the state'. The broad philosophy of the annexation, despite the detestation of Highland feudalism, was positive. The goal was

> the civilising of the inhabitants upon the said estates, and other parts of the Highland and Islands of Scotland, the promoting amongst them the Protestant religion, good Government, Industry and Manufactures, and the principles of Duty and Loyalty to his Majesty, His Heirs, and Successors, and to do no other use and purpose whatsoever.[13]

As Dr Smith explains, it was part of the mandate to render the people of the Highlands more contented with their circumstances (and therefore less prone to rebel). And, despite its ramshackle administrative machinery, it extended a well meaning paternalism to the Highlands, most notably in terms of the welfare of the tenantries. Its efforts to relieve distress in the harvest failures of 1753, 1763, 1772, and 1783 indicate an authentic and effective humanitarian concern; its record on evictions was relatively mild and the Board probably accelerated the introduction of measures against smallpox.[14] Such benevolence was the other side of the coin of repression associated with post-'45 government policy—the eradication of Gaelic, of Highland costume and the prevailing legal and political system. It was probably in the name of philanthropy that the tenants of Cromartie and Lovat were told in 1762 that the sale of alcohol would henceforth be punished by eviction. The local effectiveness of Annexation policy hinged upon the general inertia at the centre, in Edinburgh, because this left much discretion with the local agents—upon their goodwill and energy depended much of the progress of particular estates.

IV

Cromartie was the most remote of the Annexed Estates and was in 1754 still recoiling from the hammerblow of defeat in the Uprising. Its financial and economic condition was poor and it was also entangled in complex legal bonds. The Cromartie estate was under entail which, in law, limited claims on the estate to those incurred during the lifetime of the current holder. Debtors had already exercised their rights to take rents in payment of the claims—even during the rebellion. Annexation appears to have empowered the Commissioners to liquidate all outstanding debts regardless of their antiquity.[15]

The new administration began with a flush of thoroughness and commitment to its task. The factor appointed to Cromartie (and Lovat also) was Captain John Forbes of New, an Aberdonian whom Virginia Wills describes as 'an administrator ... with considerable skill, as well as tact and understanding ... responsible for creating order out of chaos in a particularly troublesome part of the country.'[16] He was immediately critical of the condition of the estates under his charge: he was a man of an improvement mentality, tutored in southern standards. He believed that the class of wadsetters and lesser gentry simply wanted to keep the ordinary people 'in ignorance and slavery'. He regarded education as the key to progress and freedom among the poor masses, and was particularly anxious that Gaelic should be eliminated. Forbes thought that no leases should be given to those who spoke no English, but he recognised the great difficulty in persuading the poor to send their children to school.[17] On one of his first encounters with the northern district, in Coigach in 1754, Forbes exclaimed: 'it is shocking to see such numbers of young ones going about in Rags, idle and without one word of English or more care taken of them (scarce so much) as of their cattle'. Forbes' views were full of the colonial arrogance of the Lowland Scot, yet rarely before had the common people been the object of such righteous concern. For many years Forbes struggled to impose order and progress on Coigach, especially among the 'insolent tenants', presumably of the larger sort. A local factor—Ninian Jeffrey, from the Borders—was appointed specifically to deal with Coigach over the years 1764-81 and this was a sign of the special problems in the populous west. Forbes himself was highly regarded locally and in Edinburgh, and in 1770 he was voted an extra £100 p.a. by the Commissioners in recognition of 'his Great Zeal and activity in civilizing the Highlands'.[18]

One of the first acts of the Board of the Annexed Estates was to commission a thorough survey and investigation in detail of the circumstances on all the estates. Elaborate questionnaires were distributed for statistical and descriptive reports and the mapmaker Peter May surveyed much of the territory of the estates. May was a professional land measurer from Aberdeen.[19] 'The Estate of Cromartie lies very much scattered and disjoined' wrote May at a later stage when he had been made ill with fatigue by these extended duties.[20] The outcome of his survey was not entirely unlike a Domesday survey of these parts of the Highlands, augmented by some of the best maps yet made of these places. The maps produced in the period of annexation show clearly the run-rig patterns of agriculture on the eastern estates and also the use of moorlands for common pasture. The surveys yielded information on a broad range of subjects: acreages, rentals, production, population, cultivation, education, religion, soils, and much else. They provide the first systematic evidence of the social and economic structures on the Cromartie estate—much objective evidence on social and economic indicators amidst a plenitude of tendentious comment about the improvability or otherwise of the people. The parallel purpose of the surveys was the need to complement the sworn Judicial Rental for the estates—a firmer base from which subsequent rents could be calculated, and a clarification of the status of existing leases, wadsetts and sub-letting arrangements. Recurrent surveys—in 1766 and 1769—produced further profiles of the estates.

The people of the estates, in these surveys, figure exclusively as objects upon which the new policies were to be imposed; they do not appear as individuals or communities in their own terms or even in their own voices. Statistical figments and objects for improvement, they nevertheless emerge in 1755 in more detail than ever before in the historical record—shadow-figures illuminated by the indirect light of the Commissioner's questions. Indeed the reports are most telling in their exposure of the values and propensities of the new managers of the Annexed Estates.

The data from the 1755 survey reveals some basic propositions about each of the Cromartie baronies—the structure of economic life, the distribution of land and wealth, the degree of anglicisation, and the relative levels of social welfare.

	COIGACH	STRATHPEFFER	NEW TARBAT
Population	896	780	372
Size of families	5.36	4.45	4.89
Rent (Sterling)	£260.7.1½	£344.0.2	£328.0.0
Rent per head	£0.29	£0.44	£0.88
Cattle per head	1.92	0.823	0.32
Population less than 10	26.7%	22.0%	26.7%
English speakers	7.5%	16.0%	33.5%

The report on Coigach stressed its remoteness, being 30 miles from Strathpeffer, itself not easily accessible. 'Nothing but necessity makes strangers resort here and for a great part of the year is almost inaccessible.' There was no resident J.P., no parochial school, and the minister seldom preached in English in a parish 15 miles by 8 which was both mountainous and rocky.[21] The barony was let out to tenants—64 in all—far less than the total number of families. Consequently, a large part of the population were subtenants or labourers, or else in some other way dependent on the tenants. Few spoke English,[22] few cultivated the land or spun wool or flax. The clearest indication of the basis of life was in the large numbers of stock—463 horses, 1413 sheep and 1728 black cattle, obviously the greatest asset of the tenantry. Remote, Gaelic-speaking, without manufacturing, with little cultivation (except for the planting of 54 pecks of potatoes),[23] Coigach was nevertheless profoundly committed to the market. As the report said, Coigach was essentially a pastoral county which sent black cattle and a 'great plenty of butter and cheese' to the markets of Easter Ross, Dingwall and Tain. It produced no flax or hay, nor even cereals which must have been imported. Fishing was a more random part of the local economy—in 1730 all of Coigach had been tacked for 15 years and tenants had found themselves in difficulties in the mid-1730s because the herrings migrated from Lochbroom, which suggests that fishing income was incorporated in the accounting of rents.

It seems that leases (or tacks) were commonly auctioned to the highest bidders and that grassums had been extracted on entry to a lease (each of which may have suggested the financial problems of the Earls of Cromartie). In 1741 all tacks had been renewed on grassum. There were other signs of inequality: for instance in the possession of cattle and in holding of land. Thus on the farm of Achiltibuie there were 11 families with 70 people, running 80 black cattle and paying a rent of £8-0-10. But at Glastullich, the farm was held by a single family, comprising 6 people, owning 100 cattle and paying £13-3-10 in rent. Peter May reported great difficulty in measuring the small holdings of the subtenants—'they are so interwoven with one another and run-ridged on sundry farms with the tenants themselves'. There were sometimes 100 holdings or ridges to an acre, 'scattered up and down like easie beds of potatoes'. May was astonished at the size of the barony and at the distance between some of the houses: on occasion he was forced to sleep in the open and indeed requested a tent: 'There is no such thing as sleeping in their houses in the summer time, they are so full of vermin. Everything is scarce and dear, my living costs more here than it does in Aberdeen although I can scarce get bear bannocks. I pay my people eight pence a day and with difficulty I can get them at any rate'.

Peter May saw great possibilities in the region—'I have not seen a country where poor people might live more comfortably than here, fish of all kinds in plenty, butter and cheese the same, with moss and firing upon every farm in great abundance, which is of no small consequence to them.' He was however especially aware of the fragile and fractious character of tenurial relations in Coigach, and this would be the greatest challenge to management: 'The tacksman and subtenants are now in a civil war; ... at present there is a bad neighbourhood among them, to present which the best plan would be to break some farms and fill them entirely with the present sub-tenants, or detach them to remote corners at some distance from the principal tacksman'. Such a solution, however, was more fundamental than he thought; it undermined the entire structure of Highland society and would be resisted tooth and nail for generations.[24]

The after effects of the Uprising were still visible in Coigach. Forbes reported 'The Tenants of Coigach were generally all in the Rebellion, and many of them were taken prisoners during that time, and were transported to America, by which means a great part of that barony was waste for several years'. Some of their lands and property had been laid waste—a tenant complained of 'the British Marines which then hovered and seized cattle and goods of your petitioner's neighbours [i.e. in Coigach] who served in the rebellion'.[25] Munro of Teanninch in 1748 had referred to 'rent and lands that have been waste and uninhabited for the time of this account.' It was claimed again that the Marines had descended on the barony and fired the Forest of Coigach. A degree of depopulation must have occurred which John Baillie, probably in 1749, had solved by letting the lease of the barony to Mackenzie of Achilty who then imported a new set of sub-tenants—'he brought tennants from the Island of Lewes and the neighbouring countys who possess there at present'.[26] It seems equally likely that between 1745 and 1749 the rental of Coigach was severely depressed but by 1756 had risen by about 20%.

Forbes described Coigach as 'the most Highland and uncivilised part of the Estate' and he recommended widescale improvements not only in agricultural practice, but also the provision of a Sheriff court, the construction of churches, schools, a new village at Ullapool and a gaol, and a road to Dingwall. There was no manufacturing, no brewing, no milling except that done by hand; only a few potatoes were grown, there were no wheeled vehicles, no grass seeded and therefore no hay, and no enclosing had been tried. Sheep production was primitive and grossly undervalued by the people. Whisky-distilling was almost universal—and under the Earls the estate had leased 'the

Liberty' of selling 'a quantity', a practice which the Commissioners swiftly terminated. There was plenty of peat and some irregular recourse to the herring fishing but this tended to create labour shortages—during a good season 'The tenants can get no servants to work for them for any hire, they throw themselves out of service, he to the fishing, she to the gutting.'[27]

A certain degree of suspicion still hung over the political loyalties of the Coigach people. As late as April 1756 John Macleod of Keanachillis was said to be harbouring a firelock in his house (in defiance of the Disarming Act), and David Ross was also thought to possess arms—which he used to destroy game, and had assisted a noted Jacobite fugitive, Ross of Pitcalnie, soon after Culloden. And although the suppression of Highland dress had taken effect generally it was not comprehensive despite repeated warnings. However rather than political subversion the estate suffered from more generalised internecine disorder and disaffection. At one moment Forbes complained:

> The Barony of Coigach is possessed by McLeods and McKenzies mixt and that there seems to be a kind of Clan Quarrel in which I am as little interested—further than doing my duty as Factor—as I am in the Disputes in Corsica.[28]

But regardless of clan, Forbes classed the community as 'a very lazy ignorant sort of people, but not at present addicted to thieving nor so poor as the people of Strathpeffer'.

The Barony of Strathpeffer was much smaller—merely three miles by one mile (excluding extensive but under-utilised mountain grazing)—but more thickly populated. It was a mixture of east and west in terms of Highland conditions. Here 780 people lived in 19 farms in somewhat smaller families than those of Coigach; rather more spoke English and there were more spinners. The number of cattle was less but the average rent per head greater—indeed Forbes remarked that 'in general the people are extremely poor and indeed I am of opinion that the lands of this barony are over-rentalled'. The economy was clearly mixed, cattle were grazed (and sent to the higher sheilings in summer) in conjunction with some cereal and potato production though the land was badly drained. Nearby Dingwall was 'a small town of little trade', while the vale of Strathpeffer was 'justly esteemed as a pretty place'. The minister preached in both English and 'Erse'.

It was sheer poverty that struck most forcibly both Forbes and May the mapmaker. Forbes said the people were 'poor ignorant and lazy' and though not thieves they were addicted to spiritous liquors and equally to leisure. Peter May, in the middle of his survey, wrote that 'The tenantry here are the poorest people I ever saw; they have neither meat nor clothes'. He elaborated: the tenantry 'for the most part [are] very poor and live in a wretched beggarly way, the cattle and they generally sleep under the same roof and have but little odds between their lodgings'. He also remarked on the heavy erosion of the soil caused by the direction of the rigs which ran down rather than across the hillsides.

The causes of poverty, according to the southern investigators, were connected with the smallness and scattered nature of the holdings, overcrowding and tenurial oppression. Plots were widely dispersed and inconvenient; rents were too high; the people had been 'formerly oppressed with servitudes' which, 'with their own indolent practices may help to account for their bad circumstances'. Forbes described the framework of life in Strathpeffer:

> The people are very numerous here and possess mostly, very small farms, which are runrigged and interfere with one another in such manner as makes it highly inconvenient for them all and impossible that they should thrive tho' the lands were set at a much lower rent.

In fact Forbes thought the people were grossly over-rented and recommended (in 1755 and 1757) a radical abatement, otherwise the land would go to waste.

Clearly at Strathpeffer there was a large stratum of marginal people—at least 160 families of subtenants or mealers, practically all of whom distilled whisky. Of the mealers, many 'have only a house, and some of them yards, for which they pay no rent but services to the proprietor', especially those at Auchterneed. Forbes and May were agreed that consolidation and enclosure were the only solution to this structural poverty, yet the solution itself would reduce many to landlessness. May said 'they must flit or live in some village by themselves', or else be settled in consolidated plots of previously barren muir at very low rents. Forbes, while advocating radical consolidation of individual family holdings noted that 'as this will occasion removing some of the most lazy and poorest of the present inhabitants, these might be employed in manufactures'. The alternative was the re-location of people on certain 'barren improvable muirs'. Here, then, was the classic eighteenth century solution to poverty and congestion—in which were contained the seeds of endless disputes about rights to land. It was a solution which drove the marginal elements of rural society to the most peripheral lands or else to distant villages.

New Tarbat, the most easterly of the Baronies, approximated most closely to the southern standards of civilisation. There were several key indicators noted in the minds of the Commissioners—a greater use of English (one third spoke the language at New Tarbat), cultivation which employed lime, many tradesmen in the population, considerable manufacturing (including 188 spinners) and a smaller dependence on the cattle trade—in fact local cattle were pastured at a considerable distance from the barony. The people were 'sober, honest and tolerably industrious'; few of them had been involved in the Rebellion and they were all Protestants—even better, the people were less clannish 'with a mixture of different names'. English was making ground and it was 'a peaceable low country'. There were obvious inequalities in wealth as reflected in the rental—for instance two families paid £116-6-8 rent while another farm was inhabited by 21 families paying £20-5-0. Peter May said of New Tarbat, 'The tenants here are in a better way than the barony of Castle Leod [i.e. Strathpeffer], though I don't think them well in comparison with Banffshire.'[29] Forbes thought the best prospect for agricultural progress would be a greater use of long leases.

The general verdict of the incoming management was that the people of the Cromartie estates were lazy, ignorant and not at all conscious of the possibilities of agricultural improvement. English was the language of the 'wadsetters and lesser gentlemen'—yet these men used their influence to keep the people in 'ignorance and slavery'—though Forbes thought they were rapidly losing their authority—'the people are already very impatient to shake off their yoke'. In too many places the smallness of undertenants' holdings forced wives and children to beg a living during some parts of the year, and the subtenants were grossly subservient to their masters, the chiefs and the tacksmen. They lacked any legal standing on the land and their total dependency was regarded as the most basic cause of Jacobitism in the north.

Forbes' prescription for progress was eight-fold—schools for the spread of English and skills in spinning; leases for tenants whose children attended school; farms to be restricted to those who spoke English; itinerant preachers to extend Presbyterian religious practice; leases with improvement clauses; the eradication of small holdings and the re-deployment of the people , those ousted to enter into manufacturing or muir improvement; the elimination of labour services and the introduction of crop rotation. Forbes also came to the view that the Highland clans lived in dangerous clusters which made them troublesome, and he recommended that strangers be settled among them to break up this dangerous cohesion. It was a set of advice which constituted a concerted assault on feudalism and the Highland way of life.

V

Eleven years after the Forbes/May reports, in August 1766, the Board's General Inspector and Riding Officer, Archibald Menzies, visited the lowland grounds of the Cromartie estates. He explained 'the season being too late for a tour through the Highland parts'. He was unable to report any great ferment of improvement, but there were some signals of change. Other indications, however, were negative or retrogressive. The problem of the smallness of farms had indeed worsened—'the possessors are daily endeavouring to make [their farms] ... less by dividing them' further among their children. The underlying reason for this practice was that of social status and family solidarity—'any other occupation than that of farmer being looked upon as beneath a person who claims his descent from what he looks upon as the first family in the kingdom'.

Menzies reported directly on the structure of society, notably the complex and subtle relations between the narrow strata of the estate community. He explained the prevailing arrangement in lucid terms. It was the custom in the Highlands for the tenant of a large farm to sublet the worst parts 'to poor people at as high a rate as he can, and makes them obliged to performing services'—all far in advance of the rent the principal tenant paid to the landlord. 'Some times he sublets so much of it in this way that he enjoys the best part of it for himself for nothing at all, and that is the case in Coygach... I don't doubt at all that these poor creatures the subtenants are frequently oppressed by the tacksmen their masters'. It was a classic argument against tacksmen (whose voice is unheard in these reports) and Menzies cited the case of George Mackenzie of Achnahaird who paid rent of £233 (Scots) for his farm and received £220 p.a. back from 17 subtenants—these however were 'not punctual payers' and, of course, it was a function of a tacksman to extract rent at this level.[30]

Forbes and May gave a picture of endless internecine conflict in the community. Many disputes concerned the demands of the tacksmen. There were claims that the tacksmen had doubled rents, imposed arbitrary fines, and evicted subtenants without proper cause. Sometimes the subtenants paid the tacksmen three times the amount he paid the landlord, and in addition they performed labour services in cultivation, harvesting, peat gathering and dyke repairs. 'They are forced to undergo the hardest slavery and perform the vilest drudgery' to tacksmen who tyrannised them. It was part of the sweeping indictment of the tacksman system: 'The true source of Rebellions and Turmoils, in the Western Highlands, is the slavish dependence in which the commons are forced to live, which leaves their properties and almost their lives at the disposal of their leading men, and it is more this day in Coigach than ever'.[31]

The reports from Coigach delivered by Forbes in the first days of his administration had reflected not only widespread social conflict but also a pervasive land hunger. He reported that the tenantry were harrying the tacksmen's sheep, breaking down dykes and pasturing their own cattle illegally. The tacksmen evicted the small tenants at the drop of a hat, for example, on the grounds that 'the possessors are so poor, idle and ignorant, as well as contentious, that there can be no hope of their being ever able to improve the place'. Forbes also emphasised the well known fact that the tacksmen 'subsett the worst part of their farm to poor people at exorbitant rates and live rent free themselves.' But his great fear was a general indiscipline:

> Permit me to tell you that several subtenants of Coigach have of late turned to be such bad neighbours of the Tacksmen that they refuse to keep their sheep or cattle off the grass or corn when the Tacksmen's cattle are in the hills or sheallings; then when they challenge them for this, and other acts of bad neighbourhood, they then reply with the most provoking and abusive language. Now, Sir, such insults from silly senseless men and scalding wives will sit very uneasy upon a man of spirit, let his temper never be so meek and peaceable, and if you do not speedily command the peace I know not what may be the consequence.[32]

The tacksmen-tenants employed labour and usually housed the accompanying family, providing a garden and some subsistence in lieu of wages. In addition the tenant might employ, for the season, cottars who 'for the rest of the year were employed in begging'. Menzies identified another class of marginal people: 'Numbers of people of late have settled on the frontiers of the annexed estates near the mosses. They just now acknowledge no master'. These people grazed their cattles informally and 'maintained themselves by beggary'. Many other people on the estates were also idle; the cornlands, in particular, were 'overstocked with inhabitants'. Yet there were specific shortages of labour, of skilled people such as millrights and masons who were imported for particular work. Technical training was required and Menzies advocated the establishment of villages and manufacturers though he was sceptical of long-term subsidisation of flax/linen production. Like his predecessor, Menzies recommended strangers as settlers: 'When any farm becomes vacant the predominant clan should be excluded from getting possession'.

Even by 1767 (when Menzies toured again) little progress was visible. Whisky smuggling continued its baneful influence; the local factors had made vigorous efforts to regularise holdings but faced the obstructive and litigious response of an unwilling tenantry. Enclosing was proceeding at a slow rate and he continued to think that the 'supernumerary inhabitants' should be settled in overspill villages. Efforts to promote manufacturing at Lochbroom and Glenmoriston were very disappointing despite large expenditures on capital works, but flax spinning at Tarbat had progressed and he held out high hopes for wool spinning in the west. He reported that sheep would succeed famously in the west and become the staple of the country—but noted that an absurd prejudice impeded its development—'Just now a farmer thinks it below his dignity to acknowledge he has any sheep or knows anything about them'. Similarly, the exploitation of the herring fishery was held back by poor technology and lack of capital.[33]

Menzies' report was scarcely a celebration of the achievements of the previous decade and a half in the administration of the Cromartie estates. Change was pitifully slow.

CHAPTER 8

State Enterprise and Infant Industries

'... we had a fine view of a most beautiful country to the west called Strathpeffer, being a Vale about a half mile wide, and a mile Deep, to the South are two rough hills; to the North a most beautiful gentle Declivity from the Hills, as if laid out by a line, and it is finely improved; at the end, exactly in the Center, is the Earl of Cromartie's Castle with woods about it, and three small valleys extending from the End of this Vale, and under Corn.' (Bishop Pococke, 1760.)

The Commissioners of the Annexed Estates, backed by government and by a small army of estate factors, was one of the first bodies to confront systematically the full severity of the perennial problems of Highland development. They were charged with the responsibility to accelerate social change and to stimulate agricultural and industrial development, to break the crust of Highland feudalism. Within the limits of prevailing technology—in terms of agricultural practise, animal breeding, new industries, roads, tenure, management—the Board pursued its set policies along the most favoured methods. The difficulties it confronted and the disappointments experienced—at Cromartie as much as elsewhere—provide an accurate measure of the scale of the objective difficulties of promoting economic change in the Highlands. In some ways the Commissioners faced less difficulties than their successors—in the sense that competition from the south and population congestion within were both, in say 1760, less severe than a century later. The relative failure is therefore doubly instructive.

I

In agriculture the failure was mitigated by the simple reality that a growing population was supported through those years. The Highlands generally, including the Annexed Estates, witnessed demographic growth by 1770—it was a consequence probably more connected with potato production than with clear benefits from agricultural improvement. However the incidence of famine and other signs of strain appear undiminished in these years. It seems likely too that more people were disconnected from the land, marginalised by both population growth and the re-arrangement of holdings and tenure. Migration siphoned off some of this displaced population, so too did the growth of domestic industry which the Board itself had promoted. There was both growth and mobility, but mainly within the old framework of economic life. The Board grappled both with the effects of its own policy and with the continuing changes in Highland society.

For instance the Annexed Estates followed a policy of agrarian consolidation in the approved enclosing manner. This, of course, required the elimination of small tenants and their redeployment in new villages and other public works. On some estates it is clear that chief tenants anticipated the policy (even as early as 1756) and began to divest themselves of their subtenants before any alternative accommodation or employment could be found. By 1762 some people on the Lovat estate had been reduced, in effect, to refugees in their own land—to 'beggary, emigration, or near starvation', in diametric opposition to the intention of the Board itself. Less is known about the impact of enclosure and consolidation on the Cromartie estate. Little seems to have been achieved in the west, but it is known that the process had reached the grounds of Castle Leod by the 1770s and that the minister at Fodderty was also consolidating his farm holdings at that time.

In Coigach the administration made some attempts to systematise holdings and to rationalise tenures, but the response of the people probably curbed the full exercise of reform. In August 1767 Peter May told Alexander Taylor that he must go to Coigach 'where there have been so many alterations made of late among the tenantry which has turned them almost mutinous; many petitions and complaints are daily received, and I am particularly instructed to examine into them'. Unfortunately the results of his examination are not to be found but it is unlikely that any further radical changes were introduced to Coigach.[1]

The experience of consolidation—a slowly continuing process in the Highlands at large—was sufficiently dislocating to cause an apparent weakening if not an actual reversal of the policy in the hands of the Commissioners. In places the changes were so precipitate that labour shortages began to affect local production. The attempt to give independence to smallholders in some places caused a dislocation of production and a deterioration in productivity. The southern managers seem eventually to have come closer to a recognition of the benefit of the much derided system of subtenancy. As Annette Smith puts it, subtenancy held advantages 'in providing a stable labour force' while the subtenant 'found himself slightly higher on the social scale and materially better off than he would have been as a hired labourer'.[2] Here indeed was one of the key impediments to radical change in the Highlands and it was reinforced by the Commissioners' explicit objection to the idea of emigration.

Another strategy for improvement was the introduction of new blood to the estates, for both economic and political reasons. The main effort of this sort was the attempted resettlement of demobilised soldiers after the peace of 1763. Several of the Annexed Estates, including Cromartie, were involved in the exercise which was seen as a reward for the soldiers' services, and as the injection of new people into the Highlands. New villages were planned and in May 1763 advertised in London and Edinburgh; houses were to be provided at a special subsidy, and the newcomers (on the three Cromartie baronies) were to be given 10 acre lots.

The Cromartie estates appear to have accepted about 70 soldiers in these schemes—at Ardvall, Auchterneed, Tullich, Polnicol and Castlehill in the east, and a further group in Coigach (at Ullapool and Ardmair). Some of the settlers were indeed strangers—one each from Armagh and Devon, but mostly they came from the Highlands and many were Mackenzies. It was intended that they should introduce useful trades to the county and they included masons, tailors, weavers and shoemakers. At Ullapool a farm was divided up for twelve men who were given a £3 bounty together with free boat and accommodation. This was consistent with Forbes' recommendation in 1755 that a fishing village be established at Ullapool.[3] The general plan had much to commend it.

It seems that the settlers' lots were carved out of already cultivated land though of the poorest sort, and this immediately caused resentment among the local people. The settlers were meant to begin paying rent by 1766 but grave difficulties had developed and the factor expressed increasing alarm. Forbes was indignant that the soldiers and sailors were sent without prior warning or time for preparation and reported 'the Universal murmurings and clamour which begins already ... among the tenants'. From New Tarbat and Strathpeffer there were heartrending petitions from the new settlers (who were called King's Cottagers) complaining vehemently about their lots, the poorness of the soil and the stony and watery land on which they were settled. One voice claimed that the men were forced 'to strip our backs to feed our bellies or else die from want'. They claimed also that the Board had not fulfilled its promises. Those in Coigach failed to pay their rent as planned in 1766 and some in the east had given up by 1768. There were local allegations in Coigach that the ex-soldiers were causing serious social disturbance and had generated problems of illicit distilling and law and order.[4] There were particularly aggrieved complaints about 'the scandalous behaviour of some prostitutes in Coigach'. Loans were not repaid and Forbes the agent lost what little hope he had for the scheme. He recommended that further assistance cease. 'Such idle fellows are not worth countenancing'.[5] In Coigach the soldiers became bankrupt, lacked seed for future seasons and left debts upon the local community. The entire unhappy episode seems to have run its course to extinction so that in 1772 Pennant reported that all the settlers' houses in Coigach were deserted. He described it as 'an Utopian project of establishing colonies' which had, within a decade, failed.[6] The whole scheme had yielded little other than prolonged frustration. Good intentions were not enough.[7]

II

The general trend of Highland rents through the period of Annexation appears to have been upwards and to this was attributed, notably by Samuel Johnson in 1773, much of the recurrent fever of emigration. The trend is somewhat obscured and complicated by the continuing process of commutation from victual/services rents to money rents. A tentative view suggests that the Coigach rent rose from £298 Sterling in 1755 to about £352 in 1772 and £380 in 1784. The combined rent of Strathpeffer and New Tarbat seems to gave grown from £672 in 1755 to £883 in 1784.[8] It is broadly clear that rents rose under Annexation but that the increase was somewhat less than the average increase in the Highlands, though at Cromartie the local agent Forbes continued (in 1770) to claim that Peter May had set rents too high back in 1755. On the Cromartie lands in the east only a small proportion of the tenantry paid money rents (though those in

Coigach had been doing so for the past century). The officials of the Board experienced difficulties in accommodating the grain derived from victual rents and in 1765 sanctioned the construction, at the cost of £300, of a new granary at Portleish for this specific purpose.[9] The process of conversion to money rents was slow, and not always welcomed by the people especially where they were required to substitute cash for their traditional labour services.[10]

Agricultural improvement under Annexation, despite the efforts of the agents and despite their relatively moderate renting policy, was hesitant. To a large extent they appear to have been frustrated by the entrenched character of Highland practice. Small improvements were certainly accomplished—such as fencing, dyking and ditching in the years 1768-71, and attempts to prevent communal overstocking by new souming rules (in 1755 and again in 1770-2). Similarly 300 acres of forest were planted at Strathpeffer in 1783. Ninian Jeffrey was notably persistent in his efforts to improve grazing techniques in Lochbroom. He advocated the introduction of sown grass and turnips for winter feeding and claimed that he had increased the size of the cattle as a result. Jeffrey also tried on many occasions to introduce commercial sheepfarming to the west and in 1765 suggested that young Coigach men be sent to the sheep-rearing districts of the Scottish borders to learn advanced methods of grazing.[11] At another time he argued that the Forest of Coigach be given to an experienced sheep farmer, rent free for a period, to demonstrate the potential of the region, and to introduce new hardy species from the south.

Jeffrey appears to have been a lone voice in the wilderness; he received neither official nor local support for his ideas, and in 1771 there still had been no start in the business. He confronted a general and barely rational contempt among Highlanders for sheepfarming. When at last a sheepfarming tenant was tempted by a long lease and low rent, his enterprise at Coigach failed—presumably because he shouldered too many costs of an infant industry which, in a few decades, would become famously lucrative. In general the era of the Annexed Estates was notable for its avoidance of large-scale clearances (for any purpose) and Annette Smith believes that such a policy would have been inconsistent with the aims of the Board 'which included ensuring a happy tenantry and did not demand a much increased rent roll as a mark of efficient management'. Clearances, she says, would have created massive social problems of re-location.[12] Thus the Board did not pursue a full-blooded policy of rationalisation. It improvised a series of piecemeal improvement rather than a co-ordinated assault on the causes of Highland poverty.

In arable farming improvements efforts were probably more successful. The management seems to have promoted the cultivation of potatoes, cabbage and turnips—in 1756 Peter May had advocated small yards specifically to promote such crops in Coigach. The managers were sensitive to the older practices—especially the use of kelp for manure—which the minister of Lochbroom explained was vital for their survival. When problems arose from the boom in kelp prices (from the industrial uses of kelp) in the late 1770s, care was taken that the letting of kelp shores allowed a proportion to be retained for local arable needs.[13] Similarly concerted efforts were devoted to the improvement of woodland for the future benefit of the estates.

Yet the rhetoric of the improvers, their scorn for the old ways, was not matched by

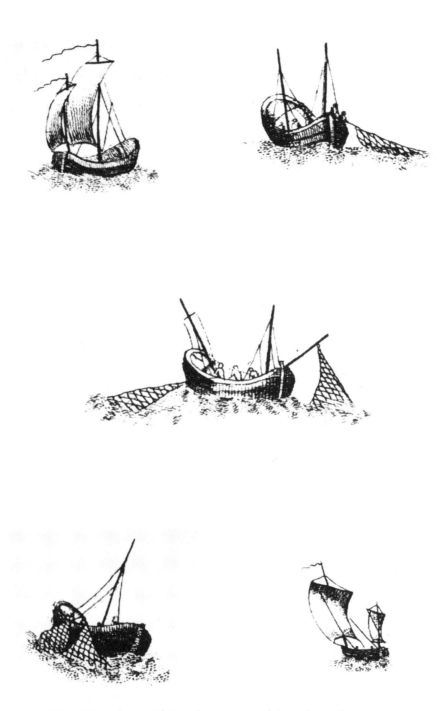

11 Fishing boats off Ross, last quarter of the eighteenth century.

action or a clear record of improvement. The broad verdict on its agricultural efforts is negative. At the beginning of the Annexation the agents said the Cromartie people were slovenly by southern standards, the tenantry 'idle', the tradesmen 'the dregs of the country', and even at New Tarbat, very few of the tenants at all were interested in improvement. At the end of the era the tone had not changed perceptibly, little advance seems to have been achieved and in its final years the Board seems to have lost much of its sense of purpose.

There were two indications of this ostensibly poor record. Famine continued to descend on the community and, indeed, the Board gained some credit for its relief efforts on several occasions. For instance in 1763 bolls of meal imported from Aberdeenshire were distributed to the poor who were *in extremis*, lacking either money or credit. In 1768 Jeffrey reported from Coigach that the people were 'in so great want that they were eating the cattle that died and few or none of them had a bit of bread to eat'. Jeffrey noted that the people were assisting each other but he felt compelled to appeal for help from the Board.[14] It is clear that, certainly in Coigach, the people continued to suffer the ancient anxieties of shortfall of food through each winter. Thus, again in the winter of 1771-2 bad weather, combined with cattle plague, created great hardship. Simon Mackenzie of Langwell lost nine-tenths of his cattle. It was a recurrence of famine on a large scale and the suffering of the people continued into 1773. The Board acknowledged its responsibility to seek supplies of potatoes, barley-bere and oats to Coigach, even from as far away as Lancashire and Ireland. Some 400 bolls of meal were distributed on the Cromartie and Lovat estates and a local report declared that

> the other day a great body of people assembled ... and begged with tears in their eyes that he [the agent] bring more yet, otherwise some of them would starve.

Such shortages were not at all exclusive to Coigach or the Annexed Estates but they were an unambiguous demonstration that concerted improvement by the Board had not solved even the primitive subsistence problems of the people.[15] There was a conspicuous lack of evidence of positive benefits: indeed the several freelance writers who toured the Highlands later in the eighteenth century paid few if any compliments to the efforts of the Board of the Annexed Estates. As Smith concludes, 'simple agricultural efficiency was not the sole, or even the first, aim of annexation'.[16]

The second indication of social breakdown and relative failure during the years of Annexation was emigration. Emigrants were flooding out of the West Highlands to America ('in epidemical fury' according to Dr Johnson) in the early 1770s and some of them were undoubtedly people from Wester Ross and Coigach. Generally, however, the movements were poorly recorded and difficult to account in the demographic and tenurial history of the region. In July 1771 a vessel with more than 80 migrants for America departed from Lochbroom, of whom 28 were indented to Kenneth Brock in George Town, Maryland.[17] It was one of many such voyages and there were contemporary allegations that too much encouragement was being given to emigration. One remarked 'What is a country without inhabitants, what are lairds without people, what is a minister's charge without parishioners?'[18] General Mackay complained 'I see numbers of people are going from our northern parts to America', but acknowledged that 'The Highlands is a growing country by nature and not for manufactures, there is no fishing for villages or towns'.[19]

In 1773 Lochbroom was the scene of one of the most celebrated emigrant voyages across the Atlantic, namely the sailing of the Hector to Pictou in Nova Scotia, sometimes referred to as 'the Scottish Mayflower', since it inaugurated the great Scottish migration to the Canadian provinces. The emigration had some of its antecedents in the famine of those years. In 1772 'The United Inhabitants' from Coigach had signed (as best they could, mainly by an 'X') a petition about their desperate circumstances: it was the first direct voice of the people in the entire history of the Cromartie estate. They referred to the fact that their cattle were dying and that the people also were starving even though they were giving each other help. They had suffered a 'prodigious loss of cattle' and were out of corn. They continued:

> In this deplorable situation some of the inhabitants had thought of transporting themselves and families to North America, but on mature consideration thought to make known their case ... But such is the scarcity at present that most of the people are in a starving condition, the more so as their horses are so weak that they could not carry loads from the low country, and no ship appeared on the coast hitherto.

They pleaded for a lower rent in return for which 'the petitioners will drop all thought of going to America.' In fact the Board refused to reduce rents but, on the other hand, sent 600 bushels of meal to Coigach for sale at cost price.

The following autumn was again ruined by bad weather and the fishing failed in the district. In December 1772 Jeffrey reported that the people were again in 'a precarious state' and needed large scale relief. By February 1773 it was evident that the weather had not improved and that there was the greatest difficulty in keeping the animals alive through to the end of the winter. In June 1773, 37 families had renounced their leases and had sold their possessions in readiness for emigration to America. The local factor had vainly refused to accept the termination of the leases and remarked that 'The spirit of Emigration makes lands difficult to sett at present rates', this being the perennial landlord anxiety after the effects of emigration.[20]

There were, undoubtedly, other precipitants at work to promote the Lochbroom emigration. In fact these people had become entangled in an elaborate land-settlement plan originating in America and facilitated by relatively sophisticated recruitment schemes operated locally by a merchant called John Ross of Lochbroom. The people were indeed responding to attractive advertisements and the enticements of emigration agents. Many of them seem also to have paid their own fares, £3.5.0 per adult, which was a substantial outlay for any Highlander. The passage money, in some cases, was probably raised by liquidating all available assets. Of the reasons given at the time, the most prominent among the 300 emigrants was that the 'landholders and Chieftains of the North have raised their rents so high and screwed their Tenants to such a degree that they were greatly oppressed',[21] and thereby reduced to indigence. Yet the degree to which the people of the Hector (and other contemporaneous Highlanders) were forced by adversity to emigrate remains a matter of contention. Professor J.M. Bumsted takes the view that 'they had sufficient capital to remain in Scotland if they had wished

... The emigration was one of rising expectations; the Highlander was less driven out of his native land than chose to leave it.'[22] It remains, however, difficult to reconcile a felicitous state of rising expectations not only with the peoples' own accounts of their motives, but also with the uncontested reality of famine at that time. One thing is entirely clear; these people, like many of their successors, were land hungry.

Emigration continued until the start of the American Revolution in 1776 and revived strongly again in the aftermath. More direct evidence from Lochbroom was provided by a voyage a year later than that of the Hector. Leaving Stornoway on 14 November 1774, was the Peace and Plenty, bound for New York. Among its passengers were the McCrans of Lochbroom, described as 'servants' leaving 'on account of their being greatly reduced in their circumstances'. They had been recruited by ship's agents under some persuasive pressure—indeed three quarters of the people who had originally agreed to emigrate did not materialise at the appointed time of embarkation. The captain had been 'so irritated that after having fired a gun as a signal to part of the Passengers who were on shore he, without further delay, weighed anchor and made off to sea, with the Passengers ... leaving several behind destitute who had paid their freights.'[23] Other shipping reports gave mention of emigrants not only from Lochbroom, but also from Strathpeffer.

The verdict on emigration offered by the ministers in the *Old Statistical Account* of the 1790s were unequivocal. There was, for instance, the report from Lochbroom

> The oppression of the landholders is a general complaint in the Highlands; and the consequence is, that great numbers of the people are forced to emigrate to America, while others go to service in the low countries and manufacturing towns.[24]

'Oppression', of course, was another word for the inflation of rents. Such landlord pressure operated in tandem with other adverse circumstances which included the rapid growth of population, recurrent food shortages and the perennial insufficiency of employment in the Highlands.

III

Beyond agriculture the Board of the Annexed Estates sought to achieve broader development, especially in industry. In most areas, including the Cromartie estate, there had existed little manufacturing for the market. But at Strathpeffer in 1755 there were reported to be 488 spinning wheels (for a total estate population of 2199) which, conceivably, reflected the promotion given in previous decades by the third Earl of Cromartie.

The Commissioners attempted to lift the whole level of textile production in the Highlands, to create a great industry, on a domestic and factory basis, which would absorb idle labour and create wealth in the country. It was based on the prevailing view that flax and linen were productions full of economic potential in the mid eighteenth century. In parallel with plans for the extension of flax cultivation at Tarbat, great schemes were hatched for a new manufacturing plant to develop flax spinning and weaving. New Tarbat was a chosen locality—particularly Milntown in Kilmuir Easter. In 1757 a comprehensive scheme was advocated to organise the entire business from cultivation to the woven product. It entailed the expenditure of £4209 and the employment of 900 girls and 192 apprentices, utilising New Tarbat House as its centre. Sadly the plan collapsed in the absence of Crown approval, and New Tarbat House itself fell into ruins. Nevertheless the spinning industry made substantial progress in the parish. William Sandeman, an influential manufacturer from Perthshire, extended his enterprise to Kilmuir Easter which, with some help from the Commissioners, flourished with growing external sales especially in London. It was said that 1000 spinners were employed in the parish in 1765—a figure difficult to take literally but a suggestion of the success of piecemeal expansion within the old framework of domestic industry. Its days were numbered, however, and eventually (at the end of the century) such 'proto-industrialization' was radically undermined by the competition of the cotton and linen factories of the Lowlands in the industrial revolution proper.

A separate effort in textile enterprise was initiated by the Commissioners in Loch Broom where a substantial linen station was established at considerable outlay. Ninian Jeffrey was involved to the extent of introducing some people from Kelso to initiate the manufacture in the late 1750s. But this scheme also failed, for unspecified reasons: the 38 Kelso people petitioned against their destitution and the expensive buildings, by 1767-8, had fallen into decay and ended up 'a woeful experience', like so many Highland ventures. The bare outline of the episode suggests a plethora of good intentions overtaken by difficulties of environment and management.

Other possibilities for development were canvassed in these years. Some attention, in the last years of the Board's aegis, was attracted to the possibilities of the modest mineral spa at Strathpeffer where the peculiar properties of the waters had long been known. The doctor at New Tarbat, Alexander Mackenzie, went so far as to report the alleged qualities of the mineral well to the Royal Society: he claimed that the waters were as potent and as recuperative as those of Harrogate. An architect was sent to inspect, and reported agreeably on the health-giving possibilities of the Strath, but once more nothing was accomplished in this period. Similarly the Board instituted a mineral survey in the hope of finding coal which 'would be a great blessing'. Lignite was again discovered at Castle Leod but was found to be useless for current purposes.

On a larger scale were several initiatives taken by the Board to develop fisheries on both west and east seaboards of the Highlands. The Board expressed the recurrent frustration of the nation about the level of local inertia amidst such obviously rich fishing grounds. There was a general lack of skill, ability, initiative and capital to develop the industry. The Board proposed the building of new villages at several locations which included Lochbroom and the Cromarty Firth. Sailors were encouraged to settle on the coasts and create a demonstration-effect for the local community. A Liverpool merchant, John Woodhouse, and Colin Mackenzie, both saw possibilities for smoked herring and kelp facilities at Isle Martin and Coigach. The local agent, Jeffrey, was equally enthusiastic and developed ideas which entailed shifting small tenants from inland to the coast for fishing work, and devoting their old grazing lands to sheepfarming: but little seems to have eventuated from these suggestions. Nevertheless Lochbroom attracted a seasonal fishing which employed local hands, but was apparently mainly conducted by non-

Highlanders. In 1776 merchants from the south began to erect houses at Isle Martin for curing herrings 'after the Yarmouth way', that is smoking them as 'red herrings'.[25] Visiting fishermen tended to generate sufficient disorder to require the hand of the militia at Lochbroom in 1756 and 1773, and a clergyman complained severely of their 'uncleanness and Sabbath profanation'. In economic terms the great problem remained— that of engaging the resident population in the prosecution of the fishing.

The Board of the Annexed Estates seems to have been better equipped to identify problems in the Highlands than to solve them. Such was equally the case on roads. Coigach, said the inspectors, had the worst roads in the Highlands: 'nothing but necessity makes strangers resort here and for a great part of the year it is almost inaccessible'. Strathpeffer also had very poor unrepaired roads and no bridges, but New Tarbat was much better provided. Forbes advocated a new road from Dingwall to Lochbroom in order to bring the benefits of civilisation to the west coast. A survey was undertaken which drew attention to the inherent difficulties, and though some small progress was made in the 1760s the bulk of the problem remained for the estate's successors.[26]

IV

The last few years of the Board of the Annexed Estates lacked all conviction and sense of continuing purpose. From as early as 1774, according to Smith, 'the writing had been on the wall' that the estates would be returned to the old families. In 1783 Henry Dundas was appointed commissioner to achieve this end. The danger of Jacobite insurrection had entirely evaporated and the purposes of the Board, to that extent, had been thoroughly achieved. In the Disannexing Act of 1784 the estates were returned 'to representatives of the original possessors upon reasonable conditions'. In fact these conditions were stringent—that the old debts which had been assumed by the Treasury be liquidated before repossession was confirmed. This yielded a total fund of £142,843 which was made available for a number of remarkable public works (including the construction of Forth and Clyde Canal and Register House). It meant, however, that some of the restored owners faced an immediate future full of debts and liabilities: for some, including the new owner of Cromartie, the clock was put back to 1745, a return to the financial difficulties of the Jacobite Earl.

Thus, by 1784, the experiment in state enterprise and administration came to a somewhat limp termination. Verdicts on the experiment have differed strikingly. In 1909 A.H. Millar concluded his reading of the evidence thus:

> the Forfeited Estates of 1746 were managed with brilliant success, and helped to bring Scotland forward in commerce, education, industry and all that tends to make a nation memorable. Thus a great disaster was transformed into a perennial benefit, and with the minimum of suffering.[27]

A more recent editor of the Papers of the Annexed Estates is also favourably impressed— 'of all the grand designs for Highland development which have been carried out over the past two centuries few have come nearer to achieving their objectives than that undertaken in the years between 1755 and 1784 by the Commissioners of the Annexed Estates'.[28]

By contrast Annette Smith offers trenchant criticisms—particularly of the economic aspects which spelt failure, demonstrating 'a conspicuous lack of results' to the expenditures. She suggests that the administration was inefficient and ineffective and that in its final years ran out of steam. She quotes the opinions of contemporaries—for instance Lord Sydney who said that the best way that the Annexed Estates were distinguished from others was 'by the almost total neglect of their cultivation'. Lord Kames, a Commissioner and notable improver of his own lands, held that the great expenditures had been like 'water spilt on the ground'. Neglect, deterioration and inadequate capitalization were the primary marks of thirty years of state intervention in the social and economic life of the Highland estates.[29]

The final years of the administration of the Annexed Estates may have negated the earlier benefits of the original efforts of the Board. Certainly when Lord Macleod retrieved the Cromartie estates in 1784 he claimed that they were 'much delapidated'[30] and Dr Smith's findings do nothing to mend this view. But incoming landowners are inveterate in the art of exaggerating the evils of the *status quo ante* since nothing could better increase the reputation of their own efforts. That the Annexed Board appeared to achieve little of concrete and permanent economic improvement is hardly surprising in the long history, both before and since, of economic failure in the north of Scotland. Few would find much glory in the record.

CHAPTER 9

Count MacLeod and the Recovery of the Cromartie Estates

I

The long decline of the traditional ways of Highland society, the erosion of local autonomies and local structures of power, prestige and social leadership had been strongly reinforced by the devastating impact of the Jacobite Rebellion and its aftermath. For the Cromartie dynasty it was almost fatal and it reduced the family to a position of grovelling humiliation and dire poverty. Its collapse mirrored the fate of the Jacobite families and the Highlands in general. Yet this undoubted devastation should not obscure the vigorous persistence of fundamental values—nothing had altered the indispensability of land, of position, of family lineage, in Highland society.

The heir to the third Earl of Cromartie, John MacKenzie, Lord Macleod, devoted, indeed sacrificed, his entire adult life to the restoration of his family's position in the Highlands. It was an *idée fixe* of obsessive dimensions, and testimony to the magic of landownership. His triumphant return to the Highlands in the 1780s was evidence of the charisma of the family in Ross-shire society. It is never quite clear why the ordinary people of the Highlands attached themselves so loyally to families such as the Mackenzies of Cromartie, nor why it was that the family could draw upon this fund in times of great difficulty. There was repeated invocation of the quasi-mystical notion of 'the Fame of Cromartie', to which each generation was 'heir and representative', and which was associated with the idea of the continuity of 'an ancient and respectable (and not long ago a noble) Family'. These were, of course, an appeal to a particular conception of society and its leadership. And beyond the idea of lost nobility, was the more mundane acquisitive spirit—the recovery of lands which could provide the remnants of the family and their descendants with an income to support a comfortable style of living commensurate with their old social and political role in the North. The restitution of the estates would provide the financial basis for a return to decent living standards for Macleod and his family. David Stewart of Garth referred to Macleod's 'invisible attachment to his native land'. That the government would recognise these claims was a measure of the *quid pro quo* (in the form of the raising of a regiment), which Macleod was able to offer at a time of national need, and a mark also of the continuity of the hereditary principle of local territorial magnates, though tainted forty years before. It was too an indication, and an accurate one, of the confidence of the government in the

12   Count MacLeod.

pacific conditions of the Highlands in the 1780s. For the people of Cromartie Estates, in simple economic terms, the restoration meant little in the short run. Their rents now were paid, once more, to the descendants of the third Earl of Cromartie instead of to the national exchequer. In social terms the change was welcome—a figure closer and more identifiable became the recipient of their rents, and a figure from whom benevolence would be expected. It is not easy to see how the restoration of the Cromartie lands in 1784 affected the people any more than this.

The single-minded determination to recover the name of the Cromartie family began in April 1749 when John Mackenzie and his brother George determined to leave their family and seek military careers in northern Europe. The decision was made a year after MacKenzie and his father had been permitted to leave the Tower but some months before the royal pardon was issued. The family was living in Layhill, Devonshire, and Cromartie's pardon specified that he should remain there at the King's pleasure. John MacKenzie's own pardon had been 'on condition that within six months of his attaining his majority he should convey to the Crown all his rights and claims to the estates of the Earls of Cromartie'.[1] The family was *in extremis*: in 1751 the Cromartie wrote 'we are most extremely pinched for want of money.[2] This was despite the fact that his wife had been voted a pension of £200 (not always paid), and despite gifts from clansmen. It is difficult to know how much, and for how long, the family obtained support from friends and relatives. It was reported that Cromartie received presents of money, smoked fish, honey and meal from loyal and charitable tenants, but these were probably mere tokens of respect rather than sources of subsistence. It is evident from Cromartie's begging letters in 1759 that whatever success his sons had by then achieved abroad it was not enough to raise the spirits or living standards of their parents in England.[3] Meanwhile the old family houses on the northern estates were now in other hands. Tarbat House fell into decay—in 1756 Peter May had said it was 'a very pretty place, but the house and gardens are already gone into great disorder and the young trees and nurseries, of which there is a great plenty, are all neglected and abused.'[4] Castle Leod was let to a Whig worthy, Mackenzie of Avoch, on a 19 year lease said to have been made on the most favourable terms.

Both sons sought a military career to revive the fortunes of the family. Both achieved good success in the long run. From Devonshire in 1749 the eldest son John proceeded to Hamburg and Berlin with introductions to the court of Sweden from Marshall Keith. By mid 1750 he had obtained a Company in a Swedish regiment after some time as a volunteer. Good connections in Sweden gave him a financial start and he served in Finland in 1754 and gained promotion in April 1755 as a major and served in Denmark and Bohemia.[5] All this seems to have been a preparation for a return to serve the British crown and application was made for entry to the British service at the time of the outbreak of war between Sweden and Prussia. Somehow the application was botched and he returned to serve the Swedes. By January 1762 he had been made a Knight in the Swedish order, and eventually was created Count Macleod.[6] By 1762 Macleod and his brother had qualified as freeholders in Ross and Cromarty and this was a sign of the direction of their ambitions.[7] But for 27 years Count Macleod earned his living under the Swedish Crown; by 1773 he was in command of a Regiment of two battalions and a founder of the Swedish Freemasons, the Timbermanns. His younger brother got a King's commission through General Murray (a relative). He was too young to have fought in the '45. He recruited and became the commanding officer for the 2nd Battalion of his brother's regiment.

A military life was not only the classic career path for the lesser sons of the eighteenth century nobility but also, by the 1770s, an indirect means of restitution of the Annexed Estates to their former owners. The Lovat family had set the pace, providing a model which Macleod himself would follow. Lovat raised a regiment of Frasers to fight for the Hanoverian Government in North America. The regiment played a large part in the capture of Quebec, and by way of reward Lovat was permitted to resume his estates which had been annexed three decades before. It may be, as some historians have suggested, that the government was already moving towards dis-annexation. The Annexation Board had generated widespread disatisfaction, its policy of long leases had made the estates unresponsive to improvement plans and many of the earlier plans for agricultural, industrial and fishing development had fallen to pieces (see Chapter 8 above). It was, by the 1780s, no very radical step to return the estates to private ownership—Jacobitism was dead, and the Treasury might gain financially by dis-annexation.[8]

It was in 1773 that Macleod's Scottish agent, Leonard Urquhart (his solicitor in Edinburgh), brought to his attention news of a possible change in Government policy towards the lost estates, news long awaited by the dispossessed heir of the Cromartie Estate. 'I am informed that there is a design to give back the Annexed Estates in Scotland to the forfeiting persons or their heirs upon payment of the sums by Govt to Creditors. I will this may prove true that I might once more see the natural born heir inhabiting New Tarbat.'[9] It was to mark the beginning of a concerted campaign to recover the estates.[10] But meanwhile Macleod continued his military operations in Finland and Denmark,[11] correspondence being much inhibited by freezing conditions on both sides of the North Sea in the winter of 1774. Already he knew that any possibility of the recovery of his estates was contingent on the repayment of debts on the estate. It is likely that an action of his uncle in 1776 was closely connected with the effort to regain the Cromartie estates. Sir John Gordon arranged that his nephew should, on his death, inherit his Invergordon estate. This estate was encumbered with debt, but his will specified that lands could be sold to pay off the debts. The Invergordon estates were not sold until after the restoration of Cromartie's own debt-burdened estates, and we do not know the net effect on Cromartie's own finances. But it is most likely that the arrangement was materially beneficial for Macleod's aspirations.

II

An even more decisive move was made in 1777 when Macleod returned to England and offered himself to the British crown for service in the colonial wars.[12] He clearly realised that the military circumstances in North America and India favoured a new approach to London. His cousin Henry Dundas smoothed the way; Macleod was received by George III and an offer to raise a regiment of Highlanders was accepted. Macleod was commissioned as colonel in the 73rd Foot a week before Christmas. In the following year Macleod and his kinsman Inchculter raised the 71st Regiment, known also as Macleod's Regiment. The extraordinary aspect of the episode was the rapidity with which he was able to recruit 840 Highlanders within a few weeks, to which were added 230 Lowlanders raised by David Blair. They were passed for service by General Skene at Elgin in April 1778. To reinforce this success a second battalion was ordered and Macleod was very rapidly at the head of 2,200 countrymen 'of whom 1800 were from the neighbourhood in which his family once had its name'. The details, the inducements, the promises which attended this astonishing feat, are not known but it is inconceivable that it could have been achieved without drawing upon the collective emotion of family loyalty and a popular identification with a social leader. David Stewart of Garth was probably not merely romantic when he cited this event 'as a remarkable example of the traditional influence of an old and respected name'. Stewart saw it as symbolic of the integrity and cohesion of the old Highland style of social relations—a spirit that survived annexation and which was now channelled towards the needs of the Hanoverian government in London:

> Finding his influence in the Highlands still considerable, although destitute of property and military consequence, he was encouraged to offer his services to raise a regiment. The offer was accepted, and so well grounded were his anticipations of success, and such was the respect entertained for his family and name, that in a very short time 840 Highlanders were recruited and marched to Elgin.... It is not in many countries that a man, without money or credit, supported only by the feelings excited by a long remembered and respected name have thus attained an honourable command over such trusty and willing followers, and laid a foundation for future wealth and inheritance.

Stewart of Garth, writing after Waterloo, regarded the entire episode as the epitome of the Highland experience, an exact measure of loyalty and allegiance and good feeling in the old Highlands. It was also symbolic of change: 'Such was the state of society fifty years ago, but there has been a melancholy change in the character and disposition of the higher and lower orders in that part of the country since Lord Macleod's time'. Subsequently sheep and improvements had been introduced:

> Instead of a faithful attached tenantry, the assistance of the Sheriff and the civil power have been called for to protect the landlords in the execution of their plans; and this being found insufficient, recourse was had to the military. Increased incomes may sometimes be procured by too great a sacrifice.[13]

Stewart's influential account, however, omitted certain recorded difficulties that arose during the recruitments. Macleod in fact found that he was unable to meet his immediate anticipations for two reasons. First, it became clear that some of his officers had rejected some recruits who were, therefore, not delivered to headquarters; some of their recruits had deserted; some had been claimed by, and delivered up to, other regiments; others were detained on various pretences common in the recruiting service. Second, 120 were discharged from service, and others 'hearing of the destination to the East India, to which they were averse, represented their being under diseases which they had carefully concealed till then', which accounted for the discharge of a further 55 men. Macleod pointed out that 1040 effective men had been raised, a greater achievement than other new corps, despite the fact that he had been in Finland and his brother in America at the time. He submitted that the outcome was 'a satisfactory justification of the Representation he had given' to the Government.[14]

Recruitment had been most successful in Coigach but the eastern lands also supplied substantial numbers. The exercise may have reflected the persistent loyalties of the people to Macleod's family, and it is true that Macleod's regiment was the only Highland regiment of the period never to be rocked by mutiny. Nevertheless there were other inducements to be considered. The story was later told that in Strathpeffer Macleod had instructed his Lieutenant to write down in a little black book the names of families who yielded forth sons for the regiment, 'and for as long as his family had any say in things, the family would not suffer'. Twenty years later one blind old woman went to Castle Leod with a written petition to ask for assistance. She said 'If I had a hundred sons I would have given them to Lord Macleod, but had the one and he did not come back from India'.

Macleod went to India with the first battalion in early 1778 and remained there until he decided to leave, probably in August 1781. The troops joined Eyre Coote's campaign. In India Macleod found himself saddled with unexpectedly large responsibilities during 'the irruption of Hyder Ali into the Carnatic'. The contribution of Macleod and his batallion was regarded as vital in the campaign. The troops themselves had suffered badly from high mortality rates in poor accommodation in barracks in Madras about which MacLeod protested vehemently. There was testimony to Macleod's reputation from the hand of the regimental surgeon, Alexander MacDougall. In August 1779 MacDougall wrote home from the Cape of Good Hope and described Macleod as the best Colonel imaginable. MacDougall had himself been promoted by Macleod which had caused some 'little jealousies among the officers of his own clan'. Macleod gave parties every evening for his Field Officers and Captains and raised MacDougall's hopes of making a fortune from 'the Gold Pagodas of the Carnatic'. But the regiment had lost its baggage, Macleod's included: 'His Lordship lost everything he had, not a shirt or a shift, money, plate or other articles remain. His loss amounts at least to 4000 Star Pagodas. He does not value the money but the loss of some papers of consequence and very old family plate distresses him much.'[15]

Unfortunately the financial benefits of Macleod's military careers are not known. His subsequent scale of living suggests they were large. But in mid-1780 there was an obscure and ostensibly trivial breach of etiquette between Macleod and Eyre Coote which terminated in the abrupt resolution of Macleod to leave for England with considerably increased military status. In 1783 he became a Major General in the British establishment.[16] His battalions had been a great success, and Macleod had developed useful connections inside the War Office. He now repeatedly petitioned the Crown for the return of his estates on the precedent created by Lord Lovat. The case was reinforced by the action of his brother in commanding the 2nd Battalion which saw service in the seige of Gibraltar in 1784 before joining the 1st Battalion in Madras. Macleod's Highlanders later became the Highland Light Infantry and were re-numbered in the Army List.

Macleod remained in an anomalous position until 1784. He had proved his loyalty and his efficiency in raising a regiment; he had retrieved his family's political and social influence in Ross-shire yet he had no estate. The anomaly was reinforced by the fact that in December 1780 (while still in India) he was returned to Parliament as member for Ross-shire, apparently amid another great show of local popularity. He remained Tory M.P. for four years. Meanwhile recruitment in his name continued. His military affairs were mainly organised by his agents Bishop and Bramwell in Piccadilly, who, in January 1782, expressed their condolences for the parlous state of the nation's affairs, particularly in North America and also India: 'O shameful disgrace to old England ... it seems at present as if we were to be quite surprised by the aggregate strength of the enemy—having nothing but Foes in every corner of the world'—even though the latest news from India was less depressing.[17] Macleod's agents were especially anxious about the problem of the debts of the army in Madras; Macleod's loss of the clothing supplies for his troops bound for India, and the unpaid accounts of the Army, were threatening to undermine all provisioning at a vital moment in the war. Macleod was exceedingly worried.[18] The financial problems in the army had a bearing upon Macleod's ambition to recover the family estates because the recovery would depend not merely on government agreement but also upon his ability to pay off the debts of his estate.

III

Macleod's campaign to regain the family's territory was, of course, in direct emulation of the success of Lord Lovat. Macleod cited the Lovat case in his appeal to Lord North when it appeared that the government was forgetting his contribution to the war and when his claim for restoration seemed to be lapsing. He reminded North that:

> Soon after General Fraser had obtained a grant of his Father's Estate I came over to that Kingdom from Sweden in hopes that, the ice being broke, the same favour might be shewn to me as to General Fraser, encouraged thereto as I had offered at different times during the last war to raise a Corps of Highlanders for His Majesty's Service, tho' it was my misfortune not to succeed, and more particularly as my family had the honour to be patronised and protected by His Majesty's Royal Father.

He continued in the same vein:

> On my arrival in this Country I was advised to follow General Fraser's line of conduct and endeavour to reconcile the leading men of different parties to the measure before I troubled your Lordship with any application. I followed this advice and they begged the Duke of Buccleugh to speak to your Lordship.

Macleod reported to Lord North that he had 'been more successful with the heads of opposition than my most sanguine hopes had been'. He now expected North to support his restoration through Parliament but complained that he had received little commitment—'The peculiarity of my Situation, my not having bread in this Country and the necessity I am under of returning to Sweden early next spring, will, I flatter myself, plead my excuse for intruding'.[19] As late as July 1784 there was still no final certainty about Macleod's case and he was consoled by one correspondent, 'I am sorry that the restoring your Family Estate is a measure not yet absolutely decided upon, but hope it will still be done during the present session of Parliament'.[20] There were worrying rumours of new opposition from the Lord Chancellor to the general policy of the restoration of the annexed estates.[21]

The resistance of Parliament eventually evaporated and on 18 August 1784 an Act of Parliament was accepted which restored the Estates. The restitution was surrounded with conditions of a financial character which required elaborate solutions. Macleod had been required to name sureties 'in the personal bond to be granted from the price of the Estate of Cromarty' which almost certainly related to the repayment of the accumulated sum of £19,000 attached to the debts (including a long-standing accumulation of Crown Rents) at the end of annexation.[22] The whole problem was compounded by the fact that substantial monies were owed to Macleod in relation to the services of his regiment in India, and by the exceedingly complex arrangement which entangled the Invergordon Estate—itself in debt but already pledged to Macleod by the terms of Sir John Gordon's will. The Invergordon Estate was indebted to Cromartie himself. At one stage there was a possibility of Macleod living in Invergordon House, partly because Tarbat House had lapsed into a ruinous condition.[23] In the outcome the Invergordon Estate was sold to Macleod of Cadboll for £29,000.[24] But it is not certain what proportion of the sale money was devoted to redeeming the debts on the Invergordon estate, or what proportion became available to Count Macleod.[25] The Invergordon free rents were barely sufficient to cover the interest of his uncle's debts, but some of the debts were probably payable to the Cromartie estate.[26] Nevertheless it is likely that the Invergordon inheritance, together with the wealth Macleod accumulated from his two military careers, provided the means by which the Cromartie estate was extricated from its ancient debts. Whatever the form of these obscure financial manoeuvres, Macleod emerged happy with the result.[27]

Macleod's campaign had yielded his ultimate reward in the form of his ancestors' estates though he did not regain his title. He was rehabilitated, he had expiated his youthful error (that is, his treason) by virtue of a life of military service. His tacit bargain with the government seemed to be complete and he retired from military service. In fact the Government pressed him hard to continue recruiting for the regiments. In July 1786 Sir George Yonge told Macleod that more recruits were required for India and that he was not to stop until told to do so. In pressing his point Yonge remarked: 'It is to be observed also that in a Climate so unfavourable as India, it is too probable that the numbers wanted are at this time considerably greater than the estimated figure.' Climate or not, some men who accepted recruitment for India were accused of doing so merely to get there free without any intention of serving in the armed forces, and of another group 39 out of 82 were rejected on medical grounds before being sent from Inverness to Chatham.[28] But the main erosion came from fatalities in India reaped by the climate and Yonge needed a constant flow of men from the Highlands: 'I think it is my Duty to represent to you the necessity of not allowing any relaxation in the carrying and the recruiting for your Lordship's Regiment; as from the nature of the climate and other causes it is not to be expected that the Regiment can be kept up in the Condition fit from service without a constant and considerable supply of recruits to be sent over in the ships of each season'.[29]

One of the few appearances of the common man of the Cromartie estates revealed in the documents surviving at this time was, not surprisingly, found in the instructions and memoranda relating to the recruitment of men for the regiments destined for the fatal climate of India, some, no doubt to replace the 126 men who, in August 1781, were held prisoner by Hyder Ali from the 1st Battalion of the 73rd Regiment. In the recruiting instruction it was specified that 'No man to be enlisted who has done growing under five feet six inches. Boys under eighteen and likely to grow may be taken at five feet five inches high'. No man older than 30 could be taken, nor an apprentice or a collier (not in any case likely in the Highlands). All men were carefully examined by a surgeon before acceptance. Each recruit received three good shirts, stock and buckle, two pairs of hose, a kilt, a bonnet, two pairs of shoes, a knapsack—'The expense of which is to be taken out of his Bounty money'. Among the instructions was the point that 'Officers are to keep their Partys as clean as possible and prevent them from rioting and quarrelling with Partys of other Regiments or with the inhabitants of the place they are quartered.' They were recruited normally by 'beat of Drum' and the agents paid £3 'for each recruit approved of by a Field Officer'. It is not clear what each recruit obtained as an inducement to join but large aggregate sums were involved in the raising and provisioning of a regiment.[30]

Of 23 recruits to the 71st Regiment who arrived at Chatham in October 1786, five were rejected as deformed or unhealthy, most were 16 or 17 years of age, the youngest 15; the tallest was 5ft 9in. At the same time another consignment yielded only ten healthy out of 26, of whom the tallest was 5ft 10in.; of another group only 15 were accepted out of 33 (the tallest was 5ft 6in). Many were rejected because they were too small, or scrofulous, or suffered from ulcerated legs and were possessed by the 'itch very bad'. The 'leprous' and undersized were dismissed and so was another, described as 'quite a miserable object'.[31]

IV

A lifetime's quest fulfilled, Macleod had only three years to live. He was already ill in 1787 and travelled to Bath to take the waters. In two more years he was dead. In that short time he made two commitments which held financial consequences far into the future. One was his marriage in 1786 to Marjorie, daughter of the 16th Lord Forbes,[32] who outlived him by 56 years, and to her he pledged a substantial income for the rest of her life. She later married the 4th Duke of Atholl whom she also outlived by many years. Obligations to relatives into the indefinite future were a recurrent drain on the Cromartie estates throughout the family's history. Equally important was Macleod's decision to revive the style of life of his ancestors—particularly the complete rebuilding of Tarbat House in Easter Ross after its dilapidation, and the remodelling of its policies. This programme of renovation and construction represented a financial commitment which strained the finances of the estates and put severe pressure on its rental. The architect, James McLeran was paid £360 in 1786, and the house cost more than £6000 to complete. The jointure to Lady Macleod was £600 per annum. But in addition, after all the financial balancing, there remained a debt of £4848 to the Government (of the original £10,000 debt) and £2880 on the debts of Sir John Gordon. Thus, almost as soon as Macleod regained his estates they were quickly burdened with extremely large fixed obligations. And since Macleod died without a direct heir he was followed in quick succession by different branches of the family who opened up new lines of dependency on the rental of the estate. The burden grew to oppressive dimensions over the following decades.

It is obvious that Macleod was aware of the danger of the burden of favoured relatives swallowing the entire revenue of the estate even beyond the claims of the nominal incumbent. He attached to his will a clause which attempted to restrict (within generous limits) the channelling of the estate income to relatives. It provided that:

> *1st*. The proprietor of the Estate for the time being to have power of settling a jointure on his widow not exceeding one fourth part of the free yearly rent of the Estate and if the Estate is in the person of a female, she to have power to make the like Settlement on her husband in case of her death.
> *2nd*. Only one years free rent of the Estate to be settled on each of the younger Children
> ...
> *3rd*. The Estate to be answerable for no debts except those I may leave at the time of my death, excepting those that may be contracted for improvements in Entailed Estates.[33]

While Macleod thus made provision for the future of his relatives and his family's restored assets, there was another great development on his estate which also had long term prospects and which by contrast cost Macleod and his successors virtually nothing. In 1786 the British Fishery Society made a decisive move to re-activate plans to exploit fishing grants from a new base at Lochbroom. It was a further echo of the proposals and investments initiated by the first Earl of Cromartie almost a century before.[34] The development that had been modestly renewed under the Forfeited Estates Commission at Isle Martin[35] was now rapidly accelerated by large investments from the Fishery Society. In 1786 the enthusiastic Highland improver George Dempster helped inspect potential sites for new fishing villages on the west coast including Ullapool. In 1787 the Company issued a prospectus which alluded to this 'very considerable part of the Coast of Great Britain [which] continues destitute of the blessings of Art, Industry and Independence though inhabited by a numerous tribe of British subjects no less capable or less inclined than their fellow citizens to become useful members of the Community.' The Society's plans were also designed specifically to deter emigration and to promote settlement for displaced people within the Highlands. Ullapool was soon singled out as an appropriate location for a large development.

Negotiations for the purchase of land at Ullapool and Isle Ristol were initiated between the Society and Lord Macleod who quickly perceived the potential advantage to his estate. Macleod saw that land values would be enhanced and recognised 'the Improvement of the Fishery to be an object of great public utility'. He agreed to the purchase[36] but was temporarily obstructed by the current occupier of the Ullapool Farm, Sergeant John Mackenzie, the sixty-year-old principal tenant (who had just married a woman of eighteen): his lease had six years to run and he refused to give it up except by force of 'a King's Letter'.[37] The matter was eventually settled and the construction of a new fishing station began in 1787.

By 1789 settlers were being recruited to Ullapool, 'making it an Asylum for those of the country people who wish to maintain themselves by labour and industry in the Fisheries'. Attempts were made to persuade the local people that a future in Ullapool would be better than any alternative in America. Moreover in the new village, and presumably in contrast to the common pattern of life in Lochbroom, every settler

13 *Pier at Tanera, Loch Broom*, by William Daniell, 1820.

'might be his own sole master, providing he worked honestly for his own daily bread'. Meanwhile, with the assistance of Thomas Telford, the basic building programme was completed by 1798. In addition there were complementary projects to develop farming and manufacturing at Ullapool as well as new communications. Dempster in 1798 exclaimed 'With what joy did I the other day see the one end of a fine road now coursed half thro between Dingwall and Ullapole.' Despite a certain amount of abrasion caused by the local agent for the Society, Melville (who was described as 'the little Emperor of Ullapool'), a great deal of investment had been undertaken. Melville alone had erected buildings costing £720. Warehouses, quays, inns, and curing houses were erected, together with 72 houses, half of them slated.[38]

At the time of the creation of the new village at Ullapool, Henry Beaufort had expressed a concern that the plots of land offered to the settlers would be large enough to render them bad farmers rather than good fishermen. He was alert to the dictates of Adam Smith's theory of the division of labour. Beaufort advocated the introduction of artificers, such as masons, carpenters, blacksmiths, boat builders, who would

> release the Highlander from the necessity of supplying with infinite toil and loss of time, his own personal wants by his own personal skill; for at present, many of the articles which he needs for the support of life, for shelter, or for cloathing, his cottage, the few accommodations which he has, and much of his dress, even to his very shoes, must be manufactured by himself.[39]

Yet Ullapool had been well established and seemed to possess a fair prospect of success. It was not however blessed with luck. It depended in the first instance, not on the sophisticated specialisation of its labour force, but on the location of the herring shoals. The fish, even in the 1790s, proved to be utterly unreliable and, in the long run, the enterprise at Ullapool would prove to be a painful disappointment. In the very process of its creation it had helped to exacerbate a continuing problem which it was designed to relieve. That is, the village of Ullapool reinforced the tendency by which small tenants were found settling on plots of land inadequate to a decent standard of subsistence. Neither the creation nor the disappointment of the Ullapool venture was in the power of Macleod to control.

Macleod had, nevertheless, achieved the central goal to which his life had been devoted since the darkest days of 1747. His estate was back in the hands of the family and he had been received with honour into the local society of Ross-shire. The debts overhanging the estate doubtless diminished the fulness of the recuperation. So also did the fact that the title was still withheld. In March 1787 Macleod, while organising the entail in his estates, sought legal opinion on the question of the effect of the attainder upon his descendents. He got a clear enough answer:

> The disability of the issue of a person attainted to succeed is a consequence of the corruption of the blood and an important part of the punishment of high treason as the Law now stands and I am clearly of Opinion that no man can exempt those he may call to his succession from this more than from any other of the pains of treason.[40]

The final prize of restoration, the cachet of aristocratic title, was clearly set beyond the reach of Macleod or, indeed, any of his descendants.

PART THREE

A Highland Estate in the Age of the Clearances

CHAPTER 10

Cromartie Restored and the Context of Change

I

Having spent most of his adult life striving to regain the family estates, Lord Macleod, the old Jacobite of 1745-6, was spared merely five years in which to enjoy the fruits of his extraordinary achievement. He died in 1789 at the age of 62. By then the future status of the Cromartie estate had been fixed and its economy set on the path of fundamental change. Throughout the Highlands new pressures were at work causing a greater involvement in the economic life of the industrialising nation.

The restitution of the Cromartie estate had been riddled with irony. Macleod's own career—in Scotland, Sweden and India—had been a close approximation of the old model of the martial clan leader in Highland society. This indeed had been the target to be destroyed by the Hanoverian government. Yet Macleod achieved the return of the estates by using the role to its utmost. In the 1770s and 1780s the London government found itself encouraging the old loyalties to clan chiefs in order to raise regiments for its own purposes. It drew upon the recently reviled patterns of social and military obligation in traditional Highland society. It was an extraordinary turnabout in official policy, an invocation of clan loyalty to raise troops which, by the government's own lights, was a return to the barbaric past. There was a degree of convenient atavism in thus calling up the forces of discredited feudalism to feed the needs of the modern British army.

The continuing loyalty to his social position enabled Macleod to raise large forces in the north. It was no doubt reinforced by the poverty of the people and the opportunity that military service gave for mobility and adventure. The glamour of the regiment fired the imagination of Highland youth. But above all else military service was integral to a more general notion of continuing social obligation. It was part of the unwritten pattern of reciprocation between landlord and people. The chief was entrusted with the security of the community, in both a military and an economic sense. In return for loyalty, the tenantry considered themselves secure in their land holdings. Land, of course, was the lynchpin of this system, as it was in all peasant societies.

Throughout the Highlands in the late eighteenth century great strains were placed on this system of social reciprocation. Population pressure, unprecedented changes in land use, and shifting expectations on the return to capital—all led to an erosion of the traditional notions of loyalty and security. Concurrently, and Cromartie is a perfect example, the demands for military service increased rapidly and were sustained over many decades. The expectation of military service[1]—the sacrifice of the male youth of the community—was revived at the very moment that the rest of society was in the throes of transformation. In this rested the central anachronism of Highland landlordism of the era.

The strength of clan loyalty is hard to measure. It is conventional to seek its decline in 'the age of improvement' in the late eighteenth century, destroyed by the calculating rationality of the new landlord system. Yet it may have been moribund long before: like the endless rise of the British middle class, the decline of the clan system seems infinitely extendable. The third Earl of Cromartie had been unable to carry all the Mackenzies into the 'Forty Five and the efforts of his successors, though successful, required much financial inducement and moral suasion. Moreover the sacrifice of a son to the regiment was often, either implicitly or explicitly, associated with a recognition that his family's tenure of land was confirmed. Each side—landlord and tenant— recognised that regimental service reinforced the mutual obligation. It enabled the tenantry to cling to the land: it was expressed in petitions—to Lord Macleod in the 1790s when tenants sought land in return for an old promise at the time of military service.[2]

The resurrection of regimental service and the old loyalties was, to a degree, against the grain of social change. As late as 1840 the minister for Kincardine in Ross-shire observed of the local people that 'They still retain a sacred regard for the clan and family they are sprung from; but it must be allowed, that this feeling is on the decline. The tale, the song, and the dance, do not, as in the days of yore, entertain the dreary winter nights.' At Dingwall, in the middle of Cromartie's eastern lands, it was reported that 'the people still retain that fond attachment to patrimonial inheritances, however trifling, which the feudal institution inspired.'[3] Yet 'feudalism' was undoubtedly in retreat, and the ministers themselves were agents for social change, offering an alternative and rival leadership to the lairds, thus producing further fissures in Highland society.

On the Cromartie estate the social standing of the laird was weakened by two further factors. First, despite the remarkable restoration of Lord Macleod in 1784, the status of the family was diminished: it was no longer an aristocratic estate and its owners were commoners. Second, the estate rapidly passed through the hands of a succession of incumbents, none of whom brought further resources to the estate. Though the income of the estate itself rose substantially, its owners, until 1849, remained relatively impecunious and dependent, unable to initiate much development from their own reserves. Indeed, the Cromartie estate was subject to an elaborate lottery of family inheritance which gave ownership to a succession of tenuously-connected relatives, most of whom knew little or nothing about the lands and their people. Lord Macleod himself died childless. (His widow, who became very wealthy, married the Duke of Atholl, whom she also outlived, and continued to benefit from the terms of the Cromartie will until her death in 1840.) On 3 May 1786 Lord Macleod had executed an entail by virtue of which he was succeeded (in 1789) by Kenneth Mackenzie—a nephew of his father, the third and last Earl of Cromartie. Kenneth Mackenzie himself died in 1796 and the estate then passed to his cousin (again by the terms of entail), Lady Isabella Mackenzie (Lady Elibank), the eldest daughter of the third Earl. She died in 1801, to be succeeded by her daughter, Maria Murray Hay-Mackenzie who, in 1820, released the estate to her son John Hay Mackenzie, thus achieving a greater continuity of control.[4]

By these complicated steps the estate descended through a series of distantly connected persons and eventually ended up in the hands of a man who happened to be the son of the daughter of the daughter of a sister of the valiant Lord Macleod. None of these people was particularly qualified, or endowed with capital or talent, to preside over the development and welfare of large tracts of the Highlands. It was a tenuous blood line not untypical of the general vicissitudes of landownership in Great Britain. More specifically, however, the process of inheritance in Cromartie was unusually debilitating for the Cromartie estate finances. Each generation soaked up capital from the estate revenues. Daughters and wives were particularly expensive—for instance Marjory Forbes, who outlived her husband Lord Macleod (to whom she was married for less than three years) by almost half a century, was paid a large annuity for the entire period. Without question the system of inheritance placed the resources of the Cromartie estate and its people at the mercy of the almost random consequences of succession and longevity.

II

Far less random were the immense structural changes of longer duration affecting Highland society in the later eighteenth century. Most fundamental was the growth of population. The exact dimensions and precise timing of the demographic increase are not retrievable but the broad outline is unmistakable.[5] Statistical fragments from the hearth tax and poll returns of the end of the seventeenth century provide a few clues; firmer footing is offered by the surveys of the Forfeited Estate Commissioners and Dr Webster respectively in the 1750s. Further evidence was yielded by the parish ministers in their reports to the Statistical Account in the 1790s. After 1801 the story was given increasing precision by each successive census poll.[6] The procedure adopted here is to take each parish within which parts of the Cromartie estate were located, which has the advantage of showing the differences of population growth between east and west (see accompanying graph).

There are some certainties but many ambiguities and unknown elements in these figures. It is clear that population accelerated at an unprecedented rate between 1750 and 1820, an experience common to most of western Europe. But the vigour of the increase was markedly greater in the west than in the east. Cautious interpretation is required to take account of internal relocation (particularly into village centres such as Dingwall and Ullapool). Some of the demographic growth may have been channelled out of the region by migration—perhaps to southern Scotland and across the Atlantic. Some parishes recorded declines between 1755 and 1801 (e.g. Tarbat and Fearn) which are not easily explained. Nevertheless there is an unambiguous and universal peak of population growth between 1801 and 1821 and a general decline, common to both east and west, after 1851. The data offers one central inescapable question—how did this region cope with such a large increase of its people in such a relatively short period of time? More particularly, how did the remote and unmodernised west, notably Coigach, accommodate a doubling of its population within sixty years?

The community had become aware of the pressure of numbers by the 1790s when

Sir John Sinclair mobilised the ministers of Scotland to produce the potted parochial information which was aggregated into the *Statistical Account*. The population of the county of Ross and Cromarty had increased 17 per cent since Webster's enumeration of 1755 and most of the parishes of the Cromartie estate reflected this increase. But in Lochbroom the increase was much greater, about 60 per cent—a growth helped by the inception of the new fishery at Ullapool (which contained perhaps 200 people at the time of the *Account*). On the other coast at Kilmuir Easter the population had increased as fast and the local minister said that the 'Population is daily on the increase'. Dingwall parish increased from 1030 in 1755 to 1379 in 1799, probably helped by annual migration to the town of that name. By contrast, the rich easterly parish of Tarbat witnessed a population decline of 1584 to 1370. The minister adduced several causes:

> One cause of the decrease of the number of inhabitants is uniting different farms into one, a practice undoubtedly inimical to population; another cause is the loss of some fishermen at sea, the removal of others from the parish, and that some crews were suffered to die out, without having their places supplied. But what chiefly contributes to the decrease of the inhabitants, is a yearly emigration to the south of young people who never return.

Here indeed were several vital themes in social and economic change in the late eighteenth century: shifting agricultural practices and the dislocation of old tenures, outward pressure exerted by landlords, the influence of alternative employment opportunities, and the quickening of mobility. A mixture of economic and psychological forces was at work.[7]

The contemporary evidence suggests that the unprecedented population increase occurred in a context of relatively adverse conditions. Indeed the Cromartie estate was passing through a period of general population growth which was partly diminished in some places by disease, hunger and migration. Geographical mobility was almost certainly on the increase and the flight to the south and to America continued in numbers which mainly passed unrecorded. One report noted that three vessels, carrying 300 emigrants, left Isle Martin in the years 1801 and 1802 but the people were mainly from Strathglass and Nairn rather than Ross. The Favourite of Kirkcaldy sailed from Ullapool in 1803, without a clearance, and arrived in Pictou on 3 August after a passage of five and a half weeks. It carried 500 passengers and landed one passenger more than the number with which it started. Two years later the Northern Friends left Ullapool 'to ship passengers for America, accompanied by consignments of oatmeal, biscuit, spades and hemp'.[8] Beyond such individual sailings little is known of these great migrations but it is virtually certain that Wester Ross remained one of the best sources of migrants after the American War. Mobility was reinforced by the policies of landlords and farmers bent upon improvement and rationalisation. More primitive forces also prevailed—for instance in Kincardine the population had fallen by 20 per cent in the previous 16 years, and the minister had no doubt about the causes:

> The chief cause of the late great decrease is, that in 1782, many were reduced to poverty by the loss of their cattle, and the almost total failure of the crop of that year, which occasioned such accumulated distress, that they were obliged to remove with their families and settle in the low country, as day labourers, or domestic servants.[9]

Nothing more vividly identifies the resolutely pre-industrial character of this society in the eighteenth century than the devastations of disease and hunger. Times of plenty—at least in relative terms—there certainly were. But smallpox, disease and famine stalked the land on at least three occasions in the eighteenth century. For each of the ministers replying to Sir John Sinclair's questions, the catastrophe of 1782-3 remained deeply imprinted on their memories. The fullest analysis came from the Tarbat parish. The scarcity in Spring 1782 had decimated the cattle resources—'neither straw nor hay could be had for any money'. The calamity was widespread and farmers were reported as quitting their farms and reduced to poverty. In December 1782 in a letter from Lochbroom to Nova Scotia it was reported that: 'The crop has failed much in Coigach having never riped fully, and some of it was damaged in the gathering. The potato crop totally lost in the ground by early frosts.'[10] The following season, 1783, was even worse and the crop 'neither was fit for meal or seed'. Hungry people roamed the countryside trying to beg or buy supplies of meal or corn: it was pitiable 'to see persons young and otherwise vigourous, in this condition, having hunger and distress of mind painted on their countenances'. The price of corn doubled and food supplies were utterly exhausted.[11]

The Highlands, therefore, remained vulnerable to the failure of the weather and the crop; in 1783 it remained isolated from the rest of Britain and the ordinary operations of the grain market were unequal to the emergency. Fortunately extraordinary efforts, locally and from London, were mobilised and special supplies were brought in to prevent a sudden surge in mortality. Landlords combined to organise and secure supplies of imports—for instance, 12,000 bolls were brought to Tarbat from the south-east of Scotland by way of Inverness. In this crisis landowners were able to fulfil an emergency role which, in some degree, helped to legitimise their dominant status in local society. On the west coast at Lochbroom, a fishing merchant, Ross, provided meal on credit to the local people. It became a matter of great pride to the grateful recipients that he was repaid—even on their deaths this was the first charge—'their whole effects were sold by auction to pay this sacred debt—there might produce on average from 6 shillings to 6 shillings and sixpence.'[12] The government also played a positive philanthropic role. Relief was channelled to Dingwall, to which place the government diverted a ship destined for America containing a cargo of pease, potatoes and oats.[13] The minister from Tarbat was able to recollect that 'not a single person died merely of famine, though diseases followed, which cut off many, whose constitution had been enfeebled by what they suffered at that period.'[14] It was the opinion of the minister that 'But for those supplies, disorder and rapine would have prevailed, and the poor, rendered desperate by famine, like so many hungry wolves would have broke loose, and laid hands on whatever they could find.'[15] Famine relief as social control could hardly have been set at a higher premium.

The severity of the crisis was compounded by its length as the great hunger persisted into the winter of 1783-4. On 10 December 1783 a meeting was held of the 'Gentlemen Landholders of the Eastern District of Ross-shire at Tain' to consider the effects of the 'General Calamity' on the tenantry in the district. The Cromartie estate was represented by Colin Mackenzie, the factor. The minutes of the meeting revealed the extreme stresses caused by the famine and voiced a remarkable degree of self-criticism of the land-owning class itself. The meeting agreed that if arrears and rents were collected in a harsh and severe manner,

> it must have the Effect of driving the Tenantry into despondency, and bring a great Majority of them to immediate and inevitable Ruin; and in so doing, will go near to lay the Country waste, which to the personal Knowledge of the Meeting, has been for these Two Hundred Years back over-rented; and if once the present Set of Tenantry are removed, there would be very little probability of getting them replaced from any other County.

The meeting therefore recommended to landlords that they offer their tenants 'the most lenient and tender Treatment, to prevent that part of the Country being depopulated and laid waste'. Specifically, they exhorted their fellow proprietors to calculate their rent conversions at pre-famine prices of meal rather than the prevailing levels which would ruin the tenantry. At the same time they drew attention to the 'frauds' perpetrated by some tenants who were selling their grain (which was contracted to the landlord) clandestinely at famine prices. The meeting agreed that unless such anti-social activity (by both landlords and tenants) was curbed 'the Consequences may be more dangerous than they are aware of'.[16]

Famine, therefore, threatened not only the subsistence but also the social fabric of estate life. In 1782-4 the action of the landowners and the government was probably more effective and sensitive than ever before. There were casualties, of course, even among the larger tenantry. For instance George Mackenzie of Meddat on the Cromartie estate lost large numbers of cattle during the crisis and found that he could not pay his rents and by 1786 was desperate for the relief of his debts.[17] Nor was the 1782-4 crisis the last famine in Highland history even in the east. In 1796 there was a further round of bad weather and scarcity which provoked food riots at Dingwall. On this occasion the Cromartie estate factor felt it necessary to intervene—he sent 30 bolls of meal to the town inhabitants 'who are becoming Riotous in one or two instances, and seem to threaten him [Mr Bertram] on account of his exportation of Oatmeal and other grain from the country'. In the following year the estate factor lost his agency and his farm because a new tenant had offered a greater rent.[18]

Famine crises had other pervasive effects. For instance the great scarcity in Dingwall in 1783 was reported to have reduced the birth rate in the succeeding few years by fifty per cent, another classic consequence of famine. At Logie Easter it was reported that 'whole families came down from the Highlands on account of the dearth, and settled here for the benefit of daily labour, and having the fuel so near them.'[19] Famine indeed seemed to accelerate the migration of people from least favoured districts. Moreover none of the accounts ascribed the famine scarcity to clearances, or enclosures, nor to the excessive dependence on potatoes (these indeed were not mentioned). The food emergency had all the hallmarks of a Malthusian crisis averted by prompt relief action. This was evidently a peasant economy still hostage to the weather and the harvest. The famine may also have accelerated the quest for more efficient agricultural techniques and tenures. Highland society had to find ways of averting further recurrence of famine; local farmers would respond to the incentive of higher prices which were also an

14 Dingwall in 1824, aquatint by J Clerk.

expression of scarcity and population growth. Famine and high prices probably induced the common people to adopt the potato as the staple crop of the emergent crofter economy.

Disease was another sword of Damocles suspended over this society. Smallpox had no respect for social class—in 1712 Inchculter referred to its grievous toll at Castle Leod itself: he reported his children being 'under it'. A child of the third Earl of Cromartie died of smallpox after being left in Tarbat House when her mother went south to join her husband in the Tower of London in 1748.[20] In the 1790s the minister at Dingwall observed:

> To periodical visits of the smallpox we are exposed in common with every part of the kingdom. It returns after unequal and uncertain intervals; but it seldom gives us a longer respite than from six to eight years. The last summer it was, in the natural way, extremely mortal.

Apart 'from nervous and putrid fevers' (probably typhus), smallpox was the only prominent killer in these parishes.[21] At Tarbat it affected children in particular—in 1757 it killed 75 children, in 1768, 46, and as many in 1791. 'Some families at those different periods lost their whole children.' At Kilmuir Easter a visit of smallpox in 1784 came close to doubling the annual death rate for the parish. At Logie Easter it was reported: 'The small pox raged here twice lately, and carried off a considerable number of children.' Unidentified fevers swept across parishes (such as Lochbroom) and carried away great numbers, but it was smallpox that was most feared.[22]

The assault on the scourge of smallpox had already begun by the time the *First Statistical Account* was published. The ministers, though not all the common people, were convinced of the efficacy of inoculation which was being introduced on a broad front in the 1780s. At Logie Easter it was reported: 'Some of the inhabitants, from a religious prejudice [unspecified], were not reconciled to the practice of inoculation; whilst others were prudent enough to take the benefit of this successful mean to save their children.' It is clear enough that smallpox inoculation was by no means universal even by 1790 and that the disease had been lethal even within the previous decade.[23] Thus the increase of population since 1755 cannot be attributed entirely to smallpox inoculation, but the eventual and decisive retreat of the disease undoubtedly contributed to the cumulative increase of population that proceeded in the subsequent three decades (see graph). The outbreak of smallpox in 1784 seems to have persuaded a high proportion of the population in this region to accept inoculation.[24] Similarly at Dingwall 'It opened the eyes of the lower classes of people to the advantages of inoculation, against which their prejudice had before been as violent as they were general.' At Tarbat the minister could write that:

> Inoculation, when tried, failed only in one instance; and there are families in the place, in which there was not an instance of recovery until this method was taken; notwithstanding which, the people still retain a strong prejudice against it, and seem deaf to all arguments used to show its lawfulness and expediency, as a mean which Providence has blessed for saving thousands of lives.

The 1790s therefore represent a turning point in the saga of the struggle against smallpox. The prejudice against inoculation was not, however, a mere function of distance and isolation. Fodderty was by no means a backward enclave, yet the minister could only observe that:

> The small-pox often rages here, and frequently proves mortal, as inoculation has never been attempted except by a very few families, who recently introduced it with success. The prejudice of the people is, however, very strong against it.[25]

The war against smallpox continued into the nineteenth century. In Lochbroom in 1812, for instance, smallpox again invaded the community and 'carried off almost all that were attacked by it.' The minister ran a campaign of inoculation and persuaded almost a thousand young people to receive the treatment from a visiting physician. Of these only five died. During the following three decades smallpox was kept at bay: the disease had thus retreated even in the remote western promontories.[26]

III

Great population growth, whatever its ultimate causes, would inevitably impose pressure on the narrow resources of this society. Moreover it was a pressure re-doubled in the years 1800-1850 for only later did total population numbers diminish. Somehow the old forms of society had to accommodate to the unprecedented augmentation of its numbers. An adjustment, in some radical form, was inescapable.

The response came in the form of a series of complex agricultural and tenurial changes under the banner of 'improvement'. In the last resort there developed a more efficient and productive use of the physical and human resources of the region. It met the burgeoning needs of Highland society—its swollen population and its greater demands for food, fuel, housing, clothing and much else. Eventually it helped to sustain the local population. 'Improvement' however was not simply a reaction to local needs; it was also a response to external stimuli, from outside the region. This of course was the great age of industrialisation in the south when the demands for many commodities—including chemicals (e.g. those derived from kelp), grain, wool, meat, whisky, fish, barley—were now much enhanced. Such incentives were not entirely novel—in the seventeenth century Easter Ross had fed the growth of Edinburgh, and Coigach had responded to the rise of the English cattle trade. But now the scale changed dramatically. The northern regions, helped by constantly improving transport methods, were converted to, indeed integrated with, the industrialising economy of south Britain. The industrial revolution offered the opportunity of great gains from the export of marketable products from the region. The entire context of economic life had become dynamic.

Such dynamism was full of hazards for the Highlands, its people and its landlords. Local needs might be overwhelmed by external incentives. Ideally the two might have coincided; in reality the maximisation of market income required a restructuring of agriculture. It required that land, the very pivot of social life, be redeployed to meet the demands of the south. Capitalist agriculture—large tenant farmers with capital—was the carrier of the new methods. Consequently profound tensions gripped society, in the form of a tightening struggle for the control of the land between each of the strata of northern society. The *Old Statistical Account* charted the genesis of these developments and voiced the anxieties to which the new methods gave rise. 'Improvement' had many faces.

One dramatic response (and some argue that it was a first cause) to the expanded subsistence requirements in northern Scotland was the cultivation of the potato. The potato was phenomenally productive in its yield of food value to labour and land. It was decisive in the resettlement of the peasant population on marginal land in very small plots. Potato production was to become the foundation of much of the crofting economy which succeeded the barley/oats/cattle economy of the mid-eighteenth century. At Lochbroom the potato had been introduced certainly by the early 1750s and, according to Pennant, was already widespread by 1772. In the 1790s potatoes and fish provided the staple diet of the west, supplemented by annual imports of meal. At Dingwall almost all the parishioners consumed potatoes. At Tarbat the minister was mindful of the recent grain famines and remarked enthusiastically that:

> Potatoes have rapidly come to supply the deficiency. There is not a farm, or small croft, a part of which is not laid out in cultivating this useful root. It would be difficult to ascertain the extent of ground employed for this purpose, or the quantities raised yearly, but both must be very considerable, as they are used in every family and constitute the principal support of some of them, during nine months of the year.

Thus there was already the spectre of a potato monoculture emerging in some parts in the 1790s. In Logie Easter it was the same story—potatoes were the support of the poor for half the year.[27]

None of the ministers offered the potato as the cause of the population increase, but none of them would have questioned its role in sustaining the accumulating increase. The potato effectively facilitated the colonization of marginal zones of arable land and the denser settlement of the common people.[28] At the same time it made feasible the release (or appropriation) of the old semi-communal grazing lands for commercial cattle and sheep farming. Here was the keystone of the structural change in the Highland economy. Kilmuir Easter is a prime example. Between 1755 and 1790 the population had doubled, much helped by immigration which had been encouraged by landlords, including the managers on the Cromartie estate during the period of the Annexation. Kilmuir Easter became a reception centre for Highlanders on the move from interior places. The minister explained: 'This increase is ascribed to the great extent of improvable waste ground in the parish, the easy access to fuel, and the encouragement given by proprietors to day labourers: these inducements led many migrants from the Highland parishes to settle here.'[29] The internal migrants successfully resettled the old soldier lots which had failed in the years after 1763.

Lotting in this fashion was integral to the rationalisation of land use in the Highlands. It helped accommodate the increments of population increase; it also provided minimum welfare for the peasantry who were displaced in the general shake-up of Highland economic life. It offered a model for much development that was already taking place in the Highlands—the close lotting of marginal land was a widespread solution to the problems of the age of the clearances. Some landowners—as in Sutherland—went further and supplemented the potato land with the development of grazing, fishing and even secondary industry. But many did not do so. Here indeed were the essential elements in embryo of the Highland problem: the superimposition of external pressures (especially for the production of wool and kelp surpluses) on top of internal demographic strains. The Cromartie estate, in common with the rest of the Highlands, had no escape from these imperatives.

IV

Before the 1780s Highland development, while palpable even a century before, had been hesitant and unsustained. A measure of the agricultural backwardness of the northern districts was offered in the unpublished remarks of the Northumbrian agriculturalists Matthew Culley and his son George, who toured the region in the 1770s. To their educated eyes even the Black Isle—normally regarded as the epicentre of northern progress—was a primitive heathland, thinly populated and only recently given roads. They could see signs of civilization emerging—'the traveller, whose curiosity leads him into these remote corners, needs no longer be afraid of losing his way, or of being plundered by Bandits'—but agricultural methods were visibly antiquated.[30]

Now, especially by 1790, there was a distinct hastening. In part it derived from a direct emulation of southern farming practice—southern farmers were introduced and became a colonising wave of innovators. As early as 1763 an English farm manager, John Baldry, was imported to the Balnagowan Estate with the declared intention of introducing the latest turnip husbandry, and of replacing oxen by horses.[31] Within a year the estate was buying new English sheep stock at the Linton market; in the next twenty years the Balnagowan estate introduced southern sheepfarmers and the lead was followed by other local landowners. Munro of Culcairn gave a Highland farm to a sheepfarmer in 1782 and the Munros of Fowlis and Novar were converting their uplands to sheep in the 1790s.[32] The landlord class was undoubtedly taking the initiative: the two pioneers in Ross and Cromarty, both possessing good lands on the east coast, were Macleod of Geannies and Sir John Lockhart Ross of Balnagowan: both sought publicly to demonstrate the benefits of modern agricultural techniques. The clear need amongst landlords was capital and it is noticeable that most exemplars of improvement possessed externally generated sources—often from the Indies—by which to galvanise their estates. In this respect Count Macleod was no exception though the actual act of retrieving his lands seems to have exhausted most of his capital.

Some Highland improvement was promoted within the basic framework of the older system, or at least without the destruction of that system. At Kilmuir Easter 300 acres of arable land had been rescued from barren muir:

> partly by mealers, encouraged by the proprietors, and enticed to build huts on the muir, in the vicinity of peats and turfs—partly by the most substantial farmers who, as they proceed to inclose their farms, trench the barren ground within their lines, and partly by the proprietors, who have set the example before their tenants.

The Kilmuir model is significant because it belongs to a pluralist phase of improvement, which incorporated each of the three strata of the society—though it effectively eliminated the peasant/communal sector. Already prominent, in this case, was the tripartite division of parts of the new Highland rural society. Its emergence helped to dissolve the older ways, but did less violence to it than the more root-and-branch methods that attended the introduction of sheep farming and large scale commercial arable operations. It was the latter development that the ministers regarded as more a threat than a promise.[33]

'Engrossing', the radical shift in land use, was the Highland variant and extension of the age old process of enclosure. It came later to the Highlands, stretching northwards by agrarian trial and error, to the remoter parts only in the late eighteenth century. For instance, the western edges of the Cromartie estate, in Lochbroom, faced the change only in the 1790s. The minister described it as 'the engrossing of farms for sheep farms' which he considered decidedly 'unfriendly to population.' The minister placed in perfect juxtaposition the confrontation of two conceptions of social welfare: of sheep versus people, of efficiency versus social harmony, of progress versus conservatism, of growth versus stability. In Lochbroom he wrote:

> This mode of farming has been introduced lately into some parts of this parish, and proved the occasion of reducing to hardship several honest families, who lived tolerably happy on the fruits of their industry and frugality. Whoever would wish to see the population of this country flourishing should do all in their power to put a stop to the sheep traffic, and to introduce manufacturing among the people. Whole districts have been already depopulated by the introduction of sheep; so that, where formerly hundreds of people could be seen, no human faces are to be met with, except a shepherd attended by his dog. It has been said, however, that these people who are dispossessed of their farms, can live much more comfortably in the manufacturing employment, than ever they could do before. But would they not be still more happy, if manufactures were introduced among them?[34]

Already, therefore, displaced Highlanders were being pushed towards manufacturing industry in the south, and already social pressures were being exerted on landlords to resist the temptation of enclosure, or else to introduce industry to give employment to the people. In many ways it was a re-play of the Tudor enclosure story. But although enclosures for sheep were probably the most effective clearing device, enclosure for arable land also took place, with the same consequence of dislodging small producers. At Tarbat it was claimed 'One cause of the decrease of the number of inhabitants is uniting different farms into one, a practice undoubtedly inimical to population.' Macleod of Geannies had introduced new rotations: 'Having his ground inclosed gives him great advantage for this, and every other improvement in farming.'[35] But it was not necessarily the landlords who were the primary driving force in the enclosure movements in this part of Scotland. Much of the land—certainly on the Cromartie estate—remained effectively in the hands of tacksmen or principal farmers (especially wadsetters) who controlled large tracts of territory which they sub-rented to smaller tenants. During the course of a long lease a tacksman could alter the disposition of his subtenancies and carve out large farms from the lease. In such cases the odium often rebounded onto the landlord who, it is possible, had the moral authority to deter a large tenant from clearance though this was not invariably the case.

In several parts the process was given greater sophistication: small farms were combined into new 50-150 acre units. Meanwhile the displaced small tenants were offered wastelands upon which they could cultivate potatoes. They would be permitted 2-3 acres rent free for seven years, and perhaps an advance of 20 shillings for a house. After seven years they began to pay a full commercial rent. Consequently the landlord gained by the release of land to new capitalist tenants and by the winning of new arable land by the displaced small tenantry. Both financially and morally it was a preferred course over outright eviction and was a solution adopted in many parts of the north (having been pioneered by Lord Kames in Blair Drummond in 1767).

Other landlords were less tender and proceeded with large scale clearances which scarred much Highland history in this period. Often clearances took place over many decades but in 1791 there was an air of imminence. At Contin, for example, it was feared that the population would soon begin to decline because 'the gentlemen are encouraging shepherds to come and settle on their properties, which must necessarily remove the present inhabitants, and force them to go in quest of bread to other countries, as there are no manufactures established here to employ them.'[36] In some parishes the 'monopoly of farms' had already begun. Mostly the people, in the first instance, were relocated within their own districts and, despite the minister's perceptions, parish population rose continuously. It affected both arable and pastoral farms. Sometimes the changes were cataclysmic and devastating for the local community (e.g. in Kildonan in Sutherland in 1814 and Strathconan in the 1840s). More typical was the gradual agrarian reorganisation which took place at the end of leases, or when a tacksman carved out a sheepfarm from the grazing lands attached to his tack. This was the most common experience on parts of the Cromartie estates.

The end results were much the same. The arable lands were rationalised and extended in a two-sector economy—capitalists on the best land in big farms, crofters on the margins ultimately dependent on potatoes but also picking up day labour together with, in some parts, part-time fishing and kelping. Easter Ross was so successful in its agrarian advance, especially its adaptation to wheat farming, that it became renowned for its productivity, a rival to the Lothians even in the 1790s. The pastoral sector showed an equally decisive shift to sheep farming which, in the hands of the commercial men, became more profitable relative to cattle. But for several decades much of the traditional cattle rearing continued in many parts, propped up by good prices in the Napoleonic Wars. In Fodderty in 1790 cattle numbers had already declined but for other parts the critical time came after 1812 when prices declined rapidly, thereby weakening decisively the old Highland economy.

The eastern baronies of the Cromartie estate were in the midst of the district which, in July and August 1792, produced the largest display of social protest and collective resistance to law and order in the Highlands since the '45. This was the extraordinary 'Insurrection' of common people in Easter Ross against the northward advance of the sheep: it involved an elaborate and concerted effort to drive out all the sheep from the territory to the north of the Great Glen. Considerable military action was required (aided by the landed proprietors of Ross-shire) to quell the revolt which, in some minds, was associated with seditious tendencies. Captain Kenneth Mackenzie of Cromartie was prominent among the rallying landowners who orchestrated the campaign to crush the rebellion.[37]

Active participation in the revolt by people from the Cromartie estate cannot be demonstrated nor is the precise sequence of land reorganisation documented. But there is clear evidence that removals were proceeding at New Tarbat during this time. In March 1792 a legal process was drawn up relating to a dispute between Captain Mackenzie and James Forbes and Kenneth McLennan who were resisting an attempted eviction by the landlord and his factor. Forbes and McLennan claimed that they had been promised continued occupation and that they 'had Captain Mackenzie's promise that they should never be removed while he paid his rent and that they were not in arrear'. Informal promises from landlords were often invoked in such cases. The defence received short shrift. The Act of Sederunt of 1756 was quoted:

> That where a tenant hath not obliged himself to remove without warning, in such case it shall be lawful to the Heritor ... either to use the order prescribed by the Act of Parliament made in the year 1555 ... anent the warning of Tenants, and thereupon pursue a Recovery and Ejection, or to bring his action of Removing against that Tenant before the Judge ordinary.

This was a widely used formula and the presiding Judge duly warned the men to get off the land. The men challenging the Cromartie estate were, respectivly, a mealer and a tenant, both of New Tarbat.[38] It is not difficult to imagine that this type of transaction created a psychology of insecurity and a propensity for collective resistance.

The two great influences therefore acting upon the Highlands in the 1790s—rising population and changing land use—worked together to reinforce each other. Except where intensive lotting arrangements were promoted, the two pressures exacerbated the employment problem, and of course the social welfare consequences, for the entire Highland region. The older agricultural economy was more labour-intensive than the new and possibly had greater powers to absorb and mask seasonal and general underemployment. Virtually all the ministers reported the need for new employment opportunities to absorb the superfluity of people. In particular they advocated manufacturing industry: it would create income, it would also deter the seasonal migration to the south of Scotland, it would reduce sloth and immorality, and the 'use of spirits'. In prolific Lochbroom 'a manufacture on a large scale, that would employ a great number of people, is vehemently desired' and there was wildly optimistic talk of manufactories for soap and woollen production to employ local women as well as local raw materials.[39]

At Fearn the problem was not so vital and military service had syphoned off some of the excess labour. The parish of Contin was not badly off but its condition could further be improved by the introduction of manufactures—'a linen or woolen one would answer extremely well. The women would be made industrious by this means.' In Kilmuir Easter such efforts had already been made—flax spinning and a stocking manufactory had been brought in—the former successfully, the latter not so. The older mode of economic life, of course, contained within it a considerable element of domestic industry—serving family or very localised demands—on to which had been grafted a marketable element in the mid eighteenth century by way of flax spinning, an eighteenth century panacea for underemployment. Tarbat parish was typical—here:

> the mistress of the house and other females are employed in preparing webs from the wool, and lint raised on the farm, partly for family use, and partly for sale, and there is scarce a house inhabited by the inferior class of people in which does not go spinning of hemp and flax, given out by persons employed for the manufactures of sail cloth and linen yarn established at Cromarty and Inverness.[40]

Expanding demand for spun yarn gave an extra lease of life to the domestic industry in the last years of the eighteenth century. But like many other domestic industries, the spinners would, within a decade, confront irresistible technological competition of flax spinners in the factories of Dundee, Dunfermline and Leeds. Long before this changing consumption tastes had already eroded the demand for the products of domestic industry in the Highlands. The general fashion to wear trousers instead of breeches and stockings (around about 1805) was damaging enough, but local demand was also shifting. In Fearn, for instance, it was reported that: 'The people have become much more extravagant in their clothing and apparel, of late years, buying these chiefly from the shops, whereas formerly they only wore their own country-made cloth.' The prescriptions of the act of 1746 were also blamed for the decline of domestic production of textiles—all the arts of dyeing, spinning and weaving tartan, were falling into idleness. The people of Kincardine, it was reported, clothed themselves like lowlanders, with flimsy lowland clothing. The restrictions upon the wearing of old Highland clothing styles were now powerfully reinforced by the attraction of cheap southern fashions for the people of the Highlands.[41]

V

The loosening of the bonds of the older social framework was more thoroughly achieved in some corners than others. The erosion of personal services and payments-in-kind represented the decline of one of the most 'feudalistic' characteristics of the society. These changes also made society more mobile and more responsive to market forces. At Fearn the minister reported the change:

> There are little or no perennial services performed by any tenants or undertenants in this parish. There were several days of servitude about 20 or 30 years ago, such as manuring and ploughing the master's farm for 2 or 3 days in the spring, cutting down his corn, and tending his peats and turf, for as many days; but all these are now converted.

Rents had generally reached a transitional position towards a total conversion to money payment. Usually in the 1790s, the farmers paid half in meal, and half in money rent. But the longstanding practice of mobilising for export the victual rents continued—in Tarbat especially, with its export surplus of grain: 'The victual rents are sold yearly, to be carried to other parts of the kingdom, or used in the country, by distillers [probably at Ferintosh], and those living in towns, or the Highlands.' At Kilmuir Easter the conversion of victual rents and customs and services was part of landlord rationalisation of agriculture, being brought in with new leases for the farmers. At Logie Easter there was a similar story—the only services which remained were those related to peat cutting and three days' assistance in harvest. The minister, with some passion, wrote:

> The servitudes which disgraced human nature, by rendering tenants almost slaves, are, in this parish, done away; and I hope the day is fast approaching, when proprietors will find it proper to have their rents paid in victual and money alone.[42]

Some forms of social change came more slowly. For instance little had been done to improve the treatment of poverty and illiteracy. Generally it was the poor who looked after the poor—individual crises were absorbed within the domestic economy, with an informal supplementation in extreme cases by benevolence organised loosely through the offices of the church. There was no organised system such as the contemporary English Poor Law. In Fearn, for instance, there were 45 poor and indigent people, and the parish provided about ten pounds per year from collections at the church, usually for the old and sickly, not for the able-bodied poor. Benevolence came from 'the gentry and farmers of the parish'. The most striking aspect of poor relief was its informality; it is clear that the poor were not often visible; they were usually submerged in the

15 Highland Mowing.

community which quietly looked after the people as best they could. In Lochbroom, with a population of 3,500, the annual collection for the poor of the parish was sometimes no more than four pounds. In Kilmuir Easter the situation differed little—the sick could expect help from church collections, those who could work got no more than a pair of shoes in which they were expected to travel from door to door begging their subsistence. At Logie Easter the able-bodied poor similarly travelled around in hope of assistance. 'They receive alms frequently from the inhabitants at their own houses.' Fines raised from fornicators and other miscreants also helped support the poor.[43]

Education was only marginally more systematic in its provision. Most ministers found much to complain of despite some assistance from the Scottish Society for Propagating Christian Knowledge [S.S.P.C.K.] teachers who were unpaid and badly housed. In Kilmuir Easter, a parish relatively well supplied, 120 children out of 450 were receiving education. In Lochbroom the minister denounced 'the stupid indifference of the people' towards the whole business of education. Education was for many still a domestic activity, achieved within the home, and only partly institutionalised. Consequently, the rise of English in opposition to the old monopoly of Gaelic could hardly be attributed entirely to schools. Gaelic, often regarded as emblematic of Highland folkways and of the integrity of the older modes of life, was becoming unseated by 1790. In Tarbat it was still the common language of the people and they preferred it to English; it was the same in Logie; in Contin Gaelic retained its dominance also. But in Dingwall most of the parishioners now understood and spoke English. Only two people in Fodderty did not understand Gaelic. At Kilmuir Easter Gaelic continued to prevail, 'but there are very few under 30 years of age in the parish, who do not speak both that and English.'[44]

The changes occurring in Highland life at this time were multi-directional. Tenurial rearrangement dislodged small tenants but probably created some extra labouring employment on arable farms. Increased rents permitted landlords to embark on building operations—larger houses and farm buildings—which would have employed more. Industrial development in the south of Scotland eroded domestic industry in the Highlands—but also created opportunities in spinning and kelp and the production of wool and cattle. It also created seasonal employment opportunities—from Fearn young men and women went each year to Cromarty, Inverness, Moray, Aberdeen, Edinburgh, Glasgow, Newcastle and even the colonies. From Kincardine,

> many of the young men and women move southward, when the day lengthens, and the weather became mild. By low living, and hard labour, they return with comfortable profits, great part of which they lend out at exorbitant interest, and during the inclemency of the seasons, they live with, and are a burden on, their friends and acquaintances, especially such as necessity has obliged to borrow their money, and who are not punctual in paying either principal or interest. There are evils to be remedied only by finding proper employment for the people at home.[45]

The emergence of seasonal migration was symptomatic of changes occurring in the structure of the economy. Labour was in total oversupply at a time when central Scotland sought such labour in growing quantities. The newer patterns of land use reduced the importance of labour and increased the capital requirements. In effect the economic entry costs in Highland agriculture rose to heights beyond the reach of the lower echelons of its society. More generally the Highland economy—in response to conditions generated in the south—now found itself with a handful of staple regional exports which promised to lead its growth. It necessarily entailed a commercialisation of the economy to a greater degree than before. The old staples—cattle and military service—were, in the main, accommodated within the traditional structure. Sheep and large-scale grain cultivation were more awkward. Kelp was also disruptive, though to a lesser extent. All this allied to population growth implied great strain in the local society. The irony and the tragedy of the situation was that while regional income rose rapidly, the export growth being very vigorous, it rendered the old structure redundant within a few decades. Social roles were revolutionised; the distribution of social welfare switched and crises emerged.

In the 1790s many of the changes were in train; the old ways predominated but were under threat. Each zone—even within Ross and Cromarty—offered a variation on the general trends. On the Cromartie estate, as the following chapters chronicle, the proprietors were embattled by their own financial problems and tended to be carried along by forces greater than themselves.

CHAPTER 11

The Broken Succession 1789-1801

I

The Cromartie estates, restored to Count Macleod (who continued to be known by his Swedish title, being disqualified from any British honour) in 1784, faced all the pressures of the new age. Inflation, population increase and accelerating economic growth and change were all visible by the 1780s. The return of the estate—an estate of considerable size and income but some distance below the greatest landed estates of northern Scotland—to private hands was associated with less formal management and accounting than the state's. The records of the time are less generous and there are no surveys of conditions and estate finances; still less are there data about the mass of the people living beneath the Cromartie managers and owners. There were nevertheless enough clues to indicate the broad changes in the framework of existence.

Count Cromartie had spent his last energies (and income) in re-establishing his family on his estate, especially his presence at New Tarbat. The irony was that he had virtually no immediate family (until he at last married, in 1786). Yet even while still in service in Sweden he had made allowances for his six sisters, one of whom was supported until her death in 1820. He rebuilt New Tarbat House in a reasonable but modest style; he seems also to have revived his political and social role in the community, and exercised his patronage in terms of appointing ministers of the church. He also gave encouragement to the development of the fishing (under the auspices of the British Fishery Society and private enterprise) on the west coast (see Chapter 9). Beyond this he had neither the capital, which he had exhausted in the re-purchase of his estates, nor the time (for he died within five years), to accomplish much else.

Macleod had done well to retrieve his estates, against all the odds. Ian Mowat has demonstrated the substantial turnover in landownership in Easter Ross—for instance that less than 40 per cent of landowning families in 1644 persisted in 1756, and that in 1862 'only about half of the estates were held by descendants of those who owned them in 1756'.[1] This indeed provides a measure of Macleod's tenacity and also his success abroad; like many other Easter Ross landowners he brought external capital to his estates. The entire region seems, in the late eighteenth century, to have been vitalised by new wealth from the East or the West Indies. Unfortunately, when Macleod expired in 1789, the Cromartie estates descended into hands which had no access to external sources of capital. Indeed the reverse applied—the Cromartie estate passed to owners who tended to drain the estate (usually towards Edinburgh) of its internally generated wealth. For them it was lucky that, from 1780 to 1820, the estates yielded greater increments of income. The new owners themselves had relatively tenuous connections with the land and people of Cromartie.

II

On the death of Lord Macleod in 1789 the terms of his elaborate will and entail came into effect, designed 'for the better preservation of his lands and estates, and to regulate the succession of the estate'. The direct male line was now depleted. Macleod had no children. His brother, Colonel George Mackenzie (1741-1787) was already dead and the estates passed therefore to the last male descendant—Captain Kenneth Mackenzie of Cromartie, son of the brother of the Jacobite Earl of Cromartie and cousin of the deceased Count. Little is known of Mackenzie. He owned the estates for seven years; he completed the building of Tarbat House and instituted several improvements in its vicinity to fulfil the intention, as he said, of his 'late worthy cousin'. There survives little documentation of these years. Kenneth Mackenzie, in April 1792, married Jane, youngest daughter of Charles Petley of Riverhead in Kent. They had no children and the widow remarried—to Donald Macleod of Geannies, an alliance which reinforced the solidarity of the local gentry of Easter Ross who, in the autumn of 1792, had faced the 'Insurrection' of the common people against the invasion of sheep. Macleod had led the resistance of the landlords in the district.[2]

The Cromartie estates themselves entered a period of rapid change which depended mainly upon external stimuli; the owners, despite improving estate incomes, confronted perennial financial difficulties. This robbed them of most of the initiative that some better placed landowners were able to exert on their Highland estates. In this respect they were more nearly typical of Highland landowners, many of whom had the greatest difficulty living even within the inflated incomes that emerged by 1815.

For the common people of the estates there were traditional problems, such as harvest failure and disease, now compounded by rising rents and increasing offspring. They also faced new opportunities—higher prices, new crops, more diversified employment within and beyond the Highlands. But mostly their story was invisible and inaudible. A single fragment, a letter of March 1789, offers a moment of illumination into the lives of these people. It was addressed to Lord Macleod's widow within days of her husband's death, and was written by the tacksman of Dochcarty. He reported that the Strathpeffer rents had 'been very indifferently paid up' and that considerable arrears had accumulated. The people had experienced difficulties,

> owing to there being no demand for their Barley, and a general scarcity of Provender for cattle all over the country, so that they are necessitate to give their Corn with the Straw to keep their cattle alive, and as the weather still continues severe with frost and snow, I am afraid that several will lose them. Among others I feel severely the want of Provender, having thrashed out all my oats and barley, so that I have the purchase of Hay to keep my Cattle alive and lay down the Crop.

The demand for barley and meal in the country was so low that stocks had accumulated and the victual rents of 1788 were still unsold. Mackenzie reported that he had not 'heard of any of the Country Gentlemen having sold their Rents as yet. Your Ladyship's wool is now spun and made into Blankets, and they are spinning lint Brought from Cromarty, as what grew at Tarbat House has not come from the Flax Dresser'.[3] Here were the salient elements of the local economy—an agriculture based upon the work of small tenants producing both black cattle and barley for a market, as well as meal. The vulnerability of the cattle in a long winter is evidence of the pre-improvement character of production and its baleful dependence on the winter weather. It was an economy in which the landlord still took much of his rent in the form of victual so that he too was greatly concerned at the level of demand. Local wool and flax production was processed in the homes of the common people who may have paid part of their rents in this way.

The formal rentals of the eighteenth century, of which the Cromartie estate is relatively well supplied, record only the direct transactions between the main tenants, i.e., mostly tacksmen or leaseholders, and the landlord. This, of course, reveals general trends in rental income, as well as the main categories of outgoings, on the estate in aggregate. Yet beneath these broad transactions was a complex and hidden structure of sub-tenancy and dependency, an intricate cobweb of relationships and obligations which connected the labouring people through the tacksmen to the proprietor. It is extremely unlikely that many small tenants held directly from the landlord, in some parts not before the mid nineteenth century. Consequently the formal rents inevitably mask the critical differentials within and between the obscure understrata of common life—at Cromartie as elsewhere in the Highlands. It is only rarely possible that the impact of general changes, for example in rents paid by tacksmen, is observable at the level at which income was generated by the common people. Moreover their tenurial rights and expectations are no less obscured, primarily because they were simply unrecorded in estate papers or in legal documents. There is, therefore, a substantial dark area in the pattern of social and economic life in this age of improvement.

The scale and timing of rent increases on the Cromartie estates was roughly the same as in the Highlands in general, and indeed in most of the British Isles. Local factors, the innovation of new crops and methods, and the disposition of lease arrangements, cast an influence on the precise moment of acceleration. Cromartie rents were particularly affected by the parallel conversion from Scots values to sterling and from victuals and service payments to money. But the general trend is clear enough (see Appendix A)— a marginal increase between 1750 and the mid 1780s, then an acceleration on all parts of the estate through to the 1820s, after which there were significant diversions between the three parts of the property. It is likely, for instance, that rents in Easter Ross all trebled between 1790 and 1815.[4] Sometimes the increases were achieved in long steps— for instance the entire Barony of Strathpeffer was set for seven years in 1787 with a 'small augmentation of victual and money'[5] components of the rental. At that point the increase was modest, though it was a mere prelude to greater increases at the end of the tack.

The aggregate rental for the three parts of the Cromartie estate was, in 1755, £932. Twenty five years later it was about £1250. In another ten years, by 1795, it had increased to £2320; by 1806 it was £4,500. At Coigach, an area described in 1795 as 'a Highland district and more suited to grass than corn',[6] the early increases in rent were owed in part to an income of £50 p.a. from the British Fishery Society and £25 for kelp shores. Only 35 tenants were enumerated, no subtenants at all though they existed in their hundreds, and all the rent was paid in cash. Elsewhere the old victual rents persisted, mainly in a mixed form with money rents. At New Tarbat and Strathpeffer the landlord received substantial quantities of barley-bere, tallow, eggs and hens, and even swine. Substantial cash income came from the rights to the Conan fishing. Out of this income the Cromartie owners had to make many payments—such as Crown Rents, Bishop's Rents, Window Duty, the levy for the navy, Ministers' stipends (for Fodderty, Logie, Kilmuir, Lochbroom, Urqhart, Kincardine and Contin), together with some schoolmasters' salaries.

In the 1780s the estate continued to negotiate leases for periods longer than seven years which may suggest a low priority for improvement. Mackenzie of Dochcarty obtained a tack for 19 years in 1787. Another tack of the same duration went to John Mackenzie of Blackhill, the rent being specified in quantities of 'good and sufficient mercantile bear and oatmeal', as well as a money addition. At a time of inflation there was often good sense in retaining the victual component of the rental. The tack signed in 1791 agreed that the victuals would be paid yearly 'at the storehouse of New Tarbat or at the sands of Nigg, and that in their own sacks and upon their own horses'. The traditional requirement that all corn for grinding should be taken to the miln remained in operation. The Milntown of New Tarbat acted as a local market as well as a centre for linen production—an advertisement for May 1793 gave notice of a market with booths, tables, etc. for sales, and the collection of rents. Tolls were to be levied on cattle, sheep and goats and a 1d on each piece of cloth—the proceeds to be directed for the repair of the streets of Milntown.[7] There was a clause in the tack which gave tangible assistance in the case of improvement—the tenant agreed to repair a house and offices, to enclose and plant certain waste lands and plant trees, and the landlord,

> as an encouragement to him to improve his farm, hereby binds and obliges him to pay to the said John Mackenzie meliorations for the forsaid improvements at the expiry of this lease, as the same shall then be ascertained by a Comprisement and Valuation to be made thereof by two or more persons to be agreed mutually by the parties.[8]

It was a compensation clause of an unusually favourable and modern character.

The most contentious aspect of rental and leasing policy was the question of rights to grazing, and the traditional character of certain quasi-communal uses of land. In the last resort it was a matter of who in the Highlands had access to the main wealth-yielding resources of the region. Charting the shifts in emphasis between collective and individualised occupation, while central to the history of the Highlands in this era, is extraordinarily difficult. Some of the tacks in the 1790s are suggestive of the tendencies. In 1796, for instance, James Mitchell, a tacksman of Achnadevach, signed a tack of 15 years duration, at £26 per annum, for the lands and grazings of Garbat near Ben Wyvis. The rent contained no victual component but indicated the presence on the land of sub-tenants.[9] Another tack, of 1790, relating to South Keanchrine in the western barony, suggests a similar continuity with past practice but with two significant provisos. It included a compensation for improvements clause and, like other contemporary leases, specifically denied any rights to subtenants covered in the tack.[10] None of the agreements empowered, or required, the tacksmen to remove their subtenants; none of them specifically prevented evictions.[11] Kenneth Mackenzie seemed to assume that the tacksmen could do as they felt best for themselves and/or the common people.

Estate income was increasing at an accelerating rate at the turn of the century but the proprietors remained financially insecure. In the last five years of his life Kenneth Mackenzie made several appeals to the government for more favourable treatment of the debts still held against the Cromartie estate. His 'memorials' expose the financial quandary of Macleod's successors. In November 1793 Mackenzie outlined the problem. When Count Macleod had repossessed the Cromartie estates in 1784 there was a debt to the government of £19,010. By November 1788 he had paid off £14,191 and the interest on the outstanding debt, being then £4,818. Macleod had originally possessed a considerable personal fortune but the rebuilding of his mansion house (New Tarbat) and the repayments to the government had left him financially exhausted.

When Captain Kenneth Mackenzie succeeded in 1789 the estate 'was indeed in a very embarrassed situation' so that he found himself 'in very narrow circumstances.' Several relatives in the large family, for many years, continued to assert their claims on the estate of the forfeited third Earl of Cromartie; one was the widow of Sir George Mackenzie who claimed that Captain Mackenzie had treated her so shabbily that she 'had to reduce her establishment'. In fact she outlived her husband by six decades and, during that time, received a government pension out of the sale of Royston.[12] Captain Mackenzie himself vainly hoped for government assistance and even entertained the idea that the family title would be restored.[13]

Mackenzie analysed the finances of the Cromartie Estate in 1793. The free rents of the estate were £1400 p.a. From this came the annuity to the widow Lady Macleod of £600, and to Lady Jane Mackenzie of £120. The debt of Lord Macleod, no interest having been paid since his death, now amounted to £6023. To this had to be added the residual debt on the estate of Sir John Gordon, now at £2461. The total debt was, therefore, £8484 which, at 5% p.a. reached £424 p.a. Thus the occupant of the Cromartie Estates was left with £255.15.4 per year on which to subsist and to maintain and improve his property. Kenneth Mackenzie's point was that it was not enough. He could not pay the interest on the loans; £255 was a miserable pittance from which 'to maintain his Family, and support, as best he can, the rank and representation of an ancient and noble family'. His assumption was implicit: it was in the nation's interest that ancient families be maintained. He pointed out that he had served as a military officer for 33 years, 21 of them abroad; that

> In 1762 he embarked for Portugal and was for some time a Captain in the Portuguese service ... [and] afterwards an Ensign Lieutenant and Captain in His Majesty's 33rd and 37th Regiments of Foot, and the greatest part of that time in the Battalion of Grenadiers.

He placed his case before the consideration of the government, in the hope of royal patronage.[14]

16 A & B (opposite page)   Roads were late in reaching Wester Ross: contemporary writers warned sportsmen about difficult conditions.

The application was evidently without success because three years later Mackenzie repeated the exercise in still more impassioned terms. He again averted to his military career, but now also to his poor health, and once more to the shocking condition of the Cromartie finances on his succession to Lord Macleod. He added some more points

> Lord Macleod had a short time before his Death entered into a Contract for building a new Mansion house, a great part of the price of which Mr. Mackenzie had to pay as well as the expense of his Lordships funeral, and a variety of family accounts.

The estate had been so encumbered that even the mains of New Tarbat were rented out, a thing unprecedented. Mackenzie had been left with a mere £381.6.6 a year 'to represent an ancient and respectable (and not long ago a noble) Family'. In 1795 Mackenzie had been able to pay off some of the government debt and the Gordon debt out of the proceeds of a small inheritance.[15] But his predicament remained serious and he had experienced 'distresses and embarrassments' in meeting his obligations. He presented himself to the government, pleading his army service by which, he maintained, he was 'entitled to some mark of royal favour'. He alluded also to the precedent of the Lovat case: Lovat had been restored to his estates without any burden of debts—'a considerable Debt due from that Estate to the Public was altogether remitted and discharged'. The 'heir and representative of the Fame of Cromartie', it was submitted, deserved similar favour. The appeal however was again ignored or rejected.

In the year of Mackenzie's death, 1796, yet another appeal was launched and once more it yielded a similarly cold response from London. From these exchanges it is evident that, for several years, Mackenzie chose not to liquidate any of the debt he owed the government in the remarkably blithe hope that it would eventually be 'remitted altogether'. His confidence had been based on the Lovat case, and he had 'flattered himself [that] there was no solid ground for making a distinction between the Heir of that family and himself.'[16]

In 1796 efforts to gain financial relief lapsed and the owners of Cromartie, facing the realities, organised a series of complex arrangements to extricate the estate from its debts. With the help of the Royston inheritance the outstanding debts were at last liquidated. This was vital breathing space. The estate remained, however, permanently burdened by its accumulating jointures and annuities, millstones draped around the neck of the estate finances on behalf of the relatives of each incumbent. The primary debts had been removed and further relief to the inheritors of the Cromartie estate came from rental income which was rising at an unprecedented rate during these years.

To a degree the estate rental was a mechanism by which the debts of the landlord, and the pressure from the estate factors, was transmitted to the working people of the estate. So also were the changes, including a new breed of tenant, to the uses made of the land itself. In the end, the tenantry itself felt the consequences of their landlord's predicaments.

When, in 1797, Lady Elibank, the new owner, wished to remove 'some tenants whose leases were expired' she found that the Title Deeds remained in the hands of the government despite the fact that the debt of £19,010 had been paid off in 1795. Her impatience about the return of the documents was symptomatic of her urgency to rearrange certain parts of the estate.[17]

III

The threat of eviction, and the fear of decline from the status of peasant to that of proletarian—from cottar to day labourer or worse—were facts of life for the people of the Cromartie estate. Apprehension was widespread and expressed itself in emigration, in introversion, even perhaps in the riots in September 1792. But rent and tenure were not necessarily the greatest concern of these people. Religion was equally important and more pervasive, though it intersected with more mundane matters too.

One of the great themes of Highland history from 1700 to 1850 was, of course, the emergence of a vigorous but introverted fervour, an alarmingly rigorous religious spirit that seemed to grip the collective psyche to such a degree that it paralysed any political or physical resistance to the landlords or the new commercial agriculture. The emergence of inspired godly men, often at odds with the established church and often bitter enemies of 'moderates' and the lairds, raised piety and spiritual austerity to the severest levels. In particular there emerged 'The Men'—laymen of influence in devout congregations, inspirational speakers who were neither ministers nor officials, but who preached with fabled fire and remarkable theological refinement. They wielded great power in their communities and always wore eccentric dress, 'old-fashioned cloaks', long uncut hair and large white handkerchiefs on their heads—this being a deliberate rejection of the 'snares of fashion'. They were merely one expression of the ferment of religious debate and antagonism which scarred the Highlands in these years, and their influence has not yet been accounted by historians.

There was a central irony in the extreme religiosity that gripped the Highlands at the turn of the century, for it coincided with the unwonted transformation of economic and social life in the north. Indeed the renewed spiritual purity of the people appeared to promote a generalised passivity in the face of extreme provocation by the landlords. In his reminiscences of the early nineteenth century, one of the most feared and respected ministers of the Free Church, the Rev. John Kennedy, gave voice to this broad interpretation of the three currents of Highland society—the work of eviction, the impact of piety, and the pacific stoicism of the people:

> ... it was at the climax of its [Ross-shire's] spiritual propensity that the cruel work of eviction began to lay waste the hillsides and the plains of the north. Swayed by the example of the Godly among them, and away from the influences by which less sequestered localities were corrupted the body of the people in the Highlands became distinguished as the most peaceable and virtuous peasantry in Britain. It was just then that they began to be driven off by ungodly oppressors, to clear their native soil for strangers, red deer and sheep. With few exceptions, the owners of the soil began to act as if they were also owners of the people, and, disposed to regard them as the vilest part of their Estate; they treated them without respect to the requirements of righteousness and to the dictates of mercy ... families by the hundred were driven across the sea, or were gathered as the sweepings of the hillsides, into wretched hamlets on the shore. By wholesale evictions wastes were formed for the red deer, that the gentry of the nineteenth century might indulge in the sport of savages of three centuries before.[18]

The timing and penetration of these doctrines of extreme pietism is not clear. Nor is it evident that they prevented all resistance to the landlords: indeed social life in many estates was punctuated by a low level obstruction of management and by open conflict over theological matters.[19] But there can be no doubting the widespread appetite for religion and education.

Coigach at all times was a relatively remote and neglected corner. In January 1793 'the inhabitants of the Aird of Coigach in Lochbroom' mounted a campaign which allowed the collective voice to be heard. It was in the form of a petition addressed to the Scottish Society for Propagating Christian Knowledge, in the Highlands, and it concerned the appointment of a missionary minister and schoolmaster, and the need for decent accommodation as a requisite condition of anyone coming to Coigach.

The petition painted a self-portrait of the district. The people laboured 'under the greatest of all possible earthly grievances: a total deprivation of every means and opportunity of religious comfort and instruction'. They lived thirty miles from the nearest church to which 'we have only access over Roads impracticable to active and vigorous Youth, and totally so to the Old, Frail and Infirm!' Their case, they believed was 'most pitiable and affecting'. They asked the society to provide a salary for a schoolmaster/minister:

> To the poor Inhabitants of this much and long neglected, dark and unenlightened corner, it is particularly distressing, when Baptizm or marriage require it, to be under the necessity of going to such an extreme distance as their parish church, which on these occasions is only practicable by Sea, and when by stormy weather they are frequently detained for many days, from their Labour, families, and homes, to their great detriment and loss.

The Coigach people argued (surprisingly in the light of the current demographic revolution) that the lack of a minister inhibited procreation:

> This is also thought to be no small check on our population, for weak children by cold and fatigue frequently loose their lives, tho' it happens for most part that they are severall months old, before they are baptised; and our youth are deterred from the honourable bonds of matrimony, from the apprehensions of the extreme expense and trouble, to which the circumstances as above related expose them.

They pointed out that they represented about 110 families, about 550 souls, 'who have not the advantage of hearing publick worship more than twice' a year,

> and during the rest of the year the poor, ignorant and illiterate inhabitants, only know the Lords day from the other days of the week, by a resting from Bodily Labour, which the Brutes in the field enjoy in common with them! How then can this poor and dark corner be said to enjoy Man's greatest boast, the comforts of religion!

The Coigach petition appears to have won the support of Dr John Kemp, secretary of the S.S.P.C.K. in Edinburgh. He confirmed the peoples' claims, and acknowledged that the problem of accommodation had driven off the previous recruit to the district. He told the society

> knowing from my own observation the miserable houses with which worthy Donald Lyon (the previous schoolmaster) was forced to put up, no successor will be appointed till a good comfortable dwelling house, and a school furnished with glass windows, tables and forms, are actually built and ready for his reception. A crop of land anent also be assigned sufficient for the maintenance of one large and two small cows all the year round.

Anyone going to Coigach, he said, would need a security from the proprietor or the tacksmen.[20] These people, of whose spiritual and educational welfare Kemp spoke, were the foundation of the estate, the source of its financial success or failure.

While the ministrations of orthodox religion were impeded for lack of funds, other sources of spiritual consolation held a grip in several parts of the Highlands. In one case in Lochbroom in 1817 religious unorthodoxy was combined with emigration as an escape from the economic and theological constraints of the *status quo*. It was led by a cantankerous and overbearing minister, Norman Macleod—a man at odds with his church, and able to inspire an entire community to uplift itself and leap the Atlantic to St Annes in Nova Scotia. There they established a rigorous theocratic community which persisted intact until the potato famine of 1847 caused Macleod to lead them yet again—in community formation—to the other side of the globe, first to Adelaide, then Melbourne in Australia, and finally to a land grant at Waipu in northern New Zealand. The solidarity of these people transcended all manner of adversity and it sprang initially from places such as Coigach, though their precise origins remain unsure.[21]

IV

On the death of Kenneth Mackenzie in 1796 the direct male line of the Cromartie family was exhausted. Thus he was succeeded by the elder sister of Lord Macleod, the dowager Lady Elibank (Lady Isabella Mackenzie, 1725-1801), already 71 years of age, a lady noted for her devoted attachment to her parents—the Jacobite Earl and his wife. The convoluted state of the estate finances was matched by the kinship and marriage interconnections and it is not surprising that the quick succession of one owner by another caused considerable bickering.[22] Lady Elibank quickly discovered the sagging financial condition of her inheritance. She brought very little apart from her own debts to the Cromartie Estate—her husband had 'failed in 1794' and her children were equally badly placed.[23] At a time when Cromartie needed an injection of external capital, it was instead saddled with a succession of heritors whose role was essentially parasitic.

Circumstances, therefore, were unpropitious for the short term of Lady Elibank's tenure of the Cromartie estate. It was not made easier by begging letters from her son-in-law Edward Hay, brother of the Marquis of Tweeddale, and the husband of the heiress of Cromartie. By 1801 he was headlong in debt and was in desperate straits for £2000 by Martinmas.[24] He made an application for help to his mother-in-law by way of their respective agents. He got a clear reply—Lady Elibank was, of course, disposed to help 'as much as possible towards Mr Hay's relief, yet from the very heavy Jointures affecting her Estate there was little in her power at present'. She could not conceivably raise £2,000; and Edward Hay had to be told that he overestimated by a long chalk the size of Lady Elibank's estate. She turned him in the direction of Lord Tweeddale as a more likely source of liquidity. In the upshot Hay appears to have raised some temporary accommodation—but his debt remained and, when Lady Elibank died in 1801, it was added directly to the Cromartie accounts—and thereby a further burden was hung upon the rental.

Lady Elibank appears to have lived in Newhall (in Midlothian) and it seems that she seldom actually visited her northern estates. Her correspondence with her factors was dominated by her demands for prompt payment of their accounts in the south and the imperative that she be exposed to no further debt. Sometimes she would arrange for a barrel of oysters to be sent to her son-in-law. More typical were the details of a hand-to-mouth administration and the petty embarrassments caused by problems of absentee management. For instance Kenneth Mackenzie's widow 'laboured and sowed a considerable part of the farm of New Tarbat in the spring of 1797'—in the mistaken belief that she had the right to do so. In fact it was not so, and she found herself in debt to Lady Elibank for £50.13.6.

The local management came under criticism: George Mackenzie was too slow and a dispute arose over the division of the rents after an annual crop calculation. The system of factoring lent itself to argument since it required the management to take responsibility for all items before squaring the account with the owner. Edward Hay was drawn into the management though mainly in a distant supervisory role on behalf of Lady Elibank. Meanwhile Hay sought new managers who would show greater energy and promptness in paying over the rents. They looked out for 'a solid sensible young man' who 'knew every foot of the estate'; they also required him 'to settle everything between tenants, but not known in the north'. Here indeed was an example of the increasing preference among northern proprietors for southern factors, men untouched by traditional inertia and able to make large changes in the working of a Highland estate.

During 1799 an acquaintance of Lady Elibank had journeyed east to west across her northern estates, possibly in search of army recruits. His report fascinated her—it alluded to the fishery at Ullapool, to the question of social hierarchy, to military recruitment, and to the behaviour of womenfolk in Coigach.

> He had been all over my property—and a very fine one it was, he had gone from Strathpeffer to Coigeach in his coach all the way, and staid a month at the village [Ullapool] government had Built there; there he made up a fine story, that going in to a house that looked better than common, he saw a very Handsome young man mending his shoes, but he was sure by his looks he was a Gentleman and he found he was a relation of the Family, upon hearing this Mrs Macleod asked him to tea, the moment she looked at him she knew him to be a Gentleman too, and Macleod told him he was very sorry he had only an Ensigns Commission to offer him he would give him the money if he could get the men, so all he could do for him at Present was to make him a Sergeant, but he hoped he would write to the Father to get the men for this fine Handsome Fellow of six foot high, as there was great plenty of men in that part of the Country. I said I was very happy to hear there was so many men on the Estate and had left it to my son Mr Hay to manage as he pleased ... its a fact that the women of Coigach whiped Macleod's Bum and sent him off Oh, Oh you may go and tell what we did to you you Plaguing our men.[25]

Though the estate administration was congested with minutia there were, nevertheless, larger shifts in the basic framework of the local economy. Indeed the tribulations of the heritors of Cromartie were translated into the lives of the working people of the estate. The years of Lady Elibank were associated with various tenurial changes which are difficult to chart.

As early as 1792 it was reported that 'Mr Ross is at this time advertising parts of the Cromarty estate for Sheep Farms and Culcairn has already Sett the highlands of his own Estate for sheep also at an increase of Rent.'[26] The report may not have referred to the Cromartie estate, but in 1798 there is further indirect evidence of the arrival of commercial sheep on the west coast. It was a petition which referred to 'a general plan of grazing, by the introduction of sheep [which] has been introduced into the north of Scotland'. The petition sought the protection of sheepfarmers from 'depredations' on their sheep: one of the signatories was Alexander MacCulloch of Badscallie, probably the tacksman of grazing lands in Coigach and whose rent had risen sharply in the previous few years.[27]

Another symptom of change in the disposition of the estate was the investigation made into wadsetting arrangements in 1799. It was found that several parts of the estate were in unredeemed wadsets dating back to the pre-forfeiture period. The wadset had been a device for raising money, and used heavily by the Cromartie family during its periodic financial crises. As an adviser noted in 1799:

> It is improbable that the sums advanced then are any thing like being adequate to the value of the wadset land now. There can be no doubt that Lady Elibank has now right to redeem any of the wadsets, if not already done.

A number of wadsets had been redeemed during the period of annexation but several remained and it became clear that, especially during the rapid inflation of rents, it was sensible to liquidate the old arrangements. In effect this required the repayment of the original account (much depreciated by the interim inflation) followed by renting out the land at a new rent. It required a capital outlay, but it also made possible the rearrangement of further stretches of the estate, perhaps for large commercial production.[28]

Concurrently the estate moved towards a greater conversion of victual rents to money payments.[29] But there was still hesitation about the wisdom of the change since it was realised that victual rents offered a genuine hedge against inflation. Even in 1799 new tacks were being negotiated which retained victual provision. For example William Chisholm of Bayfield agreed to pay 184 bolls of meal and two swine as yearly rent for the Milns of Milntown—but 'half the meal be converted/16/- per boll, and the remainder to be delivered in kind'. It was a transitional arrangement for a time of transition.[30]

Arable lands were certainly subject to new tenures during these years, and there was a widespread re-orientation of farmlands in several parts of the estate. The lotting of small plots of land was already a long tried measure on the estate. At the time of the Forfeiture, old soldiers had been given lots at Strathpeffer,[31] and Lord Macleod had also rewarded his men with lots in the same district. It was not a large step to extend the lotting system to newer ground (for improvement) which might then release other land to larger more commercially-minded farmers. These sorts of rearrangements were a widespread practice in the Highlands by the turn of the century. They undoubtedly put fear and trembling into the hearts of the common people, and a feeling of injustice and disappointment which rarely expressed itself except in sporadic resistance or sullen emigration. The scant survival of documentation for the period on the Cromartie Estate reinforces this silence.

Two letters, by chance, survive from these years, both of which speak eloquently of the popular response to the rumour (and the reality) or removal. They both relate to the lands of Auchterneed in Strathpeffer.

In November 1801 Hugh Mackenzie travelled more than 20 miles from the Heights of Auchterneed to New Tarbat House, a considerable journey as he pointed out. It was prompted by the news 'that there is a stir and removing determined to take place through the whole Estate'. He came to tell Lady Elibank that there existed an indissoluble link forged between him and the Cromartie family. This was an appeal, of course, to the tradition of reciprocation between landlord and tenantry. Mackenzie wrote 'for myself and all my Forefathers before me was ever paying Rents and following your Family for I have a small Tack where I dwell in some twenty six years ago'. He had been in India with Lord Macleod 'where I did never want while I could see his presence'. He continued:

> ... it is not my own saying I was as great a favourite of his as went ever from Strathpeffer for he took me over and he took me home and got me my pension and when I enlisted he promised me that I would get what I had for nothing he would live and more likewise for there is none alive of all the men that was ever with my Lord by myself now.

Thus claiming to be the last surviving recruit from Macleod's regiments he considered himself a trusted object for consideration in the feared 'stir and removing'. He continued '... my Lady I hope that your Goodness will never see me wanting nor being empty while I will endeavour to pay as good as another when I have none in the world to depend upon but your own honour.' He ended '... that is all from your well wisher while I live, Hugh Mackenzie.'[32] Common people rarely figured in estate correspondence except in a posture of deference and servility; in this sense they differed little from the impecunious relatives of landlords who were also compelled to petition for favours.

Another supplicant from Auchterneed was Hector Urquhart (writing through an interpreter) who was also in a state of consternation about the removal plans of the estate—that it was the intention of the landlord 'to remove me with the other tenants of Achternyde from our present Farms'. He pointed out, 'it is to me a very grievous matter, being now an old man, not much able to work ... myself and my Predecessors, Father and Grandfather, have long been in possession of my present Farm for near six score years back, old servants and dependents on your Honourable Father's Family.' He then outlined the close relations of the generations and the unbroken service provided by his family. He concluded his petition:

> From all these circumstances being made known to your Ladyship, I humbly hope and trust you will see it proper not to throw me destitute, but be pleased to order me to be continued in my Farm, as I am very willing to pay or give any raise of rent, that my neighbours will give.

It is not possible to say what happened to either Hugh Mackenzie or Hector Urquhart. The estate had the power to evict them and it is almost certain that the people of Auchterneed were pushed up the hillside to accommodate larger tenants in the strath. Similar changes had also occurred at New Tarbat. Much of the rearrangement of the lands of Cromartie, it is likely, occurred only gradually and without much drama. But there seems to have been increasing dislocation at the turn of the century. The outcome, in the eastern parts of the estate, was the creation of large arable/commercial farms and a fringe of lots or crofts. The time of the change is not yet clear and, for the most part, the only summary evidence is in the shape of maps, or in the form of pained memories expressed in the Napier Commission evidence of 1886. The voice of the people remained a distant rumbling and rarely enters the scant contemporary record.

V

The demography of the peerage and of the common landed proprietors in Britain has been the subject of important studies.[33] We know more of their vital behaviour than others because their genealogies are especially well kept. For the Cromartie family over the century after 1750 there was an outstanding demographic oddity which had a great bearing on the finances of the dynasty. The simple fact is that the women of the Cromartie marriages outlived their men by many years. Partly it was a reflection of the differential longevity of the sexes; partly it was because the male heirs married at a much later age than their spouses and/or re-married. The outcome was clear and important; females lived on and made great demands on the finances of the estate. Macleod's wife outlived him by 54 years and cost the estate an aggregate of about £32,400 (not counting interest). His descendant-cousin Kenneth Mackenzie married four years before his death and his widow also benefited by a substantial jointure. Because there were no male heirs the estate then passed to Lady Elibank, 71, whose family was in a dire financial plight. She was succeeded in 1801 by a daughter, Mrs Hay-Mackenzie, who married into debts, who outlived her husband by 34 years, and even outlived her own son by nine years. An indirect consequence was the channelling of estate income away from a re-investment in the local economy, and away from the development of the resources used by the people under the sway of the Cromartie family. In part this was the price of primogeniture and of landowning continuity, the very goal that had brought Count Macleod back to Cromartie.

CHAPTER 12

The Vicissitudes of a Highland Laird, 1801-1825

I

Lady Elibank died at the age of 77 in 1801 and the Cromartie lands then fell into the possession of her daughter, the Honourable Maria Murray Hay-Mackenzie, who, in 1790, had married Edward Hay, Esq., of Newhall, the brother of the Marquis of Tweeddale. Edward Hay had been required to incorporate the name Mackenzie into his own by the terms of the Macleod entail. He was described as a large strong man, his wife as a woman of small stature, but she eventually outlived him by 44 years. Edward Hay-Mackenzie had already been involved in the business of the estate during the last years of his mother-in-law; and he gave up his military service in order to devote himself to the affairs of Cromartie. Edward Hay-Mackenzie was the classic case of a younger son of a noble family who turned to the army for advancement and made a relatively advantageous marriage which allowed him to set up in an independent landed style. But he was quickly brought to face the fact that the Cromartie rental was, in very large part, already spoken for by way of heavy jointures, public burdens and the residue of debts from previous generations. He had also accumulated personal debts on his own account though it seems he owned a small amount of saleable property, for example, a house in Cambridgeshire, and another in Princes Street, Edinburgh.[1] Three female dependents—Lady Jane, the Duchess of Atholl (Macleod's widow) and Mrs Macleod—now cost the Cromartie Estate a total of £520 each year by way of annuities.[2]

With such expensive pensioners living off the Cromartie rental the provisions and arrangements were frequently very complex and subject to involved legal disputation. The Royston inheritance remained a continual source of contention. More favourable in its consequence for the Cromartie estate was another complicated arrangement. On the marriage of Lord Macleod, in 1786, the parents of his bride (Lord and Lady Forbes) entered a contract whereby £12,000 would be paid to the Cromartie heirs on the death of Lord and Lady Forbes (whichever lived longer). They both died in 1805 and the payment offered timely relief to the Cromartie family finances. It was a helpful return to the estate coffers to balance against the counter drain from the heavy price of annuities.[3] Annuities, of course, were a kind of insurance system for ageing and widowed spouses. Sometimes the expenses of the annuitants outreached their incomes. In March 1808 Lady Jane Mackenzie (sister of Count Macleod) experienced great difficulty making ends meet, was reported 'very much distressed for want of money, and was on this account some days ago confined to bed'. Duncan, the Edinburgh legal advisor, told Mrs Hay-Mackenzie that,

> this distress is imputed in part to an additional expense incurred by a change of habitation, but I really suspect the true cause to be a want of attention and proper arrangement of her affairs. Nothing is due to her from you till next Whitsunday—would it be agreeable to you that I should make a temporary advance to her of ten or twenty pounds for relieving her from her present necessities?[4]

Begging letters were a mark of a deference society unequal in its division of the fruits of the ownership of land and the production of its people. The estate correspondence is scattered with such requests from all strata of society. At the same time that Lady Jane took to her bed in financial despair, Mrs Hay-Mackenzie also received a letter from Tanera—the island off Coigach—from a small tenant claiming to be prostrated with rheumatism. He was, he said, 'a good old tenant', but 'proud of a distant Blood Connection' with the Cromartie family, and believed the proprietrix would 'take one of their offspring under the shadow of her wings'.[5]

The Cromarties were able to sustain their dependents, and their own style of life, only by virtue of the continuing and accelerating increase in rental income from the estate. Rents were leapfrogging at an extraordinary rate. In 1803 an enquiry into Highland emigration noted that Hay-Mackenzie's Coigach estate contained only one large and another small sheep farm, but that the estate would be out of lease within seven years.[6] In April 1807 the local western factor, John Macrae, returned home to find an offer for the Badscally Farm, at that time rented at £30. A 'good tenant' had now bid £150. 'This is no bad prospect' commented Macrae—particularly because the rental of the Coigach Salmon Fishing had just been doubled, and other rents (e.g. for Tolmich) were rising on a rack rent.[7] It is evident from tack arrangements in these years that large sheep farmers, some from southern Scotland, had entered the estate and were paying big rents. For instance in 1810 William Henderson from Selkirkshire was paying £220 for the land of Rhiddorroch.[8] The new sheep farmer class is not easily distinguished from the larger tacksmen and it is impossible to gauge exactly the dislocation brought upon the existing system by these changes. Some indication may be derived from maps made before and after the changes.

More direct illumination of changes on the Cromartie Estate is provided by a series of advertisements (typical of many Highland estates at the time) which were printed in the *Inverness Journal* in 1808 and 1809. In Coigach great territories were put up for letting—2,000 acres at Corry, 14,000 acres at Rhiddorroch, 8,000 acres at Glastullich, 6,000 acres at Langwell, 13,000 acres at Auchindrain, lots of 20,000 acres, 14,000 acres, and 2,400 acres at Altandow, and 15,000 acres at Badenscallie. Their attractions, of course, were not understated. These lands had 'all fresh water lakes attached to them, which abound in salmon and trout'. They were within 'four days sail of Liverpool' and close to 'the thriving fishing port of Ullapool [which] finds a ready market for a considerable part of the produce, and the remainder can be conveyed, either by sea or land, by an excellent road executed a few years ago at the expense of Government'. The advertisement continued: 'The lochs by which it is intersected are the annual resort

17   Maria Mackenzie, wife of Edward Hay-Mackenzie.

of the largest and finest herrings in the world and the mountains abound in game. In short, farms more desirably situated both in profit and pleasure, are seldom to be met with.'[9] No mention was made of the occupying inhabitants: the landlord was seeking the best price in the highest market.

A few months later lands in the eastern parts of the estate were put up for offer in similar terms. The lands around and about Castle Leod—'160 acres of excellent rich arable land, and about 170 acres of capital pasture' were for lease. An advertisement claimed that:

> the arable lands are capable of carrying very heavy crops of corn, and are well adapted for the turnip husbandry. The pasture affords excellent food for sheep and black cattle, and from its warm exposure, is well adapted for the cheviot and merino breeds of sheep. The situation of these farms is most desirable, being situated at the head of Strathpeffer, commanding a complete view of that beautiful valley, and the adjoining lightly cultivated country, and is only four miles from the seaport of Dingwall.

It was now possible to claim that Strathpeffer was part of the new world of 'improvement': 'In short, such a farm, from its beautiful situation, richness of soil and pasture, seldom occurs, as is well worth the attention of farmers, or of any gentleman who wishes to have a truly beautiful residence in one of the richest counties in the north of Scotland.'[10] Simultaneously more large blocks of land were advertised—in Fannich, Blackhill, Ballachgowan and also Polnicol. They were described in terms unambiguous to southern capitalists:- the eastern lands were 'in a low flat country, and well calculated for the turnip husbandry, and capable of producing any crop; and being situated close upon the shore of the entrance to the Bay of Cromarty, there is every conveyancy for shipping the produce and importing lime; seaware may also be had occasionally in great abundance.' The prominence of transport was a reference to a main consideration in the agricultural economy, i.e. export facilities. The notice continued: 'A variety of Sheep Farms upon the same Estate, being at present out of lease, and formerly advertised, they will be the objects of importance to south country farmers, who may be accommodated, at the same time, both with arable and extensive sheep farms.' Included in the lands available were the two Tanera Islands in the extreme west: 'Here there is a safe and convenient sheep walk, where the snow never lies.' A total of more than 100,000 acres was advertised.

In these public statements the Cromartie Estate left no doubt that it was on the high road to improvement, to large scale sheep farming and commercial arable production. Its blandishments were pitched directly at southern farmers, as recommended by Sir George Stewart Mackenzie in his *General View of the Agriculture of the County of Ross and Cromarty* (1813). The Cromartie Estate was typical of most Highland properties at this time. It seems that it was fortunate that it executed these plans without overt resistance from its people: and this may indicate that the change was engineered with some discretion and without excessive haste. But there is no contemporary record of the popular response to these sweeping changes at the time. Seventy years later, before the Napier Commission, the collective memory was full of accumulated bitterness (see below, Chapter Twenty-three).

The motive force behind much of the alteration in land use and rents was high agricultural prices, especially for wool. In March 1808 the Inverness Journal argued for a prohibition on the import of foreign wool in order to assist British producers. One year later the war had interrupted trade with Spain with an effect identical to an import prohibition and, consequently, wool which, it was reported:

> sold for about 4s per lb is now of 25s and still on the advance. An association is about to be entered into by several thousands of the respectable inhabitants of London, to check the infamous, unjust and unnecessary rise in the price of woollen cloth, by a resolution not to wear any woollen cloth but what is the genuine produce of this country. We trust that this laudable example will be universally followed.[11]

The sheep farmers found that their economic interest was thus opposed to those of the British consumer. The expansion of sheepfarming also ran counter to the interests of the small landholders (and some of the tacksmen) in the old system. The precise degree to which sheepfarming was disadvantageous to the common people is extremely difficult to account. It is evident that severe deprivation, for example recurrent famine, preceded the coming of the cheviots to the Highlands. Such crises continued, and were perhaps exacerbated, during the period of the expanding sheep economy. In July 1809 the editor of the *Inverness Journal* wrote:

> We are truly sorry to understand that the lower classes of the inhabitants of the West Coast of Inverness and Ross-shire, and in many parts of the Hebrides, are in a state of very great distress from want of provisions. Until very lately, a few humane and spirited individuals acquainted with the circumstances of the people, supplied them with meal on credit, until the demand should arise for their black cattle, the only commodity they have to dispose of; but these supplies being exhausted, and a necessary regard for their own security having rendered it adviseable for them not to extend their credit any farther, all the ends of want are likely to be experienced, although some cargoes of meal have been lately sent with the best intentions. Unfortunately, however, it will not be given out without Cash, and the country being completely drained of money, the miserable inhabitants may be doomed to starve even in the midst of plenty.[12]

Here, indeed, was the classic predicament of the peasant caught by the grip of poor crops with no cash surplus to draw upon to tide his family over a periodic crisis. He faced hunger and debts. It is probable that the rise of rents since 1760 had served to erode any margin of savings sufficient to insure against the hard years. It was a situation which, doubtless, reinforced Sir George Mackenzie's belief that such people should quit their lands. He was a close and influential neighbour of the Cromartie Estate and in 1808 he bought a large stock of cheviots 'for the purpose of stocking an extensive sheep walk which he has lately taken into his own hands'. Soon, it was reported, he would be able to supply the entire district with cheviots. Improvement probably helped the small producer wherever he kept his grip on his land—turnips greatly extended his ability to feed his black cattle for southern markets, and the demand for his cattle was, generally, buoyant.[13] When, after 1815, prices fell and competition intensified the small producer was more easily marginalised.

II

Despite the sparsity of detailed evidence in these years, there are enough fragments to make it abundantly clear that radical changes continued through the years of the Napoleonic Wars, accelerated no doubt by the inflation of prices for Highland commodities that coincided with the period of the war. Sir George Mackenzie's survey of Wester Ross in 1813 estimated that already two-fifths of all the rent was paid by sheepfarms, the remainder, of course, primarily from black cattle. Mackenzie noted however that 'the whole district of Coigach is about to be let'.[14]

Wool exports from Ullapool had already increased from 17 cwt in 1802 to 462 cwt in 1808. There survives a brief series of reports by the agent James Laing, which was received by Edward Hay-Mackenzie in the eight months prior to the latter's death in late 1814. Laing was at that very moment supervising the rearrangement of Coigach lands: it entailed the resettlement of people and the creation of lots for crofters, and was

18   Edward Hay-Mackenzie.

associated with 'removals' and the rapid augmentation of rents. This series of changes in Coigach coincided with similar transformations occurring in many other places in the Highlands—it was the time when the ill-famed Patrick Sellar was at large in Strathnaver in Sutherland, a time also when Highland soldiers were in service in great numbers in Europe.

In April 1814, having travelled to Coigach to oversee arrangements, Laing wrote to Hay-Mackenzie, 'I trust you will go up in the summer when the whole will be perambulated.' He remarked:

> I shall settle the small Tenants as far as in my power at present and should the Badenscallie Tenants not give £250 Badenscallie will bring more Rent and be better improved; by letting it out the same as Achiltybuie—indeed were the present Tenants or any native to have the whole, they would just subsist and enslave the poor creatures as formerly which I know is against your wish.

This document seems to indicate several points. First is that individual lots for 'crofters' were being created in Coigach (and were already fixed at Achiltibuie). Second, there was an effort to end the old system of tacksmen who traditionally took the entire land and sublet to the people in a quasi-communal fashion. Third, this policy was justified, beyond the increase of rent, by the claim that it reduced the oppression of the tacksmen upon the people. Fourth, the tacksmen were given the opportunity of bidding up to the increased (and updated) rent but the landlord clearly preferred an outsider to take the main part of the land. The document suggests also that the majority of the people were being placed in small lots, while the lion's share of the land was reserved for a large tenant at a high rent.[15] It is likely therefore that the common people, their numbers already much swollen by demographic growth, obtained reduced access to pastoral lands. They became crofters, a status which, though it provided limited grazing for their cattle, almost certainly diminished their lands. It is exceedingly unlikely that the commercial sheep economy could have been introduced without this critical effect.

Two weeks later Laing wrote again: 'I hope you have arranged matters in the west as far as possible—but it is next to impossible to please everyone.' He went on to detail the agreements that had been made so far.

> The Tenants of Rive have their possession for £60—those of Altandhu for £70—three years lease only. The Achiltibuie Tenants take in four more in addition to their present number, and pay £300 rent and will lodge in your hands, or in the Bank, three hundred pounds st. as security for the regular payment of said rent.

It is evident that heavy pressure was being placed on the tenantry for payment of increased rents, and that new lots were being marked out. Yet there also seems to have been a set of collective agreements with the people (perhaps through the agency of the old tacksmen). For instance, Laing remarked that 'the Badenscallie Tenants have agreed to given £250 and to take six more into their number.' He described how Keanchrine had been lotted out to about forty-five small tenants—'I think more could be accommodated should they come forward'. He also knew that people from Ullapool were keen to take lots—'I am glad that I reserved a larger lot for your disposal, if a person could be found to improve as an example to others it would be of great advantage'. There is no hint here of ejecting people from the estate; indeed, on the contrary, the landlord encouraged the influx of newcomers, both large and small. Improvement was a hope rather than a plan, but rents were extracted with greater vigour and precision. For the future it was intended that lots would only be obtained directly from the landlord which, of itself, indicates a greater degree of landlord control than before and a decline in what may be described as 'district autonomy' in the hands of the tacksmen. The relation of landlord and people would become more direct and systematic. Laing had reached the point where there were no arrears in the Boreraig of Coigach, but he was already aware of a recent fall in prices and the reduced opportunities for any further improvement.[16]

Laing returned to Coigach in September 1814 and reported

> I have to inform you I found everything to my mind—the new settlers on Keanchrine have got most of their houses up. I have got it all divided into lots. I hope the arrangements

will meet with your approval—there are fine crops all along the coast they never were so good—the fishing has been long and tedious, but they think upon the whole a good one.[17]

Resettlement, house building, lotting, new crops and an emphasis upon fishing were all features associated with the type of clearances which shifted people from the inland valleys to a coastal crofting existence, while large stretches of the interior were given over to sheep farmers. In effect the evidence suggests that substantial areas of Coigach were cleared, that is, radically reorganised, in the year 1814.

These great changes in the west which altered the pattern of life for the people at a time of an onset of long-term depression in the Highlands economy, were directly related to the financial problems of the Cromartie family who lived mainly in Princes Street, Edinburgh—an expensive address and, no doubt, an expensive style of life. In November 1814 (three weeks before Edward Hay-Mackenzie died) Laing announced that his collection of rent would soon enable him to send about £2,000 to the family; but he thought living in Edinburgh was an obstacle to the genuine financial recuperation for the family. He advised, 'I am confident if you and family would reside in Ross-shire you would soon be free of your Agents. I should give every assistance in my power to get free of them and I know it is practicable—what expense living in Town, furnishing everything there, paying Taxes for and keeping two Houses.'

Meanwhile however, the Hay-Mackenzies had decided to renovate their castle in Strathpeffer, making it habitable for one of the Murrays (related by marriage) and also for occasional visits by Mrs Hay-Mackenzie. The Countess of Sutherland, with a shaky grasp of Highland history, wrote a description of the work in July 1824. She referred to:

> a very old chateau of Hay-Mackenzie in Strathpeffer called Castle Leod ... it is quite a ruin, the roofing has cost £500. There is a curious old Gallery with a painted ceiling ... very beautiful in compartments, Adam and Eve etc—Q—when painted and by whom? [It is] like a Chateau de Roman, old castle of God knows who before the Mackenzies existed. It was deserted except by Crows and requires entire restoration.[17]

As always the Cromartie heirs were living beyond their means—means which derived from rents which had increased greatly in the previous fifty years but which, in common with the rest of the Highlands, in 1814 had come to a critical downturn. Prices of all commodities fell dramatically. Already adverse symptoms were visible. In November Laing reported: 'This is a particularly bad time for the letting of land owing to the fall in markets'. A farmer had been thrown off his farm because he could not pay the high rent, though Laing reckoned that 'bad management was the cause of his failure'.[19]

By 1816 tightening economic conditions in the north began to aggravate the financial difficulties of the Hay-Mackenzie family. There was, of course, nothing at all unique about the Cromartie inheritance dilemma. It was a recurrent theme in many aristocratic families. There was a parallel case even in Wester Ross, the effects of which engaged the feelings of the common people. Kenneth Mackenzie, Esq., of Dundonnell (in Little Lochbroom with lands wadsetted from Cromartie in the seventeenth century) had inherited his estate in 1816 with an income worth £1600 p.a., and he also possessed money of his own from his army service. He set out to institute far reaching improvements and spent large sums on his estate. But he died at 36, deeply in debt. His heir, a younger brother, was unable to clear the debts, and the estate was settled past him 'but burdened with a legacy to the eldest son of the heir, and still larger provisions to the numerous children of a favourite sister, of more than sufficient amount to exhaust the surplus value of the whole property.' The apparent disinheritance of the heir enraged his friends and 'operated powerfully on the characteristic attachment of the poor Highlanders; outrages were committed of an atrocious character—fire raising, destruction of property, brutal mutilation of cattle, and even deliberate attempts on life.' The heir was eventually reinstated 'amidst much rejoicings'. But, in reality, there was not enough income to pay the accumulated debts on the estate nor the annuity of £500 to the widow, her sister and her children. And so his estate was declared bankrupt and, with all its 'improvements and embellishments', was sold off to 'an intelligent stranger'.[20]

A comparable case was cited in Parliament in February 1841 by a northern M.P., H. Baillie, in a debate about poverty and emigration in the Highlands: 'He knew the case of one gentleman whose whole estate was not sufficient to pay the settlements which were made upon his younger brothers during the flourishing state of the kelp manufactures; he was in consequence obliged to give up his whole estate to his younger brothers, and he himself was only last year sent out at their joint expense as a sheep farmer to Australia'.[21] In comparison the problems of the Hay-Mackenzies remained modest, though by the 1830s the danger signs became more urgent.

III

Edward Hay-Mackenzie, who had undertaken much of the management of his wife's northern estates, died in December 1814. He was survived by Mrs Hay-Mackenzie, his widow, who lived on until 1858, and by three daughters and a son. Of the daughters, one married Sir David Hunter Blair of Brownhill,[22] another married John Buckle, and the third married the Earl of Glasgow. The son was John Hay-Mackenzie (born circa 1800, died 1849) to whom his mother conveyed the fee of the Cromartie Estates in 1822 and 1828. Outlived by his mother, he never actually owned the estates but appears to have hired them from his mother on payment of a portion of the estate. By putting her son in premature control of the estates Mrs Hay-Mackenzie further increased the net number of the family pensioned upon the Cromartie rental. John Hay-Mackenzie, in 1828, married Anne, third daughter of Sir James Gibson-Craig of Riccarton. She too eventually outlived her husband by twenty years so that, between 1849 and 1858, there were two Mrs Hay-Mackenzies, both widows and both dependent on the estate as annuitants. Already, for several decades the finances of the Cromartie Estate had been increasingly precarious. In 1849 the estate accounts reached a severe crisis. Yet, by extraordinary good chance, in that year Hay-Mackenzie's only child contracted a remarkable marriage which ultimately changed the horizons of the estate. The fact that John Hay-Mackenzie left only one child was, in terms of the previous generations, both unusual and a great saving to the estate.

19 John Hay-Mackenzie.

At the time of the French Wars the estate income had increased in parallel with the general inflation of the times, reinforced by the high bidding of big farmers for new leases. Cromartie was a middle-ranking Highland estate with perennial financial difficulties. The precise social standing of the family is difficult to gauge: it enjoyed considerable political and social patronage in Ross and Cromarty but its prestige was a pale shadow of its role in, for example, the late seventeenth century. It may have been significant that the Countess of Sutherland declined to receive the Hay-Mackenzies at Dunrobin in 1808: the families were no longer in the same league.[23] The road engineer Joseph Mitchell knew the Hay-Mackenzies in these years. 'Mr Mackenzie', wrote Mitchell in a later reminiscence, 'was an agreeable kindly man, took no great interest in country affairs, but sang a good song. His lady was cold and taciturn in manner.'[24] Mrs Hay-Mackenzie lived mainly at Newhall in the south and this was called 'their seat' though they probably summered briefly at Tarbat House.[25] Local management was left in the hands of a local agent, the longest serving being James Laing. In April 1810 Mrs Hay-Mackenzie 'conveyed all her property and the rents of the entailed estate of Cromarty [sic], in trust, for behoof of a variety of persons to whom she was at that time considerably indebted'.[26] This, of course, was a measure of the financial strain under which the estate managers laboured. Laing became answerable directly to the Trustees—a body drawn from close relatives, particularly Sir David Blair, and legal agents in Edinburgh. The Newhall connection was thereby reinforced at this time.

Under the management of James Laing (subject to the legal direction of Francis Walker in Edinburgh) a two-pronged attack was mounted on the problem of the family finances. The first was to place the income of the estate on a new footing which, for the tenantry, meant upheaval. In the west a transformation was already in process, as already described, and the small tenants were being assembled into crofting lots and sheepfarming was being extended. Rents for some of the Coigach lands were raised fivefold on the new leases. In 1813 further lands in Achiltibuie, Badenscallie and Keanachrine were being advertised as being 'especially suitable for the accommodation of sheepfarmers'. Kelp-shores and fishing were also being re-let. The chronology of these changes is significant: the Cromartie Estate was advertising lands at the end of the first great sheep and wool boom. Its plans were probably overtaken by the sudden decline of prices in 1814-16. Indeed some of the old system of landholding survived until the mid nineteenth century.[27]

The second prong of Laing's strategy was on the expenditure of the Hay-Mackenzies the success of which was probably only modest. The family was not ascetic; they continued to spend too much of their income in Edinburgh and Haddington. Their debts were of their own making, and Laing made no bones about the unwisdom of maintaining, furnishing and paying taxes on two large houses. Amongst his tasks was the provision of woodcock, grouse, cheese, onions and other produce from the Highland estate to the owners in Newhall. His main source of optimism was improving income from kelp and fishing in the west and the growth of exports southwards of barley and oats in the eastern baronies. Both were assisted by improving communications, but both depended upon the buoyancy of primary prices.[28]

Already by 1816 the precipitous fall of agricultural prices, common across the entire nation, had caused reconsideration of the prospects of any continued advance of rents on the Cromartie Estate. The estate advisors were forced to alter their leasing arrangements to take account of the rapid deflation of farmers' income. New adjustable grain rents[29] were introduced, calculated on the Fiars' prices for wheat, barley and oats. Sir David Blair advised that the adjustment should be contracted for four years only and that tenants should be bound 'strictly to a proper mode of management for that short period'. His advice was based on the assumption that prices would recover soon and that temporary alteration was all the farmers required. He also suggested that the estate provide some assistance for farm repairs, but warned against any general indemnification for improvements which he regarded as 'very troublesome and expensive'.[30] Indeed there is little evidence to suggest that the estate was heavily committed to an active programme of improvement.

It seems likely that much of the improvement that had been accomplished on the Cromartie Estate had derived from the tenants rather than the landlord. Some parts of the estate had reached the forefront of agricultural advance. In 1817 the Highland Society awarded an honorary premium to Mackenzie of Hilton for his improvement of waste ground in the Valley of Strathpeffer.[31] Some of the credit apparently, was due to Humphrey Davy. Robert Southey, in his Tour of Scotland, visited Strathpeffer in September 1819 and referred to the substantial changes in progress. A large stretch of boggy land had been recovered to great advantage though not to Davy himself:

> We entered ... upon Strathpeffer, where poor Davy persuaded the landholders to drain between 6 and 700 acres; he converted for them this extent of unprofitable marshy land into excellent growth which is a state of high cultivation, and was satisfied with five and twenty pounds for his services. Had he stipulated for a shilling or two a year upon every acre which he reclaimed, they would probably have been glad to close with him upon such terms. They ought to give him an annuity of £50 for his life.[32]

The Cromartie Trustees, meanwhile, continued to battle against depressed prices and intractable debts. In mid 1818 Mrs Hay-Mackenzie complained again that the Trust was restricting her existence to a degree which she found barely tolerable. Walker, to whom the estate was directly indebted, responded spiritedly from his office in Edinburgh. 'I am no less desirous that it should be at an end than you are', he said, 'for it has been attended with a most serious inconvenience to have had my Funds which necessarily fall under its operation, locked up for so long a period.' He continued, 'We certainly at one time had every reason to suppose that the debts would have been paid before now, but the continuance of the Trust, has been altogether owing to causes over which I had no control.' The causes over which he had no control related to the severity of the previous seasons: the near famine conditions of 1816-17 which were compounded by the collapse of cereal, cattle, and kelp[33] prices throughout the country. 'No person could have forseen the last two years the effects of which are not yet at an end, and it would have been the height of folly to have pushed the Tenants during these two years of general distress.' Mrs Hay-Mackenzie had complained about the cost of management on her estate, to which Walker retorted: 'I can only say that I have used my best endeavours to supply your Interest and to keep the Expense as moderate as possible, and I really believe that there is not an Estate in Scotland of the same Extent, where the expense of management is really so moderate as yours is'. The Trust, and the general ease of life for the Cromarties, depended ultimately on the capacity of the tenantry to yield results. Walker ventured a little optimism, 'I trust ... that things have taken a turn for the better, and if Laing [the local factor] is able to recover the arrears without being too hard upon the Tenants it will [lead] much to the extrication of your Affairs.'[34] Prices however remained stagnant through the next two decades.

The financial exigencies of the estate were both a reflection of, and in part, a cause of desperation in the tenantry already disabled by a reduction in real income which attended the post-war years. Sir David Blair as trustee had advised against proceeding to 'extremities with the tenants' since it forced them into bankruptcy.[35] But some tenants simply gave up. The pitch of competition in agriculture increased and small tenants were reduced to cottardom or migration, possibly in response to the greater efficiency of southern farmers who had entered the region.[36]

Donald Mackenzie, for example, resigned his farm at Auchterneed in February 1824, and in his bitterness told the elder Mrs Hay-Mackenzie that 'I am fully aware that had the Farm produced gold, and had been profitable to me, as it has been the reverse, for three or four years back, you would not have allowed me possess it.' He added, in irony, 'I have great pleasure in thinking that the intrinsic value of the Lands I occupy is much greater than it was when I entered into possession of them'.[37] Others, especially small tenants, found their arrears accumulated to the point where they had to beg to stay on their land. For example, a widow appealed directly to Mrs Hay-Mackenzie: 'you will have the goodness as to let me know what will be done by me as I have none to help me but I trust in the Almighty, I am affraid to be turned out of Doors every day.' Another example was John Macleod, an old, illiterate ex-soldier who owed the estate £3.18.0 and had been warned off his land in March 1824. He had already been removed from a previous holding. He found someone to write his plea: 'I have had neither horse, cow, or sheep since I was removed from Achnacall; but was always till the last two years, regular in my small rent, indeed I was only 15 or 16 years old when I first began to pay rent to your family and my predecessors have been upwards of due hundred years doing the same.' He pressed the family's reciprocal obligations further: 'Three years after my first becoming your Tenant, Col. George[38] prevailed with me to go the army and accompanied him to Gibralter, where I was wounded about forty years ago, which induced him to send me home, and how [as] soon he returned to Britain he would procure me a Pension, but his premature Death to my great misfortune prevented that.' Mrs Hay-Mackenzie indeed recognised the obligation—her annotation on the letter was categorical: 'Macleod Keanchrine went with Col. George Mackenzie, he must not be turned out.'[39]

Economic strain and anxiety about the future was not limited to the lower levels of Highland society. On the higher steps of the social pyramid advancement was equally dependent on indulgence and opportunities forged by way of family connections and then oiled by deference and marriage. This was particularly true of the younger sons of landed families. One such was John Murray who lived in Castle Leod. He was a kinsman of Mrs Hay-Mackenzie and he lacked *entré* to public life; often he lent a hand in advising on matters of estate management. In September 1819 Murray told Mrs Hay-Mackenzie that he was working on her behalf, that 'I intend that you shall be so comfortable and independent of all your tenants' that she would make Castle Leod her headquarters more often. He was about to tour Coigach 'but the expense is my dread, as they make us pay much more than in England at all the little Highland Inns.'[40]

Murray at this time was angling for a position in London and was cultivating a contact with Lord Melville and his secretary who had promised to see if he could do anything for him. He mused, 'I confess had I not seen so many affairs already passed over my head, I would have no reason to doubt the sincerity of their professions.' Mrs Hay-Mackenzie had also tried to press his case. He had become engaged:

> I only want my past rank to be among the happy married. My intended is humble in her wishes, frugal in manner of living, having been educated in the strictest economy, and pleasing in her manners, she is excellent at her needle, can make a capital pudding, and is not only a good musician as she plays well on the piano and guitar, but speaks Italian and French as well as English. She is in addition the very best tempered good hearted unaffected girl you can know, and she thinks me a perfect nonsuch, which is as it ought to be you know.[41]

Another of the same family, Patrick Murray, had made a career in Canada which had provided him with fertile opportunities to create an independent family fortune. His success in Canada helped relieve some of the problems facing the Murray-Elibank family, particularly when it was linked with the acquisition of a professional position for another son, James Murray, who had also been helped by Mrs Hay-Mackenzie. He reported in 1820: 'I conceive himself to be entitled to a grant of land not less than 5000 acres, for obtaining for Government, by purchase, for the trifling sum of £1200 in Indian goods from the store, a country on Lake Erie and Lake St Clair of 3000 square miles, this, if effected, may be of service to my Daughters.' Patrick Murray provided an instructive model for the partial extrication of families from their inter-generational financial problems. But it was not a solution adopted by the Hay-Mackenzies—while Patrick Murray colonised Canada, the Cromartie heir lived in style, travelling to Geneva at great expense, 'an occasion to see a good deal of men, manners and things'.[42]

IV

The mineral springs at Strathpeffer were often regarded as a potential object of development and a source of augmented income for the Cromartie Estate. From time to time the estate factors toyed with ideas for its promotion. The first systematic analysis of the properties of the spa waters had been published in *Philosophical Transactions* in 1772 though the Rev. Colin Mackenzie of Fodderty was commonly credited with the recognition of the reputed health-giving qualities of the spring. He is said to have erected a covered shed 'to benefit the suffering thousands' who eventually used the facilities.[43] During the time of Annexation the spa waters were already well known. In 1777 the estate factor wrote to William Barclay, Secretary of the Board of the Annexed Estates, claiming that the famous Well was 'reckoned at least equal, if not superior, to any in England. It is of infinite service to numbers in this part of the world; and I wish to God half a dozen of the Honourable Board (for pleasure only,) tried it for three weeks; they would get an appetite, a pack of good hounds, and plenty of game, goat, whey, etc.'. If they tried it they would have no doubt about the desirability of the development of the facilities. Considering these benefits it is surprising that Lord Macleod, only a few years later, chose Bath as a restorative for his own health.

The wells were located on the lands of Ardivall and country people had used the waters to cure a wide range of disorders. The publicity achieved through the Royal Society inflated the medicinal claims and also the social and geographical range of its reputation and clientele. It was, in the 1770s, reputed to be 'at least equal, if not superior, to [the waters] of Harrowgate'. The waters, it was alleged, were excellent for the digestion, improved the appetite, and offered 'a remarkable cure for scorbutic or other disorders of the blood, swellings, ulcers'. Its advocates spoke of its beneficial influence on herpes, measles and smallpox: 'some very foul faces have been quite cleared' it was claimed. It would also assist in 'curing the itch'. The water possessed a 'strong sulphurous smell' which purged the system but also 'whets the appetite and sits light on the stomach'.

In 1777 the local factor Mackenzie recorded two semi-miraculous cures, one which benefited a school teacher of Fortrose, the other a tacksman of Kincardine. Such good news created a boom for the Spa—and for five years it had 'been pretty much frequented by different ranks of people from the counties of Ross, Cromarty, Inverness, Murray and Sutherland; and last season there were some people from the town of Aberdeen'. The influx had created pressure upon accommodation at the Spa which thereby discouraged further use of the local facilities. Mackenzie felt that some form of lodging place should be built to promote the health trade. He outlined the advantages in terms which would become a theme of estate correspondence for a century to come:

> This house would not only be a great accommodation to those frequenting the well, but would be of great use to the tenants of the whole Barony of Strathpeffer. It would be the means of affording them a ready and good market during the summer and harvest seasons for what wares they have to dispose of such as butter, cheese, eggs, milk, kid, lamb, mutton and poultry; and would in general create such a circulation as to enable to pay their rents more punctually than usual, and also to rear more of the above articles than they formerly did. Nor is it improbable that in time this place might become a thriving village.

Mackenzie, in pressing the case, pointed out that 'since the forfeiture, little or rather no money at all has been laid out, or demanded, for improving this estate.' He asked for £6 to preserve the well and for authority to estimate the cost of a place for accommodation. And in 1778 the Board of the Annexed Estates empowered the factor to estimate for an inn and a village near the mineral well—'to be paid out of the rents of the said Estate', with provision for feuing (i.e. leasing) out land for a village.[44]

The spa was used considerably through the following forty years. In 1795 for instance, George Dempster reported that his friend Sandy Duncan had been drinking the waters at Strathpeffer over a period of six weeks 'for his ugly leg'. Dempster joined him 'and plied the waters assiduously and if I ailed anything it has cured me and renewed my age like the eagles'. He recommended Strathpeffer to Sir Adam Fergusson, as being superior to Harrogate, Bath, Carlsbad, Aix-La-Chappelle and Moffat.[45] Sir George Stewart Mackenzie reported in 1813 that the spa was 'much frequented by Highlanders, and by strangers', including 'women who had been disappointed in their expectations of having children'. He was concerned for the Spa on two accounts—first that it was being neglected, and second that the exercise taken by the visiting invalids was more curative than the waters.[46] Several visitors paid tribute to the attractions of Strathpeffer. The itinerant poet Robert Southey in 1819, for instance, recorded that 'about three miles from the town [of Dingwall] is a mineral spring in such repute that a neat house has lately been erected over it, and the Landlady at Dingwall says her house is frequently filled with persons who come to drink the water.'[47] Hugh Miller, the radical geologist and churchman, spent part of his formative years in the district and remembered it with great affection:

> Strathpeffer, one of the finest valleys in this part of the country, lies within five miles of Conan-side. My walks occasionally extended to it, and I still retain a vividly pleasing recollection of its enchanting scenery, with the more pleasing features of the scenes through which I passed on my way to it. There is in the vicinity a beautiful little lake, which contains a wooded island. Along the banks of this lake I have sauntered for whole hours, and from the green top of Knockfarrel, one of the hills by which the valley is bounded, I have seen the sun sink behind Ben Wyvis, without once thinking that I was five miles from my place of residence.[48]

The Inverness Courier carried occasional items about the Spa, and in 1818 it was happy to report that 'The Strathpeffer Wells have a much gayer and more numerous attendance this season than ever they had before', and expressed the hope that facilities would be given for feuing in the village.[49] In 1819 it was glad to note that a handsome Pump room had been erected by Mrs Hay-Mackenzie for the accommodation of ladies and gentlemen. The reputation of the Spa was yearly increasing and was likely to become 'a place of fashionable and beneficial resort', but the village was in visible need of a hotel.[50] The new Pump Room had been built by the Cromartie Estate for £300 on borrowed money. The immediate effect on custom and demand was disappointing—sales of fruit at the Room were poor in 1819 and other arrangements had to be made for the disposal of local produce.[51]

James Murray strongly argued against the idea of feuing out small plots of land for the creation of a resident village. In so doing he touched the problem of how the Spa was to attract the highest class of visitor while maximising the income of the Spa. At bottom it was a question of social exclusivity. Murray was in no doubts about the prospect: 'I am of opinion, that by giving feus for 99 years you will for the annual additional income of £150 or 100, create a Petty republic of Poachers, drunkards, thieves and vagabonds of both sexes in the centre of this the finest part of your property.' There was a precedent for such damage—the southern Scottish spa town of Moffat had 'been created within these forty years and the morality of its inhabitants is Proverbial as a Nest of Idle Vagabonds it is the Pest of the Country and has cost Lord Hopetoun more trouble than the value of ten times the revenue arising from it, nearer home Milntown is no bad specimen of having Independence so near your Doors'. If short feus were allocated people would be able to build cottages or fine houses for permanent residences which would detract from the aesthetic qualities of Castle Leod:

> And if a rich merchant lives there, he will of course have sauce in spite of you, if he wishes it, and the Profession of Poachers will be a profitable one, and when once established you will find you have not the power to root them out, and if Castle Leod once becomes the residence of any of your family, you will find twenty Castle Leods within a half a mile of it, and any one of those will be as well supplied, tho' at a lower rate, with game, and this for an additional £100 per annum.[52]

Poaching and undesirable merchant rivals were powerful counterbalances to the development of the village of Strathpeffer and its medical and tourist potential.

The development of the Spa was, therefore, restrained by the restrictive outlook of the Hay-Mackenzies and by their poor access to capital for building. They had delegated the management of the waters to 'a respectable servant man ... who conducts the business of the place with much decorum'. The reputation of the Spa was ascendant but, as the Inverness Courier observed in June 1819:

> nothing is now wanting to render the delightful valley of Strathpeffer a place of fashionable and beneficial resort but a few neat cottages to accommodate invalids, and a hotel or boarding-house which would perhaps better answer the purpose of fashionable visitors.[53]

From their dealings with the Spa and its future it is clear that the Hay-Mackenzies held precise views about the need for an ordered and stable society in which its own place was established. Murray could be confident that his views on the 'Radicalism' in the south of Scotland and in England in 1819 would find receptive ears among the Hay-Mackenzies. On the passing of the Six Acts, Murray wrote,

> I hope and trust that the vigorous steps the Government has taken, will stop the Radicals and all Turbulent rascals in their career of wickedness. It makes one's Blood Boil with Indignation to think that a few unprincipled and Brazen faced Blackguards should have been able to carry things to the length they have, that a whole country should have been thrown into a state of ferment by such fellows as Hunt, Cobbett and Co.

Murray was able to reassure Mrs Hay-Mackenzie (in Edinburgh) that her northerly country was free from radicalism: 'The Country is quiet, and only know such things are, by report, and I fancy even little by report.' Two years later Strathpeffer and Castle Leod were within ten miles of the most spectacular anti-clearance riots of the half century, at Culrain. But mostly the north was quiet.[54]

While radicalism was anathema in the country-house circles, the stoic and peaceful acceptance of poverty and distress by the lower orders was regarded as estimable and worthy of support and sympathy. Hence the reaction of Georgina Ann Hay-Mackenzie, wife of the Earl of Glasgow, to the problems of the Paisley weavers in 1826: 'It is terrible the distress in Paisley at present for want of work, they say there are about 1000 weavers out of work there has been a meeting about them and a subscription set going for them. Lord G. sent £100. I hope they may get work soon at all events they ought to be encouraged they are behaving so well poor creatures and are perfectly quiet.'[55]

V

Notions of deference and place in Highland society were generally clearly established, but in matters of religion there was greater ambiguity. Tension and dispute were compounded by the circulation of new theological currents through the north at the end of the eighteenth century.[56] Although the Cromartie family had in its gift the appointment of ministers in several parishes, there was a general convention that the minister, in an unspecified degree, should be also acceptable to the parishioners. Thus, within the framework of traditional practice, there was scope for the expression of popular preference sometimes in defiance of the landlords. The induction of ministers in Scotland was a common source of riotous behaviour in the eighteenth century. It was an area of social life in which landlords had been unable to establish total control: indeed the appointment of ministers was fraught with potential conflict for any landlord less than flexible in his or her views. During her brief tenure of the Cromartie estate, from 1796 to 1801, Lady Elibank had tried to re-establish ancient family rights of patronage over fourteen parishes. This generated great hostility, not only among the parishioners, but also among other landowners. Evictions and inductions were the two great sources of riot in the Highlands and some form of social protest was a predictable outcome of any such unpopular event. Recent events in both Sutherland and Ross offered serious warning to landlords in the exercise of their rights.[57]

In this sense, therefore, popular reaction set a limit to landlord authority which the rulers could transgress only at the risk of considerable unpleasantness. Church patronage was an explosive issue in the social life of the Highlands. Eventually, in 1843, the whole question split the Church—in Easter Ross during the Disruption all the members of the Tain Presbytery (with one exception) joined the secession. The Hay-Mackenzie family itself was faced with a deserted church.[58] Mrs Hay-Mackenzie had been tenacious in her hold of church patronage. For an interminable time she had fought the Crown over the right of presentation at Kiltearn. Eventually the question had been brought before the Court of Session and the House of Lords—and won the contest in the latter place in July 1814. The battle lasted for eight years during which period the financial savings from the vacancy were used to support a catechist.[59]

In the decades before the Disruption, the family's patronage remained intact, and the Hay-Mackenzies were involved repeatedly in disputes from this source. On one occasion for example, in 1816, the new minister in Lochbroom complained vehemently of the 'intolerable molestation' he received from his parishioners and the lack of support from the heritors. John Macleod, who had been presented at Lochbroom by Hay-Mackenzie, 'was so disappointed with the congregation that he returned his presentation'. On another occasion Francis Walker, the family's legal advisor and creditor, asked Sir David Blair for assistance to his brother for election to the office of Procurator for the Church: 'I hope you will forgive me for requesting of you to ask Mrs Mackenzie to use her extensive Church Patronage in favour of James.' In this case Walker was concerned that unnamed and extraneous political pressures were being excited against the normal operation of the Hay-Mackenzie influence—and, indeed, a queue of rival candidates formed, all seeking patronage.[60]

In 1820 a vacancy arose in the church at Alness which, though not within the

Cromartie Estate, was subject to the Hay-Mackenzie patronage. The landowner, Munro of Novar, wrote to Mrs Hay-Mackenzie outlining the situation. He had received a deputation of the heads of families in the parish who had already delivered a petition to Mrs Hay-Mackenzie. The petition named 'three clergymen for your choice, any one of whom would afford them peculiar satisfaction'. Novar then alluded to the distracted state of feeling in Kiltearn parish arising from an unpopular clergyman—at Kiltearn the minister was effectively boycotted, often attended by a congregation of less than a dozen people. He also referred ominously to the Culrain riot on his own estate, precipitated by a particularly insensitive eviction in that year. In the light of these circumstances, and knowing 'the great influence which a clergyman, who possesses the confidence of the people, would have in checking' such turbulence, Novar advised his neighbour to agree to the petition, i.e., 'the people's choice'. Novar indeed equated popular resistance with immorality, and evidently believed that clergymen could be expected to perform a pacifying function in the Highlands.[61]

Tension about the Alness case continued through April 1820. There was delicate diplomacy but there was also a clearly understood threat of physical resistance. One of the contenders wrote to Mrs Hay-Mackenzie that he was confident that she would not choose 'a Pastor who will be unacceptable and consequently unprofitable to the People'.[62] A John Macdonald advised that though it was imperative that the parish be supplied with 'a pure and faithful gospel ministry' it was equally vital to avoid a 'violent settlement'. He advised Mrs Hay-Mackenzie against any 'unacceptable' candidate, being anyone 'whose evangelical principles and genuine feeling' left reason for serious doubt. The attraction of Macdonald's own choice—Hector Allan—was that he could promise 'a comfortable settlement'. Another candidate wrote to Mrs Hay-Mackenzie requesting support because his current patroness had treated him insensitively:

> Lady Mary Ross has never paid any regard to my petition for additional accommodation to my family; my highland pride is such that I shall not again supplicate her Ladyship, whatever I may endure ... To your disinterested goodness, dearest Lady, I owe my advancement in my profession ... and it is to you that I look for supporting me at present.[63]

The Alness contest exposed the many lines of contemporary deference and patronage in the social fabric, especially since it was set against the background of landlord anxiety during the Culrain eviction crisis. Everyone knew that ministerial appointments such as this were commonly suspected of political corruption and favouritism. 'When men devoid of principle get into orders', warned one of Mrs Hay-Mackenzie's correspondents,

> they connect themselves in friendship and intercourse with town magistrates and county freeholders so that especially crown presentations are often lamentably made a political job of, to the great detriment of the country, and the subversion of that mutual confidence and attachment which should exist between the people and the government.

He added quickly,

> I rejoice to hear that this is not the case with you and that you are resolved only to patronise pious and evangelical young men who will be acceptable, zealous and useful, this determination is most important to Ross-shire.[64]

In the outcome Mrs Hay-Mackenzie chose a man who, though not the first choice of the people, was thought to be generally acceptable. This was candidate Flyter whose success was not announced for several months. He had the advantage of being a man of Ross and the people were told that in this choice Mrs Hay-Mackenzie had 'every occasion to believe will be acceptable to them ... This possibly may keep them quiet.' The whole business was hazardous and Mrs Hay-Mackenzie's advisor remarked, 'It was long since represented by Solomon, that wealth and power had almost as many vexations attending them as comforts.'[65] Novar reiterated that 'it is of the greatest consequence that the people should be satisfied with their clergyman.'[66] The possibility of an 'obnoxious' person was enough to make the people (and heritors) close ranks. Fortunately for the Cromartie family Flyter was acceptable and there were few qualms about his induction in October 1820: 'The settlement promises to be very agreeable and the people will receive their new minister with open arms.' An eyewitness of the induction reported:

> I was never present at a more impressive and interesting scene. The Gaelic sermon was preached without to a Crowd which no Church here [Inverness] could contain. The English sermon was preached in the Church to the most respectable and most crowded congregation I ever saw in Ross-shire—all the residing Heritors of Alness, the residing heritors and tacksmen of Kiltearn and Rosskeen with many gentlemen and ministers from great distances.[67]

The tension surrounding the settlement at Alness was not uncommon. At much the same time a similar competition occurred at Kincardine where the people 'were foolishly averse to Mr Allan's settlement among them.'[68] These parishes, it should be said, were at the centre of a long tradition of evangelicalism in the Highlands and were well known for their rowdy disputes on theological and other questions. An awkward convention pitted the independence of the parishioners against proprietorial patronage. This independence was guarded with communal solidarity and strengthened through the years leading towards the Disruption. The Disruption itself, of course, focussed these tensions perfectly. The energy of the dissident clergy was seen in the life of George McLeod, admitted to the Free Church at Lochbroom in the year of the Disruption, 1843, who was said to have travelled some 9000 miles, mainly in an open boat, in pursuit of his ministry. Moreover the tradition of congregational independence lived on. In July 1857 the Free Church minister at Fodderty claimed he and his flock were suffering discrimination over the question of preaching rights at Strathpeffer Spa, and three years later there was successful resistance to the placement of a minister at nearby Urray.[69]

VI

It is not entirely clear how far the Hay-Mackenzies were able or prepared to maintain the full extent of their position and status in Highland society. Their perilous financial position eventually forced a considerable retreat in the 1820s[70] and the same problem caused them to press their tenantry more stringently than they sometimes wished. But the yield of rental, though vital, was not allowed to become the exclusive consideration for the Hay-Mackenzies. For instance they put great store by game and the sport attached to it. Much of their correspondence was devoted to details of the despatch of grouse, woodcock, and other edibles to Newhall and elsewhere. John Hay-Mackenzie was a sporting man who, when in England (according to his mother) found 'plenty of fox hunting which he does not find easy to resist'. Fannich, the inland wilderness on the Cromartie estate, was prized for its ptarmigan, and perhaps not much else. In August 1815 the Inverness Courier announced that 'The Hon. Mrs Hay-Mackenzie, being desirous to give the game a jubilee on her estates in Coigach, Strathpeffer, and New Tarbat, in the County of Cromarty, requests no gentleman will ask leave to shoot there this season.'[71] Some of the owner's angriest words were directed at a gamekeeper. 'He is a simpleton, a coward, and moves like an Elephant, whereas the preservation of those woods requires an active and a resolute man', said Murray to his patroness, though he absolved the agent from blame—Laing was 'a most worthy good man, and one who really wishes to act up to your interest'. When a farm came up for leasing in September, Laing gave full weight to the consideration of sport. It was a farm for which he was 'not prepared to say whether Black Cattle, or sheep, will be the most proper stock for it, keeping it in view the preservation of the game, but that will be taken into consideration before letting it, you may be sure that nothing will be done without your knowledge and approbation.'[72] The importance of sporting rights for rental income increased greatly by the mid-century.

But the general thrust of leasing policy was unambiguous. Land was to be rented out without sentiment with the object of seeking the best tenants, preferably with a good capital backing, paying the best rents. Murray was glad to report in October 1819 that: 'The grazings of Knockfarrel, Balmillich, and Forester's croft will be set at Whitsunday of their real values, at least double their Present rent. I told the Major that they were to be valued, as the Present rent is far beneath their actual worth. I know he will pay their value rather than part with them although he affects to hold them cheap.'[73] A candidate for the tenancy of the big Meddat Farm had two disqualifications. As a legal adviser explained, 'I should be apprehensive that he has no sufficient capital for such a farm, but he assures me that he has about £1200 which he says will be sufficient'. This alone provides an index of the costs of entry into the newly modernised agriculture of Easter Ross and of Cromarty—it excluded from the most productive and lucrative agriculture the overwhelming majority of the indigenous population. The same point was even more true of the new sheep farmers. The Meddat contender had another disadvantage as Francis Walker explained:

> I believe he is a respectable man in his station, but I have great doubts how far it may be prudent to let a Farm to one so nearly connected with your Factor, and where it is hardly possible to suppose that some partialities may not be occasionally shewn him which would not be shewn to a stranger.[74]

Factorial nepotism was always a danger in Highland estate management and added to the problem occasioned by the fact that many factors held farms of their own. The estate appears to have taken a rigid line on rents despite the sudden fall of agricultural income; one man who asked for a reduction was told that 'his rent was fixed at 25/- per acre by his lease and that I [the factor] had no power to give him any deduction'.[75]

The most ominous and disturbing event of the immediate post war years was the eruption of resistance and violence to large and ill-managed clearances on the neighbouring Culrain estate in Easter Ross.[76] This was executed by Hugh Munro, the 'young and rakish laird of Novar'. About 600 people were involved in Strath Oykel. In February 1820 attempts were made to secure Writs of Removal to quit at Whitsunday. After the episode the minister was roundly abused for the sympathy he showed the people. The minister, in fact, wrote to Mrs Hay-Mackenzie about his conduct during the highly publicised events. He wrote: 'I am happy that you signify your approbation of my conduct ... The attack made upon me by the Sheriff was unmerited—and in vindication of myself, I have been forced to reply to it.' He continued:

> Nothing final in the way of arrangement has yet taken place for the Culrain people but I trust they shall not be removed this year. I am defending them before the Sheriff Court—and for a year at least—I expect to keep them in. The removal of so large a population in such circumstances—able and willing to pay a larger rent than the Incoming Tenant, and not a penny in arrears—is as impolitic as it is inhuman. All who know your character, Madam, are convinced that no consideration would induce you to committ such an outrage on humanity—600 souls to be turned adrift without a cot provided to shelter them.[77]

These comments reinforce the probability that the Cromartie Estate itself was not involved in large-scale evictions to be compared with the Culrain events. Nevertheless there is unambiguous evidence that the estate eased many of the common people off most of the best land on the estate, and thereby released such territory to the larger farmers. The Culrain episode was notorious because of its haste and its violence, and for the fact that Novar made no provision for the accommodation of the people dispossessed. Cromartie was lucky to escape real trouble and yet, though its policy was gentler and more gradual, there were undoubtedly casualties, few of whose voices entered the surviving record.

CHAPTER 13

Economic Malaise, Above and Below

The accumulation of debt and the narrowing circumstances of the post war years placed the Cromartie family perilously close to that widening category of Highland lairds who were forced off their lands in this period. The rapid turnover of land after Waterloo[1] saw the end of many ancient families (for instance the Reay family, Bighouse and others) who were swallowed up by families which could draw upon wealth from beyond the Highlands. The Cromartie family managed to cling on although it lost some of its prestige and its land in the process. The finances of the estate were never comfortable, despite the greatly inflated rental; the difficulties that recurred almost endlessly were consequent upon the commitments of income made to dependent relatives, and the level of consumption of the incumbents of the estate. The responsibility for the parlous state of the finances rested on the shoulders of the owners, rather than on the producers on the estate.

I

The Cromartie finances deteriorated to such an extent that bold measures were taken to shore up the estate in January 1820. A new and more vigorous Trust was established and one of the trustees, Charles Selkrig (an Edinburgh accountant) pronounced the collective determination to Francis Walker who had (and continued) to bear most of the credit burdens for the estate. Walker had extended credit to the Cromartie estate which, he claimed, repeatedly threatened his own destruction. Selkrig told him:

> It is essentially necessary that they [the accounts] be examined and everything put on a distinct and regular footing, before I commence operations under the new Trust, and especially before I proceed to make a distribution of the fund now divisible. But you may depend upon it, that no undue delay shall take place in accomplishing the object which Mrs Hay Mackenzie is very anxious about.[2]

Debts of more than £2000 owed to Mrs Hay-Mackenzie's sister had been accumulated, and a third of this was paid off, possibly by the calling up of assets in England.[3] Other debts however continued to grow and in October 1821 Walker pointed out that Mrs Hay-Mackenzie owed £5309 'exclusive of interest, law charges, commission etc.' Her son was attempting at that time to raise on bond a figure of £4000 but the bond was difficult to prove and Walker was adamant that 'it was impossible for me to advance any more money unless I receive this bond.'⁴ Little relief could be expected from other relatives, most of whom appear to have been in similarly impecunious circumstances—Lord Elibank was in difficulty for the payment of annuities, while some of the Murrays migrated to Canada to improve their prospects.⁵ Mrs Hay-Mackenzie's daughter married Lord Kelburne (later Earl of Glasgow) who had the advantage of an unentailed estate worth £60,000.

It is not known how far the entail on the Cromartie Estates restricted the sale of property to meet the tangled debts of the family, but some of the assets were reasonably liquid. It became necessary to make financial provision for the heir, John Hay-Mackenzie, who was approaching adulthood. Eventually his personal needs prompted the sale of estate assets which, in the long run, could only weaken the place of the family in northern society. John Hay-Mackenzie came of age in 1823 and his mother conveyed the fee of Cromartie Estate to him in that year and in 1828. Young Hay-Mackenzie however conducted a style of living which placed further strain on the rental income. He overspent his income at an alarming rate. Walker was agitated. The new incumbent consumed all the income from Newhall and created further debts as well. Walker, in his alarm, wrote to Mrs Hay-Mackenzie about her son:

> From the whole of Newhall rents having been paid to him [Hay-Mackenzie] for the last year, and from his having drawn his allowance as usual here, his balance was increased £1500 independent of what is due upon the amounts which were received when he came of age. This is so very serious a sum that I wrote to him in what manner he proposed to liquidate it, and to state that I presumed he was in future to provide for all the charges upon the Newhall Estates, such as the payments to you, and the public burdens etc.

Mrs Hay-Mackenzie herself owed about £1500 and Walker believed that he could no longer allow any extension 'without some arrangements being made for their gradual reduction'—the advances were so inconvenient 'as to hamper my business with my other clients .... I hope your son will see the propriety of not drawing upon me again.'⁶

John Hay-Mackenzie, often somewhat insouciant in such matters, expressed distress and surprise when Walker told him of the gravity of the financial plight of the family. Walker was in no mood to temporise and, in effect, told the heir that he had been negligent and extravagant and that the whole problem had been brought to his attention many times. Walker virtually accused Hay-Mackenzie of deceit in getting Tarbat rents paid directly to himself without telling the Trustees—he was being utterly irresponsible and foolish. Walker's tone became very firm: 'If you will excuse the advice of an old friend, I would earnestly recommend, when your leisure permits, after the shooting season is over, that you should come to Town, when we will look over matters, and see what can be done in this extremity.'⁷

Walker's judgement was that the estate finances were in a condition of 'emergency', and 'a very awkward predicament'.⁸ His analysis of the accounts left no room for doubt. Between them, Mrs Hay-Mackenzie and her son extracted from the Newhall estate a sum greater than the net income—there was indeed an annual deficit of about £127. Mrs Hay-Mackenzie drew from Newhall and Cromartie £1430 p.a. and gave her son

£400 of it. Walker's consideration of rental income gave an accurate indication of the effect of the post war deflation. Over the period 1817 to 1823 the average income from the Cromartie estate had been £3332 per annum, but taking the first three years of the new period gave an average yield of £3966; of the second triennium it was £2698—a fact of life which added great urgency to 'the present emergency'.

From the Cromartie Estate rental certain payments were deducted, on an annual basis:

Mrs Hay-Mackenzie	800
Duchess of Athol	600
Mrs Hunter	110
Royston's heirs	165
Lady Hunter Blair	100
Mr Buckle	100
Mrs Major Mackenzie	10
Premiums in Insurancing + fine	20
	£1906

Thus, after provisioning for the pensioners on the estate, and without any consideration for the maintenance of the capital stock of the estate, only £793 remained out of an average rental of £3332. Of this £450 departed for feu duty of £450 p.a., which left for 'incidental payments and expense of management' a trifling £343.1.0. At Newhall the position was worse still. Its rental came to £774; its annual charge £725 and its interest payments £182—leaving a deficit of £127 p.a. It was an extremely unhealthy set of figures on any reckoning. It led Walker to suggest the necessity of selling off property, or else obtaining a loan on the security of the Tain Acres.[9]

By 1824 it was evident to all concerned—heritors, creditors and trustees—that the debts could not be extended any further and that definitive action was inescapable. The debts would have to be curtailed. In August 1823 the total debt came to £13,500. Various alternatives were considered—the sale of the Tain acres, a new loan at 4%, or a loan 'by way of redeemable annuity'.[10] The man most exercised by the circumstances was the greatest creditor of the family—the estate owed Francis Walker £10,000 by July 1824. As he kept saying, he had no security for this amount 'except what is afforded for a part of it only, by a Trust deed'. His associates pointed out that a stop would have to be made. Mrs Hay-Mackenzie was told:

> By the heavy advances which we have made for your family we think we have given substantial proofs of our anxiety to serve every member of it; and it was with very sincere regret we found ourselves under the necessity of hesitating to pay the draft which you last made.

It was, of course, a moment of crisis—there would be no more credit.

> We believe you will find in our correspondence distinct notice that we could come under no further advance till the accounts were settled and arrangements made for the liquidation of the balances due to us .... the magnitude of the aggregate balance is such as to justify in the fullest manner the propriety of our refusing a farther advance.

Walker had now reached a position of determination—he must have security for his money. 'My advances have been very heavy for 15 years, and of course the loss I have sustained by having my money locked up for so long a period has been very great.' He suggested that relatives should be asked for assistance. The Tweeddales offered no hope at all; Sir David Blair, he noted, 'is both wealthy and prudent ... his estates are not entailed'—but he was under no formal obligation to help even though a Trustee of the Estate. Blair's advice was to sell off the Tain Acres and the Conan Fishing. The problem with this advice was twofold—the fishing was the subject of a complex dispute which had reached Parliament, and the two assets together were, anyway, worth less than £7000. Walker complained to Lord Tweeddale that Mrs Hay-Mackenzie kept avoiding the whole unpleasant subject.[11] Over and over again Walker told her of the strain: 'These advances', he wrote yet again in February 1825, 'to which I was often called upon to make to prevent legal steps being adopted, have often been the cause of considerable anxiety to me, and latterly of my considerable pecuniary loss.'[12]

The financial devastation had reached a point where a sale of assets was inescapable.[13] The Conan Fishing case reached the courts in 1825. The Cromartie Estate lost and, in the process, incurred heavy legal costs.[14] In addition to the Tain acres and the fishing rights there was the possibility of selling off the political patronage which continued to rest in the gift of the Cromartie heirs. It was undoubtedly a painful prospect since political influence was an index of social rank and esteem: its erosion or removal entailed a diminution of standing. Lord Macleod's rescue of the estate in the 1780s had been associated with a full restoration of the political clout of the family—there had been a symbolic return of the heritor to his full social, economic and political place in society. The first Earl of Cromartie on the eve of the Union had been one of the great political managers of his day. The prospect of the sale of the family influence was, therefore, a telling matter in the decline of the family. The creditors of the Hay-Mackenzies strongly encouraged the move, preferably in advance of an election:

> I would say that if your mother were to sell her spare superiorities, which are of no use to her—and which would fetch a better price now than after the Election, and likewise her Church patronage to Government, she would realise, for what is a mere name or shadow, a good tangible sum exceeding I should think, £20,000.[15]

The political influence was said to be worth £500 or guineas per vote. In the very week that she received encouragement of this sort, Mrs Hay-Mackenzie was given a timely indication of the tangible reality of her political influence. A candidate wrote asking for her support in the election, which he judged to be crucial for his success, having been surprised by the sudden development of opposition. He wrote:

> I do not wish to disturb the country with a canvass knowing as I do, it always evokes an unpleasant feeling, indeed I was so advised by my agent, as there was no hostility making its appearance, not to disturb the County; but no sooner was my back turned southward than an active and actual canvass commenced against me, back in the North and South.[16]

The pressures on the family were too great and it seems that the superiority was sold off and, if the agent's advice was accepted, the price was 'at the rate of five hundred pounds or guineas for a vote.'[17] Only part of the influence was sold. But the Hay-Mackenzies, 'Keen Tories' as they were described in 1842,[18] retained a substantial though indirect role in local politics. Their financial difficulties were also relieved by the negotiation of further loans on the security of its property in Tain and on the Conan fishing. The estate therefore remained heavily burdened with debt.[19]

This endless theme in the Cromartie story was reflected in the details of the life of the estate and its administration. For instance the pressing request for the provision of a new church in Lochbroom (where a population of 2400 had seats for only 300) was turned down. It would cost £1500 which was not possible.[20] Tenants fell into arrear and were forced off their lands. Typical was Robert Mackenzie of Leckmeln who was well behind in his rent payments and was waiting on the Inverness market for the sale of his stock. He found it difficult to believe that he would be evicted: 'I have paid many thousands pounds rent to Mrs Mackenzie' he told the factor,

> and it is not natural to suppose that either me or my family should now wish to remove unless we are forced to do so ... If a better tenant is not had for the place I will be glad to enter into equitable terms regarding it upon a new lease for five or seven years and pay my arrears by annual installments taking off the deductions formerly promised me.

He was one of the many tenants the terms of whose leases had not been adjusted to take into account the sharp deflation of prices and monies that had occurred since 1813.[21] At another level was Murdo Mackenzie of the Heights of Dochcarty—a cottar who had been given a plot of unimproved moor in 1798—'it was but a small piece of moor when I entered the same and was charged no rent for a number of years, but afterwards had to pay 26/-.' He had become a cripple and needed help after a life of improvement labour.[22] And still less secure was widow Mary Forbes who pleaded to Mrs Hay-Mackenzie: 'you will have the goodness as to let me know what will be done by me as I have none to help me but I trust in the Almighty, I am afraid to be turned out of doors every day'.[23] Begging letters were universal in estate correspondence: the ability to respond in the 1820s was restricted by the diminished income of the estate and by the financial needs of the Hay-Mackenzies themselves.

II

The rental of the estate, of course, ultimately depended on the disposition of the landed resources and the prices commanded by its tradeable surpluses. Changes in the allocation of land may be traced back almost indefinitely but there was a more radical shift from the 1780s. This had continued through the turn of the century but the precise extent and chronology is only poorly recorded. In the years 1825 to 1840 further consolidation in the new pattern of land use was achieved, i.e. the re-allocation of the best grazing and arable land to large commercial producers, and the restriction of the majority of the people to small lots or crofts on relatively marginal land, usually on the coast or on hillsides in the interior (as at Strathpeffer). This fundamental division had been in creation from the mid eighteenth century—the pattern was not, in any case, totally divorced from the pre-1745 arrangements. In the Cromartie case the change seems to have been engineered quietly and very gradually. Sometimes the change was not pressed to its fullest form—semi-clearances were possible whereby, perhaps, the lion's share of the pasture land was consolidated into one block, leaving substantial areas in the hands of the people. The existence of most of the older forms in parts of Coigach in 1850-3 testifies to the uneven and slow progression of the clearance system. It may also be emphasised that much of the reallocation of land was probably executed by the tacksmen in pursuit of their own interests. Under the system of tacks—still prevalent into the nineteenth century—the tacksmen sublet their lands virtually as they pleased, paying the aggregated rent to the landlord but collecting from their subtenants. Thus, when the landlord took over the land directly he may have found a crofter system already entrenched on the estate. By the turn of the century it would have been in the tacksmen's interest to devote much of the land to sheep farming.

In the 1820s and 1830s there was almost certainly an acceleration of the creation of a crofting system on the Cromartie estate. The creation of lots was not necessarily synonymous with a reduction of land available to the people—it certainly divided the older communal land into individual lots but there may have been no net reduction of land to the people as a whole. There is evidence that subtenants were made direct tenants progressively through the second quarter of the century, and that 'lotting of townships' proceeded *pari passu*. In 1829 Altnacraig was lotted and its rents were much the same for the following fifty years; so was Achnahaird; Altandhu was lotted in 1831 with 15 lotters paying £39.10.0; so was Canniscoil; Polbain was lotted as late as 1848 with 19 tenants paying £49.5.0; before 1848 Polbain township had been let to a tenant with the power to sublet. Isle Martin was lotted in 1831; Achindrean was lotted 'about 1828'; Isle Tanera 1846, Polglass in 1829, Keanchrine in 1825, Strathan 1829, Rhive 1829, Achanduart 1829, Achlachan 1829. What is striking about the rental evidence is the general equality of holdings among the lotters—a point which may have given the crofting community a basic sense of social cohesion, and a reduction of individualistic rivalry.[24]

Since the changes of the 1820s and 1830s were poorly accounted even in the estate records, the recollection of the re-organisation of land holdings became, later in the century, a matter of contention and public dispute. The crofters, in evidence before Lord Napier's Crofter Commission in 1884-5, made many indignant complaints of earlier evictions which were squarely rejected by the estate management of the day. Yet when, at that time, the estate officials tried to trace the history of land allocations on the Cromartie estate they were generally unsuccessful. In another search, in 1894, an agent turned up a document which demonstrated that Langwell had been reorganised in 1826. It also showed that the crofters were given at that time 'a [valuable] piece of hill ground taken from the crofters in the Coigach District—this doubtless having been done in order to put this township on the same satisfactory footing as their neighbours with regard to outrun.'[25] It suggests further that, when the sheepfarms were carved out of the old cattle lands, a certain degree of quid pro quo, even compromise, had attended the transformation.

III

The financial difficulties of the Cromartie estate, and other struggling Highland estates, were not well concealed. There was, moreover, a large predator at work in the northern Highlands, the imperial force of the great Sutherland estate. This estate, the property of the Marquis of Stafford and his wife, the Countess of Sutherland, was immensely wealthy. Its reserves were not the result of Highland enterprise: the Sutherland Estate was swollen with the profits of English canals and railways and its owners had already swallowed large stretches of Highland territory belonging previously to impecunious lesser lairds. It was like a great pike in a pool of lethargic smaller fish. In 1833 the Sutherland estate turned its greedy gaze on Easter Ross, in particular to the peninsula of Tarbatness where the Cromartie estate used to own extensive lands. The Sutherland estate dispatched an agent, George Taylor, to take a confidential assessment of the economic possibilities of the peninsula with a view to purchase by the Marquis of Stafford, very soon to become first Duke of Sutherland.

Taylor did most of his travelling by land and discovered that there were already rumours of the Sutherland interest in the locality. He travelled at an immensely hazardous time since cholera had recently reached the north. It was particularly virulent in Easter Ross: at Tain it was said to account for the decrease of the parish population between 1831 and 1836, while in the village of Inver 'above a third of the inhabitants were swept off in a few weeks' by the 'ravages' of the disease. Indeed in the following year the outbreaks proved worse and exposed the pitifully small medical provisions in the country, especially in the west. When cholera broke out in Coigach there was simply no doctor there to receive either instructions or medications. In the entire county of Ross and Cromarty, a region renowned for its dispersed population, there was only one medical officer per thousand people.

Taylor was not well accommodated during his tour of inspection. He spent a night at Portmahomack where the landlady had put him in 'a bed in which three Cholera patients died—a father and two children'. He accomplished his report 'by walking over the country, which was but child's play after Coigach'. His report was heavy with agricultural detail and demonstrated a closely calculating approach to the entire question of estate ownership. Taylor thought the filthiness of Portmahomack accounted for the recent incidence of the cholera[26]—but all could be remedied by improvement expenditure to become 'a fishing and trading place of some importance'. It was a country overstocked with poor people; it had two ruined castles, commanding a view of the Sutherland coast. Taylor noted that the local people had virtually no knowledge of the history of the district. He remarked:

> The total extinction of every recollection of the former history or traditions of these Strong holds among the Natives, and their complete apathy as to these matters formed a strong contrast to the prevalence of old traditionary core, as it even now exists, in other districts of the North. Is it probable that the repeated changes of property, and the parcelling out of the land among several small Proprietors, as has been the case, in this part of Ross-shire, has had the effect of banishing from the mind of the people all recollection of the old proprietors? Or has the abundance of Peats and Moss Fir in the more Highland districts, which enable the people of every Township to congregate during the long winter nights

20 Ballone, one of 'two ruined castles' which George Taylor saw 'commanding a view of the Sutherland coast'.

around large fires—had an influence in perpetuating tales of former times among them? It is on such occasions that the Sutherland small Tenants look over all subjects that interest them; but in Tarbat, before coal was introduced, a cheerful evening fire must have been almost unknown among the Cotters.

Taylor regarded most of the land as well improved; much that was beautiful and reminiscent of England. He noted the commercialism of the tenant farmers and their total dependence on the price of wheat; moreover their straw production could complement the Sutherland estate which was deficient in that respect. In conjunction with the other Sutherland estates including the recent acquisition of the Highland portions of the parish of Rosskeen, Tarbatness would 'be a most desirable and [rounding?] in this quarter to the Dukedom'—especially since it could be seen from Dunrobin Castle.

Taylor was less than complimentary about the ordinary people of Easter Ross against whom he made tendentious contrasts with those of Sutherland. In Easter Ross the small tenants seemed to have little ambition directed to their improvement,

and they have a prejudice against all changes, however beneficial for themselves, in their domestic or rural affairs. The Ross-shire Peasant is also more boorish—or less acquainted with all matters that do not concern himself directly than his Sutherland neighbour, and I have often been told in Ross-shire by the Country people, upon asking who lived at the neighbouring large Farm, that they did not know. They are however plodding, and, I think, industrious people—generally well behaved and moral in their conduct, and religiously inclined, having, if any fault in this respect, too intolerant and uncompromising a spirit in religious matters.

He was also impressed with the efforts they put into collecting seaweed for their pasture land—which he pointed out was inferior to that of the larger farms. He reckoned Ardivall unsuitable because too many people were settled on poor land 'and the consequent low rate of rent to be obtained'. He continued, 'connected with this is the disagreeable feeling to a Proprietor like the Duke of having so many more than ordinarily poor Tenants located on a miserable piece of ground, without the prospect that they will be able of themselves to improve their condition.' The congestion of population was a distinct disadvantage. But, Taylor pointed out, if the Duke invested heavily in the improvement, 'the consequent prosperity of a numerous group of small Tenants, under such unpromising circumstances, would give an immense *éclat* to the Duke's management in that part of Ross-shire, and would secure golden opinions from the whole class of cottagers, and the public throughout the Country.'[27]

A second report was drawn up by another of the Sutherland agents, Smith. He calculated that there were six likely estates in Tarbatness equal in all to about 6500 acres. Evidently the view from Dunrobin Castle was an important consideration—the Countess of Sutherland (soon to be the Duchess on the elevation of her husband to a Dukedom) wished to own all that she could see from her ancestral home. Smith thought the arable soil generally of good quality, much of it in a high state of cultivation. He supported Taylor's view that Tarbatness was a rich agricultural country by northern standards. 'Wheat is the prevailing, or rent paying grain raised on these soils, even by the small Tenants'. Yields were well above average for the north, and supplies of seaweed were good. 'Upon the whole of these lands there is an excellent and respectable Tenantry. The small Tenantry are considered an honest and industrious set of Tenantry and perhaps from the example which the larger farmers have set every part seems to be under a good system of husbandry.' In some parts the amount of arable land had been greatly increased since 1813.[28] In a second letter Smith was optimistic about the prospects: 'Upon the whole I think it is quite possible to get possession of these lands at a fair price if matters are properly managed which no doubt will be done by the Duke's men of business.' The total price might be about £172,000 and Smith offered the comment: 'At this a good investment would be made and the expenditure of a few thousand pounds would produce a profitable return if judiciously laid out in Improvements.'[29] Another adviser to the Sutherland family was equally positive: 'the whole put together does not amount to a very frightful sum to the Duke and certainly as desirable a purchase for his Grace is nowhere to be found.'[30]

The advice proferred to the Duke of Sutherland was encouraging and prepared the way for a substantial purchase. The Sutherland family had already bought land in Ardross and Rosskeen and elsewhere to the north and west. Their takeovers were part of a wider turnover of land in the Highlands which was itself an aspect of the mobility of land-use and population in the new age. For instance in the parish of Kincardine, between 1765 and 1840 there was a rapid alteration of landownership and the merging of small properties into larger. Thirteen landed estates shrank into eight. Only four of the original families survived as proprietors—Cromartie, Ross of Balnagowan, Munro of Fowlis and Ross of Pitcalnie.[31] But the Sutherland thrust into Tarbatness, in the upshot, was not pursued: within four months the first Duke of Sutherland was dead and there followed a radical change in the family's financial circumstances. Ironically, within twenty years, the Cromartie estate (comprising a territory much larger than Tarbat) slipped smoothly into the Sutherland empire—accomplished not by the calculating rationality of estate agents, but by the consequence of a remarkable marriage.

In 1833 therefore Easter Ross and its estates were spared the acquisitive grasp of the northern empire. The Cromartie finances however continued in their perennially parlous condition—and remained perilous for two more decades. In 1835 several parcels of land were sold off to retrieve debts of the family. The sales marked the territorial decline of the Hay-Mackenzie line; the sales also demonstrated the effects of the agricultural slump and the increasing impact of sporting leases on Highland land values.

The sales took place in Edinburgh and the *Inverness Courier* made it the occasion for a comment on the upward drift of pastoral land values in the Highlands in recent years.[32] Land in Fannich, rented at £180 per annum was sold for £6550 (37 years purchase). A second lot—in Lochbroom, sold for £9200 (34 years purchase). The sale was 'pretty sharply contested. The upset price of the two was £13,150; it rose £2000 higher, when the two lots were knocked down at £15,756, to Mr Murdoch Mackenzie, late of Ardross, then of Dundonnell'. The editor noted that a few years earlier such prices would have been considered ruinous. It reflected the value of sheep, better communications and the developing importance of sport.

> Even unconquered barrenness is now to be turned to good account. At the present moment, we believe, many Highland proprietors derive a greater revenue from the moors alone, for grouse shooting, than the whole rental amounted to sixty years since. The passion entertained by English gentlemen for field sports has been fostered by the increased means of communication, northwards, and up and down the country, from the highest hill to the deepest and most distant glen. The sportsman throws himself into a steamer at London, and in 48 hours or less he is in Edinburgh or Aberdeen. Another day, and he is in the heart of moor and mountain, where he may shoot, saunter, or angle to his heart's content.[33]

Sporting leases in the Highlands introduced an exotic element into the local economy, a juxtaposition of southern wealth and high consumption with the intractable and possibly worsening poverty of the indigenous people. Sporting tenants also introduced an extra increment of pressure on land uses, though the rich tenants also increased regional income and seasonal (and limited) employment opportunities. For Highland landlords the new craze for sport on their territories represented windfall gains. For instance in the parish of Contin sporting leases had increased the rent of one piece of land from £1400 p.a. in 1792 to £6000 p.a. in 1834. In the same parish the grazing at Fannich rose in fifty years from £12 per annum to £200 by 1834. Shooting rights began to cost more than grazing rents.[34]

The sacrifice of lands in 1835 may have given the Hay-Mackenzie family time to wrestle further with the problems of the estate. Their financial straits do not appear to have prevented considerable consumption of a conspicuous nature. For instance Tarbat House, the expensive symbol of restitution begun by Count Macleod, was maintained in substantial style. It was described, in the 1830s as 'a highly finished modern building, and the chief seat of Mr H. Mackenzie of Cromarty. The grounds surrounding it are laid out with great taste, and have of late years been highly improved'.[35]

Financial stress did not impede a relatively expansive attitude to consumption. For instance in June 1845 Hay-Mackenzie was found to be 'most comfortably established [in Paris] in a very nice house in the Champs Elysees where we are free from all stinks, and have plenty of fresh air'. Indeed from Paris Hay-Mackenzie transmitted his implacable opposition to the first steps towards railway development in the northern Highlands. He had issued an interdict against the 'Inverness and Ross Railway' preventing the surveyors access to his land. He declared he had never heard of 'a more mad speculation' which was designed simply to put money into the 'pockets of penniless speculators'. He had consulted Gladstone in London who seemed to agree that the project was 'an act of railroad fanaticism'. Hay-Mackenzie's main objection—that proprietors were prepared to 'sacrifice the privacy and comfort of their places for the sake of a little money in the mean time'—suggests a somewhat conservative attitude to economic development in the Highlands.[36]

The erosion of the territorial strength of the Cromartie family remained relatively slow. The family was clinging on. Indeed the land sales of 1835 represented a relatively small fraction of the total estate. Similarly the political influence of the family remained considerable through these years despite pressures already mentioned. At the time of the Reform Bill in 1832 there was an exchange of political correspondence which indicated the continuing importance of the Cromartie influence. In 1832 the registered electorate of Ross and Cromarty stood at 516 for a total population of 74,800.[37] In July 1832 Munro of Novar found himself as Conservative candidate challenged by a Liberal—viz. James Alexander Stewart Mackenzie, and embroiled in 'the turmoil of these disagreeable politics'. Novar was frantic for votes but Hay-Mackenzie, and the Cromartie influence, was incommunicado in the south. He discovered that the Cromartie agent, Andrew Scott, was reluctant to issue instructions without direct advice from his employer. One correspondent told him that he much regretted that:

> you do not feel yourself at liberty to do anything for the good 'Conservative' cause in Coigach. Perhaps the enclosed letter from Novar to me, which shows how completely Cromartie's feelings and wishes are in accordance with his, will prevent any further hesitation on your part from using your utmost endeavours to secure every voter of £50 and upwards for Novar.

He offered a list of likely persons in the west that the agent ought to canvass.[38] Novar had no doubt about Hay-Mackenzie's allegiances—and reported that he had just seen him,

> and had the great gratification of hearing him express the most cordial hopes for my success as a candidate for Ross and Cromarty. He told me also that his political sentiments were in complete accordance with my own. He said he had stated this generally to his Tenantry. If any of them, therefore, are still in doubt respecting his feelings and wishes,

you can have no scruple in stating to them what I have written above which will be completely confirmed by personal application by them to himself.[39]

Novar's political agents drafted several versions of a letter to be issued under Hay-Mackenzie's name. They wanted Hay-Mackenzie to support publicly 'the good conservative cause' and to associate himself with 'that side of politics which is favourable not only to the agricultural interests of the country but to the good order and well being of the state'. It would also express his opposition to 'the party called Liberal' and the Seaforth interest in the county. In fact the Cromartie estate agent Scott refused to make any written commitment without explicit instructions from Hay-Mackenzie, who appears to have been either elusive or ambivalent throughout the election. In the outcome Munro of Novar lost the election in December 1832 by 272 votes to 148. So far as the Hay-Mackenzies were concerned the episode demonstrated the survival of their influence beyond the Reform Bill, and the persistence of political deference upon which they could continue to draw.

IV

The underlying changes to the agrarian structure of the Cromartie estate continued in the 1830s. Though most of the estate papers of the period are lost, rental statements survive and provide useful indicators of the social and economic life. Indeed the estate administration became more systematic when a new factor was appointed in 1831. This was Andrew Scott, a man from Roxburghshire, a professional improver and a loyal servant whose factorship stretched from the time of the 1830s clearances in Coigach until 1869 the year before his death.

At the time of Scott's death the crofters' movement had made considerable progress in the Highlands and the Cromartie estate itself figured prominently in the agitation of the day. The crofters were mounting an unprecedented campaign to repossess land in the Highlands. Much of their eventual success (see below, chapter Twenty-One) was achieved on the basis of historical claims. They argued vociferously that, at some previous time, the small tenantry had possessed traditional rights to land, especially grazing land, which was held communally.

Crofters on Cromartie and elsewhere repeated these claims on many occasions, asserting in effect the existence of a time of communal landownership of which they had been dispossessed. It was at the heart of the dispute between the crofters and the landlords and was expressed with outrage and indignation—partly, of course, with a view to wresting control of the land from the landlords. Mostly estate administrators dismissed these historical claims outright, they were mistaken or they were myth. For instance in 1893 the crofters of Strathpeffer applied for access to the grazing lands of Glenskaith on the grounds that it 'was at a former period held by them in common—the rent they say being included in their croft rents'. The factor at that time, William Gunn, rejected the assertion. Consulting the estate ledger he traced the history of the land in question. He found that the Heights tenants, before 1834, had leased the grazing at a separate rent. They had relinquished the grazings in 1834 'when a considerable amount of arrear was written off as irrecoverable'. At that point, the entire grazings were let to one tenant—James Scott of Hawick (probably a kinsman of Andrew Scott) as a sheep farm which he held until his death in 1861. But in his denial Gunn conceded an important part of the crofters' case—that their forbears had indeed held the grazing lands until they were dislodged to accommodate a large southern sheep farmer. It was a version of a clearance—though it would not have involved physical displacement of the people from their homes. It was straightforward enough evidence that the Cromartie estate, in the 1830s, had appropriated grazing land from the people.

The Cromartie estate pursued a policy of land reallocation over many decades and, for the most part, achieved the result without much protest or public outcry. Confirmation of peaceful clearances on the Cromartie estate in the 1830s is available in the contemporary documents. In the first quarter of 1833 for instance, Langwell and Corrie districts were rearranged and the people shifted from their old grazing areas. Leases were falling in and new tenants were sought. One applicant for Langwell Farm was Gunn, a factor on the Sutherland estate to the north (it was not unusual for factors to farm privately on a regular basis). His offer of rent was not the highest but he was regarded as a very desirable tenant and the amount of rent was not to be 'the sole criterion'.[41] The previous tenants had been in arrears and the plan was to remove the leaseholders and their subtenants in order to make way for the large sheepfarmers. The legal adviser to the Cromartie estate indicated that 'It is generally understood that under a summons of Removing against a Principal tenant it is Competent at the term to Eject his Subtenants if there has not been a recognition of any kind of the subtenants, as I understand is to be the case this year in Coigach, the only safe course is to give the usual warning to all and sundry.' He advised great precision and care in the operation. The Cromartie tacks all specifically excluded subtenant rights.[42]

The correspondence between the factors at the time of the 1833 clearances demonstrates the priority and nervous energy expended in ensuring that the operation took place quietly and without commotion. It was important to avoid litigation with the parties on account of the expense involved. One incoming sheepfarmer, Walter Mundell, was told to be patient and to understand that there was some doubt about the legal timing of his entry to the lands. The law agent told Andrew Scott that it was best to avoid the 'heavy expense of extracting Decreets of Removing' and those of executing the law. It was not formally necessary to take such steps 'except in the special case of resistance to removing being anticipated, or having actually taken place. I did not understand that either the one or the other was likely in any of the cases where we had quietly obtained Decreets of Removing last March.'[43]

Scott felt it necessary to follow this elaborate procedure since he anticipated some degree of resistance. The law agent complied unhappily. He reiterated that the despatch of officers to a removal was a 'step ... seldom or ever resorted to except in cases where resistance against removal is offered or anticipated'. He had had to employ his clerks 'night and day to write out charges upon the Decreets against every individual who has been summoned as you do not mention any one in particular who is likely to resist your wishes.' He also arranged the party to proceed from Ullapool in sufficient strength in case 'it shall be necessary to resort to forcible ejection ... I shall be happy to hear that the different Tenants have removed without recourse to actual force for that purpose.'[44]

A scene was set for an event which was a repetition of innumerable such occasions in the Highlands in the nineteenth century. There was the possibility of ugly resistance, but more likely a passive acceptance of the rearrangement. In the outcome there was no force required at Corrie and Langwell in 1833; the outgoing tenant made a settlement when the time came, and the people were reported to have acquiesced quietly in the arrangements.[45] Their grazings were clearly diminished by the change and they were placed in more restricted circumstances in their coastal settlements. They became more closely identifiable with the emergent pattern of nineteenth century crofting. In the great majority of such cases there is no surviving documentation of these changes which were instrumental in reinforcing the basic trends of Highland landholding. Indeed the best documented cases are those which were resisted by the people. The leases and rentals of the Cromartie estate suggest that there was an accelerated extension of sheep farming during the 1830s.

Another case of rearrangement in Coigach concerned the return of an emigrant to his homeland after many years absence in America. The man, Macleod, made a bid for Old Dornie in 1831, as a comfortable house and a 'snug little farm'. The Cromartie factor, Laing, was enthusiastic about the suggestion and told Macleod:

> you could be of great service to the tenancy by pointing out to them habits of industry to which they are as yet strangers, and in doing so, and engaging in the fishing yourself you could enlarge your income and comforts—a person like you and having your habits is much wanted among the tenants of Coigach.

Unfortunately the introduction of Macleod required the removal of resident tenants and in June 1831 he complained that he was still unable to get possession of the house—the occupant MacCauley being totally obstructive: 'I went 5 or 6 times to see if they were clear of Old Dorney but the torrent of abuse I heard from John MacCauley's wife made me leave the place with disgust.' He told the agent:

> Believe me sincerely had I known that there were so many obstacles in my way, that no inducement would make me have anything to do with Dorney ... The house ... is not good enough for a Pig-Sty ... I cannot express in a letter the trouble, vexation and disappointment I have already met with since my return to my native Country.

He had approached the place by boat; the people were in possession with their cattle—the people simply refused to move and Macleod was in a high state of frustration: 'You know there are many drawbacks and objections to any person who saw less or more of the world to reside in Coigach and nothing brought me to the Country but my attachment to the Cromarty Family and my native Country.' Two weeks later he gained possession but his complaints then redoubled. The buildings were a disgrace

> In fact I never saw a more wretched appearance than that place made. Only one pane of glass in the house and the thatch off, sufficiently enough to admit any ordinary man to got out of one hole and came in through another, in short it was just like a playhouse for goats and kids.

He also noted that the people of the country were in great need of meal for which they were awaiting a shipment: 'There is hardly any meal to be had in the country'.[46] Coigach was inhospitable to strangers and not generous to its ordinary people.

Sometimes the old tacksman took over land on his own account—land which he had previously sublet to small tenants. Once again this adjustment entailed the dislodging of subtenants. For example in 1830 a Tack was drawn up in the name of Duncan Mackenzie; the lands were specified as 'being the same as formerly possessed by him excepting what used to be occupied by subtenants'. He bound himself, by 1835, 'to cultivate and bring under the plough the whole unprofitable waste land on the lands hereby let being sixteen acres and 3/4 an acre of the pasture in the fields marked'.[47] It was another variation on the theme of clearance. The claims made by crofters sixty years later to the crofter Commission were not inconsistent with the contemporary evidence. For instance in 1890 a group of Rieff tenants applied for authority to graze horses at Inverpolly. They remarked:

> Before the Township was formed into Crofts sixty years ago, there was a portion of the sheep farm of Inverpolly allowed by the Proprietor to graze our horses, without any rent or charge of any kind, the owners of the horses only giving 1/- yearly each to the Shepherd, so that he might take some charge about them ... When the crofts were formed that privilege was taken from the crofters, and they were only allowed to keep a bare souming of cattle and sheep.

The factor in 1890 confirmed that the changes had been fixed in 1829-33—it had been part of the erosion of land access sustained by the people over many decades.[48]

These clearances of various sorts were associated with a reciprocal development. Subtenancy was much reduced, though not eliminated, across the estate. In addition some at least of the crofter occupants were provided with leases. It was, in effect, part of an effort to regularise and systematise tenurial relations on a more formal basis, increasingly in conformity with southern practice.[49] Tolerance of tenants in arrear did not increase in this regime. John Nicholson of Tanera was removed for an accumulation of arrears in 1832. He explained that the kelp trade had collapsed and for three years 'did not in fact pay their expenses of manufacturing and sending to market' despite his own expenditure on equipment. He appealed to the justice and generosity of the Cromartie family: 'I am reduced to such low circumstances that I cannot pay any such amount, they may take my personal or my little household furniture, and they will be little better for either, and I can scarcely think that they will be so cruel.' He pointed out that it would do the proprietor no good to see him ruined in this way.[50] He received short shrift.

V

Amid the reorganisation of landholding on the Cromartie Estate in the 1830s there emerged therefore a more direct relationship between landlord and tenants. Tacksmen and middlemen of the old system were on the retreat. At the same time some crofters obtained their own leases. For instance David Munro, a slater of Milntown, received a ten-year lease in 1835 for a croft. The lease specified restrictions on cropping—and 'to manage the lands hereby let in a proper husbandman-like manner', that compensation for buildings would be paid on the expiration of the lease. Munro was a substantial crofter who paid £13 per annum. A similar tack was agreed with William MacLennan, a mealer on a croft in Auchterneed, for 11 years from 1835 for a rent of £5.5.0. His tack contained two significantly negative clauses: 'No meliorations to be given at the expiry of his lease for improvements that may be made by the said Mr MacLennan either in building of houses or any other thing whatsoever.' Subletting and assignees were expressly excluded. James Cameron also received a croft lease for his lot on the Heights of Fodderty, at a rent of £8.5.0 p.a. His lease required him to conform with the ancient obligation of carrying all his corn to the mill. He was given the right to peats. It is not clear whether such leases were general or reserved for the larger type of crofter.[51]

Larger tenants were subject to elaborate agreements which closely specified the terms of agricultural practice and compensation. Duncan Mackenzie leased the big farm of Meddat for approx £150 for 19 years in 1828. His lease subjected him to the usual restriction on white crops in successive years, and also to 'cultivate and bring under the plough the whole improveable waste land or the lands hereby let being sixteen acres'. Even tenants of large arable lands were required to take their corn to the mill of Mill Nain. And, like the crofters, Mackenzie was subject to a double rent if he continued to occupy the land beyond the term of his lease. Such leases that survive make it clear that some large tenants occupied more than one sheep farm. For example Walter Mundell and Walter Grieve held leases for several properties in Coigach. James Mitchell and William Robertson leased vast stretches of sheep farming territory. James Mitchell rented Inverpolly in 1837 for a rent which was £280 until 1841 which then rose to £300 'provided the average price of cheviot wool sold at the Inverness wool fair to be held in the month of July that year shall be twenty one shillings or more than 21/- per 24 lbs imperial weight and so all throughout the remaining years of the Tack'.[52] In July 1838 Hay-Mackenzie proposed to Major Gilchrist that he make improvements on the carse and waste lands of Meddat for the purposes of drainage for which Hay-Mackenzie would pay £150 on the expiration of the lease.[53] The impetus for improvement remained with the tenants primarily, partly because the landlord himself had no command over usable capital.

VI

A deficiency of landlord capital also restrained the development of the best known asset in the Cromartie estate, namely the Spa at Strathpeffer. The new pump room of 1819 had certainly augmented the facilities and its clientele had grown, but the enthusiasts always felt that a far greater resort was feasible if only capital and enterprise could be found.

Virtually all visitors to the district made comment on the Spa; in 1825 Alexander Sutherland described the 'beautiful and thickly inhabited' valley of Strathpeffer, renowned for its medicinal waters which were 'strongly impregnated and sulphuretted with hydrogen gas'. He said that the Spa had recently become a fashionable resort but 'accommodation for the better class of visitors is difficult to be obtained in the immediate vicinity of the springs'. Many stayed at Dingwall and commuted to the springs. Sutherland reported: 'In this way we accounted for the groups of idle dandies and flaunting belles sauntering about the streets, evidently without any other object in view than that of exhibiting their bright tartans and flashy bonnets.'[54] Thus was the leisure industry emerging on the doorsteps of Castle Leod.

Ten years later the Spa had progressed little and the accommodation remained, to expert eyes, decidedly primitive.[55] There was, nevertheless, an identifiable Strathpeffer 'season', from May to October and attendance was invited for a broad range of complaints—gout and dyspepsia, and afflictions of the kidneys and the bladder, as well as rheumatic, scrofulous and cutaneous conditions. More interestingly Strathpeffer was offering itself to the casualties and the retired servants of Empire—'for constitutions which have suffered by long residence in tropical climates'. It boasted waters as powerful as those of the Rhineland spas, waters which could be taken 'without oppressing the stomach or irritating the system'. Spas such as Strathpeffer depended almost entirely upon reputation, especially that conferred by itinerant 'medical authorities'. Strathpeffer benefited from the analysis of its waters by Dr Thomson of Glasgow in 1824 who pronounced them stronger than those of Moffat. Dr Thomas Morrison of Elsick in Aberdeenshire, who claimed to know all British spas, declared Strathpeffer's wells and balsamic air unrivalled. At his suggestion a new pump room was constructed in 1829. Wisely the local minister pointed out that 'the pure dry bracing air which circulates around the district' and scenery which activated the inert, were also therapeutic.

The organisation of the waters had emerged along commercial lines. Visitors now paid two shillings per week for the privilege of the waters with other charges for particular uses. The well-keeper lived by gratuities. The pump room opened for two or three hours per day except on Sundays. One earlier tradition survived:

> The poor have the waters gratis, and are accommodated with a comfortable room attached to the upper well. They receive unremitted and disinterested attention from John Mackenzie Esq. M.D., Kinellan, who acts in this quarter in the professional capacity of consulting physician.

Some of the basic facilities had certainly improved. A small hospital for poor invalids was opened in 1839 and new villas were also in the course of construction. Coaches ran twice daily to Dingwall which connected with a service each day from and to Inverness. (Weekly steam boats connected Edinburgh and Dingwall and there was a fortnightly service from London to Invergordon). Newspapers and the penny post were also provided by the early 1840s. The local economy was gearing up to the provision of the Spa—supplying bread, meat, poultry, eggs, vegetables and fruit during the summer season. By 1840 there were modest inns and hotels being built,[56] but the full potential of the Spa as a fashionable and lucrative resort had yet to be explored. In essence the Spa required either a landlord with capital or else a company of entrepreneurs to brighten its facilities. It also needed a clientele prepared to travel to so relatively remote a location.

CHAPTER 14

Measures of Highland Change: the 1830s

I

From 1820 to 1849 the Cromartie estate, by simple misfortune, preserved relatively few papers of its internal management. During these years, there was mounting public discussion of the problems of Highland estates. As a consequence there were published several external accounts of the shape of economic and social change, some of which related directly to the Cromartie estate.

Highland estates which had no access to outside capital tended to slumber on, often vulnerable to famine and population pressures. The problem of congestion was less pressing where estates could take consistent advantage of the market opportunities of cattle, fish, kelp and wool production. But much of the dynamic for change came in the form of external capital, often when estates changed hands and gained access to supplies of capital from outside the region. New ownership was one way by which Highland estates sometimes became connected with capital. Another was by way of marriage and a change of leadership within a proprietor's family.

Cromartie eventually experienced all these stimuli. But between 1800 and 1850 it was essentially a middle-sized Highland estate with little injection of new investment. During these years the estate scraped along; its proprietor at all times was caught between the need to re-invest estate income in new development, and the temptations of competitive and opulent consumption. Much of the estate income continued to flow into unproductive uses—into personal consumption, into sport, into building, and into the pockets of relatives. Since its restoration by the great efforts of Lord Macleod in the 1780s, the family had re-established itself in northern and Edinburgh society. The family was evidently more desirable in the sense of marital alliances with similar families but the drain on its basic resources was palpable. By mid-century the Hay-Mackenzies were again in dire financial straits, and already on the downward slide towards bankruptcy and imminent sale. Meanwhile, of course, the maintenance of the basic resources of the estate was mainly in the hands of the various strata of the tenantry and their welfare was contingent on the continuing structural changes in the Highland economy.

II

It was unlikely that Elizabeth Isabella Spence would penetrate the workings of Highland life. She was a popular novelist and travel writer touring the north in 1816. Her memoirs were generally banal and she regarded the Highlanders as exotic natives in a terra incognita, but they made good copy for her English reading public. Nevertheless she offered some simple descriptions of the eastern Highlands about Strathpeffer and Tarbat which indicate the diet and housing of the people in a year just before one of the worst subsistence crises of the century. She was surprised at the richness of the food: it was July and there was a plenty of salmon, trout, barley-broth, mutton and poultry at social levels below 'families of the first condition'. She was witness to the paradoxical natural prosperity of the Highlands which was always liable to turn into extreme privation. She was able to report,

> I partook of a truly highland breakfast, and for the first time saw the whisky-bottle present ere the meal before us was spread. Tea and coffee, the wheaten loaf, oat cakes, marmalade, honey, and other sweet meats, cold salmon, a dried fish, called spelding, cold chicken, ham and eggs. It was quite a repast of luxuries.

Such was the seasonal plentitude of the land to be juxtaposed against the recurrent need for the Highlander to go without luxury, having 'fewer wants'—for these were the 'aborigines of the country', and 'the brave remnants of unconquered Celtics' who had anciently taken to the hills rather than submit to invaders. Miss Spence dealt in stereotypes: these people were inured to hard conditions, they were renowned for their military prowess and for their 'native indolence' to which she also felt able to testify.[1]

'Out of many of the wretched hovels into which I looked have sprung many a brave soldier, whose couch was composed only of a straw pallet, and whose hard fare consisted of nothing beyond oat bread, and Kale, with a garment little more than a bare covering.' She went on to describe the huts which were 'scarcely fit for human habitation':

> They are often built without window or chimnies, a cavity in the wall admitting the light, out of which issues an abundance of smoke, and a hole in the roof supplies the want of a chimney. In the middle of an earthen floor, is a peat fire, around which often hovers a group of almost naked children. A sort of press in the wall contains the bed, which seldom has any other covering than a blanket, and is usually that of straw. These wretched dwellings look at a distance like heaps of mole hills.[2]

Miss Spence observed that since the Highlanders' comforts were so slight their aspirations to comfort were also necessarily modest and they were, therefore, content with their lot:

> They will tell you that they miss none of those things which to us appear so necessary; and that, far from envying, they rather pity us.... The highland peasantry are satisfied with the magnificence of nature: the tale, the song, the warmhearted and ardent imagination.

Elizabeth Spence was also witness to another pre-clearance scene from the eastern lands close to Strathpeffer. She described the activity of the summer months in the pastoral districts of Strathglass where

> the peasantry wander from place to place with their flocks and herds, taking their families and goods along with them, like the ancient patriarchs of old. The Shieldings they dwell in, are composed merely of wicker-work; and they repose on beds of hether, feeding their cattle, for certain periods, on the pastures adjacent to the rude habitations, removing with their utensils and small portion of furniture, carried in panniers, in which their children either travel, or are borne on their backs. Thus they wander from mountain to mountain, during the summer, in a mode of life somewhat resembling the tribes of gypsies in England.[3]

The days of such gypsy-like scenes were strictly numbered by 1816. Miss Spence conjured up a picture of a life which was anathema to the improvement mentality that was taking an iron-grip on the Highlands in these years. The squalor, the indolence and the inefficiency of the old communal ways would not survive the exhortations of the improvers. The most influential propagandist in Easter and Wester Ross was Sir George Stewart Mackenzie.

Sir George Mackenzie was one of the most robust and uncompromising of improvers and his *General View of the Agriculture of the Counties of Ross and Cromarty* published in 1813 was designed to propagate the best available thinking on agricultural practice. But it was much more than a mere textbook of ploughing and sheepfarming. It was a substantial description and indictment of the older forms of life in the Highlands, and a prescription for a new society and economy. His work is especially relevant to Cromartie since he was a landlord next door to Strathpeffer. He set a standard for the district by which his neighbours could be judged. Most seem to have fallen short of his rigour, or at least lagged behind in the imperative of wholesale change.

Mackenzie's indictment was comprehensive. His category of 'native farmers' was the prime object of his criticism. Their farms had from 7 to 30 acres of arable and promiscuous access to hill pasture to which they sent their horses and cattle after seed time:

> The occupiers of the hill pastures generally take a greater number of horses and cattle for grazing than the surface they allot for this purpose can well support. The consequence is, that the animals belonging to the native farmers are always poor looking, and stunted in growth. The practice of keeping an overstock renders it very difficult matter for the people to support their cattle during winter and the labouring season. They have nothing but the straw of the preceding crop, and what can be picked upon the sides of the highways, or stolen from some more provident neighbour.[4]

It was a very inefficient mode of occupation. The land suffered, the cattle suffered, and it did the people little good. By contrast when 'clever and experienced' farmers from Berwickshire were allowed to take over the land they revolutionised the productivity and rental value of the land. They introduced turnips, carrots and wheat, they drained, levelled, and enclosed, they reduced the number of people needed, and they prevented overstocking.

Mackenzie regarded the entire districts of Mid and Easter Ross from Strathpeffer to Tarbatness as ripe for improvement: 'Our great want is south country tenants of skill and real capital, without both of which, farming is impracticable.'[5] Highlanders themselves were constitutionally unsuited to improvement.

Native farmers had 'no capital to lay out in purchasing a proper stock'. They possessed, still, extensive tracts of the country—they had come to realise that sheep could be more profitable than black cattle—but, because of their poor access to capital, 'the steps of the Highlanders towards improvement are cramped and awkward.'[6] The hills were overstocked and there was no selective breeding. The attempt by the old native farmers to convert to sheepfarming had failed. 'Sheepfarming like every other speculation which holds out great profits, has tempted many persons to embark in it, who had not sufficient capital, and who were deficient in that skill, and patient attention, which are absolutely necessary for the good management of a sheep stock'. Rents had been forced up by excessive competition (of the speculative sort) for land; the winter of 1807-8 had been devastating; and it had been blamed for depopulation. In fact, Mackenzie asserted, there could be no denying the good sense of sheepfarming on the right basis—but he was quite clear about the effects on the native population—'in almost every case, the original occupiers have been removed.'[7]

The old system could not therefore simply be converted to the more profitable regime of sheepfarming. The native farmers could not produce enough crops for themselves or their livestock; they overstocked the grazing lands and had to sell their stock at ruinous prices at the onset of winter. They paid trifling rents for vast areas of the country and their communal arrangements were incompatible with a system of improvement since it permitted no specialisation of function or output.

The alternative was simple and imperative:

> If one man had the whole of one side of a glen, and the hills attached to it, he might lay down a system of cultivation, by which a greater quantity of winter provender might be raised, and part of the hill pasture saved, for wintering such cattle as could bear standing out. The hay and fodder of other sorts might be reserved for such cattle as were too young or too weak to bear the buffets of winter storms; a better and a larger stock than what a multitude of small tenants could have, would also be reared.

It was a prescription for clearance, for individualism, for specialisation, for efficiency, and for a few large farmers of capital and expertise as against the multitude. It was the antithesis of the old method of occupation in the Highlands. The price of improvement was clearance. Mackenzie's own estate, Balnagowan, demonstrated the economics of clearance: where, 40 years before, nine small tenants had paid nine pounds for 100 acres of meadow and the attached hill grazing, now it had become part of a sheepfarm and its value increased to one hundred pounds. It was much like a new technology in the local economy, but it required the removal of nine families. The native farmers were totally unfit for the occupation of productive land—they were constitutionally indolent and ignorant.[8]

Such severe remarks applied most tellingly to the west coast, and Mackenzie singled out Coigach for special condemnation. The west Highlands represented the worst version of pre-improvement conditions—in a striking metaphor, he described each communal farm as resembling 'a small republic in which every public measure is settled by a majority, and where often more time is spent in debate than in action.' Already, as on the Cromartie estate, sheepfarming had been introduced with great benefit to the rentals. For the rest the ancient customs remained, the people indolent and pauperised, living 'in the midst of smoke and filth, that is their choice'. At least half the population was 'superfluous' and the true solution must be their displacement and emigration. The other solution, much resorted to in the west, was a compromise: crofting.

Crofting met Mackenzie's ire because it retained the population without any discernable economic purpose. He conceded that it was possible to divide up land into crofts and small farms, but it was uneconomic and dangerous:

> To make a general system of small farms would certainly keep a great number alive, though the population would become comparatively useless, as it is now, its whole exertions being applied to supply itself with food, with little or no prospect of having any to spare for the labouring and manufacturing classes. In such a state of things, a season of scarcity would be attended by the most deplorable effects.

He castigated the current efforts being made to retain and increase population as being fraught with danger. It was unnatural and unnecessary. Population channelled itself where it was needed. Given good wages and food 'men, women and children will shoot up like mushrooms.' Crofting was an ill conceived system which foolishly retained the population in the Highlands.[9]

Crofting created, in association with sheep clearances, a new class, an attenuated cottar-class in the Highlands. Detached from the old way of life, crofters now re-attached themselves to patches of land regarded as marginally improvable by landlord and tenant. On its own it was a last resort, a final refuge for the displaced people from the glens. It was a halfway house between the old status of semi-communal peasant and that of landless labourer. It was to become the common lot of the ordinary Highlander in the nineteenth century. Crofting therefore was the compromise that reconciled sheepfarming with the retention of some of the displaced population. It was a solution adopted unsystematically on the Cromartie estate—both in the eastern and the western baronies as described in the previous chapter. Indeed the Hay-Mackenzies developed a humanitarian reputation for receiving the refugees from war service and from clearances on other estates, settling them as crofters on the Heights of Fodderty and elsewhere.

But of the critics of the crofting system Mackenzie was the most vociferous and penetrating. It was both avaricious and sentimental for landlords to encourage crofting. He said: 'The families of crofters are universally in rags, and their children are uneducated; industry is unknown to them, and their habitations are filthy in the extremity.' Crofting was absurd and totally inefficient. Crofters were extremely poor, and the improvements they produced were derisory. It took fifteen years to improve three acres. His message was clear: 'we cannot help contrasting the occupation of land in small patches, with that where some hundred acres are thrown into one farm.' Crofting did not help to increase output—it helped only the growth of population.[10] It was all the diametrical reverse of Mackenzie's belief that people could only be justified by their output—'It cannot be denied that, unless employment can be found, there is no occasion for people.' The crofting system was the negation of this principle: 'The people are useless to this community' however humane the instincts of the landlord.

Mackenzie thus offered Ross and Cromarty a gospel of clearance untempered by compromise or sentimentality. The native farmers should become plebeian employees of the new breed of 'systematical farmers from the south country', or else emigrate—'they must go to America for the chance of independence, leaving their merited curses behind them'. Landlords should themselves live in the country or else sell off to men with capital. There was the inexorable logic of political economy in the prescription and Mackenzie made no bones about the disruption involved—sheepfarming depopulated, 'in almost every case, the original occupiers have been removed' he emphasised. Nor did he obscure the total unpopularity of the measure—it was, he said, a 'struggle against the prejudices of the people, which were inveterate against the new system of pasturage'. Indeed he offered several examples of physical resistance all of which, for him, merely confirmed the ignorance and stupidity of the common people. The process was painful: 'It has been found necessary to remove a very great number of people from possessions to which they are strongly attached, and to which they considered themselves in a great measure, the rightful heirs.'

As previous chapters have shown, the Cromartie estate followed a somewhat less than full-blooded version of Mackenzie's ideas. There had been no mistaking the effects of population increase nor of the new agriculture, both arable and pasture. But a compromising policy, an ad hoc response to circumstances, had characterised the estate's administration. Comprehensive clearances had been avoided; most of the people remained. Consequently, like most of the Highlands, Cromartie experienced a co-existence of the new and the old; for the people the life of crofting had indeed emerged. It is to the impact of these changes that the remainder of this chapter is devoted.

III

The main witnesses of the effects of improvement and agrarian change were the ministers of the church in their reports to the second *Statistical Account of Scotland* drawn together in the late 1830s. These ministers, of course, were ambiguously placed between proprietors and the people and their opinions may have been influenced by their loyalties and their obligations. It became common to regard Highland ministers as creatures of the landlord class, men who aided and abetted the introduction of sheep, and prepared the ordinary people to accept peaceably the trauma of clearance. Nevertheless there was surprising candour in some of their reports. By the 1830s the impact of improvement, population growth and economic reorganisation, had become clear, the benefits somewhat less so.

None of the ministers questioned the improvement in productivity and rentals. In Easter Ross 'the large farm system' had turned the district into a wheat exporter to the south of Britain and had brought prosperity to its landlords and its large farmers, the sort of men likely to belong to the Ross-shire Farming Society for the improvement of corn and of the different breeds of cattle. Until about 1790 virtually no wheat was raised in Ross and Cromarty, but by 1830 it had become 'a staple of its agriculture'—and was associated with widespread technical improvements in agricultural practice, for example the drainage schemes at Fodderty. It is possible that the condition of labourers had improved, and the amount of employment increased, though it may not have kept full pace with population growth and immigration.

In the furthest eastern lands of the estate, in Easter Ross, agricultural improvement had reached remarkable peaks of technical advance. A report in 1844 described the arable lands as 'champaign districts' which had benefited from total change in the past half century, and now were as advanced as any part of Great Britain: 'The great majority of the farms display a neatness in the style of enclosing and the dressing of land, which is superior to the modes of most districts in England, and scarcely surpassed by the best in Scotland. The crops are always clean, often luxuriant and generally so good that Ross-shire wheat has repeatedly sold as the best in the London markets.' One half of all production was exported. Exports of wheat from Portmahomack quadrupled between 1827 and 1836.[11]

The social costs of improvement were far more contentious. Many of the parochial reports contended that the poor bore the brunt of the economic change. Hugh Miller reported from the parish of Cromarty in certain terms: agricultural change had shifted the peasantry out of agriculture to be replaced by commercial farmers served by a stratum of virtually landless labourers. The minister of Nigg drew a clear lesson:

> The improvement may be carried on, at an expense of morals and human comfort which no pecuniary advantage can counterbalance. Many families were driven from their homes, a few strangers were introduced in their room, and poverty succeeded in the train of all the actors and sufferers in the scene. The writer is passionately fond of improvement and beautifying the face of the earth. But he conceives that the earth, though beautiful as the garden of Eden, would be but a waste without moral beauty, and that the proprietors, who expel the inhabitants from their properties are depriving themselves of some of the higher enjoyments in life—the luxury of doing good, and the pleasure of being surrounded by a moral, a grateful, and a happy population.[12]

The horizontal divisions in society had thereby clarified by the 1830s. The minister of Rosskeen also reported unambiguously on the question:

> In many respects, this parish has been improved within the last forty years, but the depopulation of the country by large farms, is a serious evil, and is likely to bring along with it consequences which the landed interest seem not to have contemplated. There is no longer an independent peasantry. The morals of the people are deteriorated by the loss of independence, and their spirits embittered by what they deem oppression.

It was not unlike a premonition of the food riots of 1847:[13] 'The ties which united master and tenant are severed; and when the time comes, to which we look forward with fearful anticipation, it will, we fear, be found, that an error has been committed, by grasping too much, at the risk of losing all.' If it was an error, then by 1835 it was irreversible.[14]

In effect the agrarian changes had caused a rootlessness among the people. At Contin, which covered part of the Cromartie estate, the minister had no doubt that the circumstances of the people at large had deteriorated and had induced migration: the people had been 'swept off to make way for extensive farmers'. A few years later a rare voice of a victim of these clearances (on the estate of Sir George Mackenzie) was recorded before the Parliamentary Inquiry into the Scottish Poor Law (1844). William Stuart, aged 50, had been evicted from the Contin estate and, like so many others, shifted his family to the nearest town, in this case Dingwall. He explained his circumstances with simple dignity:

> William Stuart, aged fifty.—I have a wife and seven children, and am a native of the parish of Contin. I came here because the shepherd took from us the place that I had. I had a small croft. It, along with many others, was thrown into a sheep-walk. We have a boy ten years old, who is lame. We have been here nearly two years. We came here immediately when we were sent off the farm. We came to Dingwall because it was the nearest place in which we could get a house. We could not get a house any where else. We did not come here to obtain a settlement. I just work here and there when I can get it. About seven families went to America. When we were put away none other came to Dingwall but me. Some are at Maryburgh. My eldest son, and another, a lad, are in Mr McEwen's service. I have three girls at service. The eldest with me is a girl, twenty-one years old. My youngest child is four. I held my farm from Sir George Mackenzie. He had no factor but himself. I thought I could get work here better. I was more likely to get small jobs here than elsewhere. My rent is 2/-. We applied to the session on account of the cripple son. We received 5/- a year on his account at Contin. It is a very common notion among the people, that when they go to a new place they will receive the same as they did in the parish from which they came, and that they have no claim on their former parish. My reason for coming here was to get work—not from any idea that I would get more here.[14a]

At Kilmuir Easter, a parish dominated by the Hay-Mackenzies, the decline of population was attributed 'partly ... to emigration, but principally to the system of large farm letting, which has of late years become so general.'[15] Alness told a similar story of the baneful consequences of 'a practice now becoming too common throughout the country, of converting districts of land which have been formerly tenanted by a number of small farmers or crofters into large farms. The tenantry thus ejected are obliged either to emigrate to some of the colonies, or to congregate in the villages at home.'[16] Similarly in Rosskeen the country population had declined while the village population rose disproportionately to the total parish population:[17] 'This is to be attributed to the doing away with the middle class of tenants, and merging their small into large farms.'[18]

Certainly most of the initiative in the eastern arable lands came from the large tenants—the drainage and reclamation on the Cromartie estate at Strathpeffer was cited directly. The valley had consisted

> of swampy morass overgrown by stunted older trees, and commonly called the bog. Through this a channel was cut for the Peffery, sufficiently deep to afford a fall for drainage, but a judicious use of which, and by trenching and levelling the surface, this, which was of so little value as to be used as a common grazing, has become one of the ... farms in the parish.

The reporter noted that most of the expense had been incurred by the tenants on long leases—19-21 years. He pointed out that the 'chief obstacles to improvement on the part of the farmer here, arise from the frequent inability of the proprietor, owing to the circumstances connected with the law of entail, to render the tenant any assistance or encouragement in times of depression.' The description indicated clearly enough that arable land had been recovered from bog by the efforts of a tenant farmer which, however, entailed a loss of common grazing by the people. The small tenants were, in effect, pushed up the hillsides.

The parish of Fodderty, a parish in the barony of Strathpeffer where the Hay-Mackenzies owned half the rental, was a clear case in point. Its population had increased from 1483 in 1755 to 1730 in 1794 to 2300 in 1831. But the increase had occurred mainly in the villages of Maryburgh and Keithtown—villages on the Seaforth estate 'which are of recent formation', and on the 'heights'. These two zones were reception areas 'being resorted to from remote districts lately converted into pasturage'. It is difficult to believe that the great campaigns for improvement did not create considerable employment in capital projects over several decades—trenching, draining and levelling were highly labour-intensive activities, especially stone dyke building. But the common people had been levered off their old lands into villages or on to decidely marginal land. Two separate pressures combined to produce this classic symptom of land hunger—population growth and the altered utilisation of the land towards pasture. Unlike the enclosure movement of the south, the new land uses in the Highlands tended eventually to reduce the total labour force at a time of demographic expansion. In the east, the arable lands, this may not have been the case since improved agriculture was both labour and capital intensive. In Fodderty the outcome was visible: 'The greatest part of the parish is occupied by large farmers, who have introduced all the modern improvements in agriculture. The rest of the people consist of small tenants, crofters, a few mechanics, and the extremely poor'. It was well recognised that the rift between the great commercial farmers and the crofters was far too wide. When (in March 1850) some of the large farmers invited small tenants from the heights of Strathpeffer to dine with them, Andrew Scott, the Cromartie factor, was extremely enthusiastic for it would 'tend to promote the general happiness'.[19] In reality it was a rare gesture in a much fragmented society. Nevertheless, the land supported more people than before, the output was larger and the level of material welfare may have been better than before. But the hold of the common people on the land itself was diminished. In a peasant, pre-industrial society, such a loss of land was a matter of great moment, a social trauma.

Some of the social characteristics of the Fodderty population in the 1830s emerged in their minister's report. The average size of the family was 7.7; 506 families lived in 481 houses. Of these families 65% were chiefly engaged in agriculture, 10% in trade, manufacturers and handicraft, and the remainder outside that classification. Of the adult male population of 515 (i.e. over 20 years of age) 17 were occupiers who employed labourers—clearly a very restricted class—and 189 were employed in this fashion. Hence, even if all the employers were of equal status, they employed eleven labourers each; but they were not equal and, therefore, some of these occupiers employed very large numbers of men. Occupiers without outside assistance (and who were not dependent on other work) amount to 189—essentially the crofter class, quite distinct from the large new tenant farmers of the carse. Seventy men were employed in trade and handicraft, and 13 were non-agricultural labourers. Surprisingly there were only 70 female servants. Gaelic remained 'by far the most prevalent language', but the patterns of education reveal widespread illiteracy and inequality of opportunity. Thus 538 people above 15 years of age could read in neither English nor Gaelic. Among the children 216 boys and 162 girls were learning to read, 74 and 31 to write. It was a clear indication of the low value placed on literacy, but particularly for the females. It would seem that less than half the males were literate amongst the population, and less than half the children were being given education.[20] The minister testified to the people's attachment to the Established Church but noted at length their persisting superstitions. The Church of the parish had seating for 600 people but was considered inadequate for the needs of the parish, of which Mrs Hay-Mackenzie was patroness. A teacher had set up a school on his own initiative on the heights of Auchterneed where he obtained an attendance of 84.

In a population of Fodderty of 2300, there were 96 on the poor roll, plus 20 others who obtained occasional assistance. The poor were supported by church collections (about thirty pounds per year) which also funded various fees. They also received support by the mortification of 12 bolls of barley per year *in perpetuo* by the Earl of Cromartie in 1686—which had been directed especially to 'decayed tenants and their wives when widows'. In 1838 it was equivalent to nine pounds per annum, now augmented by the proceeds of legacies worth two hundred pounds. On this basis there was probably less than forty pounds a year to look after 116 people, and it suggests that the poor were very wretched and/or looked after by the community in a manner very informal. This evidence, together with that presented to the parliamentary inquiry into the Scottish Poor Law in 1843, revealed the lax, meagre and informal character of public provision for the poor in the Highlands. The prevalence of begging and mutual support amongst the poorest members of society was documented in vivid terms. It was a picture of bleak insecurity, of poverty persistent even when economic conditions were relatively favourable. It is evidence also that the manse and the landlord were regarded as the final resort when total desperation threatened. For instance, in the parish of Kilmuir Easter, the minister acknowledged that the Hay-Mackenzies had 'done a great deal for the poor, and that no case of destitution has ever been brought under their notice which was not immediately relieved'.[21]

One of the most important differences between the peasantry of the mid-eighteenth century and that of a century later was the number of surviving children in each household. The decline in the infantile death-rate almost certainly caused a sharp increase in the number of dependent offspring. This of course compounded the problem of land availability in the age of improvement and redoubled the pressure to migrate within and beyond the region. Many of these people were shaken off the land only to take up a more precarious residence on the margin. The process was described again in Logie Easter, where the Hay-Mackenzies were also prominent landowners and where the population had fallen marginally since 1790. The minister ascribed the decline

> to the system adopted by the northern proprietors in general (and this parish in particular) of letting large farms, and thus dispossessing the small tenants, some of whom remove to neighbouring towns, some to America, and others to cultivate waste moors where they best can. Logie Easter, it is well known has suffered more in its population from this cause, than most other parishes in the north. And though the system has greatly beautified the

> face of the country, and perhaps raised the rents of the land, it cannot be denied, that is is at the expense of the comfort (in most cases) and, I am sorry to add, the morals of the poor people in general.[22]

There is no doubt that the Hay-Mackenzies were involved in such processes. The Hay-Mackenzies were enclosers and improvers, spurred on by their financial problems, following the lead of agricultural pioneers in the region.

Fishing remained the failed panacea of the Highland economy, east and west. In Cromarty Hugh Miller noted that the fish had deserted the Firth for a dozen years and those engaged in it had 'sunk into abject poverty'. At Nigg too the benefits had been extremely doubtful:

> It is true ... that many of the fishermen were enabled by their success, occasionally, a few years since, to build nice cottages, and improve their furniture (and there was abundance of need) but the ordinary fishing for haddocks, cod, etc., was a good deal neglected—debt was in many cases incurred—high ideals were raised—and now there is a considerable degree of poverty, in consequence of the almost total failure, for some years back, of the herring fishing on this part of the coast.[23]

Within this tide of pessimism was, also, the story of the decline of indigenous industries and some of the perversity of the local response to southern industry. Hugh Miller chronicled the actual disappearance, within fifty years, of a small village, Meikle-Ferness: 'The steam looms of Glasgow and Paisley have stopped the village weaver of employment; the manufacturers of Sheffield and Birmingham have discharged the smith, the taste for fashionable furniture, to which the improved dwellings of our agriculturalist naturally led, has shut up the workshop of its carpenters; and the love of dress, so universally diffused in the present age, has levelled the domicile of its tailor, and the staff of its make of Highland shoes'.[24] This was one of the central paradoxes of Highland life in these years and the same pressure on local, traditional manufacturing was seen at Nigg. Here craftsmen's wages had been depressed; shop clothes had become popular and 'the old weavers have given up their trade'.[25] Several parishes referred to the crying need for manufacturing employment. Kiltearn repeated the refrain: 'There is no manufacture carried on to any extent. Even the home made stuffs, which the peasantry used to wear, are now nearly discontinued, as they find it cheaper to purchase than to manufacture them.'[26] Southern goods, the fruits of industrialism, were cheaper and more attractive: 'In many respects, it is very desirable that a manufacture of some kind should be established in the village of Evanton, where there are so many unemployed children, who might be enabled to assist their parents in providing for their support.' This was the reverse side of the coin of industrialisation—a perfect contrast with Manchester and Paisley.

The story of Urquhart and Logie-Wester had equally reflected these changes:

> There is no manufacturing in the parish. The machinery of the south has almost entirely superseded the spinning wheel of the industrious matron, and the simple loom of the country weaver. The good old practice of manufacturing the linen and other apparel for the use of the family, which at one time formed a principal part of the domestic employment of

the female sex, is now nearly forgotten. Our young people have accordingly exchanged the simple but comfortable woollen stuffs in which their ancestors attired their limbs, for the more gaudy but less substantial fabrics of Glasgow or Manchester.

The local minister mused on: 'Whether any benefit accrues to their health from the change may be questioned ... Is it impossible that the substitution of their cotton for warm woollen raiment in the humid climate of Britain is a main cause for the prevalence of consumption in the present day?'[27]

IV

The western parish of the Cromartie estate, Lochbroom, was the most resolutely congested and, probably, the most affected by great changes in economic life over the previous half century. Here a large crofter population subsisted side by side with large sheepfarms and the new shooting leases. In 1842 James Wilson, in his voyage around the western coasts, provided a description of the landscape of post-clearance crofting in Coigach:

> As we advanced beyond Isle Martin, there was a great sheet of this peculiar kind of cultivation, but more regularly divided by straight malls, indicating different possessions, and having a lengthened street or string of huts running along its centre, the whole squared off upon the upper or moorland side, evidently by a planner of estates. The property we believe is part of Mr Hay Mackenzie's, and the village has probably been formed for the accommodation of such of the inland people as were required to move shorewards on the foundation of the larger farms.[28]

But local industry, fishing and kelp were all in retreat. The population continued to grow and large stretches of the estate had not been fully rationalised: the work of estate reorganisation was far from complete. The poverty of the people was mainly unrelieved and the landlord was helpless to do much to improve matters.

Thomas Ross, minister of Lochbroom, offered only the slightest commentary on the changes in his parish. Before the introduction of large-scale sheepfarming the hills of his parish had been 'well stored with game of all kinds'. In his only reference to the subject he remarked that sheepfarming had had a deleterious effect on the game, the woods, 'and also on its race of heroes'.

There was no resident proprietor in Lochbroom despite its huge extent. The population, according to the minister, was substantially understated by the Census. In 1831 the Census reported 4615 (yet a count in 1824 had produced 4747). He believed that 'some hundreds of the parishioners of Lochbroom, away at sea, at the Caithness and deep sea fishings, and at south country labouring of various kinds, must have been omitted in their own, and returned from other parishes'. He claimed that the real population in November 1834 was 5206. The analysis of the population was taken directly from the census. The total population of 4615 was divided into 938 families who inhabited 947 houses. There were 572 occupiers of land, 96 in retail and like trades. The population of the barony of Coigach was 1975 (compared with about 600 in 1790).

In the parish only 1496 people could read or write and many of these not at all well; 3710 could neither read nor write—'many of the people are not sufficiently alive to the benefits of education'. Gaelic was the more widely spoken language but was losing ground. The people were both very poor and badly fed: 'Their ordinary food consists chiefly of potatoes and fish; and it must be admitted that the strength of body, and daring spirit for which the Highlanders were once justly celebrated, are greatly on the decline.' Smuggling and poaching continued.

A more revealing insight into the occupational structure of Lochbroom had been provided by the Militia List of 1827 which included 614 names exempted from the ballot on grounds of business, ill-health, deformities or the provision of a substitute: it included 24 shepherds, 170 residenters, 10 servants, 169 tenants, 13 meallers, 10 tailors, 16 labourers, 99 fishers, 6 shoemakers, 4 teachers, 6 coopers and 5 carpenters. The list suggested a low level of secondary employment beyond simply domestic production, the continuing importance of fishing (despite grave difficulties) and the meagreness of employment in the sheep industry. In contrast to the east Lochbroom had virtually no demand for day labourers. The fact that there were only two blacksmiths indicated the insignificance of metal-working in this society; there was also only one drover, but 7 tacksmen, a piper, a missionary, an excise officer, a farm manager and two fox hunters.[29]

The minister at Lochbroom dated the introduction of the blackfaced sheep to Lochbroom in the 1790s, but the blackfaced were being replaced by the 1830s by the Cheviot. The sheepfarmers obtained leases of 15-19 years. Very little landlord-initiated improvement had occurred—'The proprietors will lay out nothing on their lands, nor will they allow meliorations to their tenants, even for substantial improvement'.[30] Kelp had declined to nothing except for manure. The minister's own economic position was instructive of the general plight of the west coast. His church was so dilapidated that part of the roof had collapsed on his congregation in 1831 so that 'many of them could not be prevailed upon to enter the church again'. The Manse was also in disrepair. His glebe was mainly rugged hillside, but a lower portion he had brought into cultivation, 12 acres, 'at immense expense, which they would never repay him. The rest is let to small tenants or crofters, who labour the ground with their own hands and feet, by means of a certain implement called the cas-chrom, and for which they pay a precarious rent'.[31] His stipend, measured in meal, he regarded as inadequate and ungenerous.

The decline of fishing, concomitant with the increase of population, exacerbated the poverty of Lochbroom. The system of poor relief was similar to that in the east. In all 101 people received parochial aid, 2/- to 5/- each per year. The total income was £21 per year (£16.13.0 at the church door, £5 from a legacy). The only other source derived from fines on adultery, fornication etc.: 'In most ... cases of distress, the heritors have always resisted an assessment, which cannot be enforced without law expenses. There is a strong disposition among the poor to refrain from seeking parochial relief, which they consider as in the lowest degree degrading'. In the parliamentary inquiry into Scottish Poor Relief in 1843 evidence presented from Lochbroom revealed more serious problems especially regarding begging in the vicinity of Ullapool. The minister reported that 'There is a great deal of begging amongst paupers on the roll. The poor here live principally by begging. They beg daily; and if it were not for this resource it would be quite impossible for them to subsist. They are very miserably off.' His evidence was reinforced by a fish curer who said that the poor survived almost entirely by private charity: 'Begging is incessant—not daily but hourly; at certain seasons, however, particularly from the latter months of spring till the time when the potatoes are ready for use, the supply arising from this source is often very limited and precarious. During this season the wants of the poor are often very ill supplied—I have known cases of extreme destitution among them. Often when sitting down to my own meals, I have felt that I was scarcely at liberty to partake of them, while conscious to myself that many around me were almost in circumstances of starvation.'[32]

Fishing, once the panacea for Highland development was, on the west coast, in severe decline. Ullapool, fifty years before, had been the most ambitious of the efforts to promote herring fishing and to employ the small tenantry of the west coast. The British Fishery Society had expended more than £10,000 on public works which included a pier, an inn, and storehouses on a substantial scale. A large village population had collected but, even by 1813, Sir George Mackenzie, with great scorn, was able to denounce the whole venture as a great flop—the settlers were in a state of 'abject poverty and complete distress'. The fishing had failed and the people dispersed and what remained was 'a nest of wickedness'. In all £20,000 had been 'uselessly sunk'; a colony of 700 had been created without subsistence. The projectors, wrote Mackenzie, had been deluded into believing that the inhabitants had been oppressed by their landlords, and that they could be fully emancipated into industrious ways by a system of villages. In fact the promises only made the people destitute. The herring shoals had proved totally unreliable.

In fact, as the subsequent decades showed, the Ullapool venture was a sorry story. It suffered the fate of the entire west coast fishing industry, broken by the continuing migratory shift of the herring shoals towards the north and east coast of Scotland. Already in the first decade of the new century fishing in the Minch failed repeatedly. In 1808 the British Fishery Society had to provide meal as relief for both the settlers and the black-hutters at Ullapool and in the same year Melville (agent for the Society) became a bankrupt. Assets were being sold off in 1812, and in 1813 the Customs House was abandoned. In 1817, partly because of widespread crop failure in the Highlands, the people of Ullapool were desperately impoverished. In 1825 there were complaints about the 'utter apathy and indolence of the inhabitants' and already many of the people were leaving on an annual basis for the season's fishing at Caithness though some continued to work locally in the cod and ling fishery. An effort to promote a whale fishery collapsed in 1817.[33]

Consequently the bright expectations of the Ullapool venture subsided into long-term decay. Yet though the fishery was virtually a total failure the population of the village remained and it was a measure of the defeat that by 1838 vigorous encouragement was being given to emigrants from Ullapool.[34] For the Society this was a complete reversal of its original policy and a final admission of failure. The local people continued to fish for their own subsistence off the west coast but, on the rare occasions when they collected a surplus catch, they were unable to market their produce. In 1850, for instance, there was an abundance of herring in Lochbroom but there were no long-distance vessels available to purchase the fish.[35] The herring supply was too erratic for regular commercial production. A salmon fishing enterprise had more success in the mid-century. A London entrepreneur, Hogarth, operated seven bothies along the west coast, equipped with boiling and curing gear, to supply the London market.[36]

Visitors to Lochbroom were united in their depressing impressions of the blighted condition of the local population. In 1836, for instance, the traveller, Lord Teignmouth, wrote: 'About seven miles from Ullapool we entered an extensive green valley, sprinkled with cottages, through which a mountain-river flows to the sea, which now becomes visible, gemmed with islands of which Martin is the principal, backed by the bold promontory separating the greater from the lesser Loch Broom.' He continued: 'The cottages were wretched: none of the people spoke English.' It was, he remarked, a sad sight and Ullapool was 'the victim of herring caprice' made the more poignant by the sudden return of vast shoals which almost choked the Loch.[37] Two years later the Glasgow statisticians, Fullarton and Baird, were a degree more gloomy about Ullapool. Its only trade was undertaken by a few vessels trading with Ireland, Greenock and Liverpool: 'This constituted their only commerce and as, since the cessation of the kelp business and the fisheries, there is no other trade or manufacturing, the bulk of the people of the place are idle, and in very great misery.' They were utterly pessimistic about Ullapool's prospects and noted that there were 200 paupers in its population with virtually no poor funds to sustain them. They were too poor to emigrate and so wretched that it was not unlikely that 'their numbers may be thinned by disease or famine'.[38] The great problem, of course, was that the establishment and settlement of Ullapool in the euphoria of the 1780s had subsequently left its capital investment and its labour force entirely stranded, without utility. As a Gazateer of 1844 pointed out, Ullapool's buildings were 'greatly disproportionate to the present state of the fishing'.[39] So too was its population.

A desperate air of depression had fallen upon the village. In 1850 it was said that the Ullapool fishery had been in decay for many decades, and the buildings had become dilapidated and there was no sign of a revival. In that year the Cromartie estate let out the Summer Isles, once a fishing centre, to Alexander Mackenzie for a mere ten pounds per annum—'on condition that you clear out the squatters and keep them out'.[40]

The minister of Lochbroom in his report to the *New Statistical Account* made no effort to conceal the poverty of his parish. The people lacked employment:

> Even if a hand manufacture, on the smallest scale were introduced, which would enable the females of the parish, by any employment suitable to their sex, to purchase Newcastle or Liverpool coal for fuel for their families, instead of degrading their persons, and often losing their lives, by carrying peats upon their backs, from almost exhausted morass inaccessible to horses or to carts, it would be an unspeakable benefit to the country.

Inaccessibility was a severe problem. The road built between Dingwall and Ullapool at the turn of the century had disappointed—'the line chosen was so absurd, and the execution so wretched' that it had become useless and dangerous even to pedestrians, and virtually impassable to wheeled vehicles. A new road was indispensable, the *sine qua non* for any other type of improvement.

Though the Lochbroom report was penned in 1835, prior to the descent of near-famine in the following year, its poverty was indisputable. Indeed, the people of Coigach had already dispatched petitions to Parliament 'representing their melancholy state of almost total destitution, and imploring the interposition of the Legislature on their behalf'.[41]

V

No single measure of change or of social welfare could fully account for so radical a transformation of social and economic life in the previous half century. The 'standard of living' in these Highland communities was subject to endless complications—to population shifts, to occupational alterations, to migration into and out of many districts, to changing consumption patterns, to differing levels of tolerance and to new values. It seems unlikely that general trends of welfare improved during the age of the clearances, but the possibility cannot be ruled out.

The most elementary evidence of welfare is in what people ate. The shift towards wheaten bread had been evidenced before 1800 and so had the increasing dependence on potato consumption. Mostly the people ate oatmeal and potatoes, occasionally with fish and milk. This was true in practically all parts. 'The standard of living is exceedingly low', said the Dingwall reporter in the 1830s, 'butcher meat being to the lower orders a luxury in which they seldom indulge. Still, however, the people are social and contented, and enjoy the comforts of society in a higher degree than their slender circumstances would indicate.' Potatoes and herrings were the universal staples, butter and cheese were luxuries, and mutton a rarity in a land of sheep. In Lochbroom oysters, cockles and mussels often helped to tide people over the early summer season 'when meal is scarce or exhausted'.

Underemployment was widespread and for those in work, hours were long. Wages had increased by 20% or more since the 1790s, but prices had also advanced for most commodities. Some of the large farms in the east employed a dozen men in the harvest season and up to 80 women, but the work was inconsistent and increasingly subject to the competition of reaping machines. Nevertheless despite many adverse conditions the people seemed to be buying more commodities—tea, sugar, imported clothing and such like, and several ministers claimed that such consumption was an indicator of a decline not only in traditional manners but also in general morality.

The question that had exercised the cultural imperialists of the previous century, the survival of the Gaelic language, remained a matter of lively public discussion. In many parishes, even in the east, Gaelic was still the language of most of the 'lower orders'. English was spreading but more rapidly among 'the higher ranks'. Urbanisation was the great accelerator. The Tain minister regretted the decline because:

> The stream of traditional wisdom descending from our forefathers has been interrupted in its flow; the feelings and the sentiments of a race, distinguished for high feeling and noble sentiment, will not transfuse themselves into a foreign tongue; and the link of connection between the present and past generations has been snapped.

For some the decline of Gaelic was not rapid enough. Improvement was regarded as synonymous with the spread of English. As one minister put it:

> The English language is daily taught in the Society School in the upper district of the parish, and this affords an opportunity for acquiring it to the poorest of the people. Along with the improved education of the lowest classes, arising from her general acquaintance with the English language, there is a growing improvement likewise in their customs and habits.

It would not be difficult to detect a cultural and linguistic arrogance in such remarks.

> Those popular amusements which formerly engrossed much of their time, and dissipated their means and attention, and were the inlets to much low debauchery, are almost entirely given up, and when resorted to, occasionally, are not at all so nearly prosecuted as they used to be, in former generations.[42]

VI

The ministers' verdict on the passage of improvement was mainly negative though hardly unambiguous. Evidence of 'land hunger', for example higher rents, dispossession, migration, greater cultivation of marginal land, reclamation, new capital investment, were not necessarily inconsistent with rising levels of welfare. Some aspects of material life, even for the poor, had improved. Famine was probably more localised, less frequent and less lethal than in the previous century. Yet, even so, the belief in progress was not contrary to the reality of extreme poverty and over-population in both east and west. The economy had been dislocated and remodelled in 50 years: it had shaken out its labouring people and set them in new patterns. They had become less attached to the land, and thereby more mobile. It was a shifting basis for life.

The social consequences were undoubtedly large. Ministers feared that the linkages of society had been broken, that the social bonds had been weakened. They feared social breakdown. Symptoms of general alienation were perceived in the decline of Gaelic, the departure of young people in emigration, and the erosion of Highland traditions. The new and expanded villages seemed raw and uncomfortable as social communities. The older intricacies of deference seemed to pass. Yet there is little evidence of actual breakdown in this society—a rural revolution in the economy passed with little overt social dislocation, little resistance. The evidence is unambiguous about the re-formation of the rural economy; it is less clear about the social adjustments.

Highland society had become shifting and insecure as well as having a growing population. For the most part it had little obvious communal solidarity and little resistance to the ongoing changes. Even Gaelic was little cherished and there is evidence that the lower classes pressed their children to learn English as a means of a better future for their generation.[43] The most distinctive communities that emerged in these years were the fishing villages which created a local subculture turning its back on the arable farming community and sufficiently cohesive to mount food riots in 1847.[44]

Common to both sides of the Highlands was the dissociation of the people from the land. Large consolidated farms replaced the old semi-communal and unsystematic agriculture. The transformation undoubtedly dislocated the old society. Three possibilities faced the people ousted by these changes: they might be given crofts, they could become part of the agricultural proletariat living in the swelling villages, or they could leave altogether. Crofting in the east was a compromise between the old ways and the new—semi-subsistence, semi-proletarian. In the west it is not so easy to see the consequences—the old farms were taken over by sheepfarmers, but the people still needed large communal grazings. But it seems inescapable that the *per capita* holding of land and livestock diminished in the west. Each group, even as low as the cottars, kept a tenuous grip on a piece of land, though the grip seems to have been weakening.

CHAPTER 15

Emigration, Famine and the Impecunious Landlord

I

Emigrants had been leaving the Highlands for more than a century. There was a long tradition of mobility in many forms—seasonal migration within and beyond the region, the annual cattle droving, fishing especially in the north east, regimental service abroad, migration to villages, new crofts, to southern Scotland and England, to America and even to Australia. It was all evidence of a population far from stable and landlocked. Some of the mobility was voluntary, some in various degrees, less so. Agrarian change undoubtedly dislodged some of the population, though less in arable than in pastoral districts. Some left because they were cleared or levered out. But the mobility was insufficient to meet the needs of the economy and to satisfy the opinions of most of its landlords. Total population, especially in the west, continued to grow into the mid-nineteenth century. The crofters seemed to become less mobile and more tenacious of their precarious hold on the land. Famine recurred—notably in 1836/8 and 1847/9 and the region seemed on the brink of tragedy.

Failure of crops and the collapse of crofter income on the west coast in 1836 and 1837 triggered a great deal of public anxiety for the future of the Highlands; eventually the general apprehension persuaded the government to institute a parliamentary enquiry into emigration which was increasingly regarded as the panacea for poverty and hunger on the celtic periphery. Already in 1838 the Statistical Society of Glasgow had taken an initiative, and gathered together for publication, evidence and opinion on the problem of Highland poverty. Two members of the Society, Fullarton and Baird, reached a serious view of the dangers facing the West Highlands, believing that the region was 'overcharged' with population. It was plain, they concluded, that 'emigration is as necessary to the happiness, nay, we may say, to the existence of the present redundant population of the Highlands and Islands, as it is to the welfare of those who are destined to be its future inhabitants'. Emigration was the top priority but should also be supported by measures to prohibit subletting and by the better provision for education.

Lochbroom was a perfect example of their general diagnosis: it was backward, lacked the basic social capital of any civilized community, and was grossly over populated. Its population had increased from 3500 in 1798 to 5400 in 1838. Fullarton and Baird remarked that 'although the general aspect of the country is bleak, barren and rugged, yet there are spots along the shore, and in the glens and valleys, which redeem its character and refresh the eye of the traveller'. But conditions were poor: there were only eight schools in the parish and most of the population simply could not read. The teachers could not keep up with the growth in numbers. The authors were expressly critical of absenteeism among the proprietors—four (including Hay-Mackenzie of Cromartie) out of five did not live in Lochbroom, leaving the people 'flagrantly destitute of all the advantages of a law abiding gentry, by whose presence and example they might be led in the paths of improvement'. The problems of the west coast crofters were profound:

> It need hardly be stated that in such a parish as this there is little or no attention paid to agricultural improvement. The absence of the landlords may, to a certain degree, account for this; but, even were they present, they neither could do, nor were bound to do, much to further an art to which the country had no adaptation, either from soil or climate.[1]

The Glasgow report reinforced the growing opinion that the national government should instigate an Inquiry into conditions in the north. Many already were convinced that a massive subsistence crisis was impending and that large scale emigration was the only feasible answer. Some believed that the government should intervene directly and subsidise the evacuation of a large proportion of the population—the government however steadfastly resisted the whole idea for both financial and ideological reasons. It was reluctant even to accede to an enquiry. Eventually, in 1841, the government agreed to a Select Committee on Emigration (Scotland) though it made it perfectly obvious that expectations of substantial aid to emigration would be unjustified. The main proponent of the Inquiry was Henry James Baillie, an eloquent advocate for Highland welfare. He pointed out that some 40,000 people were destitute in the region, many of whom would be better off in Canada, though not in Australia.

> In Canada they know they would find many of their own relations and friends; they know that they would find whole districts of the country peopled by Highlanders, speaking their own language, maintaining their own manners and customs, and, above all, they know that they would find their own church established by law.

Baillie did not fail to note that the émigré Glengarry Highlanders had remained loyal in the recent Canadian troubles. Moreover, he reminded the House, that 'in spite of all their misery and all their distress, they had heard of no outrages, they had heard of no violence, they had heard of no Chartism in that country; all that they had heard of was patient endurance, of the worse, the most intolerable of evils to which humanity could be subject.' They were clearly a special case, and their conditions were worse than those of the former slaves of the West Indies who had, he pointed out, already received assistance from the British government.[2]

The 1841 Parliamentary Inquiry, though it ultimately did little to shift the government's attitude to emigration, exposed the roots of the Highland problem to public scrutiny. It revealed fully the subsistence vulnerability of the west coast: indeed to a degree it was a harbinger of the great famine which descended on the west Highlands in 1846/7. It was not entirely unlike the role of the Devon Commission in Irish pre-famine history. In particular it yielded a great deal of data about the basis of Highland poverty and thus included substantial evidence of the barony of Coigach on the Cromartie estate.

Most of the Cromartie evidence[3] came from Andrew Scott, factor to John Hay-Mackenzie for the previous ten years. Scott was a man of the Scottish borders, from Roxburghshire. His office was located at New Tarbat and much of the west coast factoring was done by a sub-agent, Kenneth Mackenzie, a local man with little training in the business of modern estate management. Scott's evidence was a systematic exposition of the West Highland problem viewed from 'the factor's office'.

Scott told the Inquiry that the Coigach estate covered 145,000 acres, equivalent to a third of the large parish of Lochbroom. It was exceedingly populous: in 1838 he had made his own count which produced a total estate population of 1512 of whom a third were less than 12 years of age. Of these 231 were tenants, and the average size of a family was 6. The average annual rent was between 65 and 70 shillings per head. The tenantry were located on 'eight lot farms'.[4] The rest of the district was in the hands of the great sheep farmers. 'Lot farms' were lands set aside for crofters (probably at a time when the sheep farms had been carved out of the ancient grazing lands) with communal grazing for their stock, usually presided over by the mid-nineteenth century descendants of tacksmen. The lot tenants possessed a mere 450 acres of arable land—presumably all for oats and potatoes. Efforts to extend cultivation had proved fruitless and no further expansion or reclamation was contemplated. Such were the basic facts of crofter statistics save for one other: in addition to the tenants and their families were 500 others—the unofficial marginal people, the squatters who inflated the dependent population to about 2000. They represented a vast under-class in this remote peasant society.

The famine of 1836/8, which is otherwise virtually unrecorded, echoed through Scott's remarks to the Inquiry.[5] The famine had been caused by potato failure and early frosts which had attacked the corn before it had had time to ripen. Its severity was unusual but every year produced its quota of distress—'I have known every year cases where families were living almost altogether on shellfish from the shore, with a little water gruel at night, and not a bit of bread or potato in their house.' Scott may have been inclined to exaggerate the plight of the common people—his own job would certainly have been easier if the people could be induced to emigrate; yet he was prepared to say that they were generally healthy. In the recent famine Hay-Mackenzie had provided his own famine relief and had allowed arrears of rent to accumulate. But reality interposed: the rent arrears were almost certainly irrecoverable and external famine relief had been decisive, notably that provided by the Glasgow Relief Committee. Indeed it seems likely that the orchestration of outside assistance was a critical element in the avoidance of fatal consequences in mid-nineteenth century famines, especially compared with periods before 1783. Though it was said that Coigach (even in 1860) was 'shut out from other parts of the country by lofty mountain ranges and was one of the wildest and least accessible parts of Scotland',[6] the record of famine relief from southern agencies indicates that one of the most ancient and tragic isolations had indeed been broken forever.

The vulnerability of the people was unquestionable—they had required relief in every year since 1835[7] and in each year Hay-Mackenzie had made arrangements to relieve distress. Coigach commonly produced less than half of its direct subsistence requirements and each year meal imports were required. The crofters raised cattle, grazed on common hill ground, to pay their rents, each tenant holding between one and three cows and between two and 20 sheep: 'The hill ground laid off to each township is common to the tenants of each township, and is from 1000 acres to 5000 according to the extent of arable land there may be in a particular township'. The land system had been stabilised before Scott's arrival in 1831; he testified that the sheep farms had been created before that time and no other changes had been made since. Small rents were poorly paid and if the people left Coigach their land would certainly be converted into sheep farms and the rental would improve greatly. But clearances, Scott indicated, were unthinkable for no man of humanity would attempt it. The land would be better utilised under sheep and the landlord had the power to remove his people if he chose to use it. The principle of humanity was the only reason for not clearing the people.

The crofters therefore continued to live by their croft, by cattle, together with the fishing and seasonal employment in the Lothians and at Wick. There had been little kelp production in the district and, unlike other parts of the west, little of the great population growth could be attributed to its artificial stimulation for the kelp industry. It was however possible, Scott conceded, that the fishing had generated demographic growth. Before 1825 it had been prosperous and Scott agreed that the landlord had indeed granted small crofts to the fishing folk. The Ullapool enterprise had been punctuated by failure and by a poor long-run record of growth. Since 1826 (with the exception of the year 1840) it had been depressed and unproductive: 'I was told by my predecessor, about fifteen years ago, that the shillings were as plenty there as pennies were when he gave up the business to me'.

Scott demonstrated the narrow limits of crofter life—apart from fishing and potatoes most of the people had no other means of subsistence—'unless they were to emigrate to the low country and work at spade work; they have nothing but their labour ... many go to the seasonal migration, but somewhat fewer than before'. The people of Coigach carried peat on their backs and the mosses were now almost exhausted. The landlord had tried to dampen population growth by preventing any subdivision of crofts but the problem of squatting was virtually uncontrollable. The prohibition on sub-letting was a means of discouraging early marriage. When asked the question, 'What happens when a young man marries and has no croft?' Scott replied, 'We do not look after him at all; he may go anywhere he pleases', but he was not allowed to squat on the estate. Yet Scott also admitted that little was done to evict even the squatters. While it was true that 'the worst should be picked out from time to time' Hay-Mackenzie had no stomach for 'any steps of a violent character'. The sheep farmers derived absolutely no benefits from the existence of the crofters and their lands 'could be turned to better account were they removed altogether' and the pasture converted to sheep land. But this would require clearances, but Scott repeated, no 'man of any humanity would attempt that'.

There was minimal official provision for the poor of Coigach. The poor looked after the poor in the assistance they gave each other—'they are very remarkable for that; a poor man would divide his potatoes with his destitute neighbour'. Some charitable funds were collected at the church doors 'and the landlords probably give a few pounds now and then as the ministers represents the cases of necessity'. The people were very poor but there were few complaints about the fate of 'the impotent poor, the blind, the halt, and the lame'—indeed Scott thought the poor of Coigach were no worse off than those of his own native Roxburghshire. The great fear of the landlords was the threat of compulsory assessment, of an official Poor Law. If this were imposed on the west Highlands the landlords would be forced to drive the people off their lands, and the sheepfarmers would be equally vociferous. All prevailing humanitarian contracts would be eliminated and evictions would become inevitable. Scott even claimed that the people were also against a Poor Law because it would rob them of their sense of independence: 'they have a decided objection to be on the poor roll.'

Thus within the general context of poverty and overpopulation, the social community operated to maintain minimum levels of security: no-one starved and the poor were looked after within the bosom of the people. The people themselves, it was said, were extremely moral and sober and there had been no outrages on property during the recent destitution.[8] The landlord consciously resisted the temptation to maximise his economic returns by way of clearance and sought to avert this final resort (though radical change had occurred in previous decades). Traditional ways of social and economic life were entrenched in contrast to the eastern quarters of the Cromartie estate where improvement had worked its course. Emigration was the great hope for the future. Scott was candid: 'I think it would be a decided benefit to the people themselves, as well as to the landlord, to get rid of the burden of the support of these people'. And if they left, their places would not be refilled in a Malthusian fashion because Hay-Mackenzie 'would make the farms into sheep grazings.' Australia was not currently popular, but whole families would go to Canada if they were given passages together with the prospect of land in the new country. Without government assistance the problem could find no real solution.

Another parliamentary inquiry at this time, into the Scottish Poor Law, also received evidence on emigration from the Highlands. Emigration was clearly subject to sudden enthusiasms and highly variable responses from the people. The reports were often contradictory or discrepant. In the east there was said to be 'no disposition in the people to emigrate. They prefer their native parish'. But from Rosskeen it was reported that a great many had emigrated even though 'no highlander wishes to leave his country if he can help it'. In the west, at Lochbroom, the recent destitution had increased interest: 'The people are tolerably disposed to emigrate but they have not the means to do so, and very few persons have emigrated from this part of the country for many years past'. Emigrants tended to be 'chiefly persons in better circumstances than those of the average of our common labourers. The labouring classes show no disposition in favour of emigration.' Several reasons were suggested to explain the reluctance of the people to emigrate. Australia was unpopular because of a fear of bushrangers and natives. But mostly the cause was ignorance—'their sphere of ideas is not sufficiently enlarged' to see the advantages of emigration. Only the provision of education and subsidised passages would achieve the goals of mass migration from the region.

The Select Committee on Emigration reported in ways sympathetic to opinion such as Andrew Scott's. The West Highlands was grossly overpopulated and unless large-scale emigration were achieved then famine must recur:

> It was established by the Evidence ... that an excess of Population existed beyond that for which the country could afford the means of Subsistence, or furnish adequate Employment, along that part of the Western Coast which includes portions of the Counties of Argyll, Inverness, and Ross, as well as amongst the Islands; and this excess of Population, who are for the most part for a period of every year in a state of great destitution, was variously calculated at from 45,000 to 80,000 souls.[9]

Hence the Committee recommended 'a well-arranged system of Emigration' which would require government assistance perhaps with the aid of colonial monies. Without emigration, famine was inevitable. Everyone in the West Highlands knew this already.

II

Scott's public testimony to the Parliamentary Enquiry of 1841 was shadowed by a fatalism for the poverty of the western Barony and the future of the people. Overpopulation was the root of the problem but a radical shake-out would require firm action. Hay-Mackenzie did not possess enough constitutional fortitude to institute radical removal policies and the government refused to sanction subsidies for mass emigration. The causes of overpopulation were in dispute: on the one hand the crofters were blamed for their inertia, their immobility, their inefficiency and their thoughtless attitude to procreation; on the other hand, the congestion of people in coastal settlements was denounced as the product of landlord policies which had expropriated land from the old farms and forced the crofters into fishing and potato cultivation. By Scott's own evidence it is clear that earlier clearances had moved people off the new sheep farms and that small crofts had been created in the unavailing belief that fishing would support such small tenants.[10] The objective fact was that on the west coast of the Cromartie estate a larger population than ever before was now subsisting on a smaller territory than their less numerous forebears. The extreme vulnerability of the crofters was a product of severe land hunger and an ungenerous environment. Moreover the owners, the Hay-Mackenzies, were in no position to finance improvement or emigration from their own resources.

The management of the small tenantry absorbed a disproportionate part of the energy of the Cromartie estate management. In the 1840s a new tension emerged in the use of west coast lands: sporting leases were now being sought by seasonal tenants from the south. Existing small tenants were even less welcome to the deer-hunters than to sheepfarmers and a further incompatability developed. Moreover the estate officials intermittently pursued individual small-scale removals among tenants in arrears or where they were found to be harbouring unofficial sub-tenants. The persistence of subletting on the Cromartie estate was evidence both of the tenacity of squatting and the survival of the remnants of the old tacksman system. The modernisation of management on the western estate was far from complete and many anomalies remained. For instance there was the case of a woman from Badenscallie who, in February 1841, travelled all the way to Tarbat—perhaps 60 miles across the mountains—to appeal to Hay-Mackenzie to save her from eviction by her over-tenant. She had no cattle or sheep but had the responsibility of maintaining her aged and bed-ridden mother on her lot. She petitioned the landlord to help pay two pounds a year to the tenant for the arable land and the old grazing land to be added to an adjacent croft. It seems that Hay-Mackenzie acceded to this request on condition that no new houses were built and that no strangers were permitted on to the land.[11]

Pressure was undoubtedly exerted by Hay-Mackenzie upon the small tenants. In May 1841 Andrew Scott asked for 'a list of tenants summoned to flit this next term. They will surely be removed unless they can give security that they will pay better than they have hitherto done besides making a good payment at this time.'[12] As always rent collections were difficult and arrears forever mounting.[13] Yet the business of removals, even on the smallest scale, was always approached with the greatest hesitation no doubt reinforced by the odium well known to attach itself to clearing landlords in the Highlands. There was a good example of such sensitivity in 1842. George Gunn, factor on the great Sutherland estate to the north, made himself candidate for the farm of Badentarbet which was to be taken over at the expense of some small tenants. Gunn made it clear that he wished it to be understood that Donald MacDonald of Lochinver would be thought of as tenant, even though MacDonald would have nothing to do with the lease or the payment of rent. The reason for this subterfuge was that Gunn 'seems a little anxious about people saying that the Duke of Sutherland's factor is going into Ross-shire and dispossessing Cromartie's old tenants there.'[14] Similarly it is equally unlikely that Hay-Mackenzie would wish to be associated with the reputation for eviction irrevocably connected in the public mind with the Sutherland estate regime.

Small-scale and routine evictions on the Cromartie estate continued annually, acting like attrition and helping to thin the population on a temporary basis without achieving much impact on the problem in general. A few tenants in arrear in Coigach and Strathpeffer were removed, and tacksmen themselves executed their own removals (at Polbain for instance). Scott maintained a policy towards the crofters designed to minimise any increase in their numbers. Tenants could build new houses on their lots only so long as their previous dwellings were converted into byres or barns, and the new dwelling possessed no more rooms than the old. It was a rule to avoid the likelihood that:

> more than one family may be lodged under the same roof and maintained in one and the same Lot—which will not be suffered. And as soon as the new House is finished and fit to be inhabited, the old one must be taken down. But if the old House be wanted for a Byre or a Barn or stable it must be fitted up for that purpose; but in no case will it be permitted the tenant to have a fine room in the end of the old house, and cattle in the other end of it—the Old House must be wholly used as an Out House after a new one has been built, or entirely demolished.

There were similar dangers in the practise of building summer bothies in the hills, and Scott issued another prohibition, mainly to prevent any individual tenant from gaining too much pasturing advantage over his co-tenants—'The whole Hill stock ought to graze promiscuously together, and without disturbance from any one—which cannot be, if this Bothy system be permitted'. All this was evidence of the continuing communalism and pastoralism of the west coast small tenants,[15] and the continuing dependence of the people and their rents upon cattle sales and prices. They were a marginal but surviving pre-industrial peasantry facing old and new pressures, still expecting to rely on the landlord's benevolence whenever famine descended.

Andrew Scott, the main factor of the Cromartie estates, was reluctant to pursue a policy of clearance and could always find reasons to delay the day. In March 1843 he wrote in these terms to a ground officer:

> In respect to the policy or utility of sending summonses of removing to any of the tenants on the Coigach Barony this year I am doubtful. It has not been a favourable season, the late one, and most of them did, I have no doubt, their best at the last Marts to stand fair with the Landlord. To send summonses therefore would only add expense rather than produce any good effect in the way of procuring better payments of rents in future—besides it might be construed into a rigour not consistent with Cromartie's method of dealing with the poor people on his estates.[16]

Scott's instruction was a substantial hint of the restraint and rationalism that coloured management on the Cromartie estate. Scott himself was sensitive to the necessary rigours of his function as agent. He knew that, on occasion, he was required to perform things 'neither agreeable to myself nor pleasant to those with whom I have to deal ... Such things must be done by some one and if I perform any not very pleasant duty with as little harshness as another wd be likely to shew there can be no causes for serious complaint agt me.'[17]

III

The costs of population growth and the failure of economic development were paid in the much-predicted famine of 1846/7 caused by the same potato blight which devastated Ireland. It was because the people of the West Highlands depended on potatoes and had little capital saved to tide them over a harvest failure, that much of the region was reduced to destitution. One of the relief committees described it as 'this great and mysterious calamity [in which] three fourths of the food of this vast population has been withdrawn from them.' The intensity of distress approached the suffering experienced in Ireland: but a catastrophe on the Irish scale was eventually averted by a series of relief measures generated from both internal and external sources.

Coigach was in the middle of the devastated region. Unfortunately direct evidence of the famine and its onset is missing from the Cromartie estate correspondence. Nevertheless it is clear that Ullapool was already in dire straits by December 1846 and in the following March the local minister reported that:

> The destitution of the people here from want of meal is truly alarming, and unless some immediately arrive, death will be the consequence. Great numbers of people have nothing to eat but herrings, as there is no store of meal, country or government, starvation is surrounding its victims.[18]

The minister reported that there were:

> a considerable number of families in absolute want of food, raiment, and money, subsisting wholly on the charity of their poor neighbours,—a great many of whom will become equally destitute in a few weeks, unless a kind Providence send some relief from some unseen source.[19]

A supply of oatmeal was the first priority. In neighbouring Assynt, to the north, there had been a total failure of the potato crop; the disaster affected crofters on the coast as well as those who had remained undisturbed in the inland zones; they were eating their seed corn and there were hundreds in the parish 'in actual starvation'. The minister warned that 'unless something is done, and that immediately, for their relief, hundreds of my poor parishioners will, ere two months elapse, be in eternity'.[20]

On the Cromartie estate the crisis was confined to the west coast. There were, it is true, rapid increases in food prices in the east, and great apprehension of local shortages resulting from large exports from the district, but there was little danger of destitution.[21] The localised character of the current calamity was emphasised by a report (in June 1847) that the eastern districts were in good cheer. From Strathpeffer, for instance, it was reported:

> This vale is now beginning to appear in all its summer beauty, the fields that have been cropped are assuming an appearance indicative of an abundant harvest, and the trees and hedgerows are fully covered in foliage. Already have some of those visitors who frequent this delightful spot for the benefit of their health made their appearance, and, in the course of a week, many more are expected.[22]

There was likely to be a record harvest.

A few months later there were three reports from Lochbroom to the General Committee of Edinburgh for the relief of Destitution in the Highlands and Islands. They confirmed the existence of a dense, vulnerable and hungry population. Two-thirds of the potato crop had been lost and the people were forced back on to a diet of herrings alone. The fate of the seed potatoes was now a critical factor in the situation. Potatoes and herrings formed two-thirds of the diet, three-quarters according to another account. The number of destitute was accelerating but no food had been imported whatsoever even though there was ample storage space. There were many able bodied people able to work for relief, but there was presently no employment to be had. The people were living in the expectation of relief, and William Cameron (a minister of Lochbroom) remarked that:

> every week's delay in sending a supply of provisions will soon tell woefully on the inhabitants of this Parish. At present they are mutually assisting each other and bearing their hard lot without murmur or complaint.

A supply of relief food was 'daily and anxiously looked for' and by the end of February 150 families would be destitute. Some of the people were searching daily for employment and would 'prefer purchasing provisions for themselves and families by the produce of their labour than receive their provisions gratuitously at the hands of the Committee'. The Free Church minister, Mr McLeod, at Ullapool, urged that 'work should be furnished without a single day's delay'. The able-bodied were desperate for work; 'it will be attended with a positive moral injury to the people who are both able and willing to work, if arrangements be not made in time to afford them employment'.

The same report said categorically that the destitution was more severe than at any former period 'in the recollection of even the oldest in the parish'. Fishing was a vital means of life even though 'a gambling means of subsistence' and many families were reduced to living off those herrings. New road construction would be the best solution to the immediate and long term problems of the district.[23]

In April 1847 a correspondent, looking for long-term causes of the crisis, pointed out to Hay-Mackenzie that the population of the Barony of Coigach had increased from 1600 in 1836 to 1760 in 1847. He asked: 'Could not means have been taken to prevent so great an increase in the population as 160 in ten years?'[24] The question was rhetorical and pointed to the attendant severity of famine in the district, as also for the common failure of Highland estates to cope with the recurrent scarcities of food.

Famine relief in the West Highlands came in various forms depending on the degree of landlord participation. There was much private relief but also large public subscription relief in the form of subsidised food imports. In both cases, however, there were usually work tests applied to the assistance given to the common people. In effect the people were required to work before relief was given; the work usually took the form of road construction or agricultural improvements. Coigach conformed to this pattern of relief regulation. Hay-Mackenzie co-operated with relief schemes and also assisted his west coast people from his own small resources.

In mid-1847 Scott reported that Hay-Mackenzie had already advanced to his west coast people in meal and seed oats the equivalent of one year's rent, 'a great part of which he will not be able to recover'. He responded promptly to the suggestion of the Board of Supervision that relief by way of road construction might be initiated in the district. Scott was asked for details of the likely time needed for construction. He answered that it would depend on the number of hands available, 'and as the natives are not accustomed to labour, it will take a little time to drill them to steady perseverance in such kind of employment. You can easily imagine that men accustomed to little else than fishing will make but indifferent spade men.' Scott argued that a road to Coigach could be made in two or three years and would be a great boon to 'so remote and neglected a country', and it would educate the people to 'the use of implements of labour and it might be [a means] of inducing habits of industry and a taste of comforts that hitherto they have not discovered the want of.' Late summer, before harvest, was the best time to raise labour, and he recommended their payment as two-thirds in meal and one-third in cash. Seedtime, harvest and mid-winter were the least practical times for labour; if work and superintendence were made available 'there would be no excuse for idleness; and families in need of sustentation unless visited by sickness would be forced out to earn their food as others do by the sweat of their brow.' He noted that there was a permanent deficiency of employment in the district, and that the people 'were obliged to husband carefully their little means from Harvest to Harvest—every season finding many of them at the starving point before the young potatoes were fit for food.'[25]

For many decades the difficulties in the way of road construction had been one of the greatest problems facing the western and central Highlands. Public financial provision for roads in Ross and Cromarty had been the source of some of the most ill-tempered disputes in the county in the early nineteenth century. As late as 1850 there were many large stretches of the county, some 'of the wildest and most inaccessible parts of Scotland, still without roads at all'. The west was always badly served both for trunk roads and feeders. Road Acts had been passed in 1825 and 1828 to connect Dingwall with Garve and Ullapool and other western districts. In fact the construction work reached only to Garve, and most of Wester Ross remained virtually roadless. Proprietors possessed the authority to use statute labour to create roads, and for their maintenance, and in 1844 further concerted efforts were made to connect the west, followed by another survey in 1847. But so far little had been achieved.

The Famine brought these plans to an unprecedented degree of co-ordination. Most decisive was the flow of money from the Central Board of the Destitution Fund[26] which acted in conjunction with the Lords of the Treasury: the relief bodies in fact raised £200,000 by public subscription and decided to use some of the funds to construct roads for the generation of income and employment as well as for the permanent improvement of economic prospects in the West Highlands. The Edinburgh section of the Central Board took charge of operations and arranged:

> the appointment of experienced officers of the army and navy to superintend the distribution of the fund, and to assist carrying out their plans. This fund was at first distributed by direct relief to the destitute population in meal and other personal necessities, but was latterly employed in aiding local efforts to get the population of the various districts to work on roads, and other works of public benefit in those districts of the country where the co-operation of the proprietors could be obtained.

Hay-Mackenzie was involved in public meetings and was prominent in mobilising Wester Ross landowners into co-operating with the Destitution Board. Eventually each proprietor acted semi-independently to take advantage of the Destitution Board grants. The money was provided on condition 'that the proprietors of the lands within the said parish should take upon themselves the burden of the support of the people on their own estates respectively,' and 'that they should undertake to complete the said road in as far as situated within the said parish'. The Road Trustees (including Hay-Mackenzie) agreed and the operations were set in motion to construct a road from Garve to Ullapool together with a further link into Coigach and Knockan.

Andrew Scott, though alarmed at the delays in the evolution of these plans, was filled with enthusiasm, partly because he envisaged that the road would permanently link the Coigach people with the Bonar Bridge district in the east 'which would consume a large quantity of Coigach fish and for which it would pay in meal, potatoes, or anything that the Coigach people might require in exchange for their produce.' Scott could see a developing division of labour between the east and west sides of the estate, especially since the Duke of Sutherland was currently sponsoring road construction north and south to Ullapool. Lacking roads the trade to the east was still transported by ponies and creels. These plans were further complemented by other expenditures undertaken by Hay-Mackenzie at the time of the famine. For instance he took advantage of the opportunities for preferential loans offered by the Drainage Commissioners: he borrowed about £10,000 over five years much of which was spent on trenching a moss at Keanchrine 'with the intent to be a creditor to the next heir of entail' to the Cromartie estate. Some of the expenditure was paid for the creation of shooting facilities at Drumrunie. Relief and improvement expenditures such as these were almost without doubt critical in sustaining the west Highlanders through the worst subsistence crisis of the century.[27]

The conditions by which the Highland Destitution Committee provided assistance to localities required local heritors to maintain the population. The people if able bodied were required to take outdoor employment; where the able-bodied were not able to do outdoor work and yet could not be placed on the roll of paupers, 'knitting or some such easy work will be required'. It seems that Hay-Mackenzie was advanced money for the construction of the road in Coigach and was then expected to look after the welfare of his people without further assistance from the Board of Supervision. It was clearly a system of relief founded upon the principle of a work test for the able-bodied.[28] The best workers on the roads could earn 10/6 a week and they were able to obtain an advance of meal on credit of two weeks wages. The relief operation was complicated by the fact that many west coast people were supported by breadwinners at the Caithness fishing who normally sent money home for the support of their families. Andrew Scott, the factor, was insistent that these people should be made to repay for any assistance obtained during the relief operations, and he kept a list of their payments.[29] The Central Committee paid for relief employment in the district and from this income the people were able to buy food to tide them over the crisis. The landlord undertook to maintain the rest of the dependent population, and he also appears to have organised supplies of meal for the small tenantry on the west, and made arrangements for clippers with meal from Banff and Aberdeen on the east coast to call at Ullapool.[30] Potatoes were also carefully preserved for distribution in late 1848.

The measures taken for relief were subject to periodic inspection which, inevitably, exposed local difficulties and anomalies. In August 1847 Captain Eliot reported from Ullapool to the Edinburgh section of the Central Board. He said that the local relief lists were 'loaded with names that should never have been admitted on to them'. The work test had been neglected and men who were totally destitute of every means of existence were being relieved side by side with 'the rent-paying tenant, the possessor of at least the amount of stock on his holding'. Nevertheless Eliot testified to the gravity of the destitution and the total failure of the potato crop and that 'but for the interference of relief, the gravest consequences would have been in fatal operation'. He gave the astonishing figure of 1671 as the number of Hay-Mackenzie's people as recipients on the roll—that is, practically the entire population of Coigach.[31]

The famine was not only severe in its intensity but also debilitating in its duration. It lingered on into 1850 when the potatoes were again rotting in their pits and stock prices were so poor that cattle were scarcely worth raising, especially because they were also very small. Scott remarked in March 1850, as he set out to Lochbroom, that he would arrange a part of the road construction and set the people to work: 'There are many of them badly off, their potatoes having wholly failed and I cannot think of advancing them meal without work'. Scott made an arrangement with the Destitution Committee to keep the Cromartie estate people in Outdoor and Indoor Relief while the Committee advanced £475 in aid of the road from Ullapool to Knockan. Thus Scott was again obliged to raise meal supplies—which he obtained for 14/- per boll—from the east coast, notably from Aberdeen and Banff. The road work was put out on squad work by contract. Much of the work involved rock-cutting and special contractors were brought in for particularly difficult sections of the road construction, including bridgework. During the fishing season many of the men on relief work departed for Caithness and Scott had to take on new hands. For the indoor work yarn and twine were obtained for the manufacture of netting. A great deal of responsibility fell on the local ground agent Kenneth Mackenzie, who was urged on by Scott thus: 'you will have to set your shoulder to the wheel and do your best to keep everything right.'[32]

The supplies of meal were normally left to the enterprise of local traders in the villages who charged prices which were high enough to present a constant source of irritation to the crofters. Andrew Scott estimated that meal could be brought from Caithness to Ullapool and sold at 5/- to 6/- a boll less than the prices obtained by the local traders. There were repeated requests from the people that a store be constructed at Ullapool to provide against severe shortages and famine prices. As late as February 1852, Scott was balancing the proposition in his mind; his concern was that the people would never be able to repay either their rent arrears or the cost of the meal. His greatest apprehension was that the people would come to expect and rely upon such assistance, and 'if they are to be helped whenever they ask for help, they will never learn the virtue of self dependence but continually rely on the proprietor for aid whenever they are in any difficulty.'[33] Opposition to the relative ease of relief came from several influential people connected with the estate. Guaranteed relief for the able-bodied would be the destruction of landed estates.[34] Scott's own view was that meal supplies and relief employment were merely temporary expedients. Emigration was the only permanent resolution of the real difficulties of the region. But the Cromartie estate, though it encouraged the rising spirit of migration in 1848, was unable from its own resources to sponsor schemes for the expatriation of the crofters.

In the spring of 1851, Scott was required to collect statistics of Coigach for Sir John McNeill's enquiry into the West Highland problem. He was, however cynical about the purpose of the exercise: 'I think this is got up to justify the government in refusing relief to the west coast Highlanders'. He thought the real object was to place the burden of relief of the able-bodied poor onto local rate-payers. He declared that 'anybody knows who has been any time in the Highlands that if the people can be made to understand by the agents of the Free Church (and they will require very little teaching) that able-bodied labourers must not be allowed to suffer in health from any cause, they will apply for relief in numbers that one cannot almost anticipate.' He said of these people that they would rather half starve than look for work, and that if the Scottish Poor Law operated in this way the burden on proprietors would be ruinous. It would be tantamount to the confiscation of Highland property.[35] In this way the impact of the Disruption and government in the famine had, together, sharpened social tensions in the region and was, in a small way, preparation for the birth of political consciousness among the crofters.

By November 1851, the Cromartie estate management was at last beginning to sound relatively optimistic about prospects in Coigach. The potato crop had been secured and was both abundant and sound: 'If it keeps in the store, sound and good, as when put in, the poor people will be well off and comfortable for it is upon the potato crop they chiefly depend'. The herring season was poor but rents were being better paid. Moreover, as Scott pointed out: 'We have by new roads opened up districts of Country that two years ago could only be approached on foot—now you may drive your carriage. This I reckon a great boon to the people of the remote localities.'[36]

The human costs of the famine are not well recorded in either contemporary documents or in oral recollection and the details of the human suffering endured on the west coast of the Cromartie estate during the famine remain unknown. It is clear enough, however, that the estate and the people were not able to cope with the crisis from their own resources: the locality was in a condition of mendicancy to a degree even greater than in 1781-2 or 1836-8. It was all symptomatic of the growing strain of the west Highland economy which contrasted increasingly with the possibilities of better circumstances beyond the region, in Britain and abroad. As always the landlord's position was under stress: his own finances were extremely perilous, but could be improved only by dislocating the life of the crofting population. The crofters' condition could only be raised by assistance from the landlord, and by a better regulation of their own fertility and agrarian practices. The unending dilemma was subject to further variation in the 1850s.

IV

The Cromartie management, ambivalent in its response to the famine, mixed its thoughts of relief with those of radical reform, which normally took the form of removal. In Coigach there were still substantial grazing areas in the hands of tacksmen and small tenants, untouched and uncleared since the alterations in the first quarter of the century. As Scott said, 'a large proportion of the Parish is in farms let on lease and a considerable extent is in townships or allotments of land to which are attached extensive hill grazings occupied in common by the tenants of the townships respectively.'[37] This, of course, was the traditional, uncleared pattern of settlement; it was an impediment to the extension of both sheep farm and sporting tenancies; it appeared also to encourage the unrestricted growth of a recurrently mendicant population. It was a challenge for management and the source of communal obduracy among the common people.

Andrew Scott adopted a gradualist approach to the problem—of piecemeal and small-scale removals which would avoid the noise and resistance precipitated by the root-and-branch methods adopted by other Highland landowners. Moreover his methods did not require complete eviction but rather the shifting of people from one spot to another within the estate. Few were left without a place on the property.

But even small clearances were approached with trepidation by the Cromartie man-

BAY OF NIGG

LANDS OF NEW TARBAT Hon ble Mrs HAY MACKENZIE

BALNAGOWN Sir Chas Ro

R E Mrs Maclea

Barbara Village

New Tarbat

Milltown Burn

SHANDWICK Charl

BURN OF

Polon Pier

and Mud Banks coverd with

Dehauts Channel

Line of Low Water

New Tarbat Channel

with My At Scalp

Nigg Channel

Remains of Old Vest

BAYFIELD Robert Mi

PITCALNIE Geo Ross Esq

NIGG Walter Taylor Esq

30 feet deep below Low Water

WESTFIELD William Murray Esq

ESTATE OF CROMARTY

Roman Camp

Market Point

The Ness

CROMARTY FERRY

Harbour

Dun Skaith

NORTH SUTER

CROMARTY

Red Rock

STEEP ROCKS

Sand Bank or Shoal

Red Burn

Mortal Den

Cromarty House

SOUTH SUTER

Dropping Cave

Cairney Gavel

Belonging to HUGH ROSE ROSS Esqr

Outer Stalks

agement. In mid 1848 ejectments were planned for the Dornies district in Coigach and Scott already feared that the people would prove refractory:

> The manager was to go among them on Wednesday last and ... to see the idle dogs [were] put out of the way and see the tenants removed that have been summoned. Should they refuse to go, an officer must be sent from Dingwall to eject them. Before I left Ullapool on Tuesday, I heard that none would remove unless compelled by law to do so.[38]

This indeed was the first act in a long struggle by the Coigach people to preserve the *status quo* and to defy Andrew Scott and his masters.[39] Scott soon became pessimistic and warned the local authorities about the long term danger of failing in an attempt to force through the eviction.

> If you have any doubts about going on ... I as acting for Cromartie hereby authorise you to proceed and effect the ejectments on these tenements [holdings]. It will not do to spend as much money on these Removings and then withdraw and confess to a defeat. The people are unruly enough as matters are at present and to succumb now and give up the point would be fatal to everything like order amongst a class so ignorant, wilful as the people you are now dealing with.[40]

It appears that Scott withdrew his attempt to force the issue in 1848, postponing the effort until the people were less defiant. It was not, in any case, a sweeping clearance which was beyond the capability of the Cromartie management. It was, however, an indication of the rising frustration with rent arrears and the financial insecurity of the Hay-Mackenzies. There was indeed a similar problem in the east; in December 1848, Scott pointed out that Strathpeffer arrears were very large despite the fact that wages were better than ever and food prices low. 'This will not be endured', he exclaimed. 'There will be a sifting this year, and those who fail to pay may begin to look about them where they will get land without paying rent, for Cromartie will not suffer this trifling any longer'.[41] As for the west coast people, he remarked that:

> The time is drawing nigh when summonses of removing must be served upon such as should be removed ... If they go on increasing their arrears they will soon take all in themselves and be more destitute than ever. The desire to clear accounts with the landlord seems to be fast giving place to a lazy indifference. I am quite puzzled what to do in regard to these people—especially the Tanera tenants. If there is no hope of their being made to do better they must be removed from the Island altogether ... We should be disgraced by allowing this state of things to continue.[42]

21   Tarbat, Nigg, part of a chart of the Firth of Cromartie from 'A survey by George Buchanan, civil engineer, Edinburgh, 1836'.

PART FOUR

Cromartie and the Aristocratic Merger, 1849-1880

CHAPTER 16

A Vital Marriage and the Seeds of Trouble: 1849-1853

I

A financial crisis loomed over the Cromartie estate as mid-century approached. The full extent of the embarrassment was not visible to the outside world and may not have been clear even to the owner, John Hay-Mackenzie. His young daughter Anne was certainly innocent of the danger to her inheritance.

The famine had taken some toll of the finances of the family: relief had been expensive, debts had been incurred, and in Coigach the small rents of several years were totally lost. It is true that the improvements on the 'champaign lands' of the eastern parts of the estate had been real enough and commercially productive too. But this had to be balanced by the continuing poverty and intractability of the crofting population in both Coigach and Strathpeffer. Hay-Mackenzie had lacked the capital to develop his assets—for instance the Spa at Strathpeffer, increasingly popular but clearly under-capitalised. Even more hazardous were the management consequences of proprietorial penury: it pushed the landlord towards greater confrontation with the crofters in an effort to raise the rental income of the hills, notably where sportsmen were ready with new money for shooting rights. Hay-Mackenzie was close to his financial limits: in normal circumstances, other things being equal, it was almost certain that the Cromartie estate would slip out of the hands of the family. As the debts of the family mounted against net income the estates would have to be sold, either in part or in whole.[1] Count Macleod's patrimony was in the greatest jeopardy.

Instead the unexpected happened. Hay-Mackenzie's daughter, with little apparent warning to the family, in 1849 married the heir to one of the largest fortunes in the Kingdom. Anne Hay-Mackenzie became the wife of the Marquis of Stafford who, in 1861, became the third Duke of Sutherland. The Sutherland family had accumulated huge fortunes in canals, railways, coal and iron, and also in lucrative landed estates in the English Midlands. They owned most of the County of Sutherland as well as great stretches of Ross-shire. Their merger with the Cromartie estate was a very neat extension of their territorial empire.[2] In other ways, however, it was a remarkably unequal alliance. The Sutherland connection in reality rescued the Cromarties from the very brink of financial capitulation. It was only after the marriage of Anne Hay-Mackenzie, and the death of her father only a fortnight later,[3] that the Sutherland family and its professional

22   Anne Hay-Mackenzie, 1848.

agents came to a stark appreciation of the financial morass into which their heir had married. For the Cromarties there was a nice irony in these developments—for much of the debt hanging like a millstone on the estate was a consequence of familial burdens contracted by several generations of financially unproductive marriages. Now, at last, the marriage stakes yielded high rewards in return. But the result for the Cromartie estate was its effective incorporation into the great Sutherland empire. It was perhaps not surprising that one of the first episodes in the new era was that the Cromartie estate became publicly associated with the Sutherland management's infamous policy of clearance. The fact that the Sutherland estate had not entertained any clearances for twenty years was a further irony in the story, and an echo of its earlier notoriety.

Anne Hay-Mackenzie (the future Duchess of Sutherland) was just 20 years of age when in 1849 she married George Granville Sutherland-Leveson-Gower. At that time he was styled the Marquis of Stafford and, while well-provided as heir, he was in no position to finance the estates of his wife from his own allowances. It is almost certain that the Sutherland family and its managers miscalculated the financial foundations of the family into which the heir married. They had no idea of Hay-Mackenzie's embarrassments. Once the full extent of the difficulties of the Cromartie estate were exposed, the Sutherland management began to express alarm and surprise at the burden which the marriage had incurred. In return the Sutherland empire was extended territorially and Cromartie became the eighth peerage (suppressed though it still was) to be connected into the family (the eight had been collected over a period of 300 years).

The wedding was followed in rapid succession by the death of John Hay-Mackenzie in July 1849, and the coming-of-age of his daughter, now Marchioness of Stafford in April 1850. Public celebrations of the heiress's majority were orchestrated somewhat laboriously by Andrew Scott. It was a matter of judging the appropriate degree of levity, familiarity and generosity in an expected public ritual. Scott had to contend with inevitable comparisons that would be made with the Sutherland celebrations arranged for the Marquis of Stafford's coming-of-age only a short time before. The Cromarty tenants were encouraged to show signs of spontaneous celebration. Scott remarked, 'I think the tenants of every Township in the Barony [of Coigach] should collect and erect a good large Bonfire'. The estate itself arranged suitable functions to mark the event. There would be a dinner for the large tenants and neighbours, Scott instructed, and drink for the common people:

> They should get whisky certainly, but not to do any of them any harm; this applies to the road squad who mostly are tenants as well as to the makers of the Bonfires. The Foresters and Ground Officers should have a dinner and a moderate supply of whisky. You cannot do it all without a Piper to play during dinner and between the Toasts and when your party tire of the Table if you can strike up a dance with the girls of the village there is nothing to hinder.

Fires were lit across the estates east to west. At Tarbat House an ox was roasted to provide a feed for the small tenants and labourers, 'and a hop after it in one of the granaries ... the Paupers in the different Baronies are to share in the general rejoicing by having an allowance distributed similar to what was made in Sutherland at the coming of age of the Marquess'.[4] A sense of place, of hierarchy and decorum, covered the whole occasion;[5] there was a curious artificiality about it, an invocation of a tradition the strength of which was unknown to the agent and probably to the people as well. Celebrations were set up in each part of the estate. In the east, at Tarbat, there were few accomplished pipers and Scott told the west coast factor that 'I have a piper here—a drunken fellow—but such as he is, I must put up with him. Still if your man will come for £3 you may send him, if not he may stay at home.' Another tradition was the distribution of half crowns to paupers (83 were distributed in Coigach). But, Scott told Mackenzie, the local factor at Leckmeln, 'above all there should be no brawling or fighting among the common people on your grand festival day—Let them make merry to the top of their bent and welcome ... Wishing you all a pleasant and joyous meeting on the day of your rejoicing.'[6]

In order to avoid any chance of marring these auspicious events all summonses against rent defaulters, 'even against the hopelessly bad on the property', were suspended. Scott explained: 'For this reason I have given them a year of grace, to try them if they will amend, and do better in the future'.[7] This indeed was a quiet prelude to a full scale conflict between the estate managers and the crofters of Coigach.

II

The marital alliance forged, realities of a financial sort soon emerged. One of the first shocks to the new owners was the revelation of the demands of Hay-Mackenzie relatives on the estate. Scott reported in May 1850: 'Lord and Lady Stafford seem amazed at so many things being claimed by Mrs Hay-Mackenzie'.[8] Within the following two years the full extent of the Cromartie debts and financial commitments were revealed and eventually radical steps were taken to relieve the crisis into which Lord Stafford had married. But before these problems were fully identified and confronted, Lord Stafford and his young wife had to be educated in the facts of the Cromartie estate. In particular they were inducted into the problems of being landlords of west Highland property. They eventually learned difficult lessons, notably about the intersection of their own financial difficulties with the needs of rational estate management among a crofting community.

Reason for measured optimism, nevertheless, could be found on the door-steps of Castle Leod. There was one legacy of the last days of Hay-Mackenzie which brought good cheer, and even a public reputation for landlordly benevolence, to the new owners of the Cromartie Estate. A project had been initiated at Strathpeffer in the last year of Hay-Mackenzie's life which reached fruition only after his death when the estate was fully under the influence of Lord Stafford and the Sutherland estate commissioners, James Loch and his son George Loch. It concerned the reclamation of a considerable tract of boggy land at Knockfarrel, a mile or so from the village of Strathpeffer. The improved land was divided into lots in 1850 and settled as the Gower township by a group of small tenants who had been evicted from the Balfour estate in Strathconan (formerly an old Mackenzie property).[9] The settlement was known as the 'Strathconan colony' for several years. The reception and settlement of these 'clearance refugees' was

23 Section from 1850 sketch of Knockfarrel allotments.

NO of LOT	Names of Occupants	Imperial Measure Ac Dec	
I	Alexander Mackay	6	087
II	John Mackay	10	
III	Kenneth Cameron	10	
IV	Murdo Maclennan	10	
V	Duncan Urquhart	10	
VI	Duncan Cameron	10	
VII	Donald Cameron	10	
VIII	William Cameron	10	
IX	Murdo Cameron	7	
X	Finlay Maciver	7	
XI	Donald Macrae	7	
XII	Kenneth Mackay	7	
XIII	John Mackay	7	
XIV	Finlay Mackay	7	
XV	Donald Macdonald	7	
XVI	Rodrick Macdonald	7	
XVII	Finlay Beton	7	
XVIII	Donald Finlayson	5	870
	Road		256
	Total Contents	145	213

24 Detail from 1850 sketch of Knockfarrel allotments.

widely praised across the Highlands as an act of philanthropy. Alexander MacKenzie, writing in 1883, described the Strathconan events in detail and stated that 24 families participated in the migration 'to the neighbourhood of Knockfarrel and Loch Ussie, where they were provided with holdings by the late John Hay-Mackenzie of Cromartie, father of the present Duchess of Sutherland, and where a few of themselves and many of their descendants are now in fairly comfortable circumstances.'[10] More fulsome was the praise of D.G.F. Macdonald writing to the Duke of Sutherland (previously Lord Stafford) in 1871. He recollected the 'forced expatriation' of the 'little band of peasants exiled from Strathconan' who petitioned the Duchess for permission to settle on 'an unreclaimed piece of moor at Knockfarrel ... The Duchess, influenced by high and generous sentiments cheerfully conceded the request.' The Duke, he wrote, had personally supervised the subdivision of the land, 'setting a noble example of turning the industry of poor Cottars to account in their own land'. The tenants were given 19-year leases which afforded them each 'that confidence to use his funds in the permanent improvement of his land'. They had been saved from emigration and by 1871 the land, originally worth three shillings an acre was now worth seven times as much and presented 'a beautiful picture of fertility, peace and prosperity'. It was a model of benevolent landlordism in the Highlands.[11]

The actual circumstances of the Knockfarrel development, though somewhat romanticised by later accounts, were indeed unusual. After all it was true that Hay-Mackenzie in his last days was close to bankruptcy. From his own resources he was in no position to undertake large-scale agrarian improvements. Moreover, on the Cromartie estate, and throughout the Highlands, there was an overwhelming tendency towards the consolidation of, rather than the creation of new, holdings. The development of a community of poor crofters, of small peasants, in the middle of the nineteenth century in the middle of the Strathpeffer estate, ran against the grain of contemporary agricultural improvement. Only a few months before the creation of the Knockfarrel settlement Andrew Scott was evicting small tenants from the Strathpeffer estate. In May 1849 he focussed on cases which he described as 'hopelessly bad' in terms of arrears and cultivation: 'I intend to dispossess them of the Lands and leave with them their Houses .... and if those going out cannot live without their Lots of land they must or rather one of them (for he is an old man) be placed on the roll of Paupers.' Consolidation of holdings and the ejection of tenants grossly in arrears was the only way that Scott could see the landlord avoiding greater losses.[12]

The Knockfarrel scheme, in reality, pre-dated the forced migration of the Strathconan refugees. Its origins were connected with the loans made available to landowners through the agency of the Drainage Commissioners.[13] The purpose was to promote the improvement of lands on preferential terms as a means of sweetening the pill of the Repeal of the Corn Laws. There had been considerable apprehension about Repeal in Easter Ross, a great wheat growing district. The local farmers' club was hotly opposed to government policy and Andrew Scott agreed with the prevailing attitude. 'Agitation has begun', he wrote in September 1850, 'and I have no doubt the Manchester School Politics will have to succumb to the more rational views of the Country Party'.[14] Such opposition did not prevent Hay-Mackenzie from applying successfully for assistance from the Commissioners.

Substantial trenching and drainage operations began at Foddertty in 1848, and they originally extended to about 145 acres costing more than £15 per acre to improve but later eventually extending further to Knockfarrel.[15] Sufficient progress had been made by May 1849 for advertisements to be considered and some of the work was to be finished by the end of the year. In the interim, however, Hay-Mackenzie died and Lady Stafford became proprietrix.

Andrew Scott believed that the reclaimed land should be leased and it is clear that he was thinking of a single large tenant. He noted that: 'If it be let in one farm, a set of

Houses will have to be built by the landlord' meaning a farmhouse, steadings and outbuildings which were normally provided by a landlord to a large tenant. A local farmer, Dudgeon, was immediately interested and, since he already lived in the district, he would require fewer buildings on the property. In the outcome, however, negotiations with Dudgeon failed because he would not agree to pay the rent set by Scott.[16]

In order to make a reasonable return on capital invested at Knockfarrel Andrew Scott had calculated a rent of 25 shillings per acre. In this expectation he appears to have been over-optimistic; fears of the anticipated effects of Repeal may have depressed the land market in the district.[17] This factor, and the need to avoid extra expenditure on farm buildings, induced the estate to advertise again in January 1850. The land was now offered in small lots between six and 20 acres, but without accommodation.[18] It is clear that Scott had experienced difficulty in locating a tenant at Knockfarrel and it was with a sense of relief that he announced, in the third week of March, that the Strathconan people had presented themselves as tenants for the reclaimed land.

Scott told Lady Stafford and Melville (her legal agent in Edinburgh) his good news. He emphasised the fact that the Strathconan people had accumulated considerable reserves of money in the bank—'made by labour on Railways in the south'. Moreover they had been:

> highly recommended to me as a Colony with not only a considerable amount of means in money and in stock, but as highly industrious, peaceable and well disposed people, 17 in all. The rent is to be 15/- per acre for the first five years, and 21/- per acre for the remaining 14 years ... No question but the rent is much higher under what I hoped to obtain for the land [i.e. as a single farm] but it is as much as I see any chance of getting; the Outlay to houses is moderate—only the price of the timber required for them—nothing else.

He consoled his superiors with the thought that, after twenty-two years, the value of the land would have increased tenfold compared with its original state.[19]

Scott's evident relief was echoed by Melville in Edinburgh: 'In the present situation of matters, and with the prospects we have, we may be thankful for a reasonable offer from men who have money.'[20] There was no suggestion in any of these proceedings that Lady Stafford was performing an act of charity towards the 'Strathconan emigrants'. It was a commercial arrangement and the settlement was christened 'Gower' in honour of Lord Stafford's family. Nor was Scott without anxiety about creating a new colony of small tenants but he felt able to say that 'If the people are once settled I would anticipate no trouble from them, but there is much to do towards their comfortable settlement'. Trouble, indeed, developed in the following year when the Gower settlers were accused of trespass on the neighbouring Seaforth estate. Scott, however, sprang to their defence and told Seaforth's representatives that the crofters' crops were in more danger from Seaforth's own trespassing deer, and he suggested that they 'devise any method of preventing this'.[21]

The Gower settlement was a success in the sense that a new community of small tenants had been created which was capable of sustaining itself for many decades. But the idea of extending the experiment by further investment in drainage in 1858 was quickly scotched on the grounds of expense.[22] Moreover, when the leases eventually ran out (after 21 years) there were anxious rumours that the settlers would be evicted to make room for a single large farmer. There were reports current that the people lived in 'constant fear of being ejected from their little homes made comfortable by their own hands'. In fact no such plans were being mooted and George Loch in 1871 had asked Scott 'would it be desirable to give these poor people [new] leases?'[23]

The question of leases was resolved but the true significance of the experiment was twofold. First it demonstrated that, in certain circumstances, crofters even in the mid-nineteenth century, could compete effectively against the rents offered by large tenant farmers. Second, the Knockfarrel settlement provided vivid evidence of the tenacity and hunger for land among the displaced small tenantry of the Highlands. It is clear that the people of Strathconan had been prepared to accept railway employment in the south—but that this was essentially a prelude to their reinstatement on semi-virgin land back in the Highlands.

Thirty years after the original colonisation at Knockfarrel, Scott's successor, William Gunn, reported the story of the Gower allotments to the Napier Commission. He said that, with scarcely an exception,

> they have proved to be excellent tenants in every respect. They are industrious, and farm systematically and well, and of this we have the best evidence in the fact that they pay their rents regularly, and that within the last few years they have substantially improved their houses, four of which have lately been seated.

Nevertheless Gunn repeated yet again the old and erroneous story that the colony had sprung into existence when the Marchioness of Stafford had yielded to the importunities 'of people who had been evicted from another estate'.[24]

Slightly more accurate was an account written in 1943 by Colin Macdonald, who had grown up as a crofter on the Heights of Strathpeffer. He referred to the people as the 'Conanachs' whose forebears had been evicted and had been 'permitted by our landlord to settle on small areas of unreclaimed land, which they had industriously brought into cultivation'. Macdonald reported that the descendants 'still lacked the homogeneity of the older community' but were known for their friendliness and hospitable disposition.[25] They had certainly fared better than their crofting counterparts on the west coast.

III

There was nothing like the Knockfarrel development in the western barony of the estate. Even in 1850, Coigach retained many of the remnants of the old economy and society. Old ways changed slowly. The management itself retained antiquated practices in its rental procedures. Even victual payments survived. When Andrew Scott offered David Purves the position of forester he was given the choice of a full money salary (together with a house and garden) or else a fraction of the salary supplemented by six and a half bolls of oatmeal per annum. In Coigach most of the population remained subject to the intermediacy of the tacksmen, the large leaseholders who sublet their lands to small tenants. It was convenient for the estate management to leave the extraordinarily difficult business of rent collection to these local men, even though the net income of the estate was thereby diminished. When in 1850 two tacksmen wished to relinquish their tack of Achiltibuie and Badenscallie the estate resisted,[26] partly because the management depended on the system.

The peasant economy was still based on cattle, oatmeal and potatoes, and seasonal employment in the east coast fishing. The old contradictions remained. When the harvest was poor the people had no meal to sell and were forced to pay high prices to cover the shortfall. When the harvest was good prices were low and they had great difficulty accumulating any income from their surplus production.

The seasonal character of their lives made it difficult even to gain advantage from the relief promised by the Destitution Board. The road construction, which involved much rock cutting, overlapped into the short herring season which was one of the main sources of cash income for the people. In 1850 the Cromartie estate found itself short of labour (which was intended as a form of relief) for the road construction and the agents had to recruit others in order to continue the work. Scott told the Marquis of Stafford that 'at this season many of the people usually go to Caithness to the herring fishing where they can gain better wages than in road making'. The money for the road would be exhausted by September.[27] The herring fishing provided much of the ready cash for rents and for meal purchases.

Scott provided his new master, Lord Stafford, with an analysis of the western problem, particularly relative to the allotment system—'and the fruit that system is surely but silently producing'. He recalled his arrival as factor in Martinmas 1831, at which time crofter rent arrears were large and irrecoverable. 'I thought at the time that something must be wrong either with the land or the occupiers of the land.' In 1832 he revalued the lots and effectively reduced rents by 15%:

> And this was intended to act as a stimulus to exertion rather than as a relief, for it was abundantly evident that the absence of any kind of remunerative employment, and not high wages, was the perpetual evil the people had to contend with, and it will always be so. The tenants of the large grazings do not require labourers, and the Lot tenants after sowing their lands are idle till Harvest; and when that is over they have nothing to employ themselves with till the time comes round again to begin labouring for another crop.

The herring alone enabled the population to survive. Even if the land were rent-free there would not be sufficient subsistence:

> And now that the potato crop has failed (and I fear the root is doomed) you are forced to make an advance to these destitute families in the shape of meal and seed oats to keep the extremity of famine from their door, and this advance is equal to seven-eighths of the whole leviable rent. Can this state of things continue?

He answered his own question

If it is suffered to do so, landlords will become impoverished, the sympathies of the Public will be worn out and become callous from there being no end to demands for help from such localities as Lochbroom, and the Land (to use a vivid Scripture metaphor) will by and by 'Spew' out its famished population.

The herring had failed for several seasons, and thus hardly half of the rents had been paid. The failure of the potato caused the reduction in the price of herrings. Yet population continued to rise despite the prohibition of subdivision and the squatting of young families. The population consisted of nearly seven to a family.

For Andrew Scott the only solution was large and liberal emigration. It would reduce the scale of the responsibility and reduce the hindrance to further improvement. He had no doubt that, if the people were removed, 'the lot farms on your property of Coigach would fetch more and would be worth more rent, as individual Holdings than as at present occupied.' Consolidation would be the best plan, though a transition would be required, costly but in the end much happier. Rents were 10/- on average: 'A subdivision of land or so ... must necessarily induce a dead level of pauperism, and the occupiers under an infliction like the present potato rot are helpless and undone.'[28]

Rent collections reflected the basic sources of the peasant economy and this applied as much to the crofters on the Heights of Strathpeffer (overlooking the richer farms in the glen) as to the people of Coigach. During the famine days of mid 1850, when potatoes rotted in their stores and the harvest promised little better,[29] Andrew Scott corresponded with James Loch, Commissioner of the Sutherland empire and perhaps the most experienced business administrator in the Kingdom. Scott told Loch that:

> I never knew the small tenants—those paying from three to Twenty pounds—pay so badly as at this audit. The small Highland cattle reared by such people are almost unsaleable, and any surplus corn that they might have to dispose of after keeping themselves in meal, brought in very little meal. Two thirds of the small tenantry did not attend. The principal tenants paid as usual.[30]

Three months later the story from the west coast was once more pessimistic:

> I am sorry to hear that the potato crop is again doomed to suffer, but I hope the loss will be less real when the crop is gathered home than appearances at present would indicate. The price too of small Highland cattle is so reduced, they are not worth rearing—indeed they can hardly be sold at any price.

The people took their cattle as far as Kincardine for sale. Scott believed that they should sell their cattle because: 'There is no chance of such stock ever improving in value or price, as they will not pay the grazier or feeder in proportion as larger and better bred Cattle will, and might now coupled with a quick return is what every body is after.' The scales were always balanced against the crofters.[31] Even when the herrings returned temporarily to Lochbroom it was usually so late in the season that the price was low with few buyers in the market.[32]

Poor rent collections were the endless despair of the estate managers and the estate itself was in such dire financial straits that further urgency and frustration were added

25 Features of the agricultural landscape in the Strathpeffer area. 1. Rough grazing; 2. Plantations; 3. Estate 'policy'; 4a. Large farm steadings; 4b. Croft houses; 4c. Ruined or empty croft houses; 5a. Dingwall-Strathpeffer road; 5b. Old Dingwall-Strathpeffer railway track. Thick black lines are existing farm and croft boundaries; broken lines indicate field boundaries; A. Village of Auchterneed; F. Fodderty; M. Millnain.

to the problem. When Scott set off in November 1850 on his regular rent collection he said he expected it would be 'bootless this year', and he told Melville, the Edinburgh lawyer for Lady Stafford:

> I look forward to a bad collection from the Lot tenants in Lochbroom at this time. I do not know what will have to be done with these people; they are every year turning worse in their circumstances, notwithstanding the work that has been given to them to do; nothing almost can be kept out of their earnings for rent, they consuming all in meal, the potato crop failing them less or more every year for the last four.[33]

Flickers of optimism crossed their minds from time to time—a show of herrings in the Loch and better keeping qualities in the new potatoes might stave off the worst ravages of famine, but it was a tight margin throughout these years.

There was, in reality, no abatement to the darkening fatalism of the estate's attitude to the crofting problem. Even when it seemed likely that the Sutherland fortune might be tapped to assist the Cromartie estate (see below), there was little sense that the crofter problem could be solved. Scott returned to his regular refrain: only wholesale emigration could relieve the west coast, and even that was fraught with difficulties. Nor did he believe, as did many of his contemporaries, that large capital projects could revive the west Highland economy. For instance the promising idea of a railway from Oban to Inverness was being circulated in early 1851, but Scott greeted it with little enthusiasm:

> The relief it would afford to the destitute would only be temporary, and after the Works shall be completed ... the population will be after all as far as ever from being a self-sustaining population. I have never been able to see in any scheme devised for the benefit of the West Coast Highlanders any thing that held out a promise of permanent improvement in their condition except in a large and liberal measure of Emigration. And to make it work well both for the poverty stricken people themselves, and those proprietors into whose very vitals they are eating, the people should be encouraged to emigrate by Families—not one of a family should be left behind that might incline to go.

Family emigration was indeed rapidly gaining ground as the prime solution to the Highland problem. The most important public expression of this philosophy was the creation, in the early 1850s, of an elaborate scheme of subsidised emigration from the Highlands to Australia, generated by the inspiration of Charles Edward Trevelyan.[34] In this scheme crofters were given free passages, from funds derived from public charity, from colonial revenues, and from the landlords themselves. The emigration of entire families, in Scott's view, was indispensable.

> It would give them courage to undertake the dangers and difficulties that might be apprehended to meet them in going forth to seek a new home in a new Country: their sympathies and affections would be less divided or disturbed, than if part of a family were to emigrate, and part were to remain at home .... Besides, were a scheme of Emigration to be restricted to the able bodied only the old and inferior would be an intolerable burden on the Land. They would not be able to cultivate it or to fish—they would be a mass of pauperism wholly dependent on the industry of others. they would ... stand in the way of Proprietors making new and better arrangements in respect to the management of their estates whereby such evils as now assail them might be effectually warded off in times to come.

Scott's exposition was an unmistakeable reiteration of the view that the crofters had no reasonable place in the west Highlands. The land must be reorganised:

> And this can only be done by occupying the land more as a pastoral than as a corn growing country. It is abundantly evident to any practised farmer that tillage in the West Highland except in a few favoured localities is a mistake. Pastoral farming is what the Country by nature, is best adapted for, its climate precludes the hope of remunerative cultivation of its soil and masses of the population, since the country became densely inhabited, have every year been on the borders of starvation.

Scott pointed out that any emigration scheme would require government assistance and would be strenuously opposed by the Free Church clergy who possessed great influence among the people. He thought that 'the pinchings of poverty' would operate to counteract clerical influence; moreover 'as it is a characteristic of Highlanders to act collectively, rather than like their Saxon brethren individually, and on a principle of self reliance, if the ground were once fairly broken it may be presumed there would be less difficulty in inducing them to follow their leaders.'

It was symptomatic of the state of the Coigach estate that Scott had little accurate data about its population. He guessed that there were about 1700 people of whom 25% were tenants who paid £825 per annum in rent. He observed that:

> This gives a very small average rent to each—less than ten shillings—a burden on the land it is inconceivable how it can bear—indeed were it not for the sea from whence they draw most of their resources it is impossible the Land could keep them if they had it rent free. This last year the Coigach lot tenantry were fortunate in having a winter herring fishing, and I hear they are better to do this season than they have been for a number of years bygone.[35]

In fact the herring fishing in that year, 1851, was especially generous and the spectre of want retraced its steps for an interim, and the crofters paid up some of their arrears for the first time in many years. Nevertheless Scott continued to complain that the people had been 'paying very badly for the last two years, disgracing themselves, the manager, and me.'[36]

IV

Large scale family emigration was Scott's favoured solution to the 'crofter problem' and was widely promoted in the years after the famine. As Scott had noticed, there were many elements in the Highland community who continued to oppose the idea and, in any case, the cost of emigration was usually beyond the capacity of either the crofters themselves or their landlords. The extent of emigration from the Cromartie estate is almost impossible to gauge though occasional episodes were recorded. In March 1842 for instance a tenant and his family were assisted to America by way of Cromarty Town at the cost of £15 to the estate.[37] Again in May 1848 the estate agreed to take the holdings of stock off the hands of departing tenants and even helped with their fares to Leith.[38]

The Cromartie estate was relatively late in its participation in the more broadly-based schemes to subsidise emigration which had developed out of national apprehension for the crofters during the recent famine. The greatest of these schemes was the emigration of five thousand people to Australia under the auspices of the Highland and Island Emigration Society. Its activities did not take effect until the famine had diminished and Scott had understood that its operations were to be restricted to emigration from Skye. When, in July 1852, Sir John McNeill asked if the people of Coigach wished to join the scheme, Scott was caught unprepared. He was apprehensive that large costs would be incurred by the estate which was required to contribute to the scheme. Moreover he was adamant that, 'if the proposed emigrations be not conducted by entire families the relief by it would be no relief at all'. He predicted that the aged would be left behind to become paupers, and 'the land would still be in their hands'. He saw emigration as a facet of the endless contest for the land.[39] In fact the Emigration Society scheme specifically addressed the problems raised by Scott.

It was not until the following year that any substantial number of Coigach families were involved in the Australian migration. In June 1853, McNeill announced that 1000 passages were available and that 50 were allocated to the people of Coigach.[40] A brief description survives of the departure of one group from Lochbroom in October 1853. They were accompanied to Glasgow by the local factor, Kenneth Mackenzie. From Glasgow they would proceed to Liverpool for embarkation to Australia. There was an inauspicious start because the boat from Coigach was partially disabled en route and lost two days on its voyage. It was forced to take a tow into Glasgow by steamer.

The emigrants were by no means happy. As Mackenzie reported:

> I parted with the Emigrants on Saturday afternoon, they were in very bad spirits; independent of the weather, I never had a more disagreeable trip in my life, there was no pleasing them, they were mostly all sea sick by the way when their families were thus distressed they thought that I could command the Boat to return or run to some harbour, they were again too ill to please in their food, and so very troublesome to the hands on Board the Steamer. At parting I got the greatest insolence and abuse from some of them for not paying Porters for putting their luggage on Board them to Liverpool, while they were going themselves with their hands in their pockets. Several of them were most

anxious to return home from here [Glasgow], I am certain if I had not been with them, that one half of them would not have come this length.[41]

The disgruntled and abusive group of Coigach migrants described by Kenneth Mackenzie were almost certainly the same 65 emigrants who left Birkenhead aboard the *Sir Allan McNab* on 28 October 1853 destined for Hobart in Van Diemen's Land. The Tasmanian historian, Hugh Campbell, has investigated this migration in precise detail. It is clear, for instance, that the emigrants had been recruited by the Highland and Island Emigration Society at a time when difficulties were being experienced in raising enough migrants to fulfil the commitments of the Society. Conditions in the Highland economy had improved sufficiently to dampen the enthusiasm for emigration.

The party of emigrants, of whom the Coigach people were part, were dispatched as 'of a very superior class—healthy, robust people—and most of them speak English tolerably well'. The Coigach people were from the villages of Dornie, Rieff, Morefield, Ardmair, Auchindrain, Tanera and Isle Martin. They were in 15 families and the total cost of their migration was £1425. They were mainly in their twenties or thirties and conformed to the Society's regulations though at least one of them obscured his true family and marital status in order to qualify. They were, by the terms of the scheme, all pledged to repay their costs to the Society, but this requirement was never honoured, partly because the Van Diemen's Land officials were unclear about the Society's regulations.

The voyage from Birkenhead to Hobart appears to have been less hazardous than that from Ullapool to Glasgow. One of their number, Susan Mackenzie, was appointed Matron for the voyage. On arrival the emigrants were described as 'accustomed to farming pursuits' and they found employment relatively quickly. They were dispersed to their various different employers. The central motivation of the Coigach immigrants was captured in a much later report of their immigrant careers. In 1880 a local Presbyterian minister spoke of their 'general hope of having a steading of their own where they and their children might live and work together'. Back in 1853 they had each started, with very meagre resources, and had separately progressed towards their goal on difficult country west of the River Tamar. They began as farm servants or house servants. Eventually, after ten years or so, some of them began to buy land of their own in the locality, that is at Wickleigh, re-clustering as though they were back in Coigach. In the interim they had saved enough money to become small landowners. But of the others, some had gone on to New Zealand or to other districts of Tasmania. It was a classic tale of social and economic aspirations transplanted to the other side of the world. In the longer-run, however, there was a marked withering of the original kinship bonds at Wickleigh and an absorption of the Coigach people into the wider world of mixed migration in Australia, as elsewhere.[42]

The 1853 emigration to Van Diemen's Land was the last occasion when the landlord (and external agencies) combined together to induce and subsidise a large scheme of emigration from Coigach. Thereafter the level of spontaneous emigration was never enough to satisfy the estate managers. Moreover the local ministers of the church continued to denounce emigration as an unacceptable solution to the problem of Highland poverty.[43]

The emigration of the Coigach people in 1853 perhaps also hinted at the tenor of social feeling in the district. Their abusive and truculent disposition on the voyage to Glasgow was certainly in character with the riotous behaviour of their fellow crofters at home in Coigach in that same year.

CHAPTER 17

Rebellion at Coigach

I

A few months after the settlement of the Strathconan refugees at Knockfarrel, in August 1850, Lord and Lady Stafford received high praise in the outspoken Wick newspaper, the *Northern Ensign*. The new landowners were, it reported, 'held in great estimation by the poorer portion of the population throughout the Highlands, and if their recent act of benevolent protection towards a few of the excellent men who were expelled from Strathconan is to be regarded as an index of their future conduct, there may be good days in store for certain parts of the Highlands yet. *Blessed are the merciful, for they shall obtain mercy.*' It was pointed out that there had been much 'eulogising' of the Staffords in the northern newspapers. The only discordant note was struck by 'The Poor Man's Friend' of Wick, who suggested that the Strathconan people would have been better advised, for their own sake, to have emigrated altogether.[1] But the overwhelming response to the recent events was favourable and the Staffords basked in a warm reputation.

The reputation lasted less than two years. It was displaced by a vigorous campaign of opposition and denunciation of the Staffords and, more specifically, the 'borderers' they employed to manage their estates. The public hostility was led by the *Northern Ensign*[2] and was occasioned by Andrew Scott's attempts to reorganise some of the small tenantry in Coigach. It precipitated some of the best recorded anti-clearance resistance and riots in the nineteenth century Highlands.

II

The estate officials on the Cromartie estate, as elsewhere, regarded the management of the crofting population as a matter of social control. There was a recurrent anxiety that, if matters were let slip, all authority would be lost not only in matters of rent-payment but also in the use of the land itself. It was a continuing contest for the control of the land. In the summer of 1848 for instance, Andrew Scott had encountered great difficulty in performing simple removals at Coigach. He told the removing officer that Hay-Mackenzie had given clear instructions to proceed and effect the ejectments required ... It will not do to spend as much money in these Removings and then withdraw and confess to a defeat. The people are unruly enough as matters are at present and to succumb now and give up the point would be fatal to everything like order amongst a Class so ignorant and wilful as the people you are now dealing with.[3]

Similarly in May 1851, Scott explained to his superiors that it was important to remove a few crofters in arrear of rent in order to retain some measure of discipline over the others. Some of the offenders he allowed to remain in their houses but denied them the use of their crofts. To do otherwise, he claimed, would be 'very hurtful to the interests of the estate'. But he realised that Lady Stafford was especially sensitive on such questions: 'I know Lady Stafford will not like ... severe measures be taken with the people there, but would I let them alone and go on without any further notice than a threat at rent time, they would get out of hand altogether.'[4]

The Cromartie estate's management of the crofters, in fact, lacked both consistency and resolution. Scott repeatedly urged the necessity of removals and the proper stocking of the lands of Coigach.[5] Yet when the execution of such policies was broached there was ceaseless prevarication and reconsideration. Scott was obviously inhibited by the fear of public controversy and also, perhaps, by a sense of humanitarianism for the hapless crofters. Lady Stafford obviously found the whole question distasteful and her husband had small appetite for it either. There was little iron in the soul of the management and when removals were eventually attempted in Coigach (in 1851-3) the crofters mounted a uniquely successful resistance to the estate administration.

The fatalism which shrouded the management was expressed in the lack of firmness of intention in administration, and in the acceptance of the inertia of arrangements in the west. In March 1851, for instance, an offer was made by a sheepfarmer, Purves, from the Borders, for the farm of Auchnahaird at a rent well in advance of the current payment by eleven subtenants. Purves was told that the farm would not really suit him because the proprietor had no intention of removing the subtenants. 'Were there no subtenants in the way', Scott averred, 'the farm would make an excellent Ewe farm and would keep about 600 as good Cheviot ewes as any in the district'. But the proprietor would not take on the task of removal. He explained (somewhat ambiguously), 'it is proposed to let the farm with power to the incoming tenant to continue the subtenants as they are at present—not to increase their number, tho' he may diminish them as it may suit his convenience.' This, of course, was an evasion of the moral, and indeed the practical, question; it passed on to the tenant the responsibility for clearance, a task which few tenants relished.[6] In the outcome the new tenant was George MacLeod from neighbouring Assynt who paid a little more for the land than his predecessor and retained the small tenants on the land.[7] In the event MacLeod took over Auchnahaird 'subject to the condition of not removing the subtenants so long as they paid their rents and conducted themselves in an orderly peaceable manner'.[8]

Within the crofting community in Coigach it was common for mutual aid to be extended to people in difficulty. But there were also bitter inter-communal conflicts in which crofter was pitted against crofter. Sometimes a crofter would evict his or her own sub-tenants. Some crofter families were riven by jealousies and opposing interests.

It was not rare for a crofter to request the estate management to evict a fellow crofter. In April 1851, for instance, there was a case in which a son took 'to himself a wife', and then pressed his way on to his father's croft with the intention of turning him and his other children out of the door. Andrew Scott was compelled to intervene to persuade the family to accept the *status quo* until the old father was removed by death. The interloping son was told to find himself another place. Scott was emphatic that there could be no double tenancy: 'If the old man allows his son to come in ... I think it is likely the whole family, and he among the rest, will be removed at the first opportunity I can have to do so.'[9]

The tacksmen themselves faced difficulties with their subtenants. In early 1850, William and Alexander Mackenzie, tacksmen of the large Achiltibuie property, made representations to Lady Stafford. They had been experiencing great difficulty in extracting rents from their subtenants. In these circumstances, they told Scott, 'we see that we cannot maintain our ground as middlemen between your Constituents and the Tenantry, [and] under the circumstances we now come forward to renounce the residue of the lease which we trust will be taken off our hands.'[10] When the tacksmen were unable to maintain their authority the problems of estate management were immediately compounded. It undoubtedly strengthened the case for removals.

Circumstances therefore emerged in the early 1850s which produced a climacteric moment in relations between the Coigach crofters and the Cromartie management. The financial difficulties of Lady Stafford, and pressures from potential sporting tenants and sheep farmers, gave a powerful incentive for more rational land use. The irremediable poverty of the crofters had been demonstrated unequivocally during the years of famine. Even the tacksmen were failing to extract rents. But the people themselves seemed to develop a new tenacity, a communal resolution to contrast with the weakness of the proprietor.

Yet Scott himself forever warned of the dangers of leniency and his fear of a collapse of factorial authority. This was graphically displayed in Scott's reprimand to the people of Auchnahaird in 1852—they had not only refused to pay their rent to the tacksman but had heaped abuse upon him. Scott told them that he had personally arranged for their retention on the land when the lease had been set, 'that you might not be driven to the wall'. He explained that it had been done on the understanding that they would pay their rents punctually and behave respectfully. 'Foolish Men! Do you imagine you can remain in your allotments and not pay rent? Whoever so counsels you is your enemy not your friend.' He wrote: 'Take my advice and settle with Mr Macleod. If you do not you will repent, when you will be driven forth of [sic] the Estate, and no one will receive you from the Character you will have made for yourselves. At least the Marchioness will not.' This threatening appeal carried little strength among the crofters,[11] and was a foretaste of events soon to come.

III

The Coigach riots of 1852 and 1853 developed out of a series of financial predicaments in the Cromartie management. In part the problem was merely an extension of previous difficulties with crofter rentals which were now heavily in arrears; in part it was also a consequence of recently incurred expenditures. The dowager Mrs Hay-Mackenzie had chosen to install herself in Castle Leod and this required the expenditure of £1700 on the renovation of buildings in the vicinity. Moreover the Cromartie estate had committed itself to road construction to an extent of £2000 beyond the assistance received from the Destitution Committee. A point was reached early in the new proprietorship at which expenditure exceeded estate income. This forced a series of economies on both Lady and Lord Stafford, and on the Cromartie factors. Lord Stafford for example was forced to give up his treasured shootings on the estate; it was decided also to sacrifice timber to raise income as sales of pit props; and the owners agreed to prune their own living expenses (see below, chapter 18).

There was also action on a second front—which eventually generated the riotous resistance of the crofters. Estate policy was directed to ways of increasing rent, and it was clear that only two sources of augmented income were possible. Land could be made over to sheepfarmers or, alternatively, to sporting tenants who were offering much higher rents. As early as 1850 Andrew Scott had hatched the plan of carving a new sheep farm from land in Coigach, surrounded by a new dyke to separate it from the crofters, some of whom would have to be shifted. Clearly it would create a degree of dislocation, even turmoil. The introduction of sporting tenancies at Coigach required the re-organisation of several groups of long-entrenched crofters. As the question evolved it rapidly became a test of the authority of the landlord and of the law. When the people resisted the re-organisation, the issues widened to a question of tenant rights and the control of the land in Coigach and indeed in the Highlands at large.

By late 1851 the ravages of the potato famine had diminished. The recent crop had been abundant and of good quality and it was thought that 'the poor people will be well off and comfortable for it is upon the potato crop they chiefly depend'.[12] Rents were somewhat better paid, but far too many crofters were still far in arrears. When several large tenants, including Mundell and the Mackenzies, began to make moves to opt out of their leases, Scott came to the conclusion that the cause of their difficulties was the proximity of crofters on the land. There was evidence that the crofters reduced the value of the land, especially by their trespassing. In January 1852 Scott explained to Lady Stafford that one of the sheepfarmers, Mundell, would not think of renewing his lease 'on account of the trouble and loss he has had to suffer since he became the tenant, at the hands of the Lot tenants on every side'. The demands of existing and prospective tenants were central in estate policy in 1852.

Scott advised the shifting of as many of the Badenscallie people to Badentarbat as possible—'then put the sheep stock on the cleared ground of Badenscallie, and make a sheep farm of it—and it would be an excellent one; and this arrangement would, in the course of two and three years, considerably increase the rental of the Barony, and ensure its being better paid.' This kind of removal would safeguard a new sheep farming tenant from the encroachments of the lot tenants. Otherwise, 'the people would drive him out'. It was a considerable enticement to a proprietor caught in embarrassing financial problems. It would, of course, require the clearing of the lotters to a new colony at Badentarbat.[13] No large tenant would take over the land until it had been in the hands of the proprietor for a few years. Mundell, who thought the plan excellent, made this a condition of any interest that he expressed. Part of Mundell's old sheep farm was to be converted to lots for the people; it would include grazing rights for the crofters.[14]

Scott was fully aware that this radical plan for the people of Badenscallie would create enthusiastic opposition. He realised that there would be no voluntary 'flitting' and that it was likely that the entire population would have to be served with summonses of removing: 'I am sure the people will not move, or submit to have their present possessions taken from them unless legal means be taken to enforce submission.'[15] He set about the difficult task of collecting the names of the people of Achiltibuie and Badenscallie—Scott still entertained the vain hope that the tacksmen would do the actual organisation for the sheriff.[16] The re-arrangements required the crofter to move about two miles, hardly a major clearance by nineteenth century standards. Scott told Lady Stafford that the legal costs might reach £100; he had also drawn up agreements to resettle for the people. However, he expressed his misgiving particularly

> as to the ultimate success of the Removings were they to be attempted through the ordinary mode of serving summonses; for there is such a number of tenants that were they to resist and set the hands at defiance, I doubt not that they would carry their point. I am therefore for avoiding compulsion, and aim to try the gentler method of persuasion.

It was not the attitude of a confident man but it was accurate in its forebodings.[17]

Scott thus set in motion elaborate plans to minimise the inconvenience of the clearance to the crofters. They would be given sufficient time to gather their crops and time to erect their new houses. But any recalcitrant tenant would be dealt with 'in a judicial manner' and turned off the estate; the co-operative would be fully protected especially if they conducted themselves 'in the spirit of a peaceful, quiet and tractable disposition, everything may be done in as amicable a manner as the nature of the changes will admit of'. He expected the people to sign minutes of agreement to the proposed change.[18] These instructions were to be conveyed to the people by the subfactor for the western part of the estate. Scott knew that even this would be a test of the people's acquiescence in the arrangements, especially the question of the signing of the forms. Unless the people signed the letter they would be completely evicted from the estate—that was the transparent threat.[19] Scott's tactics were quite explicit, but not the less irresolute in foundation—for he knew that if the crofters resisted, the law would be set at defiance 'as is too often done here in the North'—and that they would be able to keep possession. His idea was to avoid compulsion and, as he had said, 'try the gentler method of persuasion'.[20]

The first confrontation took place in the third week of February 1852, and it was immediately obvious that the people would provide active and violent opposition to every attempt at change.[21] Nevertheless, out of 93 tenants at Badenscallie 75 signed the letter and thereby agreed to depart; 18 refused and were marked for eviction. There was to be a reduction in hillgrazing and a hope that a greater effort in the direction of fishing would occur—as Scott said 'it will take a little time and much patience to induce industrious habits when at present such habits hardly exist.'[22] The 18 recalcitrant were distinctive in that they were to lose their crofts as well as their hillgrazings; the co-operating crofters only lost part of their hillgrazings.[23] It appears that the 18 crofters who faced outright eviction were able by their resistance, to block the entire scheme for resettlement.

The next stage of the process was that of serving notices of removal on the 18 non-signatories. Scott knew there was a strong possibility of a deforcement on this occasion; he therefore requested police accompaniment for the Coigach manager and the sheriff's officer.[24] The event occurred on 18 March 1852 when the small party went from Ullapool to Coigach. There they met a great gathering of people—men and women who had been waiting all night: 'The women rushed in upon the Party, tore open their clothes and searched every one in succession for the summonses'—and made a fire of the papers. They did the same for the summonses against a number of sub-tenants who were in rent arrears to the tacksman George Macleod: the subtenants said they would pay when they could.

The first act in the resistance was a clear victory to the recalcitrant crofters. The sheriff's party was forced to withdraw. Scott's reaction was adamant. The law, he exclaimed, should be allowed to demonstrate its full authority and might to the people of Coigach. He himself was fully roused and demanded to accompany the police party in the second, more organised and reinforced, attempt to assert the landlord's rights. The contingent travelled by boat to Achnahaird. Scott said that they saw several hundred people amassed as they sailed along the coast, and at both Achnahaird and Achiltibuie the legal party found themselves totally unable to present the summonses. They were entirely outnumbered by the mutinous people:

> all this was done by women but I have no doubt all the men of the place were there backing them ... there were not fewer than 250 men and as many women concerned in the riot but although the latter only were the active agents in the deforcement, had any serious resistance been offered, the men would neither have been slow nor gentle in punishing such resistance. A hundred of the best of any police force in the kingdom could not have effectively protected the officer and enabled him to serve the summonses.[25]

The stakes had now been raised by several degrees. One of the tacksmen, a party to the resettlement arrangement, was so anxious and distressed by the temper of the people that he offered to withdraw from the contract he had made with the estate administrators. Scott however persisted and another skirmish occurred—another set of summonses was seized from the officers and burnt before their eyes, and their boat was hauled and dragged over the shingle about 300 yards. Scott observed in his jaundiced state of mind that 'it is clear, if this can be done with impunity, there is an end to landlords on the West Coast collecting their rents if the tenantry, like the Achnahaird subtenants, refuse to pay.'[26] The incident was not the less embarrassing because it was reported in both the Inverness newspapers. The plans for re-settlement were postponed for 12 months.[27]

In June 1852 Scott went over to Lochbroom again, primarily to gauge the disposition of the people. Scott knew that the Stafford family were ambivalent and irresolute about the clearance. They entertained the idea that the evictions might be accomplished little-by-little, a handful each year. Meanwhile a better offer for the land had entered the question: Lord Dupplin (a *nouveau-riche* distiller from the south) wanted the land for shooting, and required a long lease (of 15 to 19 years). But it was his condition that the land would have to be cleared. Scott commented: 'there will be no use in attempting any improvement in the management if we cannot go through with it, and make the people understand that they are not to be the masters, as they at present fancy they are'. Most revealing was the report of the Coigach people that: 'They have it currently amongst themselves that the Queen will not allow military to be sent against them, and as for Civil power, they care not a straw for it'. No legal sanction had been applied against the offenders of 1852. Scott was unrestrained in his comment on the position: 'Such leniency on the part of the Civil power is not the way to vindicate its supremacy over an ignorant, simple and semi-barbarous people. It only brings it into contempt.'[28]

Scott, in November 1852, told Dupplin's representative that Lady Stafford was determined to press forward the rearrangements in Coigach. She had agreed with Scott's own concern that, otherwise, the estate would be perceived as having been 'baffled' by the popular opposition.[29] Dupplin was a highly desirable tenant (Lord Anson was also interested, though at a lower rent) and his arrangement with the Cromartie estate was directly threatened by the resistance of the Coigach crofters. Dupplin demanded the removal of all the sheep as well as the people so that he could introduce deer.[30] If Dupplin took over the Coigach shootings, and if Lord Stafford sacrificed his own hunting forest, the addition to the estate rental income might be £900 net per annum, which would have a decisive impact on the estate finances.[31] Moreover it was evidently

26 An illustration entitled 'An Interloper' from *Shooting* by Lord Walsingham and Sir Ralph Payne-Gallway, London, 1893.

the only way of increasing the rent of the estate. The resistance of the people made the land unlettable—a point made repeatedly by the outraged Scott.

The opposition of the Coigach crofters was part of an alienation of a general sort on the west coast. Resistance indeed was not restricted to the threatened clearances. In December 1852 a constable from Dingwall (in Scott's company), charged with the task of collecting poor rates on the west coast, was resisted and deforced by large groups of people. Scott said it made a joke of the law at the hands of 'turbulent riotous people; the country will not be safe to live in especially if a man asks them for his own'. Added to these repeated acts of physical resistance the people also refused to reduce their arrears despite the fact that they were relatively better off with the return of higher cattle prices in 1852. As for the Badenscallie people, Scott believed that only military force would prevail against them; the small tenantry would be unmanageable unless the law was fully re-asserted. Consequently he made plans to drive through his clearance in the early new year.[32]

In this resolution Scott seemed to receive the direct support and urging of Lady Stafford, the young proprietrix. In June 1852 she had received a petition from the Coigach people asking for a cancellation of the removals. In reply she told them to stop their resistance because the measure 'will most assuredly be finally carried into effect'. She rejected their claim that her measures would cause them 'poverty and great misery'. She told them that she was surprised to receive such a petition from them 'after the disagreeable treatment her Factor experienced in the month of March last, which cannot be forgotten by her'. She assured them the estate plans would be put into effect. Six months after, Lady Stafford was yet more adamant, instructing Scott, 'I think the sooner and the more decidedly the Badenscallie people are taught their lesson the better, and it will also be a warning to the other small tenants'.[33]

With a renewed attempt to execute the removals impending, the local officer in Coigach reported that the people were more determined than ever. No officer would even attempt to serve the summonses on them. The people had arranged a constant surveillance of all movements by the factors: 'Watching is kept up regularly every night and Scouts are at Ullapool to give warnings of our movements here on the instant'.[34] The anticipated confrontation occurred early in February 1853. The sheriff's party had travelled by boat to Culnacraig where they were violently assaulted by a large number, mainly of women. Once more summonses were wrenched from the officer, and burned; the officer was then entirely stripped of his clothes 'and was put on board the Boat in which he went to Coigach in a state of almost absolute nudity!'[35] Women were reported as the leaders.[36] 'Although women are said to have committed the outrage on the officer', said Scott, 'I have no doubt all the men of the district were present as last year ... on a similar occasion'. Scott was now intensely agitated: a military force, he declared, was imperative and there must be a Precognition into the affair. He began to talk of the people as the 'Coigach insurgents', and looked to the Edinburgh authorities to make some legal response.

Scott had come to the view that the ordinary police force of the district was impotent. Even a hundred men would be insufficient to sustain the civil authorities. Scott told Lady Stafford, 'I have taken it for granted that matters have gone so far that they cannot stop short now without giving such a superiority to these turbulent people that it will be in vain to control them in future.' It was very disagreeable and the introduction of the military would increase the Rogue money assessment in the County. There was an animus in the district, and the history of the popular resistance in 1852 had become an inspiration both locally and beyond. The law in Coigach was in rapid retreat.[37]

Melville, the estate's legal representative in Edinburgh, reported the response of the legal authorities:

> It was suggested that a party of military, or of police from Glasgow, should be sent to aid the officers in serving the summonses of removal; but the Law Officer of the Crown here [Edinburgh] thought there had been no deforcement as to justify the sending of force from a distance; and their instructions to Sheriff Cameron were to go to Glasgow for a steamer, and to arrange for the carriage of the County Police to Coigach, and not that he might take police from Glasgow. They thought it of importance to land all the officers at once from a steamer and that otherwise there might be difficulty in effecting an entrance.

If this failed, more decisive steps were then likely.[38] Melville had supported Scott's actions throughout the proceedings:

> Yielding to them [the refractory tenants] would be very bad, and ... no reasonable person can complain because of your ejecting them seeing you do not desire to expatriate them, but only to remove them to adjacent and equally good locality on the Estate in the exercise of a judicious management.[39]

James Loch, commissioner to the Duke of Sutherland (but otherwise unconnected with these events) commented in March 1853:

> The landlord's rights, it would appear, are again suspended for a year. It is to be concluded however that the Government will feel the necessity of making some enquiry into the state of things with a view of bringing the leaders to punishment.[40]

Lady Stafford herself commented: 'We are exceedingly annoyed at this Coigach business, it will certainly not do now to give in to the Refractory Tenants, if only for the sake of example'. And she asked that some explanation be put in the Inverness newspapers because their reports had said nothing of the fact that the people were to be resettled on the estate—that it was not a clearance without recourse; nor had it been made clear that the people were in arrears. She also understood that the entire business had been got up by two or three ringleaders without whom the whole rebellion would collapse. She congratulated Scott on his behaviour: 'It made me very angry to read of the summonses being burnt.'[41]

The response of the Solicitor General in Edinburgh, however, was less than decisive. He judged that the Coigach deforcements had not yet been sufficiently grave to justify the intervention of troops. Instead he ordered a third effort to accomplish the removal by the ordinary law officers further reinforced by police. The result was identical. Once more, for the third time, the law was set at nought and its officers openly humiliated by the crofters acting in communal solidarity. Yet again the estate management was both outraged and nonplussed: 'The consequence in the meanwhile is that the tenants will possess for another year.' Melville assumed that military assistance would then be given, that is, on the fourth attempt.[42] As late as December 1853 Melville was still demanding action against the Coigach tenantry, saying that 'unless decided measures are used against the refractory tenants, these parties will get beyond all management, and loss to a considerable extent will follow'. He urged a further attempt.

In the outcome the Cromartie management gave up the campaign in defeat. It did not pursue the clearance in Coigach. The adverse publicity and general unpleasantness surrounding the question eventually persuaded Lord and Lady Stafford that the game was not worth the candle. Their nerve was broken and they conceded defeat: the removal was never executed nor were the lot tenants curbed in their trespass on adjoining farms. For the people of Coigach it was a famous victory almost unprecedented in Highland history. Rarely if ever had the common people of the Highlands resisted successfully the authority of a clearing landlord. It was a victory that entered the folk memory. Thirty years later the Coigach crofters were still remembered as heroes of the land-war in the Highlands. More immediately the success of the Coigach people helped to inspire crofters in the eastern Highlands to emulate their collective resistance. But Coigach had also put steel into the minds of the landlords and police in the Highlands—and consequently the years 1853-5 witnessed bloody conflict between landlord agents and crofters in renewed clearances at Greenyards and Glencalvie.[43]

On the Cromartie estate the estate managers were forced to live with their frustrations. In 1857, for instance, the leaseholder of Badentarbat, Walter Mundell, was making the same complaints against crofters that had precipitated the original action in Coigach. Lacking any satisfaction he refused to renew his lease. Moreover, as Scott reported, 'I found it impossible to relet the farm solely on account of the annoyance given by the lot Tenants adjoining.' No commercial tenant was likely to make much profit in the circumstances, even though the advertisement for the farm stressed that the landlord had created a marches dyke at great expense to protect the ground. Scott reported the triumphant attitudes of the 'natives' or 'wretches' who taunted the shepherd, made his life a misery, and told him: 'We were here before you and will see you out and so on they go tormenting the poor fellow, yet he keeps his temper with them which is more than I could do'.[44] Scott's exasperation was almost total. In 1857 the question of the use of wire fencing was considered; Scott thought it would be very expensive. In fact the crofters then hotly disputed the line of the march and actively prevented any construction. Scott thought they were beyond reason—'There is no end to the trouble and annoyance these people give; at one time by building Houses and dividing their lots, at another by raising disputes about marches.'[45] They were literally beyond his control.

The rebellion at Coigach therefore left the Staffords with an ambiguous reputation. They clearly wished to implement a policy of removals but obviously lacked the resolution and authority with which to execute the policy. Indeed so buffeted and bruised were they by the adverse publicity that they expressly forbade their managers ever to consider any further attempts at removal. There was a great contrast between Lord Stafford and his grandparents who had been responsible for the greatest of all the clearances in the Highlands in the years 1809 to 1821. There was also a contrast in the behaviour of the rebellious people of Coigach and their grandparents who, it appears, had not raised a finger to prevent much larger re-organisations in Coigach in the period 1800 to 1830. The Highland world had changed for all parties in the continuing contest for land.

CHAPTER 18

Paradoxical Aristocratic Finances

I

The embarrassing and abortive clearances attempted in Coigach in 1852 and 1853 were the indirect consequences of the persistent financial weakness of the Cromartie estate. Had the Marquis and Marchioness of Stafford not attempted to live within the net income of their estates (in the Highlands and in the English Midlands) there would have been far less compulsion to squeeze greater rents from the unresponsive district of Coigach. Yet at the very core of their dilemma was a gross artificiality. In truth Lord Stafford was heir to one of the greatest conglomerations of wealth in the empire. In reality his family could afford to keep him and his new wife in leisurely affluence indefinitely. It was a curious principle invoked by the Duke of Sutherland (and his Commissioner) that, until he actually inherited, Stafford should live strictly within his means. His means had been determined at his majority when he was given the revenues of the substantial estate of Lilleshall in Shropshire, seat of the Leveson-Gowers and worth a gross rental of about £25,000 per annum. Unfortunately for Stafford he found that the Cromartie estate required debilitating cross-subsidies from his English property.[1]

The anxiety expressed repeatedly by the managers of the Cromartie estate was the product of the tension between two circumstances. One was the extreme difficulty in raising the income of the estate, especially in the western district. The other was the equal difficulty of reducing the expenditure of the estate, and more particularly, the outgoings of the family. These included not only the fixed charges paid to the relatives, but also the annual consumption of Lord and Lady Stafford. Much of the problem, of course, related to the very large jointures that were saddled on the estate, and great relief was anticipated from the demise of Mrs Maria Murray Hay-Mackenzie (Lady Stafford's grandmother) who required £1400 per annum from the estate. In 1853 she was 97 years old; she had been very expensive. Loch claimed that Scott had, for a matter of years, based his financial plans on the assumption that she would soon die, and that 'relief to these affairs may have been considered possible, by looking to the possible contingency of the Honble Mrs Hay-Mackenzie not long surviving'. When she at last died in 1858 it was discovered that an increase of income became due to Lady Stafford's mother (who lived until 1869) and this further depressed and complicated the Cromartie finances.[2]

But the personal expenses, plans and propensities of Lord Stafford were also to be counted in the weaknesses of the Highland property. For instance he wanted to expend capital in the development of Strathpeffer Spa. Similarly he used the shooting leases both in Coigach and Strathpeffer for his own personal sport, thereby reducing the rental income substantially: he was particularly obstinate in his refusal to relinquish the shootings at Castle Leod and Rhiddoroch. Again Stafford and his wife were reluctant to give up living in London and the Midlands, both serious drains on his income. Even their most senior advisors experienced great difficulty and embarrassment in broaching such subjects, still more in recruiting their active co-operation in such retrenchments.

The responsibility for managing these delicate matters fell to James Loch and it required all his financial acumen and tact to salvage the position and reconstruct the Staffords' budget. It particularly required him to persuade his clients to toe the line in matters of personal expenditure—to dissuade Stafford from borrowing money and buying land at a time when the revenues made the idea absurd. It took Loch (and his successor, his son George Loch) several years to bring matters to a fair balance and then only after severe financial surgery and a re-alignment of debts. The Lochs regarded themselves as the guardians of the entire Sutherland empire and they were acutely conscious of the long-term decline produced by repeated fragmentation of the colossal inheritance. Loch told Lord Stafford in July 1853, that he should take no financial decision 'independent of the Factor or Agent'. It was the Lochs' mission to save the owners from their own mistakes.[3]

Lord Stafford was, however, becoming increasingly assertive in economic matters, partly in consequence of his own maturity and the likely early death of his father. He was obviously frustrated by the comparatively pinched circumstances in which he was compelled to live, and these were mainly connected with the burdens of the Cromartie estate. His frustration brought him into conflict with Loch. Symptomatic was Stafford's vigorous suggestion that some of the best sheep farms (in Sutherland) be converted to deer forest. This idea struck horror into Loch who pointed out that it would alienate the entire sheep farming fraternity. The deer would also roam over the arable land of the crofters which would have the worst consequences for the public name of the family.

There were other obstacles towards rational change. In 1853, for instance, great consideration was given to the idea of selling off a large part of Coigach, to raise £55,000 thereby relieving pressure on estate debts. But Melville, the estate advisor in Edinburgh, pointed out two cardinal difficulties. One was a legal blockage in the way of a sale which only an act of Parliament could dislodge. Second there was the perennial problem of the resident small tenantry

> Whether your Lordship and Lady Stafford may be able to carry into effect a sale of the subjects herein referred to, may be a little doubtful seeing the Lot tenants are so numerous on that portion of the Barony, and are, besides, so turbulent and evil disposed that a person inclined to invest money in Land might fear he would not be able to keep possession or get the rents paid.

Yet again, therefore, the sheer existence of the small tenantry was tantamount to an infringement to the basic rights of property.[4]

Sometimes Lord Stafford threw up his hands and made extreme suggestions to rescue his position. In 1853 he thought of giving up residence at Lilleshall (reconstructed at great expense by his father twenty years before), and even suggested its sale. This, as Loch pointed out, was entirely anathema to the Duke of Sutherland—'as it would be abandoning your English position and your acquaintance with English habits and usefulness'. Loch was also critical of the Cromartie management. He thought Melville and Scott had relied too much on the endlessly anticipated death of Mrs Hay-Mackenzie and, even worse, 'their expectation that they could fall back upon the Duke, both now and prospectively'.[5] Melville was looking for security for the debts; Loch was near the point of blaming Lord Stafford himself for the financial disarray.[6]

Loch continued his effort to educate his young aristocratic client in the basic principles of financial management. He explained at length, for Stafford's benefit, the guidelines of the estate regime, the budgeting procedures, and especially the simple matter of separating items of income from those of expenditure: 'We will observe that the foundation of the system is, that the expenditure is settled by what the affairs can afford, not by what the Factor or Agent thinks is necessary'. He lectured Stafford on the indispensable necessity of informing his factor of every financial transaction. Vigilance was vital—'the Duke's income is considerably less than it was, and it gets less, and let me remind you that yours will be less ... from what I have written you will see that there are not the means of incurring any extra expenditure on even what you now desire'.[7] These were the facts of life which Stafford must understand, and implicit in Loch's lecture was the fact that Cromartie was now effectively controlled by Sutherland advisors. The greater empire was beginning to swallow and digest the lesser estate.

II

In the early 1850s there was widespread pessimism among Highland proprietors about the future value of their property. Some of the sheep farms, especially in the west, appeared to be suffering declining productivity perhaps from overstocking and stock losses.[8] Melville thought that the price of land would fall because of adverse expectations from foreign cattle and wool imports. In fact, as things turned out, the Highlands were entering a relatively prosperous time of good prices for both cattle and sheep; incomes rose faster than in previous decades and crofters did disproportionately well because their rents failed to keep pace with rising prices for black cattle and labour. But landlords also did well, especially from sporting tenants who bid up the level of leases faster than in any period since 1810. The extraordinary popularity, and expense, of sport in the Highlands brought some bad odour. Thus Lord Bentinck warned his brother 'that Highland proprietors are one and all the greatest Robbers, Liars and Swindlers that can possibly be and you are never safe with them unless you have tied them down by their leases even in the most minute detail'.[9]

These, however, were trends revealed only in the long run. More immediately, for the Cromartie managers, were the weaknesses of net revenue. Thus in 1853 Melville continued to regret that Lord Stafford had not let Rhiddoroch since it was leading to further financial 'perplexity' and had forced further economies in the administration of Tarbat. Some relief of finances was achieved in the following year by timber sales.

Pressure came from Stafford's London bankers who had to be persuaded that debts were being paid off before they would make any commitment for future relief. At that stage the estate continued to obtain funds from the Drainage Commissioners. But debts were a perpetual anxiety. Melville himself was owed by the estate £6000 at 5%, an arrangement which Loch criticised—he was stuck 'with the serious disadvantages of the system, so prevalent in Scotland, of transacting the affairs of great estates through persons who are half bankers as well as lawyers—who permit great debts to run up unknown to you and then charge 5 percent on the account'. Even when rents at Cromartie began to grow, as in January 1854, George Loch (who had taken over responsibility from his father) had to acknowledge that it would still create no surplus by which to discharge any of the accumulated estate debts. He told Melville: 'You are aware that with every effort the Current Income will barely suffice to meet annual liabilities and unavoidable expenditure'.[10]

By 1856 it seems that the estate at last was able to yield some net returns which could be used to pay off Drummonds Bank. Scott was cheered by the healthy remittances sent in and told Lord Stafford: 'The state of your arrears corresponds with that in Sutherland—there must have been great well doing amongst Highland populations of late.'[11] His unusual optimism reflected the growing prosperity of the Highlands by the mid 1850s. In 1857 Scott reported the best ever collection of rent from Lochbroom even though many of the tenants were still away at the Glendhu fishing.[12]

27   Castle Leod, mid-nineteenth century.

250   Cromartie

In October 1857 George Loch took a long and broad view of the state of the Cromartie estate. He was greatly impressed with Castle Leod as a residence, and the scope for its improvement. But its maintenance could only be considered within narrow financial constraints:

> The entrance would look better, were the flanking walls on either side to be rebuilt—but your Lordship and Lady Stafford would hesitate to lay out money for an object of this kind, that will merely gratify the eye, when you are compelled, however unwillingly to refrain from rebuilding cottages and notwithstanding the great care there is for doing so.

The scale of priorities could not have been more clearly stated, nor the need to restrain and correct the Staffords' consumption propensities. Loch was not prepared to put ostentatious display, or even gracious living, before the requirements of productive investment.

Loch's strictures applied equally to the development of Strathpeffer Spa which, in some eyes, offered the best prospect of lucrative investment and economic growth on the Cromartie estate. Lord Stafford had great faith in the financial possibilities of spa development and was familiar with the style and popularity of the curative waters in other continental and English health resorts. Given a free hand Stafford would have borrowed money and invested heavily in the provision of accommodation and medical facilities at Strathpeffer. It was Loch who stayed his hand, saying that any addition to debts would be a great error. Loch also imposed another basic doctrine—that a landlord should not engage in entrepreneurial tasks which were essentially the function of private capital. All that a landlord should do was to facilitate the way of private enterprisers who knew far better how to develop industry and trade. Stafford was not released from these constrictions until he succeeded to the Sutherland fortune in 1861.

III

There was a recurrent theme in James Loch's financial correspondence with Lord Stafford and his wife. In his strict professional way he repeatedly advanced the principle that Stafford should live within his current income. In no circumstances should his affairs become contingent on expectations about his princely inheritance. This of course depended upon his own longevity and the survival of his father, the second Duke of Sutherland.

Against these standards of aristocratic financial behaviour Loch drew up a series of accounts to set before his impatient masters. Thus in October 1853 the position of the Cromartie estate could be seen at a glance: for the following year the estate rents and the shootings would yield an anticipated gross income of £8036. Expenditure on the estate would be £3643 and annuities and interest on debts would absorb another £4809, leaving a deficit of £416 on the year's activities, and this allowed nothing whatever for new investment or the personal expenses of the owners. The estate was clearly uneconomic in its current disposition.

Loch made no attempt to hide his criticism of Scott and Melville for allowing this condition to develop. They had allowed the debt to mount until it was unmanageable. Indeed Melville himself was reaping 5% on the £6000 owed to him by the estate—it was, in Loch's severe view of factorial ethics, entirely anomalous. Loch told Stafford that it was all quite absurd, and that no further new expenditure could be entertained.[13] Loch determined that the rents would be paid directly to Drummonds, the bankers, in future, thereby by-passing the Edinburgh agency. Melville protested vehemently.

From these acrimonious discussions several points emerged. First, Lord Stafford received an allowance from his estates of £5000 per annum of which he regularly spent three-quarters on living expenses. He therefore had little means of buttressing the Cromartie finances from his own liquid resources. Second, large debts had been inherited from the 1820s which had been heavily augmented by new debts such as the £15,500 borrowed from the Scottish Widows Fund in 1836, as well as £26,000 from a Life Insurance company. The total debts amounted to £53,500 which simply could not be serviced out of the net revenue of the Cromartie estate.[14]

Not surprisingly there was further talk of selling off part of the northern estates to liquidate the burden of debt. Melville recommended against what he regarded as the dismemberment of the property. He said that all the shootings should be let out at the going rent and that any further development should wait until Mrs Hay-Mackenzie's annuity fell in. George Loch was more radical.[15] He told Stafford that the northern estates could not extricate themselves from debt from their own resources—'on the contrary unless some speedy steps are taken to relieve the condition it will become much more serious. A sale of land is the only remedy. I am vexed to say so, but my duty to you both obliges me to say so.' He had in mind the sale of about £55,000 of land which would pay off all the debts.

In the upshot George Loch's proposal was blocked. It was discovered that a sale of land would require an Act of Parliament which, with associated legal costs, would itself add £1500 to the debts.[16] More important still there arose powerful opposition within the Sutherland family—it was decided that no sale should take place, 'in consequence of the opinions that have been expressed unfavourable to its probable success'.[17]

CHAPTER 19

Rich and Poor on a Highland Estate: the 1860s

I

Back in 1850, when James Loch examined the financial consequences of aspects of the recent alliance of Lord Stafford with Anne Hay-Mackenzie, he mused on the extraordinarily gloomy condition of the Cromartie estate. Up to its eyes in debt, overspending its current income, tied up with heritable and personal commitments and lawyers' bills, Cromartie had been on the brink of disaster. He remarked to the second Duke of Sutherland, now father-in-law of the impecunious heiress, 'it is impossible not to wonder what must have been Mr Hay-Mackenzie's situation had he lived, or Lady Stafford had married a poor man.'[1] It was not a difficult feat for the imagination of an estate agent. Had the young Lady Anne not married Stafford, much if not all the Cromartie estate must have gone the way of many other Highland estates—on to the land market.

Instead of bankruptcy, James Loch devised ways of reconstructing the debts of the Cromartie estate and creating an even keel for Lord and Lady Stafford. He based his calculations on the fiction that Lord Stafford would be living from independent financial resources, quite separate from the fact that he would inherit the great aristocratic fortune in the kingdom. His father was 64 years old in 1850. Meanwhile on his wife's Highland estate better times emerged, certainly for the arable and large stock farmers, but even for the crofters in the west. Prices for most Highland products improved after 1850 and crofters' rents fell behind the trend of prices. There was a measure of material improvement which reduced the urgency of emigration among the Highland community.

For Lady Stafford, in 1850 so close to financial disaster, the world was even kinder. She emerged as an aristocratic star in her own right, a favourite at Court and, increasingly, an intimate friend of the Queen herself. The Sutherland family into which she had married presided over a dazzling social life in London—Stafford House was one of the most opulent private palaces in the capital and the second Duchess 'made her assemblies the most sought after in London'. Leaders in fashion and in the acquisition of art, the Sutherlands' wealth and influence were fabled. Only occasionally did their reputation as the great clearing landlords in the north of Scotland rumble across their metropolitan world. In part their glamour derived from great entertainments at Stafford House—though there was also rich hospitality in the country seats, at Lilleshall and Trentham, at Cliveden, and increasingly at the expensively refurbished, renovated and turretted fairy-tale castle at Dunrobin. Partly also their social esteem flowed from their patronage of important charities and new political causes—prisoners, paupers, coalminers, famine relief, Polish freedom, Italian unification and, most of all, the anti-slavery movement. All the fashionable and exotic seemed to be lured to Stafford House where they were lionised by the Duchess—Harriet Beecher Stowe, the Shah of Persia, the Queen of Honolulu, Livingstone, Charles Sumner and, most famously, Garibaldi.[2]

28   Countess of Cromartie, Duchess of Sutherland.

The second Duchess's daughter-in-law, now Lady Stafford, young, radiant and by all accounts full of charm, made her own way in this dazzling world. The Sutherlands themselves were generally non-political (though they controlled several parliamentary seats and Lord Granville entered the Cabinet under Gladstone). Lady Stafford did not stray from this general philosophy but she did take the notice both of Queen Victoria and Lord Palmerston. To the Queen, and in succession to her mother-in-law, she became Mistress of the Robes for the period 1870 to 1874. It was, apparently, 'a post attended by much tedium and waiting, and she had been almost the sole companion of the Queen in her years of self-seclusion after the death of Prince Albert'.[3] Duchess Anne became the Queen's closest confidante and companion and a much revered figure in her own right as well as a famed hostess to the fashionable world. To Palmerston she became a favourite (though she was hardly alone in this respect) and the recipient of his teasingly flirtatious letters. One of these exchanges of correspondence had considerable significance since it marked, at last, the full restoration of the Cromartie dynasty to its former dignity—to the aristocratic status forfeited by the third Earl of Cromartie in 1745 when he joined the Jacobite assault.

The symbolic rehabilitation occurred in late 1861 soon after the death of the second Duke of Sutherland when, of course, Lady Stafford became the new Duchess of Sutherland. At that point she had no title in her own right. This Palmerston set out to remedy. Addressing her as 'My Dear Duchess of Sutherland' he began his announcement in mock-seriousness:

> As you are fond of your Country, Scotland, it may interest you to know that I have given Directions for an immediate increase of that Part of the British Peerage which is locally connected with Scotland, by the creation of several Peeresses with Scotch Titles. I am going to make a Countess Cromartie, a Viscountess Tarbat, a Baroness Macleod, and a Baroness Castlehaven, and I shall hope to introduce these Ladies to your Acquaintance. I trust that though you are a Duchess you will not look down upon nor snub these four Peeresses for I can assure you that in Charms and attractions they would do credit to the highest Rank in the Peerage—as to myself I am badly off with regards to them. I long ago lost my heart to them, and they still have got it among them; and they will neither restore to me my stolen Property, nor make me any compensation for my Loss. I think you will admit that this is ill-treatment and I shall ask you when you have made acquaintance with them to say a good word on my Behalf. But no more at present about these strong-hearted ladies who seem to be made out of Fragments of the Caledonian granite.[4]

With this elaborate jest Palmerston announced the renewal of all the family titles forfeited a century before, no doubt a delicious moment for all concerned. The correspondence continued, Palmerston full of effusion and always playfully mocking in tone, thanking his aristocratic protégé for her political advice on all manner of subjects, and at one point saying that her sketch of the Austro-Hungarian Question should be adopted as a State Paper for the benefit of the cabinet. The banter became more serious when the details of the Patent for the new titles were being drawn up. Particular attention was given to 'Remainders and Female Succession'. Given the plurality and complexity of the accumulated titles of the Leveson-Gower family it was not surprising that great care was taken with the formulation of these new ones. In particular, stipulation was made that these titles would go, ultimately, to the Duchess's second offspring and that, specifically, they could descend through the female side. As the over-arch Palmerston remarked: 'The arrangement for Female succession is certainly an exception to general rule and practise, but then the Lady in whose case it is made is herself an exception, by her superiority to the rest of her sex, in all the qualities for which her sex is admired.'[5]

It had been a tradition in the Sutherland family, among the Leveson-Gowers, to make substantial arrangements for the second son of the family. The Cromartie elevation of 1861, a mark itself of grace, favour and wealth, now implied that some substantial means be made for the succession of the second child who, on his father's death, would (in the case of a boy) become the first new Earl of Cromartie. To the estate it was, of course, an expensive method of moderating the harsh principle of primogeniture and the model employed by the Leveson-Gowers in the past three generations. Consequently his inheritance, that is, the Cromartie estate, would have to be placed on sounder economic foundations. The third Duke deliberately channelled resources towards the Cromartie estate so that his second child would be able to sustain the needs of an earldom. This was the other half of the rehabilitation of Cromartie estate, all deriving from the fateful marriage of 1849.[6]

In her later years Countess-Duchess Anne withdrew into her shell, protecting herself with a powerful sense of religious devotion. Denis Stuart (borrowing from the fifth Duke of Sutherland) pictures her in Stafford House, 'a semi-recluse, living in two rooms, and lying on a sofa under a red silk eiderdown, surrounded by minah birds and parrots', attended 'by an ancient retainer who she bedecked with a blue ribbon as a kind of personal decoration'. Her husband had sought other female company and when the Countess-Duchess died in 1888 the Duke remarried in sensational circumstances (see below, chapter 26) which, eventually, produced yet further complications in the great Sutherland inheritance.[7]

II

Behind the glamour of aristocracy in London, and the seductive flattery of Palmerston, lay all the mundane facts of family finances and, at the end of the day, the lives of the people who inhabited the estates. Before the Staffords inherited their territorial empire (in 1861) their own finances remained, at least in the eyes of their cautious agent, endlessly parlous. Until 1861 the Staffords were meant to live off the income of their assigned estates—namely Cromartie and Lilleshall.

In some ways the expectation that the heir to the Sutherland empire be required to live off his landed estates was not only a practical arrangement but also a training in self-discipline and an apprenticeship for his later responsibilities. There was an illusion of independence. The whole process was subject to the advice, or more realistically, the superintendence of the Commissioner of all the Sutherland estates. This was masterminded first by James Loch, until his death in 1855, and then by his equally competent son, George Loch. The Lochs had made themselves into a dynasty of estate agents and the family had itself become distinguished in public life in Victorian Britain. Most influential of them was Charles Loch of the Charities Organisation Society. As overseer of the Sutherland conglomerate—a great portfolio of real and paper assets—George Loch carried great authority. His duties encompassed the balanced management of the estates and their development along the most stable and productive lines. They included the general supervision of the finances of Lord and Lady Stafford and, therefore, the Cromartie estate. Though the Cromartie estate factors, notably the ageing Andrew Scott, retained much local autonomy in day-to-day management, it was inevitable that the primary decisions fell into Loch's lap. His managerial power increased when it became clear that the Cromartie estate was inadequate to the financial demands of its owners.

At the end of 1859 Loch drew up another statement about the current status of the Staffords' account which sharply illuminated the continuing problem of the Cromartie account. He described the position as 'at present, one of much embarrassment. In the most favourable way of putting it the income of the Cromartie Estate falls short of the outgoings, taking one year with another, of £800 and upwards.' Since Lord Stafford (and still less, his wife) had no extra means of his own to meet this deficit 'it is in consequence causing an annual accumulation of debt'. Debt and its accumulation was the millstone round the neck of the Cromartie finances. Moreover the debts were being incurred at a time when gross rental income was rising steadily. By 1859 it had reached £8,200. After all normal outgoing, such as public burden, repairs, management costs and maintenance, had been deducted, there was a clear net income of about £4000 each year.

Servicing the debts swallowed the entire net income and more. Old mortgages of £20,819 were outstanding, so was a debt left by Hay-Mackenzie of £26,000, and a further £12,000 had been accumulated since his death. There were charges in favour of Mrs Mackenzie's younger children, worth £6000. The total debt was £64,819 which cost in interest and insurance £3738 per annum. Then there were annuities of £1600 per annum so that each year these outgoings exceeded the net income of Cromartie by £890. As George Loch remarked: 'It is quite impossible that this can continue—nothing but difficulty and embarrassment can be the result.'

Already the Duke of Sutherland had agreed to a loan of £8000 to his son (which required him to sell off his Virginia stock); now, in 1859, Loch suggested that the Duke take over the entire debt, by a further juggling of his funds, which would reduce the rate of interest for the Staffords' benefit. Loch told Stafford that he made this request feeling 'the greatest repugnance', but it could not be avoided. Eventually the debts of the Staffords were indeed restructured in this manner—the Duke sold off stock to the value of a further £52,819 and the debt was converted to 3%, much to the benefit of the heir and his wife's estate.

All this was done with great discretion and decorum for fear of embarrassing Lady Stafford. It was accomplished without her direct knowledge. As Loch explained the financial condition of the estate gave

> Lady Stafford much concern, and ... I have every reason for believing she would dislike the thought of going into it. One can easily understand the feelings that would cause her mortification in connection with it, at the same time she has an anxious desire to see the affairs placed on a better footing.

The arrangement, which effectively sustained the integrity of the Cromartie estate, carried two further consequences. The first concerned the long term future of the estate, eventually made more appropriate by the re-creation of the Cromartie titles. The proposition, already in the minds of the Staffords, was that of settling the Cromartie estates on their second son. This would not only provide for his welfare but would, more particularly, 'prevent them from hereafter merging in the great Sutherland property'. It would then 'make the Estate a perfectly clear and unencumbered property to him, by settling in his favour the sum of money now about to be advanced'. Thus indeed was the Cromartie estate arranged in favour of the second son.[8] In real terms the Cromartie estate had been rescued from grave financial embarrassment by a lump-sum subsidy of £68,000 from Sutherland. This was the true cost of salvaging the Cromartie estate: it had been achieved by marriage, hence the great delicacy surrounding the role and knowledge of the Lady Stafford. Yet the figure certainly understates the full benefits which accrued to the estates (not to mention its creditors and annuitants) since, during the entire period until the death of the third Duke, the Cromartie estate received developmental investment which buttressed its value and its future productive capacity.

The second consequence of George Loch's financial deliverance was the disengagement of the estate from its long-standing legal/financial agents, namely Melville of Edinburgh. About this Loch made no bones. He was severely critical of their management of the Hay-Mackenzie debts—especially the arrangements between the beneficiaries of the last will: in this the long-living widows had made very large and successful demands on the estate which created considerable antagonism within the family.[9]

The second Duke of Sutherland became very ill in January 1861. In the third week of February, Scott told of his paralysis: 'The good and gentle and kind Duke of Sutherland is I fear going the way of all the earth'. On 28 February 1861 Lord Stafford became third Duke of Sutherland and one of the wealthiest people in the kingdom. Scott did not expect the succession to create any changes in the northern management. He expected the third Duke to be a good and kind landlord 'and will look stricter into the management than his father did'.[10]

The accession of the third Duke was the moment of the formal amalgamation of the Sutherland and Cromartie estates.[11] Thereafter decisions, notably concerning estate policy and investment, were made centrally by the Duke in conjunction with his Commissioner and legal advisors. The Duke himself was personally interested in the future of the Spa and from 1860 to 1890 his direct support and investment helped its development in a material way. His attitude to crofting and agriculture is less easy to characterise. He certainly entertained sanguine notions to improve the productivity of Highland agriculture and invested heavily in novel schemes of land reclamation on his Sutherland properties. He was noted for spectacular displays of steam ploughing and the application of the latest technology to Highland bogs. But, like many others, he was frustrated by the unco-operative attitudes of the crofters and the endless intractability of the Highland problem. Apart from sport and the Spa he does not seem to have found much joy in his great Highland inheritance.

Cromartie remained as ever a set of contrasts. The big eastern farms did well for several decades and showed good increases of income; the lands of the west, increasingly valuable under deer and sheep, remained congested with crofters whose economic condition and temper remained unpredictable. Indeed the memory of the Coigach riots was kept alive through the third quarter of the century.

III

The demand for sport in the Highlands had reached an extraordinary pitch by 1860. It was reported that the grouse had been virtually extirpated by over-shooting, flood and disease, yet southerners were undiminished in their demand for the moors.[12] For landowners the most lucrative move was to convert their lands, even sheeplands, to deer. This of course simply added pressure to the contest for land between the several parties. Deer stalking undoubtedly raised the aggregate rent in the Highlands.[13] Crofters in general appear to have been able to resist, at least in part, the full effect of the upward thrust of rents. Indeed over the long run 1850-70 their incomes rose considerably more (on average) than their rents.

Relatively few landowners had the heart or the resolution to clear off their crofters in favour of deer forests. This was clearly the case on Cromartie. In 1860, for instance, George Loch toyed with the idea of converting a prime sheep farm, Inverpolly, into a deer forest; it would thereby yield substantially greater rent. Amid these deliberations Loch recollected how the idea had been bruited some years before when Lord Dupplin had made an offer for the territory. Loch remarked: 'Lord Dupplin then spoke of having some people removed; Lord Stafford would not hear of any such proposition now'.[14] The era of large scale evictions was over; the Coigach rebellion had signalled its end; from now onwards the tide moved in the opposite direction. Crofters very slowly moved towards the offensive, towards the restitution (as they saw it) of their lands.

Already, of course, the small tenants had achieved a *de facto* control of some of the land. The estate managers were no longer able even to evict individual recalcitrant crofters for fear of public disturbance. One minor case in 1858 caused Scott to warn Loch that he must proceed with the greatest caution: 'It will have a bad effect to be baffled and defeated in the matter of Removing, and if possible this should be prevented'. The frustration of the management was equalled by that of some of the large tenants. In October 1858 one of them declared that 'it would be about as difficult to get some hills and corries on the moon as the hills of Coigach from the Lot tenants. So that move ended in Moonshine.' In such a fashion the competition for the future of the land continued.[15]

Another benchmark of Highland prospects in 1860 was provided by Andrew Scott, still the factor of the Cromartie estates after thirty years' service, and an experienced observer of Highland land values. His brother William Scott was completing service in India and thinking of returning to Scotland and, in the classic mould of the expatriate, contemplating the purchase of a small farm in his homeland. Andrew Scott encouraged his kinsman by saying that some of the great Sutherland farms were likely to be broken up. Such a farm would enable his brother to retire comfortably to his native land. A few months later however, it became crystal clear that brother William entertained unattainable expectations with regard to the profitability of landed property your notion of a farmers profit upon his farm is quite visionaryfrom 50 to 100 per cent [per annum]!—Why, with the utmost care and attention to details if he can beg ten per cent he thinks himself a very lucky man. Then consider a Laird farming through the intervention of a manager cannot, in one instance out of a hundred, realise such returns from the capital invested on his farm, as a man whose sole business is to farm, and who is skilled in his calling. But at present let this pass.[16]

Andrew Scott was almost certainly correct—even in 'the age of high farming' profits could never approach Indian or colonial expectations.

IV

High farming, except in its buoyant prices, had little impact on the western Highlands. Indeed pre-industrial style subsistence crises, now less publicised than the famine of 1847-51, continued recurrently to ravage the crofting population. For instance, in 1862 crops again failed and much of the west coast was threatened with actual famine. Privation, of course, was a recurrent condition of the people and practically every year mounting arrears of rent tested the patience of the estate managers. As early as May 1861 there had been petitions from Coigach seeking indulgence in the coming rent collections. One petition from Badenscallie, signed with many crosses, claimed that the small tenants could pay no more than one third of their nominal rent. The local ground officer, Kenneth Mackenzie, recommended that cattle be accepted from the people in lieu of rent—the cattle could be used to stock the big Rhiddoroch farm. 'I must take from them anything I can get' he remarked. In the event the people would not agree on the price offered and the rent problem therefore remained unresolved. In January 1862 Mackenzie, on his annual round of Coigach, reported that the people were worse off than for several years, 'the Potatoes gone with the most of them some time ago, and consequently must be considerably out in buying meal'.[17] Arrears were mounting. Later in the year it was reported that the herrings had also failed and the potato crop was very poor. Meal supplies became imperative. The first reaction of the estate administrators was to discourage the idea among the crofters that the Duke of Sutherland would automatically and freely relieve all their wants in the crisis. But by the end of 1862 the position had clearly deteriorated into a full-scale emergency. As accounts of grave poverty in Coigach came in the question of relief became inescapable.

The story of famine relief in Coigach in 1863 was a replication of the events of 1847-9 with one exception. This time there was no external intervention by charitable and governmental agencies; instead the Sutherland administration organised its own model of relief. The west coast of the Sutherland estate was managed from the factor's office of Scourie and the Coigach factor was required to follow its methods. In January 1863 Kenneth Mackenzie visited Lochinver to observe relief measures especially in road construction and cottage development.[18] The basic premise of all relief was that the people should, as far as was possible, exchange work for any food or money they received during the emergency. It required a tight control of the financial resources by the estate and, even more, strict discipline by the estate factors.

By March 1863 relief works had been inaugurated in Coigach, administered by Mackenzie. The people were turning out in great numbers and were short of tools such as spades and wheelbarrows. There were far more applicants for work than work available.[19] The work was as usual road-building—and there was no lack of volunteers, and some of the work was recompensed directly in the form of meal. As always during famine relief the management was fearful of encouraging habits of mendicancy and dependence. George Loch was adamant that the people should at no time expect 'the Duke of Sutherland to become an Importer and Distributor or Seller of meal. His Grace is prepared to give employment to the necessitous ... and thus he will supply the people with the means of purchasing meal, but it must be supplied by others.'[20] This indeed was an invocation of the Lochian (indeed Trevelyanian) principle that landlords should not interfere in and thereby disrupt the private meal trade.

The terms of employment were that one person only from each family would be taken on. George Loch set out the conditions:

> Measures for assisting the people in their present privations may not be delayed so long as to allow of any actual destitution arising, on the other hand, there should be no over haste in commencing with them, for it would be a mistake to endeavour to protect the people from more suffering; it would not be possible to do so, nor desirable if it were possible—our duty is confined to averting absolute want and starvation.

Loch was emphatic that no abuse of the relief system should occur. On no account should wages be as much as for ordinary employment nor should anyone receive relief while already employed (for example in part-time fishing). These stringent conditions would then be a test of the people's needs—'we shall soon see who are really in need, by those who may accept and those who decline them'.

The entire relief system was subject to precise accounting and all provision of meal was to be left entirely to the private market: 'and if there be none, then you should endeavour to induce some respectable tradesman to introduce some meal'—though seed potatoes did not come into this category. Relief employment as a work-test, and the free operation of the market, were the pillars of the system. The work test would restrict relief to the genuinely destitute on the estate and the people would, in the long run, benefit by the construction of new roads. As Loch said:

> I fear that if you proceed upon a different principle you will have all the idle people of the Country flocking to you for employment, and that, at the last, you will have a very poor result in work accomplished for wages spent.

On these principles the relief was offered—with the associated promise that 'not a single person suffer from absolute starvation ... Our first duty ... is to avert actual want.' There was no question of shirking this responsibility, and Scott was told to make a personal investigation to ensure the result.

George Loch took the greatest pains to explain the principles on which the Sutherland relief system was executed. It was, of course, a policy which could easily be construed as tight-fisted and harsh, and even the local factors were perplexed by its detailed prohibition of straightforward assistance to the needy: 'The first duty to be performed is to prevent any person suffering from actual destitution, or even falling into so low a state, as to induce fever.' Only *in extremis* should the local factors involve themselves in the meal trade, possibly by way of a guarantee to the private traders because 'it would be a ruinous mistake to discourage the general trader by underselling him.' No relief could be given until the people had exhausted their own supplies of food. Moreover to receive relief employment the labourers were required to live in temporary bothies, a further disincentive to malingerers. It would help distinguish the genuine cases for relief—'the people really and truly in want of employment ... as a test of destitution'. Loch repeatedly insisted that it was no part of the landlord's duty to maintain the people 'in the ordinary state of comfort', it was his only duty to avert 'absolute destitution'. Mere relief, he conceded, 'might be attained by any description of work, useful or the reverse, even by digging holes and filling them up again.' Instead of this roads would be built for the lasting benefit of the district—a more 'permanent result than merely providing a sort of eleemosynary employment for destitute persons, for a brief period'. It was a great and remote district where new roads would generate further improvements and permanent benefits would accrue to landlord and people.[21]

It was all part of the re-education of the Cromartie management in the ways of Lochian estate administration. 'You must let no one starve. You must pay a low rate of wages, and be most rigid in exacting the stipulated quantum of work.' If relief work were done on crofts it would be clearly understood that rents would later be supplemented. It was not primarily a question of return of the Duke's capital, but ensured the avoidance of anything 'that may diminish any little feeling of independent self-reliance, that may exist among them'. All necessary funds would be forthcoming.

Andrew Scott had difficulty swallowing all this advice and ventured the idea that the Duke of Sutherland should simply import meal and provide it at lower prices. This was totally anathema to George Loch. He said he understood Scott's readiness of feeling and benevolence on the question, but these emotions were 'essentially and dangerously erroneous as guides to action, [as] all experience shows'. Loch's doctrines were indeed founded upon classical political economy, possibly by direct reference to Adam Smith's tablets. As Loch put it:

> nothing can be more injurious to the permanent interests of any community than, in periods of distress, to interpose between them and the natural, ordinary, trading machinery, by which, in ordinary times, their wants are supplied. Traders work only in the hope of making profits; if there were no profits there would be no trader. It may be taken as a rule that no trade, which is not protected by a monopoly, can in the long run yield a higher rate of profit than is commensurate with the risks attaching to, or other circumstances, connected with it.'

This was the key proposition. In the long run it was in the peoples' interest that meal traders made good prices in times of scarcity. The provision of seed however was different: 'This is a want so entirely out of the common way, that it clearly must be supplied through the direct intervention of the Proprietor—funds are at your command, wherever you require them for the purpose'.[22]

Loch conceded that his policy looked harsh to the outside world that might not understand its essential logic. For 'it requires the exertion of a cold unremitting cruel looking amount of reason to put aside the temptation [of instant relief], and to compel yourself to adopt instead, a course of proceeding which is recommended by your faith in its yielding more permanent though, at the moment, less complete looking results'.[23] The Loch policy was, therefore, put into full force despite the local advice offered by Scott and Mackenzie. The latter had advocated the sale of meal to the people at 3/- a boll less than would be charged by ordinary dealers, a course of action which Loch told him was a most 'unwise or dangerous proceeding'. He lectured Mackenzie thus:

> The profits to Dealers in an open trade, are never, in the long run, higher than the risks and circumstances of that trade deserve, and if the Meal Dealers in Coigach have been charging the people 3/- or 4/- a Boll more for their Meal than the price of which it could be imported by the farmers, I have no doubt they had good market for doing so, and that the trade could not have been carried on at all, unless they had charged that higher price. It would be madness to carry on in that way. Any interference would undermine the dealers.[24]

The doctrinaire Loch policy contrasted with the older paternalism of Hay-Mackenzie and Scott.

Following Loch's edicts, Scott made arrangements for the private dealers to supply meal at 22/- a boll (140 lbs) until August 1862. Messrs Mackay and Cameron offered to supply the work people at these prices for a period of five months.[25] By March good progress had been made with road construction. Scott had some trouble with the rules laid down by George Loch—especially the limit to full-time employment only: 'If it be carried out who is to labour the allotments and prepare the crop of this year? Then when the Caithness fishing comes on very many will leave the road working and go to the fishing. I fear this rule will not work if it is to be carried out in its entirety.' It was typical of the crofting work seasons for these difficulties to arise. In July 1863 more than 70 men were employed on the road construction.[26]

The 1862-3 crisis ended in late 1863 with improved crops and income derived from the herring fishing. Within a few months the Cromartie estate officials were weeding out tenants in arrear—especially those with no prospect of paying their rents 'either by work or the assistance of their Families'. Scott and Mackenzie drew up lists of people due for removal. Many had got themselves into debt with meal merchants, often pledging their cattle for the meal. One case was a man called McLeod who had no visible resources to support his wife and children, while he was in the south working. Alex Stewart had a cow and nine sheep and a growing son in service, but was able to pay nothing. Ken Maclean was an epileptic invalid 'with a weak family ... and not very sane', and though he owned three cattle he had no money for rent. And so the list went on—poor people with a few head of stock, no money, and in debt, often with no breadwinner in the family.[27] There were reports that many of the joint tenants wished to become independent tenants. Loch told Scott 'His Grace is quite willing to support you in having such of those as can pay and do not pay their rents removed.'[28] But Scott, still much bruised by the events of 1852-3, retreated from a full execution of such a policy. Individual cases were dealt with but most of the crofters remained fully entrenched on their crofts and in their poverty.

V

As railways extended northwards in the 1860s new advantages were opened for the Cromartie estates. Better communications particularly increased the attraction of deer forests and, by 1866, sporting tenants were effectively challenging sheepfarmers for access to land in the west. When sheep farming leases fell in the estate debated the question of converting to deer forests and rents rose rapidly.[29] In the eastern baronies there were other signs of an expansive spirit in the local economy. Thus in 1866 the great Fodderty Farm was advertised enticingly as one of the most extensive in Ross and Cromarty, with 475 acres of arable and also extensive hill grazings:

> The Farm is conveniently situated as regards roads, market towns, shipping ports and railway stations; and besides its natural fertility and well known local advantages, being in the vicinity of the Strathpeffer Spa, is in a high state of cultivation with ample buildings, and merits the attention of tenants of capital and skill'.[30]

George Loch was especially optimistic of the benefits of railways, notably for the expansion of the Spa and the tenantry at Strathpeffer. He was certainly aware of the possibilities created by the proposed Dingwall and Skye Railway Bill and the chance of a siding to Strathpeffer. A correspondent, Tulloch, pointed out that 'it would be a great advantage to the Tenants to be able to truck their Grain, Cattle and Sheep without driving them through Dingwall, and in the same way receive lime, coals, tiles and other heavy requirements without having to send into Dingwall'.[31]

The estate administration also passed through a series of changes. Andrew Scott had served the Cromartie family since 1831 and was now too old for the full responsibilities of the task. His counterpart in the western division of the Sutherland estate, the redoubtable Evander MacIver, said that Scott badly needed a rest. In 1865 Scott resigned two thirds of his responsibilities and was replaced by John Martin, about whom little is known. MacIver quickly plied Martin with advice, telling him particularly that Coigach was far behind in its development and that its people needed considerable activation. Martin however could rely on the long-serving local ground officer, Kenneth Mackenzie, who MacIver described as an excellent man. In the outcome Martin himself was removed in 1867 and replaced by William Gunn, who would govern Cromartie until the turn of the century.

Gunn at 28 was relatively young to take over the Cromartie responsibilities; he had already served an apprenticeship in estate management on the Lilleshall estate in Shropshire, one of the Duke of Sutherland's southern properties. There he had married a woman of Little Hales near Lilleshall. Already they had a son who, at the turn of the century, would continue the Gunn connection in Strathpeffer. William Gunn became a dominating presence in the Cromartie management and built up his influence in the district and became wealthy in his own right. Many years later his grandson remembered him 'as a grand old man with a long white patriarchal beard'.[32] In terms of income he received (in 1877) a salary of £300 per annum plus allowances worth £50 though this was considerably less than his Sutherland counterpart, MacIver, whose allowances were worth much more. It was Gunn who guided the estate through the crofters' crisis of the 1880s and into the later era beyond the influence of the Sutherland commissioners.

But in 1867 Gunn was second-fiddle to George Loch and followed general directives notably in the efforts to develop the crofting lands in Coigach. Plans were advanced for the subsidised reconstruction of crofting houses, based on the Sutherland model. These were instituted with timber from the east coast, glass from Glasgow, lime from Ireland—in an improved design. Some preliminary difficulty arose from the fact that many of the crofters had no carts.[33]

One of Gunn's earliest public tasks as factor at Cromartie was to appear before the Royal Commission into the Employment of Children, Young Persons and Women in Agriculture in 1867. Gunn and several of the tenantry were required to provide evidence of local conditions which, in the subsequent Report, revealed the essential features of the prevailing labour markets and agricultural conditions. For instance a tenant from Fodderty, D. Ross, testified to a considerable shortage of labour, especially that of women. Regular bothies were not provided for rural labour but temporary accommodation was made available for women during the turnip and harvest season. Ross employed west coast women in this way: despite great congestion, they were 'very well behaved, and my experience generally is that no immorality results from this arrangement'. He thought that the labour shortage was primarily a result of the scarcity of cottage accommodation. There was a continuing need for cottages for job labourers: 'it is probably that if they contained three or four rooms the young men and women who now leave their homes to go out to service might stay at home and supply the deficiency of labour on the farms. It is the crowding that drives them out.'

The evidence before the Commission demonstrated a subtle complementarity between the great arable farmers and the semi-subsistence crofting community on the fringes of the commercial farms. Ross spoke admiringly of Lord Lovat's system of placing small crofters closest to the large arable farmers and the 'large crofters, whose land was sufficient for the support of themselves and their families, at a greater distance'. Another witness said that on Lovat's estate 'the crofting system is kept up so as to supply the large arable farms with labour'. In effect, therefore, a working equilibrium had been established between the crofting and commercial sectors of the local economy. The crofters provided a settled and flexible work force—they were, to a degree, a rural proletariat on a part-time basis. Their efforts were supplemented by seasonal imports of labour from the west coast—in summer and autumn families from the west would troop across country to Easter Ross. The farmers claimed that the system worked well and of the regular labourers it was reported that:

> you won't find healthier and more contented working people anywhere. As a general rule their employers take a sincere interest in them, and the best proof of that is that changes in service are less frequent in East Ross than in any district known to me ... They are happier, healthier and better off than those in the south.

As he saw it the only problem was the insufficiency of cottage accommodation in the locality and the tendency of young people to depart the district thereby creating labour shortages.

In Easter Ross regular farm labourers were paid on a daily or monthly basis in money with supplementations in the form of meal, potatoes and other items. Wages were thought to have increased by 25 per cent in the past twenty five years though women received less than half of men's wages. Education was provided, even for pauper children, but most left school by 12 years of age and children under 13 were often found in field gangs. Crofters also made intensive use of their children's labour and the minister at Fodderty reported that the poorest crofters were unable to 'provide good enough clothing to send their children to school in'. The late Mrs Hay-Mackenzie had given great encouragement to education in the parish and literacy had improved even though the crofters could not afford to spare their children's labour in the harvest season.

Crofting was the reservoir of labour for the arable farmers and the Fodderty minister explained that: 'We have squad-labour here, but the women all come from the small crofts in the neighbourhood, and I am not aware that the practise leads to any immorality or coarseness of language. The rate of illegitimacy is comparatively low.' The 'feeing markets' at Beauly and Inverness normally absorbed any surplus labour from the district but the disengaged rural people away from home were more liable to 'moral decline'. William Gunn's opinion was that a 15 acre croft was sufficient to support a family without outside employment but many were smaller. In Coigach, he reported crofts were of 3 to 12 acres 'and possessing in addition a right of pasture for their cattle and sheep on the hill. From those, in addition to what they get fishing, they obtain a very fair subsistence'. Gunn's evidence made no reference to recent subsistence crises nor to the people's necessity to take seasonal employment away from home. The local Free Church minister was more outspoken, emphasising the poverty and congestion of the Coigach communities, their poor accommodation, their fine morality and the perennial lack of employment opportunities during the winter months.

The minister at Lochbroom (echoing his predecessor in 1842) was sure that education was a great generator of mobility and migration. It caused young people to understand the limitations of the crofter life and the possibilities of betterment elsewhere. It helped create a continuing exodus of youth from the district, both seasonal and permanent. The minister remarked:

> A very large proportion of the young people leave their homes upon growing up, and seek for employment at a distance in all parts of the kingdom, and also in the colonies. There is no opening for them here, and the accounts which I have from time to time received from many of them, both in England and abroad, have been most gratifying.

At the other extremity of the Cromartie estate, at Tarbat in the east, there was a similar refrain. Employers were fearful that the local children were being educated beyond the needs of squad work and thereby encouraged to migrate—'The girls in the district always make a point of going to the south for service as soon as they are old enough to do so, and as sufficiently well educated to obtain good situations there'. Similarly he told how 'the boys leave their homes to go to sea, emigrate, and for other lines in life,

29   Raven cottage in 1900, the last of the estate houses still to be thatched, engulfed by smart villas. The cottage was built at least 100 years earlier.

in the same way as the girls, and do not generally take to agricultural work.' Partly the cause was the poor availability of cottage accommodation, but partly it was a consequence of rising expectations among the younger generations. And so the large farmers were forced to resort to female labour from the west coast and from the spare labour of the east coast fishing villages. Walter Arras, one of the largest farmers on the Cromartie estate, built his own cottages to conserve his labour force—but even he experienced difficulty in retaining 'double man', that is a father and son working together 'as the lads always leave their homes young'.[34]

For those who remained the labour market was, until the 1880s, relatively buoyant. Even so it was often a harsh and pinched life of continual labour. A later testimony recollected the life of a woman of Kilmuir Parish who eventually died just after the First World War. She had been widowed in 1870 with four small children to support. To supplement the meagre allowance provided by the parish she took work in the fields:

> Her wages were 10d per day, her working hours being from 6am to 6pm with a couple of hours off for a mid-day meal, and in harvest time there might be a short interval for tea, served in the field at the farmer's expense. If by some mischance she had to be absent for an hour from work 2d was deducted from her day's pay.[35]

The widow of Kilmuir, nevertheless, was by all contemporary accounts, 25% better off than her counterpart of the previous generation.

VI

The policy of the Cromartie estate towards the crofters remained mildly reformist. Much effort was devoted to improving crofters' houses by way of subsidies. As time went on more subtenants became direct tenants 'and a proper value put on their lots and grazing according to the stock each holds'; overstocking, regarded as a critical problem in the crofting economy, was diminished wherever possible.[36] Individual crofters were removed on occasion without force or resistance. Sometimes eviction was blocked by the intervention of the Duchess—Widow Maclean sold liquor without a licence and should have been removed 'but a promise had been made to her father and the Duchess is unwilling to break that promise'.[37] Crofters continued to look to the factors to settle their internecine disputes.[38]

Removal remained the most sensitive issue on the estate. When Scott had taken upon himself to issue legal process for removal in 1868, George Loch was bursting with criticism. Every removal had to have the express sanction of Loch himself. He recollected that:

> Not long ago when you wrote proposing to take severe measures for the ejectment of one of these people, I wrote at once to say that nothing of the sort must be done, as it was quite contrary to the principle on which the Duke desired his people to be treated ... Let me request that all proceedings be immediately desisted from, and that the people be suffered to rest unmolested.[39]

The Duke's own influence was undoubtedly at work—he had no stomach at all for removal and doubtless suffered recurrent nightmares of Coigach in 1852-3.[40] Loch reported the landlord's attitude:

> This question gives the Duke and Duchess some concern—for they desire to avoid all risk of getting into contention with these people—and they would wish whatever steps be taken, to be adopted with much consideration, and so as not to involve the removal of the people, unless they have some place to go to—and only to do it by degrees—for there is no hurry about it, and it only be spread over a year or two.[41]

This had become the quintessence of the low-key policy of the Sutherland management towards the crofters—there would be no more rebellion, no more radical upset from the landlord side. It was virtually a confession of proprietorial impotence.

There were various signals of this managerial paralysis. For instance when the tacksman's hold on Isle Martin was relinquished in 1867 the people became direct tenants on 'very moderate' rents. It was widely recognised that there were too many people on Isle Martin and that they were very poor and that their land was very inferior. But no effort was made to reduce their numbers, no effort to rationalise the use of the land.[42] Similarly in the east of the estate, at Achterneed, a tenant successfully petitioned for clemency on the grounds that his family had been tenants for 300 years. And when the new agent Gunn recommended that interest should be charged on rent arrears Loch agreed in principle—but chose not to implement the principle. Instead he pointed out:

> Such a measure would be certain to provoke some discontent, and taking place on an Estate of the Sutherland family, would be observed upon. I don't think this of the least importance under ordinary circumstances, and when (as in this case) the proceeding would be perfectly legitimate, but just now there is so much discussion going on with respect to the relations subsisting between landlords and this class of tenants, and so much comment and criticism, that I think it may be as well to avoid taking a step not absolutely necessary, that might give rise to misrepresentation.[43]

In some respects the attitude of estate management to the crofting question was determined by the fears of generating adverse publicity enough of which had been experienced in the early 1850s. Famine also was too recent a memory to allow ideas of a more radical sort to activate the management. Relations between landlord and people were in equilibrium. Patience did not expire until the 1870s. Meanwhile the Cromartie estate concentrated its attentions on the more exotic possibilities of Strathpeffer Spa.

CHAPTER 20

Strathpeffer Spa, 1850–80

I

The third Duke of Sutherland owned about 1.3m acres in Scotland and about 32,000 acres in England, the latter yielding more income than the former. In terms of rent he was the fifth largest landowner in the kingdom. In 1861 his wife's Cromartie estate was estimated roughly at 221,000 acres in extent and produced a gross income of almost £9,000 per annum, a small fraction of the income of the Duke's assets. Together with his other assets he was immensely wealthy and was able to cultivate a range of diverse, even exotic investments. He sponsored the construction of the Highland Railway to the extent of almost a quarter of a million pounds. His portfolio of investments was hardly rivalled in that mid-Victorian age. He owned shares in railways, canals, sugar plantations, irrigation schemes, oil ventures and much more, some at home, some abroad. He took relatively small part in local and national politics and was generally regarded as socially unremarkable, and even a little bizarre in his personal enthusiasms. It was claimed by unsympathetic observers that he was 'distinguished only for his interest in suppressing fires—a useful but eccentric taste'. Certainly he was much taken by gadgets—railway trains as well as fire-engines. Like his father and grandfather, he continued to pour money into the Highlands, especially in his efforts to improve the bogs of central Sutherland. Some of his rather obsessive interests were extraordinarily expensive and some essentially unproductive.[1] Strathpeffer Spa was sometimes in danger of falling into this category.

In June 1861 Andrew Scott, the Cromartie agent, commented revealingly to a kinsman on the propensities of the third Duke:

> Since the old Duke of Sutherland's death the young Duke has come out strong in the way of building at Strathpeffer. A sum of about £2,500 is to be laid out on the Pump Room, and in building a wellkeeper's House, and a set of shops and a post office and post masters' dwelling house. Building is rather a hobby of the young Dukes as it was of his Father. It is less foolish than gambling or racing.[2]

Scott's remarks spoke volumes for the professional manager's attitude to aristocratic tendencies. The Spa was not much better than betting or horses but a Duke should be permitted his hobby, it was the way the world was ordered. Scott's comments marked also a more active phase in the development of facilities at Strathpeffer Spa. In the following three decades the Spa emerged fully from its chrysalis.

30 Lithograph of the projected Spa, and plans for the Spa feus, 1868, by William Devey.

II

Before 1850 the Hay-Mackenzies had regarded the development of the Spa with some disdain and some scepticism. Its growth had been modest, restricted to a degree by the unwillingness and inability of the family to raise capital for its facilities and its promotion. From 1850 to 1861 the Marquis and Marchioness of Stafford were also financially constrained; only in 1861 did the third Duke have full access to capital funds to accommodate his ideas for growth on his wife's estates.

Despite these proprietorial handicaps the Spa had developed spontaneously and beyond the expectations of its owners. Although development was kept on a close rein the Spa grew well in the middle decades of the century. In 1844 for instance, it was reported that:

> The various medicinal springs in the strath, particularly two in the west end, have of late years, acquired high celebrity for the cure of a great many diseases. Dr Thomas Morrison of Elsick in Aberdeenshire, who previously visited almost every other spa in the kingdom, declared the Strathpeffer wells to be unrivalled, and usually described the climate as 'the balsamic air of Strathpeffer'.[3]

Invalids were accommodated in an enlarged hospital and the season for visitors extended from May to October.

Certainly the Spa was by no means a sensation, but by 1850 Strathpeffer was a well-known place of recuperation drawing its mixed clientele from the counties which comprised the north of Scotland. Its most vigorous development as a resort however, dated from the time of the Sutherland connection. The Leveson-Gowers eventually, with the help of their friends and associates, lent the Spa ineffable aristocratic chic. Strathpeffer became fashionable during the years of general leisure resort development in Britain. Standards of living had risen to the point where the middle classes were increasingly keen to take a week or a fortnight in another place—by foreign travel or by the sea, or at a spa. Strathpeffer, in association with many other spas in Europe and England, gave the clear promise of health and beauty.[4] Its growth was part of the phenomenal development of health industries in Victorian Britain, a vast array of medical and quasi-medical enterprises which offered services and remedies to the sick (especially the tubercular), to hypochondriacs and other sufferers in the population.

Strathpeffer, of course, suffered certain disadvantages. Its extreme northerly location isolated it from the wealthy quarters of the kingdom and it was cooler and shorter in season than its southern competitors. On the other hand it was much helped by the nineteenth century glamorisation of the Highlands and Queen Victoria's own cult of 'Balmorality'. Even more immediate was the impact of railways which, eventually, brought the most affluent calibre of guest to the very doorstep of Strathpeffer. Several years later a sharp commentator on aristocratic mores observed that 'dukedoms have a habit of connecting themselves with water places'. It was unquestionably advantageous that the Dukes of Sutherland attached themselves to Strathpeffer.[5]

The third Duke regarded the Spa as a personal commitment and in this he was egged on by Scott's successor, the local factor William Gunn, and, even more, by the professional propagandisers of Spa medicine and facilities. The Duke's wife, Duchess Anne, was also an enthusiast for Strathpeffer and was familiar with the standards set in continental spas.[6] After 1861 the main obstacle to such promotion of Strathpeffer was George Loch (and subsequently his successors) who feared poor returns on capital invested in this way; they also invoked the venerable rule that landlords should not meddle in entrepreneurial territory. Such tensions enlivened the history of the Spa for half a century, during which time the popularity of Strathpeffer swelled rapidly in parallel with the Duke's expenditures on the latest Spa technology.

III

In August 1852 the Dingwall newspaper, perhaps under the influence of local patriotism or local proprietors, reported rapturously on the recent season at Strathpeffer Spa:

> This healthgiving and fashionable resort was never more gay and crowded with visitors. It is replete with beauty of all ages, from the damsel in her teens to the staid and stately matron, so that the most fastidious bachelor, we opine, can hardly maintain, in spite of the singular views, but that 'beauty is bewitching'.

The Spa water was reported to be in excellent condition and recent improvement to facilities had left little to be desired among those 'who came to partake either of its salubrious waters, or the life-giving breezes which are inhaled from the mountain tops which surround it'.[7] Warm mineral baths had recently been added. It was evident that the future of the Spa depended on its reputation and, increasingly, on newspaper reports and advertising. But its proprietors were faced with a dilemma: the success and popularity must be selective. The fashionability of the Spa depended on a certain social exclusivity and the management developed sensitive antennae for the appropriate clientele for Strathpeffer.

There was also the mystique of the waters. Information about the properties was expressed in quasi-scientific language put out to impress a generally unquestioning public. Not all the managers were believers, though Andrew Scott was. In March 1850, for instance, he wrote enthusiastically to young Lady Stafford—'a singular discovery ... has been made at the Pump Room'. Indeed during recent cleaning operations on the Spa drains 'a flow of a different coloured water with a white sulphureous scum upon it was found coming out of a choked drain'. From this inauspicious spot Scott proclaimed the discovery of the 'old original well ... right under the wall of the well house at the back of the pump room'.[8]

Despite these promising signs the Spa was far from lucrative or even glamorous. In 1858 the Spa yielded an annual rent of merely £100 and facilities were primitive by the standards of its southern competitors. George Loch was puzzled about the best way forward. At the end of 1857 he addressed the tourist potential in detail, taking together both Castle Leod and the Spa. The castle he said 'is amazingly striking—full of interest as well for what it is as for what it might be made—I never saw a place where there was greater natural suggestiveness of improvement'. Castle Leod however could hardly justify capital works since it was unlikely to yield a return on the outlay.

The Spa was a different proposition but was full of perplexity. Loch could sense that an outlay of money might improve its attraction, increase the number of paying guests, and enhance the value of Lady Stafford's property. But it was an unusual type of enterprise for a landed estate and an investment here could easily fail. As he put it 'the considerations connected with this are very interesting and much more difficult to be dealt with, for they involve of a more or less speculative character'. Speaking in the true voice of the agent, he continued:

> If an attempt were made, by the outlay of money, to bring the place more into notice, and to induce an accession of visitors, and if this attempt were to succeed, then great credit and praise would be bestowed on every man concerned.

But he feared failure, and too much risk for the Staffords' still fragile northern finances. He agreed that Strathpeffer was very beautiful and within reach of much striking scenery, and a railway would make it more accessible. And he added, with cynical realism, that 'the water is so beastly, as to prove that there must be some virtue in it'. Loch in private always referred to the Spa's main natural asset as 'the stinking water'. Moreover it was true that, in the north of Scotland, invalids had no other choice but Strathpeffer. Yet the Spa was patently in need of commercial development, especially in the provision of accommodation and general facilities.

On the central question of business promotion Loch invoked the cardinal rule of his (and his father's) estate management. All commercial speculation, all entrepreneurial tasks 'must rest with others'. Business was simply not the function of a landlord. He told the Staffords that 'it would never do for you to embark in speculative building for the purpose'. He would only advise the subdivision of land into small plots to feu 'to persons of no great wealth for the erection of small lodging houses'. The danger was the creation of higgledy-piggledy building and Loch advised Scott to employ a surveyor to set them out to 'make a compact little Cheltenham or Leamington, on a small scale'. Eventually a larger builder might be attracted to produce a better class of lodging house. Loch also advised the demolition of 'the unsightly old wooden Infirmary' and the provision of walks and outdoor facilities which together with the lure of 'the stinking water' might attract more visitors of 'a far higher kind'. For the moment he regarded these ideas as 'perhaps dreamy and speculative' though he agreed with Lord Stafford's own opinion that the spa deserved a substantial fillip.[9]

Loch was tentative about the Spa's future partly because he was unconvinced about its waters, partly because he was sceptical of the general frippery of spas. He returned to the theme in early 1858 and now somewhat more candidly. Strathpeffer, he declared, lacked 'all life and progress'. The place was at a standstill and there had been no progress for several years. All the recent building had been in inferior style 'and quite unsuited for the reception of visitors from among the wealthier members of society'. Certainly the Spa was situated in very pretty country, but there was 'an absence of occupation for the people going there in search of health or amusement'. The current construction of a railway northwards to Inverness would undoubtedly help prospects and could entice a better class of visitor who would then require better accommodation than presently available. He thought the vital thing was to attract builders and speculators to Strathpeffer particularly by offering short leases. He pointed out that the income from the consumption of the waters was relatively trivial compared with the potential benefits of new tenants on the estate rental but it was all a speculative business with no certainty of success. Nevertheless he was prepared to consider the merits of plans for 'a future Cheltenham' in the Highlands.[10]

Scott, in defence of his own management at Strathpeffer, told Loch that there was actually little demand for land because of high feu duties. There was however never any complaint about accommodation from 'among the wealthier classes' because they rarely attended the Spa.

> They come not for health but for amusement and their coming or not depends so much on fashion, on incidents over which the curative nature of the Spa has no control that the building and furnishing of Houses with large Handsome appartments and stables and coach-houses to match would I fear be a very doubtful speculation if entered upon before a railway came to Dingwall.[11]

The development of the Spa remained, in the eyes of the estate agents, an alien enterprise. The management understood the practical business of agricultural productivity and a sound return on rural investment. It did not understand the management and cultivation of fashion and style in a Highland village. But Scott had a brainwave. The Spa waters could be bottled at Strathpeffer and sent all over the country. It would create local employment and compensate for the extreme seasonality of employment at the Spa. Loch thought this a great joke:

> I shudder to think of the consequences that might ensue if a bottle of this water to be uncorked at a dinner table in the midst of a polite and refined society, in the expectation that it would prove a sort of seltzer water ... the effect would be fatal to Strathpeffer, of which the name would thenceforward 'stink in the nostrils' of all persons with tender stomachs.

Loch enjoyed mocking the waters. A few months later, after the *Inverness Courier* had remarked on the smell issuing from the medicinal waters, he remarked that 'it seems that my notion of the stink issuing from the water was not far wrong—sulphuretted hydrogen gas is very much the same sort of fragrance that arises from a common sewer'.[12]

Loch indeed adhered to severely Smithian principles in his view of Strathpeffer: 'The origin of most of these places is to be found in the activity and enterprise of men having something to gain from their exertions.' The landlord could give encouragement to such developers' enterprise but no more; it was their function, not the landlord's, to create a Cheltenham in the north. Thus, in the late 1850s, Strathpeffer continued to serve only a modest clientele. The poorest of the invalids still had access to the waters by way of a subvention from the Parochial Board. And the Spa attracted the infirm from all strata in the north—people in search of miracles which money alone could not command. Scott thought that visitors should pay for the waters though he thought an exception should be made for the 'class of poor not sunk to the dead level of pauperism who may find it not easy to pay for the water'.[13] If, however, the Spa were to grow and generate capital it would be necessary to draw upon the growing southern clientele of spa-users. As the railways approached Inverness and Dingwall the opportunities widened.

IV

When Scott in August 1861 noted that the third Duke of Sutherland was taking up the Spa as 'a hobby' it was clear that George Loch's austere principles inhibiting direct landlord investment had been breached. Two years later most of a new building programme at Strathpeffer had been completed. There had been a quickening of activity. Loch told Scott to advertise for a new tenant for the Well's facilities, someone with more vigour and who could pay a better rent. He also sanctioned an extension of the old practice by which small tenants in the village could take in lodgers during the season.[14] In 1864 there was a further burst of activity to promote development in the village.

The status of the Spa remained modest and the Duke's investments were so far decidedly unspectacular (especially by later standards). The lease of the Spa had increased to £180 p.a. but at this rent the tenant fell into bankruptcy in 1867. Scott's successor, William Gunn, recollected that at that time:

> the Pump Room was a low one storey building—and the mineral waters were served direct from the then available springs by means of jugs and tumblers—there was no verandah or other means of shelter, and there were only 3 very dirty looking copper baths—than which nothing could be more unsuitable for sulphur waters.[15]

The possibilities of investment and development at Strathpeffer were virtually limitless. Beyond the fear of accumulating capital debts for the heir, there were two particular hazards of which George Loch, the Duke's commissioner, was especially conscious. One was the extraordinary zeal of the local agent William Gunn, who was a great proselytiser of the Spa and its future prospects—he repeatedly urged developmental expenditure by which the estate could reap future revenues from the Spa. The other danger was the mystique with which the successive/medical advisors clothed the operations of the Spa. The Spa doctors and advisors, employing a sub-language of Spa technicalities, a pseudo-science of hydropathy, threatened to bamboozle the estate into endless and expensive improvements to the facilities at Strathpeffer. Loch, in particular, was very rarely prepared to suspend his disbelief and was generally sceptical of these allegedly scientific requirements. Thus, over many years, through the 1870s and 80s, there was a struggle between the afficionados and the estate managers about the future of the Spa and its funding.

Strathpeffer Spa benefited from three circumstances in the 1870s and after. One was the general enthusiasm for spas, the growing affluence of the nation which permitted a rising proportion of its citizens to contemplate 'cures', and holidays. Another was the extension of the railway system into the northern Highlands which allowed Strathpeffer to compete with Harrogate and the southern spas. The third was the discovery of much larger supplies of mineralised waters at Strathpeffer which opened new opportunities and dimensions to the spa enthusiasts.[16] Specifically the availability of water now meant that the paying public, previously limited to drinking the water, would now be able to immerse themselves bodily in the supposedly health-giving minerals. This, however, required a great expansion not only of accommodation but also of plumbing and heating facilities.[17]

The railway came closer by stages, first to Inverness (in 1859), then Dingwall (in 1862) and finally to Strathpeffer Spa (in 1885). In anticipation of great changes in the trade an estate report of 1870 recommended a greater release of land at low feus to facilitate general development. It was noted that 'the demand for Lodging Accommodation being annually on the increase every encouragement will be given to induce building—the use of the local stone quarry will be given at a nominal charge and feuars can have a supply of excellent water at a trifling cost'.[18] Increasingly the Cromartie estate took over the facilities of the Spa and the responsibility for its general development.[19] While the Spa waters were under lease it was difficult to pursue an improvement programme and this did not fall into the estate's hands until the late 1870s.

In 1872 Gunn had toured the English spas and returned with new ideas for a series of expensive changes including new spa baths and a new well. The celebrated German chemist Herman Weyber was brought in to lend his authority to the medicinal claims made for the waters of Strathpeffer. He pronounced them 'to be one of the very best effervescing chalybeate waters. He admitted he did not know of a better, or few so good'.[20] Gunn persuaded the Duke into increasing levels of investment at the Spa, often more than £1000 per annum. But Gunn's ambitions for the Spa outstripped the Duke's commitments and he began to incubate ideas for corporate investment to raise the enterprise into a much larger tourist resort.

The pump room was expanded by 1871 and then the demand for large scale luxury hotel accommodation began to mount, together with the broad expansion of the Spa in terms of promotion and a widening range of tourist facilities. Throughout 1872 to 1874 the Duke was bombarded with ideas for hotels, heating systems, advertising, and medical specifications. George Loch mainly stonewalled these ideas. In 1873 he declined to extend the advertising saying that there were already enough notices in southern railway stations, and that 'it would however be awkward for Her Grace to insert such advertisements when there is a scarcity of accommodation in the place'. He also refused further chemical analyses of the waters as being unnecessary—'the general public care very little for analysis of these waters' and they had all been done before.[21]

Nevertheless William Gunn continued to press for a more positive response to commercial opportunities at the Spa. His enthusiasm was demonstrated by the eagerness with which he was prepared to adventure his own capital in the Spa's future: eventually Gunn became a leading investor in the Spa economy. His plans matured in the mid 1870s. Already in 1872 he broached the idea of a joint-stock company to undertake hotel construction at Strathpeffer. There had been a lack of 'enterprising spirit' and capital, and he calculated that about £9000 was now required. He knew of comparable hotel investment in the north (e.g. the Caledonian in Inverness, and also at Bridge of Allan). The deficiency of hotels at the Spa was becoming notorious. 'First class English

31   The Pavilion.

32   The wells and baths, at noon.

families' had made the long journey north in the 1871 season and had been unable to get accommodation.

> If Strathpeffer is not kept advancing it will go back—it may, and no doubt will, attract mineral water drinkers, but they are not the class of people to raise the standard of the place, or to whom we must endeavour to attract to the place to grow and prosper'.[22]

Gunn had placed his shoulder to the wheel, his effort enhanced perhaps by the prospect of personal gain.

The need for large scale investment in hotels could not be long delayed and the Duke toyed with the idea for several years. But from the beginning there was reluctance. In November 1871 Loch told Gunn, 'I doubt therefore whether the Duke will himself undertake the cost of such a building. He relies on it being done by a joint stock company ... to which His Grace would be glad to contribute.' Over the following two years the idea shifted between various possibilities. Gunn himself had complained of 'a lack of enterprising spirit—but it would succeed if the Duke were behind it'. In June 1873 consideration was suspended for twelve months because of the unsettled state of the building trade.[23] Eventually, in October 1874, Loch announced the final decision

> The Duke has decided to abandon his intention of building an Hotel at Strathpeffer. The outlay would in any case, be large, and he would rather avoid incurring it at present—but his main reason is that he thinks it an enterprize more suited to a Company or to individuals seeking an investment.'[24]

He had already pointed out that 'there is no want of Capital for the work, if the work were itself more expedient'.[25]

There was no doubt that the problems of accommodation were increasing. Both 1874 and 1875 were bumper years for the Spa, and its list of visitors demonstrated that it was a great attraction to people from across the north of Scotland—for example, from Hopeman, Arbroath, Elgin, Stornoway and Aberdeen. Visitors were also journeying from the south, from Edinburgh, Glasgow and Dundee, even from Calcutta and Canada. In the spring of 1875 the *Ross-shire Journal* noted some expansion of accommodation, 'but even with the increased number and additions made to the houses in recent years there is still a lack of accommodation to contain the large influx of visitors who arrive during the summer and autumn months'.[26]

The Duke of Sutherland's reluctance to initiate the Hotel project at Strathpeffer may have been connected with the failure of a salmon fishing project in west Sutherland in that year. He had financed and established a complicated venture which required elaborate organisation involving ice-supplies, ice houses, London agencies, local managers and arrangements with fishermen. On its demise Evander MacIver, a frank confidante of William Gunn, remarked that 'His Grace should never have carried on these fishings on his own account. Dukes should never become Farmers or Fishers.' George Loch always insisted that 'some part of the necessary effort must be met by private enterprize'.[27] Whether the Duke was directly inhibited by this principle is not known, but he left the hotel project to a Company which initially found difficulty in

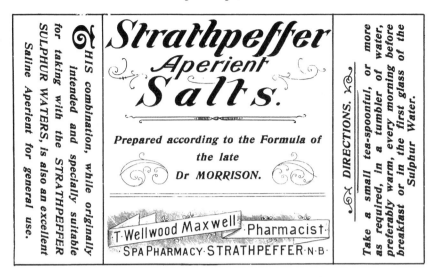

33.

raising its capital. Planned from Edinburgh its promoters complained in 1876 that 'the encouragement offered by the Duke is very cold'. They reported that 'people knowing how adventurous he is, cannot help suspecting that there must be something unsound in the arrangement, because he does not appear to be taking any part in it.' There was also another problem of credibility—'many who have never been in the locality have an idea that it is an outlandish and barren country—I do all I can to undeceive them on this and advised them to inspect and judge for themselves.'[28]

In the outcome a joint-stock company launched 'The Strathpeffer Hotel Co.' in 1876 and the Duke committed himself to £2000, almost a quarter of the initial capital. The venture drew upon other local sources of capital including the arable farmer Walter Arras and Gunn himself. Increasingly the estate looked to private enterprise for initiatives and capital. Its construction over the following two years was part of the growing sophistication of the facilities at Strathpeffer which in the course of the next ten years, brought it increasing income and the type of superior clientele necessary for its reputation and glamour and vital to its overcoming the problem of distance.[29] The Spa Hotel was completed in mid 1879.[30] Gunn was now fully attuned to the importance of publicity and requested the Duke and Duchess to visit the Spa 'in order to bring it prominently before the notice of the class of visitors whom it is specially desireable to attract to it'. Gunn knew that spas depended as much on the current vogue as on the strength and chemical composition of their waters. In 1882 the Spa was being advertised in *The Times*, on trams and in railway waiting rooms throughout the country.[31]

By 1880 the wave of popularity enjoyed by the Highlands among tourists and royalty was approaching its crest. Even the west coast had emerged into a new prominence. The Duke of Sutherland decided to build a hotel at Lochinver and attention turned to Coigach which, until very lately, said Gunn, had 'been an unknown district to tourists'.[32] At the Spa medical and quasi-scientific advisors were ceaselessly advocating expensive innovations and new investment. A doctor[33] was employed in the village, first Dr Middleton, and then Dr Thomas Manson, who spent much energy boosting the reputation of the Spa. The latter wrote a much republished book about the waters: the first edition of 300 copies in 1880 was despatched to leading medical men in both Scotland and England. Manson told Gunn that the Cromartie estate should send a person to Germany to inspect the government-managed spas in that country. He said that the waters of Strathpeffer were superior to those in Aix-les-Bains and lacked only decent facilities to take full advantage of its natural resources. Gunn reported that visitors who had also been to Harrogate and Buxton were 'discontented when they came here and find things not on equally so grand a scale'.

Life at the Spa was certainly congested at the peak of the season. In July 1878 Gunn gave a glimpse of the clientele taking the waters in the Pump Room and congregating in the adjacent waiting room: 'In fine weather they rarely went near it—but on a wet day they crowded into it with their wet umbrellas, walking sticks, etc., and the invalids with their crutches, knocking the walls and chairs, and spoiling everything.' There had been complaints and a suggestion that a charge be made for the provision of heating and newspapers, which would also 'keep the room tolerably select'. Like the other facilities, the Pump Room was simply inadequate to the needs of the trade.[34]

Renewed efforts, successful in the outcome, were devoted to the discovery of alternative sources of mineralised waters. This then became the signal for further growth. Gunn remarked in August 1880 that 'the demand for baths has never been so great as it has been ... and the inability to supply them is injurious to the reputation of the Spa as well as the loss of revenue from the Establishment.' Enough commercial success was now apparent to justify Gunn's urgent opinions. Sir Arnold Kemball, the new Commissioner to the Sutherland Estates, continued to hesitate in the manner of his predecessor, George Loch: 'I am still of opinion that in order to make success certain we should rely rather upon realised returns as a means to the end than to continue to discount the future'.[35] In effect he advocated the recruitment of private entrepreneurs; he was anxious about the reliability of the future supply of spa waters and was chary about increasing expenditure on accommodation. Operations therefore were set in motion to prove the mineral supply and to recruit the still more active financial participation of the Duke in plans for further expansion.[36]

Gunn and the medical cognoscenti were repeatedly frustrated by conservative estate officials and by the reluctance of the Duke to become involved more deeply in direct investment. Gunn's ideas for expansion were repeatedly thwarted. In 1880, for example, the total estimated revenue from the estate was £13,276 (gross) yet Gunn wanted to spend £16,925 on capital works, notably on the Pavilion, the centrepiece of the Spa. This was a time of marked retrenchment in estate finances and one of the Duke's financial advisors expostulated—'I am astonished—where in the name of wonder do you think we can get the money?'[37] The answer was clear, the Duke would not supply the money and any further investment would have to come from ordinary revenues. Somehow Gunn managed to meet the demand for improvements at the Pavilion which was opened in August 1881 together with new baths. Further development was arranged by the formation of the Ben Wyvis Hotel Company, set to construct a spectacular building close to the springs, and also to ensure the continuing success of tourism. The year 1880 was particularly successful and Kemball, in a rosier frame of mind, remarked to Gunn: 'The revenue of the Spa will no doubt cover the additional expenditure which the arrangements may occasion'.[38] Though optimistic, Kemball's opinion was premised on the notion that the Duke should be insulated from further direct investment in the Spa. But the agent Gunn was involved deeper and deeper in the hotel industry, partly on his own account, and partly responsible to both the Duke and a body of shareholders. He spent a great deal of his energy in the minutiae of advertising and organising facilities. The Ben Wyvis Hotel, for instance, offered accommodation at £3 per week which included three meals per day 'prepared by a male cook'. These were low rates but reflected the competition in the Highland hotel industry, especially in the early and later months of the season.[39]

V

There was also much competition and comparison between British and European spas. Strathpeffer depended heavily on the authority of its medical advisor, Dr Manson, and his advice often determined the direction of the development, especially about the baths and other technicalities. On his urgings there was a constant effort to maintain the latest technology to rival the installations of other spas. The year 1881 was disappointing, though the Spa operations nevertheless managed to break even. Gunn's response to recession was to advocate still more investment. He told Commissioner Kemball, 'after visiting the Dunblane and Athole Hydropathies [in Perthshire] last summer we introduced the Douche, Wave, Spray and [Seltz] Baths so much used in foreign Spas and so strongly recommended by Dr Manson'.[40] Continuing comparisons were made with other spas in which, for instance, Harrogate was declared to be decidedly inferior in various categories of mineralisation. When the prospect that a closer rival, at Croft, might be developed, Gunn assured Kemball, 'I shall do what I can to keep Strathpeffer before the public in the way it deserves and I do not think we need much fear Croft as a rival to the Highland Spa'. Indeed the waters were again 'proved' in 1882 and the Duke agreed to make a loan of £4000 to the Spa Wells Account.[41] This was intended as a self redeeming commitment and connected with a renewed wave of confidence occasioned by the approach of the proposed railway to Strathpeffer.

The main publicity for Strathpeffer Spa was written by Manson himself. He claimed, for instance that Strathpeffer was 'amongst the foremost in its class in Europe, and far beyond anything in Great Britain' in the quality of the waters. Moreover the village was now an 'easily accessible Home Spa', only 20 hours from London in 1881, and a sensible alternative to continental spas. Great improvements had been achieved under ducal patronage and 'under the able and tactful superintendance of her Grace's factor'. The main hotel at Strathpeffer was now heated by 'Taylor's system of coil pipes' and thus able to maintain a constant room temperature of 60° in the colder seasons. He emphasised that the Spa waters were equally efficacious in winter as in summer. He described the climate in scientific detail and demonstrated that the local death rate was lower than in London and that 'consumption' was a rare disease in the locality. Manson

34 Strathpeffer in summer and winter c.1907.

also catalogued the esoteric treatments available at the Spa and listed the possible benefits to the following complaints:

> misery, heavy and painful digestion, want of appetite, bilious conditions, sluggish liver, and all other curable affections of the liver, constipation, the affection called 'piles', jaundice, gall-stones, scrofulous conditions and scrofulous sores, chronic rheumatism, chronic gout, rheumatic gout, sciatica, skin diseases, syphilis, irritation or inflammation of the urinary passages, catarrh of the bladder, urinary calculi (small), white swellings, disease of the bones, and ulcers.[42]

The Highland resort attracted an increasingly exotic clientele to its waters and its bracing walks. Its patrons were perhaps the most fastidious, even hypochondriacal, that could be imagined. Nothing was good enough for some of them, and Gunn's patience was occasionally stretched to its limits. In the season of 1882 one spa-goer, endlessly complaining, penetrated Gunn's patience: 'Mr Ross Campbell', he exclaimed, 'is a humbug! Have nothing to do with him. If the Pavilion is not gd enough for him let him ....'[43] Another guest at Strathpeffer was Robert Louis Stevenson who stayed at the Ben Wyvis Hotel in 1880, hoping for a cure. Here he indulged his taste for Highland history and wrote rapturously of the pleasures of the valley, birch woods, heather and stream—'no country, no place, was ever for a moment so delightful to my soul'. Though he was much pleased with Strathpeffer he regarded his fellow clients as vile and wrote twenty-four lines of verse denouncing this 'wholly bestial crowd'.[44]

In 1884 Dr Manson, who had been the great propagandist and guru of Strathpeffer Spa for several years, died; his beloved hydropathy was unable to save him. Manson was only 45 years of age and had died of 'a bad chill which produced acute inflammation of the lungs'. Gunn said of him that although he had been dedicated to the Spa:

> his manner was blunt and not such as took readily with strangers, which told rather against him in his practice with the better class, but those who knew him best had a high opinion of his skill and sterling worth.

It was the eve of the railways at Strathpeffer by which the best in the land could travel uninterruptedly from London to the Highland Spa. The vacancy created by Manson's expiry attracted many applicants. One, a Dr Macrae of Harris, was effectively vetoed by Gunn on the grounds that he was 'a very rough diamond' and probably a 'land leaguer'.[45] Manson's successor was the redoubtable Dr Fortescue Fox and his appointment inaugurated a new phase in which the tension between growth and financial prudence was redoubled.

CHAPTER 21

The Social Volcano

I

It is difficult not to regard the history of the Highlands in the third quarter of the nineteenth century as a long preparation for the great eruption of crofter resistance in the 1880s. On the Cromartie estate and in the rest of the Sutherland Empire in the north, there appeared many hints and forebodings of the coming crisis. Looking back from the time of the crisis in the 1880s some commentators claimed that the Highlands, under the weight of landlord pressure, had reached a dangerous condition, that social relations had worsened until an explosion was inevitable. The Highlands had become 'a social volcano'. The search for such volcanic activity had a long history. Indeed an explosion had been predicted recurrently in several decades before the crofters' war. Critics of landlord policy and, especially, the clearances had often warned of the consequences, even of violence. For instance in the late 1830s a minister in Easter Ross described the desolation of a cleared landscape in which 'now nothing is heard but the bleating of sheep or the bark of the shepherd's dog'. He warned the proprietors that they had, in effect, destroyed the social cement:

> In many respects, this parish has been improved within the last forty years; but the depopulation of the country by large farms, is a serious evil, and is likely to bring along with it consequences which the landed interest seem not to have contemplated. There is no longer an independent peasantry. The morals of the people are deteriorated by the loss of independence, and their spirits embittered by what they deem oppression. The ties which united master and tenant are severed; and when the time comes, to which we look forward with fearful anticipations, it will, we fear, be found, that an error has been committed, by grasping too much, at the risk of sooner or later losing all.[1]

The eruption of social conflict in the 1880s was, in the event, relatively sudden and followed a long period of apparent quiescence. Indeed the abrupt challenge to landlord authority may have owed more to external stimuli than to the evolution of preparatory conditions within the Highlands. On the other hand it is clear that the trend in economic circumstances probably played a central part in the events. It is evident, for example, that almost all sections of the Highland economy fared more prosperously in the two decades after the famine. Landlord rents—mainly from sheepfarmers and sportsmen—rose extremely quickly. Crofters, benefiting from better cattle and general food prices, found their rents rising (if at all), less rapidly than their cash incomes. Their real incomes followed an upward tendency and it is likely that their economic aspirations rose in unison. General economic betterment probably encouraged a greater degree of harmony so long as it was maintained.

In the late 1870s the harmony was at last disrupted, primarily because primary prices and incomes began to collapse first among the sheepfarmers and then in the rest of the community. Landlords—notably on the Cromartie estates—searched for an equity of sacrifice. One consequence was that attempts were made to make the crofting sector pay rents commensurate with the rise of incomes since 1850. Landlords chose to implement such a policy at a time of wavering confidence and falling prices and it is not surprising that they precipitated opposition. The fact that the opposition cohered into region-wide political resistance is more difficult to explain. The Cromartie estate was well represented in all these events and did not escape the eruption of the volcano which, certainly until the late 1860s, had seemed perfectly dormant.

II

The management of the crofting population, even in good times, was an endless headache for the agents. Andrew Scott regarded the people as unruly and ignorant; in January 1869 he retired from the Cromartie management after 35 years service. He was succeeded by William Gunn, whose father had also been in the estate agency profession. Scott's legacy was shadowed by continuing difficulties with the west coast crofters some of whom Gunn was quickly able to settle. The long-serving Sutherland commissioner, George Loch, remarked that 'it was my impression that the difficulties that had arisen with these people were caused by want of temper and patience on Mr Scott's part. I hope now for better things.' But other factors knew better the intractability of systematic management among the crofters. At bottom was their sheer poverty and congestion on poor resources. Evander MacIver told Gunn that 'there will always be a heavy list of defaulters on the West Coast among the small tenants'. The local Coigach factor, Kenneth Mackenzie, implored Gunn to spend a few days in the district to witness the poverty and current mode of overstocking: 'your presence in trying to have better arrangements would be of the greatest importance'.[2] In 1871 George Loch himself specified the abilities required in a ground officer on the West Coast (at Assynt, north of Coigach)—he would need to be a 'very active energetic young man ... speaking Gaelic, and thoroughly up to agricultural improvements'. When Andrew Scott died—only twelve months after his retirement—Loch was able to say only that he had been 'an excellent upright man'.[3]

Prosperity, even in generally good times, was a relative matter. On the Cromartie estate, during the 1860s and 1870s the landlord—now the Duchess of Sutherland—was favoured by improving rents but experienced difficulties in raising a reasonable return on capital invested. Sheepfarmers expanded their flocks rapidly but many over-capitalised and over-committed themselves. The crofters who, in strictly relative terms, probably did best of all, remained abysmally poor by standards prevailing in the rest of mainland Britain. They were undoubtedly, on average, substantially better off than before, at least until the late 1870s; but they were still hostage to the unreliability of the seasons. And still the hungry spring too easily turned into a famished summer.

Indeed localised famine conditions recurred, even during the long secular improvement of crofter living standards after the mid century. For instance in November 1870 there were again reports from Coigach that poverty was severe and that among the crofters 'many had no potatoes since the middle of winter, [and] although food is cheap many of them have neither money nor credit'. This was the signal for the young men to search for employment along the coast, or further afield, especially towards the Caithness fishing. But the fishing had been unremunerative in 1870 and the people had become too reliant on its success to sustain them in their crofts. At one time, earlier in the century, estate planners had directed the people to the coast and encouraged them to devote themselves exclusively to the fishing.[4] Now the policy was utterly negated. As the Sutherland factor at Scourie put it, 'so long as our people depend on fishing their condition and circumstances will continue precarious. Those who stick to the land steady and never put a foot in a boat are more comfortable in every way.'[5] The reality was that their crofts and grazings were inadequate for any dependable and improving subsistence. The potato remained a lottery—as, for instance, in October 1872 when Gunn told Loch that 'the natives [sic] had got about three fourths of their crops secure and some were busy getting up potatoes of which about one half is diseased.'[6]

Little publicity was attracted by these periodic but localised disasters and the estate management did its best to cope with the problem. The effective laird of Cromartie was one of the richest men in the kingdom and possessed greater resources than most to deal with such shortfalls in the crofter sector. Crofter rents were lost by default and employment was sustained by sporadic work programmes. Each ate into the return on landlord capital; each added emphasis to the uneconomic character of crofter landholding in the West Highlands.

Road construction and seasonal employment outside the district were important cushions during each of the recurrent subsistence crises. The local agent in Coigach, Kenneth Mackenzie, believed that the building and trenching programme, financed solely by the Duke of Sutherland, would have wide consequences on the western population. It was a project which, he remarked:

> will not only afford much valuable employment to your people and afterwards tend to improve and civilise them—but it will teach many of them to work with pick and spade—which is a valuable species of education for them through life.[7]

New roads in Coigach were intended, as in the past, to open up this district, still one of the most remote in mainland Britain, to the influences of trade and civilisation. Their construction would create employment and assist fishing and other exports. Nevertheless it seems that the greatest benefits would flow to the great sporting tenants and their demands were the precipitant of such estate expenditure. It was a good time for landlords with shooting moors and their tenants were prepared to pay very high rents as well as the rates and taxes on such property.[8] In Coigach the sportsmen had been critical of the lack of bridges. Inverpolly Farm, one of the most prized of the moors, was almost inaccessible. It was said that 'the tenants of both the grazings and shootings at present suffer much discomfort and inconvenience ... There is no doubt but a road would enhance the value of both very considerably.' It was regarded as especially important that the small local port of Lochinver be connected as a terminus in the northwest for steamboat, postal and telegraph services. The contiguity of the Cromartie and Sutherland estates (by way of the Coigach and Scourie districts) gave the roads added importance for the Duke of Sutherland who also stressed aesthetic considerations in the construction question. His Commissioner, George Loch, advised that the route should follow 'the beauty of the scenery' even at the cost of making it longer. It was, however, the shooting tenants who called the tune. As a class of tenant they were often difficult, even arrogant, and required careful cultivation and handling. The Scourie factor, Evander MacIver, referring to one such, Sir Sandford Graham, remarked to Gunn in 1871, 'I hope you will be able to handle Sir G. delicately and work him satisfactorily'. MacIver was a master of the art.[9] The welfare of the crofter population was undoubtedly secondary or even incidental to these other questions.

The continuing buoyancy of sporting rents came into increasing contrast with the prospects of the agricultural tenants on the Cromartie estate after 1873. The large grazing farmers were especially sensitive to price levels, but so also were the great arable producers in the east, men who were entirely geared to the needs of southern markets. Even the crofters, dependent as ever on cattle sales, were hostage to price movements outside their region. After 1873, at different times and in different degrees, all sectors of the farming world were in economic retreat especially in comparison with the expansive years of the middle century. Sheep farmers were in some difficulty from the early 1870s, and at least one large arable farmer on the Tarbat estate gave up his land for reasons of excessive rent. When the Duke was asked for lower rents it was said that 'he would prefer doing such works of draining or other improvement as would bring it in value to the rent now paid.'[10] This was a consistent policy on the Sutherland estates throughout the nineteenth century and was only breached in times of direst difficulty.

Agricultural nerves were jarred further by a local banking crisis at the end of 1872. The Commercial Bank of Tain serviced the credit needs of the great farming community in Easter Ross. Credit had been over-extended, apparently by excessive speculation in bill-discounting, and the Bank fell into disarray dragging with it many of its farming clients. An undisclosed number of the Cromartie tenants burned their fingers and the financial consequences echoed through the community and there were general failures throughout Easter Ross. George Loch was highly critical of the 'web of speculation' that characterised local credit provision:

> It makes one anxious and distrustful to learn that even agricultural pursuits are maintained by this straining of fictitious credit. As regards Commerce one has been so accustomed to these things, as to accept them rather as matters of course—but it is otherwise when they happen in connection with farming, and it leads one to fear that the prosperity and progress of Scottish agriculture may have more to do than is desireable, with the props and aids it obtains from the artificial system of Banking which prevails in Scotland.

On this basis alone Loch predicted that less prosperous times lay ahead for the agricultural industry.[11]

Loch's subordinate, William Gunn, now factor for the Cromartie estate, concurred in Loch's view of the dangers of bank credit. Nevertheless Gunn insisted that the banks had played a vital role in the great expansion in northern farming. He argued that 'there could be no doubt but there are innumerable instances of men, who though possessed of all the qualifications that would secure success as farmers, who would never had been able to put their skills into practice or make their way in the world, had they not been helped on by aid from local Banks.' Gunn recognised that bank credit was expensive but emphasised that without it the farmers could not begin to function. For himself he preferred to celebrate the unprecedented progress and prosperity of the Highlands in the past few years, and he noted the great success of the hill farmers, especially those with a command of independent wintering facilities. Indeed Gunn emphasised the main problem that this success had occasioned—that farmers, especially on the arable lands, were beginning to feel a deficiency in the supply of field labourers. As Gunn said, 'the labour question is fast assuming an embarrassing aspect', one exacerbated by the inadequacies of cottage accommodation.[12]

In reality the Highlands in general were entering a critical moment in terms of economic welfare. In the years since the great famine prices and incomes had improved for all sectors, most notably for the small tenants whose rents remained relatively static. New levels of income and expectations had become part of the community's thinking. They had been borne along by the similar ascent of agricultural prices. After 1873 the shift was downwards, not always quickly or devastatingly, but serious enough to cause distress and pessimism. The new trend lasted two decades and required careful re-adjustment by all sectors of the estate communities. It was a great misfortune that the Duke of Sutherland and his advisors chose this moment, in the middle of the 1870s, to initiate a policy designed specifically to extract an economic return from the crofting population. This indeed was a vital element in the hardening of conflict on the Cromartie estate, as elsewhere in the Highlands, between the landlord and the common people. The long peace and prosperity of the post famine era were coming to an end.

III

Some premonition of social dispute was provided by the local elections associated with the Scottish Education Act of 1872. The Act effectively wrested control of education and schools from the landed proprietors and gave responsibility to School Boards elected by local rate-payers. It was a considerable invasion of traditional landlord authority, patronage and prestige. The Sutherland family regarded the Education Act with distaste and George Loch said of it that he 'could never see the merits which others profess to discover'. Moreover the estate adopted a severe attitude to the consequences of the new Act. The estate would remove all support from the education system on its Highland properties: henceforth the Duke and Duchess would 'withdraw all personal gifts, subscriptions or contributions to school purposes ... and occupy no other position than law imposes ... viz. those of rate-payers.' The School Boards would simply have to take over all existing responsibilities previously shouldered by the proprietor—on the

Cromartie estate, the Duchess 'will hereafter decline all expense or liability except such as may attach to her' in the capacity as rate-payer.

Having literally and symbolically abnegated all responsibility, the estate administrators nevertheless sought to influence the elections of the new School Boards. The parochial elections, by ballot among rate-payers, were arranged for April 1873. The first inclination of the estate factors was to avoid a ballot altogether—a contest would inevitably arouse 'sectarian efforts and the awakening of feelings that had much better be dormant.' The estate however wished the Boards to be controlled by 'persons of education and moderation of view'. This meant that the estate management wanted to be represented prominently in the respective parishes. Both Gunn and Kenneth Mackenzie were put up as candidates at Lochbroom and they expended considerable effort in mobilising the vote at Coigach. The elections became a focus for substantial campaigning, especially in the western parish and the Free Church ministers co-ordinated an effective contest in direct opposition to 'the laird's representatives'.

Mackenzie toured the district and spoke to most of those entitled to vote 'and gave them to understand they were expected to divide their votes equally between you [Gunn], their Minister and your humble servant, [and] I have every reason to believe they will do so'. He noted that it was 'most annoying' that so few of the Cromartie lotters qualified for a vote because their rental values were so low, and advocated some strategic amalgamation of lots to increase their voting capacity on future occasions. But it became apparent that 'sectarianism' and the 'Free Church party' were undermining Gunn's plans and in the upshot, though Mackenzie was elected, Gunn was publicly humiliated when the votes were counted. George Loch had feared that such elections would generate 'sectarian efforts and the awakening of feelings that had much better be dormant'.

Loch was right. Sectarianism and political radicalism were now forging a formidable alliance against landlord conservatism. The result was a humbling defeat for the landlord class, especially in Lochbroom where the local factor, having made the estate's wishes abundantly clear, had to report complete failure: 'The Coigach tenants have not acted as I expected or wished them to do' and the election was split by obvious sectarianism. William Gunn received the news from the election official who said: 'As returning officer I must be quiet but I must confess I never before saw so much vulgarity'. Kenneth Mackenzie, himself a defeated candidate, said that the people had been deceitful, impudent and had behaved badly and 'the Board as at present elected will be a way of strife forever'.[13]

In a restricted sense the School Board Election of 1873 represented the dawn of democracy among the rate-payers of the west coast. They at least had clearly rejected the express wishes of the proprietor and they had been led in this direction by the Free Church ministers, notably by the Rev. Kenneth McMillan. There was a measure of politicisation of the people in these events, significant perhaps in demonstrating wider potential in questions of crofter rights. But such prospects were yet undiscovered and estate relations resumed their usual patterns through the following few years. Thus in August 1873 the Cromartie estate invoked the goodwill of the small tenantry to celebrate, in the customary manner, the majority of Lord Tarbat, heir to the Cromartie estate. In Coigach the local factor arranged 'little prizes, refreshments and a first class supper for the keepers at the Hotel ... and whisky and other refreshment at the Dance after the Bonfire was lighted'. He reported that everybody behaved 'very orderly and they kept it up till about 4 a.m.' A piper was paid for his services, and scholars and paupers were provided with special allocations of food and whisky. According to Mackenzie the 'Rejoicings' were a great success and, no doubt, demonstrated the warmth of social relations on the estate.[14]

Events such as these were carefully orchestrated efforts by the landlord to stimulate good feeling among the small tenantry. Old notions of loyalty and clan solidarity may have entered their minds but the actual response of the people to these blandishments was mute and difficult to penetrate. Meanwhile however the great tenant farmers on the rich arable land of the east, men who had waxed fat in the years of 'high farming', also assumed a degree of social leadership often missing in rural society in the north. One was Walter Arras, perhaps the greatest of the capitalist farmers in Strathpeffer. In October 1875 for example, Arras gave 'a sumptuous supper to about 50 of his workers in the farm granary at Fodderty'. Celebrating the successful completion of harvest, Arras's annual supper was addressed by a missionary from China. Arras, clearly regarded as a model employer, was noted for 'his kindness' to his employees—'He takes a great interest and helps in everything that tends to their welfare.'[15] Of large affluent tenants the factors were sometimes wary. In 1874, for instance, Evander MacIver remarked that a new tenant was 'a plain vulgar man who has risen by his own shrewdness and enterprise. I do not think he can be troublesome—his agreement is fortunately plain and distinct.' Factors were jealous of their control over all classes of the tenantry and detested any direct communication between the tenants and the landlord or his Commissioner. MacIver was severely critical of direct 'intercourse with the Commissioner—who should never encourage them to go to him over the Factors'.[16]

IV

The real cutting edge of estate relations was the question of rents, the final economic nexus. While an increasing proportion of rental income came from sheepfarmers, the great arable tenants and, most notably, the sportsmen, the Cromartie estate generally chose to be indulgent towards the small tenants and the crofters. As in many parts of the Highlands (and in Ireland)[17] small rents lagged behind both general price levels and other rents. On the Cromartie and Sutherland estates the memory of crofter resistance on the west coast in the 1850s remained a scar on the memory of the Duke and Duchess of Sutherland. They remained reluctant to generate turmoil among their small tenants, particularly the Gaelic-speaking Duchess who identified more closely with the tenantry than did her husband.

Some of the estate agents were convinced that the crofters were making a mockery of a fair and reasonable management. Not only were their rents too low but they fell into arrears whenever they chose. The managers feared a total loss of control among the people, especially on the West Coast. The new generation of agents, notably William Gunn, could see no good reason to give backsliders such obvious leniency. He spoke repeatedly of the desirability of a more systematic attitude to rent arrears and the use of the Small Debtors' Court to stiffen the estate's response to recalcitrant tenants. George Loch, by now an ageing commissioner in the last years of his career, toured the estates annually, and was told of the troublesome character of the small tenants and their mounting arrears of rent. Gunn noted that the same tenants spent their income prodigally in the shops and inns at Ullapool. George Loch, however, recoiled from a sudden onslaught on crofter arrears:

> we could not adopt this peremptory course all at once having for so long, almost, encouraged irregularity, ... I have no doubt that summonses will be unpopular, and this is one reason why the tenants who receive them will avoid being in arrear, and the extra expense will be an additional incentive to prompt payment.[18]

Loch told his subordinates to proceed slowly and countermanded the idea of imposing an interest charge on all arrears.[19]

In 1874 William Gunn was again eager to press for the backlog of rents from the small tenants. He reported to Loch:

> I know that some who have been accustomed to pay at the proper time were not prepared to do so at this term, owing to them having delayed selling their spare stock in the hope of a rise in price, in which they were disappointed. But, considering the large expenditure of money, circulated in that district during this and last year, there can be no excuse for many who have neglected paying.[20]

Each rent collection required the local factor to estimate the circumstances of the people, usually relating to the price of cattle and the income from the fishing. The actual rent collection was often a question of the factors seizing their share of the crofters' annual income before the Ullapool merchants did their rounds among the people. In 1874 the merchants were late and Gunn was eager to assert the estate's rights.[21]

The Duke himself was becoming impatient. The Cromartie estate, even on its ordinary account, consumed all the net income except for £800.[22] It yielded a dismal return on capital, the more so since he also had spent more than £10,000 on roads and improvements in the west. This expenditure alone justified an augmentation of all rents. Moreover the Duke was keen to deploy more of the grazing land of the people for the use of the sheepfarmers and sportsmen who, of course, paid much better rents with far less fuss.[23]

In this mood, despite George Loch's trepidation, the Sutherland empire (including Cromartie) moved towards a complete revaluation of lands. This was a momentous and expensive programme designed, in effect, to bring rents into line with the substantial improvement of incomes since 1850. The operation was agreed in principle in 1875 but the process required three years before its completion. There were two critical aspects which caused great controversy when, eventually, it was implemented. The first was its timing—the great revaluation was designed and implemented as the fall of prices began to dampen and erode all incomes but especially those in the western districts. Second, the reorganisation of rents affected only those tenants-at-will, those on annual tenancies. In essence it was directed at the crofters and the small tenants who had neither the advantages nor the disadvantages of leaseholders. The revaluation of crofter rents would become a central dispute directed by the crofters against the estate management during the 1880s.

When the idea of a revaluation was first mooted, George Loch explained that:

> It is not of course His Grace's wish to put his small tenantry on rack rent but merely to redress the general state of manifest undervaluation that now exists—it is his belief, and I have no doubt it is a just one, that the great amount of profitable work that has been going on in the Country by the making of new lines of Railway; and as regards Coigach especially considering that it has been opened up by the formation of new and important Roads, thus affording valuable means of intercourse hitherto denied to the people—it is his belief that the condition of the Tenantry has been thus so largely benefitted as to make it perfectly just that they be now required to pay a proper rent for their holdings.

Such reasoning omitted a more cogent justification for a reappraisal of rents, namely the clear improvement of incomes derived directly from price increases in the 1850s and 60s.

In Loch's consideration of the *status quo* in late 1875 he pointed out that some crofter rents had already been revalued when they had changed hands. He also insisted on the principle that tenants should not be taxed on their own improvements 'in respect of which they have not yet reaped the full benefit', and should be clearly exempted from rent changes. On the other hand Loch was convinced that the lotters had access to too much grazing, what he termed 'the unreasonable limits of outrun now possessed by the Coigach small tenants'.[24]

The revaluation of the rents required a great survey of all tenancies on the Cromartie estate which proceeded from 1875 to 1878. A parallel exercise was accomplished in Sutherland. In the outcome the surveys produced an extraordinarily detailed account of the disposition of land on the estate, virtually a Domesday Book which was a prologue to a substantial increase of nominal rents on the estate. In October 1878 William Gunn drew up a lengthy document of 'Remarks' on the crofter valuations which provided an important benchmark in the evolution of the estate.

In Coigach for instance there were 250 Cotters who rented land between half an acre and nine acres in extent. Rents varied from 16/- an acre (for the best lots in Achultibuie) down to 7/-; the average rent was less than 10/- 'with patches of waste thrown in free'. Amongst the evidence a detailed register was drawn up of the stockholdings of the lot tenants at Coigach. This showed that the tenants, on average, owned about 11 sheep, two or three cattle, a stirk, and possibly a horse per lot. There was some variation in this movable wealth—some owned merely a couple of sheep and a cow, and a few possessed as many as 30 sheep and five cattle. But the variance was not enough to affect the basic equality of life in the west.[25] Grazing land and souming rights were related to rent and the extent of land holdings which had been stable for some time. Gunn remarked that 'one great advantage of this is that the poor man who is unable to have his full complement of stock can get value for his grazing from a well-to-do tenant who has means and wishes to keep more stock'.

Gunn discovered (to his own satisfaction) that rents had remained unchanged for several decades. He examined old rentals as far back as 1829 and found that rents for small tenants had been stationary over the intervening fifty years. By contrast the great leaseholders (the graziers and sportsmen) had experienced massive increases. He cited three large farms

	1831 £	1878 £
Inverpolly	280	850
Langwell	350	550
Drumvaich	50	140

Speaking of the small tenants, Gunn reported:

> It is right to mention that having traced the Rentals back for a period of 40 years I find there has been practically no increase of Rent during that period. At that time the Crofters of Achiltybuie and other smaller townships as far as the Big Rock were all subtenants of Messrs Mackenzie, Merchants, Ullapool, and so continued until 1853 when much to their satisfaction they became the tenants of the Propr direct at the old rents.

For William Gunn the evidence was crystal-clear and the surviving rentals tend to corroborate his view of rental trends. He was able to buttress his case by reference to other aspects of the crofters' circumstances. During the period in which their rents were stationary they had benefited from the 50% increase in wages (itself an indication of emerging but periodic labour shortages in the region). Their primary cash commodity, cattle, had increased in price by 30% in ten years and by 100% over thirty years, partly as a consequence of better breeding methods greatly assisted by the introduction of new breeding stock by the Duke of Sutherland. At the same time the main purchase item of the crofting budget, oatmeal, had actually fallen in price. Added to all this was the expenditure by the Duke on improvements. He had spent more than £10,000 on 30 miles of road of which 'ten miles may be said to be almost exclusively for the accommodation of the small tenants', not to mention new cottages and meal mills: 'For this large outlay there will be no return unless the proposed increase of Rents is imposed.' The employment generated by the Duke's outlays had been beneficial to the crofters in many ways but particularly in educating them in the use of a pick and a shovel.

On the basis of these considerations and of the great re-survey of the estate, Gunn in October 1878 made sweeping and detailed recommendations for new rents at Coigach. The changes varied—in one village the rent would actually be reduced. But generally the crofters' rents would increase by between 33% and 50%, an average of 15/- per annum additional for every crofter. In defence of this policy Gunn claimed that the Cromartie rents would still continue to be lower than virtually any other Highland estate. He recommended that some of the imposition of the new rents be delayed until the new roads reached the areas beyond Achiltibuie. He also identified some lands (mainly high corries) which were used only as summer pasture by the people: This territory he said should be cleared: 'If ... they [the people] should be very clamorous some concession can be made to them'. This remark indicates clearly that he was establishing a negotiating stance, aware that his recommendation would generate opposition.

The revaluation of rents was not confined to Coigach but the surveys at Strathpeffer and Tarbat were far less complex. There were fewer crofters and cotters (115 at Strathpeffer, 60 at Tarbat and 7 at Dornie), less hill grazing, and many of the small tenants (against Gunn's wishes) possessed leases. Their rents were already better adjusted and the people enjoyed better local markets and employment opportunities. Consequently the revaluation suggested rent increases of between 9% and 13%. Having made this recommendation Gunn pointed out that the small farmer would be paying 21/- per acre for arable land. This, he remarked, was as high a rent as paid by the best farms on the estate which were given capital investment assistance by the landlord, thus yielding less net income than the average crofter on the eastern lands:

> I have made this calculation simply to show that the industrious Crofter, who pays a pound an acre puts fully more into the Proprietor's pocket than the large farmer does and that the deserving and industrious crofter, of whom I am happy to think there are many on Her Grace's Estate, is entitled to some encouragement

—particularly in slating their cottages.

Surveying the results of the revaluation and his recommendations, William Gunn acknowledged that he 'undertook the task I confess not without some misgivings, for raising the rents on poor people, however just and right in itself, is certain to be an unpopular and disagreeable duty'. He had had ten years experience of the people so felt he was 'in as good a position to do them justice as strangers unacquainted with the district'.[26]

Yet Gunn's apparent delicacy and sensitivity to the problems of the 'poor people' was difficult to reconcile with the facts of rent increases. Indeed the whole tone of estate correspondence through the 1870s was of greater stringency in the extraction of rents of which, of course, the revaluation was the lynchpin. Already, in the spring of 1878 (prior to the imposition of the new rents) long lists of rent defaulters were drawn up. Gunn wrote to the Duchess:

> I find that the more indulgence that is shown the more careless and indifferent some of them become. The whole question was fully discussed with the Duke when lately at Dunrobin when it was thought necessary and desirable to Your Grace's interest to make an example of one or two of the worst cases.

He had in mind a widow with an illegitimate child in Gower, a well known thief in Coigach, an idler in Tarbat. Gunn, comfortably, added that things were very quiet in all three districts under his charge.[27]

The new rents were being extracted in Michaelmas 1879. Already however the estate agents were apprehensive of rejection or worse from the people. It may be that news of rent strikes in Ireland had already created anticipations in the West Highlands. But when the rent collection arrived Gunn was able to report to the new Commissioner of the Sutherland Estate, Sir Arnold Kemball, that the Coigach rents had been well paid.

He noted that the herring fishing had been successful—though he emphasised that many crofters did not possess 'the necessary appliances with which to prosecute the fishing to advantage' and prices were somewhat depressed. He added, with emphasis:

> The Duke will probably be interested to know that there was no need after all for the Police Officer on this, the first occasion of exacting the increased rents ... From the groups of Lotters to be seen in earnest discussion outside it was evident that there was to be an attempt made to plead bad times as an excuse to avoid paying the rise for this year. However a little firmness at the outset soon dispelled that expectation and afterwards I had no trouble with them. On the contrary many of them expressed themselves as perfectly satisfied with the manner in which their several cases had been dealt with.[28]

In this manner, therefore, the Cromartie management appeared to have engineered a radical increase in rents without causing any suggestion of activity within the alleged social volcano of estate relations. If the auguries were good, however, the reality would be different. Within twelve months resistance would be politicised and, eventually, profoundly threatening to the peace of Cromartie and the rest of the Highlands.

V

By the mid 1870s the status and future of the Cromartie estates, in some respects, was becoming clearer. The Coigach district, with its large crofter population and persistent poverty, seemed to consume the attention and resources of its owners and their managers. In truth the crofters paid a diminishing proportion of the rental of the Coigach estate and Coigach was merely one third of the Cromartie property which itself had become subsumed into the Sutherland empire. Over the previous fifteen years the Cromartie estate had undoubtedly benefited from the channelling of the Duke's capital into roads, railways and estate development (in addition to the expenditure at Strathpeffer Spa).

The Duke's investment policies for the Cromartie estate were guided by two essential principles. First, his Commissioner maintained the rule (with some exceptions at the Spa) that the Duke should confine his expenditures to the provision of long term fixed capital works. Roads, harbours, farm building and drainage works were basic facilities necessary to attract genuine entrepreneurs (including capitalist farmers) who would apply their own capital to the normal risk-taking enterprises for which they were better equipped. The landlord should not usurp the function of the entrepreneur. Second, the Cromartie estate was administered on the clear assumption that, on the death of the Duke of Sutherland, it would descend to his second son, Lord Francis, who would then have access to no other source of income. The Cromartie estate would then revert to the independent status it enjoyed under the Hay-Mackenzies. Consequently it was necessary to prepare the estate for its future independence when it would no longer draw subsidies from the Sutherland empire. It became imperative that the capital and income assets of the Cromartie estate be established on a footing which would guarantee a future income adequate to the needs of the second son of the richest aristocrat in the kingdom. The Sutherland heir at Cromartie would bear the old title of Earl of Cromartie and the symbolism of the restoration was to be matched by the security of his estate finances. These requirements caused the Cromartie management to regularise rent policy and to maintain a relatively austere attitude to debt accumulation on capital works, especially for the development of the Spa.

The growing care and caution therefore with which George Loch administered the finances of the Cromartie estate was prompted by the requirements of the Duke's will. Lord Francis Sutherland Leveson Gower (Lord Tarbat) had achieved his majority in 1873. Three years later, in July 1876, he married the Honorable Lilian Janet, second surviving daughter of Geoffrey William Wentworth, fourth Lord MacDonald of Sleat. Evander MacIver, ever free with his comments on his masters, said he disapproved of youthful marriages but hoped it would cause the heir to be well settled.

The implication of the marriage for the Cromartie estate was clear cut. Lord and Lady Tarbat would now be required to live off the income generated by the estate. It was the model that had governed both his father and his grandfather. Hence, in July 1876, George Loch instructed Gunn to curb all expenditure which he considered was connected directly to the recent wedding:

> from the present time all expenditure on the Cromartie Estates, that is not absolutely necessary must cease. The arrangements which have been made, in the way of settlements, consequent on Lord Tarbat's marriage, make it necessary to render every penny of Income accountable. Of course works already commenced, such as the new roads, must be completed, but nothing new must be undertaken.[29]

The Sutherland merger with the Cromartie estate in 1849 was, in the outcome, the means by which the title was ultimately restored and the estate re-established in its previous independence. It was a convoluted exercise in aristocratic recrudescence and was celebrated literally and symbolically by the publication, in 1876, of a great family history of the Earls of Cromartie. One of the marks of competitive consumption among the Victorian aristocracy was the commissioning of extremely lavish and expensive accounts of their breeding and careers over previous centuries. Sir William Fraser, a hard-working and precise antiquarian and genealogist, virtually cornered this luxury corner of the publishing market in Scotland.[30] He produced a three volume history of the Sutherland family and a two volume celebration of the Earls of Cromartie, each expensively bound, generously illustrated, and well-forested with family trees. For the Cromartie family it was another gift from the Sutherland family and another mark of the restored Earldom.[31]

Lord Tarbat, in one sense, was lucky to inherit an estate which had benefited from the prosperity that had blessed the Highlands since the death of his grandfather, John Hay-Mackenzie, in 1849. It had also benefited from the generous outlays and professional management associated with the Sutherland administration of George Loch and his father before him. But he was unlucky in two other ways. One was the decline of Highland incomes already evident by 1877, worsening sharply by the end of the decade. This meant that the recently instituted stringency in rental policy was less palatable than it might have been otherwise. Secondly Lord Tarbat—a young man with little experience of estate management and little taste for political life—would soon face the rising anger and militancy of the crofters. The social volcano, which some thought of as extinct, was about to breath.

CHAPTER 22

The Shock of the Crofters' Revolt

I

The memory of the successful revolt of the people of Coigach in 1852/3 lingered in the minds of both the estate management and the crofters not only in Wester Ross but throughout the Highlands. By the late 1870s there were visible signs of a stirring of political consciousness in the Highlands. In part it was an echo of more vigorous rebellion in rural Ireland which would become an inspiration to the Highlanders in the 1880s. Partly also there was an independent awakening in the Highlands, a new rehearsal of cultural, moral and political questions which would provide fuel for an assault on the entire landlord class. A literature emerged, including Alexander Mackenzie's influential *History of the Highland Clearances*, first published in 1881 which drew together much of the literary indignation of its day into a fiery indictment of Highland landlordism. One of the most telling accounts in Mackenzie's anthology was that of the Coigach events in the previous generation, a model perhaps for a new phase of crofter resistance.

Coigach, of course, had been quiet, if poor, for the intervening quarter of a century. Now, in 1879, after several decades of stable or falling rents, the estate administration had resolved to lever up the rental to match the improvement in prices enjoyed by the crofters for many years. When the time for the first extraction of the new augmented rent came, in November, the estate factors were braced for resistance. Their anxiety was palpable for this was regarded as the moment of truth for the resolution of the estate management and the real test of the stability of the crofting community.

In the outcome the first rental collection passed without incident, and force, though in readiness, was not required. Gunn heaved a great sigh of relief and was soon arguing confidently that a little firmness had scotched any idea of rebellion among the small tenantry. But he also conceded that the people had been in a better position to pay the rents on account of a good season in the herring fishing (which had compensated for low cattle prices).[1]

The success of the rental collection in November 1879 was temporary. Within twelve months Coigach and other parts of the Cromartie estate were rapidly drawn into the great upwelling of crofter agitation which eventually consumed the Scottish Highlands for most of the following decade. All local circumstances and arrangements between tenants and landlords were overwhelmed by the remarkable galvanising of crofter opinion: by 1883-6 an atmosphere close to revolution had been generated in the north of Scotland. It was all the more extraordinary because it concerned a population—the cottars and crofters—thought to be constitutionally docile and politically naive and inert. The furore generated was so noisy and effective that the Westminster government eventually acceded to crofter demand for a sweeping inquiry—the Napier Commission (1883)—into all aspects of tenurial organisation in the Highlands. Suddenly the Highlands became the focus of the nation's attention: the southern newspapers trained their beam on the most remote corner of mainland Britain.

In June 1880 the Commissioner of the Sutherland estates (including, of course, Cromartie) agreed with Gunn, then under some considerable pressure in Coigach, that: 'It is no easy task to keep order among large numbers of Lotters, and there is no part of a Factor's duty which makes more frequent demands on his tact and judgement'.[2] As a description of the factor's lot in the mid 1880s, Kemball's remark became a gross understatement. By then the crofters, in Coigach and elsewhere, became literally unmanageable. Soon they were refusing to pay their rents altogether; they organised themselves into political bodies with easily recognisable and effective leaders; they attracted external attention (and implicit support) and startled the government into entirely unprecedented intervention. Eventually the revolt caused the government (in circumstances of political instability which aided the crofters' campaign) to over-rule the 'sacred rights of property'. The landlords were out-marshalled and defeated by the concerted campaign of the crofters. For the administrators of Highland property, and these included those on the Sutherland estates, it was a decade of managerial nightmare when all their worst fears were realised.

The shock of the revolt—bursting open the whole moral question of landlordism to public scrutiny, combined with the open defiance of the crofters—should not be underestimated. The psychological impact on the Cromartie managers manifested itself in resignations, outrage, despair, disappointment and disbelief. For them the political turmoil, which was combined with increasing economic difficulties in estate life, threatened to overturn the old foundations of society and to unseat the existing arrangements of power and control. The crofters had become revolutionaries inflamed by skilled and irresponsible agitators who indeed attacked the fundamental assumptions and principles of society.

The Crofters' Revolt, it is now recognised, achieved unprecedented unity of purpose and coherence of demands during the 1880s. The campaign was a complex and frenetic climacteric in Highland history and has been well told many times.[3] The Cromartie version of the story is offered here in general outline primarily to demonstrate not the detailed course of political events but the broad shift in relations between landlord and people. It may be that the greatest changes eventually induced by the Crofter Revolt occurred less in tenurial adjustments than within the minds of the people, in their attitudes to the landlord and their perceptions of the world about them. There was an almost tangible modification in social relations on the estate which worked its effect over the following two decades.

Indeed the final outcome of the great contest between the crofters and the estate proprietors was a tenurial compromise—in the form of the Crofter Commission Act of 1886, sometimes regarded as the 'Magna Carta of the Highlands'.[4] The campaign against private land ownership achieved not so much a radical redistribution of property and wealth but a series of restrictions and regulations on the exercise of landlord powers.

The crofters gained a new measure of security of tenure and certain extra rights, and this shocked the proprietors and diminished their arbitrary powers of eviction and land-use. But there was no social revolution, no radical redistribution of wealth and land and no return to the conditions which were thought to have prevailed before the clearances. The outcome therefore tended to ossify the features of Highland life in the *status quo* of the 1880s; the impact was limited by the needs of political compromise.

Though the revolution may be diminished in this manner, the trauma of the Revolt should not be understated. The Cromartie estate itself was convulsed and one of the gains to posterity was the exposure of so much of the underside of estate conditions during the time of the conflict.

II

Even the most experienced factors tended to regard the administration of the small tenantry as a contest in which advantage would be taken of the slightest slip in the management. The new rental policy at the end of the 1870s, instigated by George Loch, had set the scene for dispute in advance of the general crisis in the rest of the Highlands. The intention had been simple—to bring crofter rents into line with neighbouring estates and the longstanding rise in commodity prices. Naturally the exercise was exceedingly unpopular among the crofters, but the full extent of their attitude was not revealed until poorer economic conditions fell upon the community in the early 1880s. By then, of course, extraneous influences had been set at work; in particular the influence of Free Church ministers and political activists had helped to stiffen and direct crofter dissidence to the point of revolt. Precedents of crofter resistance had been signalled in other parts of the Highlands for several years—for instance the successful resistance to evictions at Bernera in 1874 and rent-striking as early as 1877.[5] Each new act of resistance was well publicised in the northern press.

Although the first new Cromartie rent collection had passed successfully there had been worrying signs which Gunn registered in his reports at the end of 1879. Some tenants had evaded the rent officer and were seen slipping away through their back doors as he approached. More serious was a general sense of turmoil in Coigach, of the people bickering among themselves, of repeated poaching and trespassing to such an extent that the local police appeared impotent. No less disturbing was the overwhelming influence of the Free Church ministers: the people of Coigach were said to be entirely beneath their sway. Their influence was sufficient to cause the people to stop work in the middle of the harvest in 1880, simply in order to attend the summonses of the Church elders. Evander MacIver told Gunn that 'the local people were under ecclesiastical despotism when they permitted such a stoppage of their interests'.[6] The Free Church ministers were a rival control over the people and their influence caused great resentment among the estate factors.

By the end of 1880 both economic conditions and the political atmosphere had deteriorated. The local fishing had failed and rents were poorly paid: 'Many of them cannot pay' reported Kenneth Mackenzie from Coigach.[7] Similar reports were coming from other estates[8] and the large sheepfarmers were also running into financial difficulties which would eventually render many of their farms unlettable on acceptable terms. Indeed the pressure for rent concessions and reductions was accumulating swiftly. Simultaneously open political debate was being reported especially from Ullapool: it is likely that radical currents were easily transmitted between the ports, between Wester Ross and Caithness, by the great interchange of the fishing populations each season. At Ullapool, in broad daylight, the Free Church minister was heard to advocate club farms for the people, perhaps the first time a public figure had voiced such a radical proposal. At the same time he gave unambiguous support to the rebellious crofters who were in conflict with their landlord A.C. Pirie on the Leckmeln estate, a small property on Lochbroom, and therefore close to the Cromartie estate. Pirie was a new landowner in the district who was attempting to shift about 23 families off their crofts and into cottages. The minister condemned him as 'this modern evictor' who would reduce the people to 'common navvies'. Indeed the Leckmeln episode is regarded as the precipitating moment that activated the crofters into rebellion across the Highlands.[9]

The minister in question was the Rev. John MacMillan[10] who emerged as a considerable orator and leader, a voice for the people of Wester Ross and especially for Coigach, who were all Free Churchers. Gunn quickly recognised MacMillan as a threat to general order and in December 1880 he told Kemball that he was 'now ... widely known as the Champion of the Leckmeln Crofters ... He goes as lecturer all over the north.' MacMillan was further suspected of directly stirring dissatisfaction among the Coigach crofters. Correspondence had appeared in the *Inverness Courier* which resurrected the story of the Coigach riots of the 1850s. Estate factors quickly moved to contradict the accounts and to deny the allegations. One of them said that 'the Coigach battle' had lost all significance—that whenever it was referred to

> there is generally a good laugh at the expense of those who came off second best in it. The sheriff and Procurator Fiscal, at the time, were very humorous, and could entertain a company for a whole evening with their experiences.

But even this version ended with the advice not to rake the embers too much, 'for the sake of peace'.[11] MacMillan, however, clearly knew the value of the Coigach story and used it to stimulate a new level of political consciousness among the crofters. In a letter attributed to him just before Christmas 1880 it was said that 'the Coigach people should make their grievances known, and in due time they may have them remedied'. This was, inevitably, heady talk for the West Coast crofters, some of whom were increasingly used to debate in the public bars and fishermen's lodgings in Caithness.[12]

Tension was evidently mounting and the crofters were disaffected though it is important to say that this was hardly a rare attitude in the western population. But in February 1881 the local factor, Kenneth Mackenzie, noticed a worsening of the tone of dissatisfaction: there was now a distinct 'growling' among the Coigach crofters mainly because their rents were rising while crofters on other estates were negotiating rent reductions. Mackenzie remarked, 'I have no doubt they are put up to this by some ill-disposed parties. I regret to say that most of them are very ungrateful for everything that is done for them.'[13] The theme of crofter ingratitude, a perennial complaint in the factors' correspondence, rose to a greater pitch as the crisis deepened—matched by a sense of personal slight in the minds of the managers. They were men who had done their best for the crofters and they simply could not understand the crofters' behaviour. Nevertheless, Mackenzie was prepared to accept that the main reason for the accumulation of arrears was sheer poverty—'the truth is they have no money at this time'. Moreover the Coigach grievances were exacerbated by the knowledge that Sutherland crofters to the north (and under the same general management) appeared to obtain earlier and larger rental concessions than their Cromartie counterparts. In August 1881 Gunn told Kemball that he was 'beseiged with enquiries as to whether the Duke's kindness to his Sutherland tenants is to be extended to Ross-shire'.[14] The Cromartie estate was indeed sinking into financial straits worsened by its inability to lease out some of its great arable and sheep farms, often for several years or more. But conditions in Cromartie were part of a widening spread of depression in the Highlands, an important context for the evolution of the Crofters' revolt.

By the end of the following year, 1882, the crisis in relations kept the minds of the managers in a state of constant anxiety. The prospects for the new year had been savagely blighted by a disastrous storm in December 1881. Gales and the highest tide in living memory had caused havoc among the small fishing boats of the west coast tenantry: 'All suffered more or less—in Achiltybuie the principal township only one small boat escaped'. As Gunn explained the boats were indispensable not only for the fishing but also to 'procure seaware for their crops'. It was a great capital loss to the people, destroying their main asset and source of cash income. 'The disaster has fallen with more than usual severity at the close of one of the poorest fishings on record' remarked Gunn.[15] Added to this were the poor stock prices and the failure of the potato crop in 1882, creating fertile conditions for disaffection. Out of these circumstances grew 'rumours of insubordination' which were directly reminiscent of the events of 1852/3 in Coigach, enough to send a shudder of apprehension through the estate agents.

The parallel became more compelling in October when reports arrived of a deforcement in Coigach—an officer collecting School Board Arrears had been assaulted and ejected from the district. He had travelled, in the traditional way, by boat to Badenscally where he had been effectively turned away. He was told that the fishermen had returned penniless and there was no possibility of his being paid. Cattle and sheep were virtually unsaleable and the potatoes were deteriorating rapidly. There was also a fear in the community that foot and mouth disease[16] was about to strike. Soon Gunn was talking of the effect of 'ill-disposed agitators' and the idea that the event was beginning to be connected with the 'Land Movement'.[17]

III

Apprehension among the Cromartie managers mounted at the end of 1882: in retrospect it is clear that they were now entering a decisive stage in the convergence of circumstances that precipitated the Crofters' Revolt in the Highlands. The resistance to the Sheriff Officer at Badenscally in October caused the local factors great alarm and their response was extremely cautious: 'Seeing what is occurring elsewhere they are naturally anxious to avoid ... any cause for collision with the Crofter class'. Gunn did not believe 'that the Coigach people were disposed to give trouble'. But there were rumours that the people were in a 'great state for resisting rent collections'. Moreover Gunn himself began to receive anonymous letters containing 'beastly falsehoods' which may have reflected a hardening edge of conflict within the crofting community.[18]

Simultaneously the people of Coigach were preparing a large-scale petition to the Duchess of Sutherland for which they gathered a large number of signatories. In the petition they complained of the recent rent increases, but they aired wider grievances. They asserted 'that the patches of ground which are now arable were, with many years of toil and hard labour without any assistance from your Grace, scraped together by ourselves and our ancestors among rocks and stones'. As soon as the crofts were thus created rents were immediately raised and the best arable land at Achnahaird was taken from them and added to a larger farm.[19]

Making matters much worse, the west coast was about to plunge into yet another subsistence crisis at the very moment when agitation and resistance became distinctly vociferous. Consequently the question of crofter rebellion (and the emerging rent strike) became confused and entwined with the subsistence emergency which overlaid the entire political crisis. The combined total failure of the potato crop and the fishing brought an odd conjunction of demands for relief while the people refused to pay rents. Events however moved quickly and the cry of 'destitution in the Highlands' helped to attract southern attention and, eventually, considerable relief. With the spotlight turned on the condition of the crofters there was a greater effort, internally and externally, to ensure that no starvation was allowed to occur. Relief, indeed, with the help of southern philanthropy (including resources from the Mansion House Fund), was entirely successful. At the same time the demands for crofter rights developed powerfully and, certainly on the Cromartie estate, landlords generally postponed plans for the collection of arrears and the rearrangement of their estates (including selective evictions) until the trouble blew over. The estate factors sometimes regarded with frustration what they regarded as a failure of proprietorial resolution: in their frustration they denounced the people for their lack of loyalty and gratitude. By the middle of 1883 the environment was altered by the government's decision to summons a comprehensive enquiry—the Napier Commission—into crofting life in the Highlands (see next chapter). William Gunn was required to gird himself for ordeal by Royal Commission. The prospect required not only a great degree of introspection but also the gathering of basic data about the condition of the crofting population.

Gunn, who had been factor for almost 20 years, now attempted to define his general philosophy regarding the crofting economy. He took the view that the west coast people were generally industrious and thrifty but were kept poor by the smallness of their crofts and the precarious nature of the fishing. They frequently fell back on the parochial Boards. This was particularly true of widows who were supporting large young families without an able-bodied breadwinner. The widespread crop failure of 1882/3 simply reinforced this view. Even in the central and eastern parts of the estate the crofters (at Strathpeffer and Tarbat) relied chiefly on potatoes for paying their rent.[20] But Coigach was worst affected—there were, among a population of 1200, about 50 families with no workers—but having land and paying rent cannot legally be regarded as paupers. The Parochial Board is slow to move in such cases—and the danger is that cases of actual want may ... go unattended to'.

In the event the Duke of Sutherland provided substantial relief and also made temporary rent concessions. Gunn however stuck to the old Loch principles of destitution relief—a labour test was applied 'and charity should only be given in cases of real and proved necessity'.[21]

Destitution and its relief did not reduce the political temperature in any identifiable way. Indeed Gunn and his factors reported that 'rather revolutionary' opinions were being stirred among the crofters both east and west. In fact the crofters were now thoroughly activated and there were regular meetings in preparation for the arrival of the Napier Commission. The crop failure, the work of the charity organisations, the approach of the Commission and the mounting interest of the newspapers (notably the *Scotsman*) attracted widespread attention. The newspapers gave great publicity to the revelations of the crofters before the Commission and the Cromartie estate itself was heavily criticised in the *Scotsman*. Gunn found the experience personally painful and repugnant: he oscillated between indignant self-justification and bouts of despair. He

35   Pony cart, used to steady the open sack being filled with the wool-clip, Wester Ross croft, late nineteenth century.

was both angry and disappointed by the events surrounding the Commission, and he could hardly believe that the crofters had turned on the landlord and his agents and publicly denounced their betters. Kenneth Mackenzie, in his eighth decade and as old as the century, could tolerate it no more and accelerated his retirement. Gunn sent spies to the crofters' meetings and received full reports in advance of the Commission. He regarded the events as a 'collaboration' and a 'conspiracy', and the widespread participation in the rent strike gave clear evidence of crofter solidarity.

The estate factors did not deny the great poverty of many of the crofters. As MacIver conceded: 'there is a class in every Highland parish between the Paupers and the Crofters not able to work who in July and August require aid'. Poverty was perennial. The essence of the factors' disagreement with the crofters concerned the causes of their poverty and the history of their condition. Indeed much of the confrontation which reached its climax before the Napier Commission was directly historical in form and content. The crofters' case repeatedly adverted to the alleged loss of rights to land, to earlier clearances, and to rack renting over many years. Gunn, in his disappointment and frustration, told Sir Archibald Kemball in December 1883, after the Commission had passed through their estates, that:

> It matters not to these people how much their circumstances have changed for the better during the last 60 years—or how much the value of such property may have increased elsewhere during that period—or how much the proprietor has contributed to that result by a large expenditure of money on works of improvement. All these count as nothing in comparison to what they conceive to be their rights to the land and to their use of it on their own terms.[22]

Here there was a total conflict of historical, economic and moral perceptions.

Gunn was deeply troubled: 'No class of tenantry could have been treated with greater indulgence as to rent arrears' or to general concern for their welfare. Their ingratitude was extraordinary and Gunn felt disheartened at having to deal with such people. He alleged that 'there are some right thinking people among them, but they are too much afraid to act upon their convictions'. His instinct, and indeed his intention, was to make an example of the agitators on the estate, to hound them for their insolence. It was only the restraining hand of Gunn's superiors that prevented him pursuing a more robust policy. Nevertheless Gunn told the Duchess of Sutherland that her people had come 'to distrust Proprietors and those who acted for them, and to claim an equal, yea a better right to the land than its rightful owners'. In these words resided the bitterness of a managerial class that had been publicly reproved by the instrument of government.[23]

IV

The Crofters' Revolt was already complicated by the conditions of economic depression, connections with Ireland and the influence of the Free Church. It was further confused in 1884-5 by its involvement in a broader political context. This, across the Highlands, involved the Liberals and the Conservatives in a general election which suddenly gave the crofting region unprecedented leverage. Inevitably there was a struggle between Land Leaguers and the established pattern of political influence. But it was the precarious status of Gladstone's government on which, eventually, crofter county members exerted considerable sway over a balanced House of Commons in 1885.

Within the Highlands the landlords feared a total loss of authority in their dealings with their small tenantries. The withholding of rents consolidated while the widely popular demands for crofter rights to pasture, and the compulsory break-up of the great sheep farms, grew in confidence. The operations of the Napier Commission (which spanned many months), and the unclear attitude of government, simply added to the suspense which seemed likely to paralyse the north of Scotland. Estate management became a struggle for the rudiments of order and system. The rent strike was widespread in both the eastern and western baronies of the Cromartie estate though its impact was partly obscured by the effects of famine and renewed poverty. In Coigach the crofters had organised an Association which was obviously directed against the landlord. The Commissioner of the Sutherland estates and Gunn's master, Sir Archibald Kemball, was regarded as indecisive. In a tense political context he was not prepared to take any form of action against refractory crofters, primarily for fear of provoking a deforcement and violence. Landlord action was undoubtedly fettered by the fear of physical reaction among the people. In these circumstances all the landlord could do was to withhold benefits normally expected by the people. Kemball told Gunn:

> It may be that legislative action, in a sense adverse to Proprietorial rights, will entail upon crofters the forfeiture of what may be termed Patriarchal privileges; but while the law is on our side I hesitate to compromise to it by their premature withdrawal.[24]

This was a remarkable statement, revealing not only an expectation of government intervention in the rights of property, but also an adversarial attitude to the crofters. It balanced patriarchy against deference, the benevolence of the status quo against a threat of a more rigorous regime if the patriarchy was subverted.

The response of the landlords and their agents—including those of Cromartie and the rest of the Sutherland empire—was extraordinarily ambiguous and inconsistent. In the general turmoil Gunn operated a policy towards the crofters which alternated between threats and concessions. As the political and social disruption worsened, his thinking, and that of his masters, increasingly favoured a recourse to law to deal with estate problems. It represented a retreat from the advantages of discretionary landlordism: in a sense it was a view which, eventually, converged with that of government.

Such attitudes emerged slowly in a context in which the general mood of the crofters also shifted. Their collective defiance gathered strength particularly under the inspiration of the events in Skye and the famous 'Battle of the Braes' in 1885 which was, perhaps, the climax of their campaign to attract national public attention. The factors might say 'Grievances cannot be redressed by the people taking the land and the authority into their own hands', but it was plain to see that the crofters had already achieved more attention and concessions in three years of agitation than they had during the previous century of relative passivity and disunity. In particular, the man whose word was paramount on the Cromartie estate, the third Duke of Sutherland, continued to ignore the stiffening advice of his factors. He and his family had no stomach for confrontation and public odium, and were always in search of compromise even to the point of experimental concession.

The pot of discussion was kept bubbling through 1885 and 1886 by anticipation of the government's action in response to the recommendations of the Napier Report. The general political instability also cast an influence. For the Cromartie estate the local agitation centred on the demand for the abolition of the odious rent increases of 1879-80. The rent strike continued and the factors found the condition of the rental, including the income from the large tenants, a continuing abscess. 'The money for rent got wings' during the strike, said Gunn in frustration. He put the administrative problem in a nutshell: 'It is easy to deal with a few isolated cases, but the difficulty here was in dealing with several hundred tenants ... all combined'. This, of course, was an exact measure of the solidarity of the crofters' movement. According to Gunn they were abetted by the interference of the Napier Commission. Further fuel was added to factorial anxiety by the 'land invasion' at Culkein in neighbouring Sutherland in March 1885.[25] The factors held firm (but private) ideas that, in the last resort, eviction and the threat of eviction were the only means of social control they possessed. In reality the Cromartie management, in common with many others, was in rapid retreat: rents were reduced and arrears forgiven on a substantial scale. The retreat was further underscored by the sensational election results at the end of 1885 which undermined the existing structure of political control in the west Highlands.[26]

V

By 1886 therefore the community in most parts of the Highlands and Islands had been radically polarised. Estate managers at Cromartie, as elsewhere, discussed the crofter question almost exclusively in terms of how much authority over the land the landlords would be compelled to relinquish. The Crofters' Act of 25 June 1886 (modelled on the Irish Land Act) indeed altered the basis of landholding in the crofting counties and it was a direct infringement and curtailment of landlord rights. It was a great victory for the crofters and their leaders. Nevertheless it was clear to all that the Act did not adequately satisfy the aspirations aroused among the crofters during their remarkable campaign. Moreover, during the interim and prior to the actual operation of the Crofter Commission (which would arbitrate conditions between landlords and crofters), relations in the Highlands were left in a continuing state of uncertainty. Estate management remained in a state of suspense while the economic circumstances were in unrelieved depression. In particular the contentious question of arrears and fair rents remained unresolved.

The frustration of the Cromartie managers was thus compounded. Gunn continued to rail against the crofters, the government, the commissioners and the new political system. The crofter case, he said over and over again, was based upon fundamental historical errors about the condition of the people 'before the clearances'. He continued to deny that clearances had occurred on the Cromartie estate. He also rejected the notion that land was the true central issue of the problem. The crofters, he maintained, possessed neither the resources nor the capital nor the expertise to farm sheep or stock on a commercial scale. Fishing, the landlord's solution for more than a century, remained the only feasible answer to west coast poverty. But the tide was running against Gunn's way of thinking. The parliamentary elections of late 1886 put the Highlands and Islands political representation into the hands of the Land Leaguers. Gunn could only believe that the whole thing was a dreadful indictment of democracy itself.

The psychological impact of the crofters' revolt was, therefore, powerful and distressing. Yet there was nevertheless also a certain adjustment in the minds of the factors and the landlords to the new realities. They knew that some elements in the crofting community still expected to gain occupancy of the land entirely without rent and this needed further resistance. But, for the most part, the Cromartie estate administrators came to a philosophical and practical attitude to the new Bill and its likely operation. They began to perceive some possible advantage, at least in terms of their own peace and quiet, in the prospect of some form of dependable regulation of tenurial relations between the crofters and the landlords. Thus, while the Crofters' Act was initially regarded with loathing and suspicion and an exacerbation of estate problems, it began to emerge as a *modus operandi*—it was in any case a revolution averted and began to offer at least some crumbs of comfort to the landlords and their agents. These more positive attitudes in management emerged warily as the political story unfolded. In the more immediate circumstances the general turmoil persisted.

Throughout these years the crofters on the Cromartie estate had gained in confidence and political consciousness. In 1887 they continued, both in Strathpeffer and Coigach, to express defiance and dissatisfaction with the estate. They continued to organise petitions demanding more land and lower rents. Meanwhile the administrative control of the Sutherland Empire had passed from Sir Archibald Kemball to an engineer, R.M. Brereton. The new commissioner, with whom William Gunn now dealt, rejected the idea that land should be handed over to the people. Such a notion he believed was no more than an empty panacea. On the other hand he believed that renewed economic development was possible in the Highlands. Brereton helped persuade the Duke of Sutherland to embark on expensive capital-intensive works in the north, massive drainage schemes and railway development.[27] Meanwhile the Duke himself was increasingly reluctant to confront and oppose the crofters; he had no taste for public debate and obloquy. In Gunn's eyes the Duke exhibited worrying signs of weakness. In the event the Sutherland estates (including Cromartie) pre-empted the decisions of the Crofter Commission by reducing rents across the board. When the Commission came to adjudicate the rents of the Sutherland and Cromartie estates, only a few further small reductions were judged necessary. Nevertheless the existence and operation of the Commission now provided the estates with firm and consistent criteria by which the factors could press tenants and defaulters for payment. In one sense the Commission thereby strengthened the hand of the proprietors.

Within the Cromartie management the attitude of the local factors remained belligerent and highly critical of the crofters and their demands. Alex Ross, the new agent in Coigach, was particularly aggressive in his dealings with the crofters and vigorously pursued rent defaulters throughout 1888 and 1889, his temper not diminished by the defeat of estate agents in the local elections of that year.

The Crofter Commission itself became a vehicle for the continuing contest between the crofters and the landlords about the practical and moral basis of landownership in the Highlands. The actual occupation of the land, as always, was the focus of the continuing disaffection. The estate factors, increasingly jaundiced by the public assault on their reputation (and that of their predecessors), became less and less responsive to ideas of further concessions.

But the Duke of Sutherland, perhaps alert to the falling returns of commercial sheepfarming, was more inclined to experiment in the direction of the crofters' demands. His attitude was substantially more flexible than that of his managers. Moreover, despite recurring land raids in some parts of the north-west Highlands, the general atmosphere was settling down. Rents were being better paid and now much of the general antagonism of the common people was being channelled into elections. This at least allowed some visible and symbolic triumph to the crofter cause. For the managers the shock of revolt was still being absorbed.

VI

One of the effects of the Crofters' Revolt and the visitation of the Napier Commission was the floodlight it cast over the normally hidden life of the crofting community. Estates were required to provide statistics and a multiplicity of other evidence about their tenantry and landholdings. William Gunn and the other factors now provided remarkably detailed accounts of the circumstances of the poorest echelons of the Cromartie estate. Among their data were a series of, in effect, pocket biographies of some of the people from the otherwise anonymous crofter crowd. These were images created from the factor's office and through factorial eyes, but they provide considerable raw detail generally missing from the historical record. They were sketches intended to gauge the ability of small tenants to pay rent. Sometimes, in a dozen words or so, the pathos and poverty of crofter life was encapsulated.

For instance, there was Duncan McRae aged 71, a widower of many years. Born at Kintail in Glenshiel he had been a miller by trade but was now rheumatic and unable to work. He needed the aid of two sticks to walk. His son was a shepherd in Feachaskin; one daughter was married to a Gairloch crofter and another continued to live with her father together with her small, illegitimate son. McRae's son used to support his father 'but he is now about to be out of a situation on account of the ground being turned into a Forest (Deer)'.[28] Similarly John Macrae of Achiltibuie, a salmon fisher, was also without money but promised to pay his rent as soon as he could. He had stock but was unable to sell presently and like others was waiting for wages from his fishing.

In January 1887 further such evidence was gathered. Ken McLeod of Reiff was a 50-year-old crofter with a wife of 45 years and three children aged 16, 14 and 10, all at home. McLeod's parents also lived in a house on their lot with two other sons. They had five cattle and twelve sheep and McLeod had a boat for the salmon fishing; he had built his house, barn and byre about ten years before without assistance from the estate.

His father's house was thatched and had two chimneys. Macleod had possessed the lot for 25 years but was in debt for both rent and meal (presumably a legacy of the famine several years before). The rental book noted: 'Has no cattle he can sell at the moment'.

Donald McLean was a 48 year old lotter at Aultandow where he lived with his wife Christy McLeod (38) and their children: Donald (10), Mary (8), Bella (6), and three younger children. They possessed three cattle, four sheep and a horse and paid £3.7.0 rent and were 15/6 in arrear. McLean owned no boat and had 'no means apart from his beasts'. He did not know when he could pay his rent; he had built his two-chimneyed house 16 years ago, the only help for which he received 10 barrels of lime and some thatch: 'Alone as male strength in the family and heavy young family, case looks hopeless—except for legacy in prospect'.

Hugh McLeod of Reiff was 55 years old, paid £6 rent per year but was £15.12.0 in arrear. He was a bachelor living with his two sisters, one aged 72, the other 40. He owned six cattle and seven sheep, an old boat and two old nets, and could not say when he would pay his arrears. He had been unable to sell his stirks at the last market; he had made no improvements to his house or lot for generations.

> He is able bodied but devoid of energy and stock dwindling down, case does not look encouraging. Complains lot too dead, sour in temper and evidently existing in the idea and hope that the Crofters Commission will reduce his rent as well as cancel his arrears. Should be summonsed for payment of arrears which evidently he does not intend to pay unless forced.

Many of the lotters of Reiff were still refusing to pay their rents and the estate suspected they were in a conspiracy to do so.

Many of these people had invested heavily in their lots, especially in the construction of their houses. John McLean of Altandhu had built a two chimneyed, slate-roofed house nine years before with only a supply of lime from the estate: its construction had cost him £100. He was 44 years of age with six children, and owned eleven cattle and ten sheep: 'Is shoemaker, no other means. Had beast at last market and did not sell. Has beast to sell now.' Added to the description was the note—'Is Land Law Reformer and talks greatly of the injustice under the present land system'.[29]

These recurring accounts of the small tenants revealed key elements in their lives. For instance Angus McLeod of Tanera expected to pay off his arrears when his sons got their first employment with the East Coast curers. Williamina Campbell, a 70-year-old widow—'Hopes to get arrear from daughter in Australia soon but understands she had adversities recently'. Mary Kerr of Achiltibuie was a 50-year-old single woman with a brother and sister living with her. Of her the estate official wrote: 'She is independent and even haughty and quite refuses to pay rent and is under the impression the Proprietrix is bound to provide for her and her brother and sister if she is deprived of the land. She neither intends nor attempts to pay rent.' Another lotter was described as 'a Tailor but a poor Skeleton of a creature'; another was an 'Old man and unfit for hard work but industrious'; another was 'a plausible and talkative little man'. Many of the lotters had children living in Edinburgh or elsewhere in the Highlands, some in Australia; some had lost all contact with their offspring while others were clearly receiving money from their children in the colonies or America. For instance, a tenant in Keanachrine 'hopes to get money from a brother-in-law in Australia wherewith to pay arrears. Those hopes appear to have been long cherished to no practical purpose.'

The stark reality of crofter life stared out of these severe biographies. There was the man who was known to have a daughter who had emigrated to Australia. He had been unsuccessful in east coast fishing; he was married with ten children; he had had no word from his antipodean daughter for four years. Another was described as having no means of paying arrears; his father was 'old and helpless at fireside and burden on son, while aspect of the family seems poor'. There was more hope for Duncan Stewart aged 54 with his wife of 41 and their five children. They owned two cows, two followers, and 24 sheep, and shared a large boat and six nets. They owed £7 for meal and nets and possessed no other means than these. They had built a house with two chimneys eight years ago, together with a byre and a barn, helped by the estate. His rent was £4.5.0 and an arrear of £3.8.0 had developed. But he was 'a regular payer' and, with the help of cattle sales, would eventually clear his arrear.

There were several salient aspects to these crofter lives. One was the continuing poverty for many of these people who had now fallen into arrears. Another was the vital significance of external income—from the fishing, from relatives, from seasonal employment—in the maintenance of any kind of independence and tolerable living standards. Cattle sales were utterly central to their ability to pay their rents. Age and health were also critical; many of the tenants in arrear were simply broken people who had no physical strength left in them. No less evident was the impact of the Crofters Revolt on these people—most of whom were not directly political. Many of them, to the fury of the estate agents, openly voiced the idea that they could not be evicted and that the landlord was bound to support them if they were indigent. They expected to continue to occupy their crofts even if they were able to produce nothing from their possession. Their expectations were, of course, greatly strengthened by their confidence in the Crofter Commission.

The influence of the Land League was widespread. Many of the individual descriptions alluded to the effect on rent payment. For example a tenant in Polbain was described as 'the son-in-law of a Land League Reformer and is supposed to be influenced by him as to payment of rent. He should be pressed to pay. He is ruptured.' Of another it was said: 'Their loyalty to the estate or Proprietrix is open to question, as between them they might have paid arrear ... their brother Hector is an advanced Land League Reformer.' Another was under the impression that since he was poor and dependent on his lot for subsistence he could not be removed. One lotter was also described as a 'pronounced Land Leaguer, with large family mostly young. It is scarcely possible for him to overcome arrear and case does not look encouraging.' A fellow crofter 'talks greatly Land League Reform with a triumphant tone underlying his statement', of whom, said the factor, an example should be made. Another, of Keanchrine, was said to be 'able and industrious but having Land Law Reform notions in his head', was exactly paralleled by a man 'strongly tainted with Land League principles'.[30]

Land Leaguism had reached into the lowest levels of the crofter community. It had materially affected the payment of rent and had caused monumental irritation among the estate administrators. Their frustration shone through the rental commentaries.

Fortunately the representation of these people and their view of the world was not limited to chance remarks filtered through the factors' books. In the proceedings of the Napier Commission the crofters and their representatives were able to speak directly into the historical record.

CHAPTER 23

The Voice of the Crofters

I

While the factors on the Cromartie estate (and the other Sutherland properties) had regarded the approach of the Napier Commission with dismay and despair, the crofters and their leaders were organising their testimonies and their demands. The Commission moved quickly on its tour of the Highlands and indeed spent only one day in Ullapool and Dingwall respectively, 30 July and 10 October 1883. Nevertheless the hearings were extraordinarily detailed and wide-ranging and were further augmented by written submissions. They filled many pages of evidence which, *in toto*, rendered the Napier Report the most penetrating and comprehensive investigation ever undertaken in the history of the Highlands. The provenance of much of the evidence was questioned at the time, and by later commentators. Its polemical and challenging character cannot be denied: it was the climax of a century of seething ill-will in many parts of the Highlands. Although the Cromartie estate was not involved in the most vociferous hearings before the Commissioners, it nevertheless witnessed a full-scale exposure to the controversies which were electrifying the Highlands in that year.

Before 1883 the experience of the common Highlander had been either unknown, or else filtered through the medium of ministers and spokesmen, through song and story little known beyond their own world, or expressed by way of direct action (as in the Coigach Riots of 1852-3). In the Napier Commission's evidence the Highlander uttered directly into the record; perhaps for the first time the voice of the people could be heard. In earlier parliamentary enquiries, into emigration, labour questions and agricultural conditions, virtually all witnesses were experts or else wealthy members of the community. But in 1883 the Highlander spoke and his words were fully recorded: egged on by the community, organised by political elements or simply speaking directly, the testimonies are eloquent. The timing was important: this was the aftermath of the conversion of so much Highland life to a regime of crofting and sheepfarming. Inevitably the great weight of testimony was retrospective, expressing the communal bitterness at the alleged injustices and immoralities of that century-old transformation. Amid the confusions of memory and indignation it was often difficult to derive a clear picture. Moreover though many crofters and cottars spoke up, the rapidity of the Napier Commission's proceedings made it inevitable that 'representatives' and 'spokesmen'—often ministers, radicals and teachers—spoke on behalf of whole communities and districts. The sick, the broken, the emigres, the women, the old, the apathetic, had no direct voice. Despite such difficulties—which, of course, were pounced upon by the Commission's detractors, including those in the Cromartie management, there can be no doubting the importance of the evidence. The proceedings were loud with accusation, recrimination and a corrosive sense of injustice.

The evidence of the cottars and crofters on the Cromartie estates reflected the recurrent themes heard at each of the hearings of the Commission. In brief they consisted of accusations that the people had been robbed of rights to land, usually at some distant past time; there were impassioned complaints against the absence of any security of tenure or compensation for improvements, about increases of rents and the failure of the landlord to initiate capital works; there were allegations of factorial oppression and charges that witnesses who appeared before the Commission had been subject to pressure from estate officials. Over all the particular complaints was the overarching indictment of the landlord class, that the proprietors had reduced the people of the Highlands to the scandalous level of poverty which had at last been brought to the attention of the British public.

The evidence of John Maclean, a shoemaker and crofter of Altandu in Coigach immediately exposed the fundamental problems of crofter life as well as the aspirations that had been activated within the past few years. Maclean, on behalf of the Altandu crofters, presented a petition which had been written by their minister, according to their own 'composition'. Under questioning Maclean explained that a committee of about a dozen crofters had met at the minister's house and requested the minister to draw up their statement according to their directions. The petition represented 18 crofters and four cottars living in Altandu and paying a rent of £50 who, in their grandfathers' day had paid only £7: at that time the land had been tenanted by only five crofters who had access to much more pasture land which had since been made over to sheep and deer. Now the crofters occupied about three acres of arable land each, which they had tilled repeatedly for many years. All improvements and house building had been accomplished at their own expense and for which no assistance or compensation was given. Rents had increased considerably within the last few years so that now 'we can scarcely make half a boll of meal for every pound of rent we pay'. If they kept a horse it cost £1 extra in rent and any seaware they gathered as manure was also subject to extra charges. They still used the caschrom to cultivate their soil and if they were to live exclusively by the produce of their crofts they would need at least ten acres of arable land each and the use of horses without any augmentation of the rent.

Maclean's evidence testified to the continuing importance of cattle and fishing in the crofter economy. Cattle were the source of external income and the means of rent payment, but the crofters had insufficient land on which to pasture them. They were gripped by land pressure which gave them neither arable nor pasture in adequate proportions. As Maclean said: 'At present some of us are so deeply in debt that it would take nearly all our stock to pay up the debts of merchants who have advanced meal, and other necessaries of life to us'. So poor were they that, in the ancient manner, some were 'compelled to go below tide-mark and gather whelks etc to eke out a scant livelihood'. Similarly, though the people were keen to fish they had no local harbours and had no capital for boats or nets: 'We also feel that pauperism is greatly on the increase owing to the failure of the fishing, the unproductiveness of the soil, and the high rents'—which in some parts had increased thirteen-fold in one hundred years.

Poverty and its causes were at the centre of Maclean's evidence as it was throughout the Napier volumes. At Altandu, though the chronology was vague, the people claimed that they had suffered a collective deterioration of circumstances. More people now existed on a much smaller proportion of the land. They had been deprived of pasture, for instance the grazings on the Summer Isles had been taken from them; they used to be able to pasture unlimited numbers of cattle and horses at Strath Polly which was now under sheep and deer. Maclean was imprecise about clearances but he knew that many tenants were removed from Badentarbat at one time. Pauperism was increasing because of 'the smallness of the lots ... The population is increasing and the amount of land occupied by them is getting less, getting worse, and getting dearer.' He agreed that part of the problem was the *de facto* subdivision of crofts when families expanded but that was essentially a consequence of the unavailability of land. He noted that some crofters accepted their fate unresistingly, they were 'facile and pliable' and paid their rent without complaint. Others were becoming obstinate because they realised that they were worse off than their fathers had been: 'Formerly the land could just keep the tenants, and they didn't require to go to the shore to seek for shellfish, and go east and west to the danger of their lives, for work'. The solutions were indeed simple—the crofters needed larger holdings, security from eviction and from rising rents, compensation for improvements, and assistance for better housing, harbours, and fishing equipment.[1] Maclean was the man described by factor Gunn as a Land Law Reformer labouring under a debt of £10.[2]

There was a great deal of evidence from other crofters, from individuals and on behalf of villages and groups, which echoed the main grievances expressed by Maclean. Between them, both in the west and in the east, they scoured the collective memory for the origins of their poverty. Their testimonies all rested on the implicit assumption that their predecessors had been in better economic condition than they themselves. There was, almost literally, hardly a single good word for the landlord, and few for the factors. The people were oppressed by the tenurial conditions imposed from above and by the fundamental landhunger that constricted their lives. Equally, it was all evidence of a tenacious peasant life and its way of thinking. It was expressed not only in the single-minded striving for land but also in a dozen other ways. One was in the economic importance of children as in the case of the crofter from Reef who said he was getting poorer because his family had departed 'and my strength ebbed away'.[3] Another was found in the attitude to status—that it was better to be a crofter than a labourer, even though labour was in places scarce and paid well. Yet this was changing, partly because wages for labour had increased disproportionately and partly because crofting was in such poor circumstances in the 1880s. Said one former crofter, 'when I had a croft I was a greater slave than I am now'.[4] A further expression of the tenacity for the old ways was the resistance to emigration, subsidised or not. Few crofters, especially under the influence of the Free Church ministers, regarded emigration as an acceptable escape[5] from their poverty even though some of them evidently benefited from remittances for their kinsfolk abroad. For them, the solution to the Highland problem resided in a reallocation of land and rights in the Highlands, not in expatriation. Paradoxically, as living standards slowly rose, the crofting population in Coigach, as elsewhere, began to decline, partly caused by the spontaneous out-migration of the youth of the communities.

Some of the witnesses could speak of an extraordinary continuity of tenancy on the Cromartie estate. For instance, Murdo McLeod, a 52-year-old crofter and fisherman of Achnahaird, traced his ancestors in his district over a period longer than 200 years, as foresters and crofters: 'My people were here before the Union when James was King—before the Georges came to the land'. His own immediate family and neighbours had cultivated the same stretch of land continuously for 80 years and they had been deprived of a third of it 30 years previously. They no longer had access to pasture land, their houses were bad and they were forced to pay horse-rent. And although the factor Gunn had always been fair to them their rents had been increased while their capacity to pay had been diminished: 'We used to pay our rent by our stock, and now we cannot keep stock.'[6] Some of the west coast crofters still made their clothes directly from their own wool and sometimes their clothes were better than they used to be. Nevertheless it was still the case that children were unable to attend school for want of clothing. Some of the testimonies were from men who were clearly illiterate, signing their evidence with a mark. They all recounted times when their communities had more land than presently, referring to changes when (for instance) the tacksmen were replaced by direct tenancies and when their pasture lands had been diminished, referring vaguely to a period before 1840. Many believed that there was no incentive to improve the crofts since the landlord stole the benefit: 'the man that improves best will have his rent increased most'. And while rent increased and land diminished, the actual population dependent on the land was growing. Thus at Achiltibuie, in fifty years the number of families lotted on the land had increased from 72 to 104. Moreover the cottar class remained as ever a burden on the crofters.[7]

The most eloquent, challenging and vehement statement about conditions on the Coigach estate and Lochbroom in general came from the Free Church minister, Rev. John McMillan. He believed that the condition of the people had deteriorated, partly because the fishing had been in depression, but mainly because of the artificial constraints on the availability of land. A much greater human population could easily be accommodated at Lochbroom if it were not for the preference given by the landowners to animals, to sheep and deer. The only improvements made were in the form of roads but these were exclusively for the benefit of the great sporting tenants—an allegation repeated in several of the testimonies.[8] The people had no security of tenure and therefore had no independence of spirit, they were entirely cowed by their masters. As McMillan put it: 'The power of the factors and lairds appears to me as a millstone upon the people, and my soul has been frequently pained by this incubus resting upon them which they have no power to throw off'. In the same breath he described William Gunn as an excellent man: the system not the man was at fault. McMillan was convinced that the people were better off before the clearances which he dated about 70 years before. He argued that the critical basis for crofting life in the Highlands was stock and that the people simply must have more land. In particular the large pastoral and deer holdings must be broken up and re-let to the people, preferably in the form of 'club-farms': 'If the proprietor would give the hills to the people would they rise up ten degrees and more in prosperity.'9 McMillan was most articulate on the impending danger to social order and the sheer immorality of the prevailing order of society in the Highlands. Unsurprisingly his appearance turned into a sermon: it was the aim of all right-minded men 'to preach the duties of property, now that its rights are beginning to be realised as wrongs, after having served for centuries as a catch-word to justify a thousand forms of oppression'. He warned that, while the people had not become wild radical agitators, yet if nothing was done 'the people will assert their rights'. To emphasise his warning, he said: 'The radical spirit is abroad ... as Professor Blackie says, we may awake some mornings and find ourselves sitting on the verge of a social volcano.'[10]

II

It was more than two months before the Napier Commission reached Dingwall and heard the evidence of the Strathpeffer crofters of the Cromartie estate. Here again the allegations against the landlord were loud and damaging, and once more, were informed by a long historical perspective which attributed responsibility for current woes to a distant historical change in landholding. At Strathpeffer the crofters' case was largely connected to the sequence of changes which had shifted the small tenants progressively up the hillsides to increasingly marginal land. The crofters claimed that 'clearances' had been executed some 80 or more years before, but they had been gradual and there was no allegation of force or violence. Indeed their own testimony indicated that the small tenants who were 'cleared' in this fashion were, indeed, resettled on the estate.[11] But the best land, allegedly improved by the bare hands of the crofters, had been passed over to the great arable farmers. Concurrently, over a period of several decades, the lotters had also lost pasture land to both sheepfarmers and deer forests. In several of the testimonies there were unequivocal statements that living standards had fallen, even halved, within the previous generation.[12]

Donald MacDonald spoke for the people of Inchvannie on the Heights of Strathpeffer. He said the low parts of the strath, 80 years before, had been occupied by the crofters. These low, fertile acres had been made into large farms while the crofters were 'gradually turned off'. They had received no compensation. They were re-settled on reclaimed barren soil higher up the hillside together with 1200 acres of common pasture 'for which they paid no rent, and which belonged to the crofters on the heights from time immemorial'. Thus resettled they were required to cultivate the land and build houses and for 20 years they succeeded 'by ceaseless toil' in making the barren land valuable. (This was on the pattern of land reclamation widely advocated in the Highlands at the turn of the eighteenth century.[13]) At this point the landlord had made the crofters his direct tenants, reorganised and subdivided the crofts and raised the rents—without ever assisting the people to improve the land. After a further 20 years the crofters were deprived of much of their hill grazing. The land went to a sheep farmer. Another 15 years saw a doubling of many rents, beyond the real value of the land. Leases were promised but, by the imposition of a ten-shilling fee[14] by the estate, the leases were never effected. Three years ago rents were raised but had not yet been implemented 'probably because the signs of the land agitation were then becoming very manifest

36 John Rose of Inchvannie and his wife *c.*1870: almost certainly the man who gave evidence to the Napier Commission.

among the crofters in various parts of the country'. The factors were, nevertheless, entering the rents in their books and would hold it against the people at a future time.

MacDonald, who occupied 14½ acres with four cattle and a horse, claimed that he and his father had spent £400 on the croft, helped by £40 sent by a brother from the colonies. But with every improvement the landlord simply skimmed off the surplus by an augmented rent. MacDonald claimed to represent all the Strathpeffer crofters (except for three) and they had three specific demands: the revaluation of their rents by a government surveyor, the provision of perpetual tenure, and compensation for all improvements. He stated clearly that these wants were not new nor generated by external influence: twenty years previously the crofters of Strathpeffer had met to draw up a petition to the Duchess of Sutherland but were utterly thwarted by the factor –

> who stood in our way like a flaming sword so that until this year we have not ventured to give public expression to our grievances. So long, then, we have crouched under the iron heel of the oppressor without a groan.

Under questioning, MacDonald claimed that the large farmers were given much better treatment than the crofters. The small tenants were disadvantaged by the effects of game on the estate, including grouse, deer and hares, yet they were not allowed to destroy them when they trespassed on their crofts. They had lost land, its quality had declined, and if they complained they lived under the fear of eviction.[15]

Other testimony, supported by the memories of the oldest members of the community, reinforced MacDonald's account. John Rose of Keppoch referred to a time in his grandfather's life when, 80 years before, 'the mania for big farms was spreading through the country'. Evictions had shifted the people from the fertile land and they were then offered land up the hill which had 'never been touched by a plough'. The old man had had to supplement his rent by peat-carting for a big farmer; he had to sell off his stock and was reduced to poverty. He would have died destitute but for the help of his family. The proprietor had never spent a penny on improvements yet the rent had increased five-fold since 1836 and when the people complained they were threatened with removal. Rose made two particularly damaging allegations. One was that some

37 John Mackenzie, pony-man and Inchvannie crofter who occasionally helped out on the estate, outside his own croft, 1912.

of the old people were practically destitute and one woman of 80 was discovered in a roofless house with inches of snow on her bed. And though the Duchess gave the poor sugar, coats and flannel, etc., they continued to eke out an existence by 'wretched economy and untiring perseverance'. Some of the crofters, not even on the poor roll, used guano bags as bedclothes. Second, Rose stated that the estate clerk had told the people that they would be better off if they refrained from 'the agitation'. Rose emphatically denied that the crofters were under the sway of 'a professional gentleman' (meaning a political agitator), which was merely a rumour put about 'by some whose interest it is to depreciate our evidence'.[16]

III

The evidence and the demands of the Cromartie crofters were in no sense exceptional in the vast outpouring of testimony received by the Napier Commission. The Cromartie crofters made few allegations of wanton cruelty and oppression; their main indictment rested on past deprivations and on the continuing sense of the unfairness of the entire land system.

The task of countering the adverse evidence of the crofters, both at Ullapool and Dingwall, fell to the main Cromartie factor, William Gunn. He had had many months in which to organise his general defence but was unprepared for specific charges brought forth on the days of the hearings. Some of his evidence was filed later and employed in the body of an appendix to the Report.

At Ullapool he gave a good deal of statistical information about Coigach but his historical account, he claimed, was limited by the lack of estate records. At Coigach there were 19 townships occupied by 237 crofters and 5 cottars on 700 acres of arable land and 30,000 acres of pasture at an aggregate rent of £1068 per annum. (The big sheep farmers paid £1690 and sporting rents yielded a further £2700, reflecting the recent shifts in land usage values). Until 1853 most of the lotters had been subtenants of Messrs Mackenzie of Ullapool, at which time they became direct tenants to the Duchess of Sutherland but the rent was not altered.

Indeed Gunn claimed unequivocally that for fifty years croft rents had been stationary (even though farm rents had doubled or more). Meanwhile wages had improved by fifty per cent and cattle prices had almost doubled within the past twenty years, partly because of improvements in breeding stock provided by the landlord. Paying only interest on the capital cost, the people were freely provided with timber, lime and glass for their houses, and slate. The estate had spent £11,000 on roads, and further on the provision of a meal mill, a cartwright and carpenter. A modest revaluation of rents had been undertaken in 1878 in order to gain some small return on these investments.

Gunn pointed out that there were six schools in Coigach but agreed that the district was still poorly equipped in terms of communications and markets. There had been, except for one backslider, no evictions in the past 50 years, beyond which time he could not account. The people were prone to overstock the pasture to their mutual disadvantage. The small tenants already possessed all the available arable land in their district (except for about 50 acres); there was already a safe harbour at Altandu;

compensation was given to departing tenants; charges for sea-ware were illegal; the road constructed followed the only possible route in the district and was designed for the general good. Gunn conceded that the great sheep farm at Rhiddorach had been cleared of sheep for deer; but it had never been occupied by crofters. He said that Hay-Mackenzie had been extremely kind to the people: 'He would have been the last to have evicted or be unkind to any of the small crofters on the place'. He questioned the crofters' evidence heard by the Commission; the delegates he said had not called proper meetings of the people and they had failed to give proper expression to the people of Coigach. As his final response he claimed that the people were very generously provided with land: 'I have never had an application for more land since I was connected with the Cromartie estate; I never heard that the people considered they had too little land until today'. Taken literally, it was the most astonishing remark in all Gunn's evidence.[17]

At Dingwall two months later Gunn adopted a similar attitude. On the Strathpeffer property there were 83 crofters who paid a total rent of £760. He made much of the graduations of holdings among the crofting population, ranging from less than £10 rent to over £400. He stated categorically that 'the crofters of Strathpeffer property hold now every inch of arable land that they ever possessed'. Unfortunately he did not indicate whether this assertion related only to the present generation. He drew particular attention to the Knockfarrell/Gower allotments, in total 150 acres, which had been reclaimed by the landlord in 1848.50 at the cost of £2868. The lots had been intended originally for local cottars, but eventually were given to people evicted from another estate—in essence a sanctuary.[18]

Gunn had examined old estate plans dating back to 1835 which indicated that the Heights' small tenants then had access to the grazing on the southern slopes of Ben Wyvis. When the lease fell in, in the year 1839, the people were not deprived of the grazings; rather they could not agree among themselves about them. There had never been a proposal since then for the people to re-occupy the land and he was affronted that they had never mentioned it to him. He stressed the relatively favourable conditions in which the Strathpeffer crofters earned their living—good land, proximity to a railway station, and the great demand for dairy produce, poultry and eggs now generated at Strathpeffer Spa during the tourist season. The landlord had been exceedingly lenient with arrears, and rents had risen only from 12/- to £1 an acre in 60 years. The recent rise of rent was almost entirely a matter of commuting labour services (relating to road maintenance) and therefore did not constitute a true increase at all.[19] He defended his predecessor as factor, Andrew Scott, as well as the owners of the Cromartie estate, none of whom 'would do an unjust or unkind thing to any of the Heights people'. But Gunn was prepared to concede that the landlord gave more direct help to the larger tenants which was reflected in their higher rents: 'I am quite free to admit that the crofter who pays £1 or £1.1.0 per acre really puts as much into the proprietor's pocket as the larger tenant who pays the larger rent'.

Under questioning Gunn disclaimed any knowledge of events at the beginning of the century and simply repeated his conviction that the landlords were never unkind: 'Mr John Hay-Mackenzie was not the man to have disturbed tenants and removed them to a barren moor without taking the matter in consideration and dealing kindly by them.' He conceded that compensation for improvements was important but was also

38 Tarbat House, built 1796.

contingent on the level of rents; rents were higher on the large farms which occupied better land and buildings. Attacking some of the crofters' evidence and their claim to represent the entire community, Gunn was pointedly warned by one of the Commissioners, Fraser-Mackintosh, that the crofters had to be protected from recrimination, and presumably, factorial punishment. Gunn claimed that the Strathpeffer tenantry were envied for their prosperity and that they were in high demand as labour in the district at good wages[20] for which they were reluctant to serve.

In subsequent evidence Gunn answered specific charges made in the crofters' testimonies and took the opportunity further to impugn their evidence. The delegates, he asserted, were not representative of the people and were indeed, 'entirely out of sympathy with their feelings and wishes'. He categorically rejected the notion that the management had made threats against potential witnesses before the Commission. The cases of distress mentioned by the 'delegates' were personal tragedies which the estate made genuine efforts to help; they were irrelevant to the crofters' case. The estate provided much wage-labour for the people who were generally unusually well off by local standards. The Chairman regretted that Gunn did not make himself available for further cross-questioning.[21]

IV

The conflict between the evidence of the Cromartie crofters and that of the estate factors was repeated endlessly through the volumes of the Napier Commission. In the case of Cromartie there was diametrical opposition both in the analysis of the causes of the continuing poverty of crofting life and in the perception of its origins. It was symptomatic of the two mentalities that the people sought to cast a much longer historical retrospect than the landlords' men were prepared to entertain. There was however, some elementary agreement between the two sides: that there had been no evictions of any scale in recent years; and that changes in crofter circumstances (for better or worse) had been contingent on the abolition of the tacksmen's leases and the subletting system which, in some parts, had persisted into the 1850s.

William Gunn and his advisors laboured in a state of genuine ignorance of the earlier history of the Cromartie estate.[22] But it must also be said that they also adopted a cavalier attitude to the past: events 80 years ago, they asserted, were irrelevant; it was too long ago to matter any more. They were also deliberately obscurantist about the process of change which was certainly documented in old estate records, albeit in somewhat fragmentary form. Gunn simply fell back on pious assertions that the owners of Cromartie and their agents had given the people an unbroken line of beneficence and fair dealing.

In reality the claims of the people were both true and false. They were right to say that tenure, rents and land availability had been subject to vast changes over the previous century. It was objectively the case that there was a far greater population, in say, 1870 than in 1780 and that the arable land had been increased very little. It was equally true that the sheepfarmers and sporting tenants had entered the eastern and western parishes and strained the cattle-carrying capacity of the smaller tenants. On the other side it was not true that the people had been prosperous and secure before this great transformation: the history of famine alone is a great obstacle in the way of that perspective. Nor was it true that the landlord had invested nothing in the land even though the bias was towards the commercial and sporting sectors. Most of all it was not necessarily true that the old tacksmen had provided more land and lower rents than the subsequent regime. When tacks fell in and new tenants were introduced the crofters' position was more closely defined. But the exact extent of their losses, if there were any, was difficult to determine—precisely because the old system operated in an almost subterranean fashion beyond the direct knowledge of the estate managers or anyone else. None of the contemporary observers of sub-tenant life in, for instance, the 1790s or the 1830s, had much that was favourable to say for either the productivity or the welfare of the system. Mostly it was simply ignored.

None of this however impinged upon the minds of the land leaguers. Nor did the factor's testimony dampen the irritation or vigour of the resistance. The immediate sequel to the Napier hearings on the Cromartie estate was a strengthening of the solidarity and resolution of the people to resist the landlord and his agents. In December 1883, for instance, a joint letter was received from the Tenants of Achindrean:

> We the undersigned beg to say that in common with the other townships of the Barony of Coigach are not [able] to pay this year the additional rent paid by us for a few years back—we found it hard enough to pay previous to its being added to ...
>
> We complain very much that no work of any duration was carried on amongst us to give us even an opportunity to earn what would pay the potato and oat seed which was very kindly given us—for which we are grateful—neither were we permitted to work where work was carried on in other parts of the estate.[23]

The rent strike, partial in some cases, was associated with other reports that the collaborators were actively intimidating any tenant who broke the strike.[24]

The response of the Cromartie management was one of increasing anger and frustration. Gunn was stunned by the people's ingratitude and sophistry, especially in their appearances before the Napier Commissioners. He wrote to one acquaintance how

> abuse and statements grossly untrue should have been uttered is to myself personally more disappointing than I can well explain. I can truly say that I never missed an opportunity of putting in a good word for the people, recommending and pressing forward any scheme of improvement likely to be advantageous to them—but Oh! such heartless ingratitude—I cannot get over it. I am very sorry, for the people themselves will be the first to discover the mistake they have committed.

To another correspondent Gunn exclaimed similarly:

> Such ungrateful people it has not been my lot to meet before....Those lairds who have not done a thing for their people get more thanks today. I am bitterly disappointed that they should have been unjust and unfair as well as ungratefull.

He said he had spoken the absolute truth in his own evidence. Of the people of Coigach he fulminated, 'out of a population of over 1000 there was not one who had the moral courage to speak one word of acknowledgment of anything that has ever been done by that noble and kind proprietor'.[25]

Gunn's indignation and chagrin were an accurate measure of the poor state of relations between landlord and people across many parts of the West Highlands in the 1880s. But more importantly it exposed the gulf in understanding that existed in the minds of men like Gunn—factors who widely regarded themselves as the humane agents of decent landlords. They clearly had entirely misread the condition, psychological and economic, of the great mass of the people. The emotional distress expressed by Gunn eventually affected much of the response of his class to the changes eventually imposed on the Highlands by the Crofters Commission at the end of the decade.

CHAPTER 24

Managerial Attitudes

I

The management of the Cromartie estate supervised a growing and shifting population located in heterogenous agrarian communities spread almost from coast to coast across the Highlands. It was a complicated business. During the course of the nineteenth century the business became more diversified and onerous for the men selected to undertake the owners' wishes. But the Cromartie estate required a relatively modest apparatus of management compared with the great landed estates of the larger aristocratic owners in Britain. Moreover the Cromartie management was itself swallowed into the vast Sutherland administrative machine after the marriage of Anne Hay-Mackenzie to the Marquis of Stafford in 1849. Yet this arrangement, if anything, increased the responsibilities and burdens shouldered by the Cromartie estate office: the Cromartie management became part of the inter-penetration of Scottish and English land agency methods and personnel which characterised the Sutherland estate empire throughout the country.[1]

Land agents were the lynchpin of the managerial class which emerged strongly during British industrialisation. For as long as agriculture remained the greatest sector in the national economy its management—in increasingly large units of enterprise, the great estates—demanded greater professionalism and sophistication.[2] In agriculture, as in the affairs of industry and the state, the scale of operations, levels of investment, and the development of technology, all demanded new responses in organisation. On the Cromartie estate the role of the management was unusually critical because the factors tended to outlive their masters. Three of the key managers served for three or more decades and provided an extraordinary line of continuity through the Victorian age.

Their work became more difficult. For one thing the Cromartie factors were required to preside over the dissolution of the last vestiges of 'feudalism', the elimination of the tacksmen, labour services, victual rents and the like. The demise of the old leaseholders was designed to make the small tenantry directly responsible to the landlord and this alone multiplied the burden of the estate agents. Previously the tacksman had collected all rents, settled disputes, ruled the local community. Under direct tenancies the district agent became directly responsible even though he possessed no traditional authority for the role. During the same period the Cromartie owners tended to be rather more absentee than many of their predecessors and their factors were left to cushion relations between landlord and tenant, implement difficult policies, maintain order, and cultivate their employer's popularity. At the same time they were expected to promote agricultural efficiency across the diversified lands of the estate. They were also expected to develop new enterprises such as fishing among the crofters and tourism and health facilities at Strathpeffer Spa. The managers too were responsible for the maintenance of the family's political and social role at a time when the Highlands were rent by religious and political turmoil. Meanwhile little social leadership or cohesion was provided by the large capitalistic tenants who had replaced the tacksmen of the eighteenth century. As well, between 1850 and 1898, the management was required to accommodate the methods and priorities of the Sutherland organisation which itself was profoundly hierarchic and, eventually, riven by dispute.

The nature of factoring in the eighteenth century remains in shadows and it is difficult to define the precise functions of the men who ran the Cromartie estate. Men such as George Mackenzie at the end of the century, and John Macrae in the first decade of the new one, appear to have been more personally responsible for the extraction of rents than their successors, and for various legal arrangements with the tenantry. They were probably less intrusive, directive and managerial than later factors, less responsible for the promotion of agricultural technique and general improvement. They may have been kinsmen of the laird and probably farmed on the estate on their own account. Under the Annexed Estates the management was more institutional and improvement-minded. When Count Macleod resumed the ownership of the estate in the 1780s he also took over the reins of management and reduced his factor to a secondary role. In the next generation, when the Cromartie estate fell into financial difficulties in the 1810s and 1820s, its affairs became subject to trustees and creditors who exerted a greater degree of direct management over the estate.

But the main impulses towards directive estate management derived from the re-organisation of the estate in the first three decades of the new century, and the emergence of the full-time, professional agent/factor charged with the responsibility of very much more than rent collection. One of the side-benefits of the creation of a systematic estate office was the improved keeping of records and rentals and especially the retention of correspondence. Letters written between estate factors—from, for instance, Kildary in the east to Coigach in the west—provide the best illumination of the inner history of a landed estate. It is a managerial window on the world, highly partial but often extra-ordinarily candid. The first of the 'modern' agents at Cromartie was Andrew Scott.

Scott took over the management of the Cromartie Estate in 1831 and his service spanned the middle four decades of the century: he retired finally in 1869. His salary in 1835 was £150 per annum and thirty years later it was £250. His origins are obscure but he did not enter his employment through the conventional apprenticeship in a land agency. He was a southern Scot, from Hawick in the Borders, and a farmer who had fallen into bankruptcy in about 1830. Twenty years later he recalled that he had 'made a surrender to my Creditors, but not having been a trader in the legal sense of the term I could not go into Court and seek for a Discharge'. Among his creditors were uncles in Liverpool who had been notably helpful. Some of his debts were still outstanding in 1851 when he sought to discharge the remainder. One of his creditors however refused to accept the arrangement and Scott was furious when the Post Office intercepted mail which exposed his continuing embarrassment.[3]

Scott's origins were no disadvantage as factor at Cromartie. He was an experienced farmer, a good organiser, a clear pen-man and an efficient accountant. His duties required him to oversee the valuable arable lands of Strathpeffer and New Tarbat, the great sheep farms of the west, and the dense populations of crofters and cottars, especially in Coigach. The local ground officer in the west was vital to the operation of the estate but Scott needed all his energy even to remain familiar with the scattered territories in his control. It was twelve years before he first visited the island of Tanera and the problems of accessibility in the west did not diminish significantly until new roads were built after 1845, mainly under Scott's own supervision.[4] Scott's financial management was subject to the inspection of legal agents in Edinburgh (Walker and Melville's office in the 1850s) and later to the scrutiny of the Sutherland hierarchy. This was ruled by James Loch, until 1855, and then by his son George Loch. The Lochs were the immensely influential 'Commissioners' to the Duke of Sutherland and when Cromartie was subsumed into the Sutherland empire Scott, while retaining his local authority, became answerable to the Loch system of management. One of Loch's first criticisms of the prevailing Cromartie management was its 'want of any combined action between the different branches' of the owner's affairs. It led to financial 'confusion and distressfullness'. The Loch regime centralised the income and expenditure accounting in a more professional manner.[5]

The Cromartie factor was also responsible directly to the owner even though he, rather than the owner, represented the estate in public—for instance it was Scott, not Hay-Mackenzie, who appeared before the Royal Commission on Emigration in 1841.[6] The relationship between factor and proprietor was formal: Scott expected to keep his distance and to offer automatic deference; relations with other factors were friendlier and a warm camaraderie developed between Scott and his Sutherland counterpart Evander MacIver, sometimes marked by a sneaking scepticism about their superiors and even the owners. But when Scott was invited by Lord and Lady Stafford to attend the Great Exhibition at Crystal Palace in 1851 he was overcome with gratitude and accepted effusively.[7] The tenor of this relationship is to be sensed in a sample letter he wrote to Lady Stafford on Christmas Eve 1856:

> Permit me dear Lady Stafford to offer you and to Lord Stafford my most hearty congratulations on the advent of another Christmas and New Year. It is very delightful such family reunions as these you have every year at Trentham. Long, long may the honoured Heads of that happy Family enjoy the exquisite pleasure of having their loved ones about them on such jubilant occasions as the present is my sincerest prayer.[8]

Scott described his autumn duties to his son in October 1857:

> I have annually at this season to lay my Budget of Disbursement for the ensuing year of every sort and kind before Lord Stafford, and Mr Loch, the principal Commissioner of the Duke of Sutherland and also the Adviser of the Marquis in respect to expenditure. It involves a deal of trouble and forethought, and I have just got over the work and had it submitted.[9]

The chain of command was clear cut and though Loch told Scott that he regarded him as a long-time friend[10] he did not withhold his criticism. Towards the end of Scott's career Loch believed that some of the problems in relations with some crofters had been 'mainly caused by want of temper and patience on Mr Scott's part'.[11] He hoped Scott's successor would do better. As events turned out in the 1880s, this was a vain hope.

Scott, of course, had been exposed to the rough edge of conflict with the crofters of Coigach and had suffered the indignity of widely publicised defeat by riot and resistance in 1852 and 1853. There was physical danger in some of these encounters. For instance, in December 1852, Scott journeyed to Coigach to face directly the fury of the rebellious people. He reported to Lady Stafford his reception:

> In going along someone hit me a blow across the back with a stick, but it did me no hurt, and twice they attempted to trip me and throw me on my face. I don't know what the authorities will do to make the law respected, but it is evident if some decided measures be not taken with these turbulent riotous people, the country will not be safe to live in especially if a man asks them for his own.[12]

The personal dangers facing Scott may have been less severe than those of his Irish counterparts, but they were nonetheless real enough.

Over the years of Scott's factorship his instructions varied and the resolution and intentions of his masters wavered. Sometimes a firm hand was demanded, at others the most restrained diplomacy was necessary. In 1868, now an old man at the end of his career, Scott was dealing with recalcitrant crofters occupying land illicitly. Scott's inclination was to remove them but he was countermanded—Loch told him that the Duke of Sutherland was 'indisposed to enter upon a process of removing the people, for the present at any rate—he thinks it will be better to let them remain undisturbed'. The reason was clear but, for Scott, unsatisfactory:

> they [the Duke and Duchess] desire to avoid all risk by getting into contention with these people—and they would wish whatever steps to be taken, to be adopted with much consideration, and so as not to involve the removal of the people, unless they have some place to go to—and only to do it by degrees—for there is no hurry about it, and it may be spread over a year or two.[13]

Andrew Scott rightly recognised himself as an outsider in the Highlands. He thought of the crofters more as an administrative challenge than as fellow-countrymen, an attitude coloured no doubt by his unhappy experiences in the Coigach riots. He took a poor view of Highlanders in general. In 1857, when vetting possible sheepfarming tenants for Badentarbat, he remarked of one applicant—'if he is ignorant, and has to depend on a Highland Shepherd, the farm will yield him little profit'. He commended a man named Elliot (probably a fellow-borderer) on the grounds that he was 'a careful sagacious shepherd, very trustworthy and correct in keeping his accounts. He is quiet with the natives, but will abate nothing of his rights to gain or keep favour with them.' Scott referred to the people as 'wretches' who took gross advantage of weakness and would deliberately allow their cattle to trespass on a tenant in order to harrass him out of his lease saying, according to Scott: 'We were here before you and will see you out and so on they go tormenting the poor fellow'.[14] In the light of these antipathies it was the more remarkable that Scott was frequently requested to settle or arbitrate communal disputes between the crofters.[15]

In early 1859 the managerial structure of the great empire of the Sutherland estates was thrown into turmoil by the death of the principal northern agent, George Gunn. It was soon discovered that Gunn's financial affairs were in grave disorder: as Andrew Scott described it: 'his affairs were found to be fearfully wrong. The debts are said to be over £20,000 ... It is an awful smash.' Not only was Gunn's personal estate bankrupt but there was also evidence of malpractice—'It turns out that the rents of the crofting and fishing tenants to about £800 had been paid to Mr Gunn and not accounted for by him to his constituents'. There was still worse news to come: Gunn had been borrowing from his fellow agent, the redoubtable Evander MacIver in Scourie. The figure of £4000 was mentioned, thought to be 'an extent likely to ruin him'.

Gunn's private catastrophe was the nightmare feared by every landed proprietor and every professional land agent; it was the sort of hopeless mess that James Loch and his son had devoted their lives to eradicating. The astonishing aspect of this managerial crisis was the apparent leniency and generosity with which the Duke of Sutherland and George Loch responded. Perhaps they chose to minimise their own embarrassment by quickly containing the episode. MacIver, with a very large family, who had clearly been caught in the financial tangle, was retained and probably assisted over his own difficulties. Gunn's widow was given a £200 annuity by the Duke of Sutherland though she quickly vacated the agent's house at Rhives. She no doubt received further help and comfort from her eldest son, Donald Gunn, who was himself factor to Lord Falmouth.[16]

Andrew Scott was not directly affected by the turbulent events in the Sutherland management though he would have sensed the awful warnings contained in the Gunn episode. He was however asked for his opinion on possible successors to the Sutherland administration and his private responses exposed his basic attitudes to his work amongst the crofters. Scott was indeed mindful of the possibilities for considering his own son and also a nephew for the position though he concluded that it was too soon for their cases.[17] Of another candidate he considered his merits: 'He has had little or no practice as a Factor, among lot tenants or crofters, but I think him well tempered and patient in dealing with ignorant people, and as a master he is well liked among his servants'. On the other hand the man in question, Hassock, a professional land agent, had never actually set going any substantial improvement plans in his previous managements.[18]

In the outcome Scott was not able to place his kinsmen in the Sutherland vacancy—the position was filled by an internal promotion from within the existing structure. The agent from Trentham, Peacock, was chosen for the supervision of the Highland territories. Scott was sceptical, believing that Peacock lacked experience necessary for the control of a backward Highland tenantry. He confided to a relative that

> between you and me, [it is] certainly not an appointment likely to be satisfactory to himself, his employer or the small tenantry for they are the difficulty. He cannot understand their cunning and deceit, and they will not understand his English, open, straightforward way of dealing in his intercourse with them in matters connected with his office as Factor. But if he is prudent and cautious with a good mixture of energy he may do very well. As

39 MacLean, the deaf and dumb tailor and his wife c.1870. Their house on the Heights of Strathpeffer is now a ruin.

> I hear they are exceedingly unruly and difficult to manage when anything meets them which they don't like, they immediately apply to Mr Loch or the Duke, and in this way the local factor is ignored, and his influence for good or evil almost nil.[19]

Peacock's appointment left Scott's son William without immediate employment, but his father encouraged him to return home from India. He might take up one of the small sheep farms which were being considered for the Sutherland estate.[20] Andrew Scott told his son that it would 'enable you to spend the rest of your days in a better country and among better men than, as now, among steaming fields and black pagans. So the sooner you can save five or six thousand pounds to invest in a Sutherland farm the better.'[21] Scott had been anxious about the welfare of his sons especially in 1857 at the time of the Mutiny and the 'horrid cruelties of the Sepoys'.[22]

With prejudices hardened by the events in Coigach in 1852/3 Scott generally regarded the crofters as ignorant and unruly and thought many of them should be urged to emigrate. Nevertheless by 1860 there were signs of a softening in his attitudes, and certainly a less combative feeling had emerged between the proprietrix and the crofters, at least during her visit to the Aird of Coigach in the autumn of that year. Scott was very happy to report that

> the peace that was broken in 1852 is all made up now. She was received with the greatest demonstrations of joy and gladness. She slept on board the Garth [the Duke's yacht] and she told me that after dark all the houses in Achiltybuie were illuminated, making a line of lights from one end of the township to the other and continued lighted up till midnight.

When the 2nd Duke of Sutherland died in the late winter of 1861 Scott was clearly moved by the loss of his 'good and gentle and kind' employer. The Duke's death raised questions about the future of the management of the estates, but Scott was confident of the demeanour of the new Duke: 'I don't think there will be any change in the management of the Ducal Estates in the north ... I have good hopes of the present Duke. I think he will be a good and kind landlord and will look stricter into the management than his father did.'[23]

In 1861 Scott's eldest son died of dysentery, having recently returned from Calcutta; Scott's own wife was seriously ill in 1862 and he was himself becoming an old man. He had become a substantial figure in the north, a shareholder in projected railways[24] and a farmer. He seems to have been reluctant to relinquish his factorship, though he reduced his responsibilities in 1865 and finally retired from New Tarbat in 1869. He died in the following year, having served the estate for almost four decades.[25]

II

In Andrew Scott's day the main Cromartie estate office was located at Kildary in New Tarbat; his successor later moved the office to Nutwood in Strathpeffer. Both were a great distance from the Aird of Coigach which required a separate sub-agency and local ground officer. Soon after the arrival of Andrew Scott in about 1832, a new ground officer for Coigach was appointed: his name was Kenneth Mackenzie.[26] Astonishingly Mackenzie outlived Scott by many years and lived through the turmoil of the Crofters' Revolt.

Mackenzie was an insider—a native of Lochbroom and a Gaelic speaker; in 1884 in the middle of great agitation in the west, Mackenzie's daughter married a Free Church minister. Kenneth Mackenzie lived among the people where he rented a middle-sized farm called Morefield close to Ullapool. During almost half a century he presided over a difficult and poor crofter population with little assistance from anyone else in the western community: the sheepfarmers had virtually no social impact, the ministers of the church were divisive and the landowners were as distant as royalty. The geographical isolation of Coigach was extreme. When disease came to the district in 1864, Mackenzie's wife suffered the fate of many of the small tenants: her death caused George Loch to remark that: 'It is dreadful to think of a population exposed to such a scourge, without the aid of medical advice'.[27]

Mackenzie therefore lived amid the people and had to deal with difficulties large and small, to be accessible yet aloof. He clearly developed a rapport with the people even though he represented landlord authority and the fear of eviction and rent increases. For much of the time it was an exhausting cat-and-mouse game and sometimes hatred and acute frustration marked the relationship. Nevertheless Mackenzie somehow developed a *modus vivendi* with the people which survived the Coigach riots. Towards the end of his career, however, Mackenzie became embittered about the behaviour of the crofters during the time of the Napier Commission. The balance then was destroyed and all trust broken.

Mackenzie therefore was invested with great powers in Coigach and over the years his responsibilities increased. In 1881, for instance, he was a member of the School Board and held a mandate for the Parochial Board, both highly politicised by that time. He was also a Justice of the Peace. Thus he was required to exact rents from the dozens of crofters along the broken coast line while he was also charged with the maintenance of peace between them, as well as the preservation of the sheep and sport of the great tenants, especially that of the finicky and demanding sporting tycoons. It was said of him that 'he possessed in a marked degree the bearing and the instincts of the true Highland gentleman'.[28]

The qualifications of a good ground officer for a west coast property were defined by George Loch in 1871 (seeking such a person for Assynt in Sutherland)—he would need to be a 'very active energetic young man ... speaking Gaelic, and thoroughly up to agricultural improvements'.[29] Mackenzie was no longer young but he possessed an unrivalled knowledge of the problems of supervising a crofter population and the problems of the local economy. He had lived through famines and riots, improvements in living standards and several changes of landowner. When a new principal agent was appointed in 1865 he was advised by Evander MacIver that 'Coygach is far behind— and the people therefore required to be stimulated. You have an excellent man in Kenneth Mackenzie to assist you. Give him more responsibility and power and more money.'[30] Whether Mackenzie could stimulate the people into more effective economic activity is doubtful, but at least he knew the limits of their capacities and their circumstances. In many ways he was their advocate against the misunderstanding of his superiors: it was Mackenzie who explained, with evident sympathy, the real poverty and severe conditions in which the crofters lived. It was he who warned of famine, of the implications of a poor fishing, or the loss of a breadwinner.

Hence Kenneth Mackenzie possessed a profound knowledge of the community of small tenants on the west coast. He was, nevertheless, hide-bound in his attitudes and in his conservatism. He was shocked to the quick by the behaviour of the Coigach people in the 1880s and it broke his spirit. He was, after all, in his ninth decade. In 1883 he could only make sense of the crofters' agitation in the west in terms of the malignant influence of 'outsiders'. He remarked: 'I am much disappointed with the spirit manifested by the crofters here—they don't seem in the least grateful for all that has been done for them'. They had refused even to supply stock statistics despite the kindness of the Duke of Sutherland who had given them 'seed for the ground, all the Timber and Lime wanted for their Houses, Bulls annually and now giving work to such as could not leave home still; they think it the duty of the Proprietor to do so now.' At the end of his career, he felt tired and disconsolate: 'My influence with them now is all gone', he admitted. Indeed, at a critical moment in the rent strike in 1883, Mackenzie declined William Gunn's request to accompany him in Coigach to collect their rents: 'I have no desire to meet my old Coigach friends now and some of them would prefer not seeing me, I can give you no assistance'.[31]

In 1883 Mackenzie had known the crofters intimately for the last 50 years or more and was reported as saying

> they are much changed of late, and that a spirit of ingratitude and even lawlessness is becoming every day more apparent. This is what might be expected, considering the temptation now set before them to manufacture grievances, and have them aired in public.'[32]

Nor did Mackenzie accept the assumptions of the crofter revolt. He told William Gunn in 1884 that it would be better to reduce their rents than to give them more land: 'To begin to break up the Sheep Farms now here would be such a bad precedent that there would be no end to it. I only give my opinion in confidence.'[33]

Though wishing to retire as early as 1881 Mackenzie was called upon for assistance over the following several years. In fact though in partial retirement he remained on his farm at Morefield and was provided with 'a pension to the full amount of his pay' by authority of the Duchess of Sutherland.[34] Gunn remarked, perhaps helpfully, that 'he is failing very much and is not likely to enjoy for long any pension which the Duke and Duchess may feel disposed to grant him'.[35] In the event Mackenzie lived on until March 1890. Evander MacIver, who had known him since 1834, described him as 'a close and sincere friend ... an honest and trustworthy man, and I trust [he] has gone to a happier world than this'.[36]

The factor's tasks were rendered more difficult by the social context that had set hard in the Highlands by the mid-century. Most often the proprietor was absent and his agent was alone in facing the problems of poverty and discontent. The Free Church ministers frequently presented a disruptive and challenging influence among the crofters. And there was virtually no support from the large tenants who were also mainly absentees. Evander MacIver, in the middle of the crofter revolt in 1884, sympathised with his Cromartie counterpart, remarking:

> the difficulty in this management—the non-residence of Tenants ... is very unfortunate. I mean of large Tenants who would command respect and have influence over people. The Factor of this District needs them.

The loneliness of the factor in the far west was a genuine grievance for which there was no solution.[37]

At £85 per annum salary Mackenzie's successor in Coigach was Alexander Ross, apparently also a local man because, on his appointment, he also took over the farm of his father-in-law in the district. He had been an Inspector of the Poor and this had already brought him into controversy with some of the local radicals.[38] He arrived in the factorship at a time of high tension and his views were already marked by a distinct authoritarianism. He promised firm measures, for example the eviction of two crofters who were disturbing the sheepfarmers: 'to make some arrangements whereby these people may be removed which would be both beneficial and peaceful to us'.[39]

Ross soon learned the frustrations of a land agency among crofters and the growing impotence of the management. In May 1884 he declared that the current regulations of the Parochial Boards were designed 'to protect the poor from too much "proprietor" influence', yet

> circumstances are so much changed that the tables may be said to be completely turned; that the poor have become bold in asserting their legal rights; that if any one nowadays needs protection in his position it appears to be the Proprietors.[40]

Ross, of course, faced the full flood of crofter recalcitrance including defiance in the payment of rent and refusal to remove from lots. In December he complained that he could get none of them to shift without a summons of removal:

> The tone of mind prevailing among these people I am not able to understand. They think they are to hold these Lots, rent or no rent. I am suspecting that the leniency hitherto shown towards defaulters has had a bad effect on others.[41]

Ross was particularly irritated by southern sympathisers of the crofters—people who must know well 'the squalor and wretchedness of city life'. He knew from his own experience that no 'industrious Crofter' ever needed parochial assistance, and that it was an 'indelible fact' that it was only 'the indolent and the dissipated that are the malcontents and who desire to have things so shaped as to place themselves in the possession of the earnings and the savings of the industrious'. The people, he believed, wanted to 'get hold by "hook or by crook" some of Her Grace's substance': 'there is a lower tone of morality and sense of honour prevailing among the people generally'. The people were being misled by hollow champions and 'it needs a little time to cause it to blow over'.[42]

Ross's views, naturally, were part of the polarisation of Highland opinion during the crofters' revolt, yet there was some prescience in his words. Eventually a new equilibrium was achieved both in Coigach and the West Highlands in general. But it was not a return to the old ways: the crofters won remarkable concessions and relations with the lairds were put on a new footing. Eventually even Ross was required to adjust to the post-Napier realities in the Highlands.

III

After the retirement of Andrew Scott the main Cromartie estate management was taken over by the 28-year-old William Gunn.[43] Gunn thereby began another long period, 35 years in all, of factorial stability, taking the estate into the twentieth century. The new agent was a Highlander and his father came from Sutherland. He was known to Evander MacIver and had served a nine-year apprenticeship in land agency on the Duke of Sutherland's Lilleshall estate in Shropshire. He was certainly in the mould of a professional agent, claiming expertise in agricultural technique and general business methods. His initial salary was the same as Scott's, £250 plus allowances including coals for heating. One of George Loch's first exchanges with Gunn was to reprimand him for his gross over-expenditure on heating.[44] Gunn also took over the lease of Nutwood Farm in Strathpeffer and eventually centralised the agency there. He also built a handsome house there for his own accommodation.

Gunn interpreted his brief more broadly than Scott—and in any case the responsibilities had widened with the creation of new public bodies on which he represented the landlord (such as Parochial Boards, Fishery Boards and Road Trustees).[45] But Gunn also adopted an approach almost entrepreneurial[46] for the economic development of Strathpeffer Spa.[47] He forever urged investment in the resort and indeed was instrumental in its substantial growth in the late nineteenth century. The fact that he ploughed his own capital into some of these developments (as well as in his farm) caused local opinion to allege that he had nurtured a conflict of interest and had diligently feathered his own nest. He became a dominant figure in the affairs of the Cromartie estate.

Gunn's attachment to Strathpeffer was put to the test in 1885 when he was offered a considerable promotion within the hierarchy of the Sutherland empire, namely the principal factorship at Rhives, Dunrobin, in Sutherland. He declined, offering several reasons. One was that 'a factor's life has of late years been somewhat harrassing'. He had had little rest in his 26 years of duty and he was 'not so robust as he was'. More particularly however he remarked that 'My time is very fully occupied here—Strathpeffer is fast growing into a little town—and with so many farms unfortunately on our own hands and the practical knowledge I can bring to bear is needed to make the best of things'.[48] Gunn had too much at stake in Strathpeffer.

In the following year the new Commissioner of the Sutherland estate, R.M. Brereton, ran into sharp conflict with Gunn on several matters including policy towards crofters. But the greatest source of contention was the suggestion that Gunn was placing his own pecuniary interest above that of the estate, especially with regard to the terms on which he leased land at Nutwood. When confronted Gunn responded with what was termed 'a hasty and intemperate' letter in which he hotly denied the imputations against him. His superior declared that the letter merely demonstrated that Gunn had

> had his own way in the management too long, so that he tries to assume a position beyond that of a Factor .... It is not a good principle in business for a Factor to farm on his own account, as self-interest will often clash with his client's interest.[49]

Though wounded, Gunn appears not to have offered his resignation, and in September 1887 suffered the further professional indignity of being refused direct access to the Duke of Sutherland—all management correspondence thenceforth was to be directed through the central agency.[50]

The chain of command in the Sutherland management was long and tortuous, for tenants as for the under agents, and was repeatedly disturbed by changes in the Commissionership and within the Sutherland family. There were several occasions when rival factions struggled for control, sometimes in the full glare of publicity.

The authority of George Loch had never been in question. Like his father before him he made annual tours of inspection of even the most remote fastnesses of the Sutherland territories. Gunn was also urged to assert his own presence in Coigach—for instance in 1875 he was encouraged to visit Achiltibuie despite 'the additional trouble' because 'it saves so much trouble and expense' in that the small tenants would pay their rent directly rather than squandering their income at Ullapool.[51] When it was thought that Loch would retire MacIver and Gunn exchanged reactions: there had been disagreements and he had had his faults, but he and MacIver had become better friends than ever; Loch had been 'as agreeable and gentlemanly a Commissioner as we can expect any successor to be'.[52]

Loch's successor was Sir Arnold Kemball, a noteworthy but surprising appointment. He would be a man out of his element. Kemball had served in the diplomatic service with Lord Derby's government, 'unsurpassed in his knowledge of the whole bearing of the Eastern Question, and his thorough acquaintance with the Turkish, Persian and Arabic languages marked him out as peculiarly fitted for the post of Minister to Persia' which had fallen vacant. But Lord Salisbury passed him over in a painful manner. The Duke of Sutherland, besieged by applications for the Commissionership, including one from a member of the most recent Liberal cabinet, offered it to Kemball reportedly as an 'act of kindness'. It was a position which 'carries with it a handsome income and a charming country house in the vicinity of Dunrobin', said a current report, and 'one requiring exceptional tact and diplomacy'.[53]

Kemball quickly discovered that his professional training in diplomacy was fully stretched by the developing crisis with the crofters in both Sutherland and Cromartie. He tended to swing from intransigence to great open-mindedness as he confronted the frustrations of his position. He also found himself in conflict with the estate factors—MacIver told Gunn in February 1881 that he had been much bruised by Kemball's responses and henceforth their communications would be 'stiffly official'.[54] Between themselves the agents were also critical of the Duke—he treated Scourie 'as if it were no part of his extensive Estates and does not think it worth coming to', moaned MacIver. The Duke spent all his thoughts and money on the great drainage works at Shinness.[55] When the Crofters' Revolt boiled over in 1883 it was reported that both Kemball and the Duke were profoundly worried by the turn of events in the Highlands. MacIver said he was sorry to see him so bothered (he described him as grown older and stooped at the shoulders), and the Duke responded, 'I am seriously thinking of giving up the whole affair and going into a quiet retreat in California!'.[56] MacIver believed that Kemball was thought to lack decisiveness with the crofters.[57]

There was further turmoil in the management in 1886. Partly it related to tension between the Duke of Sutherland and his eldest son, Lord Stafford. Partly too it related to the resignation of Kemball which, once announced, was regretted by some of the under factors. MacIver confided in Gunn that 'if Sir A's successor be disagreeable, or wishes a different policy carried out, my retirement at once would follow'.[58] The new man was R.M. Brereton, 38 years old, son of a Norfolk squire, an engineer who had worked in Norfolk, India and America, and a man who had been strongly recommended by Lord Walsingham: 'He enters into troubled waters and a complicated state of matters and will require prudence and talent to guide him—of Scotch business he can know very little'.[59]

At the start Brereton seemed the perfect professional, all energy and attention to detail and planning. His firmness of purpose was initially contrasted with 'the Duke's passive easy temperament'. Brereton wanted to clean the slate so far as the crofters were concerned, and was open and candid with the local factors even to the point of discussing his own liberal political inclinations. The crofters would have to be treated 'kindly and generously', but should be required firmly to pay reasonable rents without the accumulation of irrecoverable arrears.[60] He was full of energy and ideas, wrote to newspapers and addressed the Golspie Literary Association. Brereton believed that the answer to the Highland problem was sea fishing along the model offered by the well-fostered industries of Norway and Sweden. His opinions were vigorously stated, and his demands for closely-balanced books insistent. Within a matter of months he came into conflict with most of the management structure beneath him and also with Lord Stafford. A rupture became inevitable and Brereton left the management in 1888 amid great recriminations. Brereton wrote a damaging pamphlet critical of the Sutherland estate and threatening legal action. Lord Stafford told his father in June 1889 that Brereton had

> wound up his commissionership by bringing a charge against you, which makes one pity the man ... he is possessed of great cunning and might make use of any writing if he got a chance ... God save us from such men is all we can pray. The very word 'commissioner' has been abused and if you get another, call him 'general manager'.[61]

The resolution of the managerial crisis was the adoption of a complicated committee structure suggested by Lord Stafford himself in 1888 and modelled on the management systems employed by some of the larger railway companies. It would be headed by a Committee of General Management comprising the Duke of Sutherland as chairman, his sons and the principal factors of the estates (including Gunn from Cromartie). They would report to a Finance Committee with plans and estimates for each year, for scrutiny by financial advisors to give co-ordination to the entire system of estate management.[62]

The new system operated for a relatively short time until the death of the Duchess of Sutherland. At that point, in November 1888, the Cromartie estate became, once more, a separate enterprise in the hands first of the young Earl of Cromartie, and then, in 1892, of the even younger Countess of Cromartie. Conflicts in the Sutherland family and the excruciatingly embarrassing dispute over the will of the third Duke in 1892-3,[63] dislocated the lives of management. Gunn found himself dealing with a quick succession of owners and trustees through the 1890s, while conducting the most important business through legal representatives, A.D.M. Black, in Edinburgh. Black and Gunn built up a close rapport—the one going deaf, the other suffering failing eyesight—and watched while the crofter problem stabilised and while the Sutherland family sorted out its internal disputes. In the late 1890s the finances of the estate began to improve and there were signs of optimism. In 1902 Gunn at last retired and the management of Cromartie was assumed by the Countess' husband, Major Blunt, and the new factor, George Wotherspoon.[64]

IV

In the last quarter of the nineteenth century the life of Highland estate agents had been overshadowed by the crisis in crofting management. William Gunn had warned newly-appointed Kemball in June 1880 that the management of the crofting population was the most demanding part of a factor's work.[65] It was not surprising that, as a class, the factors began to feel embattled: during the period of the politicisation of the crofters the agents became a prime target upon whom was released the accumulated anger of the generations. The factors were precisely placed to absorb such antagonism, an accepted part of their managerial function. Gunn found himself defending not only his own actions but those of his predecessors in the Cromartie estate office. In December 1886 Gunn warned the Duchess of Sutherland of the power of radicals and land leaguers in Ross-shire, armed with 'their newly acquired power'. He elaborated on his own position: 'The duties of a Factor, at all times onerous and often difficult, are likely [to be] an easy prey to agitators who have their own selfish ends in view, and not the good of the people'. Now, he said, there was even greater need for a factor to exercise 'prudence and discriminating judgement'.[66] Agitators, he said, 'delight in being obnoxious and disagreeable'.[67]

Gunn, who knew the Highlands intimately,[68] was unquestionably soured by the radicalisation of the crofters. Part of his response was emotional, but he also argued a broader case, that the condition of the crofters, especially in Coigach, had much improved in living memory, and that they had been well treated by their landlords. In a letter written to Lord Stafford in June 1885, Gunn stated his opinion with obvious forethought:

> It is perfectly true, as your Lordship states, that in olden times prior to the clearances, hardships quite unknown in our day had to be endured by these people. My father was a native of Kildonan, my grandfather rented a comfortable extent of grazing in that locality. My mother on the other hand was English—so that altho a native of Sutherland and naturally feel deeply interested in the welfare of the people, I'm not in the least prejudiced one way or the other ... I well remember my father telling me, as a boy, that in his young days, altho' they had plenty of stock they were sometimes reduced to great straights [sic] for want of food. On one occasion, during a severe protracted winter storm, they were known to have been reduced to the necessity of bleeding the cattle and utilising the blood for food. Meal was often very scarce, and more than double the present price.

Gunn said that the wages of common labourers had doubled in the past 20 years and that they were undoubtedly better off: 'While the few luxuries they possess could not be grudged to them, as their lot at best is one of constant toil, yet it must be admitted that many of them are less provident than of old'. He was prepared to advocate greater pasture land for them but there was little scope for extra arable cultivation. The main solution to Highland poverty was a far greater attention to fishing and the extension of railways north into the Highlands.[69]

Gunn insisted that, in 20 years, he had always treated the people 'with kindly consideration but also with firmness'. Under alien influences the people had become loathsomely ungrateful and now distrusted the proprietors and their agents, and 'claim an equal, yea a better right to the land than its rightful owner'.[70] The crofters, of course, disagreed. So also did Sir Arnold Kemball. Kemball's interpretation of the current events, *vis à vis* Gunn's administration of Coigach and the crofting population was a fresh and even discordant note in the landlord's version of events. He agreed that the crofters were behaving illegally in withholding their rents. But he then suggested that the Cromartie estate had probably helped to give fuel to the crofters' case:

> ... the fact remains that when the rents were raised their pastoral privileges were impaired, and if the above limitations of Proprietory rights furnished a motive in Parliament for the appointment of a Royal Commission we should not be deemed the best judges of our own case, nor would it be prudent to expose ourselves to the imputation of straining our own rights in respect to the very grievance, however ill founded, which was held to justify this measure.

Kemball of course abhorred the riotous behaviour of crofters (especially those in Skye) but was not prepared to reject every element in the crofters' case. Nor was he keen to see 'the same excitement and embarrassment which attended similar events in Skye' replicated in Coigach or Scourie.[71]

The experience of factorship on both the Cromartie and Sutherland estates appeared to make the men-on-the-spot more conservative than their superiors. The west coast factors were the true guardians of the status quo and the men least likely to shift their ground. They were most intransigent on questions of crofter rights often finding themselves left behind by the more flexible, more wavering, and more temporising attitude of the Commissioners and their aristocratic masters. Sometimes there was a note of desperation, or at least, of exasperation sounded from Stafford House or Dunrobin—as when the Duke of Sutherland threatened to leave for California or, as in 1896, to divide up his Sutherland empire and auction it off to the highest bidders. Lord Stafford was no less disconcerting, offering himself as a Parliamentary candidate to promote the crofters' interests. In such a topsy-turvy world the agent had great difficulty learning new attitudes; when the changes affected political allegiances the difficulties were multiplied.

V

Exerting varying degrees and varying forms of political persuasion was an expected part of an estate factor's responsibilities. It was always a sensitive and often a covert business; sometimes there were ambiguities in the meaning of the landlord's wishes and the extent to which influence should be wielded by the factors. The coming of Reform (and changes of ownership) tended to compound such ambiguities and render the factor's role the more awkward to fulfil.

Certainly the Cromartie family had always possessed some political leverage in that votes were in their gift.[72] In the 1820s much of their local influence was simply sold off to raise revenue.[73] But this did not terminate the family's capacity to persuade tenants on its own estate, nor did the Reform Bill necessarily diminish such influence. In 1832 Hay-Mackenzie was solicited for his support by the Tory candidate (Novar) for Ross and Cromarty and responded by requesting his tenantry 'to support that side of politics which is favourable not only to the agricultural interests of the country but to the good order and well being of the State'.[74] The precise degree of control applied by the landlord is unclear.

Correspondence between Lady Stafford and her advisors in 1852 undoubtedly contained the assumption that political control over voters on the Cromartie estate was possible if the proprietor wished to exert such power. James Loch, himself one of the minor architects of the Reform Bill, defined the current orthodoxy in the Sutherland regime in a letter to Lady Stafford:

> I have always thought that what a Landlord should do, on such occasions, is simply to express his own opinions and wishes, and in most instances, where a good feeling exists between him and his tenants, the bulk of them will adopt the course most agreeable to him. If any of them shall take a different line it is the Landlord's duty and it is in his interest to regard their conduct as proceeding from honest and conscientious motives.[75]

The problem in 1852 was that Lady Stafford (now in the Sutherland camp) had shifted her political allegiances[76] to the Liberal candidate against the consistent Conservatism which the Cromartie tenantry had expected of her father. The farmers were generally protectionist, the Sutherlands free traders. It would not be reasonable to persuade them to change their own loyalties overnight and Loch recommended a quiet statement of the proprietor's new position. This however left the factor Scott, and the Liberal candidate, Sir James Matheson, in an awkward position so far as canvassing on the estate was concerned. Scott himself was told to vote for Matheson or else abstain. Lady Stafford told Matheson that 'though we do not feel it right to dictate to the Tenants you have our best wishes for your success'. Matheson said he was glad that the tenantry realise that 'they are free to vote as they feel inclined, and that their voting for me will by no means be taken amiss in the quarter they naturally look up to'. Scott declared that he had 'withdrawn from politics altogether since the accession of her Ladyship and also from the Easter Ross Farmers Society' and was no longer in their 'councils'. He also reported the cynicism of the tenantry—if he canvassed them 'the first question they would ask me would be—what reduction of rent is the Marchioness to give us if we support Free Trade or even remain neutral?' He thought that type of bargain was far from her Ladyship's mind.[77]

As the electorate was widened in the later nineteenth century, and as new modes of democracy were introduced, so too did a growing sense of popular independence exhibit itself before the very eyes of the estate management. The first serious signal of the new political realities entailed in crofter solidarity were the parochial School Board elections in the spring of 1873.[78] Here, in the full glare of publicity, the estate representatives were openly rejected by the electors on their own estate. The 1873 elections demonstrated for the first time the potential strength of concerted crofter opposition. The election was the first flexing of the muscles of a stratum of society which had long been understood to be constitutionally apolitical and passive.[79]

The voice of the crofter, inside the ballot box and outside, became louder in the 1880s, and vastly better organised. Crofter radicalism across much of the north cut a swathe through the orthodox political alignments. Before long political candidates (for local, county and national elections) from within the landlord ranks began to vie for crofters' support. It was part of the social revolution of the 1880s and was fully visible from the windows of the factor's office on the Cromartie estate.

In 1880 a landowner could still expect to draw upon reserves of loyalty from much of the electorate, voting for candidates drawn from a narrow band of upper class society. It was still important to make a proprietor's favour clear as the Duchess of Sutherland did in March 1880. She sent Gunn a telegram from Torquay: 'Have just heard from Duke thoroughly approving of my support of Conservative Association let tenantry know'.[80] Shifts of family support between the Tories and the Liberals caused the agents to inspect inwardly their own affiliations and Gunn ('a staunch liberal') and Mackenzie found themselves also shifting.[81]

Four years later the polarisation of the Highland world had reached its greatest pitch. Once more the Duchess believed that she still possessed traditional influence: she asked Gunn to 'use all possible interest with my tenantry to induce them to vote for young Mr Mackenzie of Kintail, and tell them he has my best wishes, and tell them they will follow the tradition of our house in giving him their support'. But she conceded that 'my personal influence ... is not of the value it used to be'. Kintail faced an opponent, Novar, who, according to Gunn 'in his eagerness to catch the crofters has made most rash and extravagant promises' which had offended moderate people. Gunn reported back to the Duchess that the tenants at Tarbat had expressed willingness to support Kintail but 'It does not do to count absolutely on promises made at such a time when so many influences are at work, nor does it do to bring undue pressure to bear'.[82]

The election campaign in August 1884 heightened the tensions. Some of the sporting tenants came to the aid of Kintail—Alexander Ross reported that 'Braemore's yacht was at the service of the Coigach voters', and 'sumptuous political repasts' were provided by party organisers. But Ross also explained that Land Law Reform and the crofters' revolt were the dominating issues in public debate which was also notable for 'the defiant tone of the people'.[83] The result was a defeat for Kintail. The Duchess of Sutherland took comfort in the fact that the vote from Coigach was not entirely adverse.[84] Yet the tide was clearly running away from the landlord interest and this was also demonstrated at the School Board Elections in Coigach in the Spring of 1885. Ross said that 'The tone in Coigach is very raw ... I have not approached the hot radicals'.[85] Meanwhile some established interests were moving towards the radical position themselves—Evander MacIver now indeed described Lord Stafford as a 'radical' and 'very soft on the Crofter subject'.[86] In the General Election late in 1885 the crofters triumphed and four of their own candidates were elected. MacIver (and other estate officials) exploded with disgust—democracy itself was a farce: 'The intelligence and respectability of these counties are not represented—a man who pays ten shilling a year has the same power in voting for a M.P. as a Proprietor with an income of thousands or a tenant paying £1000 a year'. He blamed Lord Stafford for opening a door 'that will give much trouble vexation and expense also for many a year to come for himself and to all who may act for him or his father'.[87]

In 1886—a critical year for legislation and elections affecting the crofters—their political power strengthened further. William Gunn in December summed up the consequences of another electoral defeat in letters to the Duke of Sutherland. The defeat of Novar was 'another and unmistakeable proof of the folly of putting the franchise so low'. The success of the crofters would render them more unmanageable than ever: 'I fear Ross-shire is now much in the power of land leaguers and radicals ... this class, conscious of their newly acquired power, will probably exhibit a more defiant attitude for some time to come'.[88]

The dawn of democracy in the Highlands had been an abrupt awakening for the landed interests. Democracy itself was the cause of anarchic tendencies, according to Alexander Ross: 'I cannot think of anything that will put a stop to this shameful state of things but a gradation of votes according to rental and a reforming of the ballot Act to the effect'.[89] Two years later Gunn told the Duchess of Sutherland that conservative politics had little future in Ross-shire; the lowering of the franchise had put the lower classes, 'the majority of whom are Radical', in a position to swamp their betters; the results of the last two elections 'shows how utterly hopeless it is to fight against such numbers'.[90]

Perhaps the most extraordinary aspect of the political revolution in the Highlands was the tardiness of the established interests in girding their forces to defend themselves. It was only very late in the piece that landowner associations were formed to repel the assault on their property and political power. The Cromartie family indeed joined such bodies—for instance the Earl of Cromartie was a member of the Highland Property Association, and there was growing collusion in the landlord camp. But the horses had already bolted. The crofters and the land leaguers were far better orchestrated and continued to inflict overwhelming electoral defeats. In 1890 the young Lord Cromartie was himself defeated—a '*scandalum magnatum*' according to one advisor who said it was a pity that Cromartie 'did not come up personally to look after his own interests'.[91] In 1892 Cromartie was further disgusted by the county results saying that the electorate 'must be cracked. Hope they will swallow their new member and choke themselves'.[92]

The elections of the 1880s and early 1890s demonstrated the essential impotence of the old political interests in the new context. The common people were now offered genuine political choice—at an election canvass in 1889 Gunn remarked that 'Being able to go among the people and talk to them in their native language gives the other candidates a strong pull'. He also suggested that the tenantry responded best to candidates who supported progressive legislation for the crofters' interest.[93] But the real key to the new politics of the Highlands was the ballot box itself. As Gunn put the point to Cromartie in November 1889, many of the householders, ploughmen and farm labourers (he was referring to Kilmuir Parish) now had the vote and they were almost all land leaguers: 'And I am sorry to say, are not to be trusted in a matter of this kind—now that they have the protection of the ballot'.[94] For Gunn and his fellow factors the loss of political authority was the obvious counterpart of a more general decline in power of proprietors and their managers in the late nineteenth century Highlands.

Appendix: a month in the life of a factor, August 1882

The range, diversity, detail and sheer labour involved in a factorship such as Cromartie can be conveyed only in the day to day operations of the agency office. August 1882 was a typical month in the late Highland summer during which William Gunn dealt with more than 110 items of business correspondence.[95] Fencing at Polnicol Farm had to be paid for; the tenancy of the Ben More shootings had been taken in hand and a temporary substitute organised; the tenant of Meddat paid his half year rent and commented on the late harvest; from Langwell via Ullapool a shipment of wool by steamer was arranged together with the purchase of lambs. Leases and kennels for the Garbat Shootings were arranged as well as preparations for a visit to Tarbat by the Duchess of Sutherland who had to be warned that a fever had broken out in the district. Subscriptions were paid. An annuitant in Inverness complained of his plight: 'children almost dieing for want of food and myself and their mother no better ... Banished into a nasty dirty hole like this without a friend or acquaintance' after having served His Grace for twenty years.

Gardeners were employed, visitors catered for, dipping materials sent to Inverpolly, and Dr Manson's views about sherry considered. Rent reductions on other estates were confidentially assessed. The wine account of Ben Wyvis Hotel was paid, and, most testingly, the accommodation on the shootings inspected. Tile pipes were despatched to Tarbat and tourist fares for Strathpeffer negotiated with the Highland Railway Company. Sir Arnold Kemball sent a telegram regarding his accommodation. Insurance policies were paid; Rhiddorach Lodge was set in good condition—beds aired, fires lit, lamps provided. School inspections and bids for farms were dealt with, a bothy provided, fishing questions clarified and an invitation to the annual Dingwall Hospital meeting accepted.

At Achiltibuie there were internecine disputes about trespassing cattle, and wire fencing was ordered to settle interminable marches problems. A pauper from Badentarbat was sent to the Northern Infirmary, suffering 'the effects of poverty' but really wanted to go to the Wells at Strathpeffer. In this case Gunn was asked to 'kindly see any usual favours accorded to the poor extended to him. He has a large young family.' Spa water analyses were ordered and the danger of competition from Croft as a rival spa were considered. Strathpeffer Hotel was leased for a period to 1930; a retired grieve requested a £10 annuity; the problem of getting from Ullapool to the shooting moors was raised; Lord and Lady Tarbat arrived at Coigach for a brief visit and the piano at Ben Wyvis Hotel required repairs. One tenant was tardy with his rent: 'Morrison is supposed to be a Millionaire but if so it is very difficult to get a penny out of his hands'. The lessee of salmon fishing on Coigach complained that his rent was impossibly high.

Small tenants were accused of trespassing on Langwell Farm; negotiations about the costs of fences proved difficult; sheep farms on hand required lambs; cement was ordered for bridge work; the new season's sport was declared poor by an indignant sportsman; an 83-years-old man in Strathpeffer pleaded for a house, having just been evicted. A troublesome client at the Spa wanted a reading room established. Cattle were damaging the pheasant shelters at Castle Leod, and the Duke insisted that vermin be kept down, and a thorough record of all game taken to be drawn up each year. (Sports statistics were better than social statistics by this time.) Sheep from Inverpolly were loaded at Garve Railway Station. Lord and Lady Tarbat announced that they would now stay at Rhiddoroch for a fortnight thereby requiring four servants, linen, plate, wine, coals, peats and a cook and housemaid. A well at Strathpeffer dried up and an informant at Invergordon alleged that local fishermen were raiding and destroying oyster beds in the Firth.

All this was in the estate correspondence of August 1882. Other business would have been conducted more directly. The first typed letter in the Cromartie Papers was dated 24 October 1887.

CHAPTER 25

The Tenantry 1830-1914

I

The functions and obligations of a landed estate were manifold. In the nineteenth century they were indeed diversifying further, creating new demands and tensions in the community. Large estates, like Cromartie, were very considerable business enterprises in their own right, and they required an increasingly elaborate structure of management and capital investment. They were basic elements in the national economy responding to the pressures and incentives of the greater national and international markets. But the great estate had always been, and was still, much more than this. The landed estate remained a form of social structure, a type of community which owed much to inherited standards of behaviour as well as to the changes induced by political, economic and social currents at work since 1750. The estate remained a source of status, of political and social influence, of power and social authority, of leadership and of the continuity of communal modes of behaviour. At the top its hereditary owners expected to maintain their 'port', a certain role and living standard, amongst their peers both locally and nationally. At the bottom the labouring population expected to extract a living from the land and the sea, sufficient to keep body and soul together, sufficient also to provide for new dependents, possibly too eventually to escape the estate.

But rural life had become more complicated, cumulatively so since the early eighteenth century. Cromartie, like so many other parts of the Highlands, had become drawn into the wider, more productive and more voracious economy of the south. The estate economy invariably traded surpluses with the outside world, yielding goods and services in exchange for imported requirements, necessities and extra items of consumption. The old rural economy had led the way with long distance cattle and grain exports; by the nineteenth century its exports had diversified and so too had its appetite for imports. Even the common dress of the people offered vivid evidence of such changing consumption patterns. Altogether these pressures and opportunities emerged to cause the estate to produce more for the world, and also for itself since there was a still more elemental force at work. The population of the estate continued to mount even beyond 1851 in most parts. Thus the estate economy was required to absorb these larger demands which, necessarily, generated tensions in all parts of the farming life. To a large degree such tensions reflected the age-old but now renewed pressure on the finite landed resources of the estate.

Rent was a crude measure both of the productivity of the land and of the distribution of resources and income within the community. It was not a perfect measure because it was derived from an imperfect market in which social expectations and inertia prevented the complete maximisation of returns. The riots of 1852/3 in Coigach represented one effective form of constraint on the landlord. The landowner's own propensities also reduced rental potential at times—not merely through a fear of communal outrage but also by considerations of aesthetics, of personal comfort, of political influence, of indolence, and of posterity. Least affected by extraneous influences were the great capitalist sheepfarmers but even their pursuit of profits was sometimes compromised by matters of status and social aspiration. The common people had less options but, increasingly, they might simply walk out of the estate and opt for a different world altogether. It was a society marked by both fluidity and immobility. On the Cromartie estate, in the late nineteenth century there was great oscillation of fortune in all sectors of the estate life; by 1914 new social and economic rules were being imposed but a permanent balance had not yet been achieved. The main oscillations were recorded crudely in the estate rentals.

II

The gross rental income on the Cromartie estate in the nineteenth century shows several broad trends—the steep rise which continued from about 1780 to almost 1820, a sagging plateau to about 1850, a rise by 1880 and then a slightly falling total to 1914. In broad terms these movements were consistent with the general national tendencies in British agricultural income. The periods of relatively poor, sometimes falling income,[1] coincided with the financial difficulties of John Hay-Mackenzie and his daughter in the 1830s and '40s, and also the problems faced by the Cromartie estate toward the end of the century. Nevertheless the general shape of the aggregate rental income obscures great variation and change within the general trends. The broad movements in the rents were, in reality, the product of highly variable components some of which moved in opposing directions.

These complications, in part, were of course a reflection of the diverse conditions across the Cromartie estate, the wide spectrum of farming life in northern Scotland. The rent graphs[2] of the three baronies, Coigach, Strathpeffer and New Tarbat, reflect the contrast between extreme Highland conditions in the west and the advanced arable culture of the east coast. In the centre Strathpeffer showed the mixture of the two, but increasingly influenced by the development of the Spa in its midst. The Coigach rental showed the greatest growth and instability, Tarbat being relatively much more consistent over the long run.

Within each rental there were contributing elements in differing proportions. The small tenants were numerous in Coigach and Strathpeffer but far less evident at New Tarbat. The great sheep farmers paid big rents in the west and the centre, but not so in the east. Sporting rents became important in Coigach by the 1840s. At New Tarbat, and to a lesser extent at Strathpeffer, the great arable farmers remained the greatest rent payers.

Ideally a series of rentals over a long period of time might yield key information about the distribution of land, the differential growth of rent and income, and other central elements in the agrarian economy. Some of the quasi-political questions thrust before the Napier Commission in 1882/3 might be answered—such as the extent to which the crofters had been marginalised and exploited. It should be possible to detect the shifting balance of agricultural impact and the economic status of the contributing components in estate life. The bare bones of the rural economy should be visible in a good run of estate rentals.

In reality, in terms of detailed rentals of the Cromartie estate management, the official memory extended no further back than about 1830 from which time reasonably systematic rental records were maintained. Their records were significant in that they showed that there had been a general regularisation of small holdings (especially in Coigach but also elsewhere) in the 1820s and early 1830s. Their own evidence demonstrated that many of the townships were 'lotted out' at that time, presumably defined more carefully and, in some cases, made direct tenants to the landlord. A survey prepared in 1884 carefully charted the chronology. Thus the township of Altandhu was lotted out in 1831 to 17 tenants at £39.10.0 p.a. (in 1884 there were 15 tenants paying £52.1.0), but the rent had been reduced to £33.18.0 in 1833 at which level it remained until the 1879 revaluation. Camuscoil had the same history; Polbain was lotted in 1848, Culnacraig in 1829, Reiff in 1831, Isle Martin in 1831, Achindrean in 1828, Isle Tanera 1846, Polglass in 1829, Keanachrine in 1825. In some the number of crofters had declined, but some crofters possessed more than one croft. Mostly it was a chronicle of remarkable stability of both occupation and rent levels in which exactions remained static until the late 1870s, and subsequently showed recurrent abatements.[3]

This stability tended to argue against the loud complaints of the crofters in the 1870s and 1880s that there was a time when they had possessed great reserves of land and paid lower rents. Their collective memory, it seems likely, therefore referred to the time before the regularisation of the lots, before about 1825. Although the matter is not well documented most of the evidence suggests that between 1800 and 1825 large sheep farms (as well as the great arable farms) were carved out of the old system.[4] The process was achieved peacefully and gradually and for many years the old and the new either co-existed or merged almost imperceptibly. Some of the old leaseholders, the tacksmen, were involved in the switch to sheepfarming while retaining much of the old cattle-rearing sector within the tack. But, inexorably, the great farms emerged and, inevitably, some of the small tenants were marginalised eventually in lots with increasingly prescribed and restricted territories. The resistance of the Coigach rioters in 1852/3 was the last and least typical act in a much longer transformation. Hence the indignant recollection of former rights of pasture voiced by the crofters in 1882 referred to a vague and distant time for which neither they nor the Cromartie managers had any clear evidence. It was intrinsically a difficult proposition to verify.

The Cromartie rentals are generally in good order, providing an almost complete run, for the period from 1833 to 1914. But there are several critical difficulties obstructing total clarity. For instance the rentals do not indicate the areas and qualities of land held by individual tenants. This is particularly true in the 1830s (and indeed into the 1850s) when many crofters were still subtenants to tacksmen. Labour services and payment-in-kind were still being extracted in some places in the 1850s. Within the subtenancy arrangements it is impossible to determine the rent paid by the crofters and cottars since the final rent was paid only by the tacksman: it may however be assumed that he paid the landlord less than he received from the people in order to extract a net profit. The abolition of subtenancy radically altered the rental base and renders comparison over time difficult. The composition of the rents also changes over the long run. For example, kelp was virtually eliminated, fishing from Ullapool declined, the Spa emerged, sheep farms were converted wholly or partially into shooting properties, farms were amalgamated or broken up, and so on. Even more confusing were some of the accounting procedures of the estate: rents were not invariably collected on a strict annual basis; arrears were allowed to accumulate and then unsystematically liquidated or forgiven; some rents were raised or reduced while other tenants were allowed special arrangements for cropping or improvements. Various pieces of land were sold during these decades, thereby also shifting the basis for comparison. In the last decades of the century many sheep farms were unlettable and were operated directly by the estate. And rental income, of course, was simply a gross figure which held meaning in relation to the costs of running the estate and also maintaining the proprietor and servicing her or his debts. Consequently rental data becomes a series of thickets to frustrate the interpretation of the broad trends.

Nevertheless some cross-sections of the estate economy are possible. In the early 1830s the total nominal rents amounted to about £6500. Arrears were mounting through these years until, by 1836, practically an entire year's rent was overdue, much of which became irrecoverable. The expenses of the estate included many minor payments but the main categories were clear. Management costs in 1836 were £348, remittance to Trustees (in debt payment) and to Hay-Mackenzie £2739, Parochial and Public Burdens £1482, annuities and interest £338. These figures encompassed an elaborate structure of dependence on the Cromartie rental income: it included items such as ministers' stipends, schoolmasters' salaries, repairs to manses, whisky for peat drivers, payments to the Sheriff, Crown and Bishop's Rents, money for the ratcatcher, payments for the delivery of meal from MacDuff (probably for famine relief on the West coast), and dozens of other small and large outgoings. It was an accountant's nightmare and so convoluted were the accounts that it was difficult exactly to see how much of the income eventually dropped into Hay-Mackenzie's own pocket. It may also help explain the embarrassment into which his finances fell in the 1840s.

By the 1830s the structure of tenancy had already taken much of its modern shape, notably the sharp contrast between the few relatively large tenants and the wide base of very small holders, increasingly termed 'crofters'. At Strathpeffer, for instance, there were 155 tenants; the two largest paid £430 and £570 each per year; six tenants paid more than £100 per annum but 98 paid less than £5, representing the crofters on the Heights. At New Tarbat out of 175 tenants, four paid more than £100 p.a. and the great majority less than £5 p.a., many of them less than one pound per year, some still in victuals. The great arable and stock farmers—at, for example, Meddat, Polnicol, Fodderty, Keppoch, Inchvannie, Kinnetas—had emerged over the previous half century, part of what a Royal Commission in 1895 described as 'the great aggregation of farms under single farmers', and also 'altogether undesirable'. The Cromartie management thought otherwise—the great farmers paid an increasing proportion of the total rent and rarely defaulted. Extracting rent from hundreds of crofters was vastly more difficult and troublesome. The large farmers were on leases and the small tenants were at will, on yearly arrangements. The pattern of landholding was now relatively stable and Andrew Scott regularised rents early in the 1830s. Access to grazing, always a contentious issue, was subject to continuing piecemeal alterations which are difficult to trace. In 1834 for instance four small tenants on the Strathpeffer Heights held grazings but were falling into rent arrears; it then was let to one individual for four years and then to James Scott of Hawick who held it until 1861.[5] On the whole the changes seem to have been marginal after 1830 though there was more mobility amongst the larger tenants—and the number of southerners, including Scott, suggests a continuing northward colonisation by men of capital and agricultural skill.

In the west, at Coigach, the disposition of land was less clear because few small tenants are mentioned directly in the rental. The great sheep farmers, such as James Mitchell at Inverpolly paying £280 p.a., and Walker and Mundell at Rhiddorrach, paying £180, certainly predominated. But much of the land was still in the hands of tacksmen who sublet to small crofters and cottars. These 'lotters' amounted to a population estimated to be 1500 in 1837, paying a rent of about £750[6] which, if correct, represented only a quarter of the Coigach rent. The Cromartie estate eventually sought to eliminate the subletting system but it was a mixed blessing. A tacksman, of course, instead of the estate managers, shouldered the responsibility of collecting the rents. On the other hand it was a system which diminished the estate's control over the land, especially the increasingly valuable grazings, and gave the tacksmen the opportunity to exploit and intimidate the subtenants virtually without restraint.

Subletting was eventually terminated in the early 1850s: at Badenscallie and Achiltibuie a lease or tack had been held by William and Alexander Mackenzie over 82 small tenants for a rent of £320. In 1853 the lease expired and the small tenants were made direct tenants at will, apparently paying £374. The landlord had tried to resettle the people at the end of the lease but was successfully resisted by popular force (see above, Chapter 17). The new rent, it was claimed, represented a diminution in the amount extracted from the people by the previous tacksmen. Gunn claimed, as a general rule, that the tacksmen had 'overcharged them in rent and kind' and that when they became direct tenants their money rents increased marginally but their labour services diminished more so, thus representing a decline in real rent. Gunn and his predecessors regarded the eradication of subtenancy (finally defeated in Achnahaird in 1860) as the last gasp of feudalism in the Highlands.[7]

While the sheepfarmers' proportion of the rent continued to expand, the capacity of the small tenants shrank. Kelp in particular had virtually ceased to pay.[8]

The collapse of kelp rent also implied a collapse in wages from labour in the industry; similarly the failure of Ullapool to generate a local fishing industry also restricted income possibilities at Coigach.[9] Consequently the small tenants were constrained by their relatively slender command of economic resources. Their arable patches produced potatoes but the crop was unreliable; the small tenants' stock numbers were restricted by their reduced grazing capacity and their own lack of capital and expertise; cattle prices were generally poor. Consequently they sought employment in the Caithness fishing or in seasonal labour in the south. The accumulating growth of their own numbers gave their economic predicament greater urgency. It was well reflected in their contribution to the rent: they paid irregularly and in diminishing proportion to the total; increasingly they depended on external income to pay the rent; and, worse still, they fell into debt and destitution when their crops were poor or diseased, as in 1836/7 and 1847/8, and again, less severely, at intervals until the end of the century.[10]

The concentration of rental income emerged even more clearly by 1860 during a time when, in contradiction to all forecasts, agricultural incomes had increased powerfully for all sectors. Now, however, grazing, sporting and arable rents moved forward much more rapidly than small rents which became increasingly marginal and pestiferous for the general income-generation of the estate. This, after all, had been the logic of tenurial change over the previous century. At Coigach 13 large tenants paid £2615 out of a total of £3504, the rest paid by 252 small tenants; at Strathpeffer nine big occupiers paid £2012 out of £3133, and at New Tarbat four men paid £1021 out of £1988. The process continued, reinforced by the emergence of large shooting leases (see next section), the buoyancy of both arable and pastoral rents, and the remarkable stability of small rents. For, while the big farms yielded increasing rents, the rents paid by the crofters remained virtually static over several decades.

The disparity between large and small tenants' contributions to the Cromartie rental was at its greatest in years of crop failure or poor fishing. One such year was 1861 when there was much distress among the Coigach crofters. The pathos of crofter poverty sometimes shone through estate correspondence—in, for instance, the letter of two tenants from Badenscallie township who, in the spring of 1861, simply could not pay their rent and offered to relinquish one third of their croft by way of compensation to the landlord. The estate occasionally removed some individual tenants in arrear. In choosing the cases to be acted against, Mackenzie came across great inequalities among the crofting people, especially in their stock holdings which were really the best measure of their assets. Some of the people were in debt to local merchants usually for meal, some had large families to support and travelled great distances out of the district to find work. One man in arrears, an epileptic, 'a sickly man with a weak family ... and not very sane', possessed three cattle and no sheep, nor any cash to pay his rent, 'but willing to give Cattle'. Catherine Ross, aged 60, had left the district, leaving her son in charge of the lot and four children: 'has nothing but one cow, says he has not two weeks' food in the house'. These people were treated with leniency, but a 'sturdy able bodied man' who showed little inclination to pay his arrears was shown short shrift.[11] There were no large scale evictions but intermittent removals of this kind were common on the Cromartie estate.

The management of the small tenants was always a headache for the estate agents. Andrew Scott exclaimed in 1858: 'There is no end of trouble and annoyance these people give, at one time by building Houses and dividing their Lots, at another by raising disputes about marches'. The estate tried to impose regulations on the crofters, especially relating to subletting and subdividing, and the use of common pasturage. It was uphill work. At the same time the management was called on to settle internecine disputes within the crofting townships. Sometimes the people supported ejectments of fellow crofters—as for instance in the case of two well-known whisky sellers in Auchindrain in 1858—Scott reported that no sympathy was shown by the neighbours and no opposition was stirred: 'They are both ... held to be dishonest bad characters, which may account for the neighbours giving no countenance to them in the hour of their distress'. Scott's report implied that collective opposition was a matter to be expected in such episodes.[12]

The general policy towards the crofters was governed by the disinclination of the proprietor to generate ill-will among the people, and by their diminishing significance in the total income of the estate. The events at Coigach in 1852/3 continued to shadow attitudes, and the main problems arose where the crofters hindered the maximisation of grazing and sporting rents. Nevertheless there were recurrent initiatives to raise crofting rents in line with rising agricultural prices and general rent levels. In 1858 Andrew Scott pointed out to George Loch that the tenants on the Braes of Strathpeffer had been 'undisturbed' in their rents since 1836. The same seems to have been true in all three baronies and may be traced in the payments of the very long-lived tenants. For example, Widow Campbell of Ardmair had paid £3.2.0. in 1835 and the same amount in 1872. The initiatives to raise rents were repeatedly suspended until 1879 when the estate at last resurveyed the entire range of crofter rents and imposed increases. Some of the increases were, after almost half a century, very small. Widow Campbell was now required to pay £3.6.0. Other increases were greater. Roderick Matheson of Achiltibuie had paid £11.15.0. per annum but now had to pay £20. John McLeod, the fiddler on Lot 29, had paid £3.6.0. since 1853, but now paid £4.7.0., and was asked to pay poor rates too.

The rent increases of 1879-80 were mis-timed (see above, Chapter 21). They coincided with a radical deterioration in agricultural prices across the northern economy. More ominously still, they occurred at the moment when crofter agitation was erupting in the Highlands.[13]

III

During the optimistic years of the 1850s and 1860s, before the sharp falls in agricultural prices, farmers had been tempted to over-capitalise their farms and to contract leases which squeezed profits to narrow margins. These people were the first to feel the pinch as conditions for commercial agriculture worsened in the early 1870s.[14] In 1871 Robertson, a large sheepfarmer at Garbat, pleaded with the Cromartie estate to reduce his rent from £230 to £200, and William Gunn told the Duke of Sutherland that Robertson was undoubtedly losing money: 'I have always heard that the rent he now pays is beyond its value.' The estate resisted the full extent of the request and other complainants were given no relief. For instance when Henderson gave up his lease at the Polnicol Farm in 1873, potential applicants were told that the Duke was 'not inclined to accept from any one a smaller rent than is at present paid for the farm. He would prefer doing such important works of draining or other improvements as would bring it in value to the rent now paid.'[15] The estate indeed consistently delayed the reduction of rents for as long as possible, minimising concessions at all costs.

An estate, however, could not insulate itself from the rent policies of contiguous landowners and by 1880 few landowners could resist the collective and individual pressure of the large tenant farmers. A series of bad seasons at the end of the 1870s had exacerbated the crisis in the northern agrarian economy. Eventually both the sheepfarmers and the arable producers were begging for relief.

Some of the best informed observers were unanimous that sheepfarming profits had deteriorated severely over the years 1870 to 1880. Partly the crisis was a consequence of the collapse of wool prices, partly it was also derived from worsening returns especially on the great west coast sheep farms. Evander MacIver told Gunn in May 1880 that tenants were experiencing great difficulty: 'There is no doubt there have been serious losses during the last three or four years'. The weaker tenants were about to go to the wall. Sheep rents indeed were soon reduced by a quarter but it was clearly not enough. For instance the tenant of Langwell Farm gave up his lease despite the rent reduction though he emphasised that the 'encroachments' of the small tenants had also contributed to his defection. Even worse was the discovery that vacant sheep farms were being advertised at much reduced rents and yet produced no response. MacIver exclaimed: 'this never happened in my experience before when a Farm was advertised'. This was a true measure of the severity of the times and led directly to an even more disturbing corollary—the landowner was compelled to purchase the sheep stock of the vacated farm and manage the property on his own hands. High capital costs were thereby incurred and the Cromartie estate found itself, without choice, undertaking the entrepreneurial functions of the departed sheepfarmers. Moreover the estate managers were poor sheepfarmers and the times were against them. In the upshot the Cromartie estate sustained considerable losses on several of its unlettable sheep farms in the late 1880s.[16]

The big arable producers were also in trouble, even those on the good lands of Easter Ross. In 1881 there was a collective sense of umbrage for not getting as much consideration and concession as fellow farmers in the district or even their counterparts on the Sutherland estates. There were urgent enquiries 'as to whether the Duke's kindness to his Sutherland tenants is to be extended to Ross-shire'. The gravity of their condition was emphasised by reports that some of the biggest tenants, the most valuable and capitalistic farmers, were in the greatest difficulty. By August 1881 Gunn pressed his seniors for action on behalf of both stock and arable farmers. He was, for some time, resisted by the Commissioner, Sir Arnold Kemball—and indeed Gunn became a powerful advocate of the farmers' plight. He pointed out that arable producers had been in difficulty for the past dozen years. Yields had been declining and the price of the main staple, barley, had fallen from 35/- to 26/-, while oats were equally depressed. Barley was practically unsaleable because of foreign competition. Gunn strengthened the case by reference to rent reductions already implemented on neighbouring properties, notably those of the Duke of Richmond who had reduced rents by 20% 'and looked quite happy about it'.[17] Even so it was thought that some farmers would require seven good years before they recovered their prosperity.

Walter Arras[18] was one of the critical cases. He had come to Strathpeffer from Roxburghshire in 1867 and had taken over one of the greatest farms in the region, Fodderty, on a rent of £874 p.a. In July 1882 he tried to re-negotiate the terms of his lease, saying that £700 was the most that he could pay. Any higher rent, said Arras, would force him to leave. He suffered from the stiffness of the soil at Fodderty, from awkward gravel spots and the moss levels which rendered his operating costs unusually high; cropping restrictions in the lease also hampered his activities: 'Look at all the farms at present and lately on the market. Some of them scarcely looked at unless they have some special attraction'. He had even tried to export potatoes to America but without success.[19] Kemball was anxious not to lose such a tenant as Arras and a temporary arrangement was effected.

By late summer 1882 the Cromartie estate had recognised the long-term character of the agricultural depression. Rent reductions were extended to the arable farmers and were offered for the full life of the unexpired bases. Arras now found himself paying £720 p.a. The tenant of Priesthill expressed his gratitude saying that the remission would 'lighten the anxiety of mind'—at the same time reporting that he had gathered in a good harvest though 'there is no sale for it'. Priesthill was re-leased on more liberal conditions and its rent reduced from £180 to £160 p.a.[20]

The estate administrators hoped, somewhat despairingly, that the farmers would react positively to their adversity, reducing costs rather than rents, thereby facing competition with increased efficiency. Gunn, for instance, believed that farmers should become more modern and scientific and he was glad to see the inauguration of an experimental field club in Easter Ross in January 1882:

> It is certainly a step in the right direction, and if Farmers can be induced to take an interest in experiments much practical good will follow. Agriculture is daily becoming more scientific, and the ignorance that prevails as to the proper use and value of artificial manures and feeding stuffs is very great.[21]

The length of the depression of prices made such advice somewhat idealistic.

Pessimism deepened in the mid 1880s and there were repeated demands for further rent reductions from all quarters. Arrears accumulated so that large farmers, stock breeders and crofters, found themselves in the same boat. In April 1884, Arras was again seeking a reduction of rent, saying that conditions were worse than ever: 'I do feel that in view of the continued and increasing depression my former request might be favourably considered and a new rent fixed at £700.'[22] Concurrently wool prices had fallen further and in August 1885 Gunn told Kemball that unless rents were reduced, not only for the crofters but for all tenants, trouble would be bound to ensue.[23]

In 1884 Walter Arras had said that, at the prevailing level of rent, he could not 'see my way to hold these farms much longer. I am losing heavily every year, and this season £400 will not cover my loss.' Twelve months later he said he had lost £300 exclusive of interest on capital—Gunn reported: 'He is very low spirited about the future of farming and would clear out if he could'.[24] By December 1885 another round of reductions was implemented yet within two months Arras, now a barometer of agricultural depression, was again seeking relief. He referred to the fact that his previous farm in Roxburghshire, which he had rented from the Duke of Roxburgh for £950, was now let at £400: 'It seems to me impossible to pay present rents when things have come to such a pass that grain cannot be sold at any price unless it is first class'. He claimed to be unable to pay any rent more than £700, 'for it is impossible to get it out of the farm at these rates. Something must be done to give relief either by a revaluation or termination of holdings.' The Duke of Gordon had already taken such decisive action and Arras was perfectly prepared to open his books and accounts to inspection in order to prove his point.[25]

The farmers were speaking with one voice. In February 1888, for instance, the Easter Ross Farmers Club on their behalf demonstrated conclusively that, since 1870, barley prices had fallen 33 per cent, oats 47 per cent, wheat 37 per cent and potatoes 50 per cent. Meanwhile the wages of farm servants had virtually doubled. Walter Arras, always prominent in public discussion, declared that farmers were now suffering 'in a way they never did before. The position was strained to the utmost.'[26]

IV

Although the continuing buoyancy of sporting rents helped cushion the effects of the depression of agricultural prices on landlord income the general situation had clearly worsened. The new commissioner of the Sutherland estates, R.M. Brereton,[27] brought a show of realism to the management in 1887 and he declared that arrears would necessarily have to be liquidated, written off altogether. But the sagging rental income, and the costs of sustaining sheep farms which had fallen into the hands of the management, had created a profound pessimism about estate finances at large. In January 1887 Brereton issued Gunn clear instructions: 'The financial condition of the Cromartie Estate demands the exercise of the most rigid economy in every way, and this you must see carried out during the current year'.[28]

Brereton was impatient with the financial and social problems of the Highland estates now in his charge. Looking over past accounts he noticed that in 1887 the gross rental income for Cromartie was £12,706, merely £146 more than the figure achieved 20 years previously and this despite heavy expenditures by the landlord on improvements during the interim. Worse still the likelihood was that rents would fall still further. Gunn was profoundly wounded by these remarks and tried to tell his superior that objective conditions were responsible for the difficulties experienced by the estate finances. Brereton sanctioned the sale of parcels of land and the negotiation of further loans to cover the sheep stocks now in the hands of the estate management.[29] The frustrations of Brereton and his predecessor, Kemball, had, of course, been compounded by the endless furore with the crofters during the 1880s. Brereton's first inclination was to plunge into Coigach and recover crofter arrears by the threat of eviction. Arrears had become mountainous, especially after the retirement of Kenneth Mackenzie. As one of Gunn's correspondents said in August 1887: 'The Crofters have literally ceased to pay arrears. I don't know what is to be the end of it.'[30]

Gunn, feeling responsible for the accumulation of crofter arrears to his new master, insisted that he had always advocated firmness with backsliders in the rental. His attitude had been undermined by the operation of the Crofters Commission and the associated uncertainty regarding the future. As he described it,

> it is well to bear in mind that the whole Highlands were in a state of ferment in these years, and that attempts made by proprietors in Skye and elsewhere to recover arrears were rendered futile by the deforcement of the officers of the law sent to serve writs

for recovery. This state of affairs naturally frightened many landlords from instituting proceedings, which in different circumstances would certainly have been adopted.

The management of many estates had faced 'a general strike' against the payment of rent. At Cromartie he pointed out that many of the people had no income and many were very old; moreover there were no empty houses into which old people could be removed, 'and they cannot be turned on to the road'.[31] Eventually the energetic Brereton was compelled to come to terms with the intractability of the crofter rental and the fact that the newly established Crofter Commission would eventually arbitrate rent levels. He began to see that the operation of the Commission, initially so threatening, might ultimately operate to make some of the estate's problems more manageable.

Estate Commissioners came and went, Brereton himself resigned in 1888, but the pessimism in rural life continued even into the following decade. The pastoral sector showed little sign of recovery. In 1888 Gunn was told that 'the sheep farms in hand are the most pressing and serious matter' and if tenants could not be found on reasonable terms it should be considered clearing them altogether to make way for sportsmen whose demand was undiminished throughout these years. But many of the sheep farms remained unlettable; in February 1889 Gunn had to report that he had received no offers for any of the sheep farms (which was also true in Sutherland) rent abatements continued even though Gunn was aware that once 'rents get down it is very difficult to get them up again'.[32]

Sometimes the voice of the farmer *in extremis* reached into the factor's office. In June 1891 John Ross, the tenant of the big farm at Kildary, wrote an impassioned letter which expressed his despair:

> Years, months, weeks and days have passed and nothing has been done to help my position as regards the conditions on which I entered on the farm of Kildary but exacting money. But it is said it is a long road that has no turn in it, it can't go on any longer. No one in creation would put up with my accommodation, not only that I am losing the value of all my labour and outlay on stock and grain, but now I can't get a ploughman to stop but one year.

Ross said his turnip crop was being ruined by rabbits and his buildings were dilapidated. How much assistance the estate provided Ross with repairs is not known; his rent however had been reduced first from £247 to £200 and then, by 1894, to £150.[33]

The estate managers knew the difficulties of the farmers and were sometimes stretched in two directions by their demands and those of the proprietor. The young (and short-lived) Earl of Cromartie, in February 1893, asked Gunn why his estate did not produce a greater income for his needs as the new incumbent. Gunn quietly explained that 'the experience of all connected with land is that Farms—both arable and pastoral—have depreciated full 30 to 35 per cent in the last 10 or 12 years'. An increased rental was simply not possible. Sheep farms continued as a managerial headache—'The grazing rental is everywhere so terribly reduced that we are compelled to make the most we can out of the shooting rents'. The dilemma of the sheep farms diminished the estate's opposition to club farms and some of the re-distributive suggestions of the Crofter Commission. But there were limits to this new liberality, especially where crofter applications for grazings seemed to threaten the shootings. One such case occurred in 1893 when Glenskaich was the subject of speculation: it was one of the best shooting grounds on the estate with excellent tenants who, Gunn warned, would be lost if it were 'over-run by Crofters'.

Applications by crofters were also made for Badentarbat and Inverpolly and similarly resisted by the Cromartie estate on the grounds that they were still in lease and that the people possessed insufficient capital to operate the grazings. Gunn knew also that it was more persuasive to resist a claim by crofters before the Land Court if the lands were held by a *bona fide* farmer rather than a sportsman, and consequently it was better to extend the lease by reducing rent than have it fall in, which thereby stymied the crofter applications. It was equally clear that very low-rented sheep farms were vulnerable to the crofters' demands and the estate was prepared to keep them untenanted rather than 'be made a hurdle of against us when the Crofter Commissions come to deal with the grazings let to the Crofters'. Moreover though there was an initial improvement in the payment of crofter rentals under the regime of the Crofter Commission, arrears once again began to mount by 1892—when Gunn exclaimed: 'Something should be done to waken up the Coigach Crofters who have paid nothing since they had fair rents fixed by the Commission'.[34] Indeed the fact that the rents had been set independently gave the estate greater moral and legal leverage than before. Nevertheless the stark poverty of the people was a recurrent fact of life little relieved by the turmoil and intervention of the past twenty years. Thus even in 1898 the local agent in the west reported in terms fully echoing their timeless plight: 'There is a terrible cry of poverty in Coigach and I fear they have no money wherewith to pay cash for seed'.[35]

The point at which the rural pessimism of two decades began to lift is difficult to determine. But by 1897 the Cromartie estate recorded an improved total rental which now reached to over £13,000—partly accounted for by improved returns from the Spa at Strathpeffer, but mostly by the continuing growth of sporting rents over and beyond the return on sheep farms. The Valuation Rolls of the years before the First World War reflected the inflated value of the shooting estates which had clearly helped the estate through the decline of sheep farming. By the turn of the century rents generally were slowly recovering. The old structure of landholding remained intact. By 1910, considerable stretches of grazing had been made over to the crofters—since 1902, for instance, the crofters in Coigach had received 5241 acres.[36]

But the improvement of rents was slow and insufficient to prevent the need to sell parcels of land on the Cromartie estate during the pre-war years. There was considerable mobility in landownership which would be accelerated by the Great War and its aftermath. Partly it reflected the long-term weakness of the old estate finances. Partly it also related to the growing demand for Highland property from outside. One of the critical elements in the shift of landownership at the turn of the century was not so much pressure from the crofters as from the propensities of southern plutocracy. As Black told Gunn in November 1899, 'there are rich men from the south of England prepared to buy Highland properties'.[37] The implications for the marginal landowner, emerging out of the long depression of prices and rents, was clear enough.

V

The financial impact of the invasion of 'the Nimrods', the sporting tenants from the south, was greatest during the last two decades of the nineteenth century.[38] On the Cromartie estate sporting rents provided a counter-balance to the declining receipts from the rest of the estate's revenues. In 1896, for instance, sporting rents were 65 per cent of all Coigach income and 38 per cent of those in Strathpeffer (always being much less in New Tarbat). Without sporting rents the estate would have faced dire financial difficulties which, of course, rendered the threat of government intervention in the late 1890s so much more dangerous to northern proprietors.

The sporting sector, notably 'the shootings', had first emerged many decades before. There was, of course, nothing new in such sport:[39] the Hay-Mackenzies and their relatives often referred to their bags of game in the years after Waterloo; they were in the habit of shooting ptarmigan at Fannich and dispatching boxes of woodcock to friends in the south. Their factor in 1819, Laing, was especially sensitive to their sporting propensities and when letting a farm considered 'whether Black Cattle, or sheep, will be the most proper stock for it, keeping in view the preservation of the game'.[40] The family employed game keepers and fox hunters to manage their sport.[41]

The commercial potential of shooting leases became visible in the 1830s. By 1834 Lord Castlereagh was leasing the shootings at Castle Leod for a term of three years which allowed him 'the right of shooting over the lands and Barony of Strathpeffer and killing all kinds of game thereon'.[42] Compared with later contracts, when Highland sport had gained rapidly in demand, the conditions of his lease were remarkably liberal. By 1841 the estate management was stirring to the new income possibilities even on the west coast. Andrew Scott remarked in May that there were 'many applications for the moors' and entirely unshot lands were becoming feasible leases. The estate increasingly found itself involved in the organisation of facilities for the new class of tenant. They included the dispatch of bread supplies across country from Dingwall to the west coast. The remoteness of the sporting tenancies (one of their greatest attractions) created considerable provisioning difficulties. Potential tenants were assured that at Ullapool there was a plentiful supply of cabin biscuits, meal for their dogs as well as good supplies of whisky, but groceries 'will be got cheaper and better from the Low Country'. They were told that it was best to journey to Ullapool by steam boat and that a boat voyaged thence to Badentarbet thrice weekly.[43]

Gradually, in the 1840s, the Cromartie estate improvised facilities and regulations for the incoming sportsmen. There were costs involved: shooting lodges[44] and, later, roads had to be constructed. There were also some local tensions: the landlord himself wished to retain access to sport for himself when the real costs were being bid upwards by eager and affluent sportsmen; similarly the intrusion of the sportsmen increased competition for the land for both crofters and sheep farmers. It took many years before an equilibrium was achieved. The conversion of land to sporting tenants later became the target for special attack by the Land Leaguers in the 1880s and 1890s.

To begin with, the shootings were let on short leases on the grounds that 'they have only recently been protected and are little known to sportsmen ... The Proprietor would expect the tenant not to scourge the shootings.'[45] Nevertheless, sporting and gentlemanly behaviour was expected of the shooters. Scott explained in 1849 (after negotiating with Lord Cardigan for a lease) that the late 'Cromartie never attempted to bind a tenant to any quantity of game to be killed in any one year, or to keep down vermin ... My own opinion is, you cannot effectively prevent a tenant from injuring your Shootings.' Scott now favoured long leases because it would give the tenant a longer view of the maintenance of the game 'and the Proprietor is not plagued every two or three years in looking for a fresh tenant, and devising plans to make him act in a spirit of a true sportsman and a Gentleman'.[46] The common people also caused difficulties not merely by occupying lands desired by sportsmen but also by their own appetites for game. In Strathpeffer there was a considerable problem with poaching which Scott thought was common among the small tenantry under the cloak of rabbit killing. He remarked that 'this perpetual disturbance by trespassing with dogs and guns will render the Property of no value as a Shooting' and the gamekeeper was given rigorous instructions: anyone caught a second time would be immediately turned off the estate.[47] Sheep farmers were also under regulations under which they occasionally chafed, notably restrictions in their annual muir burning.[48]

Under the youthful Lord and Lady Stafford the demand for sporting leases promised well—as Scott said in 1851, 'if the shootings could be let, the rents of them would help well to keep the Estate free of incurring fresh debt and this ought to be the main object just now to be kept in view'. Discreet checks were made on the wealth of potential sporting tenants. There were two larger problems in the way of maximising income. One was the reluctance of Lord Stafford to relinquish his personal use of the estate—in October 1851 Scott was unable to hide his disapproval: 'Lord Stafford appears to be unwilling to forgo the pleasure and excitement of Deerstalking'. The other problem, of course, was the demand by potential tenants that the land be cleared of its people and their stock before entering a lease. The long negotiations with Lord Dupplin and his agent[49] about the Coigach shootings had stumbled on the inability of the Cromartie estate to re-arrange the small tenants to his wishes.[50] That had been the essential context of the Coigach riots of 1853 which eventually forced the withdrawal of the Staffords and Dupplin from the arrangement, at great loss of face and income to the estate administrators. Dupplin had simply refused to compromise on the question and this forced Scott's hand to the point of direct confrontation with the people.[51]

The demand for sporting leases grew wonderfully well. In 1856 Scott told Lady Stafford that 'never before was there such a season ... nor such high rents'.[52] In the following year Rhiddorach (one of Lord Stafford's favoured forests) was let out as a shooting for £300 per annum to the astonishment of Andrew Scott who noted that it had been rented at a mere £110 as a grazing.[53] In 1858 further tracts of Coigach were cleared of sheep and the current 'very disagreeable' tenant removed, Lord Stafford having insisted on breaks in leases to deal with such problems. Scott described the land made available as 'more for Deer than Grouse' and one of the best ranges in the country for deerstalking.[54] He was able to settle the lease at an increased rent of $12\frac{1}{2}$ per cent. He experienced more difficulty with the Strathpeffer shootings because they too had been 'severely handled by the last tenant and by disease'.[55]

The sporting tenants sometimes killed too much game. In 1860 Scott remarked that, with the assistance of floods and disease, grouse had been virtually extirpated from some of the leases. Nevertheless the demand for the Highland moors was unabated.[56] Even while sheep rents were high there was growing pressure to accept more sportsmen—in 1860 consideration was given to the idea of converting the great Inverpolly Farm into a deer forest. George Loch was dubious since it already fetched £688 under sheep and he still regarded deerstalking as 'a question of fancy or fashion'. He also recollected the consequences of the Dupplin affair of 1852/3. By 1866 Loch had changed his tune and was expecting to get even higher rents for the Cromartie shootings. It was now a landlord's market,[57] and the sportsmen were beginning to overtake the sheepfarmers.

Often the sporting tenants were as fastidious and as awkward as the Spa visitors. In 1869 Andrew Robertson complained about his lease at Drumruinie—the rent was exorbitant, there were very few grouse, the accommodation was dreadful, there were sheep roaming about, and he had been 'woefully deceived with regard to it'.[58] But total demand for sporting leases was so high that the proprietor could afford to ignore most complaints; sporting tenants were even required to pay local rates and taxes.[59] Evander MacIver confided with William Gunn that one tenant, Sir Sandford Graham, would require delicate handling, remarking that 'shooting tenants, as a rule, are a troublesome lot, but they are best managed by a little coaxing and humouring'.[60] In 1882 Rhiddorrach was let at the princely rent of £800 even though the shooting lodge was in very poor condition. The tenant, Starkey, proved a difficult type and relations were so poor that in December 1888 he was telling Gunn: 'If Lord Cromartie wants possession of Rhiddorrach I should be quite willing to give up at Whitsuntide as there are better forests for much less rent to be had now'.[61]

Indeed the upward movement of sporting rents reached a slightly dipping plateau by this time. The Crofter agitation[62] had reduced some of the attraction—for the deer forests had quickly attracted adverse political attention. In 1883 the small tenants on the Heights of Strathpeffer were complaining bitterly about the damage caused by deer and demanding the construction of fences,[63] and the problem of poaching seemed to worsen.[64] The Report of the Royal Commission into Deer Forests (1892) and related questions published in 1895 had faced the question of which land in the Highlands might be more advantageously occupied by crofters. The Commissioners discovered that large tracts of the Highlands—and Cromartie was a clear case—were under forests which had in the past been occupied by shielings: 'but would have had a lower standard of life than is acceptable today'. In some areas there was no desire by the people to reoccupy them. Others however were more vulnerable, as the Cromartie estate knew, and efforts were made to counter these dangerous arguments.[65]

Supply and demand for Highland shooting facilities had become more systematic. Gunn was told in January 1901 that potential sporting tenants were able to collude in their London clubs and compare rents and conditions among the Highland estates.[66] On the other hand specialist agencies had emerged in Inverness and Perth, and much later in London, which connected prospective tenants with the offering estate agents.[67] The Cromartie estate advertised nationally—as in November 1890. The Rhiddorrach Deer Forest, 50000 acres, was offered at £1200 per annum, with 40—45 stags, 100 brace of grouse as well as fishing. Salmon and trout were to be sought in rivers and lochs. The lodge which was located in the grandest scenery in the Highlands, 'possessed 2 public rooms, 7 bedrooms with further ample accommodation for servants and keepers'. It was within reach of post, telegraph and a doctor, with 'excellent anchorage for yachts'. Similar conditions at the same price were offered at Drumruinie Forest, for 20000 acres, where the Lodge was described as 'new and spacious, seven principal bed rooms, and ample accommodation for butler and other servants'. It was the late Victorian sportsman's paradise.[68]

VI

The sporting market softened by the late 1890s even though such rents remained a large proportion of the total rental. In 1897 three of the largest shootings were unlet and the balance of the Cromartie estate finances was thrown into jeopardy—'we might find ourselves in a very awkward position' remarked Black from Edinburgh.[69] In reality the market was sustained through the Edwardian years and when the Cromartie estate came to sell off some of its best shooting lands the rents were as high as they had ever been. In 1914 Rhiddorrach, with accommodation for 14 servants, was worth £1600 per annum, on which basis it was eventually sold, after the war, in 1920.

PART FIVE

Adjustments of a New Era, 1880-1914

CHAPTER 26

Cromartie Finances in Travail: the 1880s

I

For almost forty years, from 1849 to 1888, the Cromartie estate remained in the ownership of Anne, Duchess of Sutherland (1829-88) and under the general superintendance of the commissioners of the third Duke of Sutherland's empire of estates. On Duchess Anne's death, it was well understood, the Cromartie properties would again be hived off for the benefit of their second son, Francis, Lord Tarbat (1852-1893). The future of the Cromartie estate depended greatly on the provisions of the will of the third Duke (1828-1892), and on the returns to the capital investments that had been made during the lifetime of his wife. The long period of association with the Sutherland empire was, by the 1880s, about to expire. As for the Duchess, she had become increasingly reclusive and eccentric, subject to religious fervours, pictured by her grandson as a much-faded beauty now mainly confined to Stafford House, cared for by her servant who delivered chicken dinners each day to her room. It was, no doubt, a sign of her complete estrangement from the Duke, who was now leading an entirely separate life. The Duchess had become the classic Victorian figure of the 'wronged wife', isolated but also offered much moral support by relatives and, it is likely, by the Queen herself.[1]

The years of the crofter revolt had been years of substantial financial difficulty for all Highland landowners. After three decades of buoyant prices and high output, sheepfarming became less profitable and rents fell drastically. The demand for farms was so depressed that some of the great sheep runs were taken in hand by proprietors. Landlords found themselves saddled with expensive stock at a time when their net income was falling. Naturally the obvious problems of leasing the sheep farms gave the crofters' demands greater credibility; it also meant that some landlords became marginally less adamant in their opposition to reform. On the other hand the rent strikes across the Highlands compounded the financial predicaments of the proprietors.

On the Cromartie estate the position was complicated by the financial interdependence contained in the family arrangements between the Cromartie and Sutherland sides of the estate empire. Between 1880 and the end of the century there was a succession of major changes in the administration of the Sutherland territories. On top of this however were a series of dynastic changes of ownership and control which ended with the separation of the Cromartie estate from the rest of the Sutherland empire. This was, of course, anticipated in the will of the Duke of Sutherland. Less expected, however, was the sudden shift in the financial status of the heirs of Cromartie. The estate changed hands twice between 1888 and 1893 and quite suddenly it was left without the great financial underpinnings of the Sutherland millions. Meanwhile, of course, the crofters, for all their poverty and political isolation, achieved some of the most advanced legal conditions of any tenantry in mainland Britain.

II

In 1880 the Sutherland empire was still managed by Sir Arnold Kemball, the retired diplomat who had replaced George Loch (on his death) in one of the top jobs in the world of land agency. The financial constraints in the Cromartie management had tightened while the third Duke expended vast sums on speculative improvements in Sutherland and elsewhere.[2] The development of Strathpeffer Spa, close to the heart of the Duke and his wife, provided a constant temptation and drain on the funds. But in January 1880, when William Gunn presented his annual estimates to the Sutherland central agency, the response was an incredulous expostulation. The estimated revenue was £13,276 but expenditure was put at £16,925. George Scott, from the Sutherland head-office, exclaimed: 'I am astonished—where in the name of wonder do you think we can get the money?'

Much of the extra expense stemmed from plans for the construction of a new Pavilion at the Spa. The idea of borrowing £1800 against the entail was impossible because the credit source had been exhausted already. Gunn was told: 'You must not calculate the Duke advancing any [credit]—we are cutting down strongly everywhere, and after all is done (except in Sutherland) we shall barely make ends meet, and certainly not there, unless the Duke adheres seriously to the recent decision of having but few "extras".' The Sutherland estates as a whole were not breaking even, and Sir Arnold Kemball advised that the new Pavilion might have to be postponed until better times, or come entirely out of the local funds.[3] Meanwhile, the Cromartie heir, Viscount Tarbat, was himself in the gravest financial distress[4] which may have confirmed Evander MacIver's view of Tarbat's tendency to prodigality.

The investments in the Cromartie estate had been, of course, part of the strategy of his father, the third Duke of Sutherland, to render his second son financially stronger and independent when he eventually inherited the Cromartie estate on his death. It was an arrangement which deliberately echoed the provisions made in the time of the first Duke of Sutherland who had died in 1833, and designed specifically to establish his second son (Lord Francis) as a separate and formidable strand of the family.[5] Now, in the 1880s, the Duke's advisors were telling him that enough had been done for the Cromartie estate and that it should finance its own further development. It was, therefore, advice which presaged the end of the cross-subsidisation of the Cromartie finances by the larger and richer Sutherland estate.

Looking back from 1885 Gunn noted that the Cromartie estate had received considerable improvements. Before 1867 Coigach had been much neglected. From 1876 to 1884 the estate had spent more on it than anywhere in the county, particularly on farm buildings. Roads to the value of £11,000 had been built. The Cromartie rental had increased from £10,776 in 1866 to £13,600 in 1884. Gunn, keen as always to press forward with improvements, remarked to Kemball:

> Much still remains to be done in all the three districts of the Cromartie estate, in this particular direction—and now that expenditure required for Farm Building will be comparatively trifling, it is hoped that circumstances may favour a still more rapid improvement in the dwellings of the small tenantry, for which there is a growing necessity and increasing demand.[6]

By this time the campaign of the crofters for land rights and reduced rents had disrupted much of the management of the west coast estate. The crofter agitation now monopolised much of the energy of the management.

In a review of estate finances for the years 1879-1884 it became clear that the average gross revenue for the Cromartie estate was £17,933. Standing charges against this were £5,510 per annum and ordinary expenditure was £6,297, in total £11,807. The expenditure on the Pavilion was excluded from the estimates, but the average extra expenditure (including the problem of the unlet sheep farm of Inverpolly) was £8,014, giving a total of £19,821, or an average annual deficit of £3,622 which was 20% of the gross revenue. In 1885 the estate had an overdraft of £12,509 with Drummonds the family's banker, and owed another £8,000 to insurance companies, as well as £3304 on the separate Pavilion account. Another £14,000 was required for the purchase of sheep stock for Inverpolly. It was not a happy picture—the estate finances were in a state of suspended crisis cushioned for the present moment by the continuing financial support of the Duchess' husband.[7] The problem was compounded (but not caused) by the rebellion of the crofters in the west.[8]

One of the great financial drains on the estate in these years was the impossibility of letting the sheep farms which remained on the hands of the estate and thereby tied up land, capital and labour in an expensive way—it was 'a serious addition to our troubles'.[9] Meanwhile Sir Arnold Kemball had resigned and had been replaced by R.M. Brereton, an incessant worker who was appointed in the very midst of the upheaval of the Crofter Commission report. In 1887 Brereton announced a new rigour in financial relations between the estates in his charge. The Duke would advance no further money or guarantees for the Cromartie estate, for the Spa or elsewhere, and pointed out that 'Her Grace is unable to assist in providing the money required'.[10] At that time a loan of £8,000 was due for repayment to the Scottish National and Union Insurance Company; an attempt was made to extend the loan.

Brereton took a very stringent view of the estate finances and even criticised the Duchess's small personal expenditures on household items. He wrote to the Duchess to ask her not to charge the estate with these items; he pointed out that the revenue from the estate was not enough to cover them; he emphasised the point that the Duke had had to pay out more than £37,000 from his own private account in the previous five years to cover these extraordinary costs. It was becoming a matter of some delicacy.[11] Brereton instructed Gunn to exercise rigid economy. He noted that the gross Cromartie rental for 1887 (£12,706) was only £146 greater than in 1867 despite all the improvements of that period, 'and the present outlook is in the direction of a reduced rental.'

40   Francis Earl of Cromartie.

Moreover some capital had been raised by property sales—in 1868 the disposal of the Tain nursery had yielded £900, Mossfield £750, and in 1878 the Tain Brewery was sold for £2400 together with feu duties at Lochbroom for £1737. At this time £8000 had been borrowed from the Sun Insurance Company as part of a special arrangement to borrow £10,000 on entail for permanent improvements. Another £9600 had been borrowed for the purchase of the Inverpolly Sheep Stock. Brereton was highly critical of these arrangements and his outspoken comments must have wounded Gunn.

In a crucial memorandum, prepared in the central office of the Sutherland administration in July 1885, the future of the Cromartie estate was subjected to a further close scrutiny. The analysis contemplated the ultimate separation of Cromartie from the Sutherland properties and what 'course would be practicable to preserve it from ruin.' The memorandum concluded unambiguously that the only solution would be

> the rigid exclusion of all improvements, the restriction of expenditure to the ordinary estimates, and the postponement of any other consideration to the one imperative necessity of balancing revenue and expenditure. Were the Duke's aid withdrawn, and that day must come when his aid will no longer be available, such a course would be inevitable.[12]

For himself Gunn found the financial difficulties of the estate frustrating, especially since they threatened the continuing development of the Spa. Such strict measures of economy repeatedly delayed improvements which Gunn regarded as vital for the resort and the future revenue of the estate.

Anne, Duchess of Sutherland, Countess of Cromartie in her own right, died in Torquay on 25 November 1888. Queen Victoria had been much distressed by the illness of her old friend and made no secret of her displeasure when the Duke failed to return promptly to England from America to attend his dying wife. Indeed the death of the Duchess was a further episode in the longstanding deterioration of relations within the Sutherland family. In this conflict the Duke was, in effect, pitted against his heir Lord Stafford, who disapproved of his father's financial and personal behaviour. The quarrel reached fever pitch when, only three months later, the Duke re-married at Dunedin in Florida. His new Duchess was Mary Caroline, daughter of Rev. Richard Michell, Principal of Hertford College, Oxford. She was a very recent widow—only two days before her wedding her previous husband, Arthur Kindersley Blair of the 71st Highland Infantry, 'was killed out shooting'. The Sutherland family was obviously shocked and appalled at this turn of events, at the Duke's gross insensitivity. The new Duchess was effectively ostracised. Yet all this was merely a prelude to a greater sensation (with large financial consequences for the Cromartie estate) on the Duke's own death in 1892.[13]

III

In November 1888, therefore, the Cromartie estate reverted to Duchess Anne's second son, Francis, Lord Tarbat, who became the second new Earl of Cromartie at the age of 36. This was a consequence of the re-creation of the title which had been extinguished in the 1746 Jacobite Uprising. Francis Sutherland-Leveson-Gower inherited the Cromartie title:

> Provided that if the said Francis Sutherland-Leveson-Gower or any other person taking under the said letters patent shall succeed to the Earldom of Sutherland, and there shall upon or at any time after the occurrence of such event be any other younger son or any other daughter of the said Anne, Duchess of Sutherland

That is, the Sutherland and the Cromartie estates were to be kept fully separate by elaborate legislation of 1864 which was described by The Complete Peerage as 'this extraordinary proviso', which had constructed a unique 'jumping Peerage'.[14] In 1876 the Earl of Cromartie had married Lilian Janet (1856-1926) daughter of Lord Macdonald of Sleat. The union produced two daughters, Sibell Lilian in 1878 and Constance.

In effect the estate was now released from the Sutherland empire. Consequently it was expected to live off its own resources. In the previous 38 years it had received the benefits of the connection with the Sutherland fortune, in investment and management. It was calculated that, between 1853 and 1887 the Duke of Sutherland advanced £95,752 to his wife's Cromartie estates. In 1860 he had paid off £67,898 of debts then accumulated on the estate; in 1885 he provided a £14,000 loan (free of interest) for the purchase of sheep stock, and in 1887 another £14,500 was used to cover overdrafts and expenditure at the Spa.[15] By the terms of the original marriage settlement the Duke had been entitled to draw £3000 per annum from the Cromartie estate but he had never taken advantage of this provision.[16] Sadly the estate income had not increased by a commensurate amount, though its value with regard to the Spa had been considerably augmented. For the new Earl of Cromartie there were some cold financial facts of life attached to his inheritance. It seems that Cromartie had been used to an annual income of £4,000 from his father. This was now reduced to £1,500, to be augmented by the revenues of the Cromartie estate. Peacock, the Sutherland factor, estimated that £4,500 was the most optimistic possibility as free income from the estate[17]—i.e. after paying interest on loans. The estate was in poor financial shape mainly because of the depression in sheep farming and the continuing burden of sheep farms in hand[18]—tenants were needed, and if not forthcoming there was the suggestion that they could be cleared of sheep and let as deer farms. It was a common problem for the Highlands in the 1880s.

In September 1888, yet another investigation of the estate finances was commissioned. It was reported predictably that too many of the sheep farms were not let, though Gunn commented: 'it is not surprising considering the bad times, and that infinitely superior farms are in hand in Sutherland'. It was practically impossible to let sheep farms at this time and some were running at a loss. Their management was a constant anxiety to Highland factors. Highland landlords did not make good sheep farmers, at least at current wool and sheep prices.[19] In the mid 1880s the managers had already surveyed the position of sheep farms on the estate and the extent to which capital had been locked up. It was a dismal record of tenants declining to renew leases despite very substantial abatements to rents—usually about 25%. Losses on the sale of stock had also been large: 'The outgoing tenants in every case have been urged to propose their own terms for a renewal—but declined—they evidently desire to realize believing that prices are destined to depreciate still more.'[20] Another review of the time indicated that improvements of a permanent character in 1885 and 1886 had been effected on the Cromartie estate to the tune of £9,008. It was pointed out that:

> Prior to 1876 there was a very large expenditure .... It embraced the construction of nearly 40 miles of new road to open up the entire district of Coigach, connecting it with Ullapool and Lochinver. During that period there was a heavy expenditure on the improvement of Farm Buildings, the erection of slated cottages for ploughmen—the formation of young plantations and various other important and necessary improvements.[21]

The returns on these investments were poor.

Cromartie's succession had required much financial clarification and adjustment. For instance all the sheep stock belonged to the Duke of Sutherland. A life insurance policy of £26,000 was invested by trustees. Debts had accumulated on sheep stock; but the Spa, many of the stocks in Highland Railway Company, and the Strathpeffer Hotel all belonged to the Duke. Cromartie now became responsible for the payment of various annuities. The financial adviser reported mournfully to the Duke, 'I fear from the accounts which I have seen, and on going into matters generally, that Lord Cromartie's financial position in the future will be much worse than hitherto'.[22] Once again, therefore, the familial disposition of income and priorities manipulated and shaped the uses of the Cromartie income. The size of the financial constraints caused even greater borrowings to occur in May 1889; £18,000 was borrowed from Drummonds specifically to take over the sheep stocks from the Duke; but there also appears to have been an arrangement by which the Duke made up Cromartie's income to £5,000 a year,[23] though this was not regarded as a permanent solution.

In January 1887 Brereton had said quite bluntly that the Duke of Sutherland would not pay for any further work on the Cromartie estate, especially for the large plans suggested for the Spa by the perennially enthusiastic Dr Fortescue Fox. Means were strictly limited, and the management had to 'keep in view the present indebtedness to the Banks ... which must be reduced ... It will therefore be your duty to watch over the current expenditure with the utmost care, so as to prevent any further overdrafts or liabilities.' Dr Fox's extravagant plans could not be accommodated by the Duke and all expenditure had to be met with specific funds.[24]

The Cromartie finances were investigated repeatedly through these years. Brereton had reviewed the revenue figures in 1887 which showed gross income from sheep farms at £2017, arable at £3713, crofters and cotters at £4446 (but with arrears of £2816), shooting and angling at £3004, salmon fishing at £350, houses at £1414 and feu duties at £374, producing a total of £16,322. Brereton was frankly critical of weaknesses in both the revenue and expenditure accounts. William Gunn, of course, complained bitterly when his management was submitted to Brereton's robust scrutiny:

> A perusal of any statement to Sir Arnold is sufficient to show the neglected condition of the Cromartie Estates when I entered on the management in 1867. My reports from time to time, and the yearly estimates of necessary expenditure will yet, if referred to, afford ample evidence of this.

He maintained the view that estate expenditure was indispensable if land values and rents were to be improved. He expected rents to be stagnant for many years to come; that expenditure in the earlier years had paid a good return, and it 'would be a false economy to put a stop to all improvements, more especially the maintenance of buildings, fences, drains in a state of efficiency'. He estimated that from 1872 to 1886 £15,207 had been spent in Coigach—on roads, drainage, buildings, seed, mills, etc.[25]

On the death of the Duchess in 1888, elaborate arrangements were made for the division of property. The furniture, plate and jewellery at Tarbat House, and the stock, crops and implements of the Home Farm were made over to Lord Cromartie, on condition that he gave up all arrears and sheep stock to the Duke. The latter made a further payment of £4,000 to Cromartie.[26] It is clear that Cromartie's affairs were tightly circumscribed by various conditions—his debt to Sutherland, the borrowings of £10,000 against the entail, £18,819 borrowed against the 1862 Trust Deed; premiums of £462 per annum on Cromartie's life to secure £21,000 life insurance for his children. The Duke however was to pay the interest on most of these items until his death. Cromartie was obviously an estate fully burdened. The Duke however, was persuaded to guarantee Cromartie £5,000 a year income for three years, and then £4,000 a year. But it was crystal clear that such inter-familial subsidies would eventually cease altogether. The financial foundations of the estate were, therefore, again in jeopardy. For a century the descendants of Lord Macleod lived beyond the limits of their income; the marriage of 1849 had saved the estate from fragmentation. Most positive development had tended to come less from current savings than from the mortgaging of future income.

Consequently the last dozen years of the nineteenth century was a time of disorientation and readjustment for the Cromartie estate. Its management had already been thrown into disarray by the rapid succession of Commissioners Kemball and Brereton. Relations between the 4th Duke and his heir were worsening. The death of Duchess Anne cut off the reliable source of subsidy and the new Earl of Cromartie had only slight grasp of estate affairs at a time when the crofting population seemed to be entirely out of the estate's control. Many of the old certainties had been undermined.

IV

Between times, however, more than ever was known about the foundations of the estate income. The collection of agricultural statistics in Britain improved markedly in the 1880s and it became possible to document the disposition of all estates, including that of Lord Cromartie, more precisely. For instance in 1887 Gunn answered a questionnaire from the Royal Agricultural Society of England. He calculated that the estate was 180,000 acres in extent, of which sheep farms accounted 82,000 acres, deer forests 60,000 and crofter grazings 32,000. Only 4,500 acres of the estate could be classed as arable (the large farms taking 2,400, crofts 2,100), while 1,500 acres were in the form of woods on the large farms. The average size of the large arable farms was 109 acres and the largest was 520 acres. The principal rotation was a five year cycle involving turnips, barley, grass (hay), grass (pasture) and oats. The average rent per arable acre was 20/- to 30/-. For crofts the maximum size was 30 acres, and the minimum was one acre. East coast crofts averaged seven acres, west coast, three acres. On the west coast the crofts on average had 120 acres of grazing attached, on the east none at all. In the east the crofts were generally steep and difficult to work; 30 acres would keep a man and his family very effectively in most seasons, supplemented by carting in winter. On the west coast the crofts were too small and steep to justify the keeping of horses except for carting peat. (This had been a matter of controversy in the Coigach crofters' evidence before the Napier Commission.) On the west coast there were 236 crofters and only one horse to four crofts on average. The caschrom or hand plough was still used on steep crofts.

The average yield per acre of oats on the crofts was half that of the great farms in the lowlands (but two-thirds of the higher large farms). The eastern crofters kept very few sheep but they were 'near to good markets and regular work ... They use most of their oats for meal and they generally use most of their Potatoes but we have a considerable township near Strathpeffer which depends almost entirely on their Potato crop for the rent.'

Gunn gave emphasis to the fact that the management had encouraged the attendance of cattle dealers in Coigach so that the crofters would be given the full competitive value of their stock.

> They were 20 years ago very simple and ignorant on this point and were fearfully swindled by a few local sharpers who bought up their cattle and sheep a day or two previous to the great Muir of Ord markets near Inverness where they drove them quietly and sold them, often clearing 50%.

The services of the Duke's Highland bull had improved breeds significantly and had helped to produce prices 30—40 per cent better than 30 years previously. Timber and lime for house construction had been provided by the proprietor:

> Most if not all the townships, 19 in number, are situated immediately on the sea board, and all these crofters do more or less fishing. They however have no harbour and even if assistance was given them to procure large enough boats to visit the deep sea fishing stations of Stornaway, Wick, Aberdeen and Ireland, they would be of no value without harbours or quays as the coast is very rough.

In this respect Gunn's response was at odds with his opinion to Napier which emphasised the adequacy of the harbour at Altandhu. Gunn was even prepared to extol the souming system, on the grounds that the poorest people, who could not afford stock, were able to raise money from those who could.

New roads 30 to 40 miles in extent, explained Gunn, had opened Coigach to the world. Previously the only access had been by boat. The road programme, according to Gunn, had a substantial demonstration effect

> ... it has done the people good in many ways. It has taught many of them how to use a pick and spade and this has led them to seek similar employment in Sutherlandshire and elsewhere and this travelling has in turn given them an inclination to set about improving their own crofts by trenching with draining and removing boulders.

In this respect there had been a great advance during recent years.[27]

One of Brereton's innovations in the management of the Sutherland empire had been the requirement that each factor report annually on the condition of the respective estates. Their reports provided some of the best accounts of the realities of Highland estate factoring. The year 1887, for instance, was an exceptionally dry season and crops were greatly down on average. Dry, scorching weather had reduced yields and the value of pasture, though more so for cattle than sheep. For once, the disadvantaged crofters suffered less than the rest. Gunn reported of the Heights of Fodderty, Keppoch, Inchvannie and Auchterneed

> These lands being so much higher up, with a colder subsoil and the crops being later did not suffer so much as lower down the valley ... These tenants, as a rule, observe a regular rotation of crops—they work and manure the land well, and they pay attention to their cattle which are usually well bred.

The Gower tenants were the best of all and the soil was light and kindly: 'These tenants were an importation from the Strathconan estate, from which they were evicted some 37 years go. They, as well as the Cotters on the northern heights of this Valley, pay great attention to their cattle'. The potato crop remained vital. In Strathpeffer the small tenants were increasingly taking advantage of the market for dairy produce, poultry and eggs.[28]

Two years later in 1889, Gunn again reported the condition of the estate:

> Farmers and Traders generally are crying out loudly against the new Tariff Rates recently issued by the Railway Companies. These are not the times to impose fresh burdens, which fall indirectly upon the Proprietor who is obliged in consequence to accept reduced rents. Both should combine to protect their mutual interests.

Rents for crofters had been reduced. At Tarbat the small tenants had been grateful for the reduction: 'They are behaving very well in both districts and taking no part in agitation'.

For the large farms it is clear that rent arrears were partly traded for landlord-sponsored improvements. On the Kildary Farm for instance, the farmer, John Ross, had promised to pay his arrears and rent if a new steading was provided. The sheep farms were still in great difficulties. Gunn reported: 'With the exception of North Keanchilish which has been let, and of Inverpolly, no offer had been made for any of the several farms in hand in Lochbroom'. He was afraid of accepting low offers because it would create further unrest among the other sheep farmers, and would influence the attitude of the Crofter Commissioners when they came to examine small tenants' grazings—especially with regard to the application of the Rieff crofters for a portion of Inverpolly. By contrast the shootings were all well let.

Petitions had been received from Coigach crofters for fishing facilities, especially for piers: 'The proposed branch Railway from Garve to Ullapool has a most important bearing upon the fishing and other industries of that district'. Most of the crofters were fishermen and needed a ready market—'with the result that they would come to look upon the fishing industry as their chief employment instead of making it as is too often the case now entirely subservient to the working of their crofts'. For a century the idea of a small tenant class exclusively subsisting on fishing had been the dream of west coast proprietors. A new railway, from Garve to Ullapool, would make the dream reality, according to the optimistic Gunn.[29]

It was inevitable that the continuing agitation of the crofters overshadowed and compounded the problems of individual estate finances. Practically all Highland estates had felt the cold draught of falling sheep prices and rents. Concurrently the crofters, buoyed up by the recommendations of the Napier Commission, continued to withhold rents. The Earl of Cromartie in 1889 complained to the Commission that he had suffered very irregular rents for several years, and that many crofters had practically ceased to pay. The operations of the Commission were, not surprisingly, slow and unwieldy, and much of the Highlands lived in a state of suspended animation awaiting the adjudications of the Commissioners. The delay in the arrival of the Commission at Coigach had, said the Earl, exacerbated his rental problems. Unless the Commissioners arrived before June many of the tenants would have departed to the east coast fishing.[30]

The Cromartie estate, like so much else in the Highlands, had experienced a social revolution in the 1880s. The economic context in a general sense had deteriorated as a consequence of secular price shifts. The death of Cromartie's mother had cut off much of the Sutherland subsidy. Meanwhile Cromartie, like most of the Highland landlords, had lost a great deal of the residual control over the crofters. In the 1890s they sought to achieve a new *modus operandi*.

V

The continuing struggle to re-stabilise the crofting economy and relations with the small tenants on the Cromartie estate consumed a large part of the management's energies in these years. So too did the effort to regularise estate finances. These burdens greatly frustrated the main agent, William Gunn who, almost certainly, would have preferred to devote his talents to the development of the Spa at Strathpeffer. He regarded the Spa as the most exciting prospect for the future of the Cromartie estate both in terms of income and prestige. His enthusiasm for the development exceeded that of his masters and his frustration was, indeed, further compounded by the recurrent shortfall in capital wherewith to realise his visions.

In Dr Fortescue Fox, however, Gunn found a man gripped by a passion for expansion greater even than his own. Fox was the new medical officer at the Spa, the successor (amid much competition) to Dr Manson who died in 1884. Fox had been House Physician to the London Hospital as well as serving as surgeon on steamships. He had travelled as far as China and offered lectures on opium smoking. He had a London degree and good connections in the capital which had favoured his appointment. Fox made incessant demands for Spa expansion, usually couched in the arcane jargon[31] of the pseudo-science of spa therapy and hydropathy. Fox was a man at the frontier of these technologies, devoting himself to the task of keeping Strathpeffer at least as sophisticated and advanced as its southern equivalents. He voiced the rivalry that was part of the leisure and health resort industry in the late Victorian era.

The Spa had already been much enhanced by the improvement of communications with the south. Roads had been built northwards and the railway had long ago reached Inverness. The original plan to extend the network westwards by a route including Strathpeffer was blocked by a local landowner. Nevertheless in 1885 a branch line was secured to the Spa and a weekly through coach from London was inaugurated. By the end of the century it was possible to travel overnight from the capital to Strathpeffer in sixteen hours, and the Spa became, according to the hyperactive Fortescue Fox, 'adequately equipped in every way for the scientific treatment of disease by modern balneological methods', which made it 'one of the leading Spas in Europe'.[32] By then its development has been described as possessing 'the air of a prosperous Victorian suburb'[33] with its villas, pavilions, pump room, hotels, mineral water hospital, parks, golf course and other therapeutic facilities. All this was achieved against much inertia in the capital market and a certain resistance from the owner and the Sutherland factors.

R.M. Brereton, for example, had been sceptical of Fox's ideas and adopted an adamantly commercial approach to all suggestions, but sometimes conceded the need for capital expenditure. In August 1886 he noted the considerable growth in the number of visitors to Strathpeffer and expressed his concern that 'some of the visitors had remarked that the available water supply is insufficient to meet the requirements'.[34] In that year a further loan of £2000 was made available by the Duke for spa improvements. Gunn, however, felt hamstrung by the current financial arrangements. The Spa was incorporated within the general account of the Cromartie estate and this inhibited the possibilities of investment. In essence the estate's general income was falling because of depressed agricultural rents; consequently there was little surplus for investment in the Spa.[35] Nor were the longer-run prospects encouraging: for as soon as the Duke or the Duchess of Sutherland died the Cromartie estate would lose its most important source of capital.

Meanwhile Fortescue Fox continued to concoct plans for the Spa which were too grand for the Sutherland administration. In January 1887 Fox and Gunn were told plainly that the Duke would provide no further capital or guarantees for the development facilities at the Spa.[36] Henceforth Spa development would have to depend on outside funding and a limited liability company would be the best means of meeting the needs, including the operation of the Ben Wyvis Hotel.[37] Gunn protested that these vital improvements were being delayed:

> The existing accommodation is so limited that at the height of the season it is altogether inadequate—a deficiency for which at a health resort, and in the days of improved sanitary arrangements, it is idle to offer any excuse to complaining visitors.[38]

Gunn provided Brereton with a short history of the Spa to place the problem in perspective. He recollected that when he had joined the estate in 1858 the Spa had yielded an annual rent of £100. The lease had increased to £180 but the tenant had fallen bankrupt and the facilities remained in a most primitive condition. Gunn recalled a visit he made to the spas in England after which followed a series of improvements, with additional bathrooms and a new well, excavated in 1872. The celebrated German chemist Herman Weyber was consulted and he had pronounced Strathpeffer's waters to be better than those of most competing spas. However, while the lease continued there had been little further development by the estate and in 1879 the management again assumed direct control. Receipts from the Spa then doubled between 1879 and 1886. Capital expenditure had been substantial: £11,000 had been invested in a new Spa Building, the Pavilion and in new storage tanks. Nevertheless Gunn could point to a clear return of 8 per cent on the capital over the past four years. But further capital was still required: there had been a fire in 1885 which added to the general requirements. Gunn calculated that £3000 could be borrowed at 4 per cent which would yield as much as 12 per cent and perhaps more. It was, he claimed,

> a very safe and good paying investment for the Estate. Even taking the Spa at its present state of development the Estate could not afford to part with it under a clear annual rent of £1000 p.a.—which with a judicious expenditure I believe it to be capable of much greater things.

Gunn was able to produce a long roll-call of distinguished and, still better, aristocratic guests who had visited the Spa. He wanted to publicise the fact that Sir Francis Roxburgh and the Dean of Westminster had both benefited from the waters of Strathpeffer Spa. Gunn felt able to ignore occasional local complaints that the Spa was badly managed and that dirty pipes and escaping gas were rendering the water dead 'and sickening to the stomach'.[39] The guest lists at the hotels in the village gave Gunn great optimism and he resisted the idea that the Spa should be made over to a public company.[40] It was a position which could no longer be sustained after the death of the Duchess of Sutherland in 1888. At that moment the Cromartie estate was forced to rely on its own resources, the Spa included.

VI

The young Earl of Cromartie was relatively profligate in his spending habits and it was unlikely that he would forego personal consumption to provide capital for any kind of estate improvements. On his succession some of the resources at Strathpeffer reverted to his father, the Duke of Sutherland. The Spa, despite its growing popularity as a resort, could expect little investment from internal resources. For instance the estimates for 1888 predicted that the Spa would yield £1530 on an outlay of £810. The surplus, however, would be required to meet overdrafts at the Caledonian Bank and at Drummonds (the Duke of Sutherland's bankers).

Nevertheless, the fashion for Strathpeffer was sustained and there was a possibility that the Queen herself would visit the Spa and this, thought Gunn, would help it become 'more frequented by the upper classes'. The *Scotsman*, in August 1889, had carried favourable accounts, and old Evander Maciver gave Gunn further reassurance: 'Rely on it Strathpeffer has a great future before it and it will form the most valuable portion of the Cromartie Estate'.[41]

As for William Gunn he never lacked faith. He had demonstrated his personal commitment by investing on his own account in the Strathpeffer Hotel Company (in which he was a director). He also had presided over a great expansion of esoteric facilities in the Spa—douches, pine and peat baths, massage devices and new electrical equipment, together with 'second class sulphur baths for the poor class of invalids'. He was able to point to results: he told the Earl of Cromartie that revenue had increased from £653 in 1879 to £1700 in 1889. It followed, he said, that they could 'with confidence adopt such further improvements and extensions as the increasing requirements demand'. New heating facilities, as well as the latest therapeutic appliances, were essential.[42]

The reality was however that the sources of capital had practically run dry. The surplus for 1890, about £900, was swiftly swallowed by the provision of new douches. Gunn uttered his usual lament: 'If we are to do anything to develop the Spa, and to keep the establishment up to the requirements of the times, there must be periodical outlays of capital expenditure'.[43] But the estate did not possess such resources. Consequently the idea of a joint-stock company to operate the Spa was revived, much against Gunn's own inclinations.

Gunn was convinced that the Spa was the estate's greatest asset and had caused a great increase in land values in the Strathpeffer district. He resisted the loss of control that a public company seemed to imply: 'The more the Spa is developed the more prosperous and popular it becomes', and the prosperity of the Spa redounded to the benefit of the Cromartie estate by way of better land values. In 1868 site values had been £8 per acre; in 1891 they were about £20 per acre. When he took over in 1868 the Spa had been 'a poor and neglected and backgoing place'; it had become 'an important and popular place of resort'. The Spa had yielded 8 per cent per annum on investment in recent years producing not only interest but also a small profit on capital. Unfortunately some of the profits now reverted to the Duke of Sutherland under the terms of his wife's will. The importance of Spa revenues to the estate was demonstrated in 1891 when a wet season reduced the number of visitors and income to the estate rental.[44]

Simultaneously, however, Gunn faced the constant complaints and demands of Dr Fortescue Fox. Gunn was plagued by the conflict between the financial constraints of the estate and its auditors on the one hand, and the pressures of the medicos on the other. Fox regarded himself as a great innovator and authority in Spa technology. He was, specifically, an advocate of 'Aix-les-Bains douches' which were already installed at Bath and Harrogate and which gave them the edge over other British spas. Moreover the discovery of a new and more potent sulphur spring at Strathpeffer (by Dr Hayton Davis) also required the expansion of facilities.[45]

Gunn deflected many of Fox's demands. He remained sceptical of the 'analytical appliances' for testing the content of the waters, calling them 'scientific fads'. Fox countered by saying that 'there is not a medical man of any standing who does not ask for the analysis of the various waters before sending patients'. Gunn however pointed out that the estate, in the past six years, had spent £6,000[46] on new equipment at the Spa (on Fox's own recommendation) together with associated advertising campaigns. The estate had thereby built four different styles of bath together with the prescribed douches. Yet, Gunn pointed out, the demand for these facilities had remained static. Fox had caused the estate to invest heavily in sulphur baths and yet, alleged Gunn, he advised his own patients against them; the pine baths had failed to produce a profit because the local chemist sold visitors packets of pine salts which they poured into the hotel baths at no profit whatever to the Spa. Moreover neither Gunn nor his manager had ever received a complaint: 'Hundreds, I may say many thousands, [of] visitors [are] treated during a season—suffering as they do from every conceivable form and variety of ailment, and let me add, of temperament also, [and] it would indeed be very wonderful if there should be no complaint'. Gunn told Fox in no uncertain terms that any further expenditure must yield a proper return.[47]

Since the Cromartie estate was unable to sponsor further capital development (especially during the period in which the inheritance questions were obscured by legal complications), the likelihood of a public take-over of the facilities loomed larger. Overcoming his professional reluctance William Gunn became the central figure in negotiations for the radical reorganisation of the affairs of Strathpeffer Spa. In January 1893 a London-based syndicate emerged under the leadership of a Dr Morris, intent on buying the Spa for £57,000. The doctors at the Spa, Fox and Bruce, were eager for a new regime. Gunn reported their view: 'We are getting on too slowly for them—they of course go in for lavish expenditure of money—other people's money—quite regardless of whether it brings in a sufficient return'. The negotiations were complex, partly because the syndicate itself experienced problems in raising its capital. Gunn thought that £65,000 should be the starting point in the negotiations: 'We should fight hard for £62,000 and not a penny less'.[48]

The negotiations for the Spa created nervous tension among the Cromartie managers. There was a suspicion that the syndicate was merely a speculation got up by people who intended to sell it off at a quick profit as soon as they had captured the asset. The estate's financial advisors in Edinburgh, on the other hand, were concerned that Gunn might frighten off the syndicate by his adamant demands. Black acknowledged the argument that the future owners would reap the benefits of the past investment of £14,000 which was not yet reflected in current revenues and that the price should take account of this. It was rather like a compulsory purchase case, like buying land for a railway—the estimated future value was critical in striking a price. Black also pointed out that the Cromartie estate needed ready money and that the sale of the Spa would immediately reduce expenditure as well as the 'personal worry' resting on Gunn's shoulders. In spite of hesitations and nerves the negotiation was, ostensibly, completed successfully in April 1893 and arrangements were made for the sale of the Spa for £61,000. It was at this stage however that the incapacity of the syndicate was revealed—by September the sale had collapsed apparently on the ground that organisers had been unable to fill their subscription.[49] The failure of the arrangement may have been a northern echo of the great stock market and banking crisis of 1893.

Consequently the Spa at Strathpeffer remained awkwardly placed for capital investment and the estate was unable to realise liquid resources to relieve its budgetary difficulties. None of these problems was alleviated by the sudden death of the young Earl of Cromartie in 1893 or the inheritance difficulties that emerged from the sensational controversy over the will of the third Duke of Sutherland in 1892.

CHAPTER 27

The Hazards of Inheritance, 1888–1896

I

A series of three deaths in rapid succession—the Duchess of Sutherland in 1888 followed by her husband, the third Duke, in 1892, and then his second son, the Earl of Cromartie in 1893—created havoc for the future economic welfare of the Cromartie estate. The financial effects were magnified by the legal complications and controversies surrounding the will of the third Duke. His death was the signal for sensational familial strife and an unholy public wrangle over the will and the rights of the Dowager Duchess Mary Caroline (sometimes called 'the widow Blair'), whom he had married in early 1889. There was even confusion over the succession of the Cromartie title. The upshot of these unpredictable changes in the family succession was that in 1893, the Cromartie estate fell into the hands of an under-age heiress, Lady Sibell (1878-1962). She and her advisors now faced a future of diminished financial resources by which to maintain the style of the family and the efficiency of her estate.

As always over the past two centuries the three recurrent determinants of welfare on the Cromartie estate remained first the disposition of the owner's expenditures; second, the vagaries of agriculture among the large landholders (the arable farmers, the sportsmen and the sheep farmers), and third, the circumstances of the crofting population.

The crofters, of course, had been placed on a new footing on the land and much of the interest in this final period lies in the form and character of the adjustment made by landlord and people to the new arrangements by which the Highlands were to be governed. The backdrop to the argument was, eventually, the return to somewhat better agricultural prices in the Edwardian period. This favoured all classes on the land but the great arable producers recovered their prosperity most effectively of all. Better times for the small tenants seemed to accelerate, rather than curb, the drift of young people from the crofts before the First World War.

Thus after all the economic, social, familial, and political turmoil of the last two decades of the nineteenth century, the Cromartie estate sought a new equilibrium. Its owners, now separated from one of the greatest fortunes in the kingdom, returned to the relatively modest status which was reminiscent of the days of the Hay-Mackenzies. The four decades during which it had been incorporated into the Sutherland territorial empire had achieved less permanent advantage in the aristocratic pecking order than the third Duke and his commissioners had planned. And thus the Cromartie estate entered the twentieth century with only the most modest margin for any further development or expansion. It was not long before the forces of contraction were upon it. Moreover, in the lottery of inheritance, the young Countess was remarkably unlucky, as the events of the mid 1890s began to show.

II

The crofting population was now increasingly well documented. In 1890 another 'General Statement' of agricultural conditions in Coigach was drawn up by the Cromartie estate management. It was a further sign of the developing bureaucratisation of crofting in the Highlands and of the statistical demands of the Crofter Commission. The Commission was thereby beginning to fulfil its statutory functions in the north of Scotland. Gunn's management (now ensconced in a comfortable house and offices at Nutwood in Strathpeffer), in responding to the Commission's request, provided a further historical perspective on the crofter question.

According to Gunn's statement the crofting population was now spread over 25 townships with 233 crofter holdings (with four rent-paying cottars). The people occupied 700 acres of arable land and 29,000 acres of pasture and paid an average of £4.10.0 in rent, or 8d per acre of arable land. The factor with more candour and clarity than had been offered to the Napier Commission seven years before, had traced the rentals back to 1831 'as far as we have any detailed record'. He reported 'that most of the townships were lotted in 1829, and that in 1833 there was a revision of the rents and a general reduction made'. He thought that in 1838-53 most of the tenants held indirectly as subtenants of tacksmen. 'As these leases expired the tenants came to hold direct from the Proprs at the old rents.'

The townships had become directly responsible to the landlord in the following sequence: Polbain, Dorney, Altandhu and Reiff in 1848, Achiltibuie, Badenscallie and the smaller townships southward to Culvercraig in 1853, followed by Achnahaird in 1866. There had been practically no increase of rent over the period 1833-1878, and 'the revised rents fixed in 1833 showed a substantial reduction on the rents prior to that date, so that until 1878 rents were considerably below those of 1833'. In 1878 crofter rents were at last revised upwards.

In a familiar litany Gunn declared that in the previous 25 years the Duchess of Sutherland had spent £12,000 on improvements, 'and it was felt the time had arrived when some small return might fairly be expected for so large an expenditure'. Branch roads had been taken into the various townships, a total of 40 miles in all—at least 13 miles of which were mainly for the accommodation of the people. In addition an improved meal mill was provided together with accommodation for a cartwright and carpenter, altogether costing £940.

Gunn had executed the revaluation in 1878 and there had been no intention to rack-rent the crofters. He explained the principles of his revaluation:

> There being here as elsewhere in the Highlands a strong tendency on the part of the more successful Crofters to overstock at the expense of their less fortunate neighbours the first step was to fix a souming for each township and each separate holding.

Overstocking remained a problem, and the people were always reluctant to divulge information about their stock numbers: 'We generally find that those who keep an overstock and get most benefit of the hill grazings are those who have active sons who can climb the hills and look after their stock—while their less fortunate neighbours suffer because they are unable to do so.' Rent increases were not placed on such people or on recent crofter improvements. While crofter rents had been static for 50 years, farm rents had increased by more than 100 per cent though in recent years they had fallen about 30 per cent. Gunn noted that: 'Crofters as well as farmers have suffered from the fall in the value of stock during the last few years'. The reconstruction of crofters' houses had been given priority and 100 had benefited since 1867, allowances and loans being given for roof timber and slates. The tenants provided all the other materials and the labour. Slated houses were now found in every village. The number of carts had also greatly increased: 'The District is so wide and the population so scattered that there are no fewer than six schools in the Coigach Estate'.

Most of the people (except for those in one or two inland townships) lived near the sea 'and many of them are more dependent upon fishing than upon their Crofts'. Problems of transport kept the fishing industry from reaching its potential 'and consequently the people naturally clung more to the land in the present circumstances'. A railway to Ullapool and a fast coastal steamer service would alter all that. Fishing would solve the land problem in the Highlands, by encouraging the people to become less dependent on the land.

Rent arrears remained the great problem for the estate management. Before 1882 crofter rents 'were paid with commendable regularity'; some years showed less than £20 of arrears (for example in 1871-2). 1882 was a bad harvest, the potato crop had failed, and there was a great dearth of seed. The Duchess had guaranteed supplies and then £180 was still outstanding from the account. Gales in 1881 also destroyed many boats and arrears had risen: 'In 1883 [yielding to outside influences—crossed out] more than half of the tenants made no effort to pay', and the result was a rise in the arrear to £1184. The year 1885 was even worse for rent payments and since then, matters had gone from bad to worse—so that in December 1890 crofter arrears were £3147, despite a general rent abatement of £806 during that four-year period. Legal steps were not taken against the crofters because of the Duchess's natural dislike of such measures: 'It was not until 1888 when everybody's patience was fairly exhausted that Decrees were obtained against some eleven defaulters'. Some of the defaulters paid up, but others simply ignored the decrees:

> While proceedings were pending the death of the Duchess put an end to them—as her son and successor, Lord Cromartie, naturally felt a delicacy in inaugurating his succession to the estate by instituting legal proceedings against his Crofter tenantry. I only wish the tenantry reciprocated the same kindly feeling and consideration towards him.

Gunn still smarted from the hurts of the Crofters' Revolt. In the same spirit, in response to the accumulating arrears the landlord had withdrawn the services of the bulls and other longstanding privileges. Some rents were reduced—for instance, Achnahaird paid £42 in 1872 and £27 in 1890, but many tenants still would not pay. Meanwhile stock prices, both cattle and sheep, had become 'extremely satisfactory'.[1]

Most of 1890 was spent waiting for the deliberations and judgement of the Crofter Commission. There had been considerable anxiety in the Cromartie management that rents would be arbitrated to much lower levels. In the outcome however the factors were surprised and gratified by the Commission's verdict. An average reduction of 21 per cent was announced for crofter rents which was, indeed, remarkably close to the level of reduced rents already adopted by the Cromartie estate. As Gunn pointed out, it 'was only 1 per cent above the abatement we have been allowing for the last five years. This is very satisfactory and compares very favourably with other West Highland estates—even with the Assynt part of Sutherland.' The proceedings of the Commission had been much marked by further verbal jousts between factors and Land League representatives. The other business before the Commission concerned claims for extra lands, but these were dealt with separately over the following years.

There was a measure of symbolic retribution in Gunn's response to the rent reduction. He told Lord Cromartie:

> Considering the small rents fixed by the Commission your Lordship cannot be expected to provide Bulls. No other Proprietor in this Country supplies Bulls ... and although the Coigach tenants have been supplied for many years they have not shown the smallest gratitude. I have hitherto advocated this grant for Bulls, but now I consider the circumstances are entirely changed.[2]

It was a small token of the rancour and bitterness that had infected the battle with the crofters over the previous decade.

In these years the attitude of the Cromartie management became demonstrably less paternalistic to the crofters, a shift which was, indeed, implicit in the aims of the Crofters' Revolt. And in this hardening of sentiment, William Gunn and his colleagues almost certainly reflected a broader change in attitudes among the established classes in northern Scotland. It was expressed in the oddest corners. For instance, a correspondent of *Notes and Queries* in 1884 remarked: 'The ideal Highlander, whose existence (if existence it can be called which is, mere parasitical vegetation) the Crofters' Commission has brought to light, most Scotchmen are anything but proud'.[3] It was part of a social revolution in the Highlands and Gunn and his fellow factors were required to cope with its consequences, both economic and psychological.

III

In general estate matters economy ruled. The Spa continued as a problem, and repeated proposals were suggested for outside developers to take over from the landlord management. The idea was generally resisted by Gunn. Between 1885-91 £6000 had been spent on structural improvements at the Spa and endless discussion continued about the profitability of these decisions. Grazing farms also remained a source of worry; wool and sheep prices continued to be very depressed and Gunn remarked in 1891 that 'the grazing rental is everywhere so terribly reduced—that we are compelled to make the most we can out of the shooting rents'. While many sheep farms remained in hand they were, of course, a constant temptation to crofters for appeal to the Commission. Sheep farms were also a managerial nightmare. Gunn noted, 'I am quite alive to the desirability of getting the other farms let and shall certainly not miss an opportunity. Nobody knows better than I do the trouble, indeed the anxiety they are when in hand.' As for the crofter arrears, the Commission's determination of fair rents had cleared the air and reduced the annual conflict over rent collection.[4]

When, in late 1892 the third Duke of Sutherland died, he left great question marks hanging over the finances of his descendants. It was virtually inevitable that the colossal Sutherland fortune should generate legal dispute but the rancour was unprecedented and attracted the full glare of Fleet Street. It was especially juicy because of the legal contortions consequent on the late Duke's second marriage in 1889. The Dowager Duchess, his wife of only three and a half years, was able to make claims on a large proportion of the entire Sutherland fortune. This, of course, had vast consequences for the male heirs—the fourth Duke of Sutherland and the Earl of Cromartie—and therefore the will became a titanic struggle before the courts and before the nation's newspapers.

On the outcome of the battle over the Sutherland Will case depended the future of the Cromartie estate and William Gunn was profoundly alarmed at the dangers. He thought that the late Duke had made clear commitments to the Cromartie heirs. He asked the estate's Edinburgh lawyers: 'When the title was restored to the late Duchess was there not an undertaking given by the Duke that such a provision would be made as would suffice to uphold the honour and dignity of the Earldom?' He thought that this obligation was being wantonly ignored: 'I remember Mr Gadsden telling me when I met him in London after the Duchess's death, that Lord C under the Duke's Will would be entitled to the interest on such a sum (I think he said £100,000) as would bring his [Lord Cromartie's] income up to £10,000. Could the last will over-rule all this? It is very hard if it can.'[5] The great skirmish over the will therefore spilled over into the affairs of the Cromartie estate. Several years passed before the will case was settled.

At this time, too, anxious warnings came from the appointment of a Royal Commission into Deer Forests in 1892. 'A very sorry crew they are' commented Gunn, 'it is sad to think that almost the only valuable bit of property that unhappily is now left the Highland proprietors should be exposed to attack by men who with only one or two exceptions are extreme Radicals and from whom a fair or unbiased judgement need not be looked for.' He advocated that proprietors should combine 'in a united and determined effort to resist the attack of such a one sided Commission'.[6] Within a month a group representing Highland lairds was indeed formed under the presidency of Locheil. It was an association of an embattled and retreating proprietorship. Gunn advised,

> I think we should be prepared with reliable information of the actual extent of the land embraced within Deer Forests or Sheep Farms that at one time, however remote, was cultivated by small tenants—also the area of land capable of being made arable at a reasonable cost keeping in view the altitude and difficulty of access.[7]

These, of course, were central questions which neither then nor since have been accurately answered.

The tighter policy towards estate management continued. Revenue was pushed up into the region of £16,000—£16,500, assisted by timber sales from the estate. Expenditure was restricted to £8100—£8000. Gardeners were declared redundant.[8] A great deal of activity was given over to the revived proposal that a syndicate might take over the operations of the Spa. The Spa had cost £14,000 in development expenditure from 1879-1893, and a new round of negotiations stumbled along without resolution. Meanwhile prospects in agriculture were beginning to improve. In January 1893 Gunn declared that rents in the eastern parts of the estate were better, though he had to point out that,

> the croft rents arrears on the West Coast go on increasing in spite of all we can do. For the last two years the poor crops and very low prices for stock have had their effect—but the difficulty is one which will have to be faced sooner or later, and the sooner the better in the interests of the people themselves as well as the estate.

Once more the estate expenditure estimates were greatly reduced.[9]

Policy towards the land in the west, and to the pressure of crofters through the new channels of the Commission, was one of some difficulty. Land could only be applied for by the crofters on the termination of a lease. Gunn felt that, in bad times, leases could be extended on lower rents as a perfectly legitimate concession from landlord to pastoral tenant, 'and before the crofters put in their application'. Inverpolly, Badentarbat and Glenskiach were each liable to crofter incursions. Where a large stretch was tenanted by

> a sportsman, instead of by a *bona fide* farmer, altho' a very advantageous arrangement for the Estate, will not be looked at favourably by the Court ... I only hope that the prospect on the near future of having this shooting, or the best part of it over run by Crofters, may not be the means of carrying away our present excellent tenant.[10]

It was a severe problem in that both arable and pasture farm rents had declined 30—35% in the previous dozen years.[11] Agricultural recovery was excruciatingly slow.

IV

The Earl of Cromartie, Francis Leveson Gower, died in 1893 (less than a year after his father) after a long and upsetting illness following a boating accident at Lochinver on the north west coast of the Highlands.[12] He died at Stafford House on 24 November 1893 at the age of 41. Outside the family there was considerable debate about the future of the title. *The Times*, the *Daily News*, the *Graphic* and the *Illustrated London News* all thought the earldom had now become extinct, that it had 'disappeared from the peerage'. The uncertainty and confusion derived from the peculiar circumstances of the patent of its creation (or re-creation) in 1861, and by the fact that Cromartie was survived by a daughter[13]—Lady Sibell Lilian Mackenzie. In the outcome, and after an appeal to the Queen, the title was made safe. The estate finances proved to be much less secure.

Lady Sibell was only 15 years old at her succession and special arrangements were activated for the assumption by her of the title Countess of Cromartie. It was necessary for her affairs to be managed by a group of Trustees. They were her uncles, the fourth Duke of Sutherland and Lord Lorne. The operations of the Trustees were complicated by continuing legal controversy over the Sutherland Will case which remained unresolved. It would eventually have critical financial repercussions for the young Countess.

The lawyer's firm of Blacks in Edinburgh organised most of the central legal business of the estate. The Countess, Lady Sibell, was very little involved in the affairs of the estate. In 1899 she married Major E.W. Blunt of the Royal Artillery and a relative in direct line of descent from Lord Nelson and Colonel Todd, founder of the Indian Political Service and author of the *Annals of Rajasthan*. Blunt took a firm hold over much of the estate business. Before that the great uncertainty surrounding the Strathpeffer Will case hung over the estate finances, especially the conditions of the entail. In 1896 Black wrote: 'I am still inclined to hold that notwithstanding the words of the directory Clause the intention of the old Duke will prevail and that the young Countess is the heiress of Entail in possession and holds the Title she will, as she should, get the money'.[14] The question revolved about the validity of the first and second wills of the old Duke of

41   The *Lady Sibell* in which the family cruised to the Mediterranean. The Earl died of pneumonia after diving in to save a seaman from drowning.

Sutherland and the meaning of the special clauses affecting the Cromartie line and, of course, the directly competing claims of the Dowager Duchess. The financial implications were immense. A case did not go before the House of Lords until 1896.

Meanwhile the management of the crofting population on the Cromartie estate had been rendered in many ways much more straightforward by the operation of the Crofter Commission. The undefined responsibilities of the paternalistic landlord were replaced by a clearer institutional framework. Rent defaulters could now be pursued with little fear of opprobrium or agitation. The main area of concern was the claims made by crofters for additional lands. In 1896 for instance defaulters were warned of their new position; this they had disregarded, 'evidently in the expectation that they will be permitted to go on as before accumulating arrears'. It was decided to move decisively against some of them who had been in arrears between two and seven years, and, as Gunn remarked:

> They have all forfeited their tenancy under Section 3 of the Crofter Act and are liable to be removed ... I do not think any of the 6 cases will create sympathy locally, as it is well known that they have been generously treated by the Estate authorities, and that they have made no effort to get out of arrear.[15]

It was an issue of considerable importance to the management; the agents believed that they had stomached enough trouble in the previous two decades. Gunn repeated the point, 'I do not believe that any sympathy will be aroused in either case as it is well known that the greatest consideration has been shown by the Estate in all these cases'.

In many respects the Crofter Act systematised relationships in estate life. It left far less room for aristocratic liberality, discretion or misunderstanding. The reciprocal of this change was a decline in the automatic deference offered by the small tenantry. Obsequiousness diminished and a more independently-minded attitude began to emerge. The subtleties of social relations were suggested in a recommendation from Black. He was referring to the problem of keeping the crofters' dogs away from the grouse at Dornie. His solution, a clear bribe, expressed old and new frissons in social expectations in the post Crofter Commission Highlands:

> I most strongly advise and Lady Cromartie quite approved, that we should give each Crofter £1 and perhaps some tea to his wife and a little tobacco to himself if they will look after the grouse and keep their dogs off the young birds ... I find that shepherds and crofters like this to come from principals and not from keepers.[16]

The importance of the Land League nevertheless remained. In autumn 1896 an estate circular was sent to rent defaulters. Black ordered decisive action against backsliders. But, he cautioned:

> We must not give the Land League a handle by proceeding against poor Widows, and suchlike, but where a Crofter can pay and defies us, it is only fair to those who do pay that action should be taken against the non-payer in Court. If we don't do something at the proper time after issuing that Circular I am afraid that we shall lose ground all over the Estates.

42 A and B Captain Walter Blunt and Countess Sibell in the year of their marriage, 1890.

As for a request for reductions by the Tarbat crofters, he advised that the estate avoid going before of the Commissioners—another sign of the effect of the crofter legislation in indirect and informal ways.[17] The Commission, by its very existence, cast a shadow over estate management and influenced rent levels, the collection of arrears, and the security of tenure, even when it did not directly intervene. Moreover the events of the past dozen years had produced a far greater consciousness of public opinion in estate management. For instance, when Gunn advised legal action against the crofters Black was impressed by his assurance 'that these are not cases that will arouse sympathy'.[18]

There were, however, some particular difficulties. For instance, in March 1897 the west coast agent described a specific case: 'I am informed that Margaret King or Fraser, Isle Martin ... one of the cases in which the removal proceedings are pending, has gone out of her mind and that the Inspector of Poor had to take charge with a view to her removal to the Lunatic Asylum. I have not heard any cause assigned.'[19] The kid-glove approach was adopted to avoid adverse publicity. Black felt that individual cases should always be kept out of the hands of the Commissioners: 'I shall be very glad indeed if we can escape from the hands of the Crofter Commissioners'.[20] But perhaps the most telling statement of the alteration of the times, the shifting attitudes in the Highlands, and the real effect of legislation on the relationship between landlords and crofters, came from Black in a letter to Gunn on 31 March 1897:

> As to the Crofters against whom proceedings have been initiated we must endeavour to follow up these proceedings or they will make a bad impression. I note that you hope to be able to get over the difficulty of providing suitable accommodation for those who may have to be removed. I agree with you that we cannot turn them out on to the road and that we must not think of providing and selling.

Such restraints on landlord action were obviously a response to the prevailing climate of public opinion. Landlord action, such as summary eviction or wholesale resettlement, which had been possible in 1840 was, in 1897, no longer feasible. Black put it unequivocally: 'The Crofter question is a difficult one, because there is so much sentiment associated with it and on both sides there is an absence of the true grasp of the subject—each party plays for the votes of the Crofters and will sympathise with them even although they do not perform their obligations.' Removals were virtually impossible in these circumstances; and the management clearly believed the pendulum controlling social relations had swung too far towards the crofters.[21]

STRATHPEFFER SPA

43　Treatment by electricity.

44　Treatment by water c.1908.

STRATHPEFFER SPA

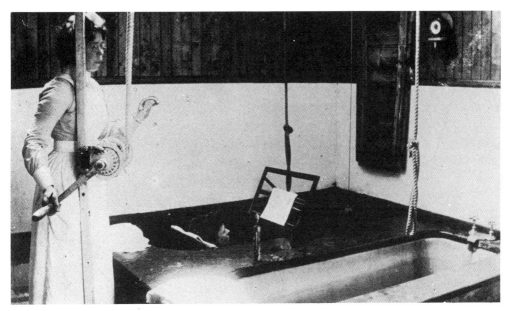

45 The Peat Bath, with a woman patient enjoying the warm wet peat and reading a paper at the same time.

46 The Douche, which followed, was designed to wash off most of the peat from the preceding treatment.

STRATHPEFFER SPA

47 The Nicholson Memorial Mineral Hospital.

48 The Pavilion, Strathpeffer, as an American convalescent hospital in 1917.

STRATHPEFFER SPA

49   Ben Wyvis Hotel, exterior.

50   Ben Wyvis Hotel, interior with electric light fittings.

STRATHPEFFER SPA

51 The orchestra gave a continental sound to the square, Strathpeffer.

52 Queen Victoria's Diamond Jubilee celebrated in Strathpeffer by the local inhabitants.

CHAPTER 28

Cromartie Alone 1896–1914

I

Between his second marriage, in March 1889, and his death in September 1892, the third Duke of Sutherland had altered his will no less than ten times. While blazing family rows raged around him the Duke had re-arranged his disposable wealth more and more in favour of his new wife, Duchess Blair, as she was termed by her disapproving in-laws. A few hours before he died the Duke added a final codicil which increased her cash legacy to £150,000. In the subsequent battle over the will Duchess Blair was gaoled for six weeks for destroying evidence. Eventually she settled with the family to receive an unspecified sum, thought to have been at least £750,000.[1] This, alone, of course, diminished the residue available for the fourth Duke and the rest of his family, especially for the under-age Countess of Cromartie.

For the Cromartie estate the critical question concerned the third Duke's intention (as interpreted from his various wills) towards the maintenance of the Cromartie earldom. The Countess's legal advisors argued that when the Earldom of Cromartie was re-created in 1861 the Duke had undertaken to provide resources to the heirs sufficient to sustain the proper dignity and social style of this branch of his family. The Will however was ambiguous and the entire question was subject to the ruling of the House of Lords. It became a matter of extreme anxiety to the Cromartie advisors and, when the decision was handed down, in May 1896, their fears were fully confirmed. The Cromartie estate received far less from the Sutherland estate than had been originally anticipated. Henceforth the Cromartie estate would have to survive on its own resources and its capital assets were far less than had been expected. The extent of the disappointment became clear in the responses to the decision of the House of Lords. The repercussions were momentous for the Countess and her successors.

According to A.D.C. Black in Edinburgh the problem arose from 'a single sentence in the will of the Duke's'. He thought it may have been a mistake because it was unlikely that the Duke 'meant it or knew the intricacies of Entail Law sufficiently to order its insertion'. Mistake or not it was, he said, 'a cruel thing'.[2] The final judgement confirmed the cruelty of fate:

> The House of Lords have reversed the decision of the Court of Session. I feared this, and to tell the truth have always been very anxious about the result ... The Lords did not see their way to read the intention of the late Duke's whatever it may have been, against the

plain meaning of the directions to the Trustees to pay the income to the heirs female of the Late Lord Cromartie ... This is a very serious decision for the Estate. We shall require to remodel our estimates, because amongst other things a considerable portion of the funds held by these Cromartie Trustees consists of bonds over the Cromartie Estates. Hitherto we have left them out of the accounts as you are aware, but now we shall have to debit the Estate with the interest and transfer one half to Lady Constance [Lady Cromartie's younger sister]. In fact it cuts down our expected income to something like £2100 a year.

The position was clarified a little more in another letter in May 1896—as Black put the bad news: 'The decision is of course disappointing from Lady Sibell's point of view. It is also a serious one for the Estate. It means about £80,000 less into the heiress's pocket and about £2200 a year less in income. You can imagine what all that means.'[3] It was a financial catastrophe for the Cromartie estate.

The whole episode—critical for the future welfare of the estate—was a prime example of the extraordinary effect of inheritance arrangements for nineteenth century landed estates. By the error of a pen in 1862 the future of the estate was decisively undermined— it was all to do with the vagaries of the aristocratic temperament and the legal smallprint, and nothing at all to do with the productivity of the land, the efficiency of management or even the general economic circumstances. It was an aspect of the total authority of the inheriting *élite*—their temperament and their errors could so easily affect the welfare of the entire enterprise. The dramatic absurdity of the position became clearer in another recounting of the events: Black came to the view that a 'trivial' error by George Loch in 1862 had caused the financial disaster

> I rather think the clause in the Cromartie Trust Deed of 1862, which has now floored us was adjusted by Mr Loch on the lines of the Peerage Patent, and that he must have attached some technical meaning to the words 'Heirs Female', forgetting that by the Law of Scotland heirs female are heirs petitioners. The direction in the Trust to the Trustees is that failing heirs male, the income of the fund is to be paid to the heirs female of the body of Lord Cromartie. The House of Lords did not see their way to override his plain direction, because an intention pointing to a probably contrary result was indicated in the narrative of the Deed.

The key appears to have been contained in the terms of the Cromartie Trust of 1862. The Trust had placed railway and hotel shares in the arrangement which the Lords' decision now shifted from the hands of the Estate. Black[4] believed that there had been negligence and ignorance among the legal advisers of the estate in the previous generation. Not only Loch, but the firm of Jameson and Gatty, had been at fault when 'they adjusted that wonderful agreement' and made over the shares to the Cromartie Trust instead of to the Heir of Entail: 'now it is past paying for'. He also complained: 'I have not had a scrap, either by wire or otherwise from Lady Cromartie. It is perplexing.'[5] It seems that only half of the vital shares descended to Lady Cromartie.[6] The decision of the House of Lords was obviously crucial. Black, a year after the fateful decision, continued to stress the financial problems that flowed from it: 'I have to look to ways and means as that unfortunate decision in the House of Lords presses very hard against the young Countess'.[7]

The financial condition of the Cromartie estate, therefore, had been seriously weakened as it separated from the Sutherland empire. Various ajdustments quickly followed the decision. Soon after Cromartie's death his yacht, Maud, was sold off for £1500 and his chambers in London were also disposed of. The young Lady Cromartie was organised to live at Tarbat. In 1894 it was decided to let out Castle Leod and its grounds.[8] The young Countess was thus required to live in far less favourable circumstances than had been anticipated. General economic conditions, particularly among the sheep farmers, created added alarm. The tightness of financial affairs on the estate was increased in 1897 by the fact that three of the great shooting leases were unlet and, from Edinburgh, Black sounded a clear warning—'If the shootings do not let, looking to the decision of the House of Lords in the Cromartie Trust case, we might find ourselves in an awkward position'.[9] The problems on the estate were not eased by persistent disagreement that punctuated the relationship between the Countess's Trustees, the Duke of Sutherland and the Marquis of Lorne which continued until the Countess reached her majority in 1899. As Henry Wright remarked: 'It is fortunate that the Trusteeship will soon come to an end' because it threatened to damage the prospects of development at Strathpeffer Spa.[10] Lorne wanted great expansion at the Spa so that it might rival facilities available at Brighton, but was frustrated by Sutherland's caution.

By the late 1890s the financial problems at Cromartie were already prompting the advisors to think of property sales. Black remarked that 'there are rich men from the south of England prepared to buy Highland properties',[11] and he knew that land sales were the ultimate solution to the problems of the Countess and her estate. Already symbolic was the sale, in October 1897, of two of Romney's portraits from the family picture gallery, for about £6000: and among the buyers was 'a very rich American, Mr Vanderbilt'.[12] Once more then, southern and foreign money was seeking opportunities to invest in the Highlands. Strathpeffer Spa was also an object of southern investment interest, even of its complete take over.

II

Strathpeffer Spa continued to attract visitors and generate revenue—for the waters and the associated facilities, especially the hotels—throughout the 1890s. Takings at the Spa itself increased steadily and the return on investment remained positive; for example in 1895 the Strathpeffer Hotel paid 8 per cent. The effort to sell the Spa in 1893 had failed and after the death of the Earl the facility was governed by the Trustees of the Countess. The fourth Duke of Sutherland sustained a personal influence in the Spa (in July 1894 he and his wife sojourned at the Spa and were joined by their guest, the Prince of Wales[13]). Small improvements were still initiated despite the underlying lack of capital.[14] The doctors were never satisfied and at one point circumvented Gunn's authority and appealed directly to the Trustees over the appointment of a new Spa manager.[15]

The special problems of managing and maximising a tourist resort continued to exercise the estate. In 1891 there were complaints about the oppressive new regulations then operating at the Spa. Previously the natives of Strathpeffer had been able to drink the waters *gratis*, but now they had to pay the same charges imposed on the visitors.

Moreover 'workmen's dwellings were tabooed at the Strath' and all the working people who serviced the Spa and its activities were 'obliged to live away a long distance from the Spa'. There was a shortage of labour—'for example, a washer-woman cannot be got for a day's washing nearer than Dingwall'. The underlying cause was the obstruction—presumably on aesthetic grounds—on the building of small dwellings at the Strath.[16] Gunn was always ambivalent about the clientele which the Spa was meant to attract. In June 1893 for instance, he tried to induce local newspapers to print all the names of visitors to Strathpeffer during the season—partly, of course, to advertise the popularity of the hotels, but also to appease the visitors themselves. As Black observed: 'Visitors like to see their names in print, at least the weaker classes do'.[17]

Similar considerations informed attitudes to the broader development of the village of Strathpeffer. There was some tension between the needs of the residents (or feuars) and the hotel users, the latter much preferred by Gunn partly because they were of a better social class and brought lustre to the Spa, and partly because he was himself an hotelier. Distinguished and opulent guests sought rural tranquillity not a bustling village. In the season of 1895 the Spa was so popular that there was great pressure on accommodation.[18] But Gunn echoed the attitudes of his predecessors in the 1810's.[19] Gunn explained his feelings in 1895:

> Our aim hitherto has been to preserve as much as possible the rural character of the place and it is this ... that makes it attractive to English visitors ... Keeping this in view we have hitherto avoided long streets, and large blocks of tenements, preferring self-contained villas each with its grass and flower plots and surrounded by a hedge.

Even so Gunn did not fully favour general residential development because 'the high class visitor almost invariably prefers apartments in one or other of the Hotels'. When the possibility of introducing electricity to Strathpeffer was mooted in 1896 it was argued that it would enhance the feuing potential of the village. But Gunn was sceptical—superior guests had no wish to build houses in Strathpeffer because the weather was too uncertain for that and 'no amount of covered verandahs or indoor amusements will induce them to do so'. Moreover feuing development would jeopardise the rural character of the Spa, its greatest attraction. For Gunn the Hotel trade was the centre piece of the resort.[20]

Revenue from the Spa maintained its upward trend reaching £2218 in 1896. Gunn continued to insist on the rural character of the resort: if it became a town it would 'no longer be the favourite place of resort it now is, with the better class of visitor, the thorough change it affords from a life in the town'. Gunn explained his philosophy further:

> It should be remembered that here we are far removed from the busy centres of population, and have no rich businessmen near us, to take up summer quarters, and go in and out of business, as they can do from Glasgow and other large towns. Those of the better class who care to come so far north, and bring their families, have no difficulty in renting comfortable lodgings here, by the month, which is what they have hitherto done. Our winter and early spring months are usually too severe and too damp for Strathpeffer ever to become a winter resort.

But the trustees, especially the Marquis of Lorne, urged on by the ever enthusiastic doctors, were keen for development and wanted to feu land at rates more competitive than currently available in Nairn, Grantown, Bridge of Allan and other Highland resorts. There was a continuing degree of dissent among the Trustees about the future of the Spa and, in the context of the great inheritance controversy, Black said that the Trustees needed to be 'most delicately handled'. Moreover though Lorne might want Strathpeffer to look like Brighton there was simply no money for such visions.[21]

Health spas, of course, depended almost entirely on reputation for their success and could not afford even the slightest hint of uncleanliness or a reduction of social chic. And despite the private scepticism of some of the Strathpeffer estate managers, the Spa continued to attract a remarkable clientele. Eminent medical men advocated the curative powers of spa treatments without apparent reservation. The treatment of George Curzon, about to become Viceroy of India, was a case in point. Agonised throughout most of his life by terrible spinal pain, Curzon eventually consulted Howard Marsh, a specialist who became Professor of Surgery at Cambridge. Among several pieces of advice Marsh told Curzon to go to Strathpeffer where, he directed,

> douching for the spine can be had. It should be douched once a day, with water as hot as can be borne without any discomfort. Rubbing after the douche could probably be useful. After a week, the douching with sea water can be carried on with a large bath sponge.

Curzon, who visited the Queen at Balmoral en route north, experienced these esoteric treatments at Strathpeffer, but still needed to encase his back in steel and leather for relief and support.[22]

Belief in the potency of the waters was, therefore, indispensable for the future of the Spa. In mid-1900 there were several related problems: there were fears that contiguous landowners would begin to tap the same source for sulphur waters and thereby break the Spa's exclusive hold on the vital asset; there was also annoyance that local youths were attending the Spa for free drinks; Gunn had to instruct the manager: 'The Refreshment Rooms are there for the convenience of visitors and not natives'.[23]

More serious were adverse rumours said to be circulating in London about the purity of the Strathpeffer waters. Fortescue Fox declared that such talk was 'likely to work very serious injury to the Spa'. Damaging reports were abroad, that there was pollution and contamination at Strathpeffer, totally anathema of course to the work of the Spa. There was a suspicion that the curative waters were being polluted from the drains. Gunn was outraged: 'During my 33 years connection with the management I have never known of a single case of fever that could be traced to the use of sulphur water polluted by leakage from sewer drains', and he observed that the source of the springs at Harrogate was actually located in the very middle of the residential district. The fears led to several actions: elaborate tests of the water were instituted; new borings were excavated; leaflets containing recommendations from visitors were circulated to reinforce the curative reputation of the Spa. Some damage may have been done for it was admitted in 1901 that 'the popularity of Strathpeffer has declined in comparison with other British Sulphur Spas'. Inevitably all this was fuel to Fortescue Fox in his demands for yet more improvements. But the estate reduced its expenditures and for a few years, from 1903 to 1907, the Spa revenues were remarkably stable.[24]

III

The Countess of Cromartie reached her majority in August 1899 and four months later married Major Blunt whom she met at a Vice-Regal Ball in Dublin. He was almost twice her age and his military career had included eight years duty in India, service in the Ashanti expedition in 1896, and also under Lord Kitchener in Egypt.[25] Rejoicings were arranged by the estate and, despite the disapproval of Black, even the crofters who were in rent arrears were allowed to participate. In October, William Gunn was sent to Harrogate for rest and recuperation (and to observe a rival spa at work) and soon there were changes in the management. Blunt, who changed his name to Blunt-Mackenzie in 1905, brought new energy and ideas to the estate and quickly assumed proprietorial responsibilities on behalf of his wife. He had visions of economic development on several fronts—at the Spa, in the creation of fish hatcheries on the west coast, in crofter progress and, most of all, in the provision of hydro-electricity in Strathpeffer and Dingwall. In much of this his enthusiasm was greater than the supply of personal and loan capital at Cromartie could match. Moreover Blunt's military career meant that he had to conduct his estate administration from a distance: his instructions to the factors flowed in from the Royal Artillery Barracks at Woolwich, from Ireland, from Sierra Leone, from Jamaica, from Norway and from France. The local factorship was modernised and the estate operated increasingly as a business; its clients and its tenantry increasingly addressed 'the Estate' rather than the 'landlord' or 'the Countess'.

There was a feeling that a new era had begun which was of course, further symbolised by the death of the Queen. The Coigach agent, Alexander Ross, like so many of his generation, gave pause for a moment of retrospection. He wrote to Gunn

> I note what you say about our national loss. Like the Blacks of Africa we are loth to believe that Queen Victoria is dead. Her memory will live. The world has not seen such an era of progress as her reign. It is difficult to believe that there is room left for the same rate of progress in a similar period in the future but changes will and must take place till the millenium but we must from the heart say God save the King.[26]

William Gunn was due to retire at the end of 1901 and in his final year he saw the financial crisis of the Cromartie estate emerge in dangerous dimensions. In June 1901 Gunn received a letter from Black in Edinburgh, marked 'Very Private' and so confidential that it did not appear in the letter book. The letter concerned Black's mounting anxiety about the estate finances. He had been negotiating a loan of £10,000 for the estate from the National Bank occasioned by the immediate need to take over sheep stock from a departing leaseholder. Black was placed in a position in which he had to provide the Bank with security for the loan and thus required the commitment of the

53 Grain stacks and the teams of horses required, on the farm of Rhinie, parish of Fearn about 1900. Courtesy of the Scottish Ethnological Archive, National Museums of Scotland.

54 Scything storm-flattened oats, about 1905, on a farm near Culbokie, Easter Ross. Courtesy of the Scottish Ethnological Archive.

55 Threshing mills did the rounds in winter in Easter Ross: a steam mill with straw-elevator at work near Conon Bridge, 1905. Courtesy of the Scottish Ethnological Archive.

56 Herring-gutters at work in Ullapool, early 1900s. Courtesy of the Scottish Ethnological Archive.

Countess's assets—farm stock, and even furniture and art-works in her own mansions. Black remarked bleakly:

> The fact is Gunn as you will see we are at a very anxious crisis and we have not the command of money as in the old days and I want to know exactly where we stand .... I don't want to frighten the Countess. But of course she and Major Blunt must soon be told how we stand as to finance.[27]

When Gunn retired at the end of 1901 he remained at Strathpeffer and continued his own interests in the Ben Wyvis Hotel and in the letting of sporting leases. His son had become factor to Lord Ashburton and leased farms on the Cromartie estate. Gunn, who had been Commissioner of Supply, County Councillor, Chairman of Fodderty Parish Council and of the Fodderty School Board, was presented with 300 guineas from the donations of feuars, tenants and employees, to mark his retirement. The local newspaper said of Gunn that 'the poorest labourer on the estates invariably receives from him the respect and courtesy due to a gentleman'. The *Ross-shire Journal* also recollected his part in the crofter revolt of the 1880s: 'He passed courageously through the tumultuous times of the land law reform agitation, and so nicely adjusted the conflicting interests of parties that the most friendly relations have been constantly maintained between landlord and tenant'. It was a generous, even rose-tinted, view of a factor's life but no one could deny Gunn's commitment to his task in the previous four decades.

Gunn's successor was George Wotherspoon who, previously, had been sub-factor to Captain Hope of St Mary's Isle and his appointment was accompanied by the announcement that Major Blunt would be taking a more active role in the estate management.[28] Gunn's retirement was followed by that of another sub-factor, Colin Fraser, in 1902 and he also looked back over a long career. He alluded to the course of rents since 1865, notably the great reduction in agricultural rents and the corresponding increase in sporting rents, paralleled also by the great increase in labour costs and taxes. He added,

> Mr Gunn and myself will never forget the dark days of the 80s, and the land agitation, when feeling ran so high, and estate officials occupied anything but an enviable position, but happily these are now matters of history, never we hope to repeat itself.'[29]

The tumult of the 1880s, it is true, had subsided and little of the earlier excitation remained. Many of the formerly contentious aspects of landlord/tenant relations were now governed by externally-imposed regulations. Government bodies ruled rents and conditions in crofting and practically all argument could be channelled into the Land Court or the Commission. None of this, however, solved the poverty which continued to shroud the crofting population; it provided little in the way of capital development or diversification in the local economy. The crofters continued to feel aggrieved at their meagre land resources and continued to bicker amongst themselves particularly about communal facilities and grazing. And they continued in their efforts to prise and lever more land out of the hands of the landlord.

Thus the contest for control of the land persisted into the twentieth century, now under new rules and under economic tendencies which still favoured sporting tenancies over the great sheepfarmers. The crofters of Coigach believed that their bargaining position for land was strengthened and that the resolution of the landlord had weakened. In 1901, for instance, there were proposals that the crofters should be given Badentarbat and Achnahaird;[30] at the same time the estate was unable to let sheep farms in Coigach, and Black lamented that there was 'nothing for but to carry them on for a little in the hope of getting tenants, but where the money to pay for the sheep stocks is to come from, I do not at present see'.[31] Pressure from the crofters meanwhile was practically continuous and while proprietors converted sheep farms into deer forests,[32] the crofters' demands were increasingly effective. Major Blunt, frustrated by the defection of sheep farmers, was prepared to relinquish more land, especially if it would 'pacify the crofters'.[33] In the following ten years the Cromartie estate made over to the crofters a total of 5831 acres of grazing in Coigach.[34]

Blunt soon learned the frustrations of what Black described as 'these recalcitrant crofters of the west coast'.[35] One of his first efforts to settle disputes about crofters' grazing limits, at Achiltibuie in 1901, ended in a typical impasse when the crofters failed to agree among themselves about common grazing rights. Blunt sighed,

> I confess I was hopeful and thought our only difficulty would be to conciliate the East Enders ... I wonder if we shall be able to persuade them some day that we really do mean well and wish to help them ... Their 'rights' are so very safe that any notion they were threatened need hardly have occurred to them'.[36]

Communal disputes among the crofters were endless and the estate managers were still expected to settle such problems. Alexander Ross remarked in 1900 that 'something must be done for these crofters to protect themselves from each other if they are to survive and till the soil ... the way they take advantage of each other is actually lamentable and disgusting'.[37] Crofters moreover still looked to the estate for direct help when they fell into economic difficulty, when illness occurred, when their boats were smashed in a storm. The estate operated as a rudimentary social welfare system and its internal correspondence was a record of human frailty, suffering, and dispute. Even so most of the day-to-day problems of the crofters were contained and settled within their own communities.

Blunt-Mackenzie co-ordinated his own thoughts on the crofter question for a speech in Glasgow in December 1907 (for the Glasgow Ross and Cromarty Benevolent Association Gathering). He believed that great progress had been achieved in the Highlands: 'Would any of its inhabitants of the present day live for a single year as did their predecessors of 100 years ago? I venture to think they would not.' He declared that there was insufficient arable land in the Highlands (the total of which had not changed since the time of Sir John Sinclair) to support a large population of small holders. The arable acreage was simply not extendable. The sporting income of Ross and Cromarty alone was £80,000 per annum, and another £80,000 was spent annually by the sportsmen in the county: 'it is a means of circulating among the population a large sum of money that would not otherwise reach it'. The people faced emigration unless more by-employment could be generated in the region. Blunt-Mackenzie noted that sea fishing had declined though there were better prospects for the artificial cultivation of lobsters and oysters. Tourism continued to create employment, and he noted the possibilities of using electrical energy for the introduction of manufacturing into the Highlands though, apart from wool, there were few raw materials for processing. His speech was not an exaggeratedly optimistic *credo* for development but a 'few suggestions' about the possibility of doing something 'to help keep in comfort at home a few of those who now find it necessary to go out into the world to work'.[38]

The population of the West Highlands was now declining and much of the discussion at the turn of the century was couched in terms of slowing the exodus. For instance in June 1912 a petition was drawn up in Achiltibuie to seek the reconstruction of a pier at Badentarbat which was practically unfit for use. It was pointed out that 'all the food supplies both for the people and for the stock on their holdings have to come by sea'. The crofters argued 'the the present tide of emigration will be probably augmented by the loss of any facilities of communication'.[39] By 1914 the Highlands had seen radical changes—the demise of many of the large sheep farmers, the invasion of southern and American sportsmen and tourists, and the transference of substantial amounts of land to the crofters. Paradoxically, after a century of continuous population increase, total numbers were declining, against a background of increasing land resources. The social complexion of the Highlands had changed radically.[40]

IV

Major Blunt entertained particular notions of literally electrifying the Highlands, starting at Strathpeffer and Dingwall and employing local water power from Rogie Falls. He became a pioneer in this enterprise and the district was one of the first in northern Scotland to receive electric lighting. Blunt threw himself into the development; the ultimate financial returns did little to relieve the continuing crisis in estate finances.

The question of private and public provision of electricity was not new. Scatwell House had possessed a supply since 1889 when, with 80 lights at work, 'a person entering a room, or lying in bed, can turn on and off the light at pleasure'.[41] In 1892 an 'electric light engineer' produced estimates for a steam-powered scheme for heating and lighting Tarbat House. Four years later there was an Electric Light Company mooted for Strathpeffer. It was thought that an electricity supply would encourage an increase in feuing arrangements at the Spa. Black, however, advised caution, pointing out that 'we must remember that the young Countess is not so rich as we had hoped she would be'.[42] In 1900 at nearby Ardross Castle water-driven dynamos were already creating electric illumination.[43]

But Blunt's plants were larger—he envisaged a scheme to provide electricity by alternating current for the entire district on a public basis. In September 1901 southern visitors had discussed 'the want of good artificial light in Strathpeffer'. They were overheard to remark: 'Look at these hills and tell me why Strathpeffer should be struggling with grease and rushes and stinking oil. There's water enough there to illuminate the whole Highlands. Strathpeffer could have all it needs at a far cheaper rate than we get it in London.' They thought the entire enterprise could be done for £4000, 'not more than one of the larger hotels might undertake'.[44] In fact Blunt had already obtained an estimate and a feasibility report from George Gordon, an electrical engineer. He calculated that electrical lighting for Strathpeffer would cost £5700, that ample water storage capacity was available, and that Rogie Falls was a suitable source for the basic power.[45]

Throughout 1901 and the first half of 1902 Blunt negotiated with engineers in London, and by May 1902 had resolved to proceed with the scheme to provide lighting to Strathpeffer. The enterprise involved a considerable capital investment—and genuine risk-taking to which Blunt committed some of his own funds. He told Gunn, 'that it is being carried through because it will help the place more than as a remunerative scheme in itself. It may not be any good to add that I am guaranteeing the outlay to some extent myself—apart from the estate—but that is the case.'[46] A public announcement was issued and the local council wished Blunt well, noting that 'he had had his doubts as to its being a financial success'.[47] Two months later Blunt offered to provide electric power to Dingwall at 3d per unit which was far cheaper than previous schemes and half the price of, and much better quality than, gas lighting. Blunt said that a cable from Strathpeffer to Dingwall would cost £2000 but a joint supply to the two towns would render the enterprise far more economical. The scheme went forward under the direction of Messrs Deacon and Sons of London, using Westinghouse equipment. Early promises that electricity would flow in 1902 were not fulfilled and the supply did not start until March 1903 when Ben Wyvis Hotel was lit up by 420 separate lights from a source ten miles distant in the mountains. Castle Leod was also well illuminated.[48] The supply was described as a '3-phase alternating current supply system, and it is the first of its kind in Scotland, if not the first in Great Britain', and was installed by the Aberdeen Electrical Engineering Company Limited.[49]

The introduction of electricity had been achieved in the teeth of considerable opposition and local political disagreement. The local councils had been divided on the issue and Blunt had been forced to accept a very low return to get their concurrence; there was also talk of the danger of a local monopoly. Meanwhile the local gas supplier had suddenly reduced rates, and the *Ross-shire Journal* commented 'the mere projection of an efficient electric lighting scheme has already had … an effect'.[50] There were other difficulties for the electrical pioneers. The first season's supply at Strathpeffer, an event in itself, had been punctuated by breaks in transmission and there were serious delays in the installation programme and in the extension of the system to Dingwall where the Council was slow to make up its collective mind.[51] In January 1904 freezing weather curtailed water power and caused embarrassing failures. In the deep of night 'the staff and sometimes the Proprietor were on the hillface in very stormy weather endeavouring to keep the supply in being'.[52] Even worse, the costs of the enterprise had 'leapfrogged to £9000' by 1904. Blunt was indeed shouldering many of the costs of innovation in his enthusiasm for electrical lighting, even in the matter of methods of charging the customers and the technology of individual lamps. He was also required to wait upon the growth of demand which lagged behind his capacity to supply current. In 1907 Blunt-Mackenzie complained of the small consumption *per capita* in the district, which was far less than in many English towns.

The financial aspects of Blunt-Mackenzie's adventure in electricity appear to have been less than lucrative. By 1909 the supply system had been amalgamated into a public company, the Strathpeffer and Dingwall Electric Company Limited, which had relieved Blunt-Mackenzie of many of his financial obligations for the sum of £6000, though he appears to have retained some debenture stock in the enterprise.[53] In 1926 a still larger company swallowed up the remnants of the pioneer. It seems highly unlikely that the Cromartie estate made any money out of its involvement in electricity; it is more likely that the estate had committed itself further into debt.[54]

V

Blunt-Mackenzie's other proprietorial passion was the Spa, the electric supply for which had been one of his first objects. Once more however the needs of the enterprise outstripped the Cromartie estate's capital capability. In March 1900 Blunt was in close discussions with the Duke of Sutherland's advisors at Stafford House in London. The Duke still owned property in Strathpeffer and it was obvious that without his or other assistance the Cromartie estate would not be able to finance the necessary improvements of facilities at the Spa. Otherwise the question of the sale of the Spa was bound to be revived, especially under pressure from the medicos at Strathpeffer. Blunt's first notion was to float the possibility of combining some of the existing interests at Strathpeffer, including the Ben Wyvis Hotel, to create a money-raising body to develop and operate the Spa. He particularly wanted to introduce electricity to the village and for the Spa to pay its own way. His initiative came in the midst of further negotiations about the termination of the Trust and the interests of the Countess's uncle, the Duke of Sutherland. Blunt told Gunn:

> Don't think I am trying to burst out into wild speculations but I want to protect the Spa from rivals and spoilers and propose that the Strathpeffer property be kept apart to pay its own expenses and take its own risks—it is not included with the rest of the estate in the settlements so this can be done easily.[55]

Despite these earnest efforts the future of the Spa remained in doubt and suspense for several more years and was denied the capital that some local experts said was imperative for its continued progress. Major Blunt increasingly took the view that the Spa had been run 'on very amateur lines' and that it was remarkable, under such circumstances, that Gunn had done as well as he had.[56]

William Gunn had advised against a public company and declared that he had spent 30 years ensuring that the Spa was 'not overweighted with capital'. And, in any case, the Cromartie estate could always provide its own security for loans at 3 per cent or less.[57] He also pointed out that Strathpeffer increasingly attracted a new category of tourists who wanted accommodation and entertainment rather than medical treatments. But the estate was caught in a pair of pincers—the demands of the doctors were increasing while simultaneously the owner was sinking into debt, 'living on overdrafts' and endlessly negotiating loans, as Blunt complained in February 1903.[58]

The Spa itself remained popular and continued to attract a fashionable clientele during its relatively short summer season. More effective advertising was begun and better railway connections developed so that London visitors could arrive directly by sleeper in under 15 hours. The early part of the season was said to be dominated by country people from Perth, Moray and adjacent counties, later attracting more exotic contingents, as the *Daily Mail* reported in 1905

> You will meet in this little northern village people from every quarter of the Empire. The veteran soldier from India rubs shoulders with the famous artist from St Ives. The white-haired dandy from St James makes himself agreeable to the army chaplain from Pretoria. Every county in England and every county in the Empire seems to have sent at least one representative to the wells of Strathpeffer.[59]

Publicity on behalf of the Spa was increasingly taken over by local medical interests. The Strathpeffer Spa Medical Guide was the most comprehensive account and justification of the *fin de siecle* facilities. The Guide argued that modern Balneology and Hydrotherapy was 'a notable example of the scientific justification of empiricism' and was especially valuable for the stresses caused by artificial life in great cities in which 'the wear and tear of mind and body engender countless functional disorders, and aggravate and intensify organic diseases'. Dr Bruce and his associates explained that a train from London departed at 8pm, delivered visitors to the Spa by 11 the next morning. By 1906 Strathpeffer had been transformed into a considerable complex of medical and hotel buildings located around the Pump Room, much enhanced by the construction of the Nicolson Mackenzie Mineral Water Hospital. The waters were now managed to provide every permutation of treatment. There were Aix baths, Scotch Douches, Russian baths, Sulphur baths, Nieheim baths, Needle baths and a local speciality, the Peat Bath. The last required unusual facilities

> Owing to the density of the semi-liquid peat, the bather does not readily sink in it, and has often to hold himself down. It is not a pre-possessing bath to look at, but this is quite forgotten when immersed in the peat, as its effects are extremely soothing. One may liken it to lying in an immense poultice.

It was particularly recommended for gout, lumbago and sciatica but necessitated a 'hot water plunge or douche' immediately afterwards. The Spa also offered a new electric treatment by which 'the patient simply reclines in a special couch and holds a metal electrode in hand', a procedure thought to be beneficial for obesity, rheumatism, anaemia and hysteria. After experiencing such a range of treatments the Spa visitors were offered 'after-cures' which included excursions to Aviemore, Kingussie and the seaside before the patients were returned to the rigours of city life.

One of the prime aims of the medical and commercial associates of the Spa at Strathpeffer was to educate the public about its broad attractions and the value of its winter season. Nevertheless the seasonal nature of its operations persisted—only in summer did the Spa orchestra perform twice daily, supported by other bands and performers in concerts. There was, also, a Lending Library, a Gallery, a Reading Room and a Post Office. Other cures for *ennui* included golf, cricket, bowling, croquet, cycling and motoring. But, the medical men stressed that the Spa existed essentially as a resting place for tired professional people, not for the 'young and foolish'. It was primarily for people rather beyond their prime. Dr Bruce acknowledged the scepticism of many observers about the medical benefits of the Spa waters, but was happy to quote the *Lancet* to the effect that Strathpeffer provided better remedial resources than the more vaunted spas of the Continent.[60]

Blunt-Mackenzie and the Countess were themselves spa-goers and their experiences in Europe gave them a sobering perspective on Strathpeffer. At Vittel (Vosges) they saw that £10,000 was spent each year to provide 'incidental amusements' while the cooking and service were up to the standards of the Savoy. Blunt-Mackenzie remarked: 'It makes one think how impossible it be for Strathpeffer to compete as the customs and climate are so very different ... It makes one rather despair.'[61]

For thirteen years in succession the Ben Wyvis Hotel published 8 per cent dividends.[62] In reality the number of visitors and level of business had fallen and expenditure had expanded between 1903 and 1907. It is not surprising that the estate began a series of negotiations, at this time, with potential buyers of the basic Spa facilities. These eventually reached a commercial focus in spring 1907 with the intervention of a syndicate of London doctors led by Dr Hastings and chaired by the Earl of Cottenham who promised: 'You won't know the place once we have finished with it'.[63] The syndicate paid £27,424 for the property. The local newspaper reported that: 'The Syndicate have satisfied themselves that despite its remoteness, Strathpeffer can be popularised in a way that has hitherto been merely dreamt of'.[64] The Strathpeffer Spa Co., particularly intended to divert spa-goers from continental watering places to the north of Scotland by 'revolutionising' its attractions.[65]

The Syndicate was reputed to have 'wide experience in purveying popular recreations and running resorts',[66] and its involvement at Strathpeffer certainly brought greater professionalism and investment to the village. There was further development in the hotel trade and the Ben Wyvis Hotel alone was employing more than 40 on its staff, and continued to pay its regular dividends until the War.[67] Yet, though the tourists continued to flow into the Spa, the Syndicate soon began to complain. In 1910 Dr Hastings virtually accused the Cromartie estate of deceit:

> We have spent an enormous amount of money that was never contemplated. We never considered the place was in such a bad state ... Perhaps we paid more for this property than we should have done, and the directors are contemplating an investigation. They propose examining the agent and also the valuers ... We feel very strongly about having paid more than we should have done for this property.[68]

Blunt-Mackenzie was angered by the imputation but it is clear that the estate, by this sale, had not only relinquished a great managerial burden, but had avoided further expenditure of its meagre capital. And, in any case, the glamorous days of this Spa, as of other spas, were already strictly numbered.

57 Patriotism was strong: the victorious tug o' war team from the Heights in 1905 and 1906 was composed almost exclusively of tenants of the Estate who were also members of the 1st Volunteer Battalion The Seaforth Highlanders.

VI

The sale of Strathpeffer Spa in 1907 was merely one symptom of the profound financial weakness of the Cromartie estate. The shadow of debt had hung over it since the 1890s. One of Major Blunt's first orders to Gunn was to put a curb on all expenditure. When sheep farms[69] fell in and sporting rents were reduced the prospects were further dimmed. Yet, at the same moment, Blunt was embarking on his electrical adventures and reconstructing Castle Leod at the cost of new capital commitments. The extensions at Castle Leod were designed for a switch of residence from Tarbat House and Blunt made clear his priorities—'I think we should take every available inch for the billiard room and make it pretty lofty'.[70] While revenues remained stagnant it was not surprising that new loans and mortgages became indispensable and that much correspondence was devoted to the possibility of lower interest rates. The majority of the estate net income was already swallowed up by the Dowager's jointure (£2500 per annum), personal expenditure (£1,150) and the interest on loans.[71]

The estate was losing money on its yearly operations and, inevitably, the limits of credit were reached. The solution, if such it may be called, was a series of sales of estate assets which began long before the First World War and continued thereafter. By 1906

58 The Countess and her sons Roderick (Rorie) and Walter at the door of Castle Leod, 1916.

the estate had decided to sell off major blocks of land. Dunie, a considerable sporting lease of 2272 acres, was sold for about £7000.[72] The estate's legal advisors in Edinburgh began further negotiations with London land agents who had clients 'who are looking out for Estates in Ross-shire to purchase'. They were instructed that 'if a satisfactory offer was made to the Countess she might be disposed to sell the West Coast property'.[73] In April 1907 there was further consideration given, now for the sale of Tarbat and some of the West Coast properties. One problem was the unpredictability of the land market. For instance Rhidorroch, once the favourite shooting ground of the Cromartie family, had been considered for sale as early as 1904 for an expected price of about £60,000. Three years later Rhidorroch attracted a bid of only £40,000 which was regarded as too little.[74] Also under contemplation were Drumruinie, Corrie, Ben More and Inverpolly, and it was decided to sell them, separately if a buyer could be found, realising that 'you do get fancy prices for sporting Estates occasionally'.[75] In 1908 the Tullich Woods were sold to enable the estate to buy deferred shares in the Strathpeffer Spa Company,[76] but the other property was not so easily disposed of and the plans to sell Rhidorroch and Tarbat were described as 'off' in February 1908.[77] Blunt-Mackenzie was still in two minds, pointing out that: 'The gain in income from 40,000 cash would be so small that it seems a pity to start breaking into the property for the money'.[78]

Nevertheless it is evident that the family had entered the psychology of land and property sales much before the War interrupted its proceedings. Badentarbat House was proposed for sale in May 1911 and by 1913 most of the Rhu More Peninsula in Coigach was added to the list, together with the possible sale of Inverpolly.[79] It is perfectly clear that the Cromartie estate was ripe for rapid dismemberment. It was the estate's misfortune that it chose not to complete many sales before the war: after the war, prices fell drastically and the estate realised less that it might otherwise have done. For instance in 1920 Rhidorroch was at last sold, to John A. Rose, the price was probably less than £30,000, half the figure mentioned originally, back in 1904.[80]

The Cromartie estate's main economic enemy was its debt burden and its poor resources. But there were also political dangers. It was perhaps symbolic, and somewhat late in the day that in 1914, the estate began to subscribe to 'The Land Union: A National Organization for the Protection of all Interests in Land, Buildings and House Property'. Its secretary described its function:

> Thanks to the steadfastness of its members and subscribers the Union has greatly strengthened its position, and is now the recognised protagonist in the fights against confiscation of private property in Land and Houses. We have fought and are fighting many Test Cases on matters of vital principle. We have won most of them, and others have served the intended purpose of exposing the injustices and worthlessness of the Land Valuation. We are doing an enormous amount of advisory work for our members, and we are making great progress in educating public opinion on the real character of Part I of the Finance Act 1901-10. We also desire to strengthen our position to enable us to fight the new proposals that Mr Lloyd George and the Land Taxers have recently brought out.[81]

It was a statement closely in tune with the mood of small and medium landowners like the Countess of Cromartie and Colonel Blunt-Mackenzie. Living in reduced circumstances, they were of a class (notably in the Highlands) which was very clearly on the retreat, and had been defending themselves without much success since 1870.

VII

In August 1914 the sounds of war reached Kildary and Cromarty Bay. Already there were stories bruited about of disabled ships, and of wounded sailors being brought ashore. The 'big guns' of the Cromarty forts were practising in earnest. Preparations were also being made for the care of anticipated wounded, and ambulance classes were inaugurated.

By the third week of August there was a great flurry of activity. Blunt-Mackenzie remained somewhat sceptical and asked his new factor Alex Taylor:

> Are the East Coast people still hearing guns and seeing crippled ships? I am thinking the seers would have had more second sight than they had realised. However there will be a fight on the sea before long and a terrible one it will be.[82]

Several batches of German fishermen had been rounded up and taken to Invergordon for dispatch southwards. And Alex Taylor told Blunt-Mackenzie: 'This will be a terrible war, both on land and sea, and it is hoped the Germans will get the severe thrashing they deserve'. Meanwhile the Countess of Cromartie had engaged a chauffeur, secured a decent supply of petrol for wartime, and moved her residence to Culmaily in Sutherland. The season at Strathpeffer had been somewhat curtailed by the sudden departure of many visitors on the declaration of war, but exceptionally good weather had kept some at the Spa. Blunt-Mackenzie, who was himself in service in Dublin when the war broke out, was particularly concerned at the predicted rise in interest rates: the burden of debt would increase and income was likely to fall. He therefore gave orders that all work on the estate should be minimised, that staff and wages be reduced, and that 'any advances to crofters must also be held over'.[83] As a gesture towards the national interest the estate offered the hill grazings on its deer forests in Coigach at nominal charges to the Ross-shire Executive Committee for Food Production. Without sportsmen and sheepfarmers the Cromartie estate found that it had little other use for its many acres.[84]

Epilogue

Epilogue

I

After 1914 the old territorial integrity of the Cromartie estate eventually crumbled. Political and economic pressures conspired to force repeated sales of land both in the east and the west. But a small central core of the estate, as well as the ancestral house at Castle Leod, remained in the Cromartie family through to the end of the new century. In comparative terms it may be said that the Cromartie family had done remarkably well to last so long. Many Highland estates had changed hands long since. Hector Mackenzie, another Highland proprietor, remarked as early as 1823: 'I am sorry to see too many Lairds gone or fast going to Pot—I shall not follow if I can but keep out of the Vortex of Style if possible and rather pull up a little in my expenses'.[1] By 1914 the method of 'pulling in expenses' was not enough to preserve the Cromartie estate from large land sales.

Nevertheless there continued a number of lines of continuity with past experience. For instance, the alacrity, the scale, and the sacrifice by which the people of the estate joined the armed forces in the Great War was reminiscent of (and possibly more wholehearted than) the solidarity of the community in the Jacobite Uprisings and in other recruitment drives. Now however loyalty and service were transferred more directly to the Crown. It is also significant that of the 'men of Lochbroom' who died in conflict many were registered as migrants serving in American or Empire forces.[2]

Colonel Blunt-Mackenzie, an experienced professional soldier, was given command of a division at Norwich in 1914, and later did service at Gallipoli and in France, until his retirement in 1919 as a Lieutenant-Colonel gazetted. He was a member of the Ross and Cromarty County Council and maintained an active and intelligent interest in agriculture and forestry until his death in 1949. His wife, the Countess of Cromartie, was an independent spirit, a woman who cultivated a career as a writer of eight mystical novels which were described as being 'pregnant with folklore'. She was thought to be the original of Tennyson's 'Airy, Fairy Lilian', and she herself wrote songs and poems. In the Second World War the Countess, now regarded as a local celebrity, was known for her work in the creation of a library for sailors in Easter Ross. The Countess and her husband, of course, had presided over the diminution of the estates and the eventual retreat of the family into Castle Leod. Land sales continued and, in 1934, a further substantial portion of Coigach was sold off, comprising 35,000 acres of prime sporting property at Drumrunie, Langwell, Keanchulish and Strathcanaird, together with the sheepstock 'which for many years has been in the hands of the Countess of Cromartie'. The buyer was Mr Clare Vyner of Studley Royal, Ripon, second son of Lord Compton, a kinsman of the Marquis of Northampton, and a retired Lieutenant in the Royal Navy. Vyner had already acquired substantial acreages in Sutherland and Lochbroom.[3]

The military tradition of the family continued. The Countess's second son, the Hon. Walter Blunt-Mackenzie, made vigorous efforts to join Franco's forces in Spain in 1936. He was trained as a Land Agent and eventually became a farmer in South Africa. His brother, Lord Tarbat, the heir, followed a distinguished military career. He was awarded the MC in France and was imprisoned in Germany during the Second World War with the rest of the 51st Highland Division. As the third Earl of Cromartie, he subsequently pursued an active public life both nationally, in the House of Lords, and locally, in the County Council. Unlike his predecessors he had studied systematic estate management and some years before his mother died (in 1962), he took over the management of the estate. His own inheritance had been subject to almost continuous decline.

There were other continuities to be observed. For instance the crofting communities persisted into the twentieth century, sustained by Crofter Commission legislation and encouraged by intermittently improving economic conditions. Yet, though living standards rose and the old bogey of recurrent famine was extinguished, the crofting communities experienced great difficulty in maintaining social solidarity and population numbers.[4] By the mid twentieth century the population of the crofting villages had declined steeply. Similarly the weaknesses in the medico-tourist trade at Strathpeffer, suspected already before 1914, became more pronounced in the following decades. The village lost for a time most of its seasonal trade and its vitality. Strathpeffer declined into genteel dormancy despite the idle dreams of spa-enthusiasts that the village might revive as the northern apex of a new spa-system in the United Kingdom.[5] In reality Strathpeffer gained new life from a totally unexpected source when, in the 1970s, it felt some local consequences of the North Sea oil boom and the village helped to service the commuters employed in the oil installations based in Easter Ross. Tourism currently enjoys a revival.

The capital weakness of the Cromartie estate had always been its greatest obstacle to survival and expansion. In the past, with some key exceptions, practically all the agricultural initiative and capital investment had derived directly from the tenantry. Most of the entrepreneurial development had been provided by the large commercial farmers whose money and energy had generated growth in rural income while also disrupting old patterns of social life. The Cromartie family had, to some degree, resisted some of the insistent logic of market forces in the mid-nineteenth century. Yet it is by no means clear that even if the family had evicted all the crofters and cottars, and raised the land to its absolute market value, this would have solved their perennial financial weakness. Like most of their kind, they always overspent their income regardless of its rate of growth. They always placed the next generation in financial straits and they always caused a haemorrhaging of capital from the future development of the estate.

In the twentieth century the owners of Cromartie were still hamstrung by capital deficiency. Lloyd George had once claimed that: 'A fully-equipped Duke costs as much to keep up as two dreadnoughts, and Dukes are just as great a terror, and last longer'.[6] Earldoms were undoubtedly less expensive, but in the case of Cromartie the old hazards of inheritance had taken severe toll. The divisions of the wealth of the estate in each generation, but especially in 1896, had gravely weakened the capacity of the estate to re-invest in its own development and to keep it safe from predatory rival landowners. A stricter adherence to primogeniture, and a less generous provision for dependent kinsfolk, might have better maintained the territory integrity of the estate. But for generation after generation the inheritors of the Cromartie estate had consumed all their income. As estate productivity rose (for example, from 1790-1850) expenditure had easily matched its rate of growth. Each succeeding generation inherited a new level of financial weakness.

In the preceding two centuries the Cromartie estate, like many others, had grown and survived on income partly derived from outside the estate—from empire, politics, industry, military service and marriage. The Cromartie estate, to a very large extent, was built by men who made their fortunes elsewhere. In the twentieth century this factor mainly ceased to operate for Cromartie as for many other traditional landowners.

Below the landowning stratum there were other changes. Over the previous three centuries the rural foundations of the Cromartie estate had sustained varying levels of population and economic welfare. Though there were clear continuities in the persistence of the small tenantries (despite radical agrarian transformation) it is evident that, despite its remoteness, this society had been deeply marked by external forces. The people of Cromartie, in no sense, had been immune from the effects of war, industrialisation, demographic revolution, religious excitations and intellectual currents from the south. For example the assault on 'feudalism' spanned one and a half centuries on the Cromartie estate and it was not until the 1860s that the last remnants of the subtenancy system were eradicated. (Road service was eliminated only in 1879.) Famine itself was eliminated over a similarly extended period. The introduction of the great sheep and arable farmers undoubtedly increased the productivity of the land and helped to provide economic surpluses for the industrial south, as well as swelling rentals for the owners. This was achieved over a long period of time during which the population of the estate, mostly unconnected with the expanding commercial sector and possessed of less land, rose rapidly and cumulatively.

The effect of very long term economic change on the ordinary people of the Cromartie estate is difficult to gauge especially since so many of them had little formal attachment to, or recognition within, the estate organisation. Generation begat generation on the estate yet little evidence was recorded of their existence until modern times. To compare the community of, say, 1870, with that of 1750, is inherently and extraordinarily difficult. Yet some points are clear enough: it is undeniable that more people lived on the resources of the estate in 1870 than in 1750; they now experienced lower death rates; crisis mortality episodes were practically removed from the demographic horizon; the common people were now able to make greater (though hardly generous) claims on the productions of the outside world; their literary rates were much higher, even if their native language was in serious retreat.

More precise measures over long historical time are problematic. It may be contended that stockholding was always a sure indicator of wealth and economic well being. Fragments of evidence on this question may be suggestive. In the 1750s for instance, contemporary evidence suggests that in Coigach, some tenants were exceptionally well placed—one owned 100 cattle, 30 sheep and 64 horses—a veritable kulak among the western peasantry. But the wealth holdings were more typical in the statistics for Ullapool where 80 peple depended on 16 acres, 12 goats, 56 sheep and 64 cattle.[7] One hundred and twenty years later a register of stock holding amongst the lot tenants in Coigach also demonstrated marked, though less severe, variations in wealth holding. But, in these post-clearance conditions, the average stock was unquestionably higher: the lot tenants possessed, on average per capita, 11 sheep, 2 or 3 cattle, a stirk and possibly a horse too.[8] Equally certain is the fact that the quality, saleability and reliability of the stock had greatly improved in the intervening years.

Such crude measures as these suggest that while great shifts had occurred in the disposition and control of the land, the crofting economy itself had also developed. None of this, however, obscures their increasing relative poverty when compared with advancing living standards in the rest of the Kingdom. Nor does such stark quantitative evidence offer any clue about the interior mental world of the crofters.

II

The elusive voice of the crofter in so much of the story, was eventually supplied in the 1930s and 1940s by Colin Macdonald (1882-1957). Macdonald was born on a croft in Auchterneed and was brought up as a crofter on the Heights of Inchvannie, Strathpeffer. He was educated at Fodderty School until aged fourteen and worked on his father's croft. He recollected that 'my chief ambition in life was to save enough money to enable me to secure the tenancy of a small farm'.[9] He later inherited, and was exceptional in that he was selected for special training: at the age of 26 he went to study agriculture at (and was later appointed to the staff of) the Aberdeen and North of Scotland College of Agriculture. He later became an agricultural lecturer and adviser in the north and west Highlands. He was a great success in the role which he described as 'missionary-lecturer and demonstrator' to the Outer Hebrides. Eventually (in 1944) he became the much-respected Gaelic-speaking member of the Land Court.[10]

In his retirement Macdonald produced four books, full of anecdote and modesty, in which he attempted to express 'the ways and daily doings of those largely unlettered but highly-intelligent and independent-minded men and women who lived in the Highlands of Scotland towards the end of the nineteenth century'. He claimed therefore, to speak on behalf of the crofting community, drawing on a memory which stretched back as far as the 1880s: 'what is written here is not culled or second-hand or fanciful but from personal experience and fact'. Amid a certain amount of bucolic whimsy the articulate Macdonald offered an eloquent and sophisticated evocation and analysis of Highland life which he was extraordinarily well-qualified to provide. His books are crammed with sentiment, humour and scepticism.[11]

Macdonald gave clear expression to many well-cherished beliefs among his kinsfolk. For example he subscribed to the catastrophe view of Highland history which regarded the Jacobite Uprising and its defeat as the end to 'the relationship between Chief and Clansmen' which 'soon deteriorated under the new regime of Landlord and Tenant'. He also believed that the crofts had been scratched out of inferior land, 'always the more fertile soil in the straths and glens is included in the big farms, while the crofts are pushed up either on to the top of the valley or to the limit of the workable soil'. Indeed contemporary records (as we have seen) tend to confirm this interpretation of the origins of crofting and also the view that productivity on the crofts was relatively high.[12]

Macdonald's account of former living standards (that is, in the late nineteenth century) tended to vary. He painted a picture of comfortable material circumstances set within rather narrow limits, but he made no reference to great privation and near famine in his own early lifetime.[13] It is probable that conditions among the Strathpeffer crofters were, in any case, more favourable than those prevailing in, for instance, Coigach. In a later account Macdonald specifically attacked the sentimentalisation of the Highland past, especially the rosy view of the condition of the people before the Crofters' Act of 1886. He said that he could find virtually no evidence of a richer past: 'The truth is that in those much-lauded old days most Highlanders lived in an atmosphere of endless strife with their neighbours and squalor and poverty in their homes—just as people in the rural districts of Scotland and England did'. Macdonald was especially scornful about 'the wealth of oratorical pronouncements in regard to the populous, prosperous, happy Highlands which existed sometime in the past when cultural attainments were the distinguishing characteristics of the Gael'.

On the nuances of social life in the Highlands, Macdonald was also revealing. He was critical of the oppressive role of the Free Church in the community and its unbending insistence of the eternal chastisement of sinners. In secular matters Macdonald recollected some of the psychological aspects of crofting life. For example, when the rent was paid up on rent day the crofter felt a surge of independence. The greatest topic of conversation was always 'how to sell the cattle'.[14] But the crofters were intensely conscious of a sense of social inferiority and lived beneath the shadow of the landlord and Castle Leod. Within the community there were other distinctions and Macdonald provided a rough analysis of these gradations. At the bottom were the farm servants, that is the sgalags who were extremely poor and often led a nomadic existence: 'only God and their mothers knew how they were clothed and fed'. Above them were the crofters who possessed the inestimable right of permanence and security. Further up the social ladder were the families of the village: the shopkeepers, feuars, estate officials and a few professional people. At the very top were the farmers' families who constituted a special elite.[15] Macdonald noted that the crofters provided occasional labour for the large farmers; he recollected that the harvest in the Strath depended entirely on the flail until the 1860s. It was the custom of the big farmers to 'bargain with the young men from the crofts to give them so many days or weeks with the flail throughout the winter'. Macdonald's own father was employed at Inchvannie Farm, earning one shilling for eleven hours' hard labour.[16]

Macdonald also recorded the patterns of social behaviour between the various groups in the Highland population. He was perceptive about the southern sportsmen who 'annually resorted to their Highland lodges for a respite from the concern incidental to the care and conservation of their millions'.[17] The crofters, claimed Macdonald, were not opposed to the sporting use of the land and acknowledged that the income so derived was essential to the needs of an impecunious landlord.[18] But the sportsmen were also figures of fun (as well as of side-income) to the crofters simply because their activities were so obviously 'a frightful waste of money'. The estate management was similarly a target of crofter feeling: 'From infancy I was brought up in an atmosphere of hot hostility to, and contempt for, landed estate factors. Such we regarded as the natural enemies of crofters! Tales of their tyrany and turpitude were in prime favour at the Ceilidh.' In his later years Macdonald began to see estate managers in a different light, as a diverse group of men who were too easily made the scapegoat of all the problems of Highland life. He also reported his father's perception of social distinctions in the Highland community. Pitted against the true crofters were 'the Haves' who voted Tory. These were the landlords, the factors, the big farmers, the moderate ministers, the school teachers. With them were the gamekeepers and the gillies, abetted by compliant stalkers, gardeners and stablemen, who were the parasites and turncoats of the crofter community, 'the dozen slaves who had sold their birthright for a mess of pottage'.[19]

Macdonald offered a picture of crofting life which allowed for more political sophistication than it is normally given credit. He believed the growth of political consciousness was greatly encouraged by the operation of a local Debating Society and by the work of the Land League.[20] Macdonald believed that the Crofter Act had been the hinge of modern Highland history. It had done more for the Highlands than any other legislative act in the past 100 years, most effectively by way of 'the special form of tenure which gives the holder the undisturbable right to remain in occupation during his own lifetime and to pass on a similar right to anyone within a specified circle of relationship'.[21] The benefits of the Act were incalculable simply because it conferred independence—henceforth 'no shadow of fear of the boss ever crosses the crofter's mind. He has no boss and is free to plan his own life and way of living.'[22] Macdonald, in his adopted career, was exceptionally well-placed to observe the use and misuse of this regulatory system (by both crofters and landlords). His general verdict was that its operation had been vastly successful. Under the arbitration of the Land Court the crofters had gained confidence in their security of tenure and had seized the opportunity to conduct their own agricultural improvements. Consequently, he wrote, the Land Question, 'so long the source of bitter feelings and conflict in the Highlands, gradually lost its venom'.[23]

Colin Macdonald's judgement on crofting life was a fine balance of realism and sentiment. Though it offered an existence still marked by poverty it nevertheless remained a remarkably fine way of life:

> despite repeated attempts to convert a free and forthright people to the status of city serfs, they are still essentially free to maintain and develop the God-given individuality in human life and outlook which elsewhere is being so ruthlessly smothered.

But this praise for crofting was much moderated by an acknowledgement of its diminishing attraction for crofter youth. Macdonald explicitly rejected the 'political philosophies which thought that depopulation was a haemorrhaging of the Highlands'. He maintained that the appropriate population for the Highlands was that number that could earn a 'sufficiently attractive livelihood there when the natural rural resources had been fully developed'. The truth was, as the mid twentieth century approached, that the Highlanders had themselves changed; they would no longer accept squalor and poverty.

THREE FAMILIES: 1, THE CROMARTIES

59 Lord Tarbat's welcome home party in 1928: Lord Tarbat had attained his majority while serving as a soldier in India.
Back row, left to right: Mr Milne, Estate Factor, Mr Grant, clerk to the Estate Factor, Mr Thomas Christie, manager of Tarbat Farm, Mr Hugh M Mackenzie, Tenant, Polnichol Farm, Mr John Ross, Tenant, Milton Mill, Mr George Mackenzie, Stationmaster, Kildary Station; Mr McCorquodale, Tenant, Meddat. Seated: Walter Blunt-Mackenzie, The Countess of Cromartie, Lord Tarbat, Col. Blunt-Mackenzie, Lady Isabella Mackenzie.

60 Family at the celebrations for Lord Tarbat's return from India: Lady Bella, Col. Blunt-Mackenzie, the Countess of Cromartie, the Duke of Sutherland, Lord Tarbat, and his brother Walter Blunt-Mackenzie, 1928.

THREE FAMILIES: 2, THE GRANTS, GAMEKEEPERS OF GARBAT, STRATHPEFFER

61 John Grant born in 1800, photographed about 1870. His wife and sister were wearing mutch caps under their bonnets and their shawls were probably hand-woven. They both have handsome brooches.

62 Colin Grant (on right with a beard) organising a big shoot on the low ground at Castle Leod.

Epilogue

63 Ian Grant (with gun) and the stalkers celebrating bringing in a Royal: taken outside the stables, Castle Leod, 1888.

64 Lord Cromartie presenting long service medals to Estate staff in 1964: to Mr John Grant, fourth generation of Keeper on Garbat, to Mr Campbell (seated), formerly Head Gardener, and to Mr Munro, Head Forester (right).

THREE FAMILIES: 3, THE MACDONALDS, CROFTERS ON THE HEIGHTS OF INCHVANNIE, STRATHPEFFER

65   The Macdonald family were originally displaced from the farm of Inchvannie when it was improved in the mid-eighteenth century, and settled on the Heights of Inchvannie on a croft. This is the third house they have built, largely with their own labour. John Macdonald, here seen with relatives at the gate, had given evidence to the Napier Commission. (His own father, he did not mention, had spent a short spell in Dingwall jail for home distilling of whisky.) The house was built about 1894; the porch and dormers were added in 1911, the year this photograph was taken. This house replaced a traditional long-house, with two rooms and a middle 'chalmer', with box beds in both. Byre and barn were built in line, all single-storeyed. This was a little to the west of the present free-standing barn, also built in the 1890s. The original croft, probably going back to the mid-eighteenth century when the first Macdonalds arrived, was just below the present 1894 house, and foundations of huge stones were found in the garden. This family can be identified in the estate papers practically continuously to the 1750s, in this place.

Epilogue

66 Colin Macdonald, son of the builder of the house, joined the Department of Agriculture after showing ability at the North of Scotland Agricultural College, later he became the Gaelic-speaking member of the Scottish Land Court, and an author and broadcaster. Here with his parents (centre) and relatives outside the croft house, about 1911. Colin is top right.

67 A family occasion on the Heights, July 1906: front: 'Grandpa, Donnie, Belle and David, Grannie, Teen and Elsie. Back: Dad (Colin Macdonald), W Thomson, Connie Munro, Baxter, Rosie Munro, George Munro'.

68 Cromartie Estates forestry staff, Castle Leod, taken at Blairninich Sawmill Yard in 1912. Left to right from horse: James Gallie (foreman carter), Donald Mackenzie, Danie Bain, Finlay Mackenzie, William Robertson, John Mackenzie (holding horse).
Second Row: James Mackenzie, Willie Macdonald, Willie Macdonald (Brae), Andy Galloway, Tom Fraser (clerk), Alick Macivor, I Smith, William Macintosh.
Third row: James Maclennan, Roderick Munro, Donald Maclennan, Charlie Macgregor (foreman), James Donald (head forester), his son Jim, Willie Cameron (carpenter), Murdo Mackenzie, Colin Matheson and Hector Mackenzie.
Also on the staff at this time, but not represented in this photograph, were the following:
Spa staff: Roderick Macdonald (Rocks), boiler man, Roderick Munro (baths attendant), Finlay Mackenzie and Murdo Mackenzie (peat baths attendants).
Electrical: Donald MacDonald (Red Donald), Glen power supply, generating station, Glenskiach.
Shepherds: Rory MacLeod and son John.
Keepers: William Fraser and William Ramsay.

For Macdonald, writing in 1947, the new reality was that

> it is becoming more and more the aspiration of intelligent young people of the farm servant class to seek emancipation from what, despite betterment in the way of wages, hours and holidays, is a hard life at best, offering little prospect of independence with advancing years.[24]

The crofters were subject to much the same pressures and alternatives as the farm servants. It was simply 'unreasonable to expect educated young people to stay contented and happy in an unremunerative calling while bigger prizes are offered elsewhere'. Politicians and sentimentalists argued in opposition to this reality and parents often asked too much in the name of filial duty. But, as Macdonald put it: 'Young people nowadays resent being talked down to, and are perfectly capable of deciding a matter of this kind for themselves'.[25] Macdonald had seen it all himself—in the dispersal of his generation in his own family—to Africa, Canada, Orkney, and, of course, in his own peripatetic career through twentieth century Scotland.[26]

Macdonald's priceless memoirs provide the essential interweaving threads of continuity and change in the fabric of Highland society. From the 1880s to the 1950s he observed the mellowing of social tensions and the erosion of social obstacles. He saw the decline of absolute dependency and deference, promoted crucially by the Crofters' Act and aided too by the growth of alternative employment beyond the Cromartie estate. It produced a world of greater security and independence. At the end of the day the landlord possessed fewer acres and less power, the crofters had won greater autonomy, and the population now declined, seemingly inexorably.

III

While the landlord's acres had diminished there seemed to be a compensatory resurgence of symbols and sentiment. As the end of the twentieth century approached the remaining lands of the Earl of Cromartie were not very different from those held by his far distant ancestor, John of Killen, who had planted two sweet chestnut trees in the park of Castle Leod to mark the royal charter for those lands, granted by Mary Queen of Scots in 1554. Those trees survive, gnarled and battered by storms, but still green each spring. The lands that remain are those of the parks and Mains farm of Castle Leod, the crofts of the Heights of Achterneed, and the forestry lands on the slopes of Ben Wyvis, to the north. The family had been persuaded to sell most of its remaining lands in 1949 and to re-invest in securities. The sale included all the remaining west coast properties, the farmlands and town of Strathpeffer, and all the property at Tarbat except the mansion house which was the Countess's home until her death in 1962 when it too was sold. Income from the investments then became the main support for the relatively modest living standards of her successors.

The prestige and standing of the family was sustained by other means. In 1979 Lord Lyon King of Arms gave his judgement, engrossed on vellum, that the Earl of Cromartie, Roderick Francis Grant Mackenzie was lawful Caberfeidh, Chief of the Clan Mackenzie. The office of Chief had lapsed at the extinction of the male line of the Mackenzies of Seaforth in 1815. In the meantime a number of lesser Mackenzie houses had also waxed and waned with the decline of landed property. The award of the Chieftainship to Cromartie was justified by the clear blood-line from the Lords of Kintail. Neither Lord Lyon, nor the custom of the Scots peerage, jibbed at the fact that the name, lands and prestige of the Mackenzies was thus seen to have been transmitted through four female heads of the family.

In 1979, therefore, Lord Lyon had given official sanction to a re-invention of tradition at Castle Leod. The honorary chieftainship now recognised the sentimental reality, that Earl Rorie and Castle Leod were the head and heart of the Clan Mackenzie. The Earl, unlike most of his forbears, made a commitment to unite the scattered clan in ties of patriarchal affection. Countless Mackenzies, from home and abroad, now make the pilgrimage to the Castle to scour family trees and old rent rolls in the hope of recognition and the hint of a former world.

Appendices

A. Rents on Cromartie Estate
B. The Population of the Cromartie Estate
C. The Oral Testimony of Morag Shaw Mackenzie, 1982
D. Maps

APPENDIX A

Rents on Cromartie Estate

The rental series of the Cromartie estates reflects all the problems involved in making comparisons of income levels over a long period of historical time. There is virtually no systematic rental data before the eighteenth century. There exist fragments of accounts in the period before the estates were forfeited in 1745. After that the evidence is intermittent, especially before 1786 and then again between 1800 and 1830. Subsequently there is a good series of rentals for all the estates though some rentals are missing for particular years.

   Long historical series are notoriously difficult to interpret. Within the Cromartie data there are special difficulties which should be enumerated. The methods of payment were heterogenous: values were expressed in Scottish currency in the early eighteenth century and subsequently changed to sterling denominations.[1] While the tenants of Coigach generally paid in cash, the eastern estates paid in victuals or services, or a combination of these and cash. Sometimes victual rents were converted into cash, sometimes not. In the long run, by the end of the eighteenth century, many of the older modes of payment were permanently converted, but others remained. At the same time there were systems of sub-renting whereby small tenants paid rent to a tacksman or large farmer who, in his turn, paid a general rent to the landlord. Often, little is known about the level and trend of rent exactions from the small tenantry, certainly until the 1850s and even after.

   In the eighteenth century and the first part of the nineteenth the estate factor was, at least partly, contracted to bring in the rent and to square the accounts in a way which was apparently legally binding. Endless complicating obligations were incurred by the landlord, the factor, and the tenantry. Equally confusing was the practice of running up arrears and then cancelling at a later point—thereby causing exaggerated peaks and troughs in the annual rent-due figures. The accompanying series is mainly (though not necessarily uniformly) comprised of 'rent received' statistics.

   Other complications included a changing land-base for the estate—over the long run the estate gained and lost land and other assets. Apart from the fine efforts of Peter May in 1755, the precise measurement of the estate was a twentieth century development. Nevertheless the Cromartie estate probably changed in scale less than most other estates in the period 1700-1914. Wadsets, the semi-permanent disposal of land, were more difficult to account and make the net-rental status of the estate far more problematical. Alterations in the uses of the estate are also significant—the rise and fall of the herring fishery, the similar career of kelp production in Coigach, and the disputed status of the Conan fishing, were all important for the estate income. The shift of land into commercial sheep farming was clearly vital at the end of the eighteenth century; so also was the reclamation and extension of arable production on the eastern lands. The variable development of non-industrial income (from, for example, the operations of the fisheries at Ullapool and the Spa at Strathpeffer) masked changes in purely agricultural income. At the end of the period the land was valued to include its sheep stock. The withdrawal of sheepfarmers created not only a loss of income but severe accounting difficulties. Simultaneously there were great changes in the organisation of the estate, its obligations, it management and its accounting procedures.

Consequently simple deductions about income, welfare and equity cannot be drawn directly from rental series. Moreover there were two other fundamental circumstances to be juxtaposed with the rental series. The first was the population base of the estates—clearly the number of people who generated the estate rental, and subsisted from the resources of the estate, varied dramatically over the quarter millenium under consideration. Secondly the values of the rental should be related to an index of relevant prices to provide a 'real' measure of comparability. Periods of deflation and inflation marked most of the series and the nominal trends are therefore quite misleading. There are, however, further problems of deflating or reflating Highland rents— primarily because no systematic price index has been constructed, partly because the bases of living costs shifted permanently over the 250 years in question.[2]

Such difficulties should not be allowed to obscure the more obvious features of the series. There is evidence, for instance, that as early as the 1660s the rentals of Coigach included payment in pairs of 'white plaids' (i.e. blankets or shawls) which were probably sold for good prices in London. In 1730 tacks and entails for Coigach indicate that rents were being paid in butter, plaids, cheese and coin, sometimes converted into merks. There is little other evidence to show the condition of the estate though the general correspondence of the first three Earls of Cromartie shows clearly enough the accumulation of debts and wadsets. At the time of Forfeiture, in 1752, an 'Estimate of the value of the Estate of Cromertie' was drawn up. According to this survey, after conversions had been made for 'grain grazings, customs, casualty etc', the gross rent was £800. This is a figure from which public burdens had been deducted. The document indicated that leases and tacks had been negotiated in 1742. It suggested that services such as 'carriage' had been abolished and the cash rent increased in the eastern baronies. The Coigach part of the estate paid grassums every fifth year, which were, in effect, a double rent every five years. The Forest of Fannich was sometimes let for grazing for deer and black cattle. Moreover 'a great part of the estate' was wadset for a sum amounting to £10,639 sterling—effectively a mortgage debt owed by the landlord to the tenantry. The redemption debt on the wadset lands was still £6600 and the rents had 'stood' for more than 200 years. This was the clearest hint in the Cromartie archives of the apparent stability of rents until the mid-eighteenth century though there had already been some upward pressure exerted in the early 1740s.

The steep ascent of rents seems to date from the 1780s though they had already shifted upwards somewhat before that date. The rental of 1784 sees the estate negotiating substantial rises—the Coigach rent was increased by one third from about £286 per annum to £380. Meanwhile at Strathpeffer and New Tarbat more than half the rents are still computed from victuals presumably supplied to the local girnels. The accounts were complicated further by the fact that Coigach rents were each year paid for a different period and at a different time from those of New Tarbat and Strathpeffer. The rentals were made up by the factor and juxtaposed with the expenses of the estate which included a wide array of costs such as: crown rents, bishop's rents, household and window tax, ministers' stipends and schoolmasters' salaries, and the salaries and wages of factors, foresters, and other estate employees. By the late 1790s rents were growing rapidly, sometimes being doubled (even where victual rents were charged). In the 1799 rental there was reference to 'new settlers' which may relate to changes in the uses of land and reclamation schemes on the eastern estates. There was repeated reference to 'old rents' and the 'new rents' which were climbing steeply, but the old victual component persisted—the estate continued to collect eggs and swine, tallow and sheaves, victual and multure rents at the turn of the century. At Strathpeffer the rent was measured in barley-bere and oatmeal. Relatively little rent was received from the kelpshores in Coigach and from sales of birchwood. The retention of victual rents by the estate—often converted into money by a complex calculation—may have been a hedge to protect the estate against inflation. In the long run the rents rose in both forms, reflecting the competition for land.

The steep rent increase had not been uniform. Using 1755 as a base, the eastern districts rose most rapidly by 1800—Strathpeffer by a factor of 3.5, and New Tarbat by 5.2; Coigach lagged behind with a growth of only 1.9, not quite doubling in fifty years. The complaints of migrants from Lochbroom during the period came from a context of much lower rent increases than in the east.

After the turn of the century the series are broken. There are enough benchmarks to indicate a continuing growth of rent in the east—by a factor of 1.28 in New Tarbat by 1830 and by 1.8 in Strathpeffer. By contrast the rents in Coigach now leapfrogged the eastern districts, growing by 4.4 by 1823, presumably reflecting the widespread introduction of commercial sheepfarming in the west. Other evidence suggests that the peak of all rents was probably reached by about 1820, followed by a decline in sympathy with the general price index in Britain at large. In 1816 the estate administration had been concerned by the collapse of grain prices and moved to a system of grain rents geared to fiar's prices.

The decline of rents after 1815 was common to all the estates but more precipitate in the west where rents remained relatively depressed until mid-century. Rents on the eastern properties were more buoyant and less volatile. More particularly, despite later recollection at the time of the Napier Commission, there appears little evidence of a general upward revision of rents in the 1830s at the time of Andrew Scott.

The recovery of rents in the 1840s was quite unexpected. By 1855 the previous peaks of the wartime inflation had been regained. But the growth of income at Strathpeffer and Coigach was greater than in New Tarbat. In the following three decades rents doubled—partly because of high wool prices, partly from the vigorous growth of sporting rents, but also from income from the Spa at Strathpeffer. New Tarbat in the lowland arable east benefited from good grain prices but possessed few sporting resources. The decline in the 1880s was most severe in Coigach, less in Strathpeffer and hardly at all in New Tarbat. The recovery rates were not uniform after 1890 but by 1910 the estate income was back to most of the earlier levels. By then land sales were beginning to affect the territorial extent of the Cromartie estates.

The rentals offer information on other subjects central to estate life. For instance in the 1830s there was a sharp increase of arrears so that by 1837 the 'debt' exceeded the nominal rent of the estate. Arrears were periodically abandoned. Payments still included certain labour services and victuals (e.g. hens and eggs) at New Tarbat. At Coigach all the arrears were in the category of 'small tenants'. Some small rent was still paid for kelp though in 1832 Scott described the kelp shores as practically worthless and the product for three years 'did not in fact pay the expenses of manufactury and sending to market'. There is evidence of large landlord expenditure on meal imports in 1837 which may account for part of the total for arrears.

The structure of tenancy is not easily adduced. In Coigach for instance the tacksman system obscured the actual occupation of land because land was sub-tenanted. Changes in the categories of rent payment were relatively slight for the other two estates.

The figures in the Table at the top of page 434 seem to suggest a relative stability of occupational sizes and, perhaps, also of tenantry.

A rough analysis of accounts in 1835 indicated that out of a gross rental of about £6850, £2739 went to the landlord and his trustees; public burdens accounted for £1472, annuities and interest £338, miscellaneous payments £1346, ameliorations £434, and £348 to the costs of management. Hay-Mackenzie seemed to take a net income of about £1300 from the first category. Little seems to have gone into landlord-financed improvements. The Home Farm seems to have been breaking even.

Tenants rent payments £	Number of Tenants					
	Strathpeffer			Tarbat		
	1836	1849	1860	1836	1849	1860
>100	7	8	9	4	4	4
75–100	1	—	—	2	—	1
50–75	3	2	5	2	4	3
25–50	1	2	5	4	5	9
10–25	10	20	23	13	5	12
5–10	19	13	30	12	9	18
<5	105	100	99	128	89	83

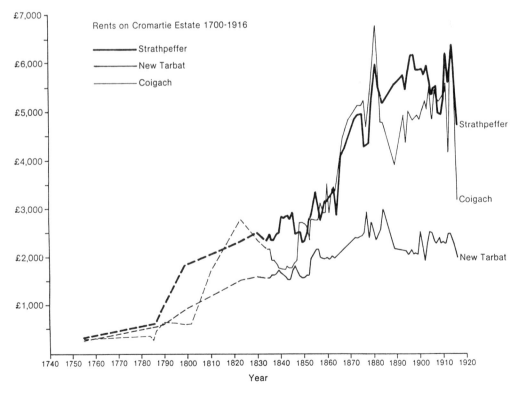

Figure 1.

Appendix A. Cromartie Rentals 1730-1914

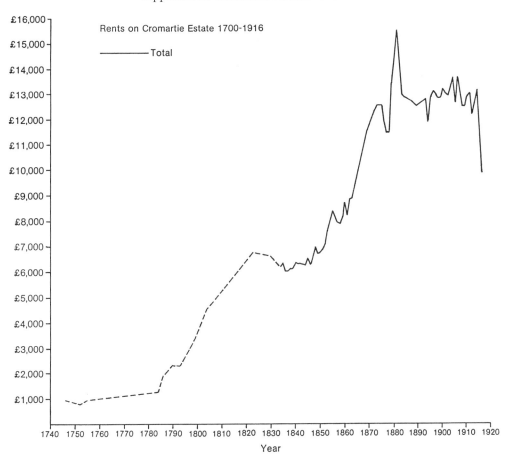

Figure 2.

Rent Income (£) 1700–1915

	Total	Strathpeffer	New Tarbat	Coigach
1700–1830				
1746	952			
1752	800			
1755	932	344	260	328
1784	1264			380
1785				281
1786	1872	626	560	466
1790	2321	1024	625	651
1793	2319			
1795				651
1799	3335	1807	902	626

Cromartie

Rent Income (£) 1700–1915—continued

	Total	Strathpeffer	New Tarbat	Coigach
1800–1830				
1800				620
1802				626
1804	4501			
1810				1703
1823	6768	2319	1537	2781
1830	6637	2508	1603	2368
1834–1916				
1834	6194	2324	1570	2186
1835	6364	2489	1575	2186
1836	6016	2341	1628	1949
1837	6031	2341	1628	1944
1838	6126	2487	1673	1853
1839	6153	2499	1740	1794
1840	6377	2818	1676	1764
1841	6306	2800	1624	1765
1842	6326	2837	1606	1766
1843	6301	2846	1531	1809
1844	6234	2790	1531	1782
1845	6538	2923	1711	1782
1846	6291	2454	1837	1882
1847	6538	2496	1718	1944
1848	6993	2502	1617	2705
1849	6695	2293	1577	2710
1850	6742	2343	1584	2700
1851	6866	2486	1638	2627
1852	7105	2787	1630	2373
1853	7672	2865	1988	2788
1854	—			
1855	8382	3350	2159	2756
1856	8159	3119	2170	2756
1857	7965	2757	1992	3103
1858	7893	2976	1902	2903
1859	8121	3146	1959	2904
1860	8735	3133	1988	3504
1861	8209	3236	1960	2904
1862	8858	3316	2029	3404
1863	8930	3464	1998	3358
1864		2859		
1865				
1866		4110		4260
1867		4189		4505
1868				
1869	11558	4460	2252	4845
1870				
1871				
1872	12339	4884	2402	5024
1873	12534	4937	2404	5132
1874				

Appendix A. Cromartie Rentals 1730-1914

Rent Income (£) 1700–1915—continued

	Total	Strathpeffer	New Tarbat	Coigach
1875	12543	4961	2449	5132
1876	12032	4294	2514	5223
1877	11499	4306	2913	4679
1878	11475	4340	2393	4741
1879	13473	5265	2735	5473
1880				
1881	15520	5978	2349	6792
1882				
1883	13001	5333	2574	4792
1884	12911	5160	2975	4774
1885				
1886				
1887	12706			
1888				
1889	12519	5554	2178	3911
1890				
1891				
1892				
1893	12805	5732	2132	4945
1894	11919	5446	2110	4362
1895	12939	5867	2047	5024
1896	13188	6160	2124	4903
1897	13049	6170	2061	4817
1898	12832	5870	2091	4870
1899	12877	5855	2074	4947
1900	13227	5878	2525	4823
1901	13069	5782	2237	5049
1902–1914				
1902	12971	5721	1929	5223
1903	13280	5919	2296	5066
1904	13659	5616	2534	5508
1905	12682	5338	2490	4853
1906	13709	5507	2337	5461
1907	13103	5536	2292	5274
1908	12553	4955	2381	5215
1909	12506	4946	2276	5283
1910	12891	5222	2314	5352
1911	13085	6227	2280	5574
1912	12215	5578	2470	4165
1913	12750	5903	2473	6122
1914	13155	6374	2347	6101
1916	9895	4732	1990	3171

Just before the First World War the general structure of tenancy on the Cromartie estate was well consolidated. At Tarbat the large farms contributed 52 per cent of rental income and the shooting a further 17 per cent. At Strathpeffer the shootings were larger, 35 per cent, and the large farms only 20 per cent. At Coigach shooting and fishing constituted 60 per cent, demonstrating the astonishing importance of sporting income to estate finances. The implication of the figures was that the crofting population (no doubt experiencing a better living standard than before but far below the national average of social and economic welfare) had become marginal in the estate economy. They had sustained their own numbers (though they were beginning to decline after 1861) and survived on a narrower base of resources. But their contribution to the commercial income of the Cromartie estate had now become very small. The logic of economic change had been remorseless. The fact that the crofters had clung on in such adversity was a testament to their fortitude and their communal solidarity.[3] By 1913 a single sportsman, for a few weeks relaxation in the Highland wilderness, paid more annual rent than several hundred crofters and their families.

APPENDIX B

The Population of the Cromartie Estate

The three parishes of Lochbroom, Fodderty and Tarbat may be used as analogues of the three main locations of the Cromartie estate (i.e. Coigach, Strathpeffer and New Tarbat) which themselves did not conform to census districts. (See accompanying graph of population trends.) None of the parishes in Ross and Cromarty had regular parish registers at the time of the first official census in 1801 and consequently there are great problems in estimating birth and death rates.

The population history of Lochbroom was complicated by the existence of the planned fishing village of Ullapool which emerged rapidly in the 1790s and then declined slowly in the early nineteenth century. In 1793 Ullapool's population was about 200 but increased to more than 1000 by 1798 which may have reflected the multiplier effect of the building activity in the village. There are conflicting accounts of its population thereafter: 1000 in 1803, 700 in 1804, 669 in 1808, an increase to 900 in 1817 but a smaller figure for 1829.[1] In 1836 the population of Ullapool was estimated at 730 which, despite long term depression in the fishing industry, seems to have been maintained at the end of the century—1871 : 752, 1881 : 897, 1891 : 868.[2]

Despite the complication created by Ullapool's immigrant settlement, it is evident that the parish of Lochbroom passed through a more dramatic population history than its eastern counterparts. Its population grew more rapidly and reached its peak in the 1850s after which it declined at an accelerating rate, especially in the 1890s. The graph for Lochbroom may understate the growth of population because the early censuses probably omitted many of the inhabitants. For instance the local minister claimed that, at the time of the 1831 census, hundreds of the parishioners of Lochbroom were absent at sea or in Caithness or the lowlands. The official figure for 1831 was 4,615 but the minister's independent count produced a 'real population' of 5206 in November 1834.[3]

The paradox of the general trend is clear: the population of Lochbroom grew most rapidly at a time of greatest tenurial turmoil, economic insecurity and famine; the population fell when crofters gained tenurial security and when their living standards unquestionably rose. The fall of the population in Lochbroom after 1871 was probably a consequence of net migration outwards and an associated fall in the birth rate. By 1911 Lochbroom's population was a mere 58% of the maximum of the years 1841-71.

The thickly populated crofter district of Coigach comprised a large part of Lochbroom parish but there is no continuous series of separate statistics for Coigach. *The First Statistical Account* in 1790 gave a figure of more than 600; the *Second Statistical Account* in 1834 gave a figure of 1975; an estate estimate in 1837 thought it was 1500. Everyone agreed that Coigach's population was increasing rapidly in the 1830s and 1840s. Andrew Scott thought there were 1760 people in Coigach in 1847, but the census yielded a figure of 1700 in 1851, 1285 in 1861, and only 1000 in 1885.[4]

On the eastern parishes the trend was similar but less spectacular: growth until 1840 was

Table 3: Populations of parishes in the County of Ross and Cromarty, 1755–1911

	1755	1801	1811	1821	1831	1841	1851	1861	1871	1881	1891	1901	1911
Tarbat	1,584	1,343	1,379	1,625	1,809	1,826	2,151	2,269	2,182	1,878	1,703	1,358	1,224
Fodderty	1,483	1,789	1,900	1,952	2,232	2,437	2,342	2,247	2,121	2,047	1,897	1,787	1,692
Contin	1,949	1,944	1,844	1,930	2,023	1,770	1,562	1,509	1,550	1,422	1,436	1,310	1,162
Fearn	1,898	1,528	1,508	1,654	1,695	1,914	2,122	2,083	2,135	2,135	1,900	1,761	1,785
Dingwall	1,030	1,418	1,500	2,031	2,124	2,101	2,364	2,412	2,443	2,220	2,576	2,758	2,898
Kilmuir Easter	1,095	1,703	1,559	1,381	1,551	1,486	1,437	1,295	1,281	1,146	1,024	985	887
Kincardine	1,743	1,865	1,666	1,811	1,887	2,108	1,896	1,746	1,685	1,472	1,417	1,265	1,198
Lochbroom	2,211	3,533	3,754	4,540	4,615	4,799	4,813	4,862	4,406	4,021	3,910	3,207	2,794
Logie Easter	850	1,031	928	813	934	1,015	965	932	912	827	870	819	700
Ross and Cromarty	48,084	56,318	60,853	68,762	74,820	78,685	82,707	81,406	80,955	78,547	77,810	76,450	77,364

Appendix B. Population 1755-1914

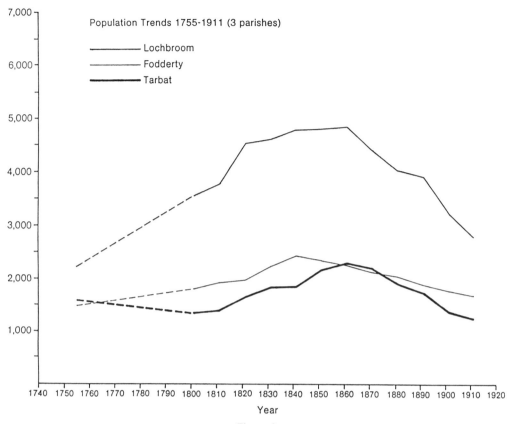

Figure 3.

continuous but less dramatic; the decline thereafter was also less precipitate. In all three parishes the population in 1910 was less than it had been 100 years before, and had been reduced by more than one third of its maximum.

Population was a key aspect of estate management. It had grown fastest in the poorest parish and slowest in the most prosperous district. The relationship between the two was, therefore, complex. But the general shape and the timing of the population loss after 1840 was not basically different from that experienced in the other rural districts of Britain.

APPENDIX C

The Oral Testimony of Morag Shaw Mackenzie, 1982

In October 1982 James N. Fraser made extensive notes derived from a series of recordings in Coigach relating to the descendants of Hector Macleod. Macleod was born about 1750 in Assynt but later lived in Achnahaird and also in Badentarbat, both on the Cromartie estate. Almost all the oral information obtained by Mr Fraser came from 'the very fine memory of Morag Shaw'. Her 'memory', indeed, though lacking dates at most points, stretched back into the eighteenth century. It is an extraordinary genealogical record associated with a great vitality of anecdote and social observation all connected with the community of the west coast.[1]

Mrs Mackenzie's oral testimony also cast light on aspects of West Highland life which commonly escape the written historical record. It was especially strong on such questions as family relations, religion, second sight, geographical mobility and emigration, as well as war service. She also recalled a great number of colourful personalities. But, like most oral recollection, Morag Shaw Mackenzie's was also highly selective and its omissions were themselves interesting, as though certain subjects were unconsciously suppressed in the folk memory.[2] Thus, in Mrs Mackenzie's testimony, there was practically no reference to political questions, to famine, to general living standards, to education, to foreigners, to death, to royalty, even to the Jacobite Uprising of 1745.

It is disappointing that Mrs Mackenzie had little recollection of relations between the people and their landlords, the Cromartie family. There was one story, however, which concerned Mrs Hay-Mackenzie in about 1820 when she

> stayed at the Big House [and] found the sight of so many peasant doorways on the Badentarbat hills so obnoxious that she made them turn the doors to the other side of their houses. This, however, proved an illusory remedy and she evicted them from Badentarbat to Tanera.

Though there exists no written corroboration for this story we do know that the Hay-Mackenzies disdained the development of inferior houses at Strathpeffer during that period.[3] Mr Fraser, recording an eviction to Tanera, suggested that the action was unusual because the Hay-Mackenzies were 'by no means bad landlords by Highland standards'.

The record, indeed, is punctuated with references to physical mobility among the community, often related to evictions both within the estate and beyond. Among the people evicted from Badentarbat to Tanera was Murdo Macleod (born circa 1795) who subsequently returned to the mainland and occupied the croft of Springwell at Polbain. Mrs Mackenzie gave the account of Angus Macleod (born circa 1800) who had been evicted from Assynt (in Sutherland) and settled at Rhu na Moine in Achnahaird; he owned a fishing boat which he and his sons used along the coast, even as far as Wick. There were other cases of evicted tenants settling at Coigach

Appendix C. The Oral Testimony of Morag Shaw Mackenzie, 1982

demonstrating the forced mobility of sections of Highland society. Thus the story of Roderick Og who (like Æneas) 'took his father on his back out of the burning village of Sionnenscaig when the people were evicted': they settled at Culnacraig. According to this recollection (which is entirely unconfirmed in any surviving evidence) Sionnenscaig, once occupied by a thousand people (sic), became totally deserted. Another Coigach person, Mary Macleod (1852-1935) became a cook on a farm in Easter Ross and attended Croick Church in Glencalvie and was able to recount stories she had heard about the clearances, and riots, at Glencalvie from the middle nineteenth century.

Perhaps the most interesting folk recollection of Mrs Mackenzie (which may be juxtaposed against the contemporary record) was that which 'involved the famous battle between the women of Coigach and the eviction officers'.[4] Her account, drawing on the folk memory, was particularly focussed on the involvement of three women—Mary Macleod, Anna Bhan (the 'hefty woman') and Katie Macleod Campbell. The story records the several efforts made to implement the eviction (in 1852 and 1853):

> The eviction officers had to serve the evictees with papers of eviction before they could legally carry out such evictions. The people of Coigach had an arrangement with someone in Ullapool who would warn them of any would-be evictions. On this occasion they received a warning and women already named and some men disguised gathered together in a barn. The purpose of the disguise was the notion that if the worst came to the worst women would be treated more leniently than men. The barn was at Culnacraig; this suggests that the evictors were coming by foot rather than boat.

On arrival the evicting officers were attacked and 'Katie Campbell took the shoes of the leader to ensure that no papers were secreted there. The officer was subsequently thrown into the sea.'

Katie Campbell was later identified and the officers demanded that the factor make certain that she never obtained living space on the estate. Consequently when she married 'she was forced to build a house below the high water mark'. It was also told that one of the evicting officers 'swore that no Coigach women would stop him. He received a blow from one of the women which did him permanent damage. He averred that the blow was so hard that it could only have come from a man.'

Mobility of various sorts is a central theme in Mrs Mackenzie's testimony suggesting much movement of people into and out of Coigach over a period of 150 years. It was seen in many changes in tenancies, but most of all in the movement induced by the search for employment—to Ipswich, to Edinburgh and Glasgow, to South Africa, America and even to Australia. There were stories of children departing and becoming cooks in Edinburgh, gamekeepers in the central Highlands, to become a coroner in Guildford, a tea planter, and to be a farmworker in Easter Ross. The last was Hector Macleod Eachinn Dragh (1828-97) from Tanera but educated at Achiltibuie who, dressed in a home-made suit, found regular work, at 5/- per week plus his keep, in Easter Ross. He sent most of his earnings home to Coigach. He later won contracts for making sheep drains and paths and managed to save £100 with which he returned to Springwell in the west. He became an elder in the Free Church: 'He was a crofter and hated the sea'.

Mobility of another sort was accelerated by press-ganging in the Napoleonic Wars though some of the recruits died soon afterwards. In another category was Mrs Mackenzie's story of Hector Macleod who received a small inheritance which allowed him to emigrate. Emigration opened wide horizons—one of the brothers of the Coigach rioters became a sheepfarmer in Australia; another Coigach man made a lot of money in Idaho and sent large amounts back home where it was 'frittered away'. Other cases included a mounted policeman in South Africa, a shepherd in Montana, a wealthy silver miner in Canada, and a soldier in India.

Mobility was balanced by other accounts of great persistence of settlement in the Coigach community—for instance the case of Allan Ban Mackenzie (born about 1780), seven of whose eight daughters married in Coigach itself. Mainly, however, Mrs Mackenzie's testimony is a series of impressionistic fragments which speak indistinctly of a half-lost world. For instance there is reference to a strong woman who:

> indulged her preference for working outside ... She knew more about crofting than her husband, and as he was away shoemaking for long periods she took charge of the croft. She kept sheep, cattle, hens and ducks. She used to gather the sheep, feed the two cows and follower.

There is similarly a fleeting acknowledgement of the great pride among the people for being able to read and write in English. Trade is mentioned—of packmen bringing supplies to Coigach, of merchants involved in trade with Ireland and even the Baltic: 'Tanera was a busy port at the end of the 18th century. One of the central parks there is known as the '*parc Eivenich*' as so much of the soil in the park is Irish. The soil was ballast taken from Ireland by the boats.' Amid much other recollection of such topics as psychic powers, body-snatching and witchery, there is also mention of sheep-stealers, millers, spinners, weavers, kelp workers and fine sailors among the crofters, and the way in which a death could reduce a family to sudden destitution. There is great clarity too in the memory of the Disruption in 1843 and the mass defection of the people from the Established to the Free Church.

The most striking aspects of Mrs Mackenzie's oral record are the strength of the genealogical memory, the selectivity of its subject matter (consistent with other Highland oral records) and its illumination of much of the material and mental world almost entirely silent in the written record. Perhaps the nearest approximation to the two sources combined comes in the books of Colin Macdonald though even his vivid Highland recollections show virtually no consideration of the inner workings of estate economies.

APPENDIX D

446 Cromartyshire.
447 Scotland, showing mainland Ross and Cromarty.
448 Barony of Tarbat, from Avery's 1727 map.
449 Barony of Strathpeffer, from Avery's map.
450 Coigach, from May's 1755 map.
451 Coigach, from May's map.

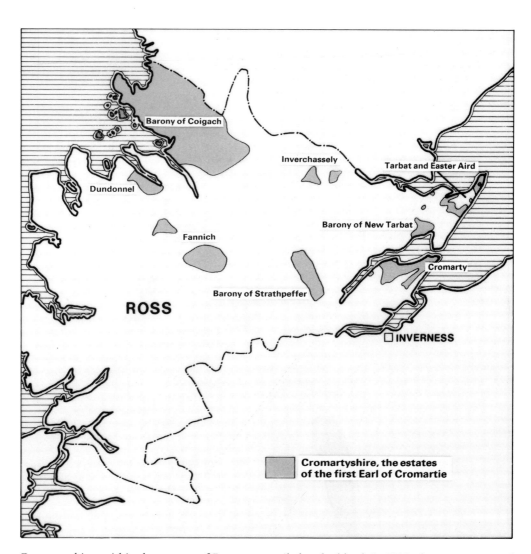

Cromartyshire, within the county of Ross was, until absorbed back in 1891, the exact extent of the Regality of Cromartie in 1686, defining the maximum landholdings of George Mackenzie, first Earl of Cromartie and his sons.

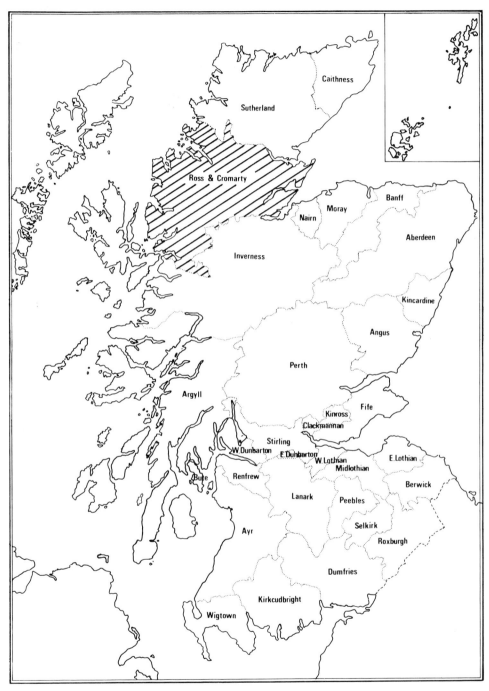

Scotland, showing mainland Ross and Cromarty, one of the pre-1975 counties.

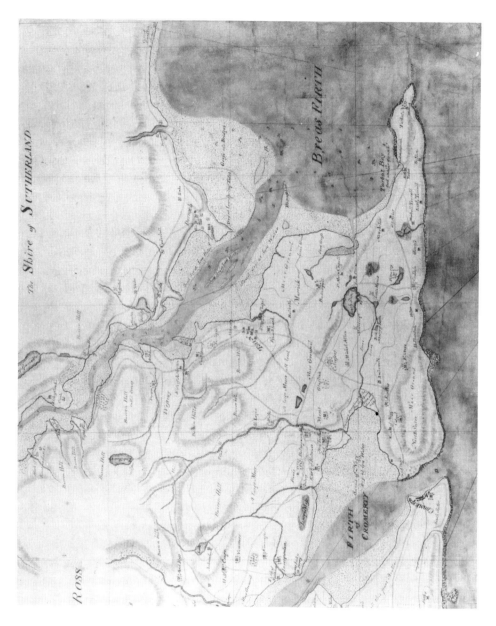

Barony of Tarbat, Easter Ross: From Avery's map of the Moray Firth 1727.

Appendix D

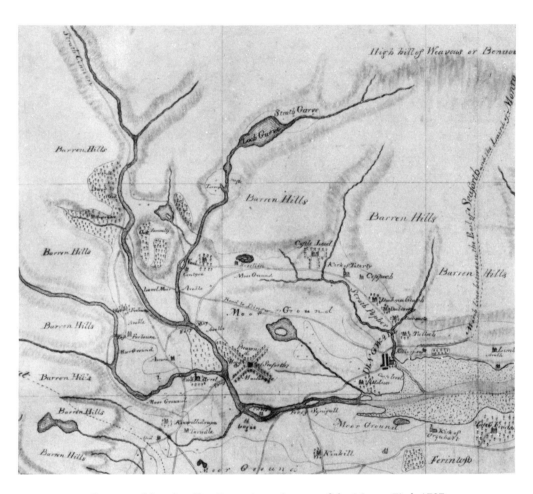

Barony of Strathpeffer: From Avery's map of the Moray Firth 1727.

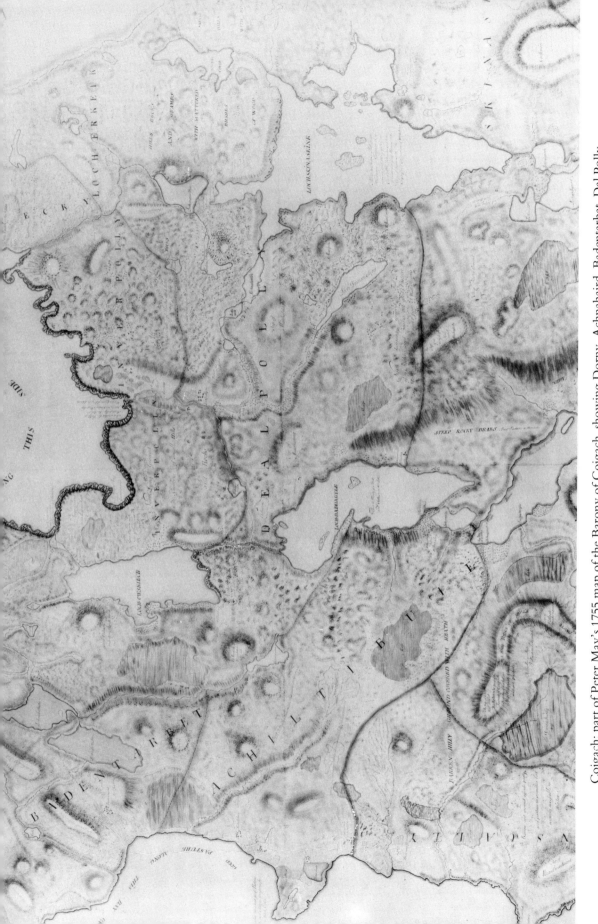

Coigach: part of Peter May's 1755 map of the Barony of Coigach, showing Dorny, Achnahaird, Badentarbat, Dal Polly and Achiltibuie.

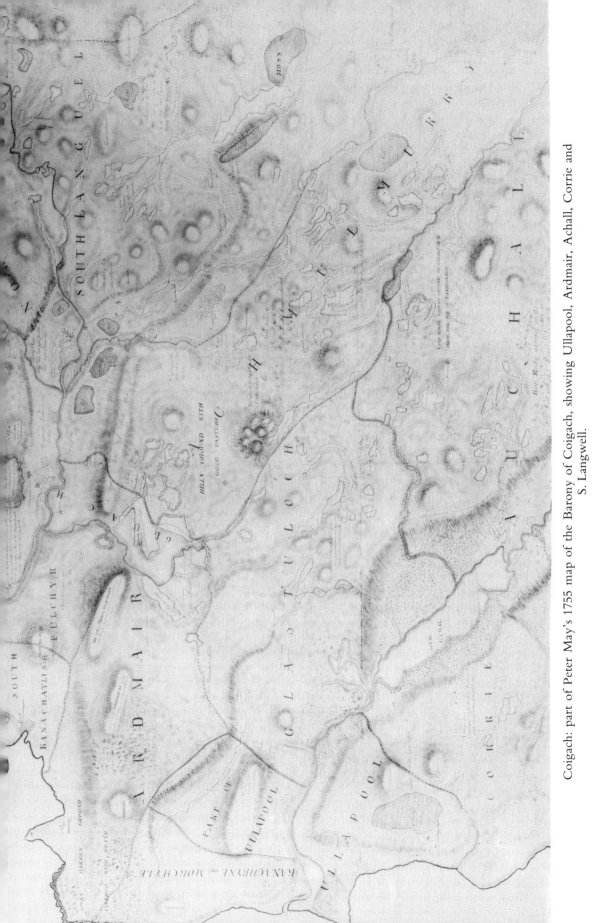

Coigach: part of Peter May's 1755 map of the Barony of Coigach, showing Ullapool, Ardmair, Achall, Corrie and S. Langwell.

Note on the pedigree and titles of the Earls of Cromartie

Specialists should of course refer to the Scottish Peerage, and to Lord Cromartie's own *A Highland History*. The family of Mackenzie of Tarbat owes its origin as a separate and senior cadet branch of the Chief of Mackenzie's line to Sir Rory Mackenzie, Tutor of Kintail, who was born before 1560 and died at Castle Leod in 1626. He was the second son of the 12th Chief, Colin 'Cam' Mackenzie. Colin's elder son, Kenneth, created first Lord of Kintail by James VII, died in 1611 leaving his infant son to the charge of his brother Sir Rory, who thus became known as 'The Tutor'. During the long minority Sir Rory successfully completed a private war in the west of Ross and in the island of Lewis, giving additional land to the chief; and Sir Rory himself married the Macleod heiress, Dame Margaret, whose dowry was the disputed Barony of Coigach. Sir Rory had already inherited the Barony of Strathpeffer, and had bought most of the lands subsequently held in the parish of Tarbat, Easter Ross, from which the family took title. The senior family of the Chief continued to flourish during the seventeenth century, becoming Earls of Seaforth. This direct line died out in 1815 and the colateral line of Humberston-Stewart-Mackenzie came to an end with the last two males falling in action in 1943. A Petition to Lyon King at Arms in 1979 has confirmed the present Earl of Cromartie as nearest in line, Caberfeidh, XXVIII chief of Clan Mackenzie.

Sir Rory's son Sir John of Tarbat was made a Nova Scotia Baronet. His son, Sir George Mackenzie of Tarbat (1632-1714) gave the second great impetus to the family, after Sir Rory. A statesman and public figure attached to the House of Stuart, he became an MP and Lord of Session after the Restoration of King Charles II in 1660, the point where this book formally begins. He was awarded the courtesy title of Lord Tarbat when he became Lord of Session, a post subsequently lost with the title. He was, however, restored and created Viscount in the Accession Honours of James VII and II, and had just acquired the lands and sheriffdom of Cromartie, later made a Regality. In the Accession Honours of Queen Ann in 1704 he was created Earl of Cromartie, Viscount Tarbat, Baron MacLeod and Baron Castlehaven. The eldest sons have adopted the courtesy title of Tarbat, and the first grandson, of MacLeod. This may explain why John, Lord MacLeod kept to this minor title, after all his titles had been forfeited.

When the third Earl declared for Prince Charles Edward Stuart in the Rising of 1745 his estates were immediately and automatically forfeited in consequence of treason to the King—George II. He was later tried for his life, pardoned but exiled from Scotland. Indeed in official correspondence thereafter he is referred to as The Former Earl, the Attaindered Person, or even more chillingly as 'The Late Earl'. The title was 'tainted' in consequence of the attainder and his son, who got the estates back, was told in no uncertain terms that the title was 'for ever extinguished'. Happily for them Queen Victoria turned the clock back, a hundred years later. The third earl's son who had also been out with his father, and was only eighteen at the time of Prince Charles's landing had used the minor courtesy title of Lord MacLeod since infancy. He continued to use it throughout the thirty or more years in which he served the crown of Sweden. His military career was distinguished, he became a Marshal of Sweden and a Count. However when he returned to Britain to raise a regiment in the Highlands, and eventually to get his estates back, the War Office wrote to him as *Mr* John Mackenzie, only slowly unbending to call him, first Count MacLeod, and eventually, after the victories in South India in which his men had been engaged, he became 'My dear Lord MacLeod' to the War Office and the Minister for War.

Note on Cromartie pedigree

The estates were restored in 1784. After his death, as he was childless, the estates passed to Captain Kenneth Mackenzie, sone of his father's brother Roderick. Also without legal offspring, Captain Kenneth was succeeded by the Lady Isabella, daughter of the third earl, who had tended her parents with loving care and only married late in life a cousin, the 6th Lord Elibank. Her tenure of the Estates was a bridge between the old regime and the new world of the nineteenth century, with the completed new mansionhouse of Tarbat as her headquarters. Her daughter and heir was the Hon. Maria Murray Mackenzie, who married Lord Edward Hay, a son of the Earl of Teviotdale. Lord Edward dutifully became *Mr* Edward Hay-Mackenzie. It is notable that the family has legally and so clearly retained its Mackenzie identity, through several female heirs, and that so long after the extinction of the peerage—a hundred years and more—a nebulous nobility hung about. The son of the Hay-Mackenzies was christened John but called Cromartie. He produced a single girl, called Anne, heiress to properties which by then were subject to severe economic pressures. She made a brilliant love-match with George Leveson-Gower, the Marquis of Stafford and later Duke of Sutherland, at the zenith of that estate's power and influence in the north. Duchess Anne was the close friend and confidant of Queen Victoria in her widowhood and, when her own marriage began to break up due to the infatuation of the Duke with another woman, Queen Victoria reluctantly accepted her resignation as Mistress of Robes, and created her Countess of Cromartie, Viscountess Tarbat, Baroness of Castlehaven and Baroness MacLeod in her own right. This revived the old family honours almost in full and is almost unprecedented in the Scottish Peerage. (The omission was old Sir John of Tarbat's Baronetage, which had been bequeathed to Kenneth, second son of the first earl, on his majority.)

The honours were to be entailed on the second son of the house of Sutherland, thus setting up the Mackenzie of Cromartie connection again, independent of any other connection. The Countess/Duchess was succeeded by her son Francis, who died as a result of a yachting accident when he went to the rescue of a drowning seaman. His only heir was, once again, a young girl, Sibell Lilias, who was born in 1878, became Countess in her own right in 1893. She lived until 1961. She married Col. Walter Blunt, a serving officer, who in the family tradition became known as Col. Blunt-Mackenzie. Their eldest son is the present earl, born in 1904, Roderick Grant Francis Mackenzie. He has a son, John, and a grandson, Colin.

It should be added, perhaps, that the family adopted the spelling of Cromartie at a time when spellings had hardly settled to definitive forms, and the spelling of Cromartie was retained with the new creation of the title to avoid too much confusion with the town and the county. However the shire and regality of Cromartyshire, stretching over fourteen blocks of land within Ross-shire did represent the furthest extent of the family's land holdings in the early eighteenth century. It was widely scattered.

The first earl made over the burgh of Cromarty and the castle there to his second son, Sir Kenneth (and the Nova Scotian Baronetage), not long after he had finally acquired it. At the same time he made over Tarbat House and barony to his eldest son, Lord Tarbat, and gave the reversion of Royston House in Edinburgh to his youngest son James. James became a lawyer, eventually Lord Royston, Lord of Session and Lord Justice Clerk. The families of neither younger sons enjoyed these estates for long. Cromarty was sold to a cadet Urquhart of the family who had owned it so long in the past; Royston was bought by the Duke of Argyll, in the 1730s.

In fact, the ownership of the town of Cromarty had, apart from the name, little impact on the family. Ownership of the harbour there was, however, another matter, and so was the Regality (which meant that all the scattered lands belonging to the family were under their own legal jurisdiction), and was a matter of great importance. Like all the Regalities this was extinguished after the Rising of 1745 through the operation of the Heritable Jurisdictions (Scotland) Act; the separately administered county of Cromartyshire continued to the end of the nineteenth century.

Bibliography

i. Archives

S.R.O. SC 34/4/6 Lybelled Summons 1792.
S.R.O. E746 Forfeited Estate Papers
S.R.O. Highland Destitution Papers vols. B10 and B11.
S.R.O. Loch Muniments GD 268.
S.R.O. Forfeited Estate Papers GD 305/E/1.
S.R.O. *Reports of the Central Board of Management of the Fund for the Relief of the Destitute Inhabitants of the Highlands and Islands of Scotland* (Glasgow 1847-50).
County Council Papers, Ross and Cromarty
Kent Archives: Petley Family Papers; Deeds and Family Papers presented by W.Hadfield Craven.
Stafford County Record Office. Sutherland Collection D593.
Cromartie Muniments originally located in Castle Leod, now in S.R.O.
B.L. Add.MSS. Mackenzie Papers.
B.L. Newcastle Papers
B.L. Mackenzie Papers
P.R.O. Home Office (Scotland)
P.R.O. TI/500 Reports of Vessels leaving with Emigrants

ii. Newspapers, Periodicals

Caithness Chronicle—Caledonian Mercury—Celtic Magazine—Edinburgh Evening Courant—Elgin Courant—Gentleman's Magazine—Highland News—Invergordon Times—Inverness Advertiser—Inverness Courier—Inverness Journal—John O'Groat Journal—North Star—Northern Chronicle—Northern Ensign—Notes and Queries—Ross-shire Advertiser—Ross-shire Journal—Ross-shire Observer—Scots Magazine—Scotsman—Scottish Highlander—Scottish Notes and Queries—The Bee—The Times

iii. Books and Articles

Adams, Ian H., *Papers on Peter May, Land Surveyor 1749-1793* (Edinburgh, 1979).
Adam, R.J. (ed.), *Papers on Sutherland Estate Management* (2 vols, Edinburgh, 1972).
Allardyce, J. (ed.), *Historical papers relating to the Jacobite Period 1699-1750* (2 vols, Aberdeen, 1895).
Anderson, George and Peter, *Guide to the Highlands and Islands of Scotland* (London, 1844).
Annand, A.M., 'Major General Lord Macleod ... 73rd Macleod's Highlanders', *Journal of the Society for Army Historical Research*, vol.37 (1959).

Anon, *The Trials of William, Earl of Kilmarnock, George, Earl of Cromartie, and Arthur Lord Balmerino* (London, 1746).
Anon, *The Life of George, Earl of Cromertie* (London, 1746).
Ayton, Richard, *A Voyage Round Great Britain* (8 vols, London, 1814-20).
Bailyn, Bernard, *Voyagers to the West* (New York, 1986).
Bain, Robert, *History of the Ancient Province of Ross, the County Palatine of Scotland* (Dingwall, 1899).
Baldwin, John R. (ed.), *Firthlands of Ross and Sutherland* (Edinburgh, 1986).
Baxter, Benjamin, *Stone Blocks and Iron Rails* (1966).
Beaufort, Henry, *The Substance of a Speech of Henry Beaufort to the British Society for Extending the Fisheries* (London, 1788).
Blaikie, W.B., *Origins of the 'Forty Five* (Edinburgh 1916).
Blake, Robert, *The Conservative Party from Peel to Churchill* (1972 ed.).
Board of Agriculture, *The Agricultural State of the Kingdom, 1816* (ed. 1970).
Boyd, J. Morton, *Fraser Darling's Islands* (Edinburgh 1986).
Boyd, W., *The whole proceedings in the House of Peers upon the indictments against William, Earl of Kilmarnock, George, Earl of Cromartie ... for high treason* (1746).
Brereton, R.M., *A Word on the Duke of Sutherland's Estate Management* (1881).
Brodie, A., *Diary of Alexander Brodie of Brodie, 1652-1680 and of his son James Brodie* (Aberdeen, Spalding Club 1873).
Bruce, W., Duncan, E.H., Kaye, H.W., Smith, J. Render, *Strathpeffer Spa Medical Guide* (Dingwall c.1910).
Buchan, John, *The Massacre of Glencoe* (1933).
Buchanan, Rev. John Lane, *Travels in the Western Hebrides from 1782 to 1790* (London 1793).
Bumsted, J.M., *The People's Clearance 1770-1815* (Edinburgh 1982).
Burns, J.H., 'Scotland and England: Culture and Nationality 1500-1800' in J.S.Bromley and E.H. Kossman (eds), *Britain and the Netherlands* (The Hague, 1971).
Byam Shaw, Christina (ed.), *Pigeon Holes of Memory. The Life and Times of Dr John Mackenzie* (Palo Alto 1988).
Campbell, Hugh, 'There is corn in Egypt. Get you down thither .... The Highlands and Islands Emigration Society and Van Diemen's Land, 1853-1854', *Tasmanian Historical Research Association*, Papers and Proceedings 34, 1987.
Cheyne, J.A., 'Reluctant Heroes: conscription in Aberdeenshire 1756-58', *Northern Scotland* IV (1981).
Clerk, Sir John, *Memoirs of the Life of Sir John Clerk of Penicuik* (1892).
Clough, Monica, 'Making the most of one's resources: Lord Tarbat's Development of Cromarty Firth', *Country Life*, 29 September 1977.
Clough, Monica, 'The Leith Glass Works c.1689-c.1708', *Scottish Industrial History*, vol.5 (1982).
Clough, Monica, 'Early Healing', *Proceedings of Tercentenary Celebrations: Royal College of Physicians of Scotland* (Edinburgh 1982).
Clough, Monica, 'The Cromartie Estate 1660-1784: Aspects of Trade and Organisation', in Baldwin, John R. (ed.), *Firthlands of Ross and Sutherland* (Edinburgh 1986).
Clough, Monica, 'Early fishery and forestry developments on the Cromartie estate of Coigach, in Baldwin, J.R. (ed.), *Ullapool and Wester Ross* (Edinburgh, forthcoming).
Colvin, Sidney, *The Letters of Robert Louis Stevenson*, vol.I (London 1900).
Cregeen, Eric, 'Oral Sources for the Social History of the Scottish Highlands and Islands', *Oral History*, vol.2 (1974), pp.23-36.
Cregeen, Eric, 'Oral Tradition and Agrarian History in the West Highlands', *Oral History*, vol.2, 1974.

Crowley, D.W., 'The Crofter's Party', 1885-1892', *Scottish Historical Review*, vol.35.
Cruickshanks, E. (ed.), *Ideology and Conspiracy: Aspects of Jacobitism 1689-1759* (Edinburgh 1982).
Culloden Papers (London 1815).
Daiches, David, *Scotland and the Union* (1977).
Dawson, J.H., *An Abridged Statistical History of the Scottish Counties* (1862).
Donaldson, Gordon, *Sir William Fraser* (Edinburgh 1985).
Dow, F.D., *Cromwellian Scotland 1651-1660* (Edinburgh 1979).
Dunbabin, J.P.D., *Rural Discontent in Nineteenth Century Britain* (London, 1974).
Dunlop, Jean, 'Some Highland Development Schemes of the Eighteenth Century', *Scottish Genealogist*, III, April 1956.
Dunlop, Jean, 'The British Fisheries Society: 1787 questionnaire', *Northern Scotland*, vol.2 (1974-75).
Dunlop, Jean, *The British Fisheries Society 1786-1893* (Edinburgh 1978).
Elphinstone, A., *The Life of Arthur, Lord Balmerino ... to which are added some memoirs of ... the Earls of Kilmarnock and Cromertie* (1746)
Extract from the Letters to the Rev. Dr McLeod regarding the Famine and Destitution in the Highlands and Islands of Scotland (Glasgow 1847).
Feenstra, Robert, 'Scottish-Dutch Legal Relations in the Seventeenth and Eighteenth Centuries' in *Scotland and Europe* (ed.), T.C. Smout (Edinburgh 1986).
Ferguson, DeLancey, & Waingrow, Marshall, *R.L.S. Stevenson's Letters to Charles Baxter* (London 1956).
Ferguson, W., *Scotland's Relations with England: A Survey to 1707* (Edinburgh, 1977).
Fergusson, James, *Letters of George Dempster to Sir Adam Fergusson* (1934).
Finlayson, Clarence, *The Strath. The Biography of Strathpeffer* (Edinburgh 1979).
Fox, Fortescue, *Strathpeffer Spa* (1889).
Fox, Fortescue, *The Spas of Britain. The Official Handbook of the British Spa Federation* (n.d.).
Fraser, A. and Munro, F., *Tarbat, Easter Ross* RCHS, Ross shire 1988.
Fraser, Hugh C., *The Land Statistics of the Shires of Inverness, Ross and Cromarty in the Year 1871* (Inverness 1872)
Fraser, Mrs. of Leckmelm, *Records of the Men of Lochbroom who fell in the European War 1914-1918* (Glasgow 1922).
Fraser, William, *The Earls of Cromartie* 2 vols (Edinburgh 1876).
Fraser Darling, F., *Island Years* (1941).
Fraser Darling, F., *Island Farm* (1944).
Fraser Darling, F., *West Highland Survey* (1955).
Fraser Darling, F., *Natural History in the Highlands and Islands* (London 1947).
Fraser-Mackintosh, C., *Letters of Two Centuries* (Inverness 1890).
Frazer, J., *A Reminiscence of the Highlands in 1843* (1873).
Fullarton, A., and Baird, L.R., *Remarks on the Evil at Present Affecting the Highlands and Islands of Scotland* (Glasgow 1838).
Gaskell, P., *Morvern Transformed* (Cambridge 1968).
Gibson, Rob., *Crofter Power in Easter Ross* (Easter Ross 1986).
Gifford, J.G., McWilliam, C. and Walker, D., *Edinburgh* (1984).
Gifford, John, McWilliam, Colin, and Walker, David, *The Buildings of Scotland: Edinburgh* (London 1984).
Gower, Lord Ronald, *My Reminiscences* (London 1885).
Grant, I.F., 'Some Accounts of individual Highland sporting estates', *Economic History* 3 (1928).
Grant, I.F., *The Macleods. The History of a Clan* (1959).
Gray, Malcolm, *The Highland Economy 1750-1850* (Edinburgh 1953).

Gray, Malcolm, *The Fishing Industries of Scotland 1790-1914* (Aberdeen 1978).
Hollingsworth, T.H., *The Demography of the British peerage* (1964).
Hopkins, P., 'Glencoe: An English Historian on a Very Scottish Subject', in *The Seventeenth Century in the Highlands* (Inverness Field Club, 1980).
Hopkins, P., *Glencoe and the End of the Highland War* (Edinburgh 1986).
Jarvis, R.C., *Collected Papers on the Jacobite Rising*, 2 vols. (Manchester 1972).
Kaye, H.M., *The Climate of Strathpeffer* (London 1909).
Kennedy, John, *The Days of the Factors in Ross-shire* (Edinburgh, 1866).
Kennedy, Rev. John, *The Days of the Fathers in Ross-shire* (1897 ed., Inverness).
Knox, John, *A View of the British Empire, most especially Scotland* (1784).
Knox, John, *A View of the British Empire*, 3rd ed. (London 1785).
Knox, John, *Observations on the Northern Fisheries* (1786).
Knox, John, *A Tour through the Highlands of Scotland and the Hebride Isles, in 1786* (1787).
Lang, A. (ed.), *The Highlands of Scotland in 1750* (1898).
Lenman, B., *The Jacobite Clans of the Great Glen 1650-1784* (London 1984).
Letters from Highland Emigrants to Australia (London 1852).
Lewis, M.J.T., *Early Modern Railways* (1970).
Livingstone, A., Aikman, C.S.W., and Hart, B.S., *Muster Roll of Prince Charles Edward Stuart's Army 1745-1746* (Aberdeen 1984).
Loch, David, *Essays and the Trade, Commerce, Manufactures and Fisheries of Scotland*, 3 vols (Edinburgh, 1778-9).
Macaulay, J., *The Classical Country House in Scotland 1660-1800* (London 1987).
McCann, J.E., 'The Organisation of the Jacobite Army 1745-6', Ph.D. thesis, University of Edinburgh, 1963.
Macculloch, John, *The Highlands and Western Isles of Scotland* (4 vols, London 1924).
Macdonald, Colin, *Highland Journey* (Edinburgh 1943).
Macdonald, Colin, *Croft and Ceilidh* (Edinburgh 1947).
Macdonald, Colin, *Highland Memories* (Edinburgh n.d.).
Macdonald, Colin, *Echoes of the Glen* (Edinburgh 1936).
MacDonald, D.G.F., *Cattle, Sheep and Deer* (1872).
Macdonald, James, 'On the Agriculture of the Counties of Ross and Cromarty', *Transactions of the Highland and Agricultural Society of Scotland*, 4th series, vol.IX (1877).
Macdonald, Rowland Hill, *The Emigration of the Highland Crofters* (Edinburgh 1885).
Macdougall, Jean, *Highland Postbag* (London 1984).
Macgill, W., *Old Ross-shire and Scotland* (Inverness 1909).
MacIver, Evander, *Memoirs of a Highland Gentleman* (1905).
MacKay, Donald, *Scotland Farewell. The People of the Hector* (Toronto 1980).
MacKay, William, *Inverness and Dingwall Presbytery Records* (SHS Edinburgh 1896).
Mackay, W. (ed.), *Letterbook of Baillie John Steuart of Inverness* (Edinburgh 1915).
Mackay, W., *Sidelights on Highland History* (Inverness 1925).
Mackenzie, Alexander, *History of the Mackenzies* (Inverness 1894).
Mackenzie, George, 1st Earl of Cromartie, *A Vindication of Robert III, King of Scotland* (Edinburgh 1695).
Mackenzie, George, 1st Earl of Cromartie, *Parainesis Pacifica, or a persuasive to the Union of Britain* (1702).
Mackenzie, George, 1st Earl of Cromartie, *A few modest reflexions perswading a just indulgence to be granted to the Episcopal Clergy and people in Scotland* (1703).
Mackenzie, George, 1st Earl of Cromartie, *An Abstract of what was spoke on Parliament, by E.C.* (1705).

Mackenzie, George, 1st Earl of Cromartie, *A letter from E.C. to E.W. concerning the Union* (1706).
Mackenzie, George, 1st Earl of Cromartie, *Letters concerning the present Union from a Peer in Scotland to a Peer in England* (1706).
Mackenzie, George, 1st Earl of Cromartie, *Synopsis Apocalyptica* (1708).
Mackenzie, George, 1st Earl of Cromartie, *An Historical Account of the Conspiracies by the Earls of Gowry, and Robert Logan of Restalrig against King James VI. To which is added a vindication of Robert III King of Scotland, and all his descendants from the implication of bastardy* (Edinburgh 1713).
Mackenzie, George, 1st Earl of Cromartie, *An Account of Hirta and Rona*, in D. Munro, *Description of the Western Isles* (1714).
Mackenzie, Sir George Stewart, *A General View of the Agriculture of the Counties of Ross and Cromarty* (London 1813).
Mackenzie, Sir Kenneth S., 'Changes in the Ownership of Land in Ross-shire, 1756-1853', in *Transactions of the Gaelic Society of Inverness* (1897).
Mackenzie, Roderick, *Tales and Legends of Lochbroom* (Ullapool 1988).
Mackintosh, James, *History of the Revolution in England* (1834).
Macleod, Joseph, *Highland Heroes of the Land Reform Movement* (Inverness 1917).
Macleod, Norman, *Reminiscences of a Highland Parish* (no date).
Macleod, W. (ed.), *List of Persons Concerned in the Rebellion* (Edinburgh 1890).
Macrae, Alexander, *The Fire of God Among the Heather* (Inverness, 1930).
Macrae, Alexander, *Revivals in the Highlands and Islands in the Nineteenth Century* (Stirling n.d.).
MacRae, N., *The Romance of a Royal Burgh of Thousand Years*, Dingwall's Story of Dingwall Records 1923 (SHS Edinburgh 1896).
Manson, D., *On the Sulphur Waters of Strathpeffer in the Highlands of Scotland, with District Guide* (London 1879).
Manson, D., *The Sulphur Waters of Strathpeffer, in the Highlands of Scotland*, 4th edition (Aberdeen 1881).
Manson, D., *Strathpeffer Spa* (Inverness 1886).
Marwick, Hugh, *The Merchant Lairds of Long Ago* (Kirkwall 1936).
Mason, Roger A. (ed.), *Scotland and England, 1286-1815* (Edinburgh, 1987).
Meldrum, H.M., *Kilmuir Easter: The history of a Highland Parish* (Inverness 1935).
Menary, George, *Life and Letters of Duncan Forbes of Culloden* (1936).
Miller, Hugh, *The Cruise of the Betsy* (Edinburgh 1858).
Mitchison, Rosalind, *A History of Scotland* (1970).
Mowat, I.R.M., 'A Society in Transition: Easter Ross 1750-1850', B.Phil. thesis, (St. Andrews, 1971).
Mowat, I.R.M., *Easter Ross 1750-1850: the Double Frontier* (Edinburgh 1981).
Millar, A.H. (ed.), *A Selection of the Scottish Forfeited Estate Papers 1715, 1745* (Edinburgh 1909).
Mitchell, Joseph, *Reminiscences of my life in the Highlands* (2 vols, 1883, ed. 1971).
Munro, Donald, 'On the Sulphureous Mineral Waters of Castle Leod and Fairburn, in Rosshire, and of the Salt Purging Water of Pitheathly in Perthshire, Scotland', *Philosophical Transactions*, vol.lxii (1772).
Munro, Jean and Munro, R.W., *Acts of the Lords of the Isles 1336-1493* (Edinburgh, 1986).
Murdoch, Alexander, 'More Reluctant Heroes': New Light on Military Recruiting in North East Scotland 1759-1760', *Northern Scotland* (1985).
Murray, David, *The York Building Company* (Glasgow 1883).
Omand, D. (ed.), *The Ross and Cromarty Book* (Golspie 1984).
Ommer, Rosemary E., 'Primitive accumulation and the Scottish *clann* in the Old World and the New', *Journal of Historical Geography*, vol.12 (1986).

Orr, Willie, *Deer Forests, Landlords and Crofters* (Edinburgh 1982).
P.P. *First Report from the Select Committee on Emigration, Scotland* (1841).
P.P. *Report from the Committee on the Funds arising from the Forfeited Estates of Scotland*, 1806.
P.P. *Reports from Her Majesty's Commissioners for Inquiry into the Administration and Practical Operation of the Poor Laws of Scotland*, 1844, XXI-XXIV.
Patrick, John, 'A Union Broken? Restoration Politics in Scotland', *History Today*, 1982.
Patterson, George, *A History of the County of Pictou, Nova Scotia* (Montreal 1877).
Pennant, T., *A Tour of Scotland* (Warrington, 1774).'Peter Patch', *Sayings and Doings in the Counties of Ross and Cromarty and District of Ferintosh* (Inverness, 1824).
Phillipson, N.T., and Mitchison, Rosalind (eds), *Essays in Scottish History in the Eighteenth Century* (Edinburgh 1970).
Pococke, Richard, *Tours in Scotland* (Edinburgh 1887).
Reports of the Central Board of Management of the Fund Raised for the Relief of the Destitute Inhabitants of the Highlands and Islands of Scotland (Glasgow 1847-8).
Richards, Eric, 'Problems on the Cromartie Estate, 1851-3', *Scottish Historical Review*, LII no.154, 1973.
Richards, Eric, 'Patterns of Highland Discontent, 1790-1850', in R. Quinault and J. Stevenson, *Popular Protest and Public Order* (1973).
Richards, Eric, *Leviathan of Wealth* (1973).
Richards, Eric, *A History of the Highland Clearances Vol.1: Agrarian Transformation and the Evictions 1746-1886* (1982).
Richards, Eric, *A History of the Highland Clearances Vol.2: Emigration, Protest, Reasons* (1985).
Richards, Eric, 'Varieties of Scottish Emigration in the Nineteenth century', *Historical Studies*, Vol.21 (1985).
Richards, Eric, 'Poverty and Survival in 19th Century Coigach', in Baldwin, John R. (ed.), *Ullapool and Wester Ross* (Edinburgh, forthcoming).
Richards, Eric, *The Last Scottish Food Riots* (Past and Present Society, 1982).
Riley, P., 'The Structure of Scottish Politics and the Union of 1707' in *The Union of 1707* (Glasgow, 1974).
Riley, P.W.J., *King William and the Scottish Politicians* (Edinburgh 1979).
Robinson, Neil, *Lion of Scotland* (1952).
Rose, K., *Superior Person* (London 1969).
Ross, Ian Simpson, *Lord Kames and the Scotland of his Day* (Oxford, 1972).
Savage, D.C., 'Scottish Politics 1885-6', *Scottish Historical Review*, vol.40.Scott, Hew, *Fasti Ecclesiae Scoticanae*, Vol.VII (Edinburgh 1928).
Scrope, G. Poulett, *Some Notes of a Tour in England, Scotland and Ireland* (1849).
Sellar, David, 'Highland Pedigree Origins, Pedigree making and Pedigree faking', in L. Maclean (ed.), *The Middle Ages in the Highlands* (Inverness 1981).
Seton, B.G. and Arnot, J.G., *The Prisoners of the '45* (3 vols. Edinburgh 1928-9).
Shaw, F., *The Northern and Western Islands of Scotland: their economy and society in the seventeenth century* (Edinburgh 1980).
Shaw, F., 'Sources of the History of the Seventeenth Century in the Highlands', in L. Maclean (ed.), *The Seventeenth Century in the Highlands* (Inverness 1986).
Sinclair, Sir J., *A General View of the Agriculture of the Counties of Ross and Cromarty* (1795).
Small, A. and Small, J.S., *The Strathpeffer and Inverness Area* (Sheffield, 1971).
Smith, A., 'The Forfeited and Annexed Estates 1752-1784', in G.W.S. Barrow (ed.), *The Scottish Tradition* (1974).
Smith, Annette M., 'Annexed estates in the eighteenth-century Highlands', *Northern Scotland*, vol.3 (1977-8).

Smith, A., *The Jacobite Estates of the Forty-Five* (Edinburgh 1982).
Smout, T.C., *Scottish Trade on the Eve of Union 1660-1707* (Edinburgh 1963).
Smout, T.C., *A History of the Scottish People 1560-1830* (1969).
Smout, T.C., *A Century of the Scottish People 1830-1950* (London 1986).
Southey, Robert, *Journal of a Tour in Scotland in 1819* (ed. 1929).
Speck, W.A., *The Butcher* (1981).
Spence, Elisabeth Isabella, *Letters from the North Highlands during the Summer 1816* (1817).
State of the Election for the County of Cromarty, in North Britain [1769 ?].
Stewart, David of Garth, *Sketches of the Character, Manners and Present State of the Highlanders of Scotland* (2 vols. Edinburgh, 1822, second edition 1825).
Sutherland, the Duchess Dowager of, *Pamphlet printed and issued by* (1892).[Sutherland, Alexander], *A Summer Ramble in the North Highlands* (London 1925).
Teignmouth, Lord, *Sketches of the Coasts and Islands of Scotland and the Isle of Man*, 2 vols (1936).
Thomson, W.A.R., *Spas That Heal* (1978).
Tivy, Joy, 'The Geography of the Strathpeffer Area', *Annual Report Scottish Field Studies Association* (1963).
Tivy, Joy, 'Easter Ross: A Residual Crofting Area', *Scottish Studies*, vol.9 (1965).
Tomasson, K., and Buist, F., *Battles of the '45* (1967 ed.).
Topographical, Statistical and Historical Gazateer of Scotland (2 vols. 1844, Edinburgh).
Walvin, James, *Beside the Seaside* (1978).
Watson, William J., *Ross and Cromarty* (Cambridge 1924).
Whetstone, A.E., *Scottish County Government in the Eighteenth and Nineteenth Centuries* (Edinburgh 1981).
White, P., *Observations upon the Present State of the Scotch Fisheries* (1791).
Whyte, Ian, *Agriculture and Society in Seventeenth Century Scotland* (Edinburgh, 1979).
Wills, Virginia (ed.), *Reports on the Annexed Estates* (2 vols. Edinburgh, 1973).
Wilson, James, *A Voyage round the Coasts of Scotland and the Isles* (2 vols. Edinburgh 1842).
Young, Kenneth, *Arthur James Balfour* (1963).
Zebel, S.H., *Balfour. A Political Biography* (1973).

Notes

Preface

1. The Cromartie Papers are now catalogued as the Cromartie Muniments, GD305. In this book we have used the old cataloguing system from Castle Leod, that is Volumes I–XXI which may be converted easily, as GD305/1/147–168. Virtually all other references to the Cromartie Papers are from estate correspondence which was arranged chronologically by the estate managers.

Chapter 1 pp. 3 to 11

1. David Sellar, 'Highland Family Origins, Pedigree making and Pedigree faking' in *The Middle Ages in the Highlands* (ed.), L. Maclean, Inverness 1981, deals with the origins of the Mackenzies in detail and is convincingly dismissive of both seventeenth century and Victorian versions. A detailed account of the origins of the Mackenzies as seen in Victorian times is given in Fraser I, pp.ix-liii. Note that Fraser draws on Lord Cromartie's manuscript *History of the Mackenzies* written in 1669.
2. William J. Watson, *Ross and Cromarty* (Cambridge, 1924), p.75; J.H. Dawson, *An Abridged Statistical History of the Scottish Counties* (Edinburgh, 1862), p.117; H.M. Meldrum, *Kilmuir Easter, A History of a Highland Parish* (Inverness, 1935), p.112.
3. Preface to the *Culloden Papers* (London, 1915), p.v.
4. The purchase of Cromarty in 1684 was a temporary gain since it soon passed to a secondary branch of the family.
5. J.H. Burns, 'Scotland and England: Culture and Nationality 1500-1800', in J.S. Bromley and E.H. Kossman (eds), *Britain and the Netherlands* (The Hague, 1971), pp.20-1.
6. S.C. D593/K/2/1/3 Fraser to George Loch 19 July 1875. The earliest item he found was a holograph letter of 1624. See Fraser I, p.xxvi.
7. S.C. D593/K/2/1/3 Lord Lovat to Lord Cromartie, 3 July 1739. See Fraser I, p.xlx.
8. W.P. Blaikie, *Origins of the 'Forty Five* (Edinburgh, 1916), p.78, fn 2. See also Fraser I, pp.xlii-xlvii, lxix.
9. Watson, *op.cit.*, p.105.
10. Fraser I, pp.lvii-lxvi.

Chapter 2 pp. 12 to 25

1. At Innerteil, Fife: his mother was Margaret, daughter of Sir George Erskine of Innerteil.
2. In July 1654 he had married Ann Sinclair, daughter of Sinclair of Mey.

3. See Rosalind Mitchison, *A History of Scotland* (1970), p.235.
4. *Ibid.*
5. In a later reminiscence Mackenzie recollected that a local 'seer' in Loch Broom had predicted the invasion of the Loch by English armies who would eat the local barley; in 1655 the prediction was fulfilled and, presumably, Loch Broom was pillaged for its foodstuffs.
5. D.N.B. under Mackenzie, George, 1630-1714.
7. For a recent analysis of some of these circumstances see J. Patrick, 'A Broken Union? Restoration Politics in Scotland', *History Today*, Nov.1982, pp.5-10.
8. D.N.B., op.cit.
9. He lodged in High School Wynd, and remained there until 1687.
10. Dated 27 Sept. 1678, Books of Sederunt vo. vii, f.120.
11. Although honours were heaped upon Cromartie his status-seeking was not easily assuaged. There appears to have been considerable dynastic rivalry over claims to the leadership of the Macleods: Mackenzie apparently petitioned the Privy Council in 1678 to prohibit Iain Brea from styling himself Macleod of that ilk, but without effect. See I.F. Grant, *The Macleods, The History of a Clan* (1959) p.31 fn 1.
12. At another time he was accused of falsifying parliamentary records for political purposes and of inventing an ancestor in order to support his claims to superior descent in the Macleod dynasty. Modern historians have been more sympathetic to his claims. See *Acts of the Lords of the Isles 1336-1493*, ed. Jean Munro and R.W. Munro (Edinburgh 1986), pp.36-7. C.P. Bundle VIII letter of W. Anstruther, 15 Dec. 1702. His intense consciousness of status and lineage caused him to claim that his family was 'the only Norwegian family remaining in Scotland'. Fraser, I, p.clxi.
13. James Mackintosh, *History of the Revolution in England* (1834), pp.109-10. John Buchan, *The Massacre of Glencoe* (1933), p.25.
14. Macintosh, *ibid.*
15. *More Culloden Papers*, ed. D. Warrand, Vol.I p.200, (Inverness 1923).
16. *Life of George Earl of Cromartie* (London 1746) p.134.
17. W. Macgill, *Old Ross-shire and Scotland* (Inverness, 1909), p.237.
18. Mitchison, op.cit. pp.285-6. Tarbat's role in Glencoe is considered by P.Hopkins, 'Glencoe: An English Historian on a Very Scottish Subject', in *The Seventeenth Century in the Highlands* (Inverness Field Club, Inverness, 1986), esp. p.160 and in more depth in P. Hopkins, *Glencoe*, Edinburgh, 1988.
19. Fraser, I, p.cliv. See John Robertson, 'Andrew Fletcher's Vision of Union', in Roger A. Mason (ed.), *Scotland and England* (Edinburgh, 1987), pp.208-14.
20. Mitchison op.cit. p.310. A defence of Cromartie may be found in Fraser, I, clxxx, *et seq.*; P. Riley, 'The Structure of Scottish Politics and the Union of 1707'in *The Union of 1707* (Glasgow 1974), p.9; D. Daiches, *Scotland and the Union* (London, 1977), pp.46-7, 60-86, 131-2, 136; W. Ferguson, *Scotland's Relations with England: A Survey to 1707* (Edinburgh, 1977), pp.193-4, 232, 300 fn.44.
21. An inventory of his books at Castle Leod after his death (C.P. Vol.XX No.45, dated 11 December 1714), suggests, like his own literary productions, an eclectic searching mind. It included many works in French, mainly Protestant in spirit but some with a decidedly Roman Catholic flavour. He possessed a useful dictionary entitled *The Marrow of the French Tongue*. He owned standard works on the *Acts of the General Assembly of the Church of Scotland* and Grotius' study of Christian religion. More thumbed was *Machivell* and *The Political Statesman*. He collected a number of vaguely salacious works (including Rabelais) together with a wide range of volumes of history, law, geography, travel and geometry.

22. Dean Swift, 'Thoughts on Various Subjects', *Works* IV, p.242, quoted in D.N.B. Further evidence of his financial decline is found in C. Fraser-Mackintosh, *Letters of Two Centuries* (Inverness, 1890), p.150.
23. There was subsequent confusion about the final burial place of the 1st Earl of Cromartie. Excavations at Dingwall in August 1875 settled the matter in a blaze of publicity. In the process the Earl was found to measure 6 feet 2 inches. *Scotsman*, 14 September 1875.

Chapter 3 pp. 26 to 37

1. The Hearth Tax returns for 1690 and 1691 gave incomplete lists of the inhabitants of the Easter Ross parishes and the Poll Tax for Coigach are still less satisfactory though the evidence of family names has potential.
2. Ian Whyte, *Agriculture and Society in Seventeenth Century Scotland* (Edinburgh, 1979), p.5.
3. The piper in rent accounts should be treated with caution as it was apparently a well-known way of increasing the Factor's remuneration, and actual pipers were much scarcer than accounts show.
4. S.R.O. E746/70.
5. Even in the eastern parish of Kilmuir, in 1792, nine out of ten elders had no knowledge of English.
6. Meldrum, op.cit., pp.32-3; Fraser I, p.cxiii. The mortification to Kilmuir was part of a larger deed, 36 bolls per annum in all, to the decayed tenants (and their widows) in the eastern lands of the Earl.
7. C.P. Bundle XII, *Letter to Alexander McKenzie*.
8. Quoted by Bruce Lenman, 'The Highland Aristocracy and North America 1603-1784', in *The Seventeenth Century in the Highlands* (Inverness Field Club, 1986), p.178.
9. See W. Macgill, op.cit., pp.44, 45, 87-90, 72. C.P. Bundle XVII, 22 June 1720.
10. C.P. Bundle XVII, 20 June 1720.
11. C.P. Bundle XVII, 22 June 1720, precognition of John Rose.
12. Rev'd John Kennedy, The Days of the Fathers in Ross-shire (Edinburgh, 1866).
13. On religious background see D. Omand (ed.), The Book of Ross and Cromarty (Golspie, 1986), chapter 8.
14. See 'Information for Colonel Robert Manor of Fowlis, John Forbes of Culloden, and Twenty Seven Others', 3 March 1722, pamphlet in the British Library.

Chapter 4 pp. 38 to 50

1. See C.P. Gorry to Mackenzie of Meddat, 8 January 1757.
2. C.P. A list of the hearthes upon the Viscount of Tarbat his landes in the Easter division of Ross (XVIII.250) dated 1690.
3. David Murray, *York Building Company* (Glasgow, 1883), p.35.
4. Macgill, op.cit., pp.234-5.
5. C.P. Bundle IV, 8 Feb. 1690 Kenneth McKenzie to Viscount Tarbat.
6. Considerable fragments of rentals survive for 1686-7 and 1703. They indicate, particularly, that in the east vast transactions were accounted in grain, that tacksmen were responsible for most payments, and that surpluses were exported after all other claims in the estate were met. The Coigach rental of 1730 shows production of butter, wedders, plaids and cheese. C.P. Vol.XVII, p.132.

7. But some lairds found the commercial disposal of their rents in kind a considerable problem and were less attached to the system. See Macgill, op.cit., p.176.
8. There is, for instance, documentation which demonstrates large exports, 10,000 bolls of bere, from Tain to Norway between 1621 and 1631.
9. See Hugh Marwick, *Merchant Lairds of Orkney* (Kirkwall, 1936).
10. W. Mackay (ed.), *Letterbook of Baillie John Steuart of Inverness* (Scottish History Society, Edinburgh, 1915), p.xviii.
11. The Tarbat measure: the bere was sold by volume, but the actual size of the boll is not known: the Great Boll of Tarbat was a copper vessel kept either at the girnel of Portmahomack or at Tarbat Parish Church. It was probably considerably larger than the Linlithgow boll which was 308lbs imperial. The trade is explained in more detail in Monica Clough, 'The Cromartie Estate, 1660-1784: Aspects of Trade and Organization', in John S. Baldwin, *Firthlands of Ross and Sutherland* (Edinburgh, 1986).
12. This included the hire of small boats and boatmen to load the ship, and the acceptance of cargo brought north on the owner's bill of lading. The turnaround usually required 'ten weather-work days'.
13. At Strathpeffer the grain was stored on the ground floor of Castle Leod, and then taken to Dingwall and Cromarty for shipping.
14. Jane Durham in Omand, op.cit., p.232.
15. Fletcher to Tarbat, 17 April 1691, in Fraser I, p.77.
16. O.S.A. Tarbat, p.433.
17. See Monica Clough, 'Making the most of one's resources: Lord Tarbat's Development of Cromarty Firth', *Country Life*, 29 September 1977, pp.856-8.
18. On wagonways, see Benjamin Baxter, *Stone Blocks and Iron Rails* (1966), and M.J.T. Lewis, *Early Modern Railways* (1970).
19. SRO E 787.18.2.
20. C.P. Vol.XVI no.211, 218, 219; Vol.VII no.32; Correspondence Norman Macleod to Cromartie, 15 August 1712, Major John Sinclair to Cromartie, 12 September 1712; SRO E 746.74 8 (3).
21. C.P. Book XXII, 51.
22. See Monica Clough, 'The Leith Glass Works: c.1689-c.1708', *Scottish Industrial History*, vol.5, no.1 (1982).
23. See Lenman, op.cit., p.179.
24. N.L.S. MS5319, Cromartie to King William, October 1705.
25. One of these gave Tarbat the lease of the Old Mills of Elgin, a profitable venture for many years.
26. Another lawyer/laird, owner of land in the southern part of the Black Isle, was author of the very early Scots novel *Arentina*, and Advocate General of Scotland.
27. Tarbat retained the services of the Urquhart chamberlain, Robert Dunbar, notary public, and tacksman of a small property near the port. In another move Urquhart's debts to a lawyer and grain merchant, John Cuthbert of Inverness, were taken over by Tarbat.
28. A generation later, in 1741, his eldest son, Sir George Mackenzie, was driven by bankruptcy to sell the estate to William Urquhart of Meldrum, suggesting that the wheel had turned a full circle. *Gazetteer of Scotland* (1844), p.310.
29. They were the Scots equivalent of a bill of exchange.
30. Bonds incorporated a rate of interest and were, often, guaranteed by the signatures of two cautioners. When the risk increased (e.g. in the declining stages of the Urquhart story) the less easy did it become to raise such signatories. The procedure was central to the Scots law system.

31. SRO E 6/5. The debt was, in fact, rejected—as 'too old a debt'.
32. Geoffrey Steel and Elizabeth Beaton, 'Local Building Traditions' in Omand, op.cit., p.213.
33. *N.L.S. Summary Catalogue of the Advocate's Manuscripts* (Edinburgh, 1971), ch.5805.
34. C.P. XIV 171
35. On Royston see John G. Gifford, Colin McWilliam and David Walker, *Edinburgh; The Buildings of Scotland* (1984), pp.603-8.
36. Surprisingly Tarbat made over nominal possession of large parts of his estate to his three sons at an early age—in 1707, for instance, Royston House was made over to James, his youngest son. Such devices may have been to prevent much of his estate being attached to his own debts. It may also have been connected with efforts to preserve the estate via a series of entails.
37. See Monica Clough, 'Leith Glass Works', op.cit., p.3.

Chapter 5 pp. 51 to 56

1. C.P. XIV 171.
2. N.L.S. Ch.5805.
3. C.P. Bundle XVI.
4. Meldrum, op.cit., p.114.
5. Fraser II, 174-5.
6. See Mackay, *Baillie Steuart's Letterbook*, op.cit., pp.325-6.
7. Fraser I, cciv.
8. C.P. Vol XVII p.118, *John MacBean's Account* 1729.
9. Fraser II, pp.176-7.
10. Rosalind Mitchison, 'The Government and the Highlands' in N.T. Phillipson and R. Mitchison (eds), *Scotland in the Age of Improvement* (Edinburgh, 1970), p.35.
11. Macgill, op.cit., p.303.
12. Fraser I, cciv.
13. Mowat, op.cit., p.45.
14. See Donald MacKay, *Scotland Farewell* (Toronto, 1980), p.39.
15. Macgill, op.cit., p.304.
16. N.L.S. MS 7059 f94; MS 7062 f69; MS 1766 f67.
17. Bruce Lenman, *The Jacobite Clans of the Great Glen 1650-1784* (1984), p.24; Mitchison, op.cit., p.43.
18. Within Cromartie's own kinship group there were inconsistencies. For instance the bankrupt Sir George Mackenzie (c.1702-48) remained loyal to the government.

Chapter 6 pp. 57 to 68

1. See *The Life of George, Earl of Cromertie*, (London, 1746), p.136. Cromartie is said to have presented himself to Sir John Cope at Inverness at the end of August 1745 and 'made a tender of all his power and influence in suppressing the Rebellion, but such assistance was not then judged necessary'. A different and contradicting version is given in Daniel Munro's 'An Account of the Late Rebellion from Ross and Sutherland', in Blaikie, op.cit., p.96.
2. Ibid., p. 137.
3. The story gains marginally more credibility from an account of a previous episode recorded in a letter of Simon Lord Lovat to Lochiel in April 1743: 'The Earl of Cromarty, after drinking excessively in this house of very good wine for five days, went to Dingwall and

fell adrinking of very bad wine, which made him so sick he had almost died there .... But I thank God he is recovered. His death would be a singular loss to his Country and to his friends, and particularly, to me...' Quoted in *Northern Chronicle*, 28 April 1888.

4. Cromartie had been angling for a Company for his son in the new Highland Regiments in May 1745, and in a letter to Lord Tweeddale had then sworn undying allegiance. N.L.S. MS 1766 f67.
5. Culloden Papers (London, 1815), pp.414-5, Cromartie to Lord President 26 September 1745; see also pp.408-9, 411, 421.
6. Culloden Papers, op.cit., p.235.
7. Ibid.
8. Culloden Papers, op.cit., p.428.
9. Baillie John Steuart, op.cit., p.xliii.
10. A contemporary print, Life of George, does however make the claim that Cromartie was about to take the first opportunity to desert the Rebellion army but was caught in Sutherland as they prepared to escape for France, op.cit., p. 138. George Menary, *Life and Letters of Duncan Forbes of Culloden* (1936), pp.221, 226, 237, 244.
11. Culloden Papers, op.cit., p.447.
12. See Mitchison, op.cit., p.43.
13. [Rev. Alexander Macbean], 'Memorial Concerning the Highlands', 1746, printed in W.B. Blaikie, *Origins of the 'Forty Five* (Edinburgh, Scottish History Society, 1916), pp. 74, 91, 98. *The Highlands of Scotland in 1750* (ed. A. Lang), pp.20-1.
14. Quoted in MacKay, op.cit., pp.14-15.
15. See Monica Clough in *Muster Roll of Prince Charles Edward Stuart's Army 1745-1746* (Aberdeen, 1984), pp.78-88, ed. by A. Livingstone, C.W.H. Aikman and B.S. Hart; and, J.E. McCann, 'The organisation of the Jacobite Army 1745-6', Ph.D. thesis, Edinburgh University, 1963; Fraser II, nos. 403-31.
16. See Macleod's Narrative provided in Fraser I, pp.379-95. Cromartie's military orders are found in N.L.S. MS 14835, f15.
17. See *Memoirs of the Life of Sir John Clerk of Penicuik* (1892), pp.199-200.
18. Fraser II, Nos. 403-31.
19. C.P. Bundle XXI, Cromartie to Meddat, 23 February 1754; Fraser, I, ccxxi, fn.
20. Trial Report, p. 5. There were conflicting accounts of the capture. See Gentleman's Magazine, XVI, August 1746; 23 April 1746 and A. McK. Annand, 'Major-General Lord Macleod, Count Cromartie, First Colonel, 73rd Macleod's Highlanders', Society for Army Historical Research Journal, vol.37 (1959), pp.21-7.
21. John Doran, *London in the Jacobite Times* (2 vols. 1877), vol.2, p.194.
22. Anon., *The Trials of William, Earl of Kilmarnock, George, Earl of Cromartie, and Arthur, Lord Balmarino* (London, 1746). Gentleman's Magazine, 23 June 1746, 29 May 1746.
23. The speech printed in Life of George, p. 142; Gentleman's Magazine. August 1746, and N.L.S. MS 2-1-15.
24. Quoted in G.E.C. *Complete Peerage*.
25. J.M. Bullock in an entry in Notes and Queries, 10th Series (13 January 1906), quotes the Stowe MSS 158, 234, Sir John Gordon to the Duke of Newcastle, 30 October 1746 about Lord Macleod's forthcoming trial—'God knows how I shall break it to his poor mother, who is now within a very few weeks of her time'.
26. Mackay, op.cit., p.18.
27. Daniel Munro, in Blaikie, op.cit., p.98 n. At the time of Uprising Glastullich was described as 'being Remarkably disaffected', The Highlands of Scotland in 1750, op.cit., p.21.
28. C.P. Meddat to Cromartie, 9 January 1747.

29. Huw Scott (ed.), *Fasti Ecclesiae Scoticanae*, vol.VII (1928 ed.), pp.157-8.
30. Macgill, op.cit., p.246.
31. *The Prisoners of the '45* (ed.), B.G. Seton & J.G. Arnot (SHS, Edinburgh, 3 vols. 1928-9).
32. *Statistics of the Annexed Estates*, p.8.
33. 'Memorial Anent True State of Highlands as to Chieftains', in J. Allardyce (ed.), *Historical Papers of the Jacobite Period* (Aberdeen, 1895), p.172.
34. W.A. Speck, *The Butcher*, 181, 185, 201.
35. Rupert C. Jarvis, *Collected Papers on the Jacobite Rising* (Manchester, 1972), Vol. II, chapter 22.
36. Speck, op.cit., 174, 181; MacKay, op.cit., calculates that 152 people from Lochbroom were transported, of whom only six ever returned.
37. Annexed Estate Reports.
38. This section is based partly on *List of Persons Concerned in the Rebellion*, ed. W. McLeod, SHS Vol. VIII (Edinburgh, 1890). Evidence given at the Trials is reproduced in J. Allardyce (ed.), *Historical Papers relating to the Jacobite Period 1699-1750* (New Spalding Club, Aberdeen, 2 vols. 1895), esp. pp.402-3, 411-13.
39. The rents of the Cromartie estates were collected for the Crown by Mr John Baillie, W.S., of Edinburgh in C.P.
40. Gentleman's Magazine, 27 February 1748. Many geneological and antiquarian details are found in a series of exchanges in Notes and Queries: 3rd series, vii, p.7-8; 8th series, i, p.475, iv, p.461, vi, pp.205-6, viii, p.8, vii, p.57, vi, p.542; 9th series, iv, pp.107, 171; 10th series, v, pp.28, 70.
41. C.P. 7 July 1748.
42. MacKay, op.cit., p.21.
43. Heavy costs had been incurred in negotiating the pardon. See Macgill, op.cit., p.247.
44. C.P. Bundle, XX, 5 November 1749, Earl of Cromartie from Northcote, Devon.
45. Fraser II, p.230.
46. Meldrum, op.cit., p.117. See S.R.O. Forfeited Estate Papers E746/17, Royal Warrant for the payment of a pension to the Countess of Cromarty. A contemporary report (Gentleman's Magazine, 5 September 1749) stated that Cromartie was given £500 p.a. out of the forfeited estates 'for the maintenance of his family' in addition to the sum arising from the sale of his estates 'to be settled on his children'.
47. B.L. Vol.cxcvi, Newcastle Papers Add. 32881.
48. Fraser, *Scots Peerage*, Vol. III, p. 80.
49. A. Mackenzie, p.550. This is confirmed by correspondence between Cromartie and his factor Mackenzie of Meddat, in which the former frequently acknowledges or solicits gifts from Mackenzie's friends in Ross. e.g.: C.P. Bundle XX, 27 March 1747, Meddat to Cromartie, repeating government pressure to pay Crown Rents; same to same May 1, 1747, 'I was going to send what money I had to Edinburgh by one of the ministers going to the Assembly. I have given Mr Colin Mackenzie Minister of Fodderty £160 sterling being all the money I could get scraped together...' Cromartie to Meddat, May 25 1754, 'I long for that remittance which Fairburn by advice from Achilty was to make to me ... I shall likewise long to hear of the cattle being well sold.' In May 1755 Cromartie thanked Meddat for the 'constant remembrance' of Cadboll (who never sent more than civil messages) and the money sent by Fairburn and Achilty, and the Pickled Pork and barrel of Loch Broom herrings and honey, 'the best that I ever ate'. Cromartie to Meddat (Bundle XXI), 31 March 1759 '...hard struggle to keep our heads above water', begging for 'Some friends in the north ... a little from several individuals would be of very great use.'

Chapter 7 pp. 71 to 84

1. Quoted in Speck, op.cit., p.164; see also p.168.
2. N.S.A., Vol.14, pp.82-3. Macgill, op.cit., p.247 quotes a letter from James Robertson written in 1749 which confirms the account of the visit of the marines three years before. They 'pillaged the country for their concern in the Rebellion' and 'one poor man ... had his house plundered and burnt, and his sheep taken away.' Hanoverian officials later confirmed the story.
3. Annette M. Smith, *Jacobite Estates of the Forty Five* (Edinburgh 1982), p.3.
4. Virginia Wills (ed.), *Reports on the Annexed Estates* (2 vols., Edinburgh, 1973), p.v.
5. Ibid, II.
6. Cromartie's own lawyer was Leonard Urquhart, in Edinburgh, who drew up petitions for Lady Cromartie's jointure and later represented John Macleod and eased his return. There is a receipt of Lady Cromartie's pension in 1755 in N.L.S. ms.295/64.
7. Some observers consider these 'yearly tributes of affection', and the alacrity with which formerly disinherited chiefs were later able to raise regiments, to be the essence of continuing clanship. See Mrs Grant of Laggan, quoted on the Lochiel estates by Rosemary E. Ommer, 'Primitive accumulation and the Scottish clann in the Old World and the New', *Journal of Historical Geography*, Vol.12 (1986), pp.121-141.
8. SRO E746.70. Murdoch Mackenzie of Achilty deposes that the factor gave him a tack in 1750, of the Barony, annually renewable. In 1755 most Coigach tenants depose they had paid him including entrance grassums. It is thus not surprising that the former Earl hoped for money from Achilty (which he generally refused to send). See note 49, Chap. 6.
9. SRO E746.72.3.
10. T.C. Smout, *A History of the Scottish People 1560-1830* (1969), p.343.
11. The extent of the debts of the Earl of Cromartie was detailed in 1764. Many of the debts dated from the beginning of the century and included amounts owed to cooks, servants and Inverness merchants. In 1752 the estate had been valued at £27,059, its debts at £8,015. The Countess was owed £6,666. N.L.S. MS.8280 Stuart Stevenson MS.ff 120-133. The Report of Francis Farquharson and David Russell, Accomplant Upon the Value of the Estate of George Earl of Cromarty (Attainted) and State of the Debts due to Creditors. Humbly made to his Lordship's remit to them dated 19 December 1764. Another report, of 1752 indicated clearly that 'a great part of the estate is wadset or mortgaged', to the unredeemed figure of about £8,600 Sterling. S.C. Rentals 1752 p.143.
12. Rosalind Mitchison, *A History of Scotland*, op.cit., p.343.
13. Smith, op.cit., p.26.
14. Smith, op.cit., p.49.
15. Smith, op.cit., p.7.
16. Virginia Wills, Reports, op.cit., p.X.
17. Smith, op.cit., p.52.
18. Smith, op.cit., p.33; also E 796.39.3. Jeffrey had a different reputation and was so unpopular in Coigach that he felt it necessary to erect his own tombstone at Achiltibuie, with eulogy, before he died!
19. See Ian Simpson Ross, *Lord Kames and the Scotland of his Day* (Oxford, 1972).
20. Papers on Peter May, Land Surveyor 1749-1793, ed., Ian H. Adams (Edinburgh, 1979), p.28. S.R.O. E.746.70.
21. The minister of Lochbroom, James Robertson, covered a parish 32 miles in length and 18 in width in which there were seven different places of worship, with a population of 2,250 souls of whom 909 were with the estate of Cromartie, i.e. Coigach. There were no papists

and no non-jurant ministers. (Judicial Rental, 1755, pp.95 et seq.) Robertson, in SRO E746.70, Judicial Rental swears population of Coigach is 909.
22. In 1756 Francis Grant, General Riding Officer and Inspector, summoned Coigach tenants to meet him and required an interpreter to convey the Commissioners plans for improvements and the development of Ullapool, Papers on Peter May, op.cit., pp.11-12.
23. Forbes' report noted that on the lots 'a good deall of potatoes' were being planted.
24. Papers on Peter May, op.cit., pp.10-11.
25. Papers on Peter May, op.cit., p.16.
26. S.R.O. T46.74.4(2/3), John McLeod of Keannichilis' petition.
27. Millar, op.cit., p.80.
28. S.R.O. E746.74.8.1.
29. S.R.O. E746.74.4(1). Mowat, op.cit., pp.35, 43-5, cites a 1755 survey which shows that all 16 holdings at New Tarbat had sub-tenants; wheat production was also evident.
30. SRO E746.70, and Papers on Peter May, op.cit., p.6; A.H. Millar, op.cit., p.80.
31. See MacKay, op.cit., p.57. There was nothing new in these disputes. The case of Murdoch Mackenzie of Achilty, for instance, showed that the lands had been in his family since a tack was arranged in 1674. S.R.O. E745.70.
32. See MacKay, op.cit., pp.54-5.
33. S.R.O. E746.74.1.

Chapter 8 pp. 85 to 95

1. Paper of Peter May, op.cit., p.81.
2. Smith, op.cit., p.67.
3. See Dunlop, op.cit., pp.40-1. See Monica Clough, Early Fishery and Forestry Developments on the Cromartie Estate of Coihach in J. Baldwin (ed.) *Ullapool and Wester Ross* (forthcoming, Edinburgh 1989).
4. S.R.O. E746.74.8.1. Wills, op.cit., p.414.
5. Smith, op.cit., p.151.
6. T. Pennant, *A Tour in Scotland* (1774 ed., Warrington), p.163.
7. SRO E 746 40-36, Correspondence of Forbes to Henry Barclay, 16 April 1763; 746.74.37, Forbes to Barclay, 5 May 1763; 746.74.39 Forbes to Barclay, 28 June 1763; E746.74.42 Forbes to Barclay, 8 August 1763; E 746.74.48 Petitions to Forbes, 14 June 1764; E 746.84.50 (3), Forbes' Return of Soldiers, Strathpeffer Station, 22 November 1764.
8. Establishing rent trends is extraordinarily difficult: arrears and commutation, changes of acreages, factors' commission, prices and conversion of currencies all combine to make a mockery of time-comparisons. However, of the Cromartie rents at the time of the restoration, in 1784, it was said that the debt, £19010, was within a trifle of 20 years purchase, suggesting an aggregate rent of about £960 sterling. See below, Appendix A.
9. Smith, op.cit. p.70.
10. Forbes also opposed the process. In 1766 he said that such a conversion was 'in effect giving an abatement of rent which is not easily be made up'. SRO E 764.74.54 (2).
11. Smith, op.cit. p.97.
12. Smith, op.cit., pp.86-7.
13. Loud disputes arose, see SRO E 746.88.4, Captain Ross to Broadly, 3 July 1770; E 746.88.1-2, Ross of Priesthill's Memorial.
14. Quoted in Mackay, op.cit. p.70. It should be remembered that the armies during the Jacobite Uprising faced extreme difficulties finding any food supplies in the Highlands—

Cope remarked in 1745 that 'the country could not afford subsistence ... it was absolutely necessary to carry a stock of bread along with us'. Cromartie himself faced problems with the granaries. See McCann, op.cit., pp.169-70, 187.
15. S.R.O. E746.74.39; Millar, op.cit., pp.82, 85.
16. Smith, op.cit., passim.
17. P.R.O. T.500 Reports of Vessels leaving with Emigrants.
18. Quoted in Macgill, op.cit., p.50.
19. Macgill, op.cit., p.158.
20. The previous three paragraphs draw on Mackay, op.cit., chapters 5 and 6, and B. Bailyn, *Voyagers to the West* (New York, 1986), chapter 14.
21. P.R.O. T.500.
22. J.M. Bumsted, *The People's Clearance* (Edinburgh, 1985), pp.61-4.
23. P.R.O. T.47/12.
24. O.S.A., XVII, p.562.
25. See P. White, *Observations upon the Present State of the Scotch Fisheries* (1791), p.58. The Cromartie rental of 1785 (C.P. Vol.XVII, p.145) includes tacks for fishing stations on the Lochbroom islands as well as for kelp making in Coigach.
26. Smith, op.cit., pp.167-70. Richard Pococke, *Tours in Scotland* (Edinburgh, 1887), p.175.
27. A.H. Millar op.cit., p.xlvii.
28. Wills, p.v.
29. A. Smith, 'The Forfeited and Annexed Estates 1752-1784', in *The Scottish Tradition*, ed. G.W.S. Barrow (1974), pp.209, 210; A. Smith, Annexed Estates, op.cit., p.226.
30. One of the Board's own factors, Colin Mackenzie, gave credence to this view when he remarked 'You will know how this estate has been harshly used since the forfeiture', Smith, p.225.

Chapter 9 pp. 96 to 107

1. *DNB*, p.599.
2. Fraser I, p.ccxxx. On Macleod's career generally, see Fraser I, pp.ccxxxvi-cclviii.
3. Fraser I, p.ccxx. See above, Chapter 6.
4. May, op.cit., p.7.
5. There is record of his departure from England for Gothenberg 5 August 1755, N.L.S. MS 295/64.
6. See S.C. D593/K Correspondence relating to Macleod between Lady Mackenzie to Gustav, King of Sweden, 3 December 1788, 27 December 1773.
7. C.P. Memo XIII 79 by Henry Dundas, W.S. 1763.
8. See Smith, op.cit., passim.
9. Cromartie Papers, Castle Leod, Bundle XXII, Urquhart to Count Cromartie, 12 August 1773.
10. Part of the campaign saw Macleod ordering and paying for an elaborate carriage in Edinburgh (via Urquhart) as a present for the Queen of Sweden who interceded on his behalf with George III.
11. C.P. Urquhart to Macleod, 20 September 1773, 5 March 1774.
12. An account is given in Robert Bain, *History of the Ancient Province of Ross, the County Palatine of Scotland* (Dingwall, 1899), pp.314-5.
13. David Stewart, *Sketches of the Character, Manners, and Present State of the Highlanders of*

Scotland (2 vols, Edinburgh, 1822), I, p.153. It was true that there were great difficulties experienced in the recruitment of the Sutherland Fencibles in 1795, see MacGill, op.cit., p.176.
14. C.P. XXVII, undated memorandum.
15. Quoted in Jean MacDougall, *Highland Postbag* (1984), pp.98-8.
16. Cromartie Papers, Bundle XXV, Sir George Yonge to Macleod, 26 November 1782.
17. C.P. XXV. Ed. Bishop to Macleod, 2 January 1782.
18. C.P. XXV. Bishop and Bromwell to Macleod, 25 January 1782, Macleod to Charles Jenkinson, 27 September 1782.
19. C.P. XXVII. Macleod to North. n.d.
20. C.P. XXV. Alex Duncan to Macleod, 16 July 1784.
21. C.P. XXV. Alex Duncan to Macleod, 20 August 1784.
22. C.P. XXV. Duncan to Macleod, 17 January 1785, 20 January 1785. See also 'Abstract of the Act for Restoring the Forfeited Estates, 1784', in A.H. Millar, *A Selection of Scottish Forfeited Estates Papers* (Edinburgh, 1909), p.357. See also P.P. Report from the Committee on the Funds arising from the Forfeited Estates of Scotland, 1806. Smith, op.cit., p.44, indicates that the £19,000 represented money expended by the Board to pay off old debts (some dating from the 1720s) and for the general improvement of the estate.
23. C.P. XXV Duncan to Macleod, 16 June 1784, Dundas to Murray, 11 May 1784.
24. C.P. Duncan to Macleod, 6 July 1785, 11 July 1785; Lewis to Macleod, 21 February 1785.
25. C.P. Duncan to Macleod, 8 September 1784.
26. C.P. Duncan to Macleod, 16 July 1784; Dundas to Sir William Murray, 11 May 1784.
27. C.P. Harrison to Macleod, 15 July 1785; Duncan Freer, 16 July 1785; Duncan to Macleod, 16 July 1785, 23 July 1785.
28. C.P. Sir George Yonge to Macleod, 5 July 1796; Bishop and Bromwell to Macleod, 30 December 1786.
29. C.P. XXVI. Yonge to Macleod, 11 May 1788.
30. C.P. XVI. Nos. 158-180. p.113. There is reference to the fact that Lots in the Heights of Strathpeffer were lotted out to soldiers—but it does not say when this took place.
31. Ibid. No.187. For a somewhat mystifying oral recollection (many decades later) see Anderson, *Guide to the Highlands* (1863), p.475.
32. The 17th Lord Forbes married a grand-daughter of the third Earl of Cromartie in 1792 and thus the families were closely tied together in a web of marriages.
33. C.P. XVIII. Macleod's will, 18 January 1786.
34. See CLough, 'Early Fishery and Forestry', op.cit.
35. See David Loch, *Essays on the Trade, Commerce, Manufactures and Fishing of Scotland* (3 vols, Edinburgh, 1778), III, pp.186-8. See also 'A Voyage to the Hebrides', in *The Bee*, 30 May 1792. John Woodhouse of Inverpool had already made considerable progress at Isle Martin where he claimed he had spent £3000 on his operations. Much of the fish was, of course, intended for the slave market in the West Indies.
36. Macleod gave access to quarries for stone for construction and, more importantly, promised the Society a lease on favourable terms for the new village. He was congratulated on his liberality by the Duke of Argyll who, in May 1788, wrote 'in consequence of the very liberal Feu right which you have given to the Fishing Society, we have received proposals from Mr Robert Melville of Dunbar for establishing a very compleat Fishing Settlement on the lands of Ullapool, and as his offer has been highly approved of, we have executed a Contract with him for carrying on all the necessary buildings which are to be begun immediately ... I am much assured it will give you great satisfaction to know that your generous and patriotic conduct, has given a beginning to this great object of National

Improvement.' C.P. XXVI, John Mackenzie to Macleod, 15 April 1788, Argyll to Macleod, 7 May 1788.
37. Kent Archives Office U116/E2 & E3 Report of a Survey of Ullapool in Ross-shire by Mr Aitken & Mr G. Mackenzie 25 January 1788.
38. See J. Dunlop, *The British Fisheries Society 1786-1893* (Edinburgh, 1978), chapters 4 and 5, Appendix pp.218-225.
39. The Substance of a Speech of Henry Beaufort to the British Society for Extending the Fisheries, 25 March 1788 (London, 1788), pp.29-32, 75.
40. C.P. Vol. XIII, no. 87, Memorial to Lord Macleod, March 1787.

Chapter 10 pp. 111 to 128

1. It is not certain that recruitment to the armed forces was easy. Useful perspectives are cast by James A. Cheyne, 'Reluctant Heroes: conscription in Aberdeenshire, 1756-58', Northern Scotland IV (1981), pp.43-50, and Alexander Murdoch, 'More Reluctant Heroes': New Light on Military Recruiting in North East Scotland, 1759-1760', Northern Scotland (1985), pp.157-168.
2. See Chapter 11 below.
3. N.S.A. Vol.14, p.420.
4. William J. Watson, op.cit., p.26.
5. Neither the estate nor the county of Cromarty corresponded to census or parish units and there is only a little incidental information about population in the estate records. As for parish data, the first census captured the problem: 'It has been found impossible to form any correct Abstract of the Baptisms, Burials and Marriages in Scotland' since only 99 out of 850 parishes had kept regular registers. There were none in Ross and Cromarty. Census 1801, Abstract of Answers and Returns, Enumeration. Part II, Scotland. See Appendix B below.
6. 'The shire of Cromarty consists of about fifteen separate parcels, locally situate in Ross-shire, and for most purposes is deemed to be united to that County, nor can its Population be distinguished.' P.P. Census 1811 Parishes Register Abstracts, p.502. On the problems of baptisms see O.S.A. Vol.III Kincardine: 'The number of births and burials cannot be ascertained; many of the children of this parish being baptised by the minister of Creich, and vice versa. And when a stranger clergyman passes through either parish, which is often the case, the parents, accompanied by one or more of the elders, wait on him, and get their children baptised. There are 5 burial places resorted to by the inhabitants, and 3 of these are in the parish of Creich. There is no regular grave-digger but at the church.' (p.508.) See also O.S.A. Vol.IV.
7. O.S.A. Dingwall, p.6., Kincardine, p.507.
8. G. Patterson, *A History of the County Pictou, Nova Scotia* (Montreal, 1877), p.234, 450-65; Mitchell Library, Glasgow, Acc.476772 Clyde Commercial List, No.485, Vol.4; N.L.S. MS 9646, p.45.
9. N.S.A. Vol.14, p.419.
10. Quoted by Mackay, op.cit., pp.166-7.
11. O.S.A. Tarbat, p.432 fn. See also W. Macgill, op.cit., p.173.
12. The Bee, 30 May 1792.
13. See Clough, Cromartie Estate, op.cit., p.91.
14. O.S.A. Tarbat, p.433.
15. In Kilmuir Easter it was reported that the people were reduced to eating shellfish while

conditions in Contin were so bad that 'no doubt many of the poorer sort must have died from want, were it not for the timely supply of corn sent by the government to the county'. O.S.A., Contin, p.167.

16. Reprinted in Appendix XC of Napier Report, pp.420-2.
17. S.R.O. E746/39/4 Sworn Statement of C. Mackenzie of Meddat, 5 October 1786.
18. Kent Archives, Petley Family Papers, V116 E4 George Mackenzie to Kenneth Mackenzie, 4 February 1796, 10 March 1797.
19. O.S.A., p.474.
20. C.P. Meddat to Lord Cromartie, 29 April 1748, 5 May 1758.
21. From Contin it was reported that 'In 1790-1 a putrid fever, which made prodigious havoc in a place called Strathbran, where it carried off more than two thirds of the inhabitants, and still continues to rage with violence there'. O.S.A., Contin, p.162.
22. O.S.A. Tarbat, p.428, Kilmuir Easter, p.190, Logie Easter, p.472.
23. On the differential impact of inoculation see Eric Richards, *Leviathan of Wealth* (1973), pp.162-3. O.S.A., Logie Easter, pp.472-3.
24. O.S.A., Kilmuir Easter, p.190.
25. O.S.A., Dingwall, p.3., Tarbat, p.429, Fodderty, p.441.
26. N.S.A., Vol.14, Lochbroom, p.75.
27. O.S.A., Dingwall, p.9, Tarbat, p.421, Logie Easter, pp.462, 470.
28. A case in point was the settlement of Murdo Mackenzie on the Heights of Dochnachar in 1798. He recalled 'it was but a small piece of moor when I entered the same and was charged no rent for a number of years, but afterwards had to pay 26/-.' In 1824 he confessed he was unable to work any longer and could no longer pay the rent. CP Bundle XXXII Mackenzie to Mrs Hay-Mackenzie, 24 August 1824.
29. O.S.A., Kilmuir Easter, p.189.
30. Journal of Matthew Culley's Tour of Scotland 1775 (typescript copy), pp.74-5, Culley Papers ZCW 43, in Northumberland County Record Office.
31. Macgill, op.cit., p.175.
32. See I. Mowat, Thesis, p.52, and R.J. Adam (ed.), *Papers on Sutherland Estate Management* (2 vols. Edinburgh, 1972), Vol.I, p.xxix fn 3.
33. O.S.A., Kilmuir Easter, p.187.
34. O.S.A., Lochbroom, p.470.
35. O.S.A., Tarbat, pp.420, 428.
36. O.S.A., Contin, p.164.
37. See Richards, *A History of the Highland Clearances* (1982), Vol.I, Chapter 9.
38. S.R.O. 34/4/6 Lybelles on Summonses of Removing 1792.
39. O.S.A., Lochbroom, pp.466-7.
40. O.S.A., Contin, p.167, Tarbat, p.433. The Cromartie estate had eventually lost its rich lands in Tarbat, first by wadsets in 1704 and 1727 and finally by the terms of the complicated transactions surrounding the marriage of the third Earl of Cromartie.
41. O.S.A., Fearn, p.300, Kincardine, p.510. The trade of Lochbroom at the turn of the century is suggested from the cargo of the ship the *Grace* trading from Greenock to Ullapool in December 1805. She carried 5 casks of refined sugar, 4 of groceries, 4 of molasses, 2 boxes of candy sugar, 8 casks of biscuit, 2 barrels of wheat flour, 2 casks of porter, 15 dozen pounds of hemp, 30 bags of oatmeal, 10 dozen pieces of earthenware, 110 lbs of rolled tobacco, 42 lb of rappee snuff, and 1000 barrel staves. Sailings out of Ullapool indicated the export of fish and wool. Mitchell Library, Glasgow, Acc.No.476772. Clyde Commercial Lists No.485, Greenock 1805.
42. O.S.A., Fearn, p.294, Tarbat, p.422, Kilmuir Easter, p.188, Logie Easter, p.474. Pennant

divined the change by 1769: 'in many parts of the Highlands their character begins to be more faintly marked; they mix more with the world, and become daily less attached to their chiefs: the clans begin to disperse themselves through different parts of the country, finding that their industry and good conduct afford the better protection (since the due execution of the laws) than their chieftain can afford, and the chieftain tasting the sweets of advanced rents, and the benefits of industry, dismisses from the table the crowds of retainers, the former instruments of his oppression and freakish tyranny.' Pennant, *Tour of Scotland*, op.cit., p.194.

43. O.S.A., Fearn, p.299, Lochbroom, p.466.
44. O.S.A., Kilmuir Easter, p.191. In 1810 the Rev. Thomas Ross said that of 4000 people on Lochbroom 'hardly seven hundred possess even a smattering of book knowledge, and comparatively few speak any English ... In a tract of ten or twelve miles ... there may not be a single individual capable of reading the Scriptures in English or Gaelic, and these, perhaps fourteen or twenty miles from the Parish Church!' Alexander Macrae, *The Fire of God Among the Heather* (Inverness, 1930), p.25.
45. O.S.A., Kincardine, p.515.

Chapter 11 pp. 129 to 142

1. I. Mowat, Easter Ross 1750-1850 (Edinburgh, 1981), pp.30, 35.
2. See Eric Richards, *A History of the Highland Clearances*, Vol.1, Chapter 9.
3. C.P. XXVII George Mackenzie to Lady Macleod, 27 March 1789.
4. O.S.A., quoted in Mowat, op.cit., p.136.
5. C.P. XIII, no.22, Notes on the Accounts of the Rents of Strathpeffer, 1787, dated 1790.
6. C.P. XVIII, Memorandum of Edward Hay Mackenzie (No. 117).
7. C.P. XIV, no.203.
8. C.P. XVI, no.331 and 332.
9. C.P. Tack of James Mitchell, 1796.
10. C.P. Tack of Margaret Macaulay, 1790.
11. See for instance C.P. Tack of Robert Meikle, 1791. See also that in 1795 Coigach was described as 'a highland District and more suited to grass than to corn' and there was a great deal of activity about the conversion of victual rents to cash at this time. See C.P. XVIII, no. 117, Memorandum for Edward Hay Mackenzie Esq., for Cromartie.
12. See C. Fraser-Mackintosh, *Letters of Two Centuries* (Inverness, 1890), pp.326-7.
13. Kent Archives, Petley Papers, V116 E4, memorials etc. of Kenneth Mackenzie Esq. of Cromartie.
14. C.P. XIII, no. 94, memorial for Captain Kenneth Mackenzie.
15. This was the Royston inheritance, some £4800, being the proceeds of the sale of Royston House. The matter was the subject of recurring legal dispute involving also Sir John Stewart of Grandtully and the Duke of Argyll. C.P. XIV, nos. 156, 157; XXIII, nos. 101, 102.
16. C.P. XIII, no.101.
17. C.P. XXVIII, letter of James Baird, 10 Feb. 1797.
18. Rev. John Kennedy, *The Days of the Fathers in Ross-shire* (1897 ed., Inverness), p.17.
19. See Eric Richards, 'Patterns of Highland Discontent 1790-1850', in R. Quinault and T. Stevenson, *Popular Protest and Public Order* (1973).
20. C.P. Bundle XXVIII, John Kemp to S.S.P.C.K., 31/1/1793, Petition, 21/1/1793.

21. See Eric Richards, 'Varieties of Scottish Emigration in the Nineteenth Century', *Historical Studies*, vol.21, no.85, October 1985, pp.473-94.
22. C.P. XIII, no. 23, Notes on the Accounts between Lady Elibank and Mrs Mackenzie, 1797.
23. C.P. XIV, no. 161.
24. C.P. XXVIII, letter dated 3/7/1801.
25. C.P. Lady Elibank to Mrs Hay, 9/?/1799.
26. R.J. Adam, *Sutherland Estate Papers*, I, p.xxix.
27. S.R.O. GD 128/36/8, Petition of Donald Macleod of Geannies and other, 1798.
28. C.P. XVIII, no. 122.
29. C.P. XIV, no. 118, Answer to Mr Duncan's notes, 1800.
30. C.P. Bundle XXVIII, Chisholm to Lady Elibank, 17 September 1799.
31. C.P. XIV, no. 117. There were lots in each of the Baronies.
32. C.P. Bundle XXVIII, H. Mackenzie to Lady Elibank, 19 November 1801.
33. See esp. T.H. Hollingsworth, *The Demography of the British Peerage* (1964).

Chapter 12 pp. 143 to 164

1. C.P. Bundle XXVIII, Walker to Edward Hay-Mackenzie, 21 February 1802.
2. C.P. Bundle XXVIII, Duncan to Edward Hay-Mackenzie, 1 May 1803.
3. C.P. Vol. XIII No. 109, Memorial for the Right Hon. James Chanacher, Lord Forbes, 25 November 1805.
4. C.P. Bundle XXIX, Duncan to Hon. Mrs Hay-Mackenzie, 11 March 1808.
5. C.P. Bundle XXIX, Duncan MacDonald to Mrs Hay-Mackenzie, 6 October 1807.
6. N.L.S. MS 9646 p.43.
7. C.P. Bundle XXIX, Macrae to Edward Hay-Mackenzie, 18 April 1807.
8. C.P. 1810 Tack of William Henderson.
9. *Inverness Journal*, 8 July 1808.
10. *Inverness Journal*, 3 March 1809.
11. *Inverness Journal*, 3 March 1808.
12. *Inverness Journal*, 8 July 1808.
13. *Inverness Journal*, 21 April 1808.
14. Sir George Mackenzie, *A General View of the Agriculture of the Counties of Ross and Cromarty* (1813), p.256.
15. C.P. Bundle XXIX, James Laing to Edward Hay-Mackenzie, 25 April 1814.
16. C.P. Bundle XXIX, James Laing to Edward Hay-Mackenzie, 7 May 1814.
17. C.P. Laing to Hay-Mackenzie, 26 September 1814.
18. N.L.S. Dep 313 Sutherland Papers II, Household and Personal Box 25, Lady Sutherland to Lord Stafford, 17 July 1814.
19. C.P. Laing to Edward Hay-Mackenzie, 16 November 1814.
20. N.S.A. Lochbroom, p.85.
21. P.P. Hansard 3rd series, Vol.56, 15 February 1841, pp.514-5.
22. See J. Barron, *The Northern Highlands in the Nineteenth Century* (3 vols, Inverness, 1907-13), vol.1, p.66. The marriage was celebrated with bonfires on the Cromartie Estate.
23. Adam, Sutherland Estate Papers, op.cit., Vol.II, p.85.
24. Joseph Mitchell, *Reminiscences of my Life in the Highlands*, 2 vols. (1883, ed. 1971), I, p.256.
25. *Inverness Journal*, 28 October 1808. The Newhall Estate yielded an income to the Hay-

Mackenzies but they consistently outspent the net revenue. Its management created problems because it was too small to warrant a full time factor. C.P. Bundle XXX, Walker to Mrs Hay-Mackenzie n.d. (1819).

26. C.P. Vol.XIII no.113. *Inverness Journal*, 1 January 1813, 29 January 1813. The advertisement was explicit: '... in dividing the Barony of Coigach, with a view to the accommodation of sheepfarmers, particular care was taken to assign each lot its due proportion of arable and pasture lands. The above farms are therefore complete, and their marches distinct.' The estate sought farmers 'of capital and skill'.
27. C.P. Bundle XXIX, James Laing to Edward Hay-Mackenzie, 25 April 1814, 7 May 1814, 26 September 1814.
28. Ibid., Bundle XXIX, Laing to Edward Hay-Mackenzie, 16 November 1814, Laing to Hon. Mrs Hay-Mackenzie, 18 November 1814.
29. I.e., money rents calculated on an index of current grain prices.
30. C.P. Bundle XXX, Walker to Hon. Mrs Hay-Mackenzie n.d. (1819), Sir David Blair to Walker, 6 April 1816.
31. Barron, op.cit., Vol.I, p.107. This work was also reported in Mackenzie, *General View*, pp.119-21, which suggests the labour-intensive nature of these arable improvements which, in the short run, may have absorbed greater amounts of labour than before. But the common people became crofters or day-labourers.
32. R. Southey, *Journal of a Tour of Scotland in 1819* (ed. 1929), p.145.
33. Kelp was produced in Coigach and the collapse of Liverpool prices created alarm among the estate factors. The estate was less dependent on kelp than other West Highland properties but Walker was knowledgeable in the trade and advised Lord Reay on the exploitation of his kelp shores—he suggested the employment of an Orkney man and the division of the shores into small lots to accommodate the dense population required as a labour force. C.P. Bundle XXXIX, Walker, n.d. The Coigach kelp shores were advertised in the *Inverness Journal*, 26 November 1819.
34. C.P. Bundle XXX, Walker to Mrs Hay-Mackenzie, 28 August 1818.
35. C.P. Bundle XXX, Blair to Mrs Hay-Mackenzie, 8 December 1818.
36. I. Mowat, *Easter Ross 1750-1850* (Edinburgh, 1981), p.140.
37. C.P. Bundle XXXII, Donald Mackenzie to Mrs Hay-Mackenzie, 11 February 1824.
38. I.e. Col. George Mackenzie, who had raised a regiment in c.1778, the 2nd Battalion, 78th Regiment.
39. C.P. Bundle XXXII, John Macleod to Mrs Hay-Mackenzie, 22 March 1824. Bundle XXXIII, Widow Mary Forbes to Mrs Hay-Mackenzie, 12 July 1825.
40. C.P. Bundle XXX, Murray to Mrs Hay-Mackenzie, 5 September 1819, 25 September 1819. Walker to Mrs Hay-Mackenzie, 26 October 1819.
41. C.P. Bundle XXX, Murray to Mrs Hay-Mackenzie, 22 November 1819.
42. C.P. Bundle XXXI, Patrick Murray to Mrs Hay-Mackenzie, 25 November 1820.
43. Alexander Mackenzie, *History of the Mackenzies*, op.cit., p.377; Fortescue Fox, *Strathpeffer Spa* (1889), quoting Donald Munro, 'Castle Leod Water', *Philosophical Transactions*, Vol.lvii, p.15. For general origins of spas see James Walvin, *Beside the Seaside* (1978), Chapter I.
44. Letter and memorials 29 December 1777; minutes of the Board of the Annexed Estates, 26 January 1778, 22 February 1778.
45. *Letters of George Dempster to Sir Adam Fergusson 1756-1813* (1934), edited by James Fergusson, p.257.
46. G.S. Mackenzie, *General View*, op.cit., p.49.
47. Southey's *Journal of a Tour of Scotland*, op.cit., 8 September 1819.

48. Bayne, *Life of Hugh Miller*, Vol.I, p.77.
49. Barron, op.cit., I, p.123.
50. Ibid., I, p.165. Fox says the Pump Room was erected by Dr Morrison of Aberdeenshire.
51. C.P. Bundle XXX, Laing to Mrs Hay-Mackenzie, 25 September 1819. Elisabeth Isabella Spence gave a useful description of Strathpeffer and its attractions to a tourist in 1866—'A sulphureous spring, in Strath Peffer ... considered very efficacious in rheumatic and scorbutic disorders, is much resorted to in summer. The situation of this spring is in the bosom of the mountains, rude and gigantic, heaped as it were one above another, in the most unequal forms, possessing an air of remote solitude and wildness, that is almost frightful when, seen one hour, blackened by dark clouds, floating over their tops, but perhaps the next illuminated by a bright sea, they were magnificent beyond description.' *Letters from the North Highlands during the Summer 1816* (1817), p.149.
52. C.P. Bundle XXX, Murray to Mrs Hay-Mackenzie, 27 June 1819. Note that the history of British holidaying is now being written as 'the progression from the preserve of the rich to becoming the annual treat of the urban working class'. Walvin, op.cit., p.11.
53. Barron, op.cit., Vol.I, pp.166-7.
54. C.P. Bundle XXX, Murray to Mrs Hay-Mackenzie, 23 December 1819; Richards, Clearances, II, Chapter 12.
55. C.P. Bundle XXXIV, Lady Glasgow to Mrs Hay-Mackenzie, 8 April 1826.
56. See Alexander MacRae, *Revivals in the Highlands and Islands in the Nineteenth Century* (Stirling, n.d.); McGillivray, *Sketches of Revivals of Religion in the North Highlands*
57. See Eric Richards, 'Patterns of Highland Discontent 1790-1850', in R. Quinnault and J. Stevenson, *Popular Protest and Public Policy* (1973).
58. See Meldrum, op.cit., p.34.
59. NSA, Vol.14, Kiltearn, p.71.
60. C.P. Bundle XXX, Thomas Ross to Jones, 26 April 1816, Walker to Blair, 23 June 1816, Ross to Hay-Mackenzie, 27 June 1816; Hew Scott, *Fasti Ecclesiae Scoticanae* (Edinburgh, 3 vols, 1915-28), VII, p.159.
61. C.P. Box XXXXI, Munro to Mrs Hay-Mackenzie, 12 April 1820.
62. Ibid., Hector Allan to Mrs Hay-Mackenzie, 13 April 1820.
63. Ibid., John Macdonald to Mrs Hay-Mackenzie, 21 April 1820.
64. Ibid., John Fraser to Mrs Hay-Mackenzie, 22 April 1820.
65. Ibid., Dr Jones to Mrs Hay-Mackenzie, 10 April 1820.
66. Ibid., Munro to Mrs Hay-Mackenzie, 10 May 1820.
67. Ibid., Munro to Mrs Hay-Mackenzie, 4 September 1820; John Fraser to Mrs Hay-Mackenzie, 13 October 1820.
68. Op.cit., Angus MacIntosh to Mrs Hay-Mackenzie, 16 November 1820. See also [Alexander Sutherland], *A Summer Ramble in the North Highlands* (1825), p.171.
69. C.P. Scott to Lady Stafford, 17 January 1860, Scott to Rev. W. Sutherland, 16 July 1858; Scott, *Fasti*, VII; See also I.R.M. Mowat, 'A Society in Transition. Easter Ross 1750-1850', B.Phil.thesis, St Andrews, 1971, pp.103.6.
70. See below, Chapter Thirteen.
71. Barron, op.cit., I, p.93. British Library, Mackenzie Papers, 39193 f27, Hay-Mackenzie to Sir James Mackenzie, 19 November 1827.
72. C.P. Bundle XXX, James Laing to Mrs Hay-Mackenzie, 25 September 1819, Murray to Mrs Hay-Mackenzie, 24 September 1819, 11 August 1815.
73. C.P. Bundle XXX, Murray to Mrs Hay-Mackenzie, 2 October 1819.
74. C.P. Bundle XXX, Walker to Mrs Hay-Mackenzie, 20 October 1819.
75. Ibid., Laing to Mrs Hay-Mackenzie, 11 December 1819.

76. See Richards in Quinault, op.cit.
77. C.P. Bundle XXX, Minister, Bonar Bridge, to Mrs Hay-Mackenzie, 21 April 1820. See Richards, *Clearances*, op.cit., Vol.I, pp.220, 255, 339, 442.

Chapter 13 pp. 165 to 181

1. See Eric Richards, *A History of the Highland Clearances*, Vol.2, chap.18. The impact of the post war depression across the Easter Ross agricultural community is documented by Donald Macleod in *Board of Agriculture, The Agricultural State of the Kingdom, 1816* (ed. 1970), pp.420-3. He drew special attention to the loss of employment for women and children in the district, and also to the invasion of southern farmers seeking the advantage of relatively low rents in the north of Scotland.
2. C.P. Bundle XXXI, Selkrig to Walker, 8 January, 1820. C.P. Vol.XIII, No.113, Memorial of the Hon. Mrs Hay-Mackenzie relative to the propriety of executing a new Trust Deed, 1818.
3. C.P. Duncan to Mrs Hay-Mackenzie, 5 April, 1820.
4. C.P. Walker to Mrs Hay-Mackenzie, 27 July, 1821, 27 September, 1821, 9 October, 1821, 2 November, 1821.
5. C.P. Douglas to Mrs Hay-Mackenzie, 9 November, 1821.
6. C.P. Bundle XXXII, Walker to Mrs Hay-Mackenzie, 5 August, 1823.
7. C.P. Bundle XXXII, Walker to John Hay-Mackenzie, 7 August, 1823.
8. C.P. Walker to Mrs Hay-Mackenzie, 22 August, 1823. Mrs Hay-Mackenzie to Sir James Mackenzie, 19 November, 1827. B.L. Manuscripts, Mackenzie Papers 39193 Add.f27.
9. C.P. Walker to Mrs Hay-Mackenzie, 22 August, 1823, 8 October, 1823.
10. C.P. Bundle XXXII Duncan to John Hay-Mackenzie, 17 May, 1824, Renton to John Hay-Mackenzie, 30 June, 1824.
11. C.P. Bundle XXXII, Walker to Lord Tweeddale, 29 July, 1824; Melville to Mrs Hay-Mackenzie, 15 November, 1824; Walker to Mrs Hay-Mackenzie, 29 December, 1824, 27 July, 1824.
12. C.P. Bundle XXXII, Walker to Mrs Hay-Mackenzie, 7 February, 1825.
13. In 1841 Hay-Mackenzie sold the small estate of Miekle Gruinard with salmon fishing rights to Murdo Mackenzie (which became a subject of dispute with Davidson), Evander MacIver, *Memoirs of a Highland Gentleman* (1905), p.46. In 1835 there were Cromartie land sales—in Barron, op.cit., III, p.175 (28 October, 1835). It may be significant that in 1817 James Balfour (a Fife landowner who had made a fortune in India) bought the 10,000 acre Whittinghame estate in East Lothian from the Hay family, kinsmen of the Earls of Tweeddale. It was near Haddington, 20 miles east of Edinburgh, and provided a net rental income of more than £11,000 yearly. In 1839 he also bought Strathconan—and cleared it substantially of its people, many of whom found refuge in Strathpeffer. S.H. Zebel, *Balfour, a political biography* (1973), p.1. Kenneth Young, *Arthur James Balfour* (1963), p.2.
14. The Cromartie estate incurred great legal costs in the fishing dispute which it finally lost, in 1825. Its opponent in the case, the Burgh of Dingwall, also ran up great debts in the process. See N.S.A. Dingwall, p.229; Mowat, thesis, op.cit., p.85.
15. C.P. Bundle XXXIII Melville to John Hay-Mackenzie, 29 January, 1825. On local political influence see E. Porritt, *The Unreformed House of Commons* (1903), vol.II, pp.4, 170.
16. C.P. Bundle XXXIII James Mackenzie to Mrs Hay-Mackenzie, 7 February, 1825.
17. C.P. Bundle XXXII Joseph Gordon to Melville; 26 February, 1825, Melville to Mrs Hay-Mackenzie, 26 February, 1825.

18. Sutherland Papers D593/K/1/3/30 Mackenzie to Loch, 9 June 1842.
19. C.P. Walker, Richardson and Melville to Mrs Hay-Mackenzie, 14 March, 1825, 21 April, 1825.
20. Ibid., Ross to Mrs Hay-Mackenzie, 2 December, 1829; Melville to Mrs Hay-Mackenzie, 30 April, 1825.
21. C.P. Bundle XXXII, Robert Mackenzie to Laing, 11 May, 1824.
22. C.P. Bundle XXXII, Murdo Mackenzie to Mrs Hay-Mackenzie, 24 August, 1824.
23. C.P. Bundle XXXIII, Forbes to Mrs Hay-Mackenzie, 27 September, 1825.
24. C.P. Crofter Statistics, November 1886.
25. C.P. Gunn to Black, 24 September, 1884.
26. N.S.A. Vol.14, Tain, p.292; C.P. G. Mackenzie to Scott, 4 August, 1832.
27. C.P. George S. Taylor to Loch, 15 April, 1833.
28. C.P. Smith to William Young, 15 May, 1833.
29. C.P. Smith to William Young, 16 May, 1833.
30. C.P. Young to Loch, 17 May, 1833.
31. There was a general tendency in the Highlands towards concentrated land ownership. As Sir Kenneth S. Mackenzie wrote in 1886, 'families who were great landowners little more than a century ago have disappeared, and others have risen in their place ... the great estates of today are made up of many small estates or parts of estates.' In the 1830s the Cromartie estate gave every appearance of being in the trend towards disintegration; it was lucky to survive. 'Changes in the Ownership of Land in Ross-shire', T.G.S.I. (1897), p.305.
32. In Rosskeen rents rose from £2000 in the 1790s to £6000 by 1838, but capital expenditure had been massive in the intervening years. On the Ardross farm alone £12,000 had been spent on liming, draining, etc. The lands were so much better that no further improvement seemed conceivable. (N.S.A. 274).
33. Barron, op.cit., vol.II, p.175, quoting *Inverness Courier*, 28 October, 1835.
34. N.S.A., Contin, p.244.
35. N.S.A. Kilmuir Easter, p.306.
36. B.L. Mackenzie Papers. Add. 39193 f 253.
37. Dod's Electoral Facts.
38. C.P. George Mackenzie to Scott, 20 July, 1832.
39. C.P. Munro to Mackenzie, 19 July, 1832.
40. C.P. George Mackenzie to Scott, 24 July, 1832, circular to K. Mackenzie, Corry, 23 July, 1832.
41. C.P. George Mackenzie to Scott, 12 February, 1833.
42. C.P. George Mackenzie to Scott, 1 February, 1833.
43. C.P. George Mackenzie to Scott, 25 March, 1833.
44. C.P. George Mackenzie to Scott, 29 May, 1833.
45. C.P. George Mackenzie to Scott, 3 June, 1833, 11 July, 1833.
46. C.P. J. Macleod to James Laing, 30 April, 1831, 17 April, 1831, 13 June, 1831, 27 June, 1831, 6 June, 1831.
47. C.P. Tack of Duncan Mackenzie, 1830.
48. C.P. Application of Rieff tenants, June 1890.
49. C.P. George Mackenzie to Scott, 14 August, 1833.
50. C.P. John Nicolson to Mackenzie, 16 February, 1832.
51. The mobility of farmers was a development of the nineteenth century and by the 1830s the movement was two-way—lowland farmers migrated north to the Highlands; some Scottish farmers moved into England, often in association with Scottish agents. One Ross-shire farmer looked for an opening on the Trentham estate in Staffordshire which belonged

to the Duke of Sutherland. His agent was, however, somewhat dubious: 'is it fair', he asked, 'to burden the country with anyone from that distant district—have they anything like distress where their rents are reasonable—have they any improved system to describe which the Southerners will not be able to detail—it is the heavy soil farmers that they wish to have.' SRO GD46/13/142 James Loch to J.A. Mackenzie 10 April 1836.

52. C.P. Tacks of the 1830s—David Munro, William MacLennan, Donald Cameron, Duncan Mackenzie, Alexander Ross, Mundell and Grieve, Jonas Mitchell, Alexander Robertson, William Mackenzie, Kenneth Mackenzie.
53. C.P. Scott to Gilchrist, 14 March, 1838.
54. Alexander Sutherland, *A Summer Ramble in the North Highlands* (1825), pp.167-8.
55. Fortescue Fox, *Strathpeffer Spa* (1889), pp.10-11. See also 'Prospectus of an Institution for the Benefit of the Diseased and Destitute Poor frequenting the Mineral waters of Strathpeffer 1833', SRO Loch Muniments GD268/363 Lady Stafford to Loch 1833.
56. N.S.A. Vol.14, Fodderty, pp.248-50. In 1839 there were about ten lodging houses in Strathpeffer as well as 'a handsome large Hotel with a fine view down the Strath to Cromarty Bay. In the season provisions and lodgings are very dear, as there are no very considerable shops in the place. There are two wells, one where the gentry go, and the other where common people drink. For scenery it is far more beautiful than Harrogate, but in size it is not nearly so much. Castle Leod, the seat of Hay-Mackenzie, is just at the entrance to the valley and village, and there are very fine moors on the hills around Ben Wyvis.' British Library, Add.MSS. Mackenzie Papers, 39193 f144, letter of 8 October 1839, Lewis Mackenzie to Mrs L. Mackenzie.

Chapter 14 pp. 182 to 199

1. E. Spence, *Letters from the North of Scotland during the Summer 1816* (London 1817), p.149.
2. Ibid., pp.156-7.
3. Ibid., pp.163-5.
4. G.S. Mackenzie, *General View of the Agriculture of the Counties of Ross and Cromarty* (1813), pp.81-2.
5. Ibid., pp.103-5.
6. Ibid., p.124.
7. Ibid., p.125.
8. Ibid., pp.103-5, 137.
9. Ibid., pp.140-1.
10. Ibid., pp.84-5.
11. *Topographical, Statistical and Historical Gazateer of Scotland* (1844); Mowat, thesis, op.cit., p.103.
12. NSA Vol.14, p.28.
13. See Eric Richards, *The Last Scottish Food Riots* (1982).
14. NSA, vol.14, p.279
14a. P.P. Report of the Poor Law Inquiry (Scotland) 1844, p.43.
15. NSA, Vol.14, p.306
16. NSA, Vol.14, p.344
17. NSA, Vol.14, p.272
18. NSA, Vol.14, p.272
19. C.P. Scott to Lord Stafford, 29 March 1850.

20. NSA, Vol.14, p.256. Evidence before the Poor Law Enquiry (Scotland), e.g. pp.21, 32, suggested a mounting interest in learning English at this time.
21. NSA, Vol.14, p.256. P.P. Poor Law Inquiry (Scotland), pp.48, 24.
22. NSA, Vol.14, p.54.
23. NSA, Vol.14, p.35
24. NSA, Vol.14, p.15.
25. NSA, Vol.14, p.17.
26. NSA, Vol.14, p.33
27. NSA, Vol.14, p.35.
28. James Wilson, *A Voyage round the Coasts of Scotland and the Isles* (Edinburgh, 2 vols. 1842), I, p.306.
29. NSA, Vol.14, p.326.
30. C.P. Militia List for the Parish of Lochbroom, 1827.
31. N.S.A. Vol.14, pp.74-85.
32. N.S.A. Vol.14, p.78; Poor Law Enquiry (Scotland), op.cit., pp.423-6.
33. This passage is based on Dunlop, op.cit., pp.144-75. The decline of Ullapool fishing was charted by visitors to the west coast. In 1814 Richard Ayton in *A Voyage Round Great Britain* (London, 8 vols, 1815-20), vol.IV, pp.71-2, noted the continuing but modest level of activity at Tanera. A decade later John MacCulloch, in *The Highlands and Western Isles of Scotland* (4 vols, 1824), vol.II, p.325, registered the sharp decline of the port consequent upon the desertion of the herring shoals. James Wilson, op.cit., vol.2, p.305, was criticalof the torpor and lack of enterprise in the village.
34. Ibid., p.180.
35. C.P. Scott to Melville, 19 November 1850.
36. C.P. Scott to Mrs Hay-Mackenzie, 5 March 1851.
37. Lord Teignmouth, *Sketches of the Coasts and Islands of Scotland and the Isle of Man* (2 vols, 1836), II, pp.59-60.
38. Allan Fullarton and Charles R. Baird, *Remarks on the Evils at Present Affecting the Highlands and Islands of Scotland* (Glasgow, 1838), p.50. P.P. Report on Emigration 1841, Q.46, 62, 991, 3233-5, Appendix, p.217.
39. *Topographical, Statistical and Historical Gazateer of Scotland* (2 vols., 1844), p.784. See also Wilson, op.cit., I, pp.310-11; S.R.O. Loch Muniments G.D. 268/137, Donald Hoare to James Loch, 15 February 1841.
40. C.P. Andrew Scott to A. Mackenzie of Dundonnell, 6 April 1850.
41. N.S.A. Vol.14. In 1850 Andrew Scott admitted that he had not visited Tanera for at least a dozen years. The facilities there were entirely dilapidated and it would never attract a tenant. 'Nothing has been done at that Station since I came to the Country in 1831, and there is no appearance just now of a revival of the Curing Trade upon that Coast'. C.P. Scott to Mackenzie and Logan, 2 February 1850.
42. N.S.A. Vol.14, pp.293, 300. A great deal more information of diet was provided in the evidence before Poor Law Inquiry (Scotland), op.cit., esp. pp.9, 23-5, 33-4, 35, 39, 46, 49, 423.
43. N.S.A. Vol.14, pp.87, 113, 222-3, 293, 259.
44. Eric Richards, *Last Scottish Food Riots*, passim.

Chapter 15 pp. 200 to 215

1. Allan Fullarton and Charles B. Baird, *Remarks on the Evil at Present Affecting the Highlands and Islands of Scotland* (Glasgow 1838), pp.49-50.

2. P.D. Hansard 3rd Series, 1841, p.17.
3. P.P. Select Committee on Emigration (Scotland), 1841-2 Report Q.1636-1828. There was further testimony from Murdo Mackenzie of Dundonnell in Gairloch which also related indirectly to Coigach. Ibid., Q.3211-3339.
4. Also called townships viz. Achiltybuie: 52 tenants; Keanchrine: 46; Badenscallie: 34; Ardmair: 26; Auchindrean: 25; Reiff: 21; Altandow: 20; Tanera: 7.
5. See Eric Richards, 'Poverty and Survival in Nineteenth Century Coigach', in J. Baldwin (ed.), *Ullapool and Wester Ross* (forthcoming, Edinburgh, 1989).
6. J.H. Dawson, *An Abridged Statistical History of the Scottish Counties* (1862).
7. In 1835 Hay-Mackenzie had imported meal to the value of £212 to a district which yielded only half of its nominal rent of £750 and for which the arrears were practically irrecoverable. Further description of the famine administration is found in Poor Law Inquiry (Scotland), op.cit., pp.424-5.
8. In nearly Gairloch there was evidence of petty violence relating to bark-stripping and sheep theft though the causes were obscure. Mackenzie of Dundonnell noted such outrages as evidence of the weakness of the forces of law on the west coast. Ibid. Q.3331-3334.
9. Ibid., Second Report, p.iii.
10. The fishing station at Ullapool in February 1841 was described as a complete failure, to such a degree that 'nothing can be made of it'. SRO Loch Muniments GD268/137 Donald Horne to James Loch, 15 February 1841. Three years earlier it had been reported that 'the bulk of the people are idle, and in very great misery. They are, at least many of them are, quite prepared to emigrate; but alas! they have not the means; and the chance is, unless they receive assistance, that, after pining a few years in their present state of wretchedness, their numbers may be trimmed by finance or disease'. A. Fullarton and C.R. Baird, op.cit., p.50.
11. C.P. Letter Book 1841-1848, Scott to Mrs A. Mackenzie, 20 February 1841.
12. C.P. Scott to K. Mackenzie, 7 May 1841.
13. C.P. Scott to Hay-Mackenzie, 22 August 1841.
14. C.P. Scott to John Hay-Mackenzie, 4 March 1842.
15. C.P. Scott to Alex Ross, n.d., Scott to James Mitchell, 3 December 1842.
16. C.P. Scott to Ken Mackenzie, 3 March 1843.
17. C.P. Scott to Capt. Macleod, 15 March 1843.
18. *John O'Groat Journal*, 5 March 1847.
19. Extract from *Letters to the Rev. Dr McLeod regarding the famine and destitution in the Highlands and Islands of Scotland* (Glasgow, 1847), p.53.
20. Ibid, p.54.
21. See Eric Richards, *The Last Scottish Food Riots* (1982).
22. *Caithness Chronicle*, May 1847.
23. Highland Destitution Papers, SRO Vol.1310/1311 Reports from Lochbroom.
24. Cromartie Papers, John Murray to Cromartie, 4 April 1847.
25. Ibid., Scott to Skene, 15 July 1847.
26. See the Reports of the Central Board of Management of the Fund raised for the Relief of the Destitute Inhabitants of the Highlands and Islands of Scotland (Glasgow, 1847-).
27. Ross and Cromarty County Council Papers in Castle Leod relating to Road Construction. C.P. Scott to Cromartie, 3 May 1848, Scott to Ross, 3 May 1848, Scott to Messrs Williamson and Ross, 15 May 1848, (Copy of Account of Money laid out by John Hay Mackenzie Esq ... in Improvements ... from March ... 1845 to March 1846).
28. Regulations specifically excluded all but the really destitute, especially 'those possessed of marketable property, or who could earn a subsistence by fishing or labour'. In August

1847 there were 1671 people on the Roll from Hay-Mackenzie's property alone. Central Board Reports, Ullapool, 5 August 1847.
29. C.P. Scott to Mackenzie, 2 July 1848, 20 June 1848.
30. C.P. Scott to Hogarth, 11 November 1848.
31. Sixth Report by the Edinburgh Section of the Central Board (1847), pp.20-1.
32. C.P. Scott to Cromartie, 16 May 1848; Scott to John Hay Mackenzie, 2 June 1848; Letterbook 1850-1, Andrew Scott to Kenneth Mackenzie, 2 February 1850; Scott to Melville, 4 March 1850. The district was visited by G. Poulett Scrope at this time, and he spoke well of relief efforts in Lochbroom—*Some Notes of a Tour in England, Scotland and Ireland* (1849), p.10.
33. C.P. Scott to Lady Stafford, 7 February 1852.
34. C.P. Melville to Loch, 24 August 1851.
35. C.P. Scott to Melville, 17 April 1851.
36. C.P. Scott to James Blake, 5 November 1851.
37. C.P. Scott to Smythe, Secretary of the Board of Supervision, Edinburgh, 22 June 1848.
38. C.P. Scott to J. Hay-Mackenzie, 2 June 1848.
39. C.P. Scott to George Mackenzie, 1 August 1848.
40. C.P. Scott to George Mackenzie, 22 August 1848.
41. C.P. Scott to John Campbell, 21 December 1848.
42. C.P. Scott to K. Mackenzie, 3 March 1849.

Chapter 16 pp. 219 to 235

1. Such, of course, had been the fate of many Highland landowners. The mobility of ownership is well charted in G.S. Mackenzie, 'Changes in the Ownership of Land in Ross-shire, 1756-1853', T.G.S.I. (1897), pp.293-324.
2. See Eric Richards, *Leviathan of Wealth* (1973).
3. John Hay-Mackenzie died 9 July 1849; his wife Anne (third daughter of Sir James Gibson-Craig of Riccarton) whom he married in 1828, lived on until 1869.
4. C.P. Scott to Gunn, 4 April 1850.
5. C.P. Scott to K. Mackenzie, 6 April 1850, 16 April 1850.
6. C.P. Scott to K. Mackenzie, 18 April 1850.
7. C.P. Scott to Laidlaw, 1 April 1850.
8. C.P. Scott to Melville, 6 May 1850.
9. C.P. A. Mackenzie to Scott, 29 January 1850.
10. Alexander Mackenzie, *The History of the Highland Clearances* (Inverness, 1883), pp.308-10. On the Strathconan evictions see *Inverness Courier*, 15 August 1850, *Northern Ensign*, 1 August 1850, *Scottish Highlander*, 24 September 1891, and Eric Richards, *History of the Highland Clearances I*, pp.393-402.
11. S.C. D593/K, MacDonald to Duke of Sutherland, 14 October 1871, and D.G.F. MacDonald, *Cattle, Sheep and Deer* (1872), pp.525-6.
12. C.P. Scott to Hay-Mackenzie, 28 May 1849.
13. C.P. Scott to Walker and Melville, 2 August 1851.
14. C.P. Scott to MacIver, 12 September 1850.
15. C.P. Contract for drainage work dated June 1848; Melville to Scott, 10 September 1849, 5 August 1851; Scott to Chalmers, 26 November 1849.
16. C.P. Scott to Hay-Mackenzie, 16 May 1849.
17. At this time Melville was anxious for the future of the small tenants—'The present is very

bad times for all connected with Land; and I fear the great expectations are now made of foreign cattle and sheep, and of foreign cured meat, will depress the value of pasture lands'. C.P. Melville to Scott, 2 July 1850.
18. C.P. Scott to Melville, 5 January 1850, 3 January 1850; Melville to Scott, 8 January 1850; A. Mackenzie to Scott, 29 January 1850.
19. C.P. Scott to Melville, 25 March 1850, Scott to Lady Stafford, 1 March 1850.
20. C.P. Melville to Scott, 27 March 1850. After the leasing of Knockfarrel the Cromartie estate made it clear that there were no further openings on the property for small tenants. Scott to Laidlaw, 1 April 1850.
21. C.P. Scott to Seaforth, 31 January 1851.
22. C.P. Loch to Scott, 9 October 1858.
23. C.P. Mackenzie to Duke of Sutherland, 14 October 1871, Loch to Scott, 19 October 1871.
24. P.P. Napier Commission 1884, p.2643. Some of the tenants testified, ibid., pp.2668 ff.
25. Colin Macdonald, *A Highland Journey* (1943), p.19.
26. C.P. Scott to William Mackenzie and Alexander Mackenzie, 14 February 1850.
27. C.P. Scott to Marquis of Stafford (n.d., c.July 1850).
28. C.P. Scott to Hay-Mackenzie, 1847, (n.d.).
29. C.P. Scott to Melville, 19 November 1850.
30. C.P. Scott to James Loch, 17 June 1850.
31. C.P. Scott to Mackenzie, 1 October 1850.
32. C.P. Scott to Melville, 19 November 1850.
33. C.P. Scott to Melville, 16 November 1850.
34. See David MacMillan, 'Sir Charles Trevelyan and the Highland and Island Emigration Society, 1849-1859', *Journal of the Royal Australian Historical Society*, vol.49, 1963.
35. C.P. Andrew Scott to Lord Stafford, 13 February 1851.
36. C.P. Scott to Mrs Hay-Mackenzie, 5 March 1851.
37. C.P. Scott to Hay-Mackenzie, 26 March 1842.
38. C.P. Scott to Hay-Mackenzie, 16 May 1848.
39. C.P. McNeill to Scott, 9 July 1852; Scott to McNeill, 12 July 1852.
40. C.P. McNeill to Chant, 3 June 1853.
41. C.P. Mackenzie to Scott, 11 October 1853.
42. These three paragraphs are based on Hugh Campbell, 'There is corn in Egypt. Get you down thither ... The Highlands and Islands Emigration Society and Van Diemen's Land, 1853-1854', *Tasmanian Historical Research Association, Papers and Proceedings*, vol.34 (1987), pp.37-50, and on personal correspondence with Mr Campbell.
43. E.g. C.P. MacIver to Gunn, 17 December 1884.

Chapter 17 pp. 236 to 245

1. *Northern Ensign*, 11 August 1850.
2. *Northern Ensign*, 24 March 1853.
3. C.P. Scott to George Mackenzie, 1 August 1848, 22 August 1848.
4. C.P. Scott to Melville, 20 May 1851; Scott to Lady Stafford, 20 May 1851.
5. C.P. Scott to Blake, 5 November 1851.
6. C.P. Scott to Purves, 4 March 1851.
7. C.P. Scott to Mackenzie, 12 April 1851.
8. C.P. Scott to MacLeod, 21 January 1852.
9. C.P. Scott to Elizabeth McLeod, 7 April 1851. There was another comparable case in

Notes to pp. 238 to 243

November 1854 when widow McLennan of Achnahaird complained to Lady Stafford that, on the death of her husband and after 49 years as subtenant the property passed to her daughter and her husband 'upon the grounds that they would support me instead of giving me the least comfort they did deprive me of everything in this world and left me quite destitute and whenever they got hold of the same left for Australia. Having paid the last rent for the Croft with my only Cow and Melioration.' She was given a gratuity by the estate. Widow McLennan to Lady Stafford, 20 November 1854. An example of a crofter requesting the eviction of a fellow crofter is recorded in C.P. Thomas McKenzie to Scott, 17 November 1853.

10. C.P. William and Alexander Mackenzie to Scott, 9 February 1850.
11. C.P. Scott to subtenants of Mr Geo. McLeod, Tacksman of Achnahaird, (n.d.).
12. C.P. Scott to Blake, 5 November 1851
13. C.P. Scott to Lady Stafford, 16 January 1852.
14. C.P. Scott to Mackenzie, 19 February 1852.
15. C.P. Scott to Melville, 30 January 1852.
16. C.P. Scott to G. Mackenzie, 7 February 1852.
17. C.P. Scott to Lady Stafford, 18 February 1852.
18. C.P. Scott to K. Mackenzie, 19 February 1852.
19. C.P. Scott to Melville, 21 February 1852.
20. C.P. Scott to Melville, 21 February 1852.
21. C.P. Scott to George Mackenzie, 28 February 1852.
22. C.P. Scott to Lady Stafford, 1 March 1852.
23. C.P. Scott to Melville, 1 March 1852.
24. C.P. Scott to K. Mackenzie, 13 March 1852.
25. C.P. Scott to James Loch, 26 February 1853.
26. C.P. Scott to Lady Stafford, 30 March 1852.
27. C.P. Scott to John Hunter, 5 May 1852. Some solace was offered by the *Ross-shire Observer*, 27 March 1852. 'This lawless proceeding places in a strong light the practical obscurity of the present law as a landlord and tenant as to removings. Why should a tenant require a warning to remove from a holding which he has not taken on lease from the landlord for the following year? It ought to be sufficient that he has not taken it, and if he should be removed contrary to his bargain, it should be on him to show that he has.'
28. C.P. Scott to Melville, 10 June 1852.
29. C.P. Scott to Coadie, 5 November 1852.
30. C.P. Coadie to Scott, November 1852.
31. C.P. Scott to Lord Stafford, 19 January 1853.
32. C.P. Scott to Lady Stafford, 4 December 1852.
33. C.P. Scott to Johnston, 24 February 1853; Lady Stafford to Petitioners of Achnahaird, 30 June 1852.
34. C.P. Scott to G. Mackenzie, 10 February 1853.
35. C.P. Scott to Melville, 11 February 1853.
36. C.P. Scott to Loch, 18 February 1853. Scott received advice from Edinburgh that the 'civil force at the command of the authorities in Ross-shire will be insufficient to enable the officers to serve the Summonses, and certainly totally insufficient to enforce removings were decrees obtained.' The only alternative was a police force from Glasgow or a military party from Fort George, the cost of which would fall on the County. More specifically Lord Stafford would need to 'stand the brunt of attacks to which he will be subjected both by the public press and in the House of Commons'. C.P. Johnston to Scott, 21 February 1853.

37. C.P. Scott to Loch, 26 February 1853.
38. C.P. Melville to Scott, 24 March 1853.
39. C.P. Melville to Scott, 24 March 1853, 17 December 1853.
40. C.P. Loch to Stafford, 31 March 1853.
41. C.P. Mackenzie to Melville, 26 March 1853.
42. C.P. Melville to Loch, 28 March 1853.
43. See Eric Richards, *History of the Highland Clearances*, Vol. I, Chapter 14.
44. C.P. Scott to J. Scott at Hawick, 18 February 1857.
45. C.P. Scott to Mackenzie, 13 April 1858.

Chapter 18 pp. 246 to 251

1. James Loch had identified many of the difficulties as early as September 1849. He predicted that Stafford, when he eventually succeeded his father, would possess a gross annual income of about £82,000, that is £10,000 less than his father. He noted 'The Cromartie estate is hardly to set itself right to any extent'. He also began to sense the state of the late Hay-Mackenzie's debts. S.C. D593/K/1/3/37 Loch to Duchess of Sutherland, September 1849.
2. C.P. Melville to Scott, 17 November 1850, 13 July 1853, 9 and 31 October 1851; Loch to Drummonds, 4 November 1853; Loch to Lord and Lady Stafford, 30 April 1853.
3. C.P. Scott to Lord Stafford, 2 June 1853.
4. C.P. Loch to Lord Stafford, 9 July 1853.
5. C.P. James Loch to Stafford, 3 June 1853.
6. C.P. Loch to Stafford, 9 May 1854.
7. C.P. Loch to Lord Stafford, 9 July 1853.
8. C.P. MacIver to Scott, 8 November 1854. There were problems also in the west coast salmon fishing in which Hogarth and Co. of Aberdeen held leases and half a dozen bothies along the shores. In 1850 they asked to be relieved of that tenancy in response to which Scott contemplated the idea of the estate operating the enterprise. This would mean taking over stock and organizing the sale of the highly perishable product. Eventually Scott threw over the notion and the lease was re-negotiated with Hogarth in 1851, and the rent was reduced from £250 to £175 p.a. Scott to Lord Stafford, 20 December 1851.
9. Quoted in Robert Blake, *The Conservative Party from Peel to Churchill* (1972 edn.), p.61.
10. C.P. Loch to Melville, 15 January 1854; Melville to Loch, 12 January 1854; Melville to Scott, 2 July 1850, 4 June 1853; George Loch to Scott, 29 September 1854; Loch to Lord Stafford, 14 September 1854, 6 November 1853.
11. C.P. Loch to Scott, 17 February 1856.
12. C.P. Scott to Lord Stafford, 5 December 1857.
13. C.P. Loch to Stafford, 21 February 1853.
14. In 1859 it was calculated that the debts on the Cromartie estate as inherited from John Hay-Mackenzie had reached the figure of £64,819. S.C. D593/P/22/1/26.
15. C.P. Melville to Loch, 31 May 1853.
16. C.P. Loch to Stafford, 24 May 1853.
17. C.P. George Loch to Stafford, 15 January 1854.

Chapter 19 pp. 252 to 268

1. S.C. D593/K/1/5/63 James Loch to Duke of Sutherland, 26 August 1850.
2. See Eric Richards, *Leviathan of Wealth* (1973), chapter 1. On the relation between the

Duchesses and Queen Victoria, see Stanley Weintraub, Queen Victoria (N.Y., 1987). See also S.C. D593/P/24/7/13.
3. Denis Stuart, Dear Duchess (1982), p.43.
4. S.C. D593/P/28/8/17 Lord Palmerston to the Duchess of Sutherland, 15 August 1861.
5. S.C. D593/P/28/8/17 Palmerston to Duchess of Sutherland, 15 October 1861. Lord Stafford agreed to the arrangement which, however, required that estates of equal value, namely the Reay estate, be settled on his eldest son by entail, namely Francis Sutherland-Leveson-Gower. D593/P/24/1/2 Loch to Stafford, 6 January 1860. *Vanity Fair* commented realistically that the marriage to the Duke of Sutherland had not only redeemed 'the burdened lands of Cromartie' but had obtained from Palmerston 'a new creation of the ancient honours of the earldom', with remainder to their second son. *Notes and Queries*, 12 November 1892. The confusions and anomalies in the succession are dealt with by G.E.C. *Complete Peerage*, op.cit., p.429.
6. There was some degree of reciprocation in 1853 when Queen Victoria appointed Lord Stafford as Lord Lieutenant of Cromarty. S.C. D593/P/22/1/3/8 Lord Aberdeen to Duke of Sutherland, 28 March 1853. In effect the Cromartie title was recreated with a remainder to the second son.
7. Stuart, op.cit., pp.42-4, based on Duke of Sutherland, *Looking Back* (1957), pp.37-8.
8. This required an Act of Parliament and careful drafting. There was good precedent in the Leveson-Gower family—when the fabulously wealthy first Duke died in 1833 his vast assets were divided between his two sons, the second Lord Francis receiving the legendary profits of the Bridgewater Trust. See Richards, *Leviathan*, passim. Note the second Duke's second son was also named Francis.
9. S.C. D493/P/22/1/26 Letters from George Loch to second Duke 1859-60, esp. 16 December 1859, 18 December 1859; Loch to James Hay-Mackenzie, 19 December 1859. D593/P/24/1/2 Loch to Stafford, 28 January 1860, 4 September 1860.
10. C.P. Scott to Andrews, 7 April 1861.
11. The third Duke's net income from his Lilleshall and Trentham estates in England alone, in 1862, was calculated at £52,095 p.a. He also reaped large returns from investments in the Funds. S.C. D593/P/24/2/4 Loch to Duke of Sutherland, 8 June 1862.
12. C.P. Loch to Scott, 30 October 1860.
13. C.P. Scott to William Scott, 23 August 1860.
14. C.P. George Loch to Scott, 8 December 1860.
15. C.P. Scott to Loch, 5 July 1858, 19 October 1858.
16. C.P. A. Scott to W. Scott, 7 January 1860, 16 April 1860.
17. C.P. Mackenzie to Scott, 1 January 1862; Scott to Nixon, 23 February 1861; Scott to Andrews, 7 April 1861.
18. C.P. Mackenzie to Scott, 5 January 1863.
19. C.P. Mackenzie to Scott, 13 March 1863.
20. C.P. G. Loch to Scott, 19 December 1862.
21. C.P. Loch to Scott, 28 December 1862.
22. C.P. Loch to Scott, 27 February 1863.
23. C.P. Loch to Scott, 1 February 1863.
24. C.P. Loch to Scott, 7 December 1862.
25. C.P. D.G. Ross of Dingwall also supplied, specially chartering vessels.
26. C.P. Scott to Loch, 3 March 1863.
27. C.P. Mackenzie to Scott, 12 June 1864, 16 March 1864.
28. C.P. Loch to Scott, 20 January 1862.
29. C.P. Loch to Mortimer, 1 October 1866.

30. Advertisement in *Dundee Advertizer*, 27 November 1866.
31. C.P. Tulloch to Loch, 20 March 1865.
32. S.C. D593/P/24/1/2 Loch to Sutherland, 10 August 1877.
33. C.P. MacIver to Martin, 18 May 1865, 18 April 1864; Mackenzie to Loch, 27 March 1863, 19 April 1863.
34. P.P. *R.C.Employment of Children, Young Persons, and Women in Agriculture* (1867), Evidence, Appendix pp.283-334. Another respondent, Campion, reported of Tanera in Lochbroom that 'Education has invariably the effect of inducing the young men of the country to push their fortunes by going both to other parts of the Kingdom and also to the colonies', ibid., p.330.
35. Meldrum, op.cit., p.70.
36. C.P. Loch to Murray, 28 February 1866.
37. C.P. Loch to Martin, 11 April 1866.
38. C.P. R. Falconer to Scott, 5 January 1864.
39. C.P. George Loch to Scott, 16 September 1868.
40. C.P. Loch to Scott, 8 March 1868. The people in question were actually squatters—which makes the case even more interesting. Scott noticed that they were very poor and a liability for the poor law and would be much better placed as day labourers. Loch believed the trouble was mainly due to Scott's want of 'temper and patience'.
41. C.P. Loch to Scott, 8 March 1868, 25 February 1868.
42. C.P. Loch to Scott, 16 February 1867.
43. C.P. Loch to Gunn, 25 November 1869.

Chapter 20 pp. 269 to 283

1. See Richards, *Leviathan*, op.cit., p.13, and Eric Richards, 'An Anatomy of the Sutherland Fortune: Income, Consumption, Investments and Returns, 1780-1880' *Business History*, vol.21 (1979), and 'The Uses of Aristocracy: The Sutherlands and Staffordshire in the Nineteenth Century', *North Staffordshire Journal of Field Studies*, vol.21 (1981).
2. S.P. Scott to W. Scott, 17 June 1861.
3. *Gazetteer of Scotland* (1844), op.cit., p.726.
4. The holiday resort industry in Britain was on the brink of rapid expansion. See E.W. Gilbert, 'The Growth of Island and Seaside Health Resorts in England', *Scottish Geographical Magazine*, Vol.55 (1939).
5. T.H.S. Escott, *Society in the English Country House* (1907), p.52.
6. According to Clarence Finlayson, *The Strath* (Edinburgh, 1979), p.77.
7. *Ross-shire Observer*, 14 August 1852.
8. C.P. Scott to Lady Stafford, 29 March 1850.
9. C.P. Loch to Lord Stafford, 25 October 1857. In September 1869 George Devey, a London architect with a reputation from his work at Virginia Water in Surrey, was advertising his services for design work at Strathpeffer. He is said to have been responsible for much of the subsequent villa development at the Spa. Signed map and lithograph in Estate office, Cromartie Estate.
10. C.P. Loch to Lord Stafford, 8 January 1858, Loch to Scott, 8 December 1860.
11. C.P. Scott to Loch, 23 January 1858.
12. C.P. Scott to Loch, 28 January 1858; Loch to Lord Stafford, 10 February 1858; Loch to Scott, 12 August 1858.
13. C.P. Scott to Lady Stafford, 26 June 1858.

14. C.P. Loch to Scott, 23 December 1863.
15. C.P. Gunn to Brereton, 5 March 1887.
16. C.P. Scott to Lady Stafford, 29 March 1850.
17. C.P. Loch to Gunn, 9 September 1872.
18. C.P. Report on Spa, January 1870.
19. C.P. Gunn to Black, 6 October 1877.
20. C.P. Gunn to Brereton, 25 June 1887.
21. C.P. Loch to Gunn, 6 June 1873.
22. C.P. Gunn to Loch, 12 January 1872.
23. C.P. Colin Mackenzie to Gunn, 24 February 1876, 1 June 1876, 14 June 1876; Gunn to Loch, 265 January 1872; Loch to Gunn, June 1873, 8 July 1876.
24. C.P. Loch to Gunn, 22 October 1874.
25. C.P. Loch to Gunn, 8 September 1874.
26. *Ross-shire Journal*, 23 April 1875; Gunn to Loch, 5 September 1874.
27. C.P. MacIver to Gunn, 19 June 1874, Loch to Gunn, 8 September 1874.
28. C.P. James Alexander to Gunn, 17 February 1876, 29 December 1876.
29. C.P. Colin Mackenzie to Gunn, 10 July 1876; Jas Alexander to Gunn, 3 March 1876.
30. C.P. Gunn to Loch, 12 January 1872, 3 September 1874; S.C. D593/K/1/3/66 Gunn to Duke of Sutherland, 5 June 1879.
31. S.C. D593/K/1/3/66 Gunn to Kemball, 17 September 1880, 6 March 1882.
32. C.P. Gunn to Kemball, 17 September 1879.
33. The doctor was paid £25 p.a. by the Duchess on the understanding 'that he should attend and prescribe to the poor crofters of the estate', C.P. Loch to Gunn, 20 March 1871.
34. S.C. D593/K/1/3/66 Gunn to Duke of Sutherland, 6 July 1878; Gunn to Kemball, 16 November 1890.
35. C.P. Kemball to Gunn, 18 September 1880.
36. C.P. Gunn to Kemball, 17 September 1879; Manson to Gunn, 30 November 1880.
37. C.P. George Scott to Gunn, 21 January 1880. Gunn said the capital could be raised at 4 per cent; eventually the Duke agreed to take shares in the Ben Wyvis venture, S.C. D593/K/1/3/66 Gunn to Kemball, 16 February 1880. In May, Gunn reported that the shares were in good demand among 'the well to do class in England', Gunn to Kemball, 10 May 1880.
38. C.P. Kemball to Gunn, 16 August 1880.
39. S.C. D593/K/1/3/66 Gunn to Kemball, 1 February 1881.
40. C.P. Gunn to Kemball, 25 February 1882.
41. C.P. Macrae to Kemball, 25 February 1882.
42. T. Manson, *Strathpeffer Spa* (1881), pp.27-8.
43. C.P. August 1882, Letter no. 91.
44. R. Masson, *The Life of Robert Louis Stevenson* (1924), p.197.
45. S.C. D593/K/1/3/72, Gunn to Kemball, 10 May 1884, 26 May 1884.

Chapter 21 pp. 284 to 296

1. N.S.A., vol.14, p.279.
2. C.P. MacIver to Gunn, 30 November 1870; K. Mackenzie to Gunn, 10 March 1871; Loch to Gunn, 23 March 1869; Loch to Gunn, 14 November 1871.
3. C.P. Loch to Gunn, 21 March 1870.
4. See Richards, Leviathan, op.cit., pp.

5. C.P. MacIver to Gunn, 14 November 1870.
6. C.P. Gunn to Loch, 19 October 1872.
7. C.P. Mackenzie to Gunn, 22 September 1871.
8. See Willie Orr, Deer Forests, Landlords and Crofters (Edinburgh, 1982), passim.
9. C.P. Gunn to Loch, 12 January 1872; MacIver to Gunn, 2 June 1871.
10. C.P. Loch to Gunn, 12 December 1872.
11. C.P. Loch to Gunn, 20 December 1872.
12. C.P. Gunn to Loch, 14 January 1873.
13. C.P. Loch to Gunn, 23 February 1873; Loch to MacIver, 9 March 1873; McLeay to Gunn, 23 April 1873; Mackenzie to Gunn, 11 April 1873, 17 April 1873, 25 April 1873, 2 May 1873, 5 May 1873.
14. C.P. Mackenzie to Gunn, 8 August 1873, 13 August, 1873.
15. *Ross-shire Journal*, 8 October 1875.
16. C.P. MacIver to Gunn, 19 June, 1875.
17. See W.E. Vaughan, *Landlords and Tenants in Ireland 1848-1904* (1984).
18. C.P. Loch to Gunn, 11 December 1872.
19. C.P. Loch to Gunn, 13 January 1873.
20. C.P. Gunn to Loch, 8 December 1874.
21. C.P. Mackenzie to Gunn, 11 November 1874.
22. C.P. Loch to Gunn, 10 March 1873.
23. C.P. Loch to Gunn, 22 August 1874.
24. C.P. Gunn to Loch, 5 October 1875; MacIver to Gunn, 12 November 1875.
25. C.P. Small memo book, dated 1873.
26. C.P. William Gunn's 'Remarks on the recent valuations of Crofter Holdings on the Cromartie Estate', October 1878.
27. C.P. Gunn to Duchess of Sutherland, 4 April 1878.
28. C.P. Gunn to Kemball, 22 November 1879.
29. C.P. Loch to Gunn, 19 July 1876.
30. See Gordon Donaldson, *Sir William Fraser* (Edinburgh, 1985).
31. C.P. Fraser to Gunn, 4 October 1875.

Chapter 22 pp. 297 to 311

1. C.P. Gunn to Kemball, 22 November 1879.
2. C.P. Kemball to Gunn, 22 June 1880.
3. See Dunbabin, op.cit., Chap.XII; H.J. Hanham, 'The Problem of Highland Discontent 1880-1885', *Trans.of Royal Hist.Soc.*, vol.19 (1960); J. Hunter, *Making of the Crofting Community* (Edinburgh, 1976); I.F. Grigor, *Mightier than a Lord* (Stornaway, 1979).
4. *Scottish Highlander*, 12 May, 1898.
5. J.P.D. Dunbabin, *Rural Discontent in Nineteenth Century Britain* (1974), pp.186-91.
6. C.P. MacIver to Gunn, 18 September 1880.
7. C.P. Mackenzie to Gunn, 11 November 1880.
8. C.P. MacIver to Gunn, 16 December 1880.
9. See Eric Richards, *History of the Highland Clearances*, Vol.I (1982), p.240.
10. See Joseph MacMillan, *Highland Heroes of the Land Reform Movement* (Inverness, 1917), pp.97 et seq.
11. C.P. P. Campbell Ross to Gunn, 30 December 1880.

12. C.P. K. Mackenzie to Gunn, 24 December 1880; Gunn to Kemball, 21 December 1880; Kemball to Gunn, 22 December 1880; Gunn to *Inverness Courier*, 24 December 1880.
13. C.P. Kenneth Mackenzie to Gunn, 24 December 1880.
14. C.P. Gunn to Kemball, 1 August 1881.
15. C.P. Gunn to Kemball, 12 December 1881, 1 January 1882, 9 January 1881.
16. In fact cattle disease broke out on Kildary Farm in April 1883, thought to have been introduced by Irish cattle bought at the Perth auction sales. It was the third outbreak in the district. C.P. Gunn to Kemball, 13 April 1883.
17. C.P. Gunn to Kemball, 6 November 1882. Reports and counter-reports of the destitution appeared in the *Scotsman*, 21 March 1883, 28 March 1883, 2, 4, 9, 12, 19, 23 April 1883. More generally see Eric Richards, 'Poverty and Survival in Nineteenth Century Coigach', in J. Baldwin, op.cit.
18. C.P. Gunn to Mackenzie, 27 October 1882; Gunn to Kemball, 6 November 1882.
19. C.P. Petition dated 29 October 1883.
20. C.P. Gunn to Kemball, 9 December 1882.
21. C.P. Gunn to Kemball, 18 April 1883.
22. C.P. Gunn to Kemball, 10 December 1883.
23. C.P. Gunn to Kemball, 22 November 1883, 16 December 1883, 31 December 1883.
24. C.P. Kemball to Gunn, 29 February 1884, 11 February 1884, 10 March 1884, 27 March 1884, 12 April 1884, 1 April 1884, 17 May 1884, 1 July 1884, 15 July 1884.
25. C.P. Gunn to Kemball, 12 August 1885; Maciver to Gunn, 3 March 1885; Gunn to Lord Stafford, 20 June 1885 (2).
26. On the crofters' electoral efforts see D.W. Crowley, 'The Crofters' Party, 1885-1892', *S.H.R.* vol.35 (1956), and D.C. Savage, 'Scottish Politics 1885-6', *S.H.R.* vol.40 (1961).
27. See Eric Richards, 'Anatomy', op.cit., passim.
28. C.P. Small Tenants Book, 4 October 1883.
29. C.P. Small Tenants Book, January 1887.
30. Ibid.

Chapter 23 pp. 312 to 323

1. Napier Commission, op.cit., pp.17-80 ff. The proceedings were reported in the *Scotsman*, 31 July 1883, 1 August 1883, 10, 11, 25 October 1883.
2. See above Chapter 22.
3. Napier, op.cit., p.1789.
4. Ibid., p.1793. when asked whether he preferred to be a labourer rather than a crofter one witness offered a Gaelic proverb: 'The flag at the doorstep of the great house is slippery', p.1793.
5. Cf. p.1788. One crofter however claimed he would emigrate if he could get compensation for his improvements (2624).
6. Ibid., pp.1805-7.
7. Napier, op.cit., pp.1807-9, 1788, 1793, 1789.
8. Estate correspondence at the time of the road construction suggests that the new roads would serve the interests of all parties. George Loch instructed that it was 'not, of necessity, to seek the shortest or the cheapest line but that of beauty of scenery or other advantages of that kind, can be obtained by talking it a little in this or that direction'. It is likely that Loch kept the convenience of the sporting tenants uppermost in his mind since, in the same letter, he spoke of the need to transfer outrun from the small tenants to the shootings.

But the road was expected to bring general advantages and it would be appropriate to 'consider what addition may fairly and properly be made to the small rents which the people at present pay'. C.P. Loch to Gunn, 22 August 1874.
9. Ibid., p.1815.
10. The idea of club farms was not automatically resisted by the established owners in the Highlands. Sheepfarming by individual crofters was generally accepted as improbable. Club farming would require a great deal of re-organisation, co-operation and capital, but was not objected to on principle. See Napier, op.cit., p.1797.
11. Napier, op.cit., p.2621.
12. Napier, op.cit., p.1784.
13. See Eric Richards, *History of the Highland Clearances* Vol.I, Part One.
14. This question was further considered in the evidence of Andrew Smith, a law agent in Dingwall, in Napier, op.cit., Appendix LXXV, pp.356-7.
15. Napier, op.cit., pp.2619-24. Nine years later some of the crofters were prepared to speak well of Gunn, describing him 'as a good factor; they never had the like of him on the estate'. They were prepared also to say that their conditions had never been better, but continued to claim that they had lost common grazing facilities during the term of Scott of Hawick. *Report of the Royal Commission* (Highlands and Islands 1892), 1895, pp.1386-95.
16. Napier, pp.2627-33.
17. Napier, op.cit., pp.1822-30.
18. This claim was clearly at variance with the evidence adduced above in Chapter 16.
19. Napier, op.cit. p.2647.
20. A large employer in the western district had testified to the increased demand for crofter labour over recent years, notably from the effect of the railway drawing tourists and sportsmen to the north west. He was at pains to emphasise that the crofters were not accustomed to southern work practices nor fed like a navvy, and therefore tended to be less efficient and well paid. Napier, op.cit., p.1796.
21. Napier, op.cit., pp.1822-30, App.p.13; pp.2642-50, 3243-50.
22. A similar vagueness had been characteristic of Andrew Scott's evidence before the Select Committee on Emigration, Scotland, 1841. He said he did not know when the great sheep farms, and the eight lot farms plus grazings, on Coigach had been formed since it occurred before his arrival, in 1831. Q.1685-7.
23. C.P., Achindrean Tenants to Gunn, 7 December 1883. Twelve signatories.
24. C.P., Gunn to Kemball, 10 December 1883.
25. C.P., Gunn to [Rae ?], 4 August 1883, Gunn to McLennan, 4 August 1883.

Chapter 24 pp. 324 to 343

1. See Eric Richards, *The Leviathan of Wealth* (London 1975), Part One.
2. See Eric Richards, 'The Land Agent', in G.E. Mingay (ed.), *The Victorian Countryside* (2 vols. London, 1981), II, pp.439-57. Some Highland lairds thought it best to cope without a factor—see Christina Byam Shaw (ed.), *Pigeon Holes of Memory* (Palo Alto, 1988), p.74.
3. C.P. Andrew Scott to Fergus Ferguson, 4 August 1851; Scott to Sir Edward Lees, August 1851.

Notes to pp. 326 to 330   493

4. C.P. Scott to Mackenzie and Logan, 8 February 1850.
5. C.P. J. Loch to Lord and Lady Stafford, 30 April 1853.
6. See above, Chapter 15.
7. C.P. Scott to Lord Stafford, 8 May 1851.
8. C.P. Scott to Lady Stafford, 24 December 1856.
9. C.P. A. Scott to James Scott, 22 October 1857.
10. C.P. Loch to Scott, 29 December 1868.
11. C.P. Loch to William Gunn, 28 March 1869.
12. C.P. Scott to Lady Stafford, 4 December 1852.
13. C.P. Loch to Scott, 25 February 1868, 8 March 1868.
14. C.P. Scott to Melville, 16 February 1857, Scott to James Scott, 18 February 1857.
15. C.P. e.g., R. Falconer to Scott, 5 January 1864.
16. C.P. Andrew Scott to Andrew Scott Jnr, 9 May 1859. MacIver fell into financial crisis again in 1861, a 'hopeless embarrassment' according to Loch, connected to debts incurred by his relatives. There was a danger that he would pass through the Insolvency Court. Loch was angry and described MacIver as stupid and dishonest: 'it is very certain that most employers would decline to retain in their employment a person who had placed himself in so false a position'. Loch had abjured such a recommendation because of MacIver's large family and 'his want of aptitude for any other employment'. In the event MacIver survived the episode and even sustained his privileges in Scourie by threatening to resign. S.C. D593/P/24/2/1.
17. His son was in India with much experience in indigo planting and had accumulated much worldly experience and also possessed a command of Gaelic; Scott put him forward for the Tongue agency in Sutherland. C.P. Scott to Loch, 18 February 1859.
18. C.P. A. Scott to George Loch, 2 May 1859. Recruitment to land agencies had by this time developed into a series of networks. A rudimentary system of apprenticeship had evolved. For instance Scott placed a likely youth from the Kildary office of the Cromartie estate as an apprentice in Evander MacIver's office at Dingwall. Perhaps it was significant that he too bore a lowland name, Elliot, and was described by MacIver as 'a promising and clever accountant'. But, instead of graduating in land agency business, he emigrated to Australia. MacIver, Memoirs, op.cit., p.184.
19. C.P. Andrew Scott to William Scott, 16 March 1859.
20. C.P. Andrew Scott to William Scott, 16 April 1860.
21. C.P. Andrew Scott to William Scott, 7 January 1860.
22. C.P. Scott to James Scott, 22 October 1857. Scott thought there was some 'radical defect in the administration of our Indian Empire'—that the Pagans were being treated like 'Christian men in this our own happy county'. Pagans were by nature liars, cheats, thieves and robbers: 'It will take centuries of time to make them fit for living under laws such as are formed for civilised communities in Europe.' Scott to Andrew Scott, 17 January 1861.
23. C.P. Scott to Andrew Scott, 7 April 1861, Scott to William Nixon, 23 February 1861. Lady Stafford had also made herself popular by her work for charity and the distribution of clothing to the poor. Scott to Lady Stafford, 31 October 1860. See also C.P. 1862 Lists of Poor People in the Barony of Strathpeffer to get article of warm clothing by Her Graces Orders (November).
24. C.P. Taylor to Scott, 7 March 1866.
25. C.P. Loch to Gunn, 21 March 1870.
26. C.P. Mackenzie had, before 1832, leased the farm of Rhinacroisk on the Tulloch estate and later was 'tacksman' of Corry and Glastullich on the Cromartie estate. *Ross-shire Journal*, 4 April 1890.

27. C.P. Loch to Scott, 4 May 1864.
28. *Scottish Highlander*, 3 April 1890.
29. C.P. Loch to Gunn, 14 November 1871. Earlier in 1859 Loch had given another definition of a local factor—'The sort of person to be desired is one having already some experience of business, and yet retaining his powers of personal activity and exertion—farming knowledge is not essential, though it would be useful—a quiet calm judgement, firmness, and yet a conciliatory manner'. C.P. Loch to Scott, 15 February 1859.
30. C.P. MacIver to Martin, 18 May 1865.
31. C.P. Mackenzie to Gunn, 2 June 1883, 24 March 1883.
32. S.C. D593 K/1/3/72G, Gunn to Kemball, 31 May 1883.
33. C.P. Mackenzie to Gunn, 24 March 1884.
34. C.P. Kemball to Gunn, 25 January 1881.
35. S.C. D593/K/1/3/66 Gunn to Kemball, 19 January 1881.
36. C.P. MacIver to Gunn, 29 March 1890.
37. C.P. MacIver to Gunn, 17 December 1884.
38. C.P. Ross to Gunn, 19 May 1884. Typical of public abuse of factors at this time was an article in the *Scottish Highlander*, 12 April 1888, which remarked 'The people of Lochbroom have now learned to distrust everything Mr Ross or his laird would recommend, and they will no doubt show this on the election day'.
39. C.P. Ross to Gunn, 19 May 1884.
40. C.P. Ross to Gunn, 16 May 1884.
41. C.P. Ross to Gunn, 29 December 1884.
42. C.P. Ross to Gunn, 3 January 1885, 4 March 1883.
43. C.P. The management was probably divided for some years with a separate sub-factor, Martin, at Strathpeffer. In about August 1867 Gunn assumed increasing responsibilities, though Scott was still involved until January 1869.
44. C.P. Loch to Gunn, 14 October 1869. In September 1873 Gunn's salary was increased to £300 p.a., plus £50 for horse and a further £30 for railway and other travelling expenses. Gunn had pleaded for the increase partly on the grounds that he had seven children to support and that the cost of living (referring particularly to the price of mutton) had increased by 50 per cent in the previous 13 years. Gunn to Loch, 2 January 1873, Loch to Gunn, 8 September 1873. *Ross-shire Journal*, 29 November 1901.
45. His 'factory' is defined in a C.P. document of 1867.
46. Gunn, chairman of the Ben Wyvis Hotel Company, was alleged in 1888 to have benefited personally from provisioning arrangements at the Spa: *The Scottish Highlander*, 15 March 1888.
47. Gunn also saw possibilities in the west, especially for hotels. 'Until very lately Coigach has been an unknown district to tourists', he said in 1879. Gunn to Kemball, 17 September 1879.
48. C.P. Gunn to Lord Stafford, 20 June 1885.
49. C.P. Gunn to Brereton, 9 October 1886, Brereton to Duchess of Sutherland, 13 October 1886.
50. C.P. Brereton to Gunn, 26 September 1887. One of the abiding anxieties of Highland factors was that the tenantry were inclined to by-pass them and communicate directly with the Commissioner, or, worse still, the landlord. As MacIver said the Commissioner 'should never encourage them to go to him over the Factors'. C.P. MacIver to Gunn, 19 June 1874.
51. C.P. Mackenzie to Gunn, 17 November 1875.
52. C.P. MacIver to Gunn, 17 August 1872.

53. S.C. D593/P/24/7/3 Miscellaneous Newspaper Cuttings 1869-1880. *Truth*, 15 January 1886 [sic].
54. C.P. MacIver to Gunn, 22 February 1881.
55. C.P. MacIver to Gunn, 5 June 1876. On Shinness see Eric Richards, 'The Anatomy...' op.cit., passim.
56. C.P. MacIver to Gunn, 28 April 1883.
57. C.P. MacIver to Gunn, 3 March 1884.
58. C.P. MacIver to Gunn, 25 May 1886; Duke of Sutherland to Gunn, August 1886.
59. C.P. MacIver to Gunn, 7 June 1886.
60. C.P. Ross to Gunn, 12 July 1886.
61. D593/24/3/2 Stafford to Sutherland, 23 June 1889; Brereton to Gunn, 17 January 1887, 27 January 1887.
62. D593/24/3/2. Lord Stafford, in effect, was Commissioner for a short time, but in 1889 his relations with the Duke broke down completely and, amid considerable recriminations, the Duke assumed direct responsibilities.
63. See Stuart, op.cit., Chapter 3.
64. See below, Chapter 27.
65. C.P. Gunn to Kemball, 22 June 1880.
66. C.P. Gunn to Duchess of Sutherland, 9 december 1886.
67. C.P. Gunn to Duchess of Sutherland, 1 March 1884.
68. In 1888 it was stated that Gunn was a crofter's son and had crofter relations. *Scottish Highlander*, 22 March 1888.
69. C.P. Gunn to Lord Stafford, 20 June 1885. Earlier he had said that, regardless of the improvement of living standards in the past 60 years, 'All this counts as nothing in comparison to what they conceive to be their right to the land and to use it on their own terms'. Gunn to Kemball, 10 December 1883.
70. C.P. Gunn to Duchess of Sutherland, 3 April 1884.
71. C.P. Kemball to Gunn, 31 March 1884.
72. See for instance, C.P. J. Ferguson to Lady Elibank, 7 June 1800.
73. See above, Chapter 12; C.P. Walker to Lord Tweeddale, 29 July 1824; Joseph Gordon to Melville, 26 February 1825.
74. C.P. Munro to G. Mackenzie, 19 July 1832, circular to K. Mackenzie, 23 July 1832, G. Mackenzie to Scott, 20 July 1832, 24 July 1832.
75. S.C. D593/P/28/10, Loch to Lady Stafford, 16 March 1852.
76. The Hay-Mackenzies were Conservatives and they and Andrew Scott had opposed James Loch as candidate in the Northern Burghs election in 1841. The marriage of Anne Cromartie with the Sutherland family created a sudden switch of political allegiances which left Scott somewhat baffled. Scott to Alex Smith, 17 May 1841.
77. C.P. Scott to Lady Stafford, 30 March 1852, 2 April 1852; Sir James Matheson to Scott, 18 March 1852; Lady Stafford to Sir James Matheson, 17 March 1852; S.C. D598/P/28/10, Loch to Lady Stafford, 16 March 1852.
78. C.P. Loch to MacIver, 9 March 1873, and above Chapter 21.
79. C.P. Loch to Gunn, 23 February 1873, 11 March 1873; Mackenzie to Gunn, 24 April 1873, 17 April 1873, 2 May 1873, 5 May 1873, 14 April 1873, 6 February 1873, 7 March 1873, 11 March 1873, 28 March 1873, 11 April 1873, 17 March 1873, 23 April 1873.
80. C.P. Duchess of Sutherland to Gunn, 2 March 1880, 23 March 1880; Colin Mackenzie to Gunn, 26 March 1880.
81. C.P. K. Mackenzie to Gunn, 27 March 1880, MacIver to Gunn, 29 March 1880; Gunn to

Mackenzie, March 1880; Gunn to MacIver, 27 March 1880; Gunn to Duke of Sutherland, 31 March 1880.
82. C.P. Duchess of Sutherland to Gunn, 18 February 1884, 26 March 1884; Gunn to Duchess of Sutherland, 7 January 1884, 1 March 1884; Ronald McCullum to Gunn, 22 February 1884; Gunn to Mackenzie, 22 February 1884.
83. C.P. Ross to Gunn, 19 August 1884, 16 August 1884, 1 September 1884.
84. C.P. Duchess of Sutherland to Gunn, August 1884.
85. C.P. Ross to Gunn, 17 April 1885; MacIver to Gunn, 24 April 1884.
86. C.P. MacIver to Gunn, 17 December 1884.
87. C.P. MacIver to Gunn, 8 December 1885; Hardcastle to Gunn, 15 December 1885; Ross to Gunn, 2 December 1885.
88. C.P. Gunn to Duke of Sutherland, 3 December 1886; Gunn to Duchess of Sutherland, 9 December 1886; MacIver to Gunn, 25 May 1886.
89. C.P. Ross to Gunn, 12 July 1886, 13 July 1886.
90. C.P. Gunn to Duchess of Sutherland, March 1888.
91. C.P. W.J. Bell to Gunn, 16 February 1890.
92. C.P. Cromartie to Gunn, 9 July 1892.
93. C.P. Gunn to Cromartie, 18 November 1889, 19 December 1889.
94. C.P. Gunn to Cromartie, 19 November 1889.
95. C.P. In letters and out letters for August 1882.

Chapter 25 pp. 344 to 359

1. Scott reduced rents substantially in 1832/3—possibly be 15%; see above Chapter 14.
2. See Appendix B.
3. C.P. Crofter Statistics 1884, sent to Kemball and Gunn.
4. See above, Chapter 12.
5. C.P. Letter of Scott dated 21 June 1843.
6. C.P. Gunn to Duncan, 26 Septemnber 1893.
7. C.P. Gunn to Kemball, 22 February 1884.
8. See above, Chapter 13.
9. In 1885 Ullapool was described as 'once a flourishing fishing town, with a large fleet of boats, an extensive yard of boat-building, a cooperage, a manufactory for herring-nets, and even a custom house, has now hardly a boat that the fishery officer would certify as seaworthy to go to the East Coast fishing. It has no carpenters, no coopers, or net-making, no industry of any kind. The village is tumbling into ruins, but still afford shelter to most of the poor of the parish of Lochbroom who number 378, and cost the rest of the parishioners £1677 a year to maintain!' Rowland Hill Macdonald, *Emigration of Highland Crofters* (Edinburgh, 1885), p.38.
10. See Richards, 'Poverty and Survival', op.cit.
11. C.P. Angus and Hugh McLeod to Scott, 14 March 1861; K. Mackenzie to Scott, 3 May 1861.
12. C.P. Scott to Mackenzie, 13 April 1858; Scott to Loch, 3 July 1858.
13. See above, Chapter 22.
14. The tenant of Garbat 'took advantage of break in his lease and quitted Farm in 1872', C.P. Lease Book.

15. C.P. Loch to Gunn, 12 December 1873; Gunn to Loch, 2 September 1871.
16. MacIver to Gunn, 28 May 1880, 16 December 1880. The scale and intensity of the individual experience was captured in brief comments in the Cromartie Lease Book. For example the sheepfarm of Achnahaird: 'Steading burnt down in 1883. Tenant left insolvent.' North Keanchillish: 'Tenant urged the taking over of this farm in 1884 which was done'. Tain Farm: tenant Shivas 'became insolvent, which terminated his lease in 1885'. Corrie Farm was similarly 'taken over' in 1885. Meddat: 'Interest allowed off to Mr George Clarke when times became bad'. Polnicol: 'Proprietrix to do £660 worth of improvements interest free' despite rent reductions already negotiating. Milntoun Mill: 'Tenant in difficulties, resigned lease in 1885'; Drumvaich Sheep Farm, taken over by estate in 1885; Badentarbat: 'allowed a further red. of 15 per cent for consideration of bad times'. By contrast sporting tenants found themselves required to pay costs of buildings on their land. See also C.P. Cromartie Estate, Factor's Report for March 1889.
17. C.P. Gunn to Kemball, 9 January 1882.
18. Arras was an exceptional tenant who contributed strongly to the local community. A borderer (from Galashiels) he arrived at Fodderty in 1867 and developed a reputation as a skilled farmer and 'an early advocate and successful exponent of advanced farming'. He was involved in the parochial Board, the School Board, the Free Church, the YMCA in Dingwall, and the Temperance movement, and was a J.P. He died in 1912. *Ross-shire Journal*, 26 April 1912. Arras held annual gatherings for his employees and promoted adult education in the parish. *Ross-shire Journal*, 23 July 1875.
19. Arras to Gunn, 20 September 1881, January 1882. In an estate advertisement placed in the *Dundee Advertiser*, 27 November 1866, Fodderty was described as one of the most extensive farms in Ross-shire, being 600 acres (475 arable) with extensive hill grazings: 'The Farm is conveniently situated as regards roads, market towns, shipping ports and railway stations; and besides its natural fertility and well known local advantages, being in the vicinity of the Strathpeffer Spa, is in a high state of cultivation with ample buildings, and merits the attention of tenants of capital and skill'. Fodderty had been leased to James Dudgeon from 1848 to 1867 at £700. In 1887 the buildings on the farm were insured for £4600 (C.P. Book of Leases). The tenant was required to pay 6% p.a. on capital expended on drainage works on the farm.
20. C.P. Milne to Gunn, 30 October 1882.
21. C.P. Gunn to Kemball, 16 January 1882; MacIver to Gunn, 23 December 1882..
22. C.P. Arras to Gunn, 23 April 1884.
23. C.P. Ross to Gunn, 26 January 1885; Gunn to Kemball, 26 January 1885.
24. S.C. D593/K/1/3/70 Gunn to Kemball, 29 August 1882; C.P. Gunn to Kemball, 29 August 1885.
25. C.P. Arras to Gunn, 3 February 1886, 23 April 1886.
26. *Ross-shire Journal*, 3 February 1888, 17 February 1888.
27. See above, Chapter 24.
28. C.P. Brereton to Gunn, 3 January 1887.
29. C.P. Brereton to Gunn, 3 March 1887.
30. C.P. MacIver to Gunn, 16 August 1887.
31. C.P. Gunn to Brereton, 20 August 1887.
32. C.P. Gunn to Ross, 22 February 1889; Gunn to Cromartie, 8 July 1890.
33. C.P. John Ross to Gunn, 25 June 1891.
34. C.P. Gunn to Cromartie, 20 March 1892.
35. C.P. Ross to Gunn, 17 March 1898; Factor's Report for March 1898.
36. C.P. Rentals. See Appendix A below.

37. C.P. Black to Gunn, 11 May 1899.
38. On the effect of sporting rents in the Highlands see I.F. Grant, 'Some accounts of individual Highland sporting estates', *Economic History* 3 (1928); Willie Orr, *Deer Forests, Landlords and Crofters* (Edinburgh, 1982).
39. In 1732 the Forest of Fannich had been let to Donald McKenzie of Kilcoy and his lease required him to supply deer to the landlord 'and to keep up the number of Deer which the Forest maintained being fifteen hundred'. (C.P. Rental 1752), p.143.
40. C.P. James Laing to Mrs Hay-Mackenzie, 25 September 1819.
41. C.P. Murray to Mrs Hay-Mackenzie, 11 December 1819. Quoted above, Chapter 12.
42. C.P. Minute of Agreement between John Hay-Mackenzie and Lord Castlereagh, 1834.
43. C.P. Scott to A. Smith, 15 May 1841; Scott to J.S. Hodgson, 3 August 1841.
44. Such building became the vehicle for the introduction of new and sometimes exotic architectural styles into Ross and Cromarty. See G. Steel and E.Beaton, 'Local Building Traditions' in D. Omand (ed.), *The Book of Ross and Cromarty* (Golspie, 1984), p.213.
45. C.P. Scott to Messrs Brooks, 25 July 1842.
46. C.P. Scott to MacIver, 29 January 1849.
47. C.P. Scott to Watson, 7 February 1850.
48. C.P. Scott to Beckwith, 31 May 1851.
49. Dupplin was offered the Achiltibuie Hills at £400 cleared of stock, or £300 'if not so cleared'. Lord Anson was also interested. C.P. Scott to Lord Stafford, 5 February 1853, 19 January 1853; Scott to Melville, 10 February 1853. Anson was no less particular about his conditions of access. Scott to Lord Stafford, 23 February 1853, 19 February 1953.
50. C.P. Scott to Coadie, 5 November 1852; Coadie to Scott, 2, 6, 10, 29 November 1852, 26 January 1853.
51. See above, Chapter 17.
52. C.P. Scott to Lady Stafford, 24 December 1856.
53. C.P. Scott to Alex Hay, 17 October 1857.
54. C.P. Scott to Newton, 3 May 1858.
55. C.P. Scott to Scott, 22 May 1858. Loch to Scott, 9 October 1858.
56. C.P. Scott to Wm Scott, 23 August 1860.
57. C.P. Loch to Scott, 8 December 1860; Loch to Martin, 1 October 1866.
58. C.P. Robertson to Scott, 12 September 1869.
59. C.P. Gunn to Ross, 6 November 1871. The tenants included men such as Walter Shoolbred who belonged to a well-known firm of London cabinet-makers who, on his death in 1905, left an estate of £607,507. *Ross-shire Journal*, 6 January 1905. The sporting tenantry included industrialists galore, many men returned from duty in India, and railway directors. Their sporting efforts were punctuated by many shooting accidents from which estate officials themselves were not secure. For instance, in 1873, Henry Wright, agent to the Duke of Sutherland, was shot in the leg. S.C. D594/P/24/7/3.
60. C.P. MacIver to Gunn, 2 August 1871.
61. C.P. Starkey to Gunn, 10 December 1888.
62. Some of the sporting tenants were marginally involved in the politics of the crofter's revolt. In 1883 one of the Cromartie tenants, Allport, volunteered the view that the people simply expected the proprietors 'to keep them in idleness' with no return nor gratitude. At Achiltibuie he said 'as far as I see ... the people get a living with the smallest amount of hard work of any place in Europe ... about 2 hours a day the year around would I should say cover all they do'. C.P. Allport to Gunn, 19 August 1883.
63. C.P. Gunn to Kemball.
64. C.P. Ross to Gunn, 19 May 1884.

65. C.P. Black to Gunn, 30 January 1896. In 1901 there was a Poaching Prevention Association established at Dingwall.
66. C.P. Ross to Gunn, 30 January 1901.
67. The earliest and best-known of the agents was Hugh Snowie, Gunmaker and Sporting Agent of Inverness. His first printed list of shootings to let, in 1838, contained eight advertisements. By 1872 he circulated 1,500 copies three times a year and he visited London himself to interview prospective shooting tenants. London-based agents came later. See R. Eden, *Going to the Moors* (London, 1979).
68. C.P. Advertisement; sixteen years later Rhiddorrach was paying £1600 p.a. and was considerably enhanced with extra bedrooms, billiard rooms and library, bathrooms, more space for servants and a croquet lawn. The estate had invested considerably in the construction of the Lodge, already £5715 by 1890 and more expenditure followed.
69. C.P. Black to Gunn, 13 December 1897.

Chapter 26 pp. 363 to 377

1. See *Looking Back*; the Autobiography of the Duke of Sutherland (1957), p.38.
2. See Eric Richards, 'Anatomy of the Sutherland fortune', op.cit., passim.
3. C.P. Scott to Gunn, 21 January 1880.
4. C.P. Kemball to Gunn, 25 May 1880.
5. See Eric Richards, *Leviathan of Wealth*, Part 2. On Lord Tarbat's marriage the terms of the settlement precipitated further action—that 'all expenditure on the Cromartie Estate, which is not absolutely inevitable, must cease' C.P. Loch to Gunn, 29 July 1876.
6. C.P. Gunn to Kemball, 13 March 1885.
7. C.P. Kemball to Gunn, 16 July 1885.
8. C.P. Kemball to Gunn, 10 September 1885.
9. C.P. MacIver to Gunn, 25 May 1886.
10. C.P. Brereton to Gunn, 28 January 1887.
11. C.P. Brereton to Duchess of Sutherland, 24 December 1887.
12. S.P. D593/K/6/7 Memo dated 13 July 1885.
13. Queen Victoria's reactions to these events is recorded in S.C. D593/P/1/23, Letter to Lady Alexandra from Queen Victoria.
14. G.E.C. Complete Peerage, p.548, fn 6.
15. S.P. D593/N/4/5/2.
16. S.P. D593/K/1/7/20.
17. Peacock to Gunn, 1 December 1888.
18. There is a helpful explanation of the system of sheep stock valuation on the departure of a tenant in Colin Macdonald, *Highland Memories* (n.d.), pp.119-20.
19. C.P. Gunn to Lord Stafford, 22 September 1888.
20. C.P. Sheep Farms: Sunday Papers, c.1885.
21. C.P. Cromartie Estate. Statement of Permanent Improvements effected during 1885 and 1886.
22. C.P. Gadsden to Duke of Sutherland, January 1889.
23. C.P. Gadsden to Cromartie, 18 May 1889.
24. C.P. Brereton to Gunn, 28 January 1887.
25. C.P. Gunn to Brereton, 2 March 1887.

26. C.P. Sutherland to Gadsden, 1 February 1889.
27. C.P. Replies to Queries by Dr J.H. Gilbert, F.R.S.
28. C.P. Gunn's Report on Cromartie estate, 1887.
29. C.P. Gunn to Cromartie, March 1889.
30. C.P. Gunn to Marquis of Lothian, Secretary of Scotland, 30 March 1889.
31. Occasionally a more common-sensical approach was heard—as in February 1888 when, at a meeting of the Edinburgh Geological Society, a member remarked that 'it was not generally known by people who drink Strathpeffer Water that they were drinking a kind of soup made from old red sandstone fishes'. *Scotsman*, 5 February 1888.
32. Finlayson, op.cit.; Fox, op.cit., p.134.
33. J. Tivy, 'The Geography of the Strathpeffer Area', *Scottish Field Studies*, 1962, p.27.
34. C.P. Brereton to Gunn, 30 August 1886.
35. C.P. Gunn to Black, 6 December 1886.
36. C.P. Brereton to Gunn, 28 January 1887.
37. C.P. Brereton to Gunn, 28 May 1887.
38. C.P. Gunn to Brereton, 5 March 1887.
39. S.P. D593/K/6/1, A Feuar to R.M. Brereton, 12 September 1887.
40. C.P. Gunn to Brereton, 25 June 1887; Gunn to Black, 6 October 1887.
41. C.P. Peacock to Gunn, 1 December 1888; MacIver to Gunn, 1 August 1889, 21 August 1829.
42. C.P. Gunn to Cromartie, 28 February 1890.
43. C.P. Gunn to Black, 13 February 1891.
44. C.P. Peacock to Gunn, 17 October 1891; Gunn to Black, 26 March 1891.
45. C.P. Fox to Gunn, 16 January 1888.
46. A total of £14,000 was spent between 1879 and 1893.
47. C.P. Gunn to Fox, 14 November 1891.
48. C.P. Gunn to Black, 13 January 1893, 17 March 1893.
49. C.P. Gunn to Black, 6 April 1893, 14 April 1893, 3 June 1893, 4 July 1893; Black to Taylor, 17 April 1893; Lean to Gunn, 16 March 1893; Report of Donald Maclean, 4 April 1893; Black to Cromartie, 10 March 1893.

Chapter 27 pp. 378 to 387

1. C.P. General Statement relating to the Crofter Holdings on the Cromartie Estate in the parish of Lochbroom 1890.
2. C.P. Gunn to Cromartie, 22 January 1891, 18 December, 28 November 1890. Annuities on the estate were also much reduced.
3. *Notes and Queries*, 1 March 1884, p.173.
4. C.P. Gunn to Black, 13 February 1891, 23 February 1891. In February 1892 rents were reported to be good but some crofters could not pay due to the unsaleability of their potatoes. Gunn to Cromartie, 27 February 1892. It was decided to go after the very worst offenders.
5. C.P. Gunn to Black, 10 October 1892.
6. C.P. Gunn to Cromartie, 21 November 1892.
7. C.P. Gunn to Cromartie, 15 December 1892.
8. C.P. Gunn to Cromartie, 27 December 1892.
9. C.P. Gunn to Black, 21 January 1893. The Langwell Farm had been untenanted since 1885. Sporting rents had been much greater than pasture rents for some time.

10. C.P. Gunn to Black, 4 February 1893.
11. C.P. Gunn to Cromartie, 18 February 1893.
12. *Ross-shire Journal*, 1 December 1893, Lord Ronald Sutherland Gower, *Old Diaries 1881-1901* (London, 1902), entry of 26 November 1893.
13. *Notes and Queries*, 9 December 1893 et seq. A son had been born in 1881 but died in very early infancy. S.C. D593/P/24/7/3. A legal opinion in 1896 states that 'Lady Sibell held a unique position, being the only Countess, in her own right, and hoped that, whenever she married she would have a son, as no daughters could bear the title, and only she had it, by special favour of the Queen, as when the title was revived for the Duchess [in 1862], it was for her, and her heirs male'. But the whole tangled question was tied up with no less than 37 clauses. The Queen had indeed taken a direct and personal interest in the matter, and would not sanction the extension of the title to a daughter. On the death of the Earl of Cromartie (in 1893) special representations were made to the Queen who acceded only for 'her dear friend's sake and name', and so the title went to Lady Sibell. But the Queen had insisted that the income, i.e. the rent roll and the fund of the Cromartie Trust, was at least £10,000 p.a. Lady Sibell's husband was required to take her name 'or no children of the marriage could inherit'. By the 1920s the Trust Funds were invested in South African, Victorian, Kenyan, Indian, New Zealand and Australian stock as well as London, Midland and Scottish debentures. C.P. Undated 'Note on Succession to Peerage: Mr A.D.M. Black's opinion, from memory'; C.M. Black to Col. Blunt Mackenzie, 3 May 1927, 8 May 1927, 28 February 1933.
14. C.P. Black to Gunn, 31 January 1896.
15. C.P. Gunn to Black, 7 September 1896.
16. C.P. Black to Gunn, 16 January 1896. The management remained nervously sensitive on all aspects of crofter affairs. In September 1892 a minor removal at Coigach was executed. Black in Edinburgh gave an audible sigh of relief that it had been 'effected without affording food for sensational paragraphs in the Highland news'. C.P. Black to Gunn, 19 August 1892, 10 September 1892.
17. C.P. Black to Gunn, 30 June 1896.
18. C.P. Black to Gunn, 9 September 1896.
19. C.P. Ross to Gunn, 22 February 1897.
20. C.P. Black to Gunn, 11 March 1897.
21. C.P. Gunn to Black, 22 October 1897.

Chapter 28 pp. 394 to 412

1. See Stuart, op.cit., pp.43-5.
2. S.C. D593/Q/2/3/2 Wright to Lord Stafford, 11 February 1893; 8 June 1894.
3. C.P. Black to Gunn, 15 May 1896, 18 May 1896; S.C. D593/L/25 Report of the Curators of Lady Sibell.
4. C.P. Correspondence of May and June 1896 between Gunn and Black. The Edinburgh firm became Mackenzie and Black in 1896. Provision had to be made for Lilian, the Dowager Countess of Cromartie; she married Reginald Frederick Cazenove in October 1895.
5. C.P. Black to Gunn, 19 May 1896.
6. C.P. Black to Gunn, 26 January 1896.

7. C.P. Black to Gunn, 31 May 1897.
8. S.C. D593/C/25 Report from the Executors of the Late Earl of Cromartie. The Earl's furniture was valued at £6,609 and jewellery at £392.
9. C.P. Black to Gunn, 13 December 1897.
10. C.P. Wright to Gunn, 15 November 1897.
11. C.P. Black to Gunn, 4 July 1897.
12. C.P. Black to Gunn, 23 October 1897. The portraits included 'Count John Macleod and his Lady' and were sold through the agency of Lord Duveen, a picture dealer.
13. *Ross-shire Journal*, 20 July 1894.
14. According to Gunn in 1893 some £20,000 had been spent on the Spa in the previous 25 years. Fortescue Fox made endless demands for expansion and always emphasised the relative potency of the Spa waters. See for example, 'Strathpeffer Spa', in *Transactions of the Inverness Scientific Society and Field Club*, Vol.IV (1888-95), pp.48, 280-1.
15. C.P. Gunn to Black, 24 September 1895.
16. *Scottish Highlander*, 13 August 1891.
17. C.P. Black to Gunn, 5 June 1893.
18. *Ross-shire Journal*, 16 August 1885.
19. See above, Chapter Twelve.
20. C.P. Gunn to Black, 25 January 1897, Black to Gunn, 24 January 1896, 5 June 1893.
21. C.P. Black to Gunn, 26 January 1897, 25 April 1899; Gunn to Black, 6 October 1897.
22. Kenneth Rose, *Superior Person* (1969), pp.329-30.
23. C.P. Gunn to MacAlister, June 1900.
24. C.P. Gunn to Blunt, May 1900; Annual Report at the Spa, 19 October 1901.
25. *Ross-shire Journal*, 5 March 1949.
26. C.P. Ross to Gunn, 30 January 1901.
27. C.P. Black to Gunn, 7 June 1901.
28. *Ross-shire Journal*, 29 November 1901, 27 December 1901, 18 April 1902, 30 May 1902.
29. *Ross-shire Journal*, 29 August 1902.
30. C.P. A.D.M. Black to Gunn, 5 June 1901.
31. C.P. Black to Gunn, 29 March 1901.
32. See *Ross-shire Journal*, 23 September 1904.
33. C.P. Blunt to Wotherspoon, 31 December 1904.
34. C.P. Blunt to Taylor, 7 January 1913; Blunt to Wotherspoon, 5 September 1909, 6 December 1913.
35. C.P. Black to Gunn, 27 March 1900.
36. C.P. Blunt to Gunn, 24 June 1901. The dispute was still unsettled in 1915 when the Land Court was asked to assist. Land Court Papers 1915, Mackenzie to Taylor, 1 September 1915.
37. C.P. Ross to Gunn, 24 February 1900; William Mackenzie to Wotherspoon, 8 December 1907.
38. *Ross-shire Journal*, 6 December 1907.
39. C.P. Petition from Achiltibuie, June 1912.
40. Blunt might have seen a parallel in Jamaica in 1904 from whence he wrote: 'This country is full of touring Americans and we find very few fellow countrymen really. The planters are almost an extinct race and their places are often in the hands of brown men or divided up amongst black ones.' C.P. Blunt to Wotherspoon, 28 March 1904.
41. *Scottish Highlander*, 10 October 1889.
42. C.P. J.C. Howell to Lord Cromartie, 3 June 1892; Black to Gunn, 31 May 1896, 11 November 1896.

43. *Ross-shire Journal*, 14 December 1900.
44. *Ross-shire Journal*, 20 September 1901.
45. C.P. Gordon to Gunn, 11 January 1901, Provisional Report by George Gordon ... on a proposal for utilising the Rogie Falls as a source of motor power 22 July 1901.
46. C.P. Blunt to Gunn, 25 May 1902.
47. *Ross-shire Journal*, 30 May 1902; see also Finlayson, op.cit., p.78.
48. *Ross-shire Journal*, 20 May 1903, 14 August 1903, 26 September 1902. It was one of the first hydro-electric schemes in Scotland and Castle Leod was the first Highland mansion to be serviced by alternating current. *Bulletin*, 4 February 1948.
49. *Ross-shire Journal*, 27 March 1903.
50. *Ross-shire Journal*, 26 December 1902, 24 October 1902, 13 March 1903, 3 April 1903.
51. An agreement was signed 20 January 1903.
52. *North Star*, 13 January 1934. Blunt wrote from Jamaica in April 1904, 'It is now a full year since we were led to expect that the plant would be in full working order and it is unpleasantly certain to me ... that the long delay, the frequent breakdowns, and long deferred completion of the work have operated prejudicially on the general adoption of the light and resulted in considerable loss to me'. C.P. Blunt to Deacon, 8 April 1904.
53. C.P. Blunt-Mackenzie retained an interest in the Electric Light Company; in May 1908 he raised a loan of £2,100 for preference shares, on the security of the entailed estate. A similar arrangment occurred at the time of the sale of Strathpeffer Spa. C.P. Black to Wotherspoon, 3 December 1909.
54. C.P. Black to Wotherspoon, 16 June 1910, 3 December 1909, 23 June 1910, 31 December 1912; Black to Blunt-Mackenzie, 23 June 1910. Further information through the assistance of Mr Finlayson of the Hydro Electric Board in Dingwall in 1975.
55. C.P. Blunt to Gunn, 31 March 1900.
56. C.P. Blunt to Fox, 28 September 1902; Fox to Blunt, 15 October 1902.
57. C.P. Gunn to Blunt, 26 March 1900.
58. C.P. Blunt to Wotherspoon, 17 February 1904.
59. *Ross-shire Journal*, 1 September 1905, 8 August 1902.
60. W. Bruce, et al., *Strathpeffer Spa Medical Guide, passim*.
61. C.P. Blunt to Wotherspoon, 2 August 1907.
62. *Ross-shire Journal*, 5 February 1904.
63. *Ross-shire Journal*, 8 November 1907; C.P. Gifford to Blunt-Mackenzie, 14 December 1905, 8 December 1905, 12 December 1905, 18 April 1907; Wotherspoon to Blunt-Mackenzie, 12 February 1906; Prospectus of Strathpeffer, Ltd 1907; Memorandum and Articles of Association of Strathpeffer Spa Limited, 1907. Revenue from the waters, baths, pavilion and rents fell from £2306 in 1900 to £1840 in 1907; expenditure rose from £1736 to £1889. By 1913 total receipts increased to £4,426 under the aegis of Strathpeffer Spa Limited.
64. *Ross-shire Journal*, 10 January 1908.
65. *Ross-shire Journal*, 21 February 1908.
66. *Ross-shire Journal*, 22 November 1907.
67. *Ross-shire Journal*, 9 February 1912, 6 February 1914.
68. C.P. Blunt to Wotherspoon, 5 August 1910, 4 August 1910, 5 September 1909.
69. In September 1902 Blunt remarked, 'It is no secret, since it appeared in the papers some 12 months ago, that we have recently had to borrow considerable sums for works on the Estate of which sheep farms swallowed up a great deal for very little return ... we are really unable to face any further capital outlay at present'. C.P. Blunt to Fox, 28 September 1902.

70. C.P. Blunt to Wotherspoon, 17 February 1904. Tarbat House was leased out in 1906 to the Countess of Moray; a sale was contemplated in 1907. But in January 1910 the 'baronial residences and shooting' at Castle Leod were again advertised for lease at £1,100 p.a. with 12 good bedrooms, 3 bathrooms, and electrically lighted throughout.
71. C.P. Black to Wotherspoon, 2 February 1907.
72. C.P. Gifford to Wotherspoon, 12 May 1906, 17 May 1906; Mackenzie and Black to Wotherspoon, 4 June 1906. Legal questions relating to sales were considered in 'Memorial for the Right Hon. Sibell Lilian Countess of Cromartie for the Opinion of Counsel', 1907.
73. C.P. Mackenzie and Black to Wotherspoon, 8 August 1906.
74. C.P. Gifford to Blunt-Mackenzie, 26 April 1907; Blunt to Wotherspoon, 27 April 1907; Gifford to Blunt-Mackenzie, 29 April 1907.
75. C.P. Gifford to Wotherspoon, 30 April 1907.
76. C.P. Blunt to Wotherspoon, 9 November 1908.
77. C.P. Blunt to Wotherspoon, 3 February 1908.
78. C.P. Blunt to Wotherspoon, 27 April 1907.
79. C.P. Blunt to Taylor, 6 December 1913, 7 January 1913; Gifford to Wotherspoon, 18 May 1913, 7 May 1913; Mackenzie to Wotherspoon, 28 May 1911.
80. C.P. Taylor to Colin Mackenzie, 5 March 1920.
81. C.P. James Hill to Wotherspoon, 15 May 1914.
82. C.P. Blunt to Taylor, 20 August 1914.
83. C.P. Blunt to Taylor, 20 August 1914; Taylor to Blunt, 25 August 1914.
84. *North Star*, 7 April 1917.

Epilogue pp. 415 to 427

1. Quoted by Christina Byam Shaw, *op.cit.*, p.124.
2. See Mrs Fraser, *The Records of the Men of Lochbroom who fell in the European War 1914-1918* (Glasgow, 1922)
3. *The Bulletin*, 9 September 1916; *North Star*, 7 April 1917; *Evening Standard*, 24 November 1925; *Daily Mirror*, 24 November 1921, *Liverpool Post and Mercury*, 24 November 1921.
4. See J. Tivy, 'Easter Ross', *op.cit.*, pp.64-84.
5. See W.A.R. Thomson, *op.cit.*, pp.135-8.
6. Quoted by C.A. Latimer in *Spectator*, 16 April 1988 (and see subsequent correspondence).
7. Quoted in Mackay, *Scotland Farewell, op.cit.*, pp.52-3.
8. C.P. Small rentbook, 1873.
9. Colin Macdonald, *Highland Journey* (Edinburgh, 1943), p.49.
10. *Ross-shire Journal*, 22 January 1947, 26 April 1957; Finlayson, *op.cit.*, p.84.
11. Colin Macdonald, *Echoes of the Glen* (Edinburgh, 1936), p.xiv.
12. Colin Macdonald, *Croft and Ceilidh* (Edinburgh, 1947), p.15.
13. *Echoes of the Glen, op.cit.*, pp.95-6.
14. *Echoes of the Glen, op.cit.*, pp.68-71; *Croft and Ceilidh*, p.126.
15. *Highland Journey, op.cit.*, pp.18-19.
16. *Croft and Ceilidh, op.cit.*, p.37.
17. *Ibid.*, p.92.
18. *Echoes of the Glen, op.cit.*, p.79.
19. *Croft and Ceilidh, op.cit.*, p.89.
20. *Echoes of the Glen, op.cit.*, Chapter V.
21. *Highland Journey, op.cit.*, p.105.

Notes to pp. 420 to 443

22. *Croft and Ceilidh*, op.cit., p.18.
23. *Highland Journey*, op.cit., p.89.
24. *Croft and Ceilidh*, op.cit., pp.135-6.
25. *Highland Journey*, op.cit., pp.53-4.
26. *Croft and Ceilidh*, op.cit., p.82.

Appendix A pp. 431 to 438

1. Until 1707 values were expressed in medieval merks of which there were three to the Scots Pound. There were twelve Scots Pounds to one Pound Sterling. The extension of a general currency for the entire Great Britain was welcomed by the first Earl of Cromartie but, in reality, the remoter regions continued to employ Scots Pounds in accounts until the latter half of the eighteenth century.
2. Important long run comparisons of nominal and real rents in the Highlands are reported in Hugh C. Fraser, *The Land Statistics of the Shires of Inverness, Ross and Cromarty in the Year 1871* (Inverness, 1872). The Cromartie estate rentals correspond remarkably well to Fraser's estimates.
3. See Eric Richards, 'Poverty and Survival', op.cit.

Appendix B pp. 439 to 441

1. Dunlop, op.cit., p.66; N.L.S. MS 9646, p.232;
2. Gazateer, op.cit., p.784, Censuses; Highland Destitution Papers: Report of Rev. McLeod of Ullapool.
3. N.S.A., p.84. He had also taken a count in 1824 yielding a figure of 4727 compared with the 1821 census return of 4540. C.P. Scott to Lord Stafford, 1 January 1858; Gunn to Lord Stafford, 20 June 1885. See above, Chapter 13. Important evidence for 1755 was provided by Rev. James Robertson of Lochbroom for the Judicial Rental in which he declared 'That he had 2,250 souls young and old, no papists no non jurant ministers and that of the above number there are 909 within the estate of Cromartie. There are two Society schools.' S.R.O. E746/70/1.
4. N.S.A., p.89, O.S.A., p.472. In the Judicial Rentals for 1755 the population of Lochbroom was given as 2250 and that of Coigach as 909 which may suggest that the 1790 figure was considerably understated. In Andrew Scott's evidence before the P.P. Inquiries into Emigration (Scotland), 1842, he stated that the population of Coigach was 1512 together with 500 squatters. At other times, in general estate correspondence, Scott estimated Coigach's population thus: in 1836 at 1600, in 1847 at 1760, and in 1850 at 1700.

Appendix C pp. 442 to 444

1. Our thanks for the typescript are owed to Mr Fraser.
2. See the penetrating remarks on similar evidence by the late Eric Cregeen, 'Oral Sources for the Social History of the Scottish Highlands and Islands', *Oral History*, vol.2, 1974, no.2. The highly selective character of this type of recollection is evident also in *Tales and Legends of Lochbroom* by Roderick Mackenzie (Ullapool, 1988).
3. See above, Chapter 12.
4. See above, Epilogue.

Index

Achanduart, lotting, 170
Achiltibuie, 78, 148-9, 153, 379
Achilty, Mackenzie of, 74, 79
Achindrean, lotting, 170, 346
Achlachan, lotting, 170
Advocates Library, 20
agriculture:
    Coigach, 18th century pattern, 38
    depression in, 350-4
    engrossing of farms, 122
    improvements, 184-5, 187-8, 198
        1st earl of Cromartie, 43
        3rd earl of Cromartie, 54-5
        annexed estates, 85-6, 88-90
        by Cromartie tenants, 154
        late 18th century, 119-23
        social costs, 188-92
    labour supply, 264-6
    production, 17th-18th centuries, 41-6
    traditional, 184, 185
    see also crofting
Alness, appointment of minister, 160-2
Altandhu (Altandow, Altandu) 144, 379
    crofters, 313-14
    lotting, 170, 346
Altnacraig, lotting, 170
Anne, Queen, 22, 24
annexation of estates, 72, 74-6
    see also estates, annexed
Arboll, 7, 50
Ardmair, 86
Ardvall, 86
army:
    military service, 111-12
    quartering of troops, 40
    recruitment for, Macleod's Highlanders, 99-101, 103-4

Arras, Walter, 279, 290, 351-3
Auchindrain, 144
Auchnahaird (Achnahaird), 170, 237, 238, 379, 380
Auchterneed, 86, 141-2
Australia, emigration to, 231, 233-4

Badenscallie, 144, 148-9, 153, 379
    clearances, 239-40, 243
Badentarbat, 239, 245
Badscally, rent, 144
Baillie, Henry James, 151, 201
Baldry, John, 121
Ballachgowan, 146
Ballone, castle of, 7, 172
Balmerino, Arthur Elphinstone, 6th Lord, 62, 63
Balnagowan, 121
    Ross of, 34-5, 40-1
banking:
    bank credit, 287-8
    Commercial Bank of Tain, 287
barley, bere, 41, 42
baron baillies, 32
barony courts, 32, 34
Bayfield, William Chisholm of, 140
Beaufort, Henry, 107
begging, 194-5
Ben Wyvis, 7
Ben Wyvis Hotel, 280-1, 283, 374, 391-2, 408
bere-barley
    as rent, 41, 42
    trade, 42
Billeting Act (162), 16
Binning, Sir William, 44
Black, A. D. C., lawyer, 336, 394-6, 399-402
Blackhall farm, 7

Blackhill, 146
　John Mackenzie of, 132
Blacks, of Edinburgh, lawyers, 384-7
Blair, David, 99
Blair, Sir David, 153, 154, 155, 160, 168
Blair, Mary Caroline, duchess of Sutherland, 367, 378, 382, 394
Blunt (later Blunt-Mackenzie), Edward Walter, 336, 384, 386, 399, 410, 409-12, 415, 416, 421
　and crofters, 403-4
　introduction of electricity, 404-6
　and Strathpeffer Spa, 406-8
bonds, financial transaction by, 47-8
bowmen, yeald, 32
Brereton, R. M., 307, 334, 335-6, 353-4, 365, 369
British Fishery Society, 105, 107, 132, 195
Brodie, Alexander, 46

Cadboll, Aeneas Macleod of, 32-3, 48, 49-50, 52
Camuscoil (Canniscoil), lotting, 170, 346
Castle Leod, 10, 17, 427
　decline, 52
　lease to Mackenzie of Avoch, 98
　mid 19th century, 249–50
　quartering of troops at, 40
　reconstruction, 409
　renovation, 150
Castlehaven, 7
Castlehill, 86
cattle:
　rearing, 123
　thieving, 35-6
　trade, 41
chamberlains, 17th-18th centuries, 30-5
charity payments by 1st earl of Cromartie, 34
Charles II, 11, 14, 16, 18
children, employment in agriculture, 265
Chisholm, William, of Bayfield, 140
cholera, 171
Church:
　and the community, 18th century, 34
　Disruption, 160, 162
　parochial conflicts, 18th century, 34-6
　patronage, 160-2, 168
civil wars, 12, 14
clan loyalty, 112

clearances, 123, 169
　Coigach, 147-50
　Cromartie, 164, 170, 177-9, 205-7, 213-15
　economics of, 185
　Knockfarrel resettlement, 222
　resistance to, 178, 258
　　Coigach riot, 240-5
　　Culrain riot, 164
　sheep farming and, 123, 185, 239-40
　social effects, 188-92, 198-9, 284
　sporting leases and, 357
coal, 54, 93
Coigach:
　and 1745 Rising
　　aftermath, 64-5, 66, 72, 79
　　raising of regiment, 60-1
　administration under Annexation, 77, 86
　agricultural conditions 1890, 379-80
　agriculture in, 38
　barony of, 7-8
　clearances, 147-50
　crofting, 292-3, 299, 319
　　revolt, 298, 299, 305
　emigration from, 234-5
　famine, 90-91
　lotting, 149-50
　Macleod of Cadboil and, 52
　mid 19th century, 227-9, 348
　petition for appointment of minister, 137
　population growth, 113
　rents, 41, 79, 87-8, 131
　　collection, 30
　resettlement of demobilised soldiers, 86-7
　riots, 238-45
　social structure, 82-3
　survey of 1755, 78-80
　timber from, 43, 52
　way of life, 38
Coigach Charter, 7
Commercial Bank of Tain, 287
communications:
　early 18th century, 39-40
　see also railways; roads
Conan, fishing, 44, 168-9
consolidation, agrarian, 86
Corn Laws, repeal, 225

Corrie (Corry), clearances, 144, 177-8
Coull, Mackenzies of, 61
courts, barony, 32, 34
crime, 17th-18th centuries, 35-6, 37
Crofter Commission (Napier Commission), 298, 302-8, 312
    Act (1886), 298, 306, 307, 385, 420
        and crofters' rents, 381, 385
    crofters' evidence, 312-19, 322
    Cromartie estate's evidence, 319-23
    effect on estate management, 307, 385-7
crofters/crofting, 186
    challenge to landlords, 176, 297, 304, 313-19, 322-3
        political, 340-1
        rent strike, 302, 306, 323
    Coigach, 292, 295, 299, 319, 379-80, 403
    Colin Macdonald's view, 418-20, 425-7
    critics of system, 186
    Cromartie estate, 237, 290-3, 319-20
        introduction, 149, 170, 186
        management, 237-8, 267, 285, 290-1, 298-9, 307-8, 349-50, 353-4, 379-81, 385-7, 402-4
        Napier Commission evidence, 313-23
        rents, 290-4, 307, 319-20, 381
        revolt, 297-301
    economic problems, 228-31, 285-6
    factors and, 337-8, 420
    as farm labourers, 264-5, 314, 419
    leases, 179-80
    rents, 286
        Cromartie, 290-3, 307, 319, 350, 353-4
        Napier Commission and, 381, 385
        refusal to pay, 302, 306, 323
        revaluation, 291-4
    revolt, 304-8
        effects, 308, 310
        precipitating events, 297-303
    status of, 149, 186
    Strathpeffer, 316-19, 320
    20th century, 402-4, 416
    way of life, 308-10, 313, 419-20
crofters/crofting Cromartie estate, rents, 290-4, 307, 319-20, 381
Cromartie earldom:
    history of Sir William Fraser, 296
    recreation, 295, 367, 383
    see also Mackenzie, Sir George, 1st earl; Mackenzie, John, 2nd earl; Mackenzie, George, 3rd earl; Sutherland-Leveson-Gower, Francis, 2nd new earl; Mackenzie, Sibell Lilian, countess; Mackenzie, Roderick, 4th new earl
Cromartie estate:
    in 19th century, 344-53
    reports of 1887 and 1889, 370-2
    in 20th century, 402-4, 427
    advertisement of land for rent (1808, 1809), 144-6
    amalgamation with Sutherland estates, 221, 257
        release from 367, 368
    annexation to Crown, 62, 71, 72
        administration during, 73, 77-8, 81-4
    clearances, 123, 145-6, 164, 169-70, 177-9, 187, 205-7, 213-15, 239-40, 267
        Coigach riot, 240-5
    crofters *see* crofters/crofting
    documentation, 26-7
    evolution of, 6-8
    extent of, 6, 10
    finances, 416-17
        17th-18th centuries, 28-30, 45, 48
        effects of female longevity on, 142, 143, 151, 246
        effects of political unrest, 40-1
        following 1745 Rebellion, 76
        late 18th-early 19th centuries, 112, 130-5, 138, 143-4
        Sutherland estates and, 221-2, 256-7, 291, 295-6, 363-9
        under 1st earl, 24, 29, 40-1, 48-50
        under 2nd earl, 52-4
        under 2nd new earl, 368-70, 381-3
        under 3rd earl, 55
        under Blunt-Mackenzies, 399-402, 409-11
        under Count Macleod, 104-5
        under Hay-Mackenzies, 219, 347
        under Lord and Lady Stafford, 239, 248-51, 256-8
        will of 3rd duke of Sutherland and, 382, 394-5
    forestry staff, 426
    forfeit after 1745 Rebellion, 62, 71, 72

improvements, 154
inheritance in late 18th-early 19th centuries, 112-13, 129-30, 138, 142
management, 324
    17th-18th centuries, 27-8, 30-4
    Committee of General Management, 336
    crofters, 79-81, 237-8, 267, 285, 290-1, 298-9, 307-8, 349-50, 353-4, 385-7, 402-4
    factors' role, 324-41
    under 1st earl, 24, 25, 40-1
    under 2nd new earl, 296
    under 3rd earl, 54-5
    under Blunt-Mackenzie, 399
    under Hay-Mackenzies, 150, 153-6, 165-9, 174
    under Lady Elibank, 138-42
production:
    17th-18th centuries, 41-6, 78
    late 18th century, 130-1
rental, 346-8
rents:
    17th-18th centuries, 41, 48, 55
    18th-19th centuries, 125-6, 130-2, 133, 135, 140, 144, 148-9, 163-4, 345-56
    following 1745 Rebellion, 73, 74
    revaluation, 291-4
    under Annexation, 87-8
resettlement of demobilised soldiers, 86-7
restoration to Mackenzies, 96-7, 102-3, 111
sale of assets, 174, 409-11, 415-16, 427
sequestration, 53
sheep farming, depression in, 350-1, 354-5, 368
social structure, 38-9
sporting leases, 356-9
surveys, during Annexation, 77-81
tenancies, 55
transport through, 7
wadsets on, 29, 48, 55, 140
Cromartie Trust, 395-6
Cromarty, burgh of, acquisition by George Viscount Tarbat, later 1st earl, 42-3, 47
Cromwell, Oliver, 14-15
Culcairn, 121

Culnacraig, lotting, 346
Culrain, eviction riot, 161, 164
Culvercraig, 379
Cumberland, William, duke of, 66
Cunningham, William, 9th earl of Glencairn, 14
Curzon, George, 398
customs (service rents), 30, 125-6

Dallas family, lawyers, 28, 29-30, 46
Dallas, George, 29
Dallas, Hugh, 28-9
Dallas, William, 29-30
Darien Scheme, 45-6
Davis, Dr Hayton, 376
Davy, Humphrey, 154
deer forests:
    Royal Commission into, 358, 382
    turning of land to, 258, 263
Dempster, George, 105, 107
Derary, Nicholas, 45
diet, 183, 197
Dingwall:
    in 1824, 117
    food riots, 116
    induction riots, 34-5
    population growth, 114
Disannexing Act (1784), 94
disease, 18th century, 118-19
Dochcarty, Mackenzie of, 132
Dorney, 379
Drumruinie (Drumrunie), 359, 415
Drumvaich, rent, 293
Dunbar, Robert, factor, 40-1
Dundas, Henry, 94, 99
Dundonnell, Mackenzies of, 150-1
Dunie, 410
Dunrobin Castle, capture of 3rd earl of Cromartie at, 62
Dunsterfield, George, plasterer, 48
Dupplin, Lord, 241-2, 258, 357

Easter Aird, barony of, 7
    chamberlains, 32
economy of Highlands:
    late 18th century, 130-1
    early 19th century, 150, 153-5
    mid 19th century, 228-31, 248
    late 19th century, 287-8, 299-301

economy of Highlands—*continued*
  effects of sheep farming, 146-7
education, 127, 265
  Scottish Education Act (1872), 288
    elections to School Boards, 289, 339-40
electricity, introduction of, 404-6
Elibank, Lord, 50, 52, 53
Elibank, Lady Isabella, 112, 135, 138-43, 160
emigration:
  late 18th-early 19th centuries, 90-2, 114
  Norman Macleod and, 138
  Select Committee on Emigration (Scotland), 201-5
  subsidised, 231, 233-4
  to Australia, 231, 233-4
enclosure, 86, 122
engrossing, 122
estates, Highland:
  19th century, 344
  annexed to Crown, 72, 74-6
    admistration of 73, 75-7, 86-95
    agricultural improvements, 88-90
    consolidation in, 86
    rents, 87-8
    resettlement of demobilised soldiers on, 86-7
    return of, 94, 98-9
    surveys of, 77
  management system, 17th century, 26, 29
  social structure, 82
  see also Cromartie estate

factors:
  17th century, 29
  annexed estates, 73, 75
  and crofters, 337-8, 420
  Cromartie:
    18th century, 325
    a typical month's work, 342-3
    see also under individual names
famine:
  1741, 43, 55
  late 18th century, 90, 91, 115-16
    effects of, 115-18
  early 19th century, 147
  1836-8, 200, 202
  1846-7, 207-8, 211, 213
  1850, 229-30
  1862-3, 259
  1870, 286
  relief, 209-12
    18th century, 115, 116
    19th century, 202-3, 209-12, 259-62
    George Loch's policy, 260-2
Fannich, 146
  forest, management of, 32
  sale of land, 174
Fearn, 124, 125
fishing boats, 89
fishing industry, 44-5, 105
  1830s, 192, 195
  advocacy by 1st earl of Cromartie, 44-5
  British Fishery Society, 105, 107, 132, 195
  development, annexed estates, 93-4
  herring, 228-9, 401
  Ullapool, 195
flax:
  cultivation, 92
  spinning and weaving, 92-3, 124-5
Fodderty:
  in 1830s, 190-1
  advertisement, 263
  clearances, 190
  rent, 351
  Rev Colin Mackenzie of, 156
Forbes, Duncan, of Culloden, 59, 61, 66
Forbes, Captain John of New, 77, 79-81, 87
Forbes, Marjorie, wife of Count Macleod, 104, 143
  annuity to, 104, 142, 143
forests, Strathpeffer, 88
Fortrose, Lord, 59, 61
Fowlis, 121
Fox, Dr Fortescue, 283, 369, 373, 374, 376, 398
Fraser, Anna, third wife of 2nd earl of Cromartie, 52
Fraser, Colin, factor, 402
Fraser, Simon, 11th Lord Lovat, 54, 57, 59-60, 62, 63
Fraser, Simon, son of 12th Lord Lovat, 98-9

Gaelic language, 127, 197-8
Gairloch, Mackenzies of, 61
Garbat, 132

Geannies, Donald Macleod of, 121, 122, 130
glass, Leith Glass Works, 45
Glastullich, 79, 144
Glencairn Rising, 14-15
Glenskaith, grazing rights, 176-7
Gordon family of Invergordon, 73
Gordon, Adam, advocate, 62
Gordon, Lady Elizabeth, wife of 2nd earl of Cromartie, 52
Gordon, Isabel ('Bonnie Bell Gordon'), wife of 3rd earl of Cromartie
    see Mackenzie, Isabel, countess of Cromartie
Gordon, Sir John, 99, 103
Gordon, Sir William, 53-4
Gower, township of, 222-7, 320
grain:
    as rent, 30, 41, 42
    trade, 42-3
grazing:
    improvements, 88
    rights, 132
Gunn, George, factor, 338
Gunn, William, factor, 176-7, 206, 263-4, 285, 333-4
    and Crofters' Revolt, 304-7
    and crofting community, 302-4
    estate management, 333-8, 351-4
        a typical month, 342-3
    evidence to Napier Commission, 319-23
    rents revaluation, 292-4
    retirement, 399-402
    and Strathpeffer spa, 271, 275, 276-8, 334, 373-7, 397-8

Hastings, Dr, 408
Hay, Edward *see* Hay-Mackenzie, Edward
Hay-Mackenzie, Anne, Lady Stafford, duchess of Sutherland and countess of Cromartie, 220-1, 252-5, 363
    and clearances, 236, 243-5
    coming of age, 221-2
    death of, 367
    marriage to earl of Stafford, 219
    restoration of Cromartie titles to, 254
Hay-Mackenzie, Edward, 138-9, 143, 147-8, 149-53
Hay-Mackenzie, Georgina Ann, countess of Glasgow, 151, 159, 166

Hay-Mackenzie, John, 112, 151, 152, 163, 166, 175
    administration of Cromartie, 204, 206
    financial problems, 219
    and Knockfarrel settlement, 222-5
    poor relief, 203, 209, 210-12
Hay-Mackenzie, Maria Murray, 112, 143, 145, 153
    church patronage, 160-2
    financial problems, 142-5, 151, 153-6, 165-9
Hector, emigrants' ship, 91
herring:
    curing, 93-4
    fisheries, 228-9, 401
Highland and Island Emigration Society, 233-4
Highland Light Infantry, 101
Highland Property Association, 341
Hilton, Mackenzie of, 154
housing, 183
    farm labourers, 264-6

Inchculter, Mackenzie of, 49-50, 99
Inchvannie, crofting, 316-19
industrial revolution, 119, 192-3
industry:
    1st earl of Cromartie, 45
    development, annexed estates, 92-4
    domestic, 124-5
    indigenous, decline of, 192-3
    late 18th century, 124-5
    see also under specific industries
Inverchassely, timber from, 43
Invergordon estates, 99, 103
Inverness, proposed university, 45
Inverpolly, 179, 180, 286
    rent, 293, 348
Isle Martin:
    emigrant sailings from, 114
    fishing industry, 93, 94, 105
    lotting, 170, 346
    tenancies, 267
Isle Ristol, 105

Jacobite rising of 1745, 57-8
    3rd earl of Cromartie and, 56-62, 65
    aftermath, 64-8, 72
    see also annexation of estates

Jacobite rising of 1745—*continued*
    Cromartie regiment, 65-6
        fate of men, 64-7
        raising of, 60-1, 65
    economics and, 56
James VII, 19, 20-1
Jeffrey, Ninian, 77, 88, 90, 91, 93

Keanchrine (Keanachrine), 153, 346
    lotting, 149, 170, 203, 346
Keanchulish, 415
Keithtown, 190
kelp:
    agricultural use, 88
    income from, 132
    industry, 348
Kemball, Sir Arnold, 280, 281, 294, 305, 335, 338, 364-5
Kennedy, John, Free Church minister, 136
Kilmarnock, 4th earl of, 62, 63
Kilmuir Easter:
    agricultural improvement, 121-2
    population changes, 120, 189
Kiltearn, appointment of minister, 160, 161
Kockfarrel:
    land drainage, 225
    resettlement of clearance refugees, 222-7, 320

Laing, James, 147-9, 153, 163
land:
    communal use, 132, 170, 176
    drainage, 225
    tenure, direct tenancies, 55
    tenure and leases:
        late 18th century, 131, 132, 135, 140-1, 169-70
        19th century, 346-9
        Coigach, 227-8
        Crofter Commission, 298, 307-8, 313
        Crofters' Revolt, 298, 304
        lotting, 140-1, 149, 170
        subtenancy, 82-3, 86, 122, 133, 348
    use:
        changes in, 120-3, 127-8, 141-2, 145-6, 169-70
        sport and, 174
        values, mid 19th century, 248

Land League, 305, 307, 310, 385
Land Union, 411
landowners:
    effects of absence, 40-1
    political influence, 27, 98, 168-9, 175-6, 338-9
    decline, 339-41
    relationship with tenants, 111-12, 141, 155, 289-90
        effect of Crofters' Revolt, 298
        effect of Napier Commission, 385-7
    social influence, 96
landownership, Highlands, 3-4
Langwell, 144, 351
    clearances, 170, 177-8
    rent, 293
    sale of, 415
Lauderdale, John Maitland, 2nd earl and 1st duke, 16, 19
law:
    barony courts, 32, 34
    enforcement, 17th-18th centuries, 36, 37, 40
Leckmeln, 300
Leith Glass Works, 45
Lillieshall, 246, 248
linen industry, 93
Loch, Charles, 255
Loch, George, estate management, 247, 249-51, 255-6, 258, 326-7
    famine relief, 260-1
    rent revaluation, 291-2
    Strathpeffer spa, 272-6
Loch, James, 229
    estate management, 247-8, 250-2, 255, 326
Lochbroom:
    in 1830s, 193-7
    emigration from, 90-1, 92, 138, 233
    fishing industry, 44, 93-4, 105-7
    grazing improvements at, 88
    introduction of sheep farming, 122
    linen industry, 93
    population growth, 114
    sale of land, 174
Lochinver, communications, 287
Lorne, marquis of 384, 396, 398
Loudon, earl of 61, 72
Lovat, Lord *see* Fraser, Simon

MacBean, John, 53
McCrae, John, episcopalian minister, 35
McCulloch, Roderick, laird of Glastullich, 64
Macdonald, Colin, 418-20, 425-7
Macdonald, Hon, Lilian Janet, 296, 367
MacDougall, Alexander, regimental surgeon, 101
MacIver, Evander, 263, 264, 287, 328, 335
Mackenzie, —, of Meddat, factor, 68, 73-4
Mackenzie family, 4
    and 1745 Rising, 60-1
    allegiance to Stuart monarchy, 10, 11
    Cromartie branch, 4-6
    of Kintail, 4
    of Meddat, 33-4
    of Scatwell, 60, 61
Mackenzie of Achilty, 74, 79
Mackenzie, Alexander, *History of the Highland Clearances*, 297
Mackenzie, Sir Alexander, of Gairloch, 68
Mackenzie, Colin, of Fodderty, 156
Mackenzie, Constance, 367
Mackenzie of Dochcarty, 132
Mackenzie, George, 3rd earl of Cromartie, 54, 63
    and 1745 Rebellion, 56-60
        military involvement, 61-2
        raising of regiment for, 60-1
    entail of estate to, 50
    estate management, 54-5
    exile in England, 66-8
        support from Cromartie tenants, 68, 74
    financial problems, 5-6
        in exile, 68, 74, 98
    marriage to Isabel Gordon, 53
    trial, 62-4
Mackenzie, George, factor, 325
Mackenzie, George, of Meddat, 116
Mackenzie, George, of Rosehaugh, 20, 46
Mackenzie, George, Colonel, son of 3rd earl of Cromartie, 98, 101, 130
Mackenzie, Sir George, 1st Viscount Tarbat and 1st earl of Cromartie, 12-14, 15, 18, 23
    absence from Cromartie, 40-1
    acquisition of Urquhart estates, 46-7, 48
    as agriculturalist, 43
    financial difficulties, 24-5, 29, 40-1, 46, 48-52
    and fishing industry, 44
    and Glencairn Rising, 15
    political career, 25
        under Anne, 22-3
        under Charles II, 16-20
        under James VII, 20-1
        under William and Mary, 21-2
    trade and commercial ventures, 42-3, 44, 45-6
Mackenzie, Sir George, cousin of 3rd earl of Cromartie, 56
Mackenzie, Sir George Stewart, 146, 147, 184
    General View of the Agriculture of the Counties of Ross and Cromarty, 184-7
Mackenzie of Hilton, 154
Mackenzie of Inchculter, 49-50, 99
Mackenzie, Isabel, countess of Cromartie, 53, 62, 63-4
    pension, 68, 73-4
Mackenzie, Lady Isabella (Lady Elibank), 112, 135, 138-43, 160
Mackenzie, Lady Jane, sister of Count Macleod, 143-4
Mackenzie, Lady Jane, wife of Count Macleod, 143
Mackenzie, Jane, wife of Kenneth Mackenzie, 130
Mackenzie, John, 2nd earl of Cromartie, 33, 51
    disinheritance from estate, 50
    financial imprudence, 49, 52-4
    trial for murder, 51
    wives, 52
Mackenzie, John, of Blackhill, 132
Mackenzie, John, Lord Macleod, son of 3rd earl of Cromartie (Count Macleod), 71, 97
    and 1745 Rebellion, 59, 62, 64, 67
    and Cromartie estate, 129
        campaign to regain, 99, 101-3, 111, 129
    as member of Parliament, 101
    military career:
        British army, 99, 101
        financial benefits of, 101, 103
        Swedish army, 98
    raising of regiment by, 99-101, 103, 111
    refusal of commission in Hanoverian army, 59

Mackenzie, John, of Meddat, 34
Mackenzie, Sir John, of Tarbat, 10-11
Mackenzie, Captain Kenneth, 112, 124, 130, 133-5
Mackenzie, Kenneth, Coigach factor, 259, 262, 263, 289, 304, 330-2
Mackenzie, Kenneth, of Dundonnell, 150-1
Mackenzie of Kintail, 4
Mackenzie, Roderick, brother of 3rd earl of Cromartie, 62
Mackenzie, Roderick, Lord Prestonhall, 46
Mackenzie, Roderick Grant Francis, 4th new earl of Cromartie, 410, 416, 421, 423
    as clan chief, 427
Mackenzie, Sir Rorie, of Tarbat, The Tutor, 8-10
    marriage to Margaret Macleod, 7, 8-9
Mackenzie of Scatwell, 60, 61
Mackenzie of Seaforth, 2
Mackenzie, Lady Sibell Lilian, countess of Cromartie, 367, 383-4, 386, 399, 415, 421
    financial problems, 395-6, 399-40
Macleod, Aeneas, of Cadboll, 32-3, 48, 49-50, 52
Macleod, Count *see* Mackenzie, John, Lord Macleod
Macleod, Donald, of Geannies, 121, 122, 130
McLeod, George, Free Church minister, 162
Macleod, John, of Talisker, 48
Macleod, Margaret, marriage to Sir Rorie Mackenzie, 7, 8-9
Macleod, Norman, minister, 138
Macleod's Regiment, 99-101
McLeran, James, architect, 104
McMillan, Rev. Kenneth, 289
MacMillan, Rev. John, 300, 315-16
McNeill, Sir John, 233
Macrae, John, factor, 325
Manson, Dr Thomas, 280, 281-3
manufacturing *see* industry
Martin, John, 263
Maryburgh, 190
Matheson, Sir James, 339
May, Peter, 77, 78, 81, 87
Meddat, 7
    — Mackenzie of, factor, 68, 73-4
    George Mackenzie of, 116
    John Mackenzie of, 34
    reclamation of low-lying land, 43

Meddat, Mackenzies of, 33-4
    chamberlaincy of, 33-4
Meikle-Ferness, 192
Melville, —, agent for British Fishery Society, 107, 195
Melville, —, lawyer, 231, 244-5, 247-9, 251, 257
Menzies, Archibald, inspector to Board of Annexed Estates, 82-4
Merchant, Alexander, of Wilkhaven, 32
Middleton, Dr —, 280
Middleton, John, 1st earl, 14, 16
migration:
    seasonal, 127, 200, 203
    see also emigration
Milns of Milntown, rent, 140
Milntown:
    linen industry, 93
    market at, 132
Milton, 7
ministers:
    appointment of, 160-2
    Free Church, and Crofters' Revolt, 298, 299-300
Mitchell, James, 348
Monck, General George, 14
Mundell, Walter, 240-1, 245
Munro of Culcairn, 121
Munro, Daniel, minister of Tain, 60
Munro, Hugh, of Novar, 161, 162, 164, 175-6
Munro, Hugh, of Teannich, 73
Murray, James, 156, 158, 159
Murray, John, 155-6
Murray, Hon Mary, wife of 2nd earl of Cromartie, 52
Murray, Patrick, 156

Napier Commission *see* Crofter Commission
New Tarbat *see* Tarbat
Newhall estate, 153, 166, 167
Nicolson Mackenzie Mineral Water Hospital, 390, 407
North, Frederick, Lord, 102
Nova Scotia:
    emigration to, 91, 114, 138
    Mackenzie lands in, 10

Novar, 121, 340-1
    Munro of 161, 162, 164, 175-6
Nutwood farm, 334

Old Dorney, 178

Palmerston, Lord, 254
Paper Manufactory of Scotland, 45
Parliaments, Union of, 23
patronage:
    Church, 160-2, 168
    political, 168
Peacock, —, factor, 328
Pettey, Jane, 130
Pictou, Nova Scotia, emigration to, 91, 114
Pirie, A. C., 300
Polbain, 379
    lotting, 170, 346
Polglass, lotting, 170, 346
political influence of landowners, 27, 98, 168-9, 175-6, 338-9
    decline of, 339-41
Polnicol, 86, 146
poor/poverty, 194
    late 17th century, 39
    18th century, 80-1, 115
    Coigach, mid 19th century, 227-9
    crofters, 304, 313-14
    relief, 126-7, 191, 194-5, 203-4, 302-3
    see also famine
population growth in Highlands, 113-14, 119, 200, 205
Portmahomack, 7
    17th century reconstruction at, 32, 35, 42, 49
ports, grain shipment, 42-3
potatoes:
    blight, 207
    introduction, 120
Prestonhall, Roderick Mackenzie, Lord, 46
Priesthill farm, 7

quartering of troops, 40-1

railways, 276
    benefits of, 263, 271
    opposition to, 175

Reform Bill, 38-9
Reiff, 379
    lotting, 346
religion:
    appointment of ministers, 160-2
    and the community, 18th century, 34
    extreme piety in, 136-7
    sectarian conflicts, 18th century, 34-6
    'The Men', 136
rents:
    17th-18th centuries, 41, 79, 80, 81
    late 18th-early 19th centuries, 130-2, 135, 140-1, 144
    Coigach, 41, 79, 87-8, 132, 144
    collection:
        17th-18th centuries, 30-2
        Coigach, 30
        crofters, 291, 294-5, 297
        during sequestration of Cromartie, 53
        following 1745 Rebellion, 73-4
    crofting, 290-3, 307, 319, 350, 353-4
        Crofter Commission and, 381, 385
        refusal to pay, 302, 306, 323
        revaluation, 291-4
    Cromartie *see under* Cromartie estate
    Crown, 55
    during Annexation, 72, 74-6
    New Tarbat, 81, 87
    service (customs), 30, 135-6
    sporting, 174, 356
    victual, 30, 41, 42, 88, 125-6, 132, 140
    see also Cromartie estate, rents
Rhiddorrach (Rhiddorroch):
    rent, 144, 348
    sale of, 410, 411
    sporting lease, 357, 358, 359
Rhive, lotting, 170
riots:
    Coigach, 238-45
    eviction, Culrain, 161, 164
    food, Dingwall, 116
    induction, 36
        Dingwall, 34-5
roads:
    construction, 210-12, 228, 287
        Coigach, 286
        and famine relief, 209-12, 260, 261
    late 18th century, 94
    to Coigach, 210

Robertson, James, minister of Coigach, 60-1, 64-5
Rogie Falls, 404-5
Rose, John A., 411
Rosehaugh, George Mackenzie of, 20, 46
Ross, Alexander, factor, 332-3, 399
Ross, Sir John Lockhart, 121
Royston estate, 20, 48
    sale of, 56
Royston House, 19, 20, 22, 24, 50
Royston, Lord, 50

Sandeman, William, 93
Sasins, Register of, 20
Scatwell, Mackenzies of, 60, 61
schools, 127
    elections to School Boards (1873), 289, 339-40
Scott, Andrew, factor, 176-7, 190, 202, 206-7, 210-13, 325, 329-30
    attitude to Highlanders, 327-8, 329-30
    and Coigach riot, 236-45, 327
    estate management, 221-35, 262-3, 326-8, 339
    relationship with employers, 326
    and Strathpeffer spa, 273-5
Scott, William, 329-30
Scottish Education Act (1872), 288
Scottish Society for Propagating Christian Knowledge (SSPCK), 127, 137-8
seasonal migration, 127, 200, 203
Selkrig, Charles, 164
Sharp, James, archbishop of St Andrews, 18
sheep farming:
    advertisements of land for, 145-6
    and clearances, 123, 185, 239-40
    depression in, 350-1, 354-5, 368
    effects of, 122, 146-7, 185, 188-9
        on rents, 144
        see also clearances
    enclosure for, 122
    introduction:
        attempt by Jeffrey, 88
        Cromartie, 145-6
        popular rebellion against, 123-4, 130
    late 18th century, 121, 140
    see also wool
shipping of grain, 42-3
shooting leases *see* sporting leases/tenancies

smallpox, 118-19
    inoculation against, 118-19
social conditions, 1830s, 190-9, 200-4
soldiers:
    demobilised, resettlement on annexed estates, 86-7
    Macleod's Highlanders, 103-4
    military service, 111-12
South Keanchrine, 132-3
spinning industry, 92, 93
sporting leases, 163, 174, 239, 248, 258, 287, 353, 354-9
    crofters' view, 419-20
    importance of communications, 286-7
    facilities and services for, 356-7
Stafford, marquis of *see* Sutherland, George, 3rd duke
Stevenson, Robert Louis, 283
Strathan, lotting, 170
Strathcanaird, 415
Strathconan, resettlement of clearance refugees, 222-7
Strathpeffer, 7
    agricultural landscape, 230
    crofting, 316-19, 320
    development of, 157, 158-9, 181
    estate, 7
        Macleod of Cadboll and, 49, 52
        survey of 1755, 78, 80-1
    forests, 88
    land improvement, 154
    rents, 131, 132
        under annexation, 87
    spa, 156-8, 180-1, 271, 275, 277, 280, 375-7, 388-93, 398, 406-8
        development, 269-83, 364, 373-6, 397-8
        hotel at, 276-9, 281, 374, 408
        introduction of electricity, 404-6
        investigation by Board of Annexed Estates, 93
        late 20th century, 416
        Nicolson Mackenzie Mineral Water Hospital, 390, 407
        sale of, 408, 427
    timber, 55
Strathpeffer and Dingwall Electric Co. Ltd, 406
Strathpeffer Spa Co., 408

Stronach, Alexander, builder mason, 49
Stuart monarchy:
    Mackenzie allegiance to, 10
      1745 Rising, 56-62
      Sir George Mackenzie of Tarbat and, 12, 14, 15, 18
      Sir John Mackenzie of Tarbat and, 11
    see also Jacobite rising of, 1745
Stuart, Prince Charles Edward, 59
subtenancy, 82-3, 86, 122, 133, 348
Sutherland, 4th duke, 384, 396
Sutherland, Anne, duchess of see Hay-Mackenzie, Anne
Sutherland estate, 171
    and education, 289
    interest in acquiring Tarbatness, 171-4
    land revaluation, 291-2
    merger with Cromartie estate, 221, 257
Sutherland family, 252
Sutherland, George Granville Sutherland-Leveson-Gower, 3rd duke, 221, 269, 367
    assets, 269
    and clearances, 245, 267
    as Lord Stafford, 221
      financial problems, 246-51, 255-6
      marriage to Anne Hay-Mackenzie, 219, 221
    and shooting leases, 357
    management of estates, 257
      famine relief, 260-1
      investment of Cromartie estate, 295-6, 367-9
      marriage to Mary Caroline Blair, 367, 382
    and Strathpeffer spa, 269-72, 275-8, 364, 369
    will, 382, 384-5, 394-5
Sutherland-Leveson-Gower, Francis, 2nd new earl of Cromartie, 366
    coming of age, 289-90
    death, 383
    financial problems, 364, 368-70
    inheritance of Cromartie estate, 296
    marriage, 296, 367

tacksmen, 82-3, 132-3
    decline of, 149, 179
Tanera, 146
    lotting, 170, 346
    pier at, 106
Tarbat:
    barony of, 7
    composition, 39
    estate, 8
      survey of 1755, 78, 81
    flax cultivation and linen industry, 92-3
    population decline, 114, 122
    rents, 81, 132
      under Annexation, 87
Tarbat (New Tarbat) House, 7, 31, 38-9, 175, 321
    building of, 43
    decline, 93, 98
    restoration of, 48, 104, 129
    sale of, 427
Tarbatness, survey by Sutherland agents, 171-3
Tarrell farm, 7, 50
Tasmania, emigration to, 234
Taylor, George, agent of Duke of Sutherland, 171
Teanninch, Hugh Munro of, 73
Telford, Thomas, 107
tenants:
    relationship with landlords, 111-12, 141, 155, 289-90
      effect of Crofters' revolt, 298
      effect of Napier Commission, 385-7
    see also land tenure
textile industry:
    development, annexed estates, 92-3
    domestic, 124-5, 127
timber:
    Coigach, 53
    sale of, 43
    Strathpeffer, 55
tourism:
    19th century, 279
    see also Strathpeffer spa
trade:
    cattle, 41
    Darien Scheme, 45-6
    export, 42, 44
    fish, 44-5
    grain, 41-3
    industrial revolution and, 119
transport:
    early 18th century, 39-40

transport—*continued*
    wagonway, 43
    within Cromartie estate, 7
    see also railways; roads
transportation, following 1745 Rebellion, 66-7
Tullich, 86, 410

Ullapool:
    emigration from, 114
    fishing industry, 44, 105, 107, 195
    population growth, 114
    resettlement of demobilised soldiers, 87
    village, 105-7, 195-6
Union of Parliaments, 23
university at Inverness, proposal for, 45
Urquhart family estates, acquisition by George Mackenzie of Tarbat, 46-7, 48
Urquhart, Leonard, solicitor, 99
Urquhart, Sir Thomas, 46
Urquhart, William, of Meldrum, 56

Urray, appointment of minister to, 162

Victoria, Queen, 254, 367
Vyner, Clare, 416

wadsets, 29, 48
    Cromartie estate, 29, 48, 55, 140
wagonway, 43
Walker, Francis, 153, 154, 160, 165-8
Wilkhaven farm, 7, 50
William III and Mary II, 21-2
witches, 36
women, employment in agriculture, 264-6
wool:
    export, 147
    prices, 146
World War I, 411-12, 415
Wotherspoon, George, factor, 336, 402

Yonge, Sir George, 103